THE COMPANY OF WORDS

Northwestern University
Studies in Phenomenology
and
Existential Philosophy

THE COMPANY OF WORDS

Hegel, Language, and Systematic Philosophy

John McCumber

Northwestern University Press
Evanston, Illinois

1993

Northwestern University Press
Evanston, Illinois 60201-2807

Copyright © 1993 by Northwestern University Press
All rights reserved. Published 1993
Printed in the United States of America

Library of Congress Cataloging-in-Publication Data
McCumber, John.
    The company of words : Hegel, language, and systematic philosophy
/ John McCumber.
        p.   cm. — (Northwestern University studies in phenomenology
and existential philosophy)
    Includes bibliographical references and index.
    ISBN 0-8101-1055-5 (cloth). — ISBN 0-8101-1082-2 (paper)
    1. Hegel, Georg Wilhelm Friedrich, 1770–1831.   2. Language and
languages—Philosophy.   3. Knowledge, Theory of.   I. Title.
II. Series: Northwestern University studies in phenomenology &
existential philosophy.
B2949.L25M35   1992
193—dc20   92-30052
                                                                        CIP

To my Aunts

Janet Eisner
Mary Louise Snively

It would go ill indeed for our cognition if we had to surrender exact conceptions of such objects as freedom, justice, morality, and even God himself, making do with vague generalized images whose details were left to the whim of each individual— just because those objects cannot be measured or calculated or expressed in a mathematical formula. The ruinous practical consequences of such a theory are immediately obvious.

—Hegel, *Encyclopedia* #99

What is valuable in humanity is that we know what we are and that we know it in the purest way, i.e. that we arrive at the *thought* of what we are.

—Hegel, *Einleitung in die Geschichte der Philosophie*

Knowing what we say is much rarer than we think.

—Hegel, "Review of Solger"

Contents

Preface

Alcibiades had the answer all along. From his youth he knew that philosophy begins, not in my doubt but in our need: not with ignorance, but affliction. His privation flared so brightly no *elenchos* could refute it.

But Socrates, in the slackness of his years, recalled that our needs are sharpest when they are forgotten. And so our one most basic need is for memory. Of what?

The most forgotten need, the one that cuts us open and makes us human, cries at us unspoken from the pages of Plato and Locke, and Kant and Heidegger, and Hegel most especially. It is the need for a company of words.

Acknowledgments

Many people have helped this book along during the eighteen years of its gestation. I can mention only a few of them here. Emil Fackenheim, H. S. Harris, and Kenneth Schmitz taught me Hegel and much more, back when chapters 7 and 10 were parts of my dissertation at the University of Toronto. I still have much to learn from them and from Reginald Allen, Graeme Nicholson, and Thomas Robinson, who showed me in very different ways what the philosophical spirit could be. Because of Anton Pegis, I became a philosopher; in spite of him, I became a Hegelian.

Paul Thagard showed me connections between my views on Hegel and cognitive science. A reader for Northwestern University Press provided very generous and helpful criticisms, as did Stephen Toulmin, whom I am most proud to have as a colleague. Françoise Lionnet has sustained this project for an unconscionable period of time. The men and women of the IPNN Collective provided warm encouragement and grounding in what is most real.

Dr. William Hohengarten provided immensely valuable help with the "logical" rewriting in chapter 4, and with related sections of the book. I am very grateful to him. Like the others I have mentioned, he is not responsible for the innumerable defects that remain in this book. J. B. Sadoff provided help with the title. The office staff of the Northwestern University Philosophy Department—Kathleen Beckerman, Donna Chocol, and especially Kristina Houston—were indispensable in this as in everything.

I am indebted to the President's Fund of Northwestern University for the fellowship that enabled me to complete this book, and to the chairs of the Northwestern philosophy department, Thomas McCarthy and especially Kenneth Seeskin, for tirelessly juggling my teaching schedules. I doubt that this book could have been written anywhere else.

Finally, this book is dedicated to my aunts, who are the very best. And I am dedicated to Jonathan and Danielle, who teach the most profound lessons.

A Note on the Texts

For the sake of consistency and accessibility, I have whenever possible cited the Suhrkamp edition of Hegel's works, edited by Eva Moldenhauer and Karl Markus Michel, 20 vols. (Frankfurt: Suhrkamp, 1970-71). References are to volume and page number; for works with numbered paragraphs, those are included as well. In the case of those works, "Anm." denotes one of Hegel's own remarks to a numbered paragraph; "Zus." designates further material appended by his earlier editors. Citations of translations follow a slash ("/"). All translations in this book are my own, but for frequently mentioned works of Hegel, I have used the following abbreviations and cited the following translations:

III (*PHG*) *Phenomenology of Spirit.* Translated by A. V. Miller. Oxford: Clarendon Press, 1977.

V, VI (*WDL*) *Science of Logic.* Translated by A. V. Miller. New York: Humanities Press, 1969.

VIII (*Enz.*) *Hegel's Logic.* Translated by William Wallace. Oxford: Clarendon, 1975.

X (*Enz.*) *Hegel's Philosophy of Mind.* Translated by A. V. Miller. Oxford: Clarendon, 1971.

XII *Lectures on the Philosophy of History.* Translated by J. Sibree. New York: Dover, 1959.

XIII (*Aesth.*) *Hegel's Aesthetics.* Translated by T. M. Knox. 2 vols. Oxford: Clarendon, 1975. (All references are to vol. 1 unless otherwise noted.)

XVIII-XX (*Hist. Phil.*) *Lectures on the History of Philosophy.* Translated by E. S. Haldane and Frances H. Simson. New York: Humanities Press, 1974. (All references are to vol. 1 unless noted.) For the Berlin transcription of the Introduction, *Introduction to the Lectures on the History of Philosophy,* translated by A. V. Miller. Oxford: Clarendon Press, 1985.

I have also made use of the following editions:

Einleitung in die Philosophie der Weltgeschichte (*EGP*). Edited by Johannes Hoffmeister. 5th ed. Hamburg: Meiner, 1955. Translated by J. Sibree, under the title *Lectures on the Philosophy of History.* New York: Dover, 1959.
Vorlesungen über die Philosophie der Religion. Edited by Walter Jaeschke. Vol. 1 (*Phil. Rel.*). Hamburg: Felix Meiner, 1983. Translated by Peter C. Hodgson, under the title *Lectures on the Philosophy of Religion.* Berkeley: University of California Press, 1984.
Vorlesungen über die Philosophie der Weltgeschichte (*PWG*). Edited by Johannes Hoffmeister. Hamburg: Meiner, 1955.

Titles to sections and subsections of Hegel's works are capitalized and enclosed in quote marks; moments and stages of his System are capitalized. Words neither capitalized nor enclosed in quote marks are used in their American acceptation. Thus, Hegel wrote only one Objective Logic and two "Objective Logics," neither of which has much to do with logic.

References to Plato give Stephanus pagination; to Aristotle, Bekker pagination.

References to Locke are, where possible, to Book, Chapter, and Section of the *Essay Concerning Human Understanding.* Where this is not possible (e.g., in the "Epistle to the Reader," I have cited Locke, *An Essay Concerning Human Understanding,* edited by Alexander Campbell Fraser, 2 vols. (New York: Dover, 1959).

References to Kant are to Kant, *Werkausgabe,* edited by Wilhelm Weschedel, 12 vols. (Frankfurt: Suhrkamp, 1978); references to the *Critique of Pure Reason* (*KRV*) are to the B edition of the Akademie-Ausagabe.

Other bibliographical details are in the notes.

Introduction:
The Need for System

W hy should philosophy try to constitute itself as a system? Why should thinkers attempt general treatments of the cosmos, of humanity or history, indeed of anything at all?

The question makes more sense to us than it would have to Hegel. Virtually every philosophical movement since his death has, often enough by its very name, proclaimed its antipathy to the idea of philosophical system. Indeed, the antipathy is usually to some aspect of what is thought to be the specifically Hegelian way of philosophizing. If Marx proclaimed himself a "dialectical materialist," for example, it was partly in opposition to what he saw as the dialectical idealism of Hegel. Kierkegaard's existentialism was an early proclamation of the inevitability of rupture, of irreducible "Either-Or's," as against the philosopher of "Both-And"—Hegel. When Auguste Comte started calling himself a "positivist," a term fated to historical adventures from Vienna to Los Angeles, he was reacting against the "negativism" towards science that he found in metaphysicians such as Hegel. The Neo-Kantians were "Neo," rather than just Kantians, because they were going, not forward with Kant, but back to him—back, that is, from the metaphysical excesses of Hegel. Analytical philosophy began, famously, in the revolt of Russell and Moore against the British "Hegelians." Adorno's negative dialectics opposed the pompous failure of Hegel's "positive" dialectics. Heidegger's *Abbau* of philosophy, which Derrida translates into French as *déconstruction* and Foucault as *généalogie*, was aimed at freeing philosophy and science from the seamless narrative imposed on them, most fatefully, by Hegel.

Rejections of Hegel are usually couched in the language of epistemology and logic: philosophical system, they hold, is (for one reason or another) impossible. But a moral tone often creeps in: System is not only impossible to achieve, but ought not (for one reason or another) to be undertaken. This double antipathy to System is, then, a keynote of philosophy since Hegel, and we remain defined philosophically by our rejection of his thought.

But have we *understood* what we reject? Even among Hegel's expositors there is no consensus on the basic meaning of his work.[1] Among his opponents, it is more than remarkable that the rejections I have noted did not all occur at once but represent an ongoing process, in which each new "refutation" implies the inadequacy of earlier ones. When the beetle is squashed, we cease to stomp. If Marx and Kierkegaard have crushed Hegel, why do Derrida and Foucault have to do so as well? If Hegel is well and truly dead, why does his corpus still twitch so tantalizingly?

What if the "real" Hegel were different from all these all too real "Hegels"? What if (the real) Hegel was not an idealist or a metaphysician, but simply developed the empirical side of Kant's philosophy in a way that took seriously history and the science of his day?[2] What if he were neither a "realist" nor an "idealist," in the usual acceptations of those terms, but sought to develop an ontologically neutral philosophical vocabulary?[3] What if those exemplary "idealists," the British Hegelians, were so far removed from Hegel's real thought that their enemies, Russell and Moore and analytical philosophers generally, were in fact closer to him than they were?[4] What if Hegel did not deny the reality of rupture at all, so that his narrative of Spirit, far from seamless, is compatible with all kinds of breaks and demarcations? What if Heidegger, Foucault, and Derrida all undertake to deconstruct something that Hegel never constructed, and thereby leave his real achievement untouched?[5]

In that case we are defined by our *mis*understandings of Hegel. In that case his system is radically other than what we have taken it to be. It is then a System not idealistic or materialistic, neither affirming nor denying rupture, neither canonizing nor ignoring the results of science. At the limit—which is precisely where I will place it—it would assert nothing, resolve nothing, lay no claim at all on reality. But what kind of "system" might this be? And what good might it be to anyone?

I

Hegel's world contained two answers to the question of why philosophy should be systematic: because reality itself was a giant system, and because it was not. The former answer was of ancient provenance, devolving from Aristotle's regimentation into a "cosmos" of an empirical world that, for Plato, was largely an ungovernable chaos of material energies. By postulating that form is in things, rather than in its own heaven and related to things by a mysterious relation sometimes called "participation," Aristotle was able to conceive of reality as a set of interlocking microcosms. Each was structured by its own kind of form: in the human individual reason prevailed, in the household the father, in the polis the council, in the heavens the Prime Mover, and so on.[6] Though the details varied, some kind of systematic order to the universe was postulated by every single metaphysician after Aristotle, for the possibly excellent reason that such postulation was essential to their project: you cannot seek out the basic principles of reality if reality is too chaotic to have any. Hence, on this ancient view, the effort to be accurate about reality—to achieve a correct view of it—required systematic thinking.

The second answer, pursued by Kant after his awakening from dogmatic slumber, conceded to the Empiricists—notably to Hume—that our experience is far too disorganized for any systematicity to be found in it. Any philosophy which seeks to be accurate to the universe as we experience it must forsake all system and eventually resolve itself into a series of unrelated reflections on passing states of affairs (as with Montaigne or Richard Rorty). And this holds, in Hume's view, for our experience of ourselves as well of nature: we are to ourselves mere "bundles of perceptions."[7] Philosophical system, as an accurate depiction of reality, is epistemologically nonsensical: you cannot mirror fragments with a system.

Kant's objection to this is, ultimately, that it makes moral action impossible. His solution is to abandon accuracy to reality as philosophy's single criterion and goal. As the "Transcendental Doctrine of Method" makes clear, the traditional content of metaphysics is henceforth to belong to an exclusively moral enterprise, in which people talk about God, the soul, and immortality, not because these things can be known to exist but simply in order to strengthen their moral will. Philosophy is subsumed, not into science, but into the "culture of reason."[8] Even Kant's own transcendental critique, which is another of his replacements for philosophy, has therefore an unstable status as descriptive. When Kant, for example, writes at the beginning of ¶22 of the *Prolegomena* that "the sum of the matter is this: the business [*Sache*] of the senses is to intuit, that of the understanding to think,"[9] he knows that he is not, strictly, describing how things are. For in fact, all around him, minds are not keeping to their business: people are trying to intuit with their understandings—that is, to posit unreflectively the reality, outside the mind, of concepts formed within it (dogmatism). They are also trying (as Locke did) to make their sensations yield categorical truths. That is why philosophy, along with the rest of Kant's modernity, is in such a parlous state. The only hope lies in our learning how to restrict each faculty to its proper business: to systematize the mind. Hence, Kant's transcendental philosophy is not a description of the mind's faculties but, as Gilles Deleuze has written, an *état civil* of them. It not only describes but regularizes the phenomena it treats, and to that extent has a performative, as well as a constative, dimension.[10]

The ultimate point of this performance, I have noted, is moral. The will is the most unitary of faculties. It has but one basic concept, that of freedom, and it realizes this (in all senses) by willing the moral law, which turns out to be nothing other than its own unitary, universal nature. Such self-willing must be one and the same for all people, at all times, in all circumstances; room is made for it by the systematization of the cognitive faculties mentioned above. The unity of the mind is thus a moral unity, and need for system is a moral need. True, our experience, even of ourselves, is primally chaotic: but it ought not to be.

There are then two characteristics of the sensory realm that require for Kant a turn to systematicity. One is only indirectly moral: it is that in its confusion and chaos, the manifold of sensory data does not allow itself to be known with certainty. To ground our cognition we must turn from accuracy to coherence—a coherence that we ourselves supply through the organized workings of our understanding, via the twelve categories (themselves conveniently arranged in four groups of three).[11] As we do this, our mind comprehends its own organization, and this enhances its self-integration—all in response to the second characteristic: that the localized and fragmentary nature of sensory experience makes moral action impossible, since it must be one and the same always and everywhere.[12]

These two defects lead in turn to two different kinds of system. In the latter case, it is what may be called a system of governance, which is what Kant has in mind when he writes, "I understand as a 'system' the unity of the manifoldness of cognitions under an idea. This idea is the rational concept of the form of a whole."[13] Such systems, established under what Kant here (in "The Architectonic of Pure Reason") calls the "governance of reason" (*die Regierung der Vernunft*), begin with an "idea," a concept of form, and then extend themselves methodically to everything which has that form. The form in question, being conceptual, serves as a principle which can be articulated and subdivided. But it can never be transgressed. An example of it would be the Categorical Imperative, which covers and prescribes to all our actions in virtue of their common form as moral actions. Morality for Kant is, par excellence, a matter of systematic governance.

But the Kantian "system of governance," advanced in an attempt to salvage morality, eventually came to seem inherently immoral. For the untransgressable specifications with which such a system begins appear, precisely because they are beginning points for reason itself, to be arbitrary. Their claimed governance over human beings then seems to be the imposition of an arbitrary essence. Such an imposition can only be an act of will, and it is as a reaction against such systems that we can interpret Nietzsche's famous remark that the *will* to System is a want of probity.[14]

Even as Kant discusses systems of governance, however, he is aware that this is not all there is. For there is also the genesis of system— that is, systems temporalized:

> Systems appear, like worms and other low animals, to be constructed by spontaneous generation [*generatio aequivoca*] from the mere flowing together [*Zusammenfluß*] of collected concepts.[15]

It is unfortunate (Kant writes), but true: systems do not develop, in our cognition, in accordance with their structures. Scientists do not in fact begin with the formal specification of a field and then work from that to ever more concrete applications and empirical corollaries. Rather, they begin with various concrete experiences that are somehow relevant to each other, that "flow together" to form concepts which themselves "flow together" to form systems, ultimately converging into the overarching architectonic of all human cognition. In systems as such—the final, atemporal systems—the formal specification comes first, and those are what I call systems of governance. The temporal development of a system to this stage, then, is the progressive instatement of an *état civil* in the mind, an organizing not merely of facts but of cognitions and capacities for cognition.

In the system in time, the system as it appears, the fundamental specification comes last. To be sure, this is because (Kant hastens to inform us) it was there, latently, all along. But this latency is its existence, not in the facts themselves, but in "reason merely explicating itself"; it *could* exist as no more than an investigator's eye for such connections and mutual relevance as may eventually establish themselves. In fact for Kant it also exists as an absolute demand of reason, at which point the underlying issues of moral governance break forth.[16] Such absolute demands are not, however, necessary for the scientist. The organization of nature can be viewed, independently of its moral significance and grounding, as merely a very basic hypothesis, to be verified where possible through investigation. Such verification would be attained whenever experiences and concepts "run together" into larger wholes: whenever our knowledge, over time, establishes patterns in nature.

This second kind of system, which I will call "reflective system," is further contrasted with systems of governance in the first Introduction to the *Critique of Judgment*. The concept of an empirical system of nature—of the unity of all empirical natural laws—is, we read there, completely foreign to the Understanding.[17] The variety of nature, in our manifold experience of it, is simply too great for the Understanding to conceive of such submission in any very detailed way. It is, rather, the faculty of Judgment which hypothesizes that nature provides us with a rounded totality of forms and laws. And since reflective judgment, in particular, begins without concepts (or laws), articulating them as it goes along, such a system must be a system without an "idea": without an initial, unitary formal specification under which everything in it is to fall. It starts, in fact, with no imposition of form upon experience, other than the empty aesthetic notion of form as such—with the hypothesis, that is, that some more concrete sort of form will become evident at some point. This sort of system is no different in structure from its own genesis. It is a wholly temporal phenomenon, the gaining of form, the appearing system.

The chasm between these two sorts of system yawns wide indeed: it amounts to the difference between seeing the universe in terms of the second *Critique*, as a law-governed whole, and in terms of the third, as a beautiful object: as like a state or like a work of art. I will discuss below how Fichte, in Hegel's view, developed his philosophy as a governing system whose basic principle, "the ego posits itself," is a near paraphrase of the Kantian view of the will as willing itself. Did Hegel himself, as is so often thought, follow Fichte in this?[18] Or is his system of the reflective type? Does Hegel, from a position outside time, impose unities on experience and identities on people? Or does his thought, itself a developing temporal whole, merely extend and further articulate unities which have somehow established themselves? If the latter, does the articulation alter what it articulates? Or does it remain accurate to the phenomena from which it begins? And if the System is not the willed imposition of an arbitrary essence, what is so morally objectionable about it?

These questions will take the rest of this book to answer, if answers they obtain. I will begin here by asking what sorts of need philosophy, in Hegel's view, is to fill. How does Hegel think that his kind of system can help us in our larger tasks?

Hegel would not be pleased to admit that there are any larger tasks. With his Aristotelian affinities, he thinks that philosophy is an end in itself, and the highest there is:

> If, as Aristotle says, theory is the most blessed and the best
> among good things, those who participate in that pleasure
> know what they gain from it—the satisfaction of the necessity
> of their spiritual nature. They can hold back from making de-
> mands on others, and can content themselves with their own
> needs [Bedürfnisse] and the satisfactions which they obtain for
> them.[19]

In other words, reason's self-realization as a necessary unity is for Hegel, as for Kant, an end in itself. Other passages where this end is decked out in reams of Hegelian encomium are not hard to find—indeed, are often hard to avoid. But Hegel knew that philosophy would always be a primary interest of just a very few people.[20] There are places where he thinks of philosophy, not as the culmination of the entire human enterprise, but as part of it. One such is in his remarkable essay of 1828 on the religious writer and cultural *Ungeheuer* Johann Georg Hamann, whose views on language I will discuss in chapter 9. According to Hegel, Hamann was unusual partly because, though an obvious genius, he felt no need (*Bedürfnis*) of philosophy:

> The need for scientificality itself, the need to become conscious
> of one's ideas [Gehalt] in thought, to see that content develop
> itself in thought, and just as much to confirm itself in that
> form, to satisfy itself as thought itself, was completely foreign
> to him.[21]

We will see later what it is for Hegel to have a "content" develop and confirm itself in thought; suffice it here that the thought in question is not that of an individual but of a community. As the word *Geschmack* ("taste") in a similar passage on p. 280 indicates, what Hegel has in mind has something in common with Kant's principles of enlarged thought. In such thought, we undertake to test the results of our judgment against the views of others (and indeed against the possible views of those whom we cannot actually consult), ready to learn from them and revise our views if need be.[22] Unwilling to submit to this, Hamann "persisted in the profound concentration of his particularity"—that is, indulged himself in the purest, and hence most idiosyncratic, forms of self-expression: "he, who should have become one of our best writers, was seduced by the desire to be original and became one of the most reproachable." Full of private jokes and allusions, Hamann's writings are incapable of reaching a broad public: some love them, others hate them, none understand them.[23]

Hamann's lack of interest in the concrete expression of his thought allowed its core to remain very abstract indeed. His version of Christianity was intensely and deeply meaningful for him, but was without any doctrine, community, or moral guidance, bereft even of the command to love:[24]

> Hamann utterly failed to appreciate that the living reality of divine Spirit does not keep itself in such contraction but is its own development [Ausführung] to a world and a creation, and is this only by way of the production of distinctions whose limitations, yes, but also whose legitimacy and necessity in the life of finite spirit must be granted recognition.[25]

Hamann's reduction of Christianity to his own rhapsodies—to the "actuality of [his own] individual presence"[26]—was in a sense liberating, for it enabled him to see through all sorts of fixed dogma, including various separations and distinctions Kant claimed to have established as ultimate. But it deprived him, we have seen, of a public. And this meant that he relied greatly on his private circle: on his friends.[27]

But here, too, Hamann's unreceptivity to philosophy caused him trouble. In his earlier years, he took it upon himself—as a "divine vocation"[28]—to help his friends to self-knowledge by scolding them for their every failing. This project produced a series of wrecked relationships, which Hegel recounts in several places and at painful length.[29] Eventually—aided by the abstract and nebulous nature of his Christianity, which enabled him to tolerate a great many things more sober Christians regard as failings—Hamann abandoned his scolding. But this meant that his inner, nebulous core did not come to expression at all: it remained foreign to his own everday life, and hence foreign to his friends.[30]

The keynote of his later life was that his friendships dissolved, no longer in dispute, but in mutual incomprehension. Hegel's portrait of this is crucial to the present interpretation of his philosophy:

> And incomprehension is in this perhaps worse than disagreement, that it is [always] connected and afflicted with misunderstanding of oneself, while disagreement may be directed against others alone. . . . If sentiments, thoughts, representations, interests, principles, beliefs, and perceptions [*Empfindungen*] are communicable among human beings, in the view of [Hamann's] circle there remained, *beyond* and *behind* all such concrete individuality, the naked and concentrated intensity of feeling, of faith. This simple and ultimate element alone was supposed to have absolute worth, and could only be found, known, and enjoyed through the living presence [*lebendige Gegenwart*] of a trustful interiority that held nothing back, gave itself wholly.
>
> Those who have established such a distinction in their view of things and have connected to it their concept of the beauty, indeed of the splendor of the soul, cannot content themselves with the reciprocal exchange of thoughts and deeds, of the objective side of emotion, faith, perception. But only by these can the inner allow itself to be revealed, shown, communicated.
>
> Since in this kind of relationship the distinctiveness and particularity of various viewpoints comes to the fore—and does so in unclarity, since the entire situation here is unclarity itself—and since this appearance as such does not correspond to the supposedly *ineffable* interiority which is sought for and demanded to be seen, the soul does not yield itself to comprehension and the result is *indéfinissable*, an incomprehensibility and unsatisfied yearning: a mood in which people, without really being able to say why, find themselves separate and foreign to one another, instead of having found one another—which they thought was the only possibility.[31]

The problem with Hamann and his circle, then, was a failure of dialogue: they were unable to discuss what was important. The opinions and representations they shared were considered by them to be trivialities, while their deeper natures were manifested in mute devotion or in the immediate, idiosyncratic "expectorations" found, for example, in Hamann's writings on Kant.[32] There was no attempt to find a common ground of intelligibility, no effort to articulate words in which, though we may disagree, we can at least understand one another and ourselves.

Systematic philosophy, if it is what Hamann so deeply lacked, is in the first instance necessary for a certain type of friendship. As such it is directed, not against disagreement, but against a more profound malaise: the separation and foreignness which remains a mere feeling because people "cannot really say why" they find themselves in it. Systematic philosophy is thus a temporal process in which participants gain the words they can use to understand one another: in which they create for themselves, and for their community, a company of words.

Misunderstanding is, Hegel notes, to be distinguished from disagreement. If you and I disagree, it is possible for me to be wholly clear about my own opinion, and even perhaps wholly justified in it. But if I do not understand you, it is because I do not have words which would enable me to do so. And to be missing the right words is, for the *zoon logon echon*, always a problem: it means to be incapable of articulating not only another's, but one's own thoughts on certain issues; unable to formulate, let alone decide, certain questions; barred from entering into certain communal practices, from playing certain games.

This does not mean that philosophy has no role in resolving disagreements. In the year of the essay on Hamann, Hegel writes (with reference to C. W. F. Solger):

> Most, indeed all disagreements and contradictions [*Widersprüche*] must be resolvable through the seemingly easy tactic of setting before oneself what one has actually said, simply examining it, and comparing it with the rest of what one similarly maintains. Knowing what one is saying is much rarer than we think.[33]

This of course is exaggerated, and Hegel knew it. Two pages earlier he had written:

> There is one species of incomprehension which, it can be directly demanded, ought not to exist, namely incorrectness [*Unrichtigkeit*] as regards what is actually the case. . . . Philosophy must at least complain, where justified, about the false statement of the facts, and if one looks closely this species [of incomprehension] is, surprisingly, the most common, and sometimes attains unbelievable dimensions.[34]

Empirical disagreements exist, indeed predominate. But the philosophically more respectable and interesting controversies result from "not knowing what one says." They are to be overcome, not by empirical investigation, but by what we would call the analysis of the terms in which those controversies are couched.

I am, in Hegel's view, what I can say: for Hamann and his circle to have the kind of friendship they wanted, they needed a different kind of language, which meant that they needed to be a different sort of self. They needed to be the kind of person who neither identifies so utterly with one's own opinions and values that to reject them is to reject oneself (as with the younger Hamann), nor holds one's ownmost essence aloof from interaction (as with the older Hamann). To enter into the kind of friendship which Hegel here advocates is thus to have a self which is able (1) to articulate itself completely, and (2) to abandon wrong or unintelligible ideas, habits, practices, and the like, without abandoning itself.

The completeness claim in (1) needs qualification. Hegel does not believe that everything about us and our experiences is articulable. The opening pages of the *Phenomenology* teach that the sheer immediacy of sensory experience is not.[35] And since Hegel, like a good Empiricist, holds (as the *Encyclopedia*'s Introduction puts it) that *nihil est in intellectu quod non fuerit in sensu*,[36] this ineffability continues to shadow all articulation—all the way, as I will argue subsequently, to the System itself. Where Hamann went wrong was not in recognizing that certain aspects of himself were ineffable, but in positing that ineffable dimension as his own essence and making it the governing factor in his relationships with others.

It is easy to recognize the kind of self that Hegel implicitly advocates here as the "consolidated self" I have elsewhere argued was the *telos* of the *Phenomenology*:[37] a self which is in harmony between the unity which makes it "a" self at all and the multiplicity which makes it a rich and dynamic one. The consolidation of the self is thus an achievement of harmony over diversity or, as Hegel puts it in the *Lectures on the Philosophy of Religion*, of healing a rupture (*Entzweiung*).

> [The need for truth] presupposes that in subjective spirit the demand is present to cognize absolute truth. Such need means immediately that the subject is [presently] in untruth; as spirit, however, the subject is something over and above this untruth, and hence its untruth is something that is to be overcome. The untruth [of the soul] is, more precisely, that the subject is split within itself, and need expresses itself to the extent that this rupture be sublated . . . and this reconciliation can only be reconciliation with the truth.[38]

If we accept the view which Anthony Storr attributes to a broad spectrum of psychoanalytical and other forms of psychotherapy, that mental "health and happiness depend entirely upon the maintenance of intimate personal relationships,"[39] we can see that a consolidated self is also an analytically mature one: its friendships are intimate because everything can be articulated in them, and they are sustainable because they are always changing.

Such consolidated selves are a condition for the formation of all sorts of human groups, as well as for society itself. As Jürgen Habermas has maintained, and more clearly than Hegel, language is not merely a private affair but is the fundamental social means by which we coordinate actions. The nature of a society and the groups it contains can be understood from the sorts of interaction it, and they, sanction and seek.[40] A self which is to any degree inarticulate is then, like the older Hamann, asocial, while one which cannot give up old beliefs and old ways is, like the younger Hamann, antisocial.

In particular, a self that can articulate its own individual situation and needs in ways that others can comprehend, and who can understand others when they do the same, is the only kind of self that can function politically within a modern society. For only such a self can come to form any sort of intelligent picture of the overall social situation, and of the scope and weight of its own personal interests within that situation.[41] Hence, Hegel saw in the activity of systematic philosophy, in the articulation of a company of basic terms, a way to provide a basic guidebook for the citizens, and especially the functionaries, of the complex web of productions and practices that make up modern society. Wolfgang Sünkel has pointed out that one very basic dynamic of Hegel's thought—that of "externalization"—is to be understood as a brutally honest picture of education:

> Education [*Bildung*] is the transformation of the subject—
> more exactly, its self-transformation, through which it loses itself in an objective material which is not itself; makes itself at home there; and, in that it appropriates and becomes versed in what at first seems alien to it, finally recognizes itself, Spirit, in that alien form.[42]

Alienation (*Entäußerung, Entfremdung*) and indeed the "toil of the concept" itself,[43] are thus pedagogically relevant phenomena. The pedagogy to which they are relevant is difficult and painful—poles apart from the simple amassing of facts and skills, and anything but the painless broadening of horizons which the young are so often, and so misleadingly, promised.

One important set of social groups in the modern state is what we call "science," and which Hegel calls "empirical science." Here, too, philosophy as Hegel conceives it has a role to play. As David Hull has shown, science is fruitfully regarded, not as a set of methods or as a static if provisional body of results, but as a temporal phenomenon: as a process.[44] One salient feature of that process is that scientific cooperation is the same thing as scientific competition: all scientists strive to get other scientists to adopt their own views, even when this requires them to give up their own. A second salient feature, according to Hull, is that scientists do not understand the significance of their own insights and discoveries: they do not know what they have done, even what they have said, until other scientists tell them. Scientific communication is thus not merely an exchange of facts, any more than is education. It a process of self-articulation on the part of scientists. It is not without irony that Hegel, as we saw, refers to what Hamann lacked as a need for "scientificality." Science, too, like politics and human society generally, needs the consolidated selves which Hegel thinks systematic philosophy can help produce.

While Hegel's philosophies of religion and art are the subjects of an enormous and growing literature, his views on science remain mysterious.[45] Without attempting any serious discussion of Hegel's philosophy of science (which would have to begin with the remark that for him the phrase is pleonastic), I can point out three ways in which he thinks his kind of systematic philosophy can be of service to scientists:

1. By supplementing science with the investigation of a sphere of "objects" which are scientifically unknowable, not because they inhabit a transcendent realm beyond the empirical domain but because they organize that very domain: because, empirically underdetermined themselves, they make empirical investigation possible. An example of this is freedom, of which no undisputed empirical examples can be given but which all scientists know is absolutely essential to their work.[46] On this level, philosophy aims to give scientists a deeper comprehension of themselves.

2. By organizing the basic concepts of science (or by clarifying the organization they already embody), philosophy seeks, in Hegel's words:

> To overcome the form in which the richness of [the sciences']
> contents are offered, as something merely *immediate* and *found*,
> a manifold of components which are merely placed next to one
> another, and therefore are completely contingent.[47]

As with the reflective systems of Kant, the aim here is to highlight and enhance the coherence and order of what would, if left to itself, appear as a heap of unrelated data and theories, stored in ever more massive quantities but accessible only to diminishing groups of ever more specialized workers: to help scientists comprehend each other.

3. To relate science to the rest of human life, lessening the incomprehension between scientist and nonscientist. In this connection, the Introduction to the Suhrkamp edition of the *Lectures on the History of Philosophy* contains a passage worth quoting in full:

> The forms of thought, and further the viewpoints and principles which have validity in the sciences and constitute the ultimate touchstone [*Halt*] for the rest of their material, are for all that not peculiar to them, but are common to the culture of a time and people. . . . Our consciousness contains these representations, it allows them validity as final determinations, it moves forward on them as its guiding, connecting concepts. But it does not know them, does not make them themselves into the objects and interests of its examination.
>
> To give an abstract example, every consciousness has and uses the wholly abstract determination, "Being." "The sun *is* in the sky," "the grapes *are* ripe," and so on forever. In higher culture there are questions of cause and effect, force and expression, etc. All [our] knowing and representing is interwoven with such metaphysics, and governed by it; it is the net in which is caught all the concrete material that occupies us in our ways and doings. But for our ordinary consciousness, this web and its knots are sunken in multilayered material. It is the latter which contains the interests and objects which we know, which we have before us. Those universal threads are not set off and made objects of our reflection.[48]

So philosophy is the analysis of "forms of thought" and their interconnections. The Preface to the second edition of the *Science of Logic* explains further:

> The forms of thought are proximally displayed and stored in the *language* of people; in our day it cannot often enough be recalled that what distinguishes humans from animals is thinking. Into everything which makes thinking something internal . . . there has penetrated language, and what we make into language and express in language contains, whether concealed, confused or elaborated, a category.[49]

These forms of thought are the previously acquired material of philosophy, that out of which it is constructed, and are to be "gratefully acknowledged" by philosophers as a necessary condition for their work—even though what they present is sometimes a spindly thread and a lifeless skeleton, with its bones disordered.[50]

In general, then, for Hegel it is the job of philosophy to clarify the nodes in the web of metaphysics that underlies and governs, and is accessible through, our discourses—including those of science and politics. To do this is to relate those nodes to one another. And because thought is our human identity, and because we have learned to think in the language of some particular web, we are what that web is: to understand the basic interconnections established by our language, what might be called the "deep ecology" of our languages, is to understand ourselves.

It was in that task that Hamann failed. Unable and unwilling to uncover and explicate the basic words that could have articulated his situation in a public way, he could aim no higher than private friendships—and because friendship too requires words, his all dissolved in disputes and misunderstandings.

That this was not just a psychosocial peculiarity of Hamann and his crew, and that Hegel believed his kind of philosophy could have effects in domains far more abstract than the psychological and social ones that I have discussed so far, can be seen by noting the resemblances between what Hegel says about Hamann and what the *Phenomenology* says about the Beautiful Souls.[51] But another dimension to Hegel's sort of systematic philosophy makes it not only useful but—stunningly, achingly—urgent. To see this, we must appreciate that Hegel's account of Hamann makes use of the categories and modes of analysis of his *Faith and Knowledge*, written twenty-six years before.

The "faith" in question there is faith in the final unification of basic oppositions. Such unification is a matter of faith precisely when it is not a matter of knowledge or demonstration,[52] and an important example of this is Fichte. In Fichte's case, the supreme opposition that faith tells us will be overcome is that between the absoluteness of the self or ego and its empirical conditionedness. The Ego gains this double status for Fichte—it is both absolute and empirically conditioned—because he takes it for his "principle." Pursuing a logic that Derrida will later attribute to Rousseau,[53] Hegel argues that such a principle must, since it is first, be in need of nothing else: it must be conceivable, and conceivable as existing, solely in terms of itself. But since it is *only* first, it must also be radically defective, so as to require later development into the system which it founds:

In this way the principle plays the double role of being, now
absolute, now totally finite and, as such, able to become the beginning point for the totality of empirical finitude.[54]

On one level—where Hamann had his empty Christianity—Fichte
has his empty but absolute ego, formed by abstraction from all content—
an abstraction that in fact is a supremely free self-positing.[55] The other
level, where Hamann made and lost his friends, is for Fichte's philosophical comprehension the level on which we experience ourselves as empirical individuals at the mercy of others, inhabiting cultures and a universe
we have not made and which to some degree make us. The unity of these
two levels is never explained: the fundamental, "all-dominating principle"
engaged here is just that each side is what the other is not.[56]

Philosophy, for Fichte, is the carrying through of a principle; for
Hegel, philosophy is "nothing but a struggle against its own beginning."[57] The consequences of the "principled" approach are even more
serious for Fichte's social theory than Hamann's problems were for his
social practice. Hegel draws them most cleanly in *The Difference between
Fichte's and Schelling's System of Philosophy*, published the year before
Faith and Knowledge. Each rational being, he claims, is present for Fichte
in a twofold way: as a free and rational self-positing being; and as mere
matter to be manipulated and formed. This dichotomy, moreover, is ab-
solutized: each side of it is what the other side is not, and it cannot be
transgressed.[58]

Because of the absoluteness of this dichotomy, society and in particular the political realm must be founded on one principle or the other:
the individual must be either a free being of infinite worth, or mere matter. To take the latter course is to locate rationality not in the individual
but above the individual, in the community—more specifically in the rational community, the state. As *Faith and Knowledge* puts it:

According to the principle of the system, the lawful, and the
erection of the lawful as of the state, is a being-for-self, absolutely opposed to liveliness and individuality. . . . Individuality
finds itself under absolute tyranny. The law ought to prevail
[*das Recht soll geschehen*] not as inner but as external freedom
of individuals, which is just their being subsumed under a completely alien concept.[59]

The individual thus sinks under a mass of laws and regulations, each rationally enacted for the greater good of the whole. Such a state, the *Differenzschrift* tells us, is a "machine."[60]

Also countenanced by Fichte's system, according to Hegel, is the other side of its basic opposition, in which the individual as such is immediately accorded infinite worth and full civil rights. In such a state, according to *Faith and Knowledge*, morality assumes the form of "raising all moral contingencies into the form of the concept and giving immorality [*Unsittlichkeit*] justification and a good conscience."[61]

The only reason for doing anything in this kind of social order, the *Differenzschrift* concludes, is my personal arbitrary insight, in which I pick and choose my moral principles to coincide with my own wishes:

> So, if self-determination is to come about, everything depends on reckoning out a verdict on the preferability of one duty to another and choosing among these conditioned duties according to one's best insight. . . . In this way self-determination passes over into the contingency of insight and, with that, into unawareness of what it is that decides a contingent insight.[62]

Hegel's presentation of this alternative ought to be startlingly familiar today. Isaiah Berlin has noted that none of the great social thinkers of history, on whose intellectual capital we continue to draw, foresaw any of the "great ideological storms" that raged through the first half of the twentieth century.[63] But it seems that the 31-year-old Hegel foresaw with frightening accuracy the ideological rigidity that marked the century's second half. For the two societies which have dominated the world since World War II are easily recognizable as the two approaches Hegel has contrasted here, blown up to enormous size and pushed to preposterous lengths, but never violated in their basic logic.

On the one approach, society is dominated by a relentlessly "rational" state structure, which multiplies law and regulation into state control of all expression and conduct. With opposition impossible, the state's powers of manipulation become immense. It throws up cities and factories in the wilderness, and prison camps as well, and millions disappear into them. It discharges pollutants in the air to poison those nearby, in the name of those far away who need what the polluting factories produce. It recognizes no human needs beyond the material or economic, and its leaders are proud to refer to their followers as "the masses."

The contrasting society grants to each individual, no matter how childish, ignorant, ill, or depraved, the right to determine his or her own life. Such a society cannot, therefore, keep its criminals and insane off its streets, where they have the right to wander and plunder; it is unable, even, to educate its young, who with their parents have a spectrum of "rights." Because individual insight is the only criterion of right and wrong, such a society is incapable of uniting for a sustained attack on any social problem. Its leaders, secure in a well-paid individuality which they seek at all costs to preserve, grow sleeker and more self-satisfied as the chaos proliferates, and strut their good conscience in the slogans of the moment.

Hegel was also aware that each approach generates its own internal opposition. On the one side, says the *Differenzschrift*, the overwhelming disciplinary apparatus of the state silences and isolates its inhabitants, until the people "is . . . an atomistic multitude without life, elements . . . whose connection is endless domination": tyranny breeds the purest individualism.[64] On the other hand, reliance on individual insight leads as we saw to "unawareness" of moral criteria, and beyond that to atrophy of moral and political argumentation. The clash of individual standpoints becomes more and more superficial, relativism achieves complacency, and the individuals in society grow more and more homogenous, their minds effectively identical in their closure.

The whole logic of the postwar era was what Hegel would call Fichtean. The dilemma laid out in his early writings encompassed political thinkers from Georg Lukács to Milton Friedman, and was sustained by political actors from Leonid Brezhnev to Ronald Reagan. It was a *philosophical* dilemma, and Hegel diagnosed it on a philosophical level. He uncovered its logic, showed that logic to be supported by and expressed in a certain sort of philosophy, and proposed a remedy: himself.

Who, Hegel?

II

None of the above problems—problems of friendship and ego development, of citizenry and science, of politics itself—can be solved by what I have called a system of governance. For the willed imposition of an essence—even if it is a self-imposition—is always the silencing of that upon which it has been imposed. These problems, however, call not for silence but for words: for adequate vocabularies, rather than for true principles. A vocabulary is "adequate," it appears, if its central concepts can articulate what its users think is important about themselves, and if those terms have been defined—that is, related to one another—in ways everyone can understand. What is needed, then, is a procedure for producing such definitions that will be comprehensible in itself; wide-ranging enough to include the basic terms it needs to include; and flexible enough to be revised as new experiments—in life and politics as well as in science—lead to new words and thoughts. Hegel, I maintain, aimed to produce such a system—such a company of words—and came very close to success.

This is almost the reverse of the common wisdom. Hegel is usually held, in Kierkegaard's words, to have "willed something great, though without having achieved it."[65] My divergence from this view requires me to separate myself from, though not to deny the usefulness of, two large and variegated families of Hegel interpretations.

One of these is the standard Anglo-American, and to some extent the prerevolutionary Russian, Hegel: an enormously overblown metaphysician who proffers a theory of some metaphysical reality. This reality may be as J. N. Findlay thought: a sort of depersonalized pantheistic godhead called the Absolute. It may also be, as Charles Taylor has advocated, a developing, suprapersonal subject of history. In any case, it is large.[66] The other family sees Hegel as a philosopher of consciousness, in the direct line from Kant through Descartes—a view advanced by Heidegger and ably articulated by Rodolphe Gasché and Alan White.[67] On this view, what Hegel is analyzing is not some reality independent of us, but the historically formed categorial structure of our own minds.

Each of these two families has hundreds of members beyond the few I have mentioned. The main problem with both is that they take Hegel's System to be about something other than it—about the Absolute, about history, about the structure of the mind. This accords poorly with the multitude of places where Hegel refers to his System as the *self*-development of thought, entirely within its own sphere and without input from elsewhere. Consider the following fairly strong statement from the *Science of Logic*:

> It [logic] has nothing to do with thinking *about* anything, with any basis for thought which itself existed on its own account outside of it . . . but [deals only] with the necessary forms and internal [*eigenen*] determinations of thought as its content and the highest truth itself.[68]

But if the Logic, and hence the rest of the System, is not "about" anything but itself, what can it be about? Like all philosophy, Hegel's System is, of course, a linguistic undertaking: a whole of words, once largely spoken and now solely written. To be about itself is then to be "about" its own language: the System must be some sort of self-contained linguistic whole, one which nonetheless (as Hegel also says at many places) relates in a concrete way to the variegated nature of life and history around us.

So, I will argue, Hegel is a philosopher of language: the first major philosopher to have made what Richard Rorty has called the "linguistic turn."[69] Like Wittgenstein, Moore, and Austin—indeed, like Carnap, Russell, and Quine—Hegel holds that all philosophical problems are problems of language, and that they can all be resolved, if at all, either by reforming language or by understanding it better. By "understanding it better," I will suggest, he means understanding language's capacities to reform itself: the rational improvement of words is, so to speak, the object of his philosophy, the point at which it plugs into extraphilosophical reality. Linguistic reform also characterizes Hegel's own philosophical project. The System is, I maintain, nothing more than a further reform, and organization, of certain words by certain procedures to which Hegel himself gave birth—and which, sadly, appear to have died with him.

Philosophy, then, is to keep company with words, rather than with extralinguistic realities. The rational reform of language is a relatively modest project compared to those with which Hegel is usually saddled: to give a final account of metaphysical reality or of the panoply of concrete conditions and categories of human thought. It becomes still more modest when we see that his "reform" amounts, in his own practice, to the reconstruction, very definite in its method, of just a few hundred basic terms. And yet, in all the metaphysical and transcendental modesty I will impute to it, Hegel's philosophy remains very ambitious and enormously difficult. Clearly it was too difficult for Hegel himself, who failed to do the one thing that would have given it a chance of success: to call it by its rightful name. Instead of "language," he talks about "Spirit"; instead of "description" and its conditions, he talks about "consciousness"; instead of "language reform," he talks about "reason in history"; instead of "rationally reformed discourse," he talks of "the Absolute." And so on. Translation of Hegel into terms apparently so foreign seems, I am aware, wholly misguided if not impious. Much will unavoidably be lost, though I am inclined (see below) to suspect that the loss will not be as damaging as it will be massive. Ultimately, I can ask only, as Hegel himself asked, that my views not be dismissed until they are understood. But here at the outset, a few points can be made about the strength of my interpretation and the confidence with which I advance it.

What will emerge from this book, if it succeeds, is at once a sketch of a philosophical paradigm, of a different way of doing philosophy, and an interpretation of Hegel. As a paradigm, this one can be judged on its own merits, as worth engaging in or not. As an interpretation of Hegel, it may or may not be faithful to him on a variety of levels. These judgments should be independent of each other; I will argue for each throughout the book.

The main merits of the paradigm, I will argue, are that it is a way of doing philosophy of language that supplements the currently traditional truth-based methods, is socially aware and critical, and can complement (not replace) approaches now current among Hegel's closest descendants—today's "analytical" philosophers. It opens a way to construct philosophical systems that will do all the good things mentioned in the first part of this introduction without being closed, essentialistic, or otherwise oppressive.

The value of the book as an interpretation of Hegel is a subtler matter, and I am tempted in this regard to distinguish maximal from minimal claims. The minimal claim would be that I advance here a set of ideas, coherent in themselves and consistent with certain texts of Hegel, but not necessarily faithful to his own project or intentions. The maximal claim would be to have revealed at last the "secret of Hegel"—to have discovered what he was trying to tell us but simply could not quite find the words. These claims present, not an alternative, but a continuum. Given the variety of the Hegelian corpus—lecture outlines, essays, posthumous notes, sui generis productions like the *Phenomenology*—it is quite usual for readings of Hegel to be illuminating on some texts and less so on others, and my own surely falls into this.

The *Philosophy of Religion*, for example, will be largely absent from my pages and this is partly because my approach, as far as I can tell, would not contribute very much to its understanding and appropriation. The Preface to the *Phenomenology of Spirit*, with its opaque but suggestive discussions of philosophical language, is largely irrelevant to what I will draw from Hegel's later writings and must be relegated, like the stew of words in the book's final chapter, to the status of a hasty, confused, and generally inferior early work.[70] Together with these limitations in textual scope goes the need to dismiss many of Hegel's standard claims for his System as rhetoric and salesmanship: as the studied expectorations of a man seeking disciples, influence, and the appeasement of a sometimes hostile sovereign.[71] Hegel is always telling the reader that he has expounded the eternal essence and truth of things, the absolute foundation of the universe, even "God before the creation of nature and of finite Spirit."[72] Dismissing such passages—or, in some cases, explaining them as saying merely that world is revealed through the languages we create for it—pushes my interpretive claim towards the minimal side of the continuum.

In any case, Hegel never yields all his secrets, and certainly has not yielded them to me. For all its length, the present work discusses only the general form and shape of his System, a few of its guiding ideas. Most of the content of the System, including such basic distinctions as that between the Logic and the *Realphilosophie*, the Philosophies of Nature and of Spirit, had to be disregarded.[73] If my interpretation is plausible, it will need to be measured in some detail against all Hegel's texts, not just those that I discuss here. So the present book, if successful, is by no means an end, an answer, a disposing of questions about Hegel. It is at most the beginning of a new way of reading him.

Hegel's thought is truly poetic in that it can be understood in many ways; it is up to readers to make of it what they will and can. The proliferation of readings of Hegel—which, like it or not, almost amounts to the history of philosophy since Hegel—is a good and fruitful thing, and I hope to contribute to it. Hence, this book is intended to stand beside approaches with which it is incompatible: if John Findlay and I cannot both be right about Hegel (and we cannot), it does not follow that either of us is so close to the truth that the other should be thrown out. But as a matter of discipline, it has seemed best to me to take as my regulating aim the discovery of the inner Hegel, the true Hegel, the one who has for so long eluded us all. And so I have tried to push my interpretation as far as it would go in the direction of actually uncovering Hegel—without deluding myself that I have gone very far.

The present interpretation has, I think, two signal merits. First, the losses from my interpretation of Hegel, I suggested above, would be more extensive than damaging. Indeed, what is lost is for the most part well lost. For by placing Hegel on our side of the linguistic turn, we can dispense with many of the philosophically most objectionable features of his thought—such as the supposed hypostatization of some suprahistorical Absolute, of a historicized consciousness, of an intellectual hyperintuition, even of a final standpoint in history. Indeed, we will be able to dispense with such "obvious" Hegelianisms as totalization and presence, at least as those have come to be understood today. *All* passages that emphasize these can be read, I suspect, not merely as rhetoric but as what I have called salesmanship.

Second, my interpretation presents a view of Hegel which is not only consistent with (many of) his texts, but makes him consistent with himself. It enables us, in fact, to overcome the infamous Left-Right split among Hegelians. In this split, which began almost at Hegel's burial,[74] the Right—including not only the "Old Hegelians" such as Erdmann, Hotho, and Marheineke but such "Neo-Hegelians" as F. H. Bradley and J. M. E. McTaggert—tends to ignore history—even (to use a word of Emil Fackenheim) to "flee" from it.[75] Hence, Right Hegelians remain fixated upon Hegel's System, with all its claims to universality and necessity; their basic texts are the *Science of Logic* and the later lectures. Left Hegelians, on the other hand, insist—with eyes to the *Phenomenology* and Hegel's other Jena writings—that thought is conditioned by history, and this means by the web of social practices that Hegel call *Sittlichkeit*. For without any claim to universality, human thought reduces to social practice, and philosophical discourse becomes a reflection on such practices. Because it is itself a practice—part of the very web on which it reflects—philosophy becomes a sort of *sittliche* reflection on *Sittlichkeit*. This leads to a renunciation of Hegel's final System as a "poetic of Being" in which Hegel "accepted the specific historical form of reason reached at this time as *the* reality of reason." Hegel's achievement is "not universal" and has "nothing, nothing, nothing to do with existence."[76]

A few quotes or paragraphs cannot hope to do justice to philosophical movements which contain thinkers as diverse as Hotho and Bradley, on the one hand, or Marx and Kierkegaard on the other. The Hegelian Left and Right are not in fact "schools" at all, but ways of reacting to a tension in Hegel's own writings. For he seems to agree with *both* sides. With his Left hand he writes:

> Philosophy is completely identical with its time. It does not
> stand over its time, it is the knowledge of what is substantial
> within its time . . . no one can really get out of his time, any
> more than out of his skin.[77]

And with his Right he tells us that his *Logic* is:

> The truth as it is, without husk, in and for itself. . . . When it is
> said that understanding and reason are in the objective world,
> that Spirit and Nature have universal laws, according to which
> their life and transformations produce themselves, then it is admitted that the determinations of thought likewise have objective worth and existence.[78]

This tension has signficance beyond Hegelianism. For the Hegelian Right puts forward as the essence of Hegel, in a complex and grandiose way, the kind of a priori thinking that David Hume called "relations of ideas"; while the Left would interpret Hegel as dealing with history as an enormous Humean "matter of fact."[79] Hume's conclusion, which I will discuss in chapter 6, was that reasoning about relations of ideas was empty, while reasoning about matters of fact was empirically conditioned, hence contingent and nonuniversal. It is impossible for there to be a thought which is at once informative and universal, which is exactly what philosophy was supposed to be.

The Humean aporia was not explicitly answered by Hegel. Certainly the discussion of Hume in the *Lectures on the History of Philosophy* is more of a dismissal than a treatment, and the discussion of "Empiricism" at *Encyclopedia* ##37–39 seeks to contrast it with Hegel's own System, rather than to answer its challenge directly.[80] The debate between those who believe philosophy can, or can only, be a kind of situated reflection, and those who think it should go after timeless truths, continues today: on the one hand we have Heidegger and Dewey, Rorty and Moore and Austin, the later Wittgenstein; on the other, Husserl, the Logical Positivists, the earlier Wittgenstein, many logicians.

If Hegel finds a middle way between the Left and Right, or rather outflanks both, then he will overcome as well the aporia with which Hume left philosophy, providing the answer to Hume, which eluded Kant. On the interpretation I will offer here, Hegel can do this because he is not trying to bring together, in that solution, two separate realms. He is not trying to reconcile God and history, for example, or time and eternity. He is simply trying to coordinate two different sets of words: those actually in use around him, belonging to a historically developed and continually developing language called High German; and the reformed company produced by his System itself, a vocabulary constructed according to procedures and warrants available at all times and all places. On pain of making the linguistic turn, then, we—following Hegel—can have our cake and eat it too: we can have both timeless truth and concrete relevance, both the *Phenomenology* and the *Logic*.

If the present interpretation cuts away much that is objectionable in Hegel and harmonizes the rest with itself, it seems to lodge somewhere in the middle of the continuum referred to above, perhaps approximating what Bernard Williams, in his *Descartes*, calls "rational reconstruction" of the philosopher.[81] There will, however, be at least one major difference between my treatment of Hegel and Williams's reconstruction of Descartes. For Williams, to reconstruct Descartes "rationally" means, in part, to show his thought to have bearing on contemporary issues and questions; the current state of philosophical discussion is assumed at the outset. Such recuperation of Hegel for contemporary issues can be fruitfully pursued, but I will not pursue it. On my reading, Hegel will in fact have relatively little to tell today's philosophers of language about the specific issues with which they deal—about reference and causality, about truth and holism. He presents instead a wholly alternative approach to philosophy: a different set of topics to treat and of ways to treat them. He cannot even, if I am right, tell us that what we do today is wrong. Like a good pluralist, he will leave the philosophical terrain, from Davidson to Derrida, essentially intact. He will provide, however, ways to organize it: to allow what seem to be incommensurable paradigms to understand their own commonalities, of approach as much as of doctrine. And as he does this, Hegel will point to other tasks and modes of investigation, will show their importance, and will ineluctably pose the question of why they should be deferred.

One question which this book cannot defer is that of why Hegel has been misunderstood for so long. The answer, I will argue, is a certain philosophical tendency to assert the conjunction of two claims: that truth is the single basic goal of inquiry, and that it comes packaged as "S is P" and derivatives (that it adheres only to propositions, sentences, statements, beliefs, and the like). I will call all such entities "assertions," and the general tendency "assertionism." Assertionism is of ancient provenance; as will be seen in chapter 2, in the writings of thinkers like Quine its double claim has the status of an obvious or trivial truth. It is, however, anything but trivial. The history of philosophy exhibits widespread rejection of its second component, by thinkers who claim that while truth in general adheres to assertions, the goal of *philosophical* inquiry is somehow different. Hegel is among these, but he is wrong. I claim here, as far as I am aware for the first time in the history of philosophy, that it is really the first component which ought to be rejected. The term "truth" should be reserved for whatever it is that distinguishes sentences which inform us about the world from sentences which misinform us, and philosophy should at last recognize that it has goals which are generically different from this. Among them, his own opinion to the contrary notwithstanding, is Hegel's. I will discuss that goal, and give it a name, in Part 1.

Granted that no reading of Hegel is ever more than one among many, the merits of the present one can be summed up in terms of Michael Inwood's sophisticated, threefold classification of norms for Hegel scholarship.[82] My interpretation, I suggest, is *intelligible* because it both explains how the System works, in greater detail than previous interpretations, and makes Hegel consistent with himself. It is *interesting* in that it absolves Hegel of several monstrously untenable ontological commit-

ments; reveals hidden relations among our own contemporary paradigms; and exposes their unsuspected historical affinities (such as those
between Hegel and Wittgenstein and Davidson, to be discussed in chapters 8 and 11). And it is as *correct* as I can make it, though certainly no
more so.

Finally: the present effort belongs within a body of thought first
adumbrated in my *Poetic Interaction*. I there argued, among other things,
that in important texts of the philosophical tradition reason takes three
forms: unsituated, situated, and situating. Unsituated reason attempts to
find timeless universal truths: Humean relating of ideas, along with
Kantian transcendental investigation, and what is traditionally called
"theoretical reason" generally—all belong to this form of reason. Situated reason, by contrast, makes use, for its premises, of truths that do
not hold always and everywhere but only here and now. Such truths are
important because such reason is also here and now: situated in a group
of human beings. When states of affairs repeatedly call forth a single
pattern of behavior in humans who confront them, I call their common
core not a "truth" but a "parameter." Situated reason recognizes the
parameters constituting a particular situation and acts accordingly. It
has affinities for what the philosophical tradition has, misleadingly I
think, called "practical reason."[83] The third form of reason, situating
reason, does not assume such contingent states of affairs and use them
for practical premises, but attempts to clarify and articulate them in the
first place, *together with their implications for practice*. In so doing, situating
reason, which has its historical basis in aesthetic reflection (especially in
Kantian reflective judgment), attempts to clarify parameters as parameters.

A "parameter" is a state of affairs, or more precisely the general
form common to a number of states of affairs, which can change in ways
that have implications for our practice (but do not end it altogether). To
understand how a parameter can change, we must relate ourselves to its
past: we must establish probable trajectories and mappings for how,
through what series of transformations, it reached us. The present situation must, in other words, be projected into the past, in a way which
highlights the differences of the past and the present without breaking
their continuity. I call such situating projection "narrative." Its aim is to
establish links between the unknown (because no longer extant) plenum
called the past, on the one hand, and present parameters on the other.
In the case of philosophy (as opposed, say, to the novel), those links are
to possess a certain loose plausibility. If I say (as I did earlier in this Introduction) that Aristotle relocated Plato's forms in things, what I say is

not strictly true. Aristotle's philosophy, rightly understood, does not exactly do that (it is possible that Aristotelian *noemata* exist, in purified form, in the mind of the Prime Mover, the way some Platonists think the Forms exist in the mind of Plato's God). And it is not all that Aristotle did: his philosophy has many dimensions beyond its transformation of Plato. Indeed, it is questionable whether Aristotelian *eidê* and the Platonic variety (to say nothing of the "things" in which they do or do not inhere) are really the same things anyway, given their very diffcrent ontological status. But it is *possible* to look at the Plato-Aristotle relationship as I have done; it is *roughly* correct to do so, even if far from true. And doing it that way shows us that Plato's and Aristotle's ways of thinking about *eide* each has an alternative: the concept of *eidos*, together with its associated practices, is something which changes parametrically. Narrative—telling a certain sort of story about a situational limit—is not the only way of articulating parameters as such. At least one other way is possible, which I call demarcation (and will touch on in a moment). But narrative is an important one. I will examine Hegel as the first and greatest sustained attempt to explore the capabilities and conditions, and especially the criteria for success, of philosophical narrative.

But precisely because Hegel is the most rigorous exploration we have of the narrative side of situating reason, he leaves out its third, demarcative side. This is the side that deconstructs, or as I prefer to call it demarcates, the narratives it spins. No situating narrative makes a truth claim: there are always discrepancies between the narrative and what it is about, discrepancies which manifest themselves when we compare the narrative with the original texts about which it presumes to tell its story, or with its own different stages. Hegel withholds all such demarcative gestures, with the result that his narrative becomes absolute in two ways: it installs a seamless web between the present and the past, so that the present can (in principle) be wholly understood through the past, as its result; and its plausibility claim is in this blown up into a truth claim: it claims no longer "this is one useful way to look at things as having happened," but "this is how it happened." In both cases, as I argue in the General Introduction to *Poetic Interaction*, freedom is destroyed. The Absolute, developing through history, is no longer a convenient point around which to organize an enormous variety of historical insights, but an actual thing that exists and governs us. That Hegel held back from this himself is something I hope to establish in this book; that he did not make it easy for others to do so is evident from some of the Hegel interpretations I have alluded to above, and many others as well.

In order to prevent this—in order to appropriate Hegel without being absorbed into him and his absolutization of narrative—we need demarcation. The ways and means of demarcation, in turn, have I believe been most rigorously explored by Heidegger. In order to be able even to write an introduction to situating reason, it will be necessary to examine Heidegger's practices of demarcation, and to do so in the light cast on them by such thinkers as Derrida, Foucault, and Rorty. I hope to do this in a future book tentatively entitled *Diakena: Heidegger's Challenge*.

Situating reason, then, must make use of three different strategies. In no particular order, these are narrative (keyed to and establishing the past), demarcation (keyed to and opening up the future), and a third, analysis—the simple effort to speak the truth about what presently exists. This book, then, can be construed as the second part of a three-part preface to an eventual introduction to situating reason. But it is also an instance of such reason, and hence makes use of its threefold rubric. In the "analyses" that follow, I seek to clarify Hegel's views on the basic concepts and dimensions of his system—its goal (truth), its form (thought), its material (words), and finally the dynamic interplay of all three. My maxim in these sections, as I have noted, is "expound Hegel." Though I cannot have gotten him quite right, I have done my best. Given the purposes of the present work concerning the Left-Right split, I have opened each Analysis with an aporia presented by secondary writers who interpret Hegel from one or the other of those camps, and show how his texts, carefully read, place him in the middle. Beyond that, while I have tried not to neglect major trends in the voluminous secondary literature, I have made no heroic efforts to be complete. My interpretation is only tangentially related to most others, and it seemed better to concentrate on its strengths rather than on their weaknesses.

The ensuing "demarcations" are designed to open up a future for Hegel by relating him to his nearest philosophical descendents, who are among today's Analytical philosophers. Indeed, in their concern for language and practice, philosophers such as Davidson, Quine, and the later Wittgenstein are not strictly speaking "descendants" of Hegel at all, for they have not thought through or gone beyond him. Somewhat as birds are considered to be not descendants of dinosaurs but smaller and more successful dinosaurs, so Davidson, Quine, and Wittgenstein are really smaller and more successful Hegels. The question is whether the larger Hegelian program, which occupies a different ecological niche, can be rescued from its perceived extinction and placed beside theirs. I argue that it can.

Each section concludes with a "narrative." Construed linguistically, Hegel may seem a strange creature indeed: it is as if the cold-blooded, all devouring tyrannosaur of philosophical legend had been transformed into a hot-blooded but peaceable diplodocus. But even when thus reinvented, Hegel has his antecedents. His views of truth, thought, and language all respond to writers before him, however little echo they may have found since. The purpose of the narratives, then, is to render my own interpretation of Hegel more plausible by showing that there was a tradition leading up to it, and to clarify aspects of that tradition for those who are, as I was until a few years ago, unaware of them.

PART   1

TRUTH AS
SYSTEMATICITY

1

Hegelian Truth:
Analysis

Aporia

One hundred forty-five years after his death, the issue of whether Hegel had a "theory of truth"—an argued set of criteria which specifies properties common to all and only bearers of truth—was still undecided. Admittedly, neither participant in the exchange I have in mind—that between Michael Inwood and Robert Solomon in the *Review of Metaphysics* in 1975 and 1977—denied the theory's existence.[1] But the possibility that there was no "Hegelian theory of truth" emerges clearly from their articles. Also emerging are some lessons which afford a hermeneutical basis for discussing Hegel's own obscure and idiosyncratic views of truth and its bearers.

There are several senses in which Hegel might not have had a theory of truth. One, alluded to as we will see by Inwood, is that he had a theory of some kinds of truth which leaves other kinds aside. Another is that Hegel has an account of truth which, for some reason, does not qualify as a "theory." And a third is that the account he gives is not of "truth" at all, but of something else. Without claiming to be exhaustive, I will organize Inwood and Solomon's discussion, and my comments on it, around three main issues.

The first of these concerns the relation of Hegel's putative theory of truth to more traditional theories. Of special importance, since Hegelian truth is usually understood to be some sort of coherence, is its relation to that philosophical congeries traditionally called the "correspondence theory of truth." Solomon claims that Hegel had a unified theory of truth which synthesizes, or sublates, elements of both the coherence and correspondence theories. Only so, Solomon argues, can Hegel's critiques of mathematical and historical knowledge in the Preface to the *Phenomenology* make sense.[2]

Inwood responds to this with the observation that Hegel is not, in that passage, appealing to a single view of what truth is and arguing that history and mathematics fail to meet that universal standard. He is, rather, claiming that historical and mathematical assertions are "true" but in nonphilosophical ways. In addition, as Inwood has it, Hegel wants to claim that mathematical truth, rather than containing any appeal to correspondence, is for various reasons too incoherent to be philosophically true (though coherent enough to be true in some other sense).[3] The correspondence theory of truth has already disappeared from mathematics for Hegel, and so will be of little use in understanding his views on truth in general: Hegel clearly, in the passage under consideration, refers to mathematics and history as containing types of truth different from the philosophical variety ["but the nature of such a so-called truth is different from the nature of philosophical truths"], so Solomon's point fails as regards scope: Hegel is not offering an overall theory of everything which happens to be called true. Perhaps, however, we can save Solomon's point that Hegel's concept of truth must incorporate features of both correspondence and coherence by reformulating it more localistically, so that it applies not to all truth but (say) to truth's specifically philosophical variety.

This revised claim must still be defended against Inwood's argument, noted above, that mathematical truth is not deficient in a way that requires, of philosophy, anything resembling a correspondence theory of truth; but such defense is not impossible. For one thing, Solomon's general suggestion that Hegel's view of truth (or, as now revised, of philosophical truth) ought to combine features of both the correspondence and the coherence theories is a highly plausible one. As Inwood remarks, Hegel "does not straightforwardly reject any conceptual system or any category. Rather, he preserves it in a modified form and a subordinate position (*aufhebt*)."[4] This general insight ought to hold for the correspondence theory of truth, for which Hegel, as we shall see, has high regard. Though the relation of his own view of philosophical truth to the correspondence theory is (as we shall also see) extremely vexed for Hegel, it is unlikely that he intended simply to cast the correspondence theory of truth out of philosophy without a trace.

Moreover, mathematical propositions are not for Hegel true, because they are coherent, though insufficiently; they are not, in the sense which makes for truth, coherent at all. The movement of mathematical proof is "subjectively" incoherent in that the person following the proof is told to make certain inferences and draw certain lines without having a clue as to how these will contribute to proving the theorem at hand. Its "objective" incoherence, apparently, is shown in that once the theorem is at hand, inference can stop: no theorem in mathematics pushes us on to prove the next one. Nor, we may add, does any theorem compel us to stop: we can always continue to combine earlier theorems with the present one to produce new ones. Hence, what warrants us to stop with any particular theorem—to content ourselves with proving *that* theorem and none other—cannot be its place in a larger chain of inferences. It can only be that, once derived, our final theorem has some other property, independent of that chain, which makes it valuable in and of itself. That property, if not its relation to other mathematical truths, must be its relation to some reality outside mathematics itself—in other words, its correspondence to such reality.

As Hegel puts it, a mathematical theorem itself is a "lifeless proposition":

> What is lifeless, since it does not move itself, does not reach
> the level of distinction proper to essence, does not come to es-
> sential opposition or unlikeness, and so does not reach the . . .
> qualitative or immanent [dimension], or self-motion.[5]

I will not stop to expound the Hegelian vocabulary here, for its words themselves—whatever their precise meaning—suffice to show that the passage is a strong denial of (philosophical) truth to mathematical propositions. Just earlier in the Preface Hegel has said that falsity, as the "unlikeness" between knowing and its substance, is the activity of "distinguishing" itself and an "essential" moment in truth, which is the "likeness which has come to be."[6] If Hegel's theory of philosophical truth is a strict coherence theory, rather than some amalgam of coherence and correspondence, then "distinguishing," "likeness," and the "essentiality" of both must be part of what "coherence" for Hegel is. But they are precisely what is denied here of mathematical truth. Thus, if Hegel's conception of philosophical truth is entirely restricted to coherence, then mathematical truth is a quite different kind and must presumably be correspondence (pragmatic theories of truth being as yet, as Solomon notes, unformulated).[7]

The situation now gets dialectical: Hegel's radical contrast between philosophical and mathematical truth means that denial of the correspondence theory for philosophy only reawakens it in mathematics. The dialectic continues: if it is present in mathematics, the correspondence theory ought, again, to be present as well, though sublated, in philosophy: for there is no discourse, however radically different from Hegel's System, that is supposed to remain unsublated by it. In typically Hegelian fashion, then, the sharp distinction between philosophical and mathematical truth turns out to mean that they have something in common; if philosophical truth is purely coherence, then what they have in common must be some form of correspondence. The view that for Hegel philosophical truth has nothing to do with correspondence thus refutes itself, and it seems that philosophical truth will for Hegel will indeed retain components of both correspondence and coherence.

The second issue of present concern throws Hegel up against contemporary logic. Solomon argues that, for Hegel as for Tarski, the theory of truth is expressed in a meta-metalanguage:[8] We talk about the world in some language, L; we make assertions about L (such as, in particular, that some proposition P is true in L) in a meta-language; and we talk about predicates in the metalanguage (such as "true in L" itself) in a meta-metalanguage. To "talk about" something is here presumed to mean making assertions that claim to be true of it, and it is the concept of truth that in the last instance produces the paradoxes that themselves call forth the hierarchy of metalanguages. In order to block out such paradoxical assertions as "this assertion is false," we claim that *no* assertion can refer to itself, that the assertion and what it is about must be in two different languages: the object language and the metalanguage.[9]

Solomon claims that Hegel employs this sort of distinction with respect to belief-sets rather than languages, and that in fact the entire *Phenomenology* is a series of what we might call metadoxastic reflections on earlier levels of belief. Among the difficulties that Inwood points out with this is that in recent logical theory there is an infinite hierarchy of metalanguages, since as Tarski showed the truth-predicate for any language L of order n must belong to a language of order, n+1—that is, to a metalanguage for L.[10] It seems then that the assertion that the System is true must be of a higher order than the System itself.[11] This leads in turn to two possibilities, both highly uncongenial to Hegel: either there is some further level of reflection beyond the System—indeed, an infinite number of such levels, each of which asserts the truth of the previous one. Or the System, which as we will see is intended to contain the totality of what can be philosophically true, is unable to assert its own truth—which would make that truth something nonphilosophical, at worst a mere "holding-for-true" or belief and at best a sort of religious faith.[12] It thus appears that the System cannot be a set of beliefs about beliefs, or indeed of assertions about assertions. But the System is clearly in *some* sense "about" beliefs and assertions, among other things, and we arrive at the apparently absurd suspicion that it is somehow "about" such things without claiming to say anything true of them.

The third issue has to do with the bearers of truth. Solomon attempts to extend epistemic and semantic concepts of truth developed in recent analytical philosophy to apply to beliefs rather than just to sentences and propositions, claiming that for Hegel it is in fact primarily beliefs which are the bearers of truth. Against this Inwood quotes *Encyclopedia* #172 Zus. to the effect that beliefs cannot, in Hegel's sense, be "true" at all. Hegel has, Inwood claims, two arguments for this, both of which Inwood characterizes as "unimpressive." One is that the content of beliefs is itself "untrue." The other is that belief purports to be an identity statement and is not. When I say "the rose is red," in Hegel's example, I am suggesting that there is an identity between the rose and redness, a suggestion refuted by the consideration that the rose is many other things besides red, while many things are red besides the rose.[13]

Unfortunately, *Encyclopedia* #172 Zus. concerns not beliefs, but what Hegel calls "qualitative judgments." Inwood's use of it to show that Hegel thinks beliefs are not true is more than slightly problematic. In any case, the arguments referred to remain "unimpressive" only as long as they are taken out of context. The second of them can be habilitated via Hegel's famous distinction between a "judgment" (*Urteil*) and a "proposition" or "sentence" (two possible meanings of *Satz*; I will translate it as "assertion" to capture both). While an "assertion" simply unites any subject and predicate, a "judgment" claims to present the same object twice: once under the form of an individual, and again as a universal. We may rephrase this by saying that a judgment, unlike a mere assertion, claims to give a *complete* account of what an individual thing is. The subject presents the thing as a mere *denotatum*; the predicate presents its complete nature.

This completeness claim seems to make judgments bizarre creatures indeed; but Hegel explains that the completeness of the account of an individual thing offered by a "judgment" is in fact relative to purposes at hand. Such judgments do not only occur in ordinary speech, but play a distinctive role in the fixation of belief: "that is a wagon," for example, is a judgment only if the nature of the thing has previously been put into doubt. That it is in fact a wagon is then a complete account of its nature for the purposes at hand: the judgment assures us that the wagonhood of the object is all we need to know about it; acceptance of it ends our present inquiry into its nature.[14]

Because the account is supposed to be complete, the thing is implicitly claimed to be nothing other than what the predicate asserts it to be: it has no additional properties that illuminate its nature. Because a complete account must include features that differentiate the individual in question from other individuals, the predicate must, when fully explicit,[15] be a concatenation of universals which, in conjunction, apply only to that single individual. Hence, there is indeed for Hegel, at minimum, a sort of extensional identity between subject and predicate in any "judgment." An immediate assertion such as "the rose is red" obviously states no such identity.

Hegel's argument is thus somewhat more impressive than Inwood allows. But Hegel's disdain for mere immediate assertions, evident in the passages where they are distinguished from judgments, indicates that, if qualitative judgments are not true, assertions certainly cannot be. Given Solomon's case that the "bearers of truth" must be either linguistic phenomena or beliefs,[16] *Encyclopedia* #172 Zus. might suggest that in fact Solomon is right: assertions cannot be true, and so beliefs must be. On the other hand, "the rose is red," standing alone, does seem to be the kind of immediate statement which expresses a belief, and Hegel's criticisms of it go to what is expressed, not to the expression. Other passages also suggest that beliefs (in the nonreligious sense) are not, for Hegel, true.[17]

But if neither propositions, nor sentences, nor beliefs can be the bearers of truth, what can? The puzzle is deepened by looking at Hegel's first "unimpressive" argument. This is not, as Inwood has it, that "the states of affairs that such judgments report are 'untrue,'"[18] but simply that the "content" (*Inhalt*) of the belief is untrue. And Hegel regularly, in fact, refers to "content" as the bearer of truth.[19] But what is "content"? What sense can it make to call it true? How does "content" relate to things like assertions and beliefs?

In Hegel's Logic, "content" signifies the determinate substrate (*Grundlage*) of some form and is opposed to "matter," which is the indeterminate substrate.[20] As this obviously Aristotelian terminology suggests, content is what distinguishes from one another individuals which are identical in form. We can expect, then, that what distinguishes *Urteile* from one another is for Hegel their content, and this would be not their form, but the specific subjects and predicates they contain. In fact this is the case: the content of a judgment is given, he tells us, in its predicate: it is the concatenation of universals with which the judgment accounts for its object.[21] It is thus tempting to see Hegel's account of truth as one of some property predicates have independently of their inclusion in judgments. But such is not the case, because for Hegel there are no predicates except in judgments.[22] Something else is going on, and the task of this chapter—and this book—is to find out what.

Though neither thinker discusses the issue, Solomon's and Inwood's positions align themselves along the famous Left/Right dichotomy in Hegel interpretation. Solomon's Hegel has a theory of truth which is universally applicable and in its own way timeless, sharing features with the pragmatic and semantic theories of the twentieth century as well as with Aristotle, Leibniz, et al. It is a theory which, on Solomon's reading, allows Hegel to condemn even mathematics as "untrue." Whence the warrant for this we are not told, but it can hardly be drawn from empirical experience and usage, especially in post-Kantian Germany.[23] True, Hegel's theory, in the final pragmatic turn that Solomon gives to it, leaves truth decisions largely up to the context and purposes of the moment; but those concerns themselves are projected by the overall set of human beliefs. This, Solomon suggests, functions as a sort of Kantian transcendental consciousness in that only by its operation do we have a "world" at all.[24] We may say that the necessary conditions of that overall belief set would constitute a sort of trancendental a priori cognitive grounding outside history, and that Solomon implicitly attributes this to Hegel.

Inwood's Hegel is much more situated. He accepts the history and mathematics he finds around him as "true" in their ways. In claiming that those ways are deficient, Hegel is criticizing not abstract theories of truth, but actual truths—and the mathematical and historiographical practices which produce such truths.[25] We could go even further and claim that Hegel's critiques of mathematics and history are "immanent" in the same way that the self-critique of consciousness in the *Phenomenology* in general is,[26] and in the way that the greatest of Left Hegelians would apply to capitalism. Hegel shows, we could say, that historiographical practice contradicts itself because it aims at "naked truth" but can reveal this only by investigating and reasoning; while mathematical knowledge is supposed to be, not merely of the theorems, but of the proofs which verify them—proofs which, we have seen Hegel argue, cannot do precisely that, because of their subjective and objective incoherence.

This discussion has led to no hard-and-fast conclusions about Hegel's theory of truth, but it does yield some suspicions in terms of which to approach Hegel's very difficult texts. The first of these is that Hegel's theory of truth is to a degree what Arthur Fine would call a "local one": there are different kinds of truth, and Solomon's attribution to Hegel of a "desire for a single all-embracing theory of truth" is at best suspect.[27] Second, Solomon appears to be correct in claiming that Hegel's theory of philosophical truth must contain sublated components of both the correspondence and the coherence theories. Third, truth must be applicable to (predicable of? manifested by?) the System without paradox. Fourth, the primary bearers of truth cannot, it seems, be assertions or beliefs, and we must understand what they are. And fifth: resolving the issues surrounding Hegel's views on truth requires us to deal with the Left-Right split.

Hegel's Account of Truth

We have already seen three different kinds of truth for Hegel—historical, mathematical, and philosophical. But his accounts of truth are still more localistic than that. Throughout the *Phenomenology*, Hegel uses "truth" to mean, simply, the result of each stage.[28] The usage is not foreign to his later works: as Hegel puts it in the *Philosophy of Religion*, "What stems from [rational development or] mediation shows itself to be the ground and truth of that from which it stemmed."[29] And yet Hegel also, we will see, talks about "truth" as if it were a single, definable property. Common to this talk is the basic point I have just adduced: that truth is a rational result or goal of some kind. Indeed, truth is the goal, we read, of reason; of Spirit as consciousness; of the Germanic world of modernity; of Hegel himself. In particular and repeatedly, he asserts that truth is the goal of philosophical inquiry.[30] Moreover, it is a goal that can be reached. That truth cannot be had even in philosophy was a common view in Hegel's time. His battle against it is the major theme of his early *Faith and Knowledge*, and the cudgels are taken up again later.[31] We can thus, in a preliminary way, characterize truth as *the actually attainable goal of inquiry*.

The different, localisic senses of "truth" are not, then, wholly heterogenous for Hegel. Even philosophical truth is a species of a wider genus. For, says the Introduction to the *Lectures on the History of Philosophy*, it is part of a single historical *telos* (*Zweck*) that philosophy be:

> The *concept* of the entire [historical form of spirit], the consciousness and spiritual essence of the entire situation, the *spirit of the time*, as spirit, present to itself in thought.[32]

How far that genus extends—whether it covers everything we might want to call "true"—remains open. For the moment, it is clear that other forms of truth not only exist, but are necessary to philosophy. Philosophy always remains directed upon its time, and on the extraphilosophical truths—the terminations of rational processes—contained in that time. This means that, though philosophical truth is distinct from other varieties, it cannot be considered apart from a broader account which I will call Hegel's view of "truth as such." My account of the nature of philosophical truth for Hegel begins with a discussion of those broader views on truth.

Those views are given most importantly in the sections on "The Concept" and "The Idea" in the *Encyclopedia* and in the *Science of Logic*, and in the Preface to the *Phenomenology of Spirit*. Hegel's standard definition of truth, there and elsewhere, is that it is the "correspondence of a thing with the Concept."[33] This sounds traditional enough, and testifies to Hegel's high regard for the correspondence theory of truth. For it seems to say that truth is nothing other than the *adaequatio intellectus et rei*, the correspondence of a mind (or, more specifically, of a mental content—an assertion or judgment) with a reality outside that mind; indeed, the only place it seems obviously to transgress that view is in the substitution of "Concept" (*Begriff*) for "intellect" (*intellectus*). But I will argue that Hegel intends, by that substitution, to attack the concepts of "mind" and "thing" that he thinks the traditional view presupposes, with the aim of showing that the thing in question cannot be "outside" the mind in question (which is not the same, of course, as showing that it must be "inside" that mind). Hegel thus attempts, to use his own word, to "sublate" the traditional view, critically transforming it into one philosophically acceptable, while retaining what he finds to be of value in it. I will discuss the three terms in which Hegel couches his definition, beginning with what he means by "the Concept."

Hegel's Concept

None of Hegel's terms can be understood straightaway in terms of a single definition and without reference to the whole of his thought; and this is particularly true, he warns,[34] of "the Concept" (*der Begriff*). In the *Encyclopedia* Logic, though, Hegel does give a brief (and difficult) characterization of what the term designates; I will use this text (paragraphs 158 and 160) as a starting point.

The fact that this characterization occurs in the Logic already tells us something about the Concept. As H. S. Harris has shown, from 1803 on, Hegel's entire system consisted in three main parts: Logic, which is the philosophical comprehension of thought taken purely for itself; Philosophy of Nature, which examines thought in the meaningless spatio-temporal dispersal which is the ultimate "other" to thought; and Philosophy of Mind, which considers thought insofar as, in human history, it gathers itself together out of this dispersal.[35] As part of Logic, then, the Concept has no immediate connection, as do moments of the other two parts of the system, to the things we stumble across in our observations (scientific and otherwise) of nature and the human world. It remains, Hegel says, "in perfect abstraction."[36] As logical, however, the Concept is also one of the fundamental structures of thought. It forms part of the indispensable *prius* to these other, more concrete activities of the human mind, which must make use of logical determinations if they are to be "thoughtful" at all.[37]

The Concept is not, moreover, prior merely to more concrete thought. It is prior as well to concrete reality: for what is permanent and substantial about things in the world is merely the rationality which manifests itself in them. The Concept is not, then, only "logical," as being one of the fundamental structures of our thought; it is "metaphysical" as well in that it also provides the fundamental structures of reality itself.[38] Hegel simply tosses this claim out here, as if it were something to be verified in the construction of the System itself; the one place where he gives a warrant for it is notably linguistic, and indeed Wittgensteinian, in flavor:

> What a real thing [*Wirkliches*] is truly supposed to be, if its
> Concept is not in it and if its objective nature is not at all ap-
> propriate to this Concept, is ineffable; for it would be
> Nothing.[39]

Avoiding (for the moment) issues of language and expressibility, it is clear that if Hegel discusses the Concept as a determinate phase in his

Logic, it must be a determinate, yet still abstract, form of thought which is manifested in both the "subjective" and "objective" worlds, forming part of the abstract basis of those worlds. To be "true" then is to conform to an abstract systematic structure.

There is more. Hegel's logic, like his system as a whole, has three parts, and "the Concept" is the last. It is preceded by "the Logic of Being" and "the Logic of Essence." These three main divisions can be distinguished, for present purposes, by the kinds of transition they contain. In all three, each individual determination is developed out of what went before, and itself develops into what comes after (in ways I will discuss in chapter 4). But in the Logic of Being these determinations cannot coexist: when one appears, the previous one vanishes, or (as Hegel puts it) "goes over" into its successor.[40] In the Logic of Essence, coexistence of a sort is possible. Each new determination is what it is because of a relation to another determination, and the relation to this other is then part of that determination itself. But the other is relegated to the position of mere *Schein*, appearance, while the determination itself is the "essence."[41] The coexistence is then one of overt antagonism and covert interdependence.

In the Logic of the Concept, finally, true "speculative" relations appear among the determinations: each individual determination relates to its other as other than it, and yet as essential to its own nature. Here we have a first, rough hint of what logical "content" is for Hegel. The content of a moment of the System is all those moments which are other than, yet essential to, it—as my heart, brain, and liver are other than, yet essential to, my body. What Hegel, in the first instance, calls "the Concept" is then, somehow, the totality of this type of thought.

Or, rather, this type of thinking. For the Concept is fundamentally dynamic, and at *Encyclopedia* #158, Hegel characterizes it as

> the independence, which is its own repulsion from itself into
> separate independent [things, *Selbstständige*]; as this repulsion,
> it is identical with itself, and as this reciprocal movement which
> remains *by* itself, it is only *with* itself.[42]

The "self-repulsion" referred to here is presumably the sort of logical transformation I will discuss in chapter 4. It results, not specifically in assertions, but generally in independent things, each of which is then the "other" of the whole. It is only by this process that the Concept itself is; its own development of otherness is, then, the generation of its content and the maintenance of its self-identity. Thus, the whole, its develop-

ment of individual things, and the things developed are all ultimately
unified into a single identity. I will express this by saying that logical
content is "narrative" in nature: it does not simply exist atemporally, but
is generated in a rational sequence. Because the sequence is rational, *post
hoc ergo propter hoc* is not a fallacy.[43] Hegel's philosophy is largely a profound and exhaustive investigation of reason as, in this limited sense,
narrative.

This enriches my characterization of Hegelian truth: to be true is
to conform, not to a static abstraction, but to a complex story in which a
number of determinations which make up the contents of some single
other determination are constituted as such by a certain sort of development. That other determination is "other" than its contents because it has
developed out of them, and they are "essential" to it for the same reason.

Constituting independent things via this narrative process of self-
repulsion, the Concept, Hegel tells us in *Encyclopedia* #160, is

> what is *free*, as *substantial power* which exists for itself, and is *to-
> tality* in that *each* of its moments is the *whole* that *it* is, and is
> posited as an inseparable unity with it.[44]

For present purposes, this means two things. First, as the organized
whole of thought, the Concept is to form the *complete* basis for both objective reality and thought itself: only so can it possess what Hegel calls
"substantial power."[45] Because it is such a complete basis, there is nothing outside it which could be said to limit it; if there were, it would not be
the fundamental whole that it is.[46] If it is in this sense "free," then none
of its moments can be brought to it, so to speak, from without: all its
determinacy must develop from within. Not that all determinacy has yet
developed in the Concept: the Concept, we have seen, is purely logical,
and hence abstract. The "completeness" of the Concept is just the guar-
antee (ultimately, I have suggested, linguistic in nature) that all determinate content is already implicit (*an sich*) within thought. Because its
determinacy is implicit within it, thought has no more need to "go over"
into otherness, or to define itself antagonistically to what is other. It has
only to develop itself, rendering its content explicit (*für sich*).[47]

In addition to *completeness*, the Concept also claims a sort of *necessity*. For its determinations are self-determinations, and because it is logical they will be brought forth in their necessary order by the process of
self-repulsion I have already mentioned.[48] In being brought forth in this
manner, each such moment itself performs that same kind of self-
repulsion. It is this necessary development which gives the Concept its

unity. For in stepping forth from what has gone before, each moment posits that as its "other"; but it recognizes that it could not be what it is without that other, and recognizes itself as being inseparable from (and hence as necessitating) its other. In its self-repulsion, then, the Concept as a whole maintains its own self-identity: each determination is the same kind of activity that the whole is, all are in that sense identical, and the whole is a "totality."

The Hegelian Concept has thus turned out to be a self-determining totality of thought. Its determinations are produced in accordance with dialectical necessity, and it is, in their determinacy, complete. The ways in which the Concept determines itself, the nature of the material that it organizes in so doing, and the necessity in accordance with which that determination operates, will all be discussed later. For the Concept sounds very much like Hegel's System itself, the subject of this book.

Hegel's View of Finite Entities

In the *Science of Logic*, Hegel says that the Concept, insofar as it attains to a free existence, is

> nothing other than the ego or pure self-consciousness. I do indeed have concepts, i.e., determinate concepts; but Ego is the pure concept itself.[49]

When I produce a determinate thought—when I think of something— my thought *is* myself, it is part of me, and I am determinate by its determinacy. Yet I remain also, always, the same self-identical thinking ego. In the same way, then, the Concept is identical with its determinations and yet remains the same in all of them.[50] Independent "things" would be contents of the Concept the way thoughts are contents of the mind.

But that way, as G. E. Moore pointed out, is mysterious.[51] In any case, such analogies, says Hegel (whose brand of idealism was unenvisaged by Moore), only begin to understand the Concept. They compare it to egos which are "finite" and find themselves confronted by a world which is other than they and yet determines them. Such egos are to be assimilated, not to the Concept, but to self-consciousness, which Hegel characterizes as a "return out of otherness" in that it moves back from, and reflects upon, the world as sensed and perceived. Insofar as it is finite, self-consciousness takes that from which it returns to be other than it, and is thus determined by its other—the natural and cultural worlds.[52] If those worlds determine me they must preexist me; they are not constituted as my others through any rational process of my own. If, for example, I happen never to have seen a desert, I am different from someone who lives in a desert; if I have grown up in one culture, I am different from those who have grown up in other cultures. I am inescapably situated in my environment and culture, and the brute facticity of this is without before and after: without narrative development.

This brute facticity is essential to the System itself. Hegel, in his Logic, uses the term "Concept" in two main senses. It is, first, the entire final section of the Logic, in which thought develops itself from within itself, in the speculative relation to its "other" that I have described above. The first of the three divisions of that section is, in the *Encyclopedia*, again called "Concept": it is "the Subjective Concept." In the *Science of Logic*, it is called "Subjectivity," and its first section, a general overview, is also called "the Concept." The succeeding sections are "the Object" (or, in the *Science of Logic*, "Objectivity") and "the Idea." There are thus a more and a less restricted meaning, for Hegel, of "Concept," and the question arises of which he has in mind in his definition of truth as the corresponding of a thing to the Concept. In "the Idea," as will be seen, the correspondence of thing to Concept is already present. If Hegel were using "Concept" in the larger sense it would include the Idea, and nothing could ever be false.[53] Hegel's formula must then refer to the "subjective" concept; and we can understand what he means by "subjectivity" here if we consider the nature of those things which, to be true, must correspond to the Concept.

We have seen that the Concept, for Hegel, is not limited from outside; and yet I have asserted that there are some things which must be outside it, in the sense that they do not correspond to it and are untrue. How can they confront it from outside without limiting it? Must it not stand over against them, as self-consciousness stands against its object? Hegel's answer is given most succinctly in the *Lectures on Aesthetics*:

> Indeed, the Concept, the truth in itself, is one thing, and the existence which does or does not correspond to it is another. In finite reality, the determinations which belong to truth appear as an externality, as a separation of that which, in its truth, is inseparable.[54]

The "existence" in question thus does not confront the Concept as something other than it because its determinations are the *same* (in several senses, to be discussed in chapter 10) as those produced by the Concept. Because the Concept must, when completely explicated, contain all essential determinations, Hegel can as we saw claim that these finite things are, in truth, "nothing" other than the Concept they have in them. What differentiates them from the Concept is the "externality," or separateness, which constitutes the form of their appearance.

As has been seen, a determination of the Concept is unified, both with the whole and with other individual moments. The separation which characterizes finite things is then separation both from other finite things and from the totality: what from a philosophical perspective are interruptions in the rational narrative. The result of such interruptions is that the metaphysical situation, if we may so call it, of the finite thing is one of isolated individuality, on the one hand, and external essential determinacy (in the Concept) on the other:

> Finite things are finite because they do not have the reality of
> their concept in them completely, but have need of others for
> this—or, conversely, insofar as they are presupposed as ob-
> jects, have the Concept in them as an external determination.[55]

This can be explained as follows. The content of any moment of the System, I argued, is a set of other such moments. Though other than the original moment itself, these determinations are essential to it and are related to it by a narrative process we saw Hegel style "self-repulsion." In a finite thing, self-repulsive unity is to some degree absent: some of what is essential to such a thing is other than it to the extent of belonging to other entities, whose relation to the thing is causal in character.[56] As causal, this relation is contingent: the finite thing stands at the intersection of a number of causal chains, any of which may at any time be broken. Whether the breaking of one of these chains destroys it or not, such a thing lacks the kind of narrative necessity to be found in the System.

If we abstract from these causal chains, considering the finite thing as an object on its own, then it is incomplete. Some of the content which the Concept specifies for it is missing (because it resides in other finite things). In addition, its causal relations have resulted in its having a manifold of properties not contained in its Concept. The finite thing thus exceeds its Concept in some ways, and falls short of it in others; it is "external" to its concept. That is why judgments about finite things can, I have noted, achieve only relative completeness.

Some examples may help at this point. One "deficient" concept is the animal species, which remains abstractly opposed to the individual.

At the end of the *Philosophy of Nature*, Hegel shows how the animal organism can resolve this opposition only by its death.[57] The highest form of unity with another that the animal can achieve is sexual congress. This affirms not the mating animals themselves as individuals, but only their species, that subset of their properties which comes to be in new individuals—their offspring—just as it was in them. Because Hegel does not accept, or indeed conceive of, the theory of evolution, for him the animal passes on its genetic material just as it received it: there is no narrative, no development. The species, correspondingly, is static and abstract; once it has played its part in maintaining that species, the animal dies. It, and its concrete life, are of no further use to nature.

In order for the externality between individual and Concept to be overcome, the individual must be set, not into a static genus, but into a dynamic network of concrete relations to other individuals; and this network must be such as to realize that individual's identity with its Concept, or its own "true" nature. A human being, whose essence for Hegel as for the tradition is thought, is able, unlike the animal, to realize that essence without dying herself.[58] But she can do so only in the context of relations to others. In the *Phenomenology of Spirit*, consciousness separates itself from nature and becomes truly human only in the act of recognizing, and being recognized by, another consciousness.[59] A human being alone from birth on a desert island would for Hegel never develop into a true human; she would remain animalistic, indifferent and external to her own humanity. If she is placed into human relationships, but into merely antagonistic ones (such as, in the *Phenomenology*, those between master and slave) she will also be prevented from realizing her true humanity—as are both master and slave.[60] It is only insofar as she can identify with her community—not surrendering her otherness to the community, but putting it, so to speak, at the service of the whole—that the human individual can fully realize her own humanity.

A human being in relation to her community can then approximate to the kind of self-repulsive unity with the whole that a moment of the System has with respect to its content. As a unique individual, she is other than her community. Because it provides her with language and values, her community is essential to her. And to the extent that she sustains and transforms her community, which in fact is nothing other than the common effort of the individuals who comprise it, that community is not a separate entity that somehow *causes* her to be the way she is: there is an unbreakable bond between such an individual and her community, and both will vanish together. Not all human individuals, of course, reach such a relation to their communities; and all of us remain animals and will finally die. When an individual has truly contributed to her community, however, her achievement will remain after her death, and that contribution is her real nature as human. The highest form of such contribution is the self-knowledge of the rational community: philosophy.[61]

A human being, as a Hegelian finite entity, is then a story. This is the key to Hegel's answer to the Fichtean social logic we saw him criticize in the Introduction to this book. For a human being does not *possess* rationality: not from the beginning of her life, or from the age of reason, or from the age of majority. Nor does the collective *possess* it, as something over and above the individual and capable of dictating to her. Rationality for Hegel is a process rather than a possession: it is what arises out of the transactions between the individual and her community, as the individual contributes something uniquely hers to the overall story of her culture. The Fichtean social logic behind the cold war, then, will not dissolve until such transactions, rather than economic production or military initiative, are seen as the heart of society.[62]

These examples and considerations, like much in this chapter, anticipate themes which must be developed later. For the present, they should enable us to see that the Concept, as subjective, is not truth: it is not yet its own correspondence with finite reality. The properties of finite individuals, such as humans, are in truth determinations of the Concept. But until this is made explicit, both in the development of the Concept and (in my example) in the development of those individual humans to the point where they can grasp their own identity with the totality, that content will appear in the separation and externality characteristic of finitude.

Because the Concept is implicitly the rational whole, finite things which are "opposed" to it are mere appearances; they are as Hegel puts it, "something subjective, contingent, arbitrary,"[63] lacking the permanent substantiality of beings which manifest the necessary totality of the Concept.[64] Furthermore, since the necessary whole is for Hegel not merely true but good,[65] such finite beings are not merely untrue but, in their finitude, bad (*schlecht*), inadequate in themselves.[66] Such finitude is then something which ought to be overcome. It can be overcome, for Hegel, because the Concept contains in itself all possible determinations, if only implicitly,[67] and thus guarantees the eventual correspondence of finite reality to itself. This brings us to the third major term in Hegel's characterization of truth: the "correspondence" of finite things to Concept.

Hegel's View of "Correspondence"

I have argued that for Hegel the Concept could be other than finite reality, without being opposed to it, only if the essential determinations of
the Concept were the same as those of finite reality. I have also argued
that, for Hegel, the finite thing can realize its own nature only by being
set into a network of relations to other finite things; so it would seem that
the finite thing can be resolved into the properties constituted in it by
those relations. If a finite being can be resolved into its properties, and if
those properties are the same as the determinations brought forth in the
self-development of the Concept, does it not seem plausible for Hegel to
say that correspondence of finite being and infinite Concept is, ultimately, their identity? It is, then, unsurprising to find Hegel saying that
nothing can exist "completely without *identity* of concept and reality,"[68]
or to find him speaking interchangeably of a thing corresponding to its
concept and a content corresponding to itself.[69]

Correspondence for Hegel thus seems to be some sort of identity,
as opposed to such modes of "corresponding" as isomorphism or resemblance. This only moves the question a step back: instead of understanding "correspondence," we now must understand "identity." We can
come to understand it if we ask ourselves this: Is it possible ever to attain
complete identity of reality and Concept? This question poses a classic
Hegelian dilemma: if on the one hand such complete identity is not attainable, then reality must always remain, to some degree, recalcitrant to
thought. Thought, for its part, will remain "subjective" and opposed to
reality, the "objective." Such was Fichte's view, and Hegel, seeking to go
beyond Fichte, disowns it.[70]

On the other hand, if the identity in question *can* be perfected, a
large price must be paid: because thought is necessary, contingency—
the inexplicable residuum of natural, brute fact—must be denied. Nature, which because of its contingency is "impotent" to display the Concept,[71] must be annihilated. Further, all human activities (except,
perhaps, pure thought) are to some extent enmeshed in contingency;
even religion contains a contingent, sensuous element in its myths, and
retains it even (as something which must be overcome) in its representational thought.[72] The attainment of truth would then be the instatement
of pure thought as the only reality; all else must either be destroyed or
(less apocalyptically) reduced to the status of mere appearance, with no
reality of its own.[73]

Once again we have the Left-Right split, this time in ontologized
form: for the perfected-identity position, the Right, the Absolute exists

and nothing else; for the other position, the Left, there is no absolute, not even in our knowledge. But these are not the true alternatives for Hegel; both depend upon a view of truth which he criticizes in the Preface to the *Phenomenology*. Taking truth to be the fully attained identity of thing and Concept would either mean that nothing, ever, was untrue or would admit the untruth of finite reality only as mere appearance, to be simply dispensed with in the final result—thrown away, says Hegel, like dross from pure metal.[74] Taking the partially realized identity of the two for truth would be merely the recognition that "in everything true there is something false"; and this, Hegel says, means regarding truth and falsity as "like oil and water": they can interpenetrate but not truly combine.[75]

Hegel's ground for rejecting both these alternatives is another invocation of narrative. Truth, he says, is not a static state of "identity" or "correspondence," but is itself a process which necessarily starts in noncorrespondence and moves towards correspondence.[76] This suggests that Hegel's use of the German *Übereinstimmung* ("correspondence") is best translated participially, as "corresponding," or even as "coming to correspond."[77]

Truth is not then for Hegel the simple identification, partial or full, of concept and thing; it is, rather, the complex movement from the one to the other, in which both degrees of identity are equally necessary and which cannot be understood in terms of either alone: in his early formulation, it is the "identity of identity and non-identity."[78] In conformity to Hegel's localistic views on truth, this process takes different forms for different types of individual—as, in my above examples, animals and human beings come to correspond to their respective Concepts in very different ways. In Hegel's view, the overall process itself, as opposed to the various concrete shapes it assumes, is not more perfectly present at one point in nature or history than at another. It is always present as just what it is: as the "eternally self-perfecting and perfected coming-to-correspond" of finite reality and the Concept. As such, he tells us, it is "the Idea," and "only as such is the Idea truth and the whole truth."[79]

Thus we find that the Idea, in addition to the ideal (*ideel*) content provided it by the Concept, has a real (*reel*) content as well: its "presentation," or the process of its development, which it gives itself in the form of externality.[80] This "real content" has then no true determinacy which the "ideal content" does not have. But it possesses as well, as the process in which the Idea realizes itself, the whole external dynamics of nature and history. *This entire process,* and not the "completed" system (as set forth in the *Encyclopedia*, for example), is what Hegel means by "whole" in the dictum that "the true is the whole."[81] The finite thing is *in truth* nothing other than its role in this process—but part of that role is to stand *in untruth*: to take a stand against the whole process, isolate itself, and assert itself as a moment against the whole. Only thus can truth be the process of its own development.

A moment of the System, similarly, is nothing other than its role in this process, which from that point of view is the Concept's generation of content, continuing until what is generated is adequate to capture the phenomena of empirical reality. "Corresponding" for Hegel is thus the convergence of two very different types of process: the systematic generation of content and the setting of individual finite things (in the climactic case, human beings) into contexts which increasingly approximate to the systematic narrative. This means that Hegelian truth, in addition to necessity and completeness, exhibits a further characteristic. It is the overcoming of oppositions: "the highest truth, the truth as such, is the resolution of the highest opposition and contradiction."[82]

This discussion of Hegel's view of truth has the following results. Truth is for him the corresponding of finite reality and the self-developing totality of thought. "Finite reality" consists in beings—sensory objects, representational universals, historical events, religious truths—insofar as they are isolated from that totality and external to each other. As such, they are not merely "untrue," but are contingent, inessential, and possibly evil. Their correspondence (or coming-to-correspond) consists in their arriving at a position in the necessarily determined network of the whole. In this they come as well to their own true identity—that is, achieve the content their Concept specifies for them. That correspondence is thus a process of identification—that a thing achieves its self-identity only in achieving its proper position within the totality—brings us to the heart of Hegel's thought. For it encompasses the entire sweep of his claim to be able to "do justice" to the actual world in his philosophical reconstruction of it.

This is a strange account of truth; its strangeness is further indicated by some of the terms to which Hegel opposes that word. These include epistemological concepts such as "certainty" and "opinion," which for him designate unverified and hence subjective cognitions. They also include "need" (*Bedürfnis*), which as I noted in the Introduction is the "untruth" of the subject and awakens in it the drive to truth.[83] Hegel's complaint against all of these, as characteristics of the subject in which truth is supposed to reside, is that they have not undergone the *process* of objectification which could render them "true"—just as correct representations have not undergone the process of evaluation of content that will show them to be concepts.

Truth is also opposed to bad (*schlecht*), inadeqate in itself. Something is "inadequate in itself," we are told, if it contains properties that are opposed to its concept. A sick body, for example, is "untrue" in the sense of *schlecht* because it has properties that do not conform to the rational concept of the human body; a bad man is "untrue" in that he acts in ways a human being ought not to.[84] Looking to Hegel's accounts of disease and crime respectively, we find that in them one part or aspect of a larger whole acts in ways detrimental to that whole: an inflamed part of the body, for example, or a criminal (who always, for Hegel, injures the whole of society, not merely the victim).[85] Truth is for Hegel also opposed to appearance, which for him is only some abstract side or other of the totality of a thing, perceived independently of the rest (as when a coin viewed from certain specific angles "appears" to be oval, though the totality of my perceptions of it indicates that it is "really" round).[86] In these cases, then, to be "untrue" is to be disunified or incomplete. To be true then means for Hegel to be a complex and complete whole, whose parts function in harmony. "Parts" here is to be understood diachronically: each phase of the existence of a true thing is such as to harmonize with its other phases, so that as the thing develops, its "truth" increases.

Philosophical Truth in Hegel

In the above quote from the *Aesthetics*, Hegel equates "the highest truth" with "the truth as such," and this gets us part of the way towards understanding the question of scope bequeathed to us by Inwood and Solomon. In giving an account of the "highest" truth, Hegel claims to be giving an account of "truth as such"—just as Aristotle, investigating the paramount being, claims to investigate being itself.[87] In order to understand Hegelian truth, then, we must look to that case in which the convergence of systematic moments and finite things is the most complete, and this is philosophy. In discussing Hegel's view of philosophical truth, I will contrast it with his views of religious and artistic truth, as presented especially in the *Lectures* on Aesthetics, on the History of Philosophy, and on the Philosophy of Religion.

Philosophy is the *highest* truth, first, in the sense that it is truth which knows itself, in its totality, to be truth. Nature, though it shows evidence of rational order and of the Concept, is hardly aware of this, or indeed of itself. In history, the human spirit is conscious of itself, but only of aspects (*Arten*) of itself. Only in philosophical science does the developing rational totality know itself in its entirety, or as absolute spirit.[88] This self-knowledge of absolute spirit must then contain all the determinacy to be found in the other manifestations of the Concept, and must contain it without externality and the resultant admixture of contingency.

The ordinary view of truth in art, says Hegel, is concerned with the correctness of artistic portrayals: the "truest" art would be the art which most closely imitates nature. Hegel finds this view of artistic truth to be no more than "correctness," or the traditional *adaequatio*. Philosophically speaking, artistic truth is nothing other than beauty itself, and this is the "immediate union" of the Idea and sensuous reality.[89] The work of art, in other words, expresses—straightaway and without the need to reflect upon it—the totality of truth.

Such expression, again, is a process of coming-to-correspond in which a finite thing—a stone or a quantity of pigment and some canvas—is shaped into a work of art. But the sensuous reality manipulated by the artist is, of course, an individual material object; and this means, says Hegel, that it is incapable of expressing the totality of truth as such. At best, the ideas expressed in art can only be the distinctive spirit of a particular historical people.[90] The development of art is an attempt to overcome this limitation, and one side of it is a succession of media, from the brick and stone of architecture to poetic language. When art takes language for its medium and becomes "the art of speaking" (*die Kunst der Rede*) or poetry, it becomes able to express "everything which consciousness conceives."[91] Truth gains the capacity to be complete—to cover all aspects of human experience—when it is expressed in language: for what cannot be expressed is for Hegel nothing.[92] In adopting language for its medium, however, truth leaves the purely sensory sphere and begins to sublate itself into religion.[93]

In religion, the Idea is able, in its universality, to find expression in consciousness: religious consciousness is an awareness, not of various properties of individual objects, but of the absolutely true as universal, containing everything within itself.[94] But religious truth, though it has true content, has it in the finite form of "religious representation," the highest form of what Hegel calls *Vorstellung*, or representation, in general.[95] Three aspects of the finitude in the religious expression of absolute truth will be of particular importance here.

In the first place, religious representation is still bound up with sensory or sense-derived content. But this connection is antagonistic. Truth, the religious meaning, is something to be freed from the sensuousness of its expression; and this sensuousness is to be dispensed with in the understanding of such representations. Thus, says Hegel, when Christianity speaks of the "Father" "begetting" the "Son," we are not to understand it literally, but to take it as a mere figure of imagination.[96] In contrast to art, where the Idea was in immediate union with the sensuous, in religious representation the meaning and its sensuous expression are thus distinct, even antagonistic; there is what we might call a "symbolic distance," a failure of convergence, between the sign and the signified. The religious standpoint itself is aware of this symbolic distance when it takes the sensuous element as something to be fought against. But in its struggle against the sensuous, it defines its own form: it reveals its dependence upon what it fights, and therefore points to its own finitude and contingency. It is, says Hegel, only (philosophical) thought itself which is able to achieve true liberation from the sensuous, not by merely fighting against it but by "lifting up the sensuous qualities of the content to the region of universal thought-determinations."[97] True freedom from the sensuous comes only from its sublation into thought—not from the struggle carried on against it by representation.

The second aspect of the finitude of religious representations of importance here is that, as finite, they are separate from one another. In the language of theology, says Hegel, we find that God is "all-wise, good, righteous," and so on. But these determinations are, he says, joined together merely by the empty "and": within religion, we do not find out how they are related to one another. Indeed, we find, upon examination, that they contradict one another, for if God is truly one, only one of them can apply to God, and to predicate any other of God is contradictory. It is only (philosophical) thought which is able to overcome these contradictions, by seeing God in the Concept of God, as a self-determining unity of finite and infinite.[98]

Finally, in finite representation, the object known—God—is presented as separate from the knowing self, which is finite and belongs to the finite world. This, too, is overcome in the philosophical view of God as the "union of finitude and infinitude."[99]

From these three aspects of finitude in religious representation, we can begin to grasp what philosophical truth is for Hegel; for it will be, in part, the overcoming of these externalities. First and foremost, it will overcome the abstract separation of knowing subject from object known—here, of man from God. Second, it will overcome the abstract separation of religious representations from one another—by setting

the determinations of God, for example, into their proper place within
the System. Third, it will overcome the separation—incompletely
achieved, yet always struggled for—of representation from the sensuous
with which it is bound up.

In order to achieve the last, philosophy must descend beyond religion to art. For in art, there was no separation of the Idea and the sensuous; the two were in immediate unity. Thus, in *Encyclopedia* #572,
philosophy

> is the unification of art and religion, to the extent that the for-
> mally external mode of intuiting of the former . . . is, in the *to-
> tality* of the latter . . . not merely held together in a single
> whole, but is raised also into simple spiritual *intuition* and
> thence into *self-conscious thought*.[100]

Philosophy, then, does not merely join together the dispersed
contents of sense-intuition into a totality of thought. It also retains
something of the mode of cognition to be found on the sensible level as
well—specifically, the type of cognition found in art. This is the cognition of the Idea in immediate unity with sensuous material. In philosophy, it becomes "spiritual intuition"—presumably, then, cognition of
the Idea in immediate unity with a spiritual reality.

Intuition, for Hegel, is the process of exteriorization of mental
contents, in such a way that the intuiting subject remains concerned with
them.[101] If there is such a thing as "spiritual intuition," it must be an
exteriorization *of* spirit which remains *within* spirit. Is there any such?
Language, says Hegel, is the only one:

> We know about our thoughts and have determinate, real
> thoughts only when we give them the form of *objectivity*, of *be-
> ing distinguished* from our *interiority*—only, then, when we give
> them the form of *externality*—of such an externality, to be
> sure, as bears the imprint of the highest interiority. The only
> such interior externality is the *articulated tone*, the *word*. . . .
> The word therefore gives to thoughts their worthiest and truest
> existence.[102]

Hegel's statement at *Encyclopedia* #572 that philosophy must retain "artistic intuition," but as transformed into a "spiritual intuition,"
seems then to point to intuition as linguistic: to mean that philosophical
language must stand in the same immediate unity with the Idea that the

work of art stood with it. Indeed, such "simple spiritual intuition" is
necessary for Hegel in order to remove, in philosophy, the symbolic distance to be found in religious representation between sign and signified.
We must be able, philosophically, to "think in names" without having to
think *about* them as we must in symbolic language: "he who hides
thoughts in symbols has no thoughts."[103]

The other two forms of finitude to which I have alluded in religious representation can be overcome by reconceptualizing God as the
Concept: as the self-repelling, self-determining rational totality.[104] The
grasping of this, as philosophical, is according to Hegel nothing less than
the development of the entire system from Logic through Philosophy of
Mind. It is then the presentation of the inner development of thought
itself, in such a way as to be a reinstatement and transformation of the
concept of God in its entire determinacy. This includes, ultimately, all
the determinacy of the actual world: for, as Hegel says, "without world
God is not God."[105] The adequate philosophical exposition of the latter
must include the former. In this process, the manifold representations
will be set into their proper places, and will thus attain their "true" identities. The System will exhibit the necessity and completeness found in
the Hegelian Concept, but in their most fully realized form.

I will sum up by saying that philosophical truth for Hegel, the goal
of his System, is the necessary and complete self-determination of the
Concept, not in nature, social structure, or artistic and religious symbolism, but in words. In this process, both (religious) representation and
words themselves must come to be somehow identified with that
thought. This entire development is then truth in its philosophical form,
and we may say that philosophical truth is, for Hegel, the necessary and
complete self-development of thought in words that somehow capture
representation. The nature of this self-development will be discussed in
chapter 4; the nature of the words and representations in which that
development takes case will be discussed in chapter 7; and the nature of
their final identification and "capture" in chapter 10.

If philosophical thought is able to appropriate both philosophical
language (words) and representational content without remainder, as
Hegel claims, then it can be said to be "complete" truth in the sense that
it is the complete subordination of these two spheres of finite being to
the Concept. It is, moreover, the *only* subordination of this type to be
found. In his discussion of Eubulides the Megaric in the *Lectures on the
History of Philosophy*, and building on his statement in the *Phenomenology*
that when language and immediate sensory experience diverge, language is the truer, Hegel goes so far as to assert that "when word and

matter [*Sache*] are opposed to one another, the word is the higher: for the unarticulated thing is an irrational thing [*Ding*], the rational exists only as language."[106] Art, even as poetry, was unable to achieve the correspondence of reality and Concept without violence to the latter, and religious representation itself points to its own failure to achieve correspondence with its still sensuous expression. Philosophical expression, Hegel claims, succeeds in this. But because it remains within the realm of thought, never getting beyond the "internal externality" of language, such expression is only the "grey on grey" of the thinker, which can produce a remedy for the world in thought only, and is only a "partial reconciliation" of thought and religion.[107]

The issues between Inwood and Solomon can now be resolved. Hegel recognizes various forms of truth, and to that degree his accounts of truth are localized. In its most general sense, to be true means to have passed through a development which fits one into a larger, more variegated and harmonious, context. The bearers of truth in this sense are not assertions (propositions or sentences), but simply things in general. Beyond this relatively empty characterization, accounts of truth must be very concrete indeed: for such things, developments, and contexts are many and various.[108] The highest, because most comprehensive and ordered, of human contexts is philosophy, in which thought develops itself so as to capture and organize the whole range of (relevant) representations. In this sort of truth, the "hierarchy of metalanguages" is replaced by stages of development: later stages, such as the System, are "about" earlier stages, not in that they claim to assert truths about them, but in that they can be shown to have developed out of them in certain ways yet to be discussed. It is with this notion of rational development-out-of (*Aufhebung*) that Hegel aims to replace, in philosophy, the traditional view of "correspondence"; while the organizing power of the System replaces the traditional view of truth as "coherence."

2

Hegelian Truth: Demarcation

The gulf between Hegel's conception of truth and conventional ones such as correspondence and coherence seems vast. How vast we do not yet know; nor do we know what must be transgressed if we are to demarcate that distance and achieve what Hegel apparently did not: to put his own account of truth into illuminating relation to traditional theories. A necessary task, because until we have a sense of that distanced relation, how can we even sketch the realm within which Hegel's views of truth, and his thought as a whole, belong and come to be? Without such a sketch, how can we understand either Hegel's thought or those of our own limitations which have prevented us from understanding it for so long? (For misunderstanding, we saw in the Introduction, reflects on both parties.) We must see what Hegel has to say about truth in the traditional sense of *adaequatio*; try and name—however provisionally—the space opened up by his own very different theory; and inquire why recent philosophers have failed to address that space. I will undertake these tasks here. The ensuing narrative, in chapter 3, will situate that space historically, showing that Hegel's views are the outcome, not of traditional thought on truth, but of a different philosophical story altogether.

Correctness

It is clear that a belief or assertion (*Satz*) can for Hegel correspond to the facts—or, as he prefers to call it, be "correct" (*richtig*)—without being "true" at all.[1] Hegel's usual characterization of the correspondence theory is that it takes truth to be the "correspondence of representation with the object."[2] "Representation" here fills the role that "concept" played in Hegel's own account of truth, as "object" fills that of "content;" but its signification, I have argued, is quite different. A "representation" is, to begin with, something defined as internal to the subject; the Concept can also, to some extent, be found in reality.[3] The nature of a representation, as its name (*Vorstellung*) suggests, is to present something other than itself. In contrast to the Concept, which is the result of stripping away inessentialities from external givens, representation aims at accuracy, to exhibit its object in all its "contingent and unessential existence."[4]

Because its business is thus to present something from outside, representation in general exhibits, in milder form, the three forms of finitude I have noted in its religious variety. Though nonreligious representations do not necessarily contradict one another the way Hegel claims theological ones do, a representation is constituted through its relation to its object, rather than through its relations to other representations. That object, the *Encyclopedia*'s general discussion of the topic tells us, is ultimately sensory, for representations generally derive from sensation; but as an abstract universal, over and above the passing sensations from which it is derived, a representation is not necessarily in the kind of conflict with the sensuous that we saw to characterize religious representation. Finally, the objects of representations are external to the subject as well as to the representation itself: I may have, writes Hegel, a representation of a house and beams—but that does not mean that I am a house and beams.[5] The gulf between myself and a beamed house is undeniable; but it is presumably not so wide as that between myself and God.

The "object" of a representation, then, is something other than it, something replete with all the contingencies and obscurities of our sensory experience. That object is simply "presupposed," not created or indeed even questioned, by the representation which presents it.[6] In virtue of that presupposition, the relation between an object and the perceiving subject which forms a representation of it is wholly one-way. While the subject actively constructs the representations by which it cognizes the world, the content of those representations thus appears to be entirely drawn from the world as cognized: there appears to be a one-to-one correspondence between the similarities that objects exhibit and the representations that the subject forms. The subject is viewed as merely passive, receptive of the content that comes to it from the object.[7]

The first point to note about this account is its sketchiness. Hegel does not specify the nature of the object of a representation, or that of its correspondence to the representation of it; and his account of representation itself is hardly very informative. Indeed, Hegel's treatment of correctness is not really part of his systematic thought at all, but is given in a series of asides or remarks, drawn mostly from student transcripts of his lectures and occasionally from his own marginalia. Hegel's own publications are remarkably silent on the subject: when he comes to his thematic discussion of "the Idea of the True" in the Logic, for example, he indeed treats various forms of finite knowing; but the discussions make no reference to truth as correspondence and in fact cover, not what makes such cognition true or false, but simply how it proceeds.[8] Similarly, when Hegel ends the *Phenomenology* in "absolute knowing,"[9] we have the overcoming of the subject/object dichotomy and so, presumably, of truth as correspondence. But the "truth" that is discussed in those knotty and elliptical pages is already Hegel's own sense of the term: "truth" as the outcome of previous stages, rather than correctness.

Does Hegel, then, tell us enough that we can know why he rejects the correspondence theory? In general, we could say that that theory, in Hegel's terms, presupposes an unbridgeable distinction between subject and object, between mind and thing. For that reason, it applies only to finite mind, not to the Concept; and what it calls "true"—adequate contents of a finite mind—cannot ultimately be so. Hegel wants, then, to replace the irreducible distinction of subject and object with the claim of their ultimate identity, and to make "truth" into the process of attainment of that identity. The fragmented stasis presupposed by the correspondence theory of truth yields to a dynamic of unification; the fragmentation is not denied, but overcome.

But *Hegel* has nowhere told us all this. As I have noted, he makes no systematic attempt to sublate correctness into his own concept of truth.[10] As far as Hegel's explicit treatments are concerned, the two concepts of truth are merely contrasted and his own concept is asserted to be "deeper" or, more happily perhaps, a "completely different meaning" from the ordinary one.[11] The assigning of "truth" to content and mere "correctness" to beliefs and assertions (*Sätze*) is not systematically justified but almost an obiter dictum, and this in spite of the fact that

Hegel's thought (as we shall see) offers a complex set of criteria for making stipulations of just this kind.

A new and perhaps bizarre suspicion begins to dawn. What if Hegel's own account of truth is so alien to the correspondence theory that it does not even compete with it? Swimmers, after all, can compete with swimmers; they cannot compete with skiers. What if Hegel's theory is so different from traditional theories of truth as to share with them nothing more than the word "truth," which names them? And yet swimming and skiing belong in a common space, a common domain of sport and recreation, where they can compete for our time and interest. Does "truth" name a larger space than we are accustomed to think, one in which both Hegel's and the correspondence theory can belong? What is it?

Let us investigate, first, whether Hegel's account of truth really is incompatible with what we might now call the correspondence theory of correctness. Because Hegel does not sublate the latter theory or even discuss it carefully, there is little hope of finding in him compelling arguments against it. He makes in fact two objections to it, neither of which shows that it is in any way "incorrect" (*unrichtig*) or even seems intended to do so. First, we saw that the correspondence theory for Hegel presupposes that cognitive mind is passive, merely receiving various properties and comparing them with what is contained in its representation. This account of cognition, he believes, is in the last analysis false, as is shown by the fact that many things go on around us of which we are not aware: even the most passive "reception" of external stimuli is dependent on our paying attention to them. So the mind is always, at least to that extent, active in perception.[12] This sounds like the sort of view Solomon attributes to Hegel, on which, as Solomon puts it, "it is the world that makes our beliefs true, but it is our beliefs . . . together with our desires, practices, etc. that give us the world."[13] Here, we would say that a representation is true if it corresponds to an object—but, at minimum, our attention is a necessary condition for us to have objects in the first place. Unlike Solomon, however, Hegel seems to be claiming that by "presupposing" objects, the correspondence theory denies this condition and hence must be factually incorrect.

But that incorrectness does not invalidate the correspondence theory. To "presuppose" something, in Hegel's Logic, means not to deny that one has posited that thing itself, but to ignore or sublate one's positing of it: "reflection in its positing immediately sublates its positing, and thus has an immediate presupposition."[14] The correspondence theory, understood in Hegel's terms, does not deny the activity of the mind in cocreating the world. It merely prescinds from that activity. Such pre-scission may indeed have its place—namely, when it is irrelevant whether we have posited the original content or not. Comparison of a representa-tion with the sensory object from which it is derived is surely a case of this, for whether we have somehow in the first place created or cocreated that sensory object is immaterial to questions of the object's agreement with our representation of it. By presupposing the objects of representa-tion, correctness merely refuses to ask where those objects—and repre-sentations—come from. It presumes that they have been constructed so as to enable true assertions to mirror reality.

This means that truth as correctness has limits, and this—not its falsity—is Hegel's real objection to it.[15] Those limits can be clarified from the nature of "experience" itself. That term (*Erfahrung*), Hegel tells us in his early essay on natural law, is ambiguous: it can mean either immediate intuition, a raw manifold (which I will call "experience$_1$"), or it can mean sensation which is supposed to be informative, to tell us how things are ("experience$_2$"). The objects with which representations are to correspond must be ingredients in experience$_2$, since they must give us enough information to enable us to judge our representations by them. But such experience contains, as constitutive features, universals: its objects present us with general properties, and alter according to gen-eral laws. We may say that such universals are for Hegel applied, in a quasi-Kantian way, to experience$_1$ to yield experience$_2$.[16] Hence, the cor-respondence theory, taking those "universal laden" objects as given, presupposes the validity of the laws and general properties in terms of which they are structured and experienced.

In other words, the main problem with the correspondence the-ory of truth is that it presupposes, does not question, the concepts, cate-gories, and laws in terms of which we view objects, merely accepting them as valid—the way we accept, on its terms, the objects themselves.[17] The correspondence theory, then, ignores certain types of question; Hegel's own kind of truth will presumably allow them to be asked. We are close here to the first of Marx's theses on Feuerbach, which asserts that Feuerbach remains content with merely postulating the category of the "sensuous," failing to ask where the contents of the sensuous world come from. We are also very far indeed from it, for while we can see that Feuerbach's category of "sensuousness" is very close to the formal objecthood presupposed by the correspondence theory, we do not yet know Hegel's analogue to Marx's productive human activity.[18] What is the origin of our categories?

The correspondence theory does not ask this question, for Hegel, because it is merely "formal." Is this formalism not implicit in its being a "theory" of truth at all? Does the problem not reside in its claim to give a set of criteria which will apply to any and every case of truth, which cases will differ from one another only as regards something immaterial to their truth, called their "content"?[19] Is the correspondence theory of truth not, then, both too abstract and not "formal" enough? For, as we have seen, content in general for Hegel is not wholly bereft of form, since it must have some characteristics which make it fit to receive the particular form that it has: to call something "content" is not to call it wholly indeterminate. Hence, though claiming to be a formal account of truth, the correspondence theory in fact deals only with the first and most abstract sort of form a *Satz* has, while ignoring the various concrete "forms" that are given by its predicates (and, in a *Satz*, by its subject)— viewing them as "matter," not as "content" in their own right. It needs to be more concretly formal, not less.

If this is right, the correspondence theory needs, not refutation, but supplementation. I conclude that Hegel believes that assertions and beliefs are valid insofar as they correspond to reality: he *accepts* the correspondence theory for them, with the single stipulation that it not be called a correspondence theory of *truth*. What Hegel thought about the coherence theory in its usual formulation—the view that what makes assertions, beliefs, and the like "true" is their coherence with other assertions or beliefs—we will never know. *For he never, not once, even mentions it*—except, perhaps, in his treatment of mathematical truth in the Preface to the *Phenomenology*, a passage which we saw denies that such truth is of Hegel's own sort. That the coherence theory should have been so persistently misattributed to Hegel[20] points, as I will suggest later in this section, to a fundamental parameter of our culture—one which we must transgress to understand him and ourselves.

The question of "truth" for Hegel is not that of whether a representation (or assertion) agrees with the object from which it is drawn, but of whether its content exhibits the sort of narrative identity with the Concept that I discussed above. Once we see this, says Hegel, our inquiry turns away from things and representations and toward the matter at hand (the *Sache*), which for philosophy is the concept of things. For the correspondence of thing to the Concept (in its Systematic generality) must work, I have suggested, in both directions: the question of whether some entity is becoming identified with its concept cannot be asked without raising the question of whether we know what that concept is, of whether it itself meets the standards for being a "concept." It is with the latter question, irrelevant to the correspondence theory of truth, that philosophy must for Hegel deal: an investigation into philosophical truth does not ask whether a concept applies to reality, but whether we are dealing with a concept at all.[21] Hegel says as much when he says that the business of Logic, and as will be seen of the rest of the System, is not to consider concepts in relation to the things of which they are the concepts but to regard them with sole reference to what is bestowed upon them by thought—that is (since thought issues concepts), to other concepts.[22] And the System evaluates those concepts, not in terms of what they can tell us about the world, but with respect to how they can grasp or relate to the true itself: to the developing system of concepts that constitutes, on its abstract side, *the* Concept, and in connection with history, the Idea.

Let us take an example: one of Hegel's, concerning the metaphysical debate over whether final causes exist in the world.[23] This debate, he tells us, was conducted without any investigation of the concepts of mechanical and final causality, at least with respect to their "truth." Once such examination has taken place:

> The objective world *may* [*mag*] present mechanical and final
> causes; their existence is not the measure for what is *true*;
> rather, the true is the criterion for deciding which of these ex-
> istences would be [*sei*] the world's true [*wahrhaft*] one.

The presence of examples of both purposive and mechanical causality in the world is a possible outcome of empirical investigation; the subjunctive *sei* in the above quote marks it as merely possible, as one among (say) four possible outcomes (both; either; neither). If that is the outcome, then both concepts are "correct"—that is, can be used to assert true propositions. The only question would be which concept applied where. But prior to that for Hegel is the question of which concept is the "truer." And this, he claims here to have proven, is final causality, which is the more complex and developed phenomenon, following systematically upon mechanical causality and hence constituting its "truth."[24]

We began with the question of whether or not Hegel has a theory of truth, and understood this to ask whether he has a general theory which is to apply to all and everything that can legitimately be called "true." It turns out that he does not, in several senses. For one thing, what he has is not a "theory" at all, but some sort of immanent conceptual construction which is to inform us of the relation of "truth," not to entities in the world—such as bearers of truth—but to other concepts. Whether we call it a "theory" or not, Hegel's account of truth excludes

from its domain almost everything we would ordinarily call "true"—
things like sentences, propositions, and beliefs. The exclusion, moreover, seems to be merely semantic: Hegel is willing to admit that sentences, propositions, and beliefs are bearers, but of "correctness," a quality
which coincides with what the correspondence theory calls "truth."[25]

But "truth" is not for Hegel a mere sound that has traditionally
designated one thing, and which he now wants to make designate another. It designates for Hegel—as for philosophers since the Greeks—
the goal of inquiry, and more precisely the goal of his own type of inquiry, philosophical inquiry. This sense of "truth" is more general than
the traditional senses; I will give more specific examples later. It names, I
suggest, the general area into which both Hegelian and traditional notions of truth fall: they designate the goal of inquiry, in this case philosophical inquiry. If this were *all* "truth" could be said to mean, then
Hegel does not want to change its meaning at all. He merely wants to
seek a new and apparently different sort of rational goal, and what he
really stipulates is not a new meaning for a property called "truth," but
the goal of his own inquiry. We may agree that philosophers ought to be
free to formulate the goals of their own inquiries, and that these may be
quite heterogenous in nature: philosophical inquiry has in general been
asserted to make us morally better, freer from trivial things, more se-
rene, wiser, and so on. If Hegel's goal can be articulated clearly enough
(a point yet to be settled), there is no reason for him not to pursue it. But
it does not follow that he is right to call that goal "truth." For "truth" in
the Western tradition, and in ordinary language, does mean more than
simply "the goal of philosopical inquiry." It designates, in general and
traditionally, that characteristic of assertions which inform us about the
world which distinguishes them from assertions which misinform us.
Hegel seems to have disregarded this entirely. Is he right to do so?

One way to argue this, with which English speakers are familiar, is
to measure Hegel's account of "truth" against ordinary language. I will
discuss this below, but with a different purpose from much of what is
commonly called "ordinary language" philosophy. For I will not consider Hegel's account of truth to fail merely if it diverges from ordinary
uses: divergence from ordinary language is a necessary condition, among
other things, of science and literature—neither of which is exactly foreign to philosophy, and neither of which would exist in its present form
(i.e., after Joyce and Einstein) without wholesale abandonment of ordinary language. But such abandonment is not a sufficient condition for
either science or literature, and needless innovation is usually better
avoided. Hegel's innovations with regard to "true" will be shown as

needless if there is another term which could convey his meaning better—that is, comes closer than "true" to capturing Hegel's account of truth. More precisely, since my investigation will be in and about English rather than German, what will be shown to fail will be the warrant for translating his sense of *wahr* by the English "true."

The other way to argue this will be pursued in the next chapter. It is to investigate whether Hegel's account of truth captures more from the history of philosophy than just the idea that truth is the goal of philosophical inquiry. Perhaps Hegel's views are not so new after all, and his innovations not so questionable.

"Real"

I will in what follows offer three words, all of which I will suggest more closely model what Hegel conceives as the goal of philosophical inquiry than does "truth." None of them is a perfect model; the first two, which I will discuss here, come from ordinary language, more particularly the King's English as expounded by J. L. Austin. The third, which comes from the history of philosophy since Plato and Aristotle but has been largely forgotten in the modern era, will emerge at the end of the next chapter as the winning, though imperfect, candidate.

In *Sense and Sensibilia*, Austin considers at length the adjective "real" as used in such locutions as "she's a real friend," or "these diamonds are real."[26] In the course of this, Austin manages to attribute to "real" a number of characteristics that Hegel attributes to "true." The first of these is that the term is substantive-hungry: we cannot know whether something is real unless we take into account just what sort of thing it is. "Real," then, does not for Austin denote a predicate that can be applied to any and every thing. As with the Hegelian "true," which assumed very different forms as the coming-to-identity of thing and concept, no general criteria can be laid down for what we might call an entity's "realness," and we can put Hegel's point about the heterogeneity of different sorts of truth in Austinian fashion by saying that truth for Hegel is "content-hungry."[27]

Secondly, the issue of the realness of a thing is raised, Austin says, only after doubt: we do not assert that the diamonds are real unless someone has questioned whether they are in fact diamonds.[28] This example not only fits Austin but parallels Hegel's claim, noted in chapter 1, that judgments are made only after the nature of a thing has been called into question. Austin expands this point to call "real" a "trouser-word;" such, he says, are pairs of words which function as do male and female (or as they apparently did in Austin's England): they are opposites, but one is primary, "wears the pants." In this case, the pants-wearing word is not real but "unreal:"

> A definite sense attaches to the assertion that something is real
> . . . only in the light of a specific way in which it might be, or
> might have been, *not* real . . . . the function of "real" is not to
> contribute positively to the characterization of anything, but to
> exclude possible ways of being *not* real.[29]

So for Hegel. It is one of the most general theses of the *Phenomenology* that consciousness begins in "untruth," which is in the saddle and drives humankind—fortunately, toward truth. And, in its progressive separation of the essential from the inessential, especially as the *Phenomenology* progresses, Hegelian thought would seem to be excluding various ways of being untrue, similarly to the way Austin's "real" functions.

In general, it appears that Hegel thinks we *should* use "true" the way Austin thinks we *do* use "real": to say, of a specific thing at least one of whose properties has been called into doubt, that it in fact has that property. But we are a long way from Hegel's conception of truth, as may be seen by substituting "real" for "true" and "reality" (or "realness") for "truth" in almost any of the Hegelian passages cited above. Three points, two of them left implicit by Austin, need to be stated.

The first is the general point that "real" (like "true") does not go with any and every substantive. Austin points out, as against what Hegel sometimes says,[30] that to say of someone that she is a "real" friend is not simply to say that she satisfies the criteria for friendship. The Big Bang satisfies the criteria for being a big bang, but we do not refer to what cosmologists talk about as the "real Big Bang" because there is nothing else that can even seem to satisfy those criteria. The fact that we use "real" (or "true") of "friend" means that the noun in fact covers two very different sorts of people: those who in fact satisfy the criteria of friendship, and those who do not but seem to. Like others of our categories, that of "friends" divides into the true and the false, albeit with a presumption in favor of the former when the term is used alone.

Moreover, in order for someone to be a false friend, certain things must happen in a certain order: the person in question must, at one time, have exhibited qualities I associate with friendship, and at a *later* time shown other, definitely unfriendly ones. It makes no sense to say of someone, then, that "she was a false friend at time t;" what we need to say is that she *turned out to be* such a "friend" at time t, which means that at previous times she exhibited qualities indicative (but, alas, not conclusively) of true friendship. Conversely, then, for the "true" friend: she is in the simplest instance one who exhibited qualities indicative of friendship at some time prior to t, and who continues to exhibit them at t (which will usually be a time when our acquaintance places demands on her).[31] Again, the appropriate verb with "true friend" is not the copula, but "turned out to be" (or "acted like," which imports other issues to be discussed later).

"Genuine"

Hegel, in the better moments we have seen, captures this with his insistence that "truth" is a diachronic predicate, referring to the entire development of a thing (or concept). In English, such diachrony is perhaps well captured by the word "genuine," which is related to "generate" and "genesis" and means that a thing actually comes from its alleged source or origin. A "genuine" friend is one whose friendliness comes from inside, or from the heart; to avoid hypostasizing such innerness, we can say that she is someone who has acted friendly from the start, or who has become more (not less) friendly as time has gone on and the stakes were raised. "Genuine" thus seems to serve better than "real," and certainly better than "true," to translate Hegel's *wahr*.[32]

The second characteristic, implicit as well in Austin's claim that we only use "real" after an entity's possession of a certain property has been called into question, is that "genuine," like "real," is what I will call an interactional predicate: the criteria for its use involve, not only properties of the thing to which it is ascribed, but properties of those who do the ascribing; and those properties themelves are developmental. On Austin's view, the use of "real" would entail, not only that the entity in question has the property ascribed to it, but that there has just been doubt among those to whom the ascription is made that the entity actually has those properties. And this means that the people in question have previously had a knowledge of the entity that was incomplete, perhaps even wrong in various ways. We thus cannot use "genuine" without committing ourselves to a number of propositions about ourselves and our interlocutors, about what we know and what we want to know, about where we are and where we want to go.

There is a third feature of Hegel's account of truth which Austin not merely leaves inexplicit, but denies. This is its positive side: Hegelian truth is not merely a means of ruling out the false, but (at least in Hegel's view) has a positive, specifiable nature of its own—even if this cannot be spelled out in a few short clauses. This positive side is not without relation to everyday language: when we say someone has "acted like" a true friend, we are implying that we know what a true friend acts like, that we have some stereotype or description of what makes a person a true friend. For Hegel, this description or stereotype is, of course, the Concept of the thing in question, and is given through the self-repulsive determination of *the* Concept, to be investigated in more detail in chapter 4. "Genuineness" makes no reference to such rigorously systematic criteria, any more than does our notion of "real." At the end of the next chapter I will introduce a philosophical term which makes good this particular lack. For the moment, we can say that Hegel's account of truth seems to be allied to the English "genuineness" rather than to the English "true" (or, perhaps, to German *echt* rather than *wahr*). May his System, which is to achieve the goal of philosophical inquiry and not merely talk about it, not be intended as a "genuine," rather than a "true," discourse? Would it not be validated, then, with regard not to what it talks about (and how truly it does so) but with regard to how it manifests and remains "true" to its own origins, however contingent these may be? Is not the Hegelian replacement of "talking about" by "developing out of," which I mentioned at the end of the previous chapter, an effort to render the System genuine in the sense just sketched?

The common space for Hegelian and traditional senses of "true" is that of goals of philosophical inquiry. They occupy, I have argued, very different spaces within that common field. But this has not been recognized: Hegel has persistently been viewed as seeking a set of assertions which will inform us about something (rather than misinform us). Why? Why does it seem so paradoxical that his discourse might not be after "truth" at all? Why are we so in the dark about what a nontruth oriented discourse might be, or about how it could possibly function? What limit has kept us from this, from understanding Hegel?

Assertionism

It appears that Hegel's choice of "truth" for the goal of his thought was misleading. But it has proven so in part, I suggest, because it contravenes

a view about truth and inquiry which, though rarely formulated, has
been deeply influential, in this century and throughout the history of
philosophy. I will call this view "assertionism"; articulating some of its
variants, if only in the rough and provisional way I will undertake here, is
a necessary step in demarcating the traditional theory of truth (of which
it is a variant) from Hegel's account. For assertionism is not only problematic in itself but blocks the very conception of Hegelian truth. It is
formed by conjoining two theses which themselves are susceptible of varying formulations.

(a) The inquiry being conducted at any given time by the assertionist belongs to a particular genre which has truth as its single goal. This
genre may be designated, in different types of assertionism, as "philosophical," "rational," "scientific," "logical," and so forth.
(b) Truth itself comes packaged in the form "S is P" or one of the various
logically sanctioned analyses and compounds thereof.[33]

As I have formulated (a), it is self-reflective: it concerns, not general truths about the object of inquiry, or even general truths about inquiry itself, but the nature of the current inquiry and the genre to which
it belongs. It is, in most cases, widely recognized to be counterfactual:
inquirers usually want something more than mere truth, such as money,
fame, power, recovery of their original relationships to their mothers,
and so on. These motives, however, are often regarded as base, which
explains the appeal to a genre. For insofar as the inquiry belongs to a
particular *type* of inquiry, the base motives of the investigator do not
matter: what qualifies *this* inquiry as belonging to *that* type is the way in
which it seeks truth.

An "assertion," as I use that term, is anything which in our ordinary speech looks or sounds like "S is P" or some logically sanctioned
compound thereof. Propositions, judgments, statements, sentences, beliefs, opinions, theses, descriptions, theories, and many other expressions are all "assertions" or sets of them. Many things are not: a sunset is
not, a bicycle is not, riding a bicycle is not, love is not, freedom is not.
According to (b), unless something is an assertion, it is not a candidate
for a truth-value: the truth or falsity of a thing cannot be investigated
unless that thing to some degree resembles "S is P." "S is P" here is a
package, not a form: it is what analysis ordinarily starts from, not what it
arrives at.[34] The architectural dictum that "less is more," for example, is
clearly packaged assertionistically, whatever its propositonal form may
turn out to be.

An assertionist need not hold that all true or false entities are from the outset packaged as "S is P," but will at minimum claim that they must be put into it, packaged that way, before their truth-claims can be determined. Thus, an utterance such as "a rabbit!" may be true or false, but we cannot know this (or which) unless we transform it into "this [entity] is a rabbit,"[35] with "this" perhaps amplified by various nonindexical ways of specifying spatiotemporal location. Similarly, as Frege's *Begriff-schrift* shows, an assertionist need not claim that such conversion or transformation of an utterance is sufficient of itself to uncover that utterance's truth-claim: an utterance may need to be transformed out of the packaging "S is P" into some other form in order for its truth-claim to become transparent.[36] It was a major discovery of analytical philosophy (which is not the same thing as assertionism) that our utterances often hide their logical grammar. But whether the actual logical structure of an assertion is best symbolized as ϕ (x), or as $\exists$ (x) or as something still different, assertions ordinarily come forward in our speech as looking or sounding similar to "S is P": "There is a cat," "Socrates is pale," and so on. Assertionism as I characterize it holds that truth applies to that sort of package, whatever is inside.

In sum, the assertionist holds that the packaging "S is P" is at least a necessary, if not a sufficient, condition for an utterance to make a truth-claim. Since by thesis (a) truth is the single goal of some genre of inquiry (to which the present inquiry, philosophical or other, belongs), all such inquiry primarily treats utterances which resemble "S is P": what I call "assertions." It seeks to discriminate the true from the false.

Assertionism is broader than the correspondence theory of truth: the coherence theory is also ordinarily couched in assertionistic terms, as maintaining that coherence is what makes a judgment, proposition, or belief true. (In this sense, as I have noted, it is not a theory Hegel even discusses.) And in his first statement of what he calles the "identity" theory of truth, Thomas Baldwin characterizes it as the view that "the truth of a judgment consists in the identity of the judgment's content with a fact."[37] (Hegel would of course disagree: such identity could at most be the criterion of a judgment's correctness, not of its truth.)

Assertionism is also more than a mere doctrine. According to (a), its self-reflexivity is mediated: the present inquiry, whatever it is, has truth as its single goal not through itself but in virtue of the genre to which it belongs. That genre can be specified more or less widely, and as the specification widens, assertionism assumes a sort of Foucauldian disciplinary function for discourse. If, for example, I say that my investigation has assertionistic truth as its goal because it belongs to the genre of language-oriented Hegel interpretation, the claim I make does not carry far beyond my own project. But if the relevant genre becomes "philosophy," or even "rational inquiry" in general, then I risk making simple claims about complex domains, and this is a way of disciplining those fields—of excluding certain types of inquiry from them. One of the most chastised fields, in this respect, has been philosophy itself; for as I will show later in this chapter and the next, philosophers have not generally viewed themselves as seeking assertionistic truth. To claim that they do reduces them, in most cases, to nonsense, and Hegel has often suffered from this.[38]

Assertionism also has effects beyond the disciplines in terms of which it is formulated because our beliefs about ourselves tend to color our beliefs about the universe; this is perhaps especially true of philosophers, who tend to regard themselves as exemplary rational animals. Given the exalted status of inquiry within philosophy and the Western tradition in general, (a) is easily generalized and reified to yield a variety of familiar views. If inquiry is, as philosophers like to think, the preeminent business of the human mind, then the overriding aim of reason itself is to get hold of inquiry's result, true assertions—rationality shrinks to the evaluation of arguments. The basic component of the "mental" realm, in which rationality resides, is then the psychologized assertion, or belief. If inquiry is exemplary for language as well as for mind, then the basic unit of language is, correspondingly, the linguisticized belief, the sentence. And if, as Aristotle surmised in the *Categories*, the structure of reality can be read from the structure of language, then the basic unit of ontology must be, not the thing, but the fact or state of affairs. The basic moral phenomenon, similarly, becomes choice: the undertaking to make true one of a variety of possible descriptions of the world. Communities and societies are then to be viewed as aggregates of such individual choices. And so on, through numerous themes that are perhaps too familiar to too many philosophers to call for argument, or even for detailed statement. Each such theme has its own warrants, of course. But they also, I suggest, have a global warrant in that set of views about inquiry I call assertionism—together with certain very traditional beliefs about the privileged, indeed exemplary, status of philosophy among all human activities.

So understood, assertionism, as well as its components separately, has been a powerful force in twentieth-century philosophy, particularly in the English-speaking world. Some of the forms it has assumed there can be indicated with a few quotes. Consider the first sentence of Quine's *Methods of Logic* in every edition from 1959 through 1982:

> Logic, like any science, has as its business the pursuit of truth.
> What is true are certain statements; and the pursuit of truth is
> the endeavour to sort out the true statements from the others,
> which are false.[39]

The genre of Quine's present inquiry, then, is "logic," with "science"
itself as the next higher level. That highest genre pursues truth which is
not only packaged in assertions but applies only to sentences. So, then,
does logic, its species; and so does Quine's book. The importance of assertionism for Quine is further indicated by the first sentence of the
book's first chapter, which is a lucid rephrasing and corollary of (b):

> The peculiarity of *statements* which sets them apart from other
> linguistic forms is that they admit of truth and falsity, and may
> hence be significantly affirmed or denied.[40]

In his 1973 defense of the coherence theory of truth, Nicholas
Rescher begins as follows:

> Philosophical theories of truth in general deal exclusively with
> the truth of statements or propositions—or, derivatively, such
> complexes thereof as accounts, narratives, and stories. Other
> uses of "true" in ordinary language (such as its adjectival use
> in contexts like "a true friend" or "a true line" or "a true art-
> ist") are beside the point of concern.[41]

Why other senses of "true" are "beside the point" is left unargued; but
since Rescher's claim is about theories of truth in general, it seems that
in his view no other type of truth has been articulated by philosophers,
so that if philosophers have pursued other types as goals they must have
done so without knowing what those other types are. Pursuit of an unknown goal hardly qualifies, it would seem, as "philosophical," and so
Rescher is saying either that the goal of philosophers in general is assertional truth, or that philosophers in general are not very philosophical.
In either case, assertional truth stands for Rescher as the goal of philosophical inquiry. This is the kind of claim I earlier characterized as "disciplinary" in that it makes a simple generalization about a complex field.
I will present some important counterexamples to it later in this chapter
and in the next.

Alfred Tarski's "The Semantic Conception of Truth" (1943–44)
holds (b) from its second page:

> The predicate "true" is sometimes used to refer to psychological phenomena such as judgments or beliefs, sometimes to certain physical objects, namely, linguistic expressions and specifically sentences, and sometimes to certain ideal entities called "propositions." . . . For several reasons, it appears most convenient to apply the term "true" to sentences, and we shall follow this course.

Nonassertionist uses of "true," such as those adverted to by Rescher, are not even on Tarski's list. A weak version of (a) is asserted near the end: "As soon as we succeed in showing that an empirical theory contains (or implies) false sentences, it cannot any longer be considered acceptable."[42] (Tarski's own theory of truth, of course, is intended to be empirically adequate to certain facts of usage.)

Tarski's "The Concept of Truth in Formalized Languages" (1931) is restricted from the second sentence to defining truth as predicated of sentences: "[My] task is to contruct . . . a materially adequate and formally correct definition of the term 'true sentence.' " That truth is the goal for setting up formalized languages—that is, for at least part of Tarski's own inquiry, is stated a few pages later:

> The sentences [in formalized languages] which are distinguished as axioms seem to us to be materially true, and in choosing rules of inference we are always guided by the principle that when such rules are applied to true sentences the sentences obtained by their use should also be true.[43]

The second paragraph of Frege's "Thoughts" (1918), which I will quote at length, reads:

> First I will attempt to sketch, in a wholly rough way, the confines [Umriß] of what I want, in this context, to call true. Uses of our word which lie beyond [abseits] these may then be rejected. That word should not be used here in the sense of "veritable" [wahrhaftig] or "truthful" [wahrheitsliebend], nor yet as sometimes happens in treating artistic questions, e.g. when one speaks of truth in art, when truth is represented as the goal of art, when one speaks of the truth of a work of art or of a true sensation [Empfindung]. People also prefix the word "true" to another word, in order to say that they want to know the word is understood in its authentic, unspurious [unverfälschten] sense. This use too lies off the path to be followed here; what is

meant here is the truth, cognition of which is set before science as its goal.[44]

Here, Frege advances the thesis that the kind of truth science pursues
(and which comes packaged as "S is P") is what "truth" will be as far as
his own project is concerned. Thesis (b) is thus advanced as a conscious
stipulation, by way of the exclusion of other possible senses of "truth."
Frege is not reporting a fact about his present project, here at its outset,
but defining that project.

   Assertionism is not always, however, so openly evident. Many
philosophical texts simply presuppose it unmentioned. More interesting,
in this regard, are texts in which it functions, not as a wholesale presupposition but as a definable, though not obvious, structuring factor. The
project of Carnap's *Aufbau*, for example, is superficially very similar to
the present reading of Hegel:

> The main problem concerns the possibility of the rational re-
> construction of the concepts of all fields of knowledge. . . . By
> rational reconstruction is here meant the searching out of new
> definitions for old concepts. The old concepts did not ordinar-
> ily originate by way of deliberate formulation, but in more or
> less unreflected and spontaneous development. The new defini-
> tions should be superior to the old in clarity and exactness,
> and, above all, should fit into a systematic structure of
> concepts.[45]

This aim is to be accomplished by using earlier concepts to construct
later ones, yielding a "genealogy of concepts" in which "each one has its
definite place."[46] The similarities with Hegel's project, as I have begun
to expound it, are already impressive; they will become clearer as my
account of Hegel continues. But the similarity masks illuminating differences.

   Assertionism informs Carnap's project from beginning to end, in
that it provides what he calls the "overall form" of his constructional
system. That form, Carnap says, is given by what he calls "reducibility."[47]
A later concept is constructed out of earlier ones if it can be "reduced"
to them, and this is accomplished by definition; it is in fact the business of
a definition to show how the sign it defines can be eliminated.[48] If, for
example, I define "man" as "rational animal," I have in effect shown
how every occurrence of "man" can be replaced by "rational animal,"
and have "reduced" the concept of man to the other two concepts.

Carnap has in this one important constraint which (as will be seen in the sequel) Hegel avoids. This is that a definiendum and its definition must "mean the same," which for Carnap means that they must both be satisfied by the same objects.[49] This, in turn, means that definition and definiendum must distribute truth-values equivalently: if inserting the definition into a propositional function yields a true sentence, then the same must happen when the definiendum is inserted instead, and similarly when the resulting sentence is false. The "meaning" of a concept is thus a function of the set of objects of which it can be truly asserted, and Carnap has in effect defined clarity and exactness as precision in the distribution of truth-values.[50] His undertaking thus construes concepts, including those used in its own construction, as having the sole function of allowing true or false assertions to be formulated, and is what I call an assertionistic enterprise. Hegel's System, by contrast, will view concepts (or words) in a more Wittgensteinian spirit: insofar as they cue or trigger certain patterned responses.[51] This means that, in spite of appearances, Hegel's project is *toto caelo* removed from Carnap's problematic and from Carnap's tools—so far removed that it cannot even criticize them. This basic difference leads to a number of others, of which I will discuss four.

First, since Hegel does not construe concepts as functioning like names, he is not concerned with the ontological status of whatever objects they might name if looked at differently. Thus, as he baldly states in lecturing on the philosophy of religion in 1831 (the year before his death), whether God actually exists is beside the point of concern:

> We do not, like natural theology, here consider God by himself, but in conjunction with the knowledge of God in religion; so all we need to prove is that religion exists.[52]

Second, the relations that may obtain among the objects designated by concepts constructed in the system will be of similar unconcern. Carnap's procedure of "definition in use," which is central to his constructional procedures, is concerned with how to reduce talk about, say, psychological objects to talk about physical objects without being committed to any particular views about how molecules in the brain may produce, or be, thoughts.[53] For Hegel, the issue is not how to construct one concept out of others without constructing the corresponding objects out of one another, but has to do purely with the way we speak. When we call an object "psychological" we mean something different from what we mean when we call it "physical," whether psychological objects are somehow compounded out of physical ones or not; and the important thing for Hegel is to establish just what those differences are. Hence, as Tom Rockmore has noted, reduction is not on Hegel's agenda: the various sciences are equally entitled to talk, and need not be legitimated by being reduced (or shown to be reducible) to, say, physics.[54]

Third, because Hegel is not concerned with issues of truth, and hence of scientific objectivity, he is also not concerned that the basic level of concepts denote experiences which are immediately given.[55] The notion of the empirical given, which was to be heavily criticized by philosophers after Carnap,[56] is doubly troublesome in the *Aufbau*. For one thing, as Carnap notes, our experience is actually more a concrete flow than a succession of discrete givens; we reach "elementary experiences," which give us the basic level of conceptual constructions, via abstraction.[57] This leads to the problem of how abstraction can do this without itself being guided by general concepts and laws, as is Hegel's experience$_2$, or how in the presence of such concepts and laws (themselves largely the historical deposits of abstractions performed and accepted by previous generations) it can be foundational.

Fourth: more puzzling than this grounding of the empirical given upon intellectual operations is the nature of the elementary experiences thus reached. As elementary, says Carnap, these are unanalyzable and hence have no "constituents or properties or aspects"; they are given, "as it were, only in point form."[58] So construed, elementary experiences cannot, it would seem, be distinguished from one another, since any distinction could only be made in virtue of some property that some such experiences had and others did not. Without such distinctions, only the most general predicate would, it seems, apply to elementary experiences: of each we could say only that it "is." The domain of elementary experiences thus begins to resemble the impoverished indeterminacy that Hegel, at the beginning of his Logic, calls Being.[59] Since Being marks the beginning of his own System, Hegel must agree that conceptual construction, of some sort, can begin from "point form experiences." But Carnap wants the beginning of conceptual construction to be, not a single concept, but a plurality of different experiences. How can there be a plurality of indistinguishable entities?

Carnap is saved from this problem by an absolute distinction between properties and relations. We normally view the relations into which an object enters as a reflection of properties that it has independently of them: if x is earlier than y, that is because both are temporal objects (or events); if y is between x and z, that is because all three are spatial in character. Carnap maintains that some attributions of relation convey no information whatever about the objects in that relation: that a "relational description" of a set of objects is possible which "does not make any assertions about the objects as individuals."[60] To say that an object is "temporal," then, is merely a way of saying that it enters into relations of priority, posteriority, and simultaneity with other objects (or events), and so on. This sort of distinction between properties and relations may or may not be problematic; it is certainly counterintuitive. In any case, Carnap's problems with the given do not arise for Hegel, who is concerned not with reducing concepts to an empirical foundation but with tracing their relations to other concepts. This is why Hegel, finally, does not have any of the problems that arise from Quine's arguments that "the given" is too indeterminate to bear the kind of foundational weight that Carnap wants to give it.[61]

It may seem that, if Hegel's project avoids these highly problematic features of Carnap's, it could provide an alternative to Carnap: another, less truth-oriented route to Carnap's overall goal of vindicating the unity of science.[62] Hegel would accomplish this by showing how scientific concepts mutually define one another, while not worrying overmuch about how the objects they (may) designate are related. There are, however, at least two problems with this view. One is that it supposes that Hegel's project will not encounter serious problems of its own, an issue which could be decided only by an attempt actually to carry through the Hegelian program. As such it is beyond the scope of the present book: all I can do here is argue that Hegel's project, on my understanding of it, escapes some of the problems that have traditionally been thought to infect it.

The other reason is perhaps already clear from my Introduction. In undertaking to examine the basic concepts of science, Hegel takes the view that those concepts are not themselves exclusive to science: they are shared with the larger culture. Hegel's own "unified science," as presented in the *Encyclopedia* for example, goes far beyond what we call empirical science to encompass domains associated with statecraft, religion, and art. A possible lesson is that science cannot be "unified" with itself unless it is also unified with the culture as a whole: that what unifies, say, high-energy physics with psychology may also turn out to unify it with abstract art and welfare reform. If such were the case, the *unity* of science would not have to be wholly sacrificed in the name of individual research programs or any such smaller units. But it would no longer be the unity merely of *science*.[63]

Stipulative and Commonplace
Assertionism

We have now seen several dimensions along which versions of assertionism can vary: they can be more or less global in characterizing relevant genres, more or less disciplinary with regard to those genres, more or less overt in expression, and may play more or less definite roles in structuring individual texts. I take it as established that behind these variations, assertionism is a basic influence structuring intellectual debate, for the philosophers I have discussed and many others. These versions of assertionism sound so different from Hegel's view of truth that it is worthwhile to note three features they have in common with him. The first of these is thesis (a): all the philosophers I have discussed, including Hegel, hold that truth is the goal of the present inquiry, be that inquiry "logical," "scientific," or indeed "philosophical." Second, all hold that what makes an assertion valid is its correspondence to reality: Hegel never even discusses coherence as contributing to the validity of assertions, and as far as many contemporary writers are concerned, coherence could be only (as it is for Rescher) a criterion of or test for the truth of assertions, rather than the definition of it.

The third similarity brings up another type of variation among forms of assertionism. It is that the writers I have quoted, again like Hegel, do not *argue* for their views on truth. In this, Hegel differs from thinkers such as Husserl and (the early and middle) Heidegger, who share his aversion to assertionism but argue for their views;[64] the assertionist philosophers I have discussed here, all of whom are "analytical" philosophers, also differ in this (as will be seen) from some of their forerunners among the British Empiricists and German logicians. When we ask why there are no arguments, reasons differ. Hegel himself, as the next chapter will show, has historical warrant for his rejection of (b). The other authors appear to have two sorts of reason why assertionism is itself merely asserted, rather than argued for: one is that it results from a stipulation; the other, that it is a commonplace.

Frege's acceptance of (b) takes the form, in the passage quoted above, of a conscious exclusion: the view that "truth" will mean what scientists (and not artists or "people") mean by truth leaves certain senses of the term outside the investigation, and thus amounts to stipulating that, as far as the present project is concerned, only assertions can be true. Frege assumes in this that the kind of truth which is the goal of science can be understood without discussing the kind which is, say, the goal of art, but his endeavor does not stand or fall with this assumption:

it invites itself to be judged pragmatically, by its fruits. Tarski, too, views (b) as a matter for stipulation, as he makes clear in "The Semantic Conception of Truth":

> I hope nothing which I said here will be interpreted as a claim that the semantic conception of truth is the "right" or indeed the "only possible" one. I do not have the slightest intention to contribute in any way to those endless, often violent discussions on the topic. . . . Personally, I should not feel hurt if a future world congress of the "theoreticians of truth" should decide—by a majority of votes—to reserve the word "*true*" for one of the non-classical conceptions, and should suggest another word, say "*frue*," for the conception considered here.[65]

This, of course, is exactly what Hegel did—though by decree rather than vote, and with "correct" doing duty for "frue." I will call Frege and Tarski's variety of assertionism "stipulative" assertionism. In such assertionism, (b) is advanced as a local convention: the view that the goal of inquiry comes packaged as "S is P" helps define the present project, and is not viewed as stating a fact either about assertions or about truth itself.

Stipulative assertionism seems to survive in Rescher's explicit dismissal of the "adjectival" use as "beside the point of concern."[66] In fact it does not, because the concern in question is not Rescher's own but that of "philosophical theories of truth in general." Rescher is not making a stipulation, but reporting what he believes to be a fact; since no evidence or argument is offered, the fact is presumably apparent to all (which perhaps renders it unique among facts about philosophy). In the passages quoted from Quine, all trace of stipulation is absent. The restriction of the goal of inquiry to packages of the form "S is P" needs only to be stated, apparently, for its truth to be accepted. In both these more recent writers, then, assertionism is presented as an obvious fact, or (as Gerold Prauss has noted) has the status of a commonplace.[67] We thus have two varieties of assertionism: the kind which stipulates (b) as holding for the present investigation, and the kind which presents it as a fact in need of no argument. I will call the latter type of assertionism "commonplace assertionism."

It is not new with Quine. It is at the root of Schelling's famous attacks on Hegel, which simply presuppose that Hegel's System is a science of essences, which according to Schelling means that it treats ultimately of God: in any case it must "treat of," claim to be true of, something.[68] Commonplace assertionism has continued to play its role in

the Hegelian secondary literature: in fostering the myth of the "speculative sentence," which I will discuss in a footnote to chapter 4, and in the
recent spate of attempts, which I will discuss in chapter 4 itself, to capture the dialectics of Hegel's System in variants of contemporary propositional calculi.

Commonplace assertionism seems to suggest that assertionism is
trivially true; but we may take it that such is not the case. It was not the
case when Frege and Tarski wrote, or they would not have been so self-
conscious in their stipulating. It is (in fact) quite easy to think of inquiry
as having goals other than a set of true assertions, such as emancipation,
moral betterment of one sort or another, personal enrichment, fame, or
any of a variety of nonassertionistic construals of truth (such as artistic
truth).[69] Indeed, few assertionists would deny that philosophy and other
forms of inquiry have such goals; they would claim, however, that those
goals are ulterior to the first and main one, which is the securing, if possible, of true asssertions.

Granted that assertionism is not trivially true, what sort of warrant does it have? The question is ill-posed: since by definition a commonplace is not argued for, warrant for it will not be found in the texts
of commonplace assertionists and we must ask, not what that warrant is,
but what it might be. It might be, for example, that commonplace assertionists think that "truth" is a property which can simply be immediately
known to apply only to assertions. But that places them in the position of
claiming that at least some nontrivial, and indeed nonempirical, propositions can be established by immediate intuition (for who has ever seen
truth itself?).

A more respectable reason for failure to question such a commonplace is, I think, that we hold issues concerning it to have been settled previously: we appeal, not to intuition, but to tradition. If there is a
hidden appeal to tradition, or to history, at the base of commonplace
assertionism, it seems that it could take one of three forms:

(1) First, we might say that the issue has been argued sufficiently, that the
debates are a matter of accessible scholarly record, and that the record
shows one side to have won. In this regard, I will consider the arguments for assertionism recorded in two earlier writers, one Hegel's
predecessor, the other his immediate successor: Locke and Bolzano.

(2) A second sort of historical appeal might be to the tacit set of unknown
decisions and unrecovered debates that has, over time, constituted our
culture and language. I will discuss this in connection with Locke's appeal to ordinary language as criterion for the philosophical uses of
"true."

(3) The third stategy would be a hybrid of the other two: an appeal to the history of philosophy, not as a record of recoverable debates, but as a repository of general consensus among philosophers. Assertionism is then the result of an unknown decision, on unrecovered grounds, which is a condition not of the general culture but of an expert tradition within that culture.

I will discuss these three types of appeal in turn, arguing that none of them can establish assertionism. It is not the business of demarcation to prove assertions, and I will not attempt to demonstrate that assertionism is false; indeed in its stipulative variety it *cannot* be false. But it may be questionable, and that question will show us room for Hegel.

(1) Locke and Bolzano's common claim is that statements claiming genuineness (a concept related, we saw, to Hegel's sense of "truth") can be reduced to propositions which can be assertionistically true or false: they argue that "S is a genuine P" can be rewritten in such a way as to eliminate "genuine." Thus, Locke, in his *Essay Concerning Human Understanding*, discusses something he calls "metaphysical truth."[70] In this sense of the term, all things are said to be true insofar as they are what they are—that is, insofar as they exist. If this were all there is to metaphysical truth, then it would simply be the same thing as being (or existence) itself; the concept would indeed be useless. But more is at issue for Locke because we sometimes, he thinks, judge the truth of things against our ideas, "looked upon as a standard for that truth"—which, he says, amounts to making a "mental proposition" about them, though a usually unnoticed one. The ideas against which we evaluate things for their metaphysical truth are, presumably, our ideas about what those things should be, and this assimilates the concept to Hegel's view of truth as the corresponding of thing and concept.[71] To have metaphysical truth, we can say, is "genuinely" to be some sort of thing; and any sentence which asserts that "S is a genuine P" turns out to mean "I (the speaker) have certain ideas about what it is to be a P, and S matches them."

Bolzano argues similarly in §24 of his *Wissenschaftslehre*.[72] He begins there with the traditional view of truth and derives three more senses of the term from it: that in which we say of a true proposition that it is a "truth"; that in which we say of the judgment (*Urteil*) that expresses such a proposition that it too is a "truth"; and that in which we say of a totality of such propositions that they are "the truth" (as in Christ's claim that he came into the world to bear witness to the truth). In addition to this orderly tetrad, however, there is a fifth sense: one which applies "true" not to propositions or sentences, but to any object at all, "when one wishes to express that such an object really is what it ought to be in accordance with the name we are giving it at the time."

This meaning of "true" (which enables us to come up with locutions such as "a true lie") is merely a short way of asserting a propositional truth: it functions as a "mere abbreviation" (*bloße Abkürzerung*). For if I say, "this is the true God," what I am really asserting is "the proposition that this entity is God does not merely seem to be true, but really is true." As with "real" on Austin's account, and "true" on Hegel's, this sense of the term is appropriate when it has been questioned whether or not an entity really has some property. As with Locke's metaphysical truth, it claims that the entity in fact measures up to a standard, though the standard in question is given for Bolzano (as for Hegel) in language, not in our ideas.

On both the Lockean and Bolzanean accounts, these standards are presupposed: whether the criteria for the "true God"—that is, the criteria for God—are themselves the right criteria is not questioned, and so Hegel would claim that they do not touch his concept of truth.[73] As regards not the criteria but the objects which come under them, the Lockean and Bolzanean accounts have difficulty in capturing the temporal and interactionist aspects of Hegelian truth. The difficulty can be shown, I think, to make the capture impractical, if not impossible. We can see this by considering what would be required to put "x is a genuine q," in its Hegelian sense, into an unsophisticated version of second order predicate calculus in such a way as to eliminate "genuine." Here, as elsewhere in this book, I will keep my "formal" rewritings as close as possible to the original English they rewrite, at the cost of strict adherence to logical convention. My claim is that if these minimal departures from natural language cannot capture certain of its features, further advance into the symbolic economy will probably not help.

Let {c} be the set of necessary and sufficient properties for an entity's possessing the complex property q, and let "p" designate any property. Then we may write "qx" in a way which captures the complexity of q by writing:

1. $(x) \{q(x) \text{ iff } (p) [(p \ \varepsilon \ \{c\}) \rightarrow p(x)]\}$

meaning that if any property p belongs to {c}, then x has p.

One function of "genuine" in such a case would be to indicate that x has, over time, come to exhibit more and more of the properties belonging to {c}. We can capture this by saying that there is some subset {k} of {c} such that the members of {k} together give a set of necessary but not sufficient conditions for something being q. We can begin to capture the developmental aspect of genuineness ("gen") by writing:

2. (x) gen q(x) iff (p) {[(p ε {k}) → (p(x) at time t)] • [(p ε {c}) → (p(x) at t+n)]}

The development here would be from manifesting some of the criteria for q to manifesting all of them. This is already rather complex, but fidelity to what we mean by "genuine" will require still more complexity in three major respects. Since my main point is not that capturing these respects in a formal structure like the predicate calculus is impossible but that it is too cumbersome to be worth the effort, I will not make that effort: I will keep my discussion colloquial (though sufficiently detailed, I hope, to state the case).

The first two of these respects derive from the work of Eleanor Rosch.[74] First, observed qualities of an object are often attributed to that object only if they are observed in certain sorts of context. Thus, if a person always greets me with a wide smile, I may take this as evidence that she is a friend—unless, for example, she is the regular stewardess on the airliner I take as part of my weekly commute, in which case the smile is (probably) a mere part of her job. In neither case is the smile either a necessary or a sufficient condition of friendship, though in the right circumstances it doubtless indicates it. We cannot, therefore, simply take "greets me with a smile" and place it as a member of {k}; we must also specify the context in which the greeting occurs, in such a way as to exclude such possibilities as professional courtesy. No doubt this can be done; but to do it will require supplementing each member of {k} with a number, perhaps a large number, of further sentences specifying the contexts in which it counts as a member of {k}.

Second, it appears from Rosch's work to be an empirical fact that people do not know all the components of {c} for the various properties they attribute to people and things, and hence are at times unsure whether an observed quality of another person, regardless of the context in which it is observed, belongs to {k} or not. In such cases, they must ask themselves whether that quality is to be admitted into {c}: making genuine friends often involves forming, or revising, one s personal concept of "friend," and so then does asserting that someone is a "genuine" friend. In such cases, capturing that sort of assertion will require us to enumerate, for each case, those qualities that we did not at first take as indicative of friendship, specifying that they have subsequently come to be included in {c}. If we want to escape such cumbersome enumeration, we will have to find some general rules for such inclusion, and include them as part of our formal apparatus, since part of what is meant by "genuine" is that {c} was itself formed in accordance with those rules. Neither of these strategies would be very easy or simple, however.

Third, once we have loosened {k} to include, not necessary conditions for friendhood but indications relevant to it, {k} may not in fact be a subset of {c}. Indeed, {k}, as the earlier set of properties relevant to friendliness, may contain properties that suggest, not friendship, but the reverse (this is the qualification promised in footnote 29): consider "I thought my new superior was going to be a tyrant when I first met her, but she has turned out to be a real friend." This is fully and quickly intelligible, but what it says is that the process of turning out to be a friend began, not with a set of properties that inconclusively indicated friendhood, but with a set that in fact inconclusively indicated unfriendliness. Some of those properties may, on better acquaintance, cease to be ascribed to the person in question: what appeared to be an angry grimace may turn out to have been a mere nervous tic or the result of a major provocation; others, such as a curt greeting, may continue to be attributed to the person but be given less weight than other, deeper factors. {k} itself, in other words, changes over time, coming eventually—perhaps—to coincide with {c} (which itself may be changing); and to capture "x is a genuine q," we need to specify those changes, which are not changes in x but in our view of what constitutes q.

To capture this, we either need a further set of sentences, specifying which members of {k} have over time became falsified or unweighted, and perhaps as well what other qualities of the person have been admitted to {k}. Or we must (as in the second example above), resort to writing rules. For if our weightings are to be rational, those properties we come to reject or overlook must have been falsified in certain regular ways. The random presence or, later, absence of a scowl, for example, will not lead us to overlook that scowl in assessing the friendliness of another. We need some sort of general explanation of the scowl which shows that it is not indicative of the other's character or deeper feelings. Hence, we must include in our formal statement a set of general rules for weighting properties as indicative of friendship.

The weighting is done by the individual who is coming to know the other. This brings us to an entirely different set of issues that would have to be considered in completing the formalization envisaged: for a member p of {k} to "indicate" q to another person, that other person must know (or think) that p(x). We never know other people (or even ourselves) completely, and any assertion that someone is a "genuine friend" is always conditioned by the incomplete sum-total of the knowledge I happen to have acquired about that person. There will have to be further propositions added into {k} or elsewhere, which specify what we do not yet know about the putative friend, yet think would be relevant for assessing her friendliness—default slots, as it were, to be filled by further acquaintance.

It seems that Bolzano and Locke, not viewing "genuine" as either interactive or temporal, are overly sanguine about the possibilities for eliminating it from sentences in which it occurs. Eliminating "genuine" from "x is a genuine q" in fact seems, if possible at all, immensely complex. "x is a genuine friend" (or, better: "x has turned out to be a genuine friend") turns out to entail that there has been a process by which I have come to know x, and that this process has exhibited certain characteristics, indeed whole families of characteristics, that are difficult to capture in a standard formal representation—not merely because they vary widely from individual to individual, as Quine suggests on occasion,[75] but also because they are developmental in nature. "Genuineness" is not simply a matter of what propositions *are* true of a given entity, but of how they *become* true, in the eyes of certain beholders of x; of how in some cases they *become* false; of the *patterned* ways in which they do both; of the *rational* significance of each of these for the overall property in question; and of what the beholders think they still do not know about the entity.

Eliminating "genuine" from "S is a genuine P" may well be possible but not worth the trouble—just as reducing advanced computer languages to machine language is possible, but not worth the trouble (except for the computer). And this may be the most radical way to deny the eliminability thesis, just as it is more radical to assert that the reducibility of the mind to the brain is of no importance than to deny or assert that reducibility.

(2) Ordinary language has evolved over history, but not always as the result of philosophical debate—certainly not of philosophical debates we can recover today. Locke appeals to it in connection with the question of the truth of ideas.[76] An "idea," as Locke uses that term, is "whatsoever is the *object* of the understanding when a man thinks," and the term covers "phantasms, notions, and species."[77] An idea, then, is not necessarily in the form "S is P." But any idea said to be true or false, Locke argues, has some negation or affirmation in virtue of which this is said to be the case, because all cases of truth and falsity involve the relation of what is in the mind to something extraneous.

As thus presented (e.g., at *Essay* 4.5.1ff.), the argument seems to beg the qustion. Roughly sketched to bring this out, the argument would run:

(1) Truth lies in the relation of things in the mind to other things.
(2) Such relations are affirmed and denied in propositions.
(3) Therefore, only propositions can be true or false.

How do we know that truth, "that which all mankind do, or pretend, to search for" (ibid.) consists in the relation of things in the mind to the things they signify? As presented at 2.32.1–4, the question is not begged because "true" in (1) refers to the "ordinary acceptation," which is presumably what warrants it. We can then replace (1) above by:

(i) Philosophers ought not to stray from ordinary usage.
(ii) The ordinary use of "true" restricts it to a property of the relation of things in the mind to other things.
(iii) Such relations are affirmed and denied in propositions.
(iv) Therefore, only propositions can be true or false in the philosophical sense.

Both (i) and (ii), however, are patently invalid. The former prescribes to philosophy, and if philosophy today were to restrict itself to the ordinary meanings of terms, it would be the only intellectual discipline to do so. After Joyce and Einstein, and probably well before, departing from ordinary language is not merely a characteristic of both literature and science, but a virtual condition for them. *Contra* (ii), ordinary English in fact persists in using "true" in nonpropositional senses: both the *Oxford English Dictionary* and *Webster*'s 2d edition (1979) list a healthy variety of other contemporary meanings of "true." And even if ordinary language spoke unambiguously about the nature of "truth," there would be nothing to prevent us from taking some other word—for example, "frue" or "genuine"—and using it for nontraditional designations of the goal of inquiry.

(3) One further appeal might be made: to the history of philosophy itself. There is a view—apparently held by Tarski, and perhaps also by Heidegger—that the history of philosophy exhibits adherence to what the former calls the "classical Aristotelian conception of truth," and what the latter calls the "traditional concept of truth."[78] Neither cites any record of overt debate on the matter, so their claim is what I suggested above to be a sort of hybrid of the other two types of appeal: an unknown decision, on unrecovered grounds, constitutive of philosophy itself.

This sort of warrant for the correspondence theory of truth is undermined by the fact that an analogous case can be constructed for "truth" in Hegel's sense of the term, as I will argue in the next chapter. In any case, the view that the philosophical tradition exhibits some sort of consensus that truth comes packaged as "S is P" or something similar is perhaps easier than that to explode; what the history of philosophy really exhibits seems to be more a tradition of lip service to the idea. Does not Plato, who often enough refers to truth as correspondence,[79] continually use *t'alêthê*, "the true things," to refer, not to assertions, but to the Forms themselves (which are assuredly not packaged as "S is P")? Does not Aristotle, the founder of the tradition of correspondence, have (as we will see) several mysterious discussions of the sense in which things, rather than propositions, are true? Does not Augustine go so far as to say, in his *Soliloquies*, that truth is being—in which Anselm's *de Veritate* would follow him?[80]

Despite Proclus's use of an apparently mathematical procedure in his *Elements of Theology*, and some of his formulations of the nature of truth,[81] we find a rather different view in his commentary on Plato's *Parmenides*. There he comes to distinguish falsity from error: if S is P, and I say "S is not P," I have asserted a falsehood, because S is P. But *both* "S is P" and "S is not P" are in "error," because in them the mind moves (*errare*) from the subject to the predicate of the sentence. Neither true nor false assertions are adequate to the truth of the One, and it is that truth which is the ultimate goal of Proclean inquiry.[82]

Question I, article II of Thomas Aquinas's *de Veritate* begins with the assurance that truth is located, not in things, but in the intellect properly perceiving reality. But the intellect may be God's, in which case a thing is "true" insofar as it "fulfills the end to which it is ordained by God."[83] With respect to the human intellect, truth is indeed found in the conformity of intellect to thing; but this, Thomas teaches, follows from the previous sense:

> Since everything is true according as it has the form proper to
> its nature, the intellect, insofar as it is knowing, must be true
> according as it has the likeness of the thing known, which is its
> form as a knowing power. For this reason truth is defined as
> the conformity of intellect and thing; and to know this con-
> formity is to know truth.[84]

Truth is primarily in the intellect—not as a proposition or set of them, but as the form of the intellect itself. When the human intellect has its proper form, it contains propositions it knows to be true, but that is subsequent.

The first definition of truth in Spinoza's *Ethics* is "adequate to its object," which again sounds traditional enough. But "adequacy" turns out to mean, not corresponding to an object, but existing as in the mind of God.[85] Kant, in his first *Critique,* "granted" the view that truth is correspondence; but the grammar of the sentence, as Gerold Prauss has shown, is complex; Kant really means to say that the old definition is no longer adequate.[86]

This cursory glance suggests that *the history of philosophy does not present us with a sustained search for true propositions, but with a set of heterogenous projects for attaining goals that are themselves extremely diverse, perhaps even mutually incomprehensible.* Is it possible, then, that "philosophy" itself perhaps names nothing but a sort of discursive space within which wholly diverse forms of discourse play past rather than against one another, disseminating themselves in such a way that each paradigm, within itself, may still display consistency and intelligibility? Is it possible that the positivist critique of the history of philosophy—that traditional philosophical activity is wholly inadequate to provide us with verified propositions—is to be maintained but deprived of its force, since finding such propositions was never the point of philosophy?

Commonplace assertionism, when ranging beyond certain highly specific fields such as logic, cannot be true. That the single goal of inquiry comes packaged in the form "S is P" is neither a logical nor an empirical truth. History provides no support for it: arguments that "true" in the sense of "genuine" can be reduced to assertionistic truth are not persuasive, and it is not the object of either a philosophical or a more generalized cultural consensus. The result is that commonplace assertionism must be, at least provisionally, declared to be, at worst, mistake hardened into dogma. At best, it is a variety of stipulative assertionism: that variety which does not make its stipulative character clear.

And that is as it should be: for the general space within which we are to understand both Hegelian and traditional truth is the space of goals of rational inquiry. To claim, in the words Tarski abjures, to have discovered the "right" conception—indeed, to claim even to have discovered, once and for all time, any characteristics of that conception, and thus to lay down in advance criteria for what sort of goal a rational inquiry has to have—is an interference with intellectual freedom, or (what is the same thing for Hegel) an attempt to stop history.

3

Hegelian Truth: Narrative

The considerations at the end of the previous chapter were intended to suggest that Hegel's rejection of assertionism has historical precedent within philosophy. The aim of the present chapter is to show that his use of "truth" and "true" stands within a rational development: that it is warranted by, and to some degree improves upon, previous uses. Such narrative warrant is basic to Hegel's own way of philosophizing, which consists in large part in the construction of a single, overarching narrative of all past philosophy—a story of which his own System is the only possible outcome. But my style of narrative is different from Hegel's: I will take up just a few of the manifold phenomena presented in the philosophical tradition, weaving them together into a story which can plausibly show rational development without arguing that Hegel's is the only possible response to previous philosophers, or that my own narrative is the only way to link them together.

The considerations at the end of the previous chapter indicate that the history of the concept of truth is not in very good state at the moment; indeed, the usual view of that history holds that it is not developmental at all but exhibits a general agreement on the nature of truth since philosophy began (or at least since Aristotle); departures from that consensus have presumably been merely idiosyncratic or unwarranted. That they are not such but exhibit the rational development of alternative conceptions of the goals of inquiry can only be shown historically, by

weaving those conceptions into a story; but given the scope of the project and the lack of secondary material, a complete narrative of even a few
strands within the philosophical conception of truth is impossible. I will
confine myself to a few stages which suggest one overall development
leading to Hegel. Those stages are presented by Plato's *Philebus*, Aristotle's *Metaphysics*, Descartes's *Principles of Philosophy*, Leibniz's "Meditation on Knowledge, Truth, and Ideas," Locke's *Essay Concerning Human
Understanding*, and Kant's *Logic*. In general, the narrative will follow the
broad pattern established in my previous *Poetic Interaction*. Plato will
make a promising but troubled beginning to the problematic, which will
then be occluded by the Aristotelian emphasis on assertional truth and
recovered, laboriously, only in the modern era.

Plato's *Philebus*

We begin with a proposition which, Socrates says, is "wondrous"
(*thaumastos*): that many are one, and that one is many (*hen . . . ta polla
einai kai ta polla hen*; 14c7). The wonder is not that this holds for the
vague and changing world of coming-to-be (for that puzzle was resolved
long ago),[1] but that it seems to hold as well for the unchanging "monads" of the supersensible realm—especially if each of those monads is
held to come to be "in" an indefinite number of transient (sensory) beings.[2] The supersensible world of Forms, the sensory world of flux, and
the relations between these worlds all exhibit this wondrous interplay of
one and many; indeed, the identity of one and many is not only *a logos*,
but is characteristic of *logos* itself—of everything which is or has been
said (15d4ff.). One example of this has already been given: that a single
sound—for example, "pleasure"—can designate many different things
(12c6ff.). Those different things are not only unlike each other, but may
even be opposed—as white and black are both designated "color" and
the delight of good and bad men are both called "pleasure" (12c6ff.,
d6f.).

If ambiguity is the type of one-many relation Plato attributes to all
things said, then every single utterance ever made (up to now) has been
ambiguous, and it is a "wonder" that we can ever understand one another at all. Perhaps, indeed, we do not: the first set speech of the *Phaedrus* hints at such a possibility.[3] Fortunately, this state of affairs, however
widespread, need not continue into the future, for there is a remedy: the
monads, or units, are not in direct relationship to a chaotic manifold.

Rather, the many's are related to the one's in definite, organized ways. Thus, if we find a unity, we can divide it into a determinate number of more specific units—that is, canvas and organize the different meanings of a single word. After that has been completed—and only then—we can worry about the relations of the smallest of these units to the many. Similarly in the other direction, for Plato is here talking about a process of inquiry: we can start with the unlimited many and pass through ascending series of monads; this process is essential to "dialectic" (16d–18a), which thus aims at overcoming the chaos of ambiguities resident within language itself by setting forth the determinate variety of meanings that a language associates with each of its terms. Ambiguity is not to be eliminated but mapped and thereby mastered. Such a map of ambiguities would then be the goal of dialectic: truth in words. It would also yield a set of words with what Plato might call their "meanings" fully explored and explicated: a company of words, ready to do duty in our human interactions.

The Phileban formula *hen kai polla* sounds enough like the *hen kai pan* about which the young Hegel corresponded with Hölderlin.[4] The relationship to Hegel is sharper than that, however: Socrates, like Hegel, is no assertionist, for Protarchus, his interlocutor, is one (36d6) and Socrates wants to show him he is wrong. There are in fact three senses in which pleasure, which is not in the form "S is P," can be false. The first and least serious of these (the account of it is couched in metaphor) is that pleasure can be taken in an object which is not good for you: the pleasures of a bad man (e.g., a miser, who contemplates the possession of much gold) are false (because gold is not really good for you, and its possession will disappoint you: 39a seq.). Such false pleasure, then, is really based on a false belief: there is, as Locke would say, an assertion at the base of it.

Or, rather, as Socrates does say, an opinion *preceding* it. The relation of pleasure to belief is not that belief is a component of pleasure or that pleasure follows logically from belief. A pleasure is rather (in a sense I will not attempt to unpack) the *depiction* of a belief (39b seq.). A false pleasure attempts to picture a deceptive thing. It does so, not only because the belief itself is false, but because the soul which holds it is defective—not dear to the gods (40a). A false pleasure may then be quite "true" in the sense that it correctly portrays the belief which is its object; but if that belief is itself a false one, the pleasure has arisen in the wrong way and is nonetheless false. As Cynthia Hampton puts it, the good man "is good because he has true beliefs that lead to true pleasures and which are preceded by right desires."[5] The pleasures of the bad man are produced by a different process, one which moves from wrong desires through false belief. The pleasure itself, to be sure, is pleasant (cf. 40d5f.); but it has arisen in the wrong way. Its spuriousness will become evident when it inevitably gives way to pain. A false pleasure, in this first case, is thus one which is not (in the sense discussed in the previous chapter) genuine: it is pleasant for the moment, but its "before" is deception and its "after" is disappointment.

The same emphasis on how a pleasure comes to be is present in Socrates' second sense of false pleasure, which is couched in terms of how we normally do things: one step up from mere metaphor, but still, we may say, confronting the images of the *Republic*'s cave. Pleasures, on this view, are not merely things we feel; they are things we get to know. And getting to know a pleasure may misfire, for it is something we do in part by comparing that pleasure with other pleasures and with pains. But pleasure compared with a pain will appear greater than it is, and conversely (41b–42c). Here, the process by which the pleasure comes to be known is a defective one, whence it results that the pleasure is (in part) only apparent. That defective process has been an interaction between the pleasure itself and the person who reflects on it, and this reflection, because it is a process of comparison with pains, is unlike the kind of "getting to know" another person discussed in chapter 2: it cannot help misleading. Apparent friendliness, we saw (in the case of the airline stewardess), can derive in part from occupational necessity: so also can apparent pleasure derive in part from its surroundings—here, the pain with which it is compared. The false pleasures so produced are "false" in a stronger sense than the first, for they are fake as pleasures—that is, because of their relations to other mental states, and not because of any false belief they may depict (42a seq.).

The third sense in which pleasures can be true or false—the strongest of all (42c7)—is also the strictest, for it is presented, not in terms of metaphor or of ordinary practice, but in those of how philosophers operate when investigating the Forms. The argument, which is double, can be sketched as follows.

Pleasures are of different intensities, and if we want to investigate the single thing which makes them all pleasures we must fix our attention on the highest and most intense (*sphodrotatos*) pleasures we can find (44d seq.). According to some theorists, pleasure is necessarily preceded by desire, which is a painful state, and hence is nothing more than an escape from pain—a point about whose generality Socrates is dubious, but which he accepts for some cases (42d–44d). Other pleasures—many of them—are mingled with pain as they occur (46b–51a). The double con-

clusion is that (a) some pleasures are quite unreal, being merely cessa-
tions of pain, and (b) other pleasures are "false" in that they are mingled
with their opposites. The first of these clearly uses the criterion of what I
call genuineness, but in strengthened form: not merely the intensity of
the pleasure, but the fact that it seems to be a pleasure at all, is nothing
more than the result of the preceding pain. The second requires a new
concept for its articulation: that the true is the pure, is that which is
unmixed with its opposite (51a seq.).

This criterion of purity is to replace the ordinary criterion used in
evaluating pleasures, that of magnitude; for the greatest pleasures are
mixed with pain.[6] This revision in ordinary beliefs is, like other such revisions in Plato, metaphysically warranted, not in the sense that it follows
from a metaphysical doctrine, but in that it enables one. We can certainly
undertake to evaluate pleasures with respect to their purity rather than
their magnitude no matter what our metaphysics (unless ours goes with
an epistemology that denies the existence of such pure awarenesses altogether); but there is no purpose in advocating the total replacement of
the one by the other except as a prelude to the dismissal of the sensible
world, where things can be large but never unmixed.[7] True pleasure is
then pleasure in which the prior pain or lack is minimal but the feeling of
its removal is maximal (51b). The sort of truth this exhibits is occasioned
by objects which are beautiful (kala), again not in the ordinary but the
philosophical sense: as applied, not to pictures or living creatures but to
simple geometric forms (53a9f., b5, c1). This concept of truth is also
generalized to knowledge (epistêmê): true knowledge will be precise—
that is, unmixed with its opposite, ignorance; and it will be knowledge of
the purest objects, those which never change.[8] The two sorts of purity of
concern to the passage, then, are beauty for the senses and accuracy for
knowledge.

As Hampton and others have noted,[9] this view of truth as purity
in knowledge joins with the passage on the sun at Republic VI, where
truth is asserted of the object of knowledge, upon which it is bestowed by
the Form of the Good.[10] The reference to light in that passage further
ties the concept of truth to what Rudolf Schmitz has summarized as a
whole archaic tradition, going back beyond Greece, according to which
some things can be understood (and are "light"), while other things cannot (and are "dark").[11] In that tradition, for an entity to be or to be
intelligible it must possess a certain degree of purity—for if it were
wholly mixed with its opposite, it would not be what it is rather than that
opposite, and nothing could be asserted of it.[12] Hence, the universe must
be such that opposites are not uniformly distributed: each member of a

pair of opposites must be able to predominate in certain sections of space and time. This sort of predominance is then the "mixing" of truth with the sensible universe, and is a necessary condition for anything's existing at all (64b2f.).

We may now ask what this account of truth as purity, which the *Philebus* has developed at such length, has to do with the one-many interplay announced with such fanfare earlier in the dialogue. The final passages of the *Philebus* (61b seq.) contain a pair of subtle and difficult cases of "mixture" which bring the two together. In the first of these, the interlocutors construct an overall characterization of the good life by mixing together knowledge and the truest, or purest, sorts of pleasure (61e–63b). To this compound must be added truth itself, for wholly without truth (in the sense of purity) nothing can come to be—that is, we may say, the mixture should be as pure as the components of which it is made (64b), in the sense that the opposites of those components should be excluded from it.

This recipe for a well-ordered human life is then generalized: what makes the arrangement (and, presumably, other such arrangments) good is its mixture of measure (*metriotês*) or virtue, and symmetry (*symmetria*) or beauty: the Good, which is measure in the supersensible realm (66a), resolves into beauty in the sensory world.[13] Mixing measure and symmetry together and again adding truth or purity (i.e., presumably, excluding the opposites of these) achieves a formulation for the Good, and with that in hand the interlocutors can examine pleasure and reason to see which of them is most akin to the Good so defined.

Truth, then, is what is added to each mixture and makes that mixture what it is and not another thing; when truth, as purity, comes to a concatenation of "monads," it renders them, like good, a single measure for sensibles; when it comes to sensibles it renders them in their own way combinations of one and many—that is, beautiful. Truth, so understood, is not necessarily something that imposes itself objectively: it is the *interlocutors* who do the mixing, adding truth itself to their mixtures; even among the monads, it is they who take together beauty, measure, and truth, and out of them constitute the good (*syntrisi labontes*, 65a2). The mixing, in other words, is somewhat like the intentional construction of a definition out of component words.

As with the previous accounts, "truth" means here to come to be, or to be perceived, in a certain way: here, by a process of "mixing," which results in a complex whole not characterized by its opposite. Such truth is, then, what binds together other concepts into a whole. Apart from what it thus binds, it can be given only a very abstract and formal characterization—that is, as unaffected by its opposite. Plato calls those other concepts (or monads) "ingredients" of the Good; we could in Hegelian terms call them "content," for they are a set of forms unified by an overarching one.

Phileban truth, like Hegelian, is not only content-hungry but narrative in nature: just as true pleasures (in all three senses) are those which arise in the proper way, so complex wholes cannot come to be without a process of mixing, and this process is important enough to bring about a revision in the Platonic concept of purity itself. In the *Phaedo* and *Sophist*, for example, "purity" is equated with simplicity and separateness from other things.[14] Here, by contrast, something can be "pure" even if compounded of other things, providing that they themselves are pure and, presumably, that none of them somehow contradicts the whole. Something thus pure can retain its purity if it becomes itself a component of other, higher-order mixtures.[15]

I have recounted here a development in the *Philebus*, one which moves us progressively away from truth as a property of assertions and toward a view of it as what unifies a plurality of monads or sensory qualities into a single supersensible measure or beautiful thing. The mixing is presented as the doing of the dialogue's interlocutors, and hence not as necessarily mirroring in detail the way things are. It is perfectly possible, for example, that the Good itself is not *simply* compounded out of beauty, measure, and truth, but stands in much richer relations to a much wider set of Forms, only two of which, plus truth, Socrates and company have admitted into their mixture.[16] To that extent, the unified mixture does not "correspond" to reality, and as a goal of inquiry must have another kind of truth. But even when at the discretion of humans, such mixing must be guided by the structures of metaphysical reality— that is, by the monads themselves which it compounds; truth itself, for example, is presented as a preexisting entity which the interlocutors simply add into their mix.

The view that the composition of a multiplicity of Forms into one is accomplished by human beings and their words[17] is in obvious tension with the Theory of Forms. For it is a basic point of that theory that the standards for our uses of words are not of our own making, but ontologically independent entities. This runs into difficulties unless qualified, however: for either the Forms, as meanings, are wholly independent of each other, indefinable, and the nature of each ineffable, a state of affairs which (as *Sophist* 260a points out) would destroy discourse; or else the Forms are related to one another in a way relevant to their function as providing word-meanings, and those relations must be fully mapped out before we can have any such meanings.

Aristotle's *Metaphysics*

The *Philebus* thus presents a tension between the capacity of a word to refer (in the first instance, to a Form), and its capacity to unify a set of heterogenous entities. The Aristotelian texts solve this tension in favor of the referential function by generally locating truth in the knowing mind as a property of judgments, and by eschewing the use of the term in other senses, thereby providing the history of philosophy with the "classical Aristotelian conception of truth" appealed to, we saw, by Tarski and Heidegger. Aristotle's usual formulation of this, from *De Interpretatione* on, is in terms of separation and combination: words are symbols for mental experiences (in the sense of *pathêmata*), which themselves refer to things (including properties). When two such experiences are combined into a proposition we are asserting that the referents of those experiences are themselves combined in reality.[18]

It is in terms of such separation and combination that we are to understand the famous and mysterious discussion of truth and being, with reference to composites and incomposites, that occupies *Metaphysics* 9.10. This must, as Joseph Owens has argued, be read as fulfilling a promise made at *Metaphysics* 6.4 (1027b28).[19] There it is asserted that the combining and separating involved in the being-true of composite beings is itself to be found in the mind, not in the things (1027b29f.). To assert that a thought-combination is true is then to assert that it has itself being (in the mind), and that the complex object to which it refers exists in reality. The former is a relatively trivial sense of "being" as "being true": it tells us only that a true proposition *is* true. The latter characteristic is nothing other than what recent philosophers call the "disquotationality" of truth, the fact that " 'S is P' is true" tells us no more than "S is P."[20] The discussion never—at least not in any usefully clear way—leaves the terrain of the traditional view of truth.

Metaphysics 5.29 uses Aristotle's standard account of equivocation[21] to dispose of two senses in which things are said to be "false." A false thing is false, on the one hand, if it follows from a false belief: for example, the "fact" that the diagonal of a square is commensurate with its side is false, because such diagonality and commensurability are never found together. The fact is then false in the sense that it was produced in the wrong way: it gained such qualified "existence" as it may have from a wrong combination of ideas or names.[22] On the other hand, a thing can be false if, instead of following on false beliefs, it produces them. This is the case for what we may call natural dissimulators—beings whose nature is to appear to be something else, such as dreams or fool's gold.

Nonetheless, true discourse is not entirely to be explained by activities of the mind; it must, as Pierre Aubenque has written, be in Aristotle's view "prefigured" by certain characteristics of things.[23] The fact that the diagonal is incommensurable results, not merely from mental experiences which stand for these things being always found in our minds, but from the fact that real diagonals are always incommensurable. In general, a true combinatory judgment—one that truly asserts "S is P," the kind of judgment that Aristotle (like the philosophical tradition in general) privileges, must have a complex object, one which has the properties associated with both "S" and "P." And it must be a unified object, since the combination of *pathêmata* in the mind can be true only if the properties those experiences designate are combined in reality.[24] The true judgment is thus prefigured by, requires for its existence and truth, an object which is, in the terms of the *Philebus*, a one and many. But the unity of such an object is not due to any abstract quality like Phileban "truth," and still less to any "mixing" that we humans may be doing. It is due to the substantial form of the thing itself, the metaphysical reality which unifies the matter in that thing and which the knowing mind can only behold, not create. Hence it is that Hegel can say, in the *Lectures on the History of Philosophy*, that his concept of truth captures the Aristotelian concept, not of *alêtheia*, but of *ousia*:[25] not "truth" but "substance" is the Aristotelian forerunner to Hegelian truth. For it is in Aristotelian terms *ousia* which, unifying various complexes of proximate matter (which Hegel would call "content"), gives objects what might be called their "genuine" natures.

Thus, both the *Philebus* and the *Metaphysics* convey the general notion of a unity which brings together a plurality of other things, so that they can be treated as one. For Plato, such unity can be sensible or supersensible, one which exists in reality or which we ourselves constitute. When it is supersensible, the entities unified can be of the same type as the unity they compose—as the good is the same sort of monad as virtue and beauty. For Aristotle, the unifying factor in question is strictly a part of reality, which our thoughts and words—even our definitions—can only mirror: the unifying function portrayed in the *Philebus* is displaced from *logos* onto *ousia*, and what gets unified is twofold: first, the proxi-

mate matter which comes under the unifying form; and second, the generic forms under which that form itself comes, and which are contained
in the definition of that substance.[26] Because Phileban truth is no longer
associated with the capacity of discourse to sum up and take as one thing
a heterogenous set of other things, but is wholly achieved by the same
thing which makes an entity exist at all—its substantial form—it becomes, for Aristotle, virtually synonymous with "being."

But it does so only in virtue of the equation of "being" with "substance" that is central to the entire Aristotelian metaphysics.[27] And that
equation, in its *locus classicus* (*Metaphysics* 4.1–3), is advanced as a step in
specifying the proper object for first philosophy itself: what sort of thing
it is to study. Hence, the Aristotelian goal of inquiry is indeed, assertionistically, a set of propositions; but those will be propositions about entitites which unify multiplicities—that is, about forms in matter or
substances. What for the *Philebus* was simply a kind of truth is for the
Metaphysics what makes truth (in the assertional sense) philosophical: being itself.

Descartes's *Principles of Philosophy*

In this Aristotelian sense, the concept of "truth in things" did not survive the transition to the modern era. Hobbes, for example, would dismiss it as "nugatory and puerile": for who would deny that "man," "one
man," and "truly a man" express the same thing? Leibniz would call it a
"thoroughly useless and almost senseless attribute," and Spinoza would
write that those who approved of it were "thoroughly deceived"; Locke
would dismiss it and Descartes never mention it at all. Kant would condemn it in the first *Critique* as the dogmatic mistaking of a sort of qualitative multiplicity, really grounded in the categories of the mind, for a
universal property of things.[28]

Any opinion held in such contempt by such a diverse array of
thinkers has doubtless met, not one destructive fate, but several. However, one characteristic of modern thought can be seen as a common
element in the various dooms of the concept of the truth of things. We
have seen that the strict analogue of the Phileban truth of a thing was,
for Aristotelian metaphysics, the substantial form which made that thing
into a substance. To understand a thing as true then meant to understand it as a substance—as the kind of thing about which true judgments
can be made. For if a true statement is a combination of terms, its objec-

tive correlative must be a combination of qualities, and that combination must ultimately refer back to the archetype of all combination, the inherence of something in a substance, so that all true judgments are somehow about substances. But the modern philosophers I have mentioned take the view that substantial forms, if they exist at all, are not properly speaking knowable: what we know in the first instance are not substances but ideas. Thus, Descartes, in *Meditation* 1, formulates the possibility that my ideas of things do not tell me anything about entities external to me at all; for they may have been implanted in me by an evil demon.[29] Locke argues at length against the view that "the simple ideas we receive from sensation and reflection," which for him are the bedrock of our knowledge, can give us any knowledge of the substances of things.[30] For Spinoza, there is only one substance; individual things as such cannot be accurately known by us, for they are but modes of God.[31] While Leibniz hardly denied the existence of individual substances, he followed Descartes in making the immediate objects of our perceptions, not external substances, but our ideas (*apparitiones*).[32] Finally, for Kant substance was merely one of the categories the mind uses to structure the sensory manifold into appearances, rather than a property of things themselves.[33]

If, then, substantial form was necessary to the Aristotelian version of truth in things; and if such form is viewed as unknowable; then talk of truth in things becomes, not false, but just what the present writers agree it is: useless, foolish, childish. But we are entitled to ask: If truth in things is dismissed because substance is unknowable, what about the things we *can* know—"ideas" themselves? Can they be said to exhibit truth and falsity? We cannot, to resolve this, turn directly to the passages where these writers discuss the issue of truth in ideas. For those discussions, as we will see, generally operate with the correspondence view of truth: an idea will be true if it corresponds to reality.[34] The task here, however, is to be guided by the meaning of "true" which has emerged in the narrative so far, and to ask about the capacity of a single idea to unite a multiplicity of other things, so that they can be taken as one. Since ideas are our cognitive bedrock, there will be for these thinkers, in the first instance at least, only one sort of thing for an idea to unify: a multiplicity of other ideas.

The first paragraph of Descartes's *Principles of Philosophy*, quite traditionally, posits truth as the ultimate goal of cognition and inquiry.[35] But all I can know is my ideas, and I cannot tell simply by inspecting them which of them might be true (except in the case of the single idea of my own existence). However, goes the argument, once it is proven that God exists and is no liar, I can take it that any idea which I perceive clearly and distinctly will also be true: for God to allow in me an idea which was clear and distinct but did not correctly represent reality would be for God to deceive me.[36] Hence, the proper goal for rational inquiry becomes clear and distinct ideas, the truth of which will automatically follow by divine veracity. It is then the clearness and distinctness of the idea, not the truth of the thing, which "prefigures" true discourse about the world.

The *Principles* contains Descartes's fullest discussion of clearness and distinctness, and tells us that an idea is "clear" when it is "present and manifest to the attentive mind." It is "distinct" when its content is precise enough to enable it to be distinguished precisely from other ideas. The "clarity" of an idea, we may say, is its presence before the mind as a unity; its "distinctness" is the clear presence of the multiplicity of constituent ideas that make it up. These two properties together are what is crucial to Descartes, and I will refer to the combination of them as clarity-and-distinctness.

While clarity-and-distinctness is not to be conflated with truth, the latter notion is the key to the problematic in terms of which the former is introduced. For the basic issue is whether there is any (intrinsic) property that can be perceived in an idea that can establish the (extrinsic) relation of that idea to reality, or its truth; clarity-and-distinctness, taken together, constitute such a property. This connection with the conception of truth as correspondence in effect truncates Descartes's discussion of clarity and distinctness. For, we may say (though Descartes does not), just as God will not give me a clear-and-distinct idea which is false, God will also not allow me to mistake for a clear-and-distinct idea one which is in fact obscure and confused. In any case, and for whatever reason, Descartes—and, after him, Spinoza—consider themselves absolved from giving any very careful account of what clarity-and-distinctness really is.[37]

Leibniz's "Meditation on Knowledge, Truth, and Ideas"

The "Meditation," to which I will turn for such an account,[38] criticizes the sketchy presentation earlier writers (Descartes and Spinoza are meant) gave the matter, in particular asserting that, on their account, it is left up to the individual to decide whether an idea is being clearly and distinctly perceived or not. The "Meditation" by contrast asserts that a "clear" cognition is one which enables me to cognize (*agnoscere*) the object it represents. The text suggests two criteria for such cognition: I must be able to recognize (*recognoscere*) the idea when it is before me again, and I must be able to distinguish it from other ideas.[39] The latter, in particular, requires we may say that the idea be different from other ones, and this in turn means that it must be pure: a color is distinguishable from other colors if, like "white" in the *Philebus*, it is without admixture of them. We thus find the "Meditation" continuing to rely on the Cartesian view that the clearness of an idea is constituted through its presence to the mind: but that presence is attested by what the mind can do with the idea.

A "marker" (*nota*)[40] is a constituent of an idea, and is itself an idea which can have further markers. An idea is "distinct" if the various markers which distinguish it from other ideas are all clearly cognized themselves, so that I can enumerate them: they are then a multiplicity constituent of a single idea, as the Phileban many is a multiplicity taken to be constituents of a monad. An idea is known "adequately" if those markers, and their markers, are all known distinctly—if it has been analyzed to its most primitive components, which for Leibniz will be absolute properties of God. Such perfection in analysis is then the ultimate goal of philosophical inquiry.[41]

Clearness-and-distinctness thus has here a systematic pull which it lacked for the *Principles*: to have all our ideas clear and distinct means to understand them all as properties of a single being or as compounded from such properties, and to make any individual idea adequate means seeing it the same way. The systematicity is limited, however: the "Meditation" is doubtful that such a perfect analysis of concepts is within human capacity. In Leibniz's main attempt to show that it is possible, the "Two Notations for Discussion with Spinoza," he is able to argue only that the primitive concepts do not contradict one another and hence could in principle inhere in a single perfect being.[42] He does not apply the other great principle of human reason, that of sufficient reason, to show that those absolute properties entail one another. Nor could he, since the proof that the primitive properties are compatible relies on their simplicity, which means that they cannot be built out of one another or analyzed into one another.[43]

In the absence of such completeness, we may note, even partial analysis of an idea is asserted to be useful for us here and now. Because ideas may be known clearly but not distinctly, they may on analysis prove to have markers which are incompatible with one another—to combine, in Aristotelian phrasing, what cannot be combined. Such an idea is, in the terminology of the "Meditition," false: one that is "true" is noncontradictory and thus affirms, if not that any object actually corresponds to it, at least the possibility that one does. To say that an idea is "adequate" is thus to say that it is known, in this attenuated sense, to be true.

Locke's *Essay Concerning Human Understanding*

The "Meditation," as I have outlined it here, has two innovations on Descartes: the more rigorous discussion of clearness-and-distinctness and, concomitantly, the attenuation of the concern with truth in the formulation of it. The *Essay*—written by the man who, with Leibniz, is for Hegel the other great figure of philosophy between Spinoza and Kant[44]—also criticizes those who have written on clear and distinct ideas, and in fact seeks (in the "Epistle to the Reader") to have new words applied to those concepts:

> By *determinate*, when applied to a simple idea, I mean that simple appearance which the mind has in its view, or perceives in itself, when that idea is said to be in it. By *determined*, when applied to a complex idea, I mean such an one as consists of a determinate number of certain simple or less complex ideas, joined in such a proportion and situation as the mind has before its view, and sees in itself, when that idea is present in it, or should be present in it, when a man gives a name to it.[45]

Clarity, or determinateness, is once again a form of pure presence to the mind; distinctness, or determinedness, is the clear presence in a complex idea of less complex ones. The reference here to naming is not trivial, for as chapter 9 will show Locke emphasizes language in a way that Descartes and Leibniz do not: ideas and names stand in a relationship which is as antagonistic as it is crucial:

> Words interpose themselves so much between the understanding and the truth which it would contemplate and apprehend that, like the medium through which visible objects pass, the obscurity and disorder do not seldom cast a mist before our eyes, and impose upon our understanding.[46]

Such imposition can take three forms.[47] First, an idea might be insufficiently distinct—that is, lacking in component ideas sufficient to distinguish the objects it refers to from others. This is not, strictly, a problem with the idea itself, for any idea "can be no other but such as the mind perceives it to be; and that very perception sufficiently distinguishes it from all other ideas."[48] The problem is that an idea in the mind of one person may not have enough components to enable her to make the distinctions that others do: the *Essay*'s example is of someone whose ideas of "leopard" and "lynx" merely designate an animal with spots. If she then goes on to use those terms, her usage—and, we may say, her idea of leopards and lynxes—is confused, though simply as an idea it is perfectly clear. This sort of thing "renders the use of words uncertain," and may be occasioned by the practice of defining words in general or abstract terms: for a term formed by abstraction, by definition, leaves out certain characteristics of the original perception whence it arises.[49]

When the component ideas of a term are sufficient in number but disorganized among themselves, it is "not easily discernible whether it [the idea] more belongs to the name given it than to any other." This problem, like the previous one, is the result of the names given to the idea. For the components of the idea are all present—that is, "plainly discernible as they are"; it is only by virtue of being ranked under a name which seems arbitrary that those components can unite to form an indistinct, or confused one. Finally, our complex ideas may change in that we allow into them or exclude from them various simple ideas—as do those who use words before they have learned their exact meanings. Such unstable ideas cannot, again, be reliably named, "and so lose the distinction that distinct names are designed for."

For Leibniz, ideas can be confused and indistinct on their own account; there is no need to appeal to language in order to explain these matters, and while the abuse of names leads to real problems with thought, it is not the only source of them: there is no essential antagonism, then, between language and idea, and the only problem with language is to make it conform to our ideas.[50] For the *Essay*, the leeway we have in compounding simpler into more complex ideas is often a good thing: it serves for convenience in communication, and "settles and completes" the combining of simpler ideas into a mixed mode.[51] But the mind must use its freedom correctly: the ideal for Locke is not simply to analyze ideas into their components, but to take care to have as many component ideas as possible on each level of the explication, and to have them as organized as they can be:

> That name is the more distinct, the more particular the ideas
> are, and the greater and more determinate the *number* and *or-*
> *der* of them is, whereof it is made up.[52]

A clearer statement of Phileban truth or of Leibnizean perfection—
couched, of course, in terms of ideas and names rather than of Forms or
the cosmic order—could not be given. Part of the reason for this is that
the *Essay's* discussion of clarity and distinctness of ideas is wholly independent of the problematics of truth in terms of which both the *Princi-*
ples and the "Meditation," as we saw, approach it: clarity and distinctness
are articulated on their own as norms, not merely for our perception of
an idea (whose only task, qua idea, is to conform to reality), but for at
least some of our ideas themselves.[53] Those norms hold independently,
not merely as intrinsic signs of extrinsic truth: language is measured
against them, not they against truth. But the *Essay* does not wholly escape
the problematics of truth: unlike Plato, for whom the knowledge of the
Forms, the one-and-many's, was the goal of intellectual inquiry, for
Locke it is but a means. The goal is always truth in the assertional sense:
the "joining or separating of signs in conformity with things signified"—
that is, with ideas.[54]

Kant's *Logic*

In the Introduction to his lectures on logic, edited at Kant's request by
his colleague Gottlob Benjemain Jäsche, Kant discusses, in addition to
truth, three other "perfections of cognition" (*Erkenntnis*): universality,
certitude, and distinctness (*Deutlichkeit*). The last of these is particularly
important to Kant. It so happens that Aristotle provided logic with
pretty much its full complement of true content. Even Kant's famous
reassignment of logic to the role of canon, rather than organon, of
thought—to providing only the proper form for presenting truth, rather
than itself generating truths—contributes only "exactness, determinacy,
and distinctness" to Aristotle's achievement.[55] Kant improves upon Aristotle, then, by being more "distinct." Distinctness must be a goal of rational inquiry—for surely Kant intends his own *Logic* to incorporate a
rational inquiry—and no small one.

All the perfections of cognition, Kant writes, exhibit a harmonious unification of multiplicity and unity. In the case of logical perfection
(as opposed to "aesthetic" perfection, which I will not discuss here),

unity in a cognition comes through its relation to an object—that is, through truth:

> Mere multiplicity without unity cannot satisfy us. And therefore truth is the chief perfection of all, because it is the ground of unity, through the relation of our cognition to an object.[56]

Distinctness of ideas (and clarity in them as well) thus arises for Kant (as for Descartes and Leibniz) in connection with truth, upon which for him the other perfections repose.[57] But the problematic, as we will see, is very different, for, as the quote above indicates, Kant thematizes explicitly the roles correspondence and unity are to play within the larger concept of truth.

I will briefly summarize Kant's rather traditional views on clearness and distinctness, partly in order to introduce the Kantian acceptation of a number of terms Hegel will transform. A representation is "clear" (*klar*) when it is in our minds and we are conscious of it; obscure (*dunkel*) otherwise. Logic, then, can deal only with clear concepts, and its business is to make them into distinct ones. A distinct (*deutlich*) concept is one which contains a manifold whose members are also clear.[58]

This manifold is one of markers (*Merkmale*). A marker (in Leibniz's term, *nota*) is for Kant a representation which applies to a plurality of things and makes the characteristic it represents into a ground of cognition of an object.[59] A marker is thus different from a perceived property of a thing, for we can have the awareness of such a property without taking it as the "ground of cognition" of the thing; we can be aware of the heat of a sultry day without taking that sensation as informing us about the air, for example.

No single marker is sufficient to give us complete cognition of a thing (unless that thing is simple, in which case we know it intuitively rather than discursively—that is, not through "markers" at all).[60] Hence, in order to be grounds of cognition, markers must come in sets of more than one member. A set of markers is a "concept" (*Begriff*); all our concepts are composed of markers, and any marker which itself has markers is a concept.[61] When a concept gives us cognition of a thing, it is in virtue of the markers which are "contained" within it.

The markers "in" a concept can, broadly speaking, be related in two ways: by coordination and by subordination.[62] A set of markers is "coordinated" when each is taken as an immediate marker of the matter at hand—for example, in a simple enumeration of its properties. Markers exhibit "subordination" when some of them can be attributed to a thing only in virtue of others (e.g., when I attribute color to an object in virtue of its being extended). Coordinated markers are connected into a concept by the fact that none of them contradicts any other, and so their connections obey the law of contradiction. It is always possible to extend a set of coordinated markers, then, by simply adding in compatible new ones, thereby "synthesizing" a new concept. Such a concept (which, since its markers are only contingently connected, can be given only in experience) has greater "extensive distinctness" the more markers it has. Subordinated markers by definition exhibit grounding relations, and hence come under the principle of sufficient reason. We can, by recursively analyzing the markers of a concept into their markers, eventually reach simple concepts, where analysis stops. In this, we increase the "intensive distinctness" of the concept.

When all coordinated markers in a concept are clear, that concept is extensively perfectly distinct or "comprehensive"; when all subordinated markers are clear, it is intensively perfectly distinct or "profound." If a marker suffices, for given purposes, to distinguish a thing from all other things, it is "sufficient." If it is a marker which must be found in the thing, it is "necessary." Necessary markers are essential; and the set of all the necessary markers of a thing that serve as grounds for further markers, but are not themselves grounded in other markers, is the "logical essence" of that thing.[63] Such a logical essence is then the purest form of cognition we can have of a thing: but for other purposes, we may presumably make markers which are not parts of a thing's logical essence into grounds of its cognition, and distinguish it from other things by nonessential features.

A "distinct" concept, then, contains a multiplicity of markers. Its unity—what makes it *a* concept at all—is to be found, not in the concept's presence to an attentive mind or even in what that mind can do with it, but in the way those markers are related to one another. The law of contradiction is negative: any concept which turns out to have markers that are mutually contradictory is impossible (in Leibniz's sense, untrue). The principle of sufficient reason requires that any cognition have grounds and consequences, and for a marker, as we have seen, these will be, in the first instance, not facts about objects of cognition but facts about other markers. Hence, we may say a "concept" is a marker which unifies a set of other markers, so that we can take them as one; and it does so in virtue of the relations those other markers have to one another.

We have, here, the first major Kantian innovation on the earlier modern thinkers I have mentioned: the unity of an idea is not to reside merely in its clear presence to the mind, but in the logical relations of its markers to one another. The question arises of what this innovation can have to do with truth, which as we saw was what provided the unity of concepts and therefore was the ground of all cognitive perfection. This poses in turn the question of what truth, for Kant, is, and leads us to his second major innovation on the tradition he received. This innovation has been often unremarked, for it is usually held that he had a traditional correspondence theory.[64] But the situation is more complex than that, in the first place because Kant questions whether any correspondence "theory of truth" is in fact possible. In order for our cognition to correspond to a thing, it must fail to correspond to other things: any proposition which is true of some objects will be false of others. But a truly universal criterion of truth would have to treat of the correspondence of cognition to objects in general; and this concrete—or, as Kant calls it, material—dimension of truth would escape it. On a charitable interpretation, Kant is arguing that the relation of correspondence is an interplay of truth and falsity, too concrete to be susceptible of treatment in a general "theory of truth." Fortunately, truth has another side—a "formal" side. For in order to have a (specific) cognition corresponding to a specific object or set of objects, you must have (among other things) a cognition at all. There are certain necessary conditions for a cognition's being a cognition, and these we can examine in abstraction from all objects and from all distinctions among objects. This will give us, if not a complete definition or "theory" of truth, at least a formal criterion by which to judge logically the truth of cognitions.[65]

Cognitions are for Kant activities of the Understanding guided by Reason, and the necessary conditions for something's being a cognition are the general laws of the understanding. Hence, formal truth consists solely in the agreement of cognition with itself, in total abstraction from all objects whatsoever and from all distinctions among them. And the universal formal criteria of truth are, accordingly, nothing other than the universal logical markers of the correspondence of cognition with itself, or—what is the same—the universal laws of the Understanding and Reason.[66]

As for Leibniz, there are two such universal laws: the principle of contradiction and that of sufficient reason.[67] Therefore, "truth" in the sense which makes for the unity of a concept is the interrelation of the markers of that concept in conformity to those two laws—and has nothing to do with correspondence to objects (other than being a necessary condition for it). As such, truth is no longer an "extrinsic" relation between an idea (or concept) and a thing, but an immanent characteristic of the relations the markers of an idea have with one another. Hence, as far as a philosophical "theory of truth" is concerned, the problematic of correspondence as an extrinsic relation has been replaced by the concept of truth as the immanent unity in a concept. And this leads the way to Hegel, who calls Kantian formal truth "truth," and Kantian material truth—that of which there can be no theory—"correcteness."

Conclusions

The above narrative has shown that, in the philosophical tradition, "truth" did not *merely* designate a property of assertions. Such assertional truth has always been viewed against the kind of truth defined in terms of the one-many problematic of the *Philebus*. The common feature was that both were goals of inquiry; and in the authors narrated here that goal was the possession, not merely of a set of propositions that corresponded to facts, but of a set of entities which in one way or another unified determinate manifolds of other entities, so that all could be treated as one.

While assertional truth by definition applies to entities that come packaged as "S is P," the nonassertional truth whose development I have narrated ranges more widely: any sort of thing, and perhaps indeed any thing, can be viewed as somehow unifying a set of other things. Thus, for Plato (in the epoch of metaphysics) such truth could be attributed to Forms; for modern thinkers (in the epoch of consciousness) it was attributed to ideas, and entitled "clearness and distinctness"; and for Kant, finally, it was attributed to concepts. Both goals of inquiry are defined in terms of relations, and the relation proper to assertional truth is, again obviously, the one that holds between an assertion and the reality it refers to. The relation between the one's and the many's of nonassertional truth is by contrast of various sorts: the many's may be the same in kind as the one's (as when one idea or Platonic Form is compounded of others), or unlike them (as when an Aristotelian individual substance is compounded of form and matter). And they may be more or less similar to one another—though they always, following the lead of the *Philebus*, constitute a determinate multiplicity and cannot therefore be identical with one another.

Finally, depending on the types of entity it relates, nonassertional truth may have different relations to the assertional variety. It may be, as with Aristotle in particular, that the kind of unity it conceptualizes is one which itself mirrors the nature of the unities we find in the universe, in which case nonassertional truth turns out to be a constraint upon the assertional variety: the goal of inquiry is a set of propositions about realities which themselves are unities of determinate pluralities and hence are the truest things. Or it may be, as with the *Philebus*, that the kind of unity sought by philosophy is in fact *produced* by philosophy, in which case it need not correspond to anything outside itself.

Hegel will respond to the developments in this narrative as follows. He will agree with Plato that the unity of one and many is a goal of inquiry, and will accept the modern view that the unities thus sought are not metaphysical entities existing in some supersensible realm. Following Kant, he will call them, not "ideas," but "concepts," though his meaning will be rather different. The Hegelian concept is, I will argue, a totality of words, not of "grounds of cognition." In constructing his Concept and the whole System, Hegel will further develop the systematic pull that clarity and distinctness had in Leibniz, while retaining the linguistic emphasis of Locke. Because of this, Hegel's philosophy presents a global change in the object of philosophy: as the moderns had replaced the order of things with the order of ideas, so Hegel will replace the order of ideas with an order of words. To the concept of such order he will add his own great original contribution, that of narrative development, so that the Concept, like everything "true" in his sense, is not something existing in a static state to be inspected but develops itself dynamically, as the systematizing of a company of words which themselves, as utterances sounding in time, are radically dynamic.

This narrative relation to previous philosophers, then, is Hegel's warrant for adopting the quality I have so far called "genuineness" as the goal of his inquiry, giving it the name "truth" while allocating to what is usually called "truth" the word "correctness." But the reception of Hegel's system has shown that this particular philosophical warrant has not been strong enough to resist the pull of assertionism, which has been so powerful as to be recurrently attributed to Hegel himself. I have argued that "real," and then "genuine," would be less misleading as a term for what Hegel is after than would "truth." But "genuine," like "real," failed to convey the systematic character of Hegelian truth: the fact that it is necessary and yet comprehensive, that in virtue of the latter it is concrete enough to have adumbrations among all sorts of phenomena of the world whose "true" nature it specifies, and that as the former it is a goal, not merely of Hegel the man and thinker, but of large-scale developments in history. We can, I think, do a bit better; and I will turn, for my third and final (though still imperfect) candidate for a name for this particular conception, to the first thinker who sharply distinguished it from "truth": Aristotle.

Nobility

Substance is not the only kind of unifying force appealed to in the Aristotelian works. A weaker sort of unity is present in the state and, indeed, on the level of the entire universe, both of which are unities of mutually heterogenous substances.[68] As unifying, not mere matter, but independently existing substances, this sort of unity perhaps comes closer to what Hegel means by truth than does *ousia* (his own opinion to the contrary, cited above, notwithstanding). It is manifested, according to the Aristotelian texts, in an observable feature of the cosmic order; a quality referred to by various forms of the adjective *kalos*.[69]

The translation of this term poses major difficulties. In Plato's *Phaedrus* and *Symposium, kalos* designates the Beautiful, the force which draws lovers together. But there is a problem with applying this sense to, for example, the Aristotelian ethical writings, where the term is of exceedingly wide application. Virtuous acts are there said to be *kalai* and for the sake of the *kalou*. The *kalon* is the telos of virtue, and to be good simply means to perform *kalai* acts; even acts which are not themselves *kalai* are for the sake of the *kalou*. The soul of the good man is put into harmony with itself through his deliberative power, and this is *kalon*. The virtues themselves are *kala*, because each is a balance between excess and defect, and is thus an ordering of right amounts: courage, for example, is the mean between too much fear and too little.[70] In sum, everyone does everything for the sake of either the pleasant or the *kalon*.[71]

The same importance and breadth are evident in the political domain as well. The state exists for the sake of living *kalos; kalai* acts are the criterion of membership in it, and when it is well-ordered it is *kalê* itself. The *kalon* is in fact sort of a political panacea:

> If all men strove towards the *kalon*, and extended themselves to
> do the *kallista* things, then everything would be as required for
> the community; and in private affairs each individual would
> have the greatest of goods.[72]

The *kalon* is not only found on both levels of individual and community, but in fact binds them together: good men are friends because they seek the *kalon*, and the state is a "network of friendships."[73]

So far, *kalon* seems, like Hegelian "true," to designate the out-come of a diversity of rational developments. It is clear that, if "beauti-ful" was an acceptable translation for the Platonic *kalon*, it cannot be for the Aristotelian; the moral significance and breadth of the term in the latter texts has led Joseph Owens to translate it, in one place, as "the morally good."[74] But the term is of even wider application than that. At *Metaphysics* 12.3, for example, the Good is not coextensive with but part of the *kalon*: for the Good (and in particular, we may add, the moral good) is always found in actions, while the *kalon* can be found as well in unmoved things, in mathematics, and in the heavens. The *kalon*, while indeed a final cause of action, thus extends beyond the purely moral domain: laws "order" a city. The heavens, and indeed all works of na-ture, are "ordered," and anything made of parts can exhibit the *kalon*, which is thus a *natural* property of things.[75]

I have referred to *kalos* as a quality of the observable universe, one which manifests a unifying principle among substances. But Aristotle tends to use the term of the unifying force itself, as the persistent use of the substantive form (*to kalon*) in his texts indicates. Indeed, the *Metaphys-ics* tells us the *kalon* is itself a cause. Though the promised discussion of this causality never comes, it is clear that it is a final cause, not merely of action, but of many other things as well: of many cognitions and, indeed, of many "motions."[76] As a cause, it is both eternal and divine:

> Some things are eternal and divine, others are capable of being
> or not being; and the *kalon* and the divine is, in accordance
> with its own nature, always a cause of the betterment of those
> things able to receive it.[77]

The *kalon*, so reified, seems to be the Prime Mover itself. *Metaphysics* 12 tells us that the Prime Mover is an unmoved mover of the cosmos itself, and hence akin to the *kalon*:

> The object of desire and of reason moves without being
> moved. And the first among these [two categories of object]
> are the same. For what is desired is the apparent *kalon*, and
> what is wished for rationally is the genuine kalon. . . . [The
> Prime Mover] exists necessarily, and quâ necessarily, *kalos*, and
> thus it is a source [*archê*].[78]

Hence, not merely humans and their communities but the uni-verse itself has a natural tendency, akin to a desire, toward the *kalon*.

This, for its part, would be not merely a manifested quality nor a unifying force, but the goal toward which that force moves: the highest manifestation of the quality, the Prime Mover itself. But there is a problem with construing the Prime Mover as *kalon*, for it is also wholly simple (cf. *Metaphysics* 12.7 1073a3–13). The *kalon*, I noted above, has an ordering function, as laws order a city and teleology orders the cosmos. But the Prime Mover has no parts, and therefore nothing to be ordered; it would seem that it cannot be *kalon*. The above quote goes on to suggest that we construe the *kalos* of the Prime Mover, not as a characteristic it possesses in and of itself, but as the quality of its rule (*archē*) over the universe. Its own simplicity, when "imitated" by the "desiring" universe, would become the unifying *kalon* of the cosmic order.[79]

But this possibility is vigorously rejected by *Metaphysics* 12. Speusippus and Pythagoras denied *kalos* to the source of all things, on the grounds that in plants and animals the source is the efficient cause, and beauty and completeness are only to be found in the effects of those causes—that is, in the things themselves. Accepting their position would be to assert that, though the Prime Mover is not *kalos*, its primary effect—the order of the universe—is. But their position, the *Metaphysics* continues, was wrong: no quality can be found in an effect which is not in its cause, and thus the Prime Mover itself must be the most *kalon* of things (*Metaphysics* 12.7 1072b30 seq.).

But the term means different things when applied to the Prime Mover and to natural beings (including the cosmos itself). *Metaphysics* 12 asks whether the nature of the whole possesses its greatest good "as something separated and off by itself [*kechorismenon . . . kai auto kath hauto*] or as [its] order." The answer is both, and the point is clarified with political analogies: just as the general of an army is both a part of the army and an individual in his own right upon whom the army's organization depends, so with the Prime Mover. Or it is as in a household: each of the slaves lives "for the most part at random" yet still, if in a small way, contributes to the common good. Similarly, then, with the universe as a whole: individual living things pursue their own ends and when they achieve them are *kala* in one sense. In so doing they integrate themselves into the order of the whole, sustain it as, in a second sense *kalos*; and by so doing they also sustain the position of its chief part, which is *kalon* in the third and strictest sense: the Prime Mover.[80]

In the *Philebus*, sensory items were said to be "true" in that they fit into the right kind of development; terms were true in virtue of the purity of their mixture, itself the result of a different, dialogical process. For Aristotle, sensibles are *kala* in virtue of a more global process, one by which the individual thing comes to occupy its place in the cosmos, while the final cause of that cosmos is *kalos* in a mysteriously higher sense. In its status as universal goal, the Aristotelian *kalon* has an important affinity to Hegel's conception of "truth" as rational result. For Aristotle, the cosmos generally is in a constant process of seeking the *kalon*, just as for Hegel it is in a constant coming-to-correspond of thing and Concept; the preeminent "truth" of Hegel's Concept would then stand to finite things somewhat as the preeminent *kalon* of the Prime Mover stands to the Aristotelian cosmos—as goal and paradigm. True, Aristotle's *kalon* seems to be reified as the Hegelian system should never be, in particular by being attributed to the Prime Mover. But it is precisely this attribution which enables us to see how Hegel's account of truth links with the Aristotelian conception of the *kalon*. For the *noêsis noêseôs*, the "thought on thought" which Aristotle attributes to the Prime Mover, is at the very end of the *Encyclopedia* attributed to Hegel's System itself.[81] Hence, in its function as a universal goal, and indeed as a (final) cause of things, Hegel's System is to exhibit—with differences, three of which will be noted below—the kind of universal final causality that the Prime Mover exemplifies for Aristotle.

Before I attempt a final translation let us see how, in general terms, Aristotle characterizes the *kalon*. *Metaphysics* 13.3 (1078b1f.) asserts that the three main species of the *kalon* are order, symmetry, and definiteness (*to hôrismenon*). Symmetry is clearly a species of order, and to "define" (*horizein*) a term other than nominally is to place it into the Aristotelian causal order, that of genera and species.[82] So I will take "order" as one side of the Aristotelian concept of the *kalon*. Also essential to the *kalon* is size. A very large or small animal, however well-organized, cannot for example be *kalon* to the eye, and a state that is too large cannot be ordered at all: the *kalon* thus exists "in size and order," *en taxei kai megethei*.[83] I will, then, define the *kalon*, in its Aristotelian conception, as order over size. When this quality is apparent in a sensible object, it corresponds roughly—as in the *Poetics*—to the English "beauty." In the case of a state, or the character of an individual, "harmony" and "moral goodness" are perhaps more appropriate. But none of these captures the full Aristotelian sense, which sees "beauty" and "moral goodness" as, so to speak, sensible and nonsensible species of the same genus, of order over size, and as the goal of human ethical and political life, of everything living, and indeed of the cosmos itself.

The English language, in fact, has no obvious translation for this notion, not merely because we have abandoned the Aristotelian conception of a teleologically ordered cosmos but also because we have lost the

Aristotelian (and Hegelian) view of the unity of soul and body: what is good for the one, we tend to think, must be bad for the other. Thus, if I call a woman "beautiful," I am all but imputing personality problems to her; to use the term of a man is to risk evoking some of the worst of Anglo-Saxon prejudices. I can of course refer to someone as a "beautiful person," but that again conveys a degree of simplemindedness. The other main translation, Joseph Owens's "moral goodness," leaves the sensory dimension behind and in our culture suggests the following of commandments.

I will, with reservations, translate *kalon* as "Noble." I capitalize this word to show that I take it, not in its unfortunate medieval connection with purity of birth (a meaning from which I seek to rescue it), but as denoting, in the first (Aristotelian) instance, order over size. In that sense, "Noble" does have some recommendation. When we say that a person has a noble bearing, we mean that she organizes the various components of her gait and posture in a dynamic and admirable way. When we say she has nobility of outlook, we attribute to her a wide range of knowledge, aptitudes, and concerns which she can bring to bear on individual concrete issues. And a person who possesses nobility of character has not just one virtue or two, but many, all cooperating in her life and relations with others.

If the term's recent history has been unfortunate, its ancient provenance is distinctly more congenial. The *nobiles* of ancient Rome were precisely not those of high birth, but those who by their own efforts had raised themselves from humble background to a point where they had to be taken account of: *nobilis* was a shortening of *notabilis*, notable. So with the company of words Hegel treats in his System: they begin, like all words, in confrontation with the grit and chaos of sensation. Then, via a historical process to be discussed in chapter 7, they rise to the heights of philosophical and scientific generality and exactitude. In this trajectory, they retain traces of their sensory origin, and are able to harmonize sensation with reason. Moreover, when they reach the level of what I will call "expert discourse," they can be defined by other terms: unpacked into their markers, or into what Leibniz would have called their *nota*. So the Nobility of a word is its capacity to sum up, in an organized way, a variety of other contents: other words, sensory phenomena, and in the final analysis social practices. The Nobility of words is in this way their *nota*bility.

In what follows, I will refer to the goal of Hegel's System—Hegelian "truth"—as Nobility. The Hegel of the Right claimed, we saw, necessity and universality for his System; the Hegel of the Left demanded that the System not be merely an abstract play, but that it have enough content to be concretely informative. That is why the development of the Concept, as I presented it in chapter 1, had to be both immanent, on the one hand, and complete on the other. *Hegelian truth as Nobility is nothing over and above this conjunction of immanence and completeness.* In claiming that his System is true, Hegel is not claiming that it informs us about anything other than itself; or, to put it in our present terms, Hegel's System—the Concept—is Noble, in the strictest sense, because its internal development is necessary and complete; finite things exhibit Nobility insofar as their development can be said to be the same; and the Idea is Noble insofar as it exhibits the necessary and complete coming-to-correspond of the Concept and finite things.

This processual nature of Hegelian Nobility provides a first contrast to Aristotle's static conception, where order over size could be as motionless as the Zeus of Praxiteles. For Hegel, Nobility is a characteristic of narrative, of coming-to-be. When the components of such a narrative are not only multiple but contrast with each other in some important way, Nobility becomes, not just order over size, but harmony over diversity. When they do not merely contrast but tend away from each other— in conflict or contradiction—Nobility becomes the reconciliation of opposites, which Hegel emphasizes so resolutely.[84]

These further dimensions are important, not least because as has been seen there are senses in which Hegelian coming-to-correspond, or truth, remains incomplete: to complete it would be to abolish it as a process. Hence, there are always finite things which do not wholly correspond to their Concepts, and contingency has a large place in Hegel's world, if only a small one in his System.[85] For the British Hegelians, who do not clearly distinguish the necessity and completeness of thought from its referential capacities, the world is itself a necessary and complete referent; as for Leibniz, philosophy should be a system because reality itself is one. Hegel stands on this issue with Kant: whether or not the world is systematically organized, our thought—if it is philosophical—should be.[86]

Also in contrast to Aristotle, the Nobility of Hegel's System must, I have argued, be linguistic in nature. If we apply Aristotle's conception of Nobility, not to the cosmos or to ideas but to words, then we have a conception in which one sort of discourse—the System, perhaps—is *kalon* in the strict sense, while other types of discourse contribute to this and approximate it. Given the Hegelian dynamism, we get the linguistic *kalon* as evolving to comprehend other forms of discourse, and those as developing toward it: of different types of discourse keeping company with each other. As thus linguistic, Hegelian philosophical truth must be the ability of a word to serve as the convergence for a determinate multiplicity of other words, so that they can define it and it can designate the unity they are capable of forming. This ability, exhibited by Hegel's System, is I will argue its goal and form: it is the Nobility which constitutes the company of words.

The linguistic nature of Hegel's System is a second sense in which he differs, then, from Aristotle. It leads to a third. For Aristotle, the unifying principle in any ordered whole is prior to the order itself: the army is an army because it has a general, and the household is a household because it has a paterfamilias—but not vice versa.[87] But language for Hegel, even the language of his System, always retains a bearing on the realities it articulates. For all its immanence and freedom, the System is (in a variety of senses to be discussed in chapter 10) "dependent" on the world it comprehends. The governing foundationalism that Aristotle codified and consolidated, and which was represented for the young Hegel by Fichte, has no place in Hegel's own conception of Nobility.

PART   2

DIALECTICS

4

Hegelian Thought: Analysis

Aporia

Scholarly literature on the basic figures and procedures of Hegel's way of thinking has become wholly unassimilable in extent. The writing on his category of "contradiction" alone would be appropriately measured in shelf-inches, if not shelf-feet.[1] It is also unimaginably diverse in content: in the beginning of the 1980s, at a symposium on Hegelian dialectic and formal logic, Jaako Hintikka counted over twenty different senses given to "dialectic" by the participants alone.[2] For present purposes the vast bulk of the literature may be ignored, for its divergence from my own approach will be clear. What I will not wholly ignore is the spate of attempts, during the 1960s and 1970s, to formalize Hegel's dialectic. Hegel himself would hardly have approved of it; formalization requires symbols, and Hegel eschewed symbolism altogether, for what he thought were good reasons.[3] This is partly because for Hegel, thinking—and especially philosophical thinking—is basically a highly sophisticated way of remembering—or, as Hegel puts it, intelligence is cognitive only insofar as it is recognitive.[4] Like many workers in recent cognitive science, Hegel views thought as noncombinatorial in the sense that thought processes cannot run without accessing memory. No step in the dialectic is wholly warranted solely by general rules known at the outset, as is the case in "combinatorial" views of thought. Given the narrow scope of rules in

Hegelian dialectic, we can expect then that a general account of it will be of very limited use.

Not, however, of no use at all. Unless it is strictly a series of improvisations, Hegelian thought must have a "form" of some sort: there must, at minimum, be certain basic gestures which are repeated as the System develops, and against which individual moves can be judged. "Formalization," as the presentation of these basic moves in a set of arbitrary symbols, rather than the words Hegel actually used, has thus had a plausible claim to give a normative representation of certain general features of Hegelian thought.

The strategies adopted by efforts at formalization have been diverse. Clark Butler and Yvon Gauthier have attempted to capture Hegelian dialectic in traditional predicate calculus, while F. J. Asenjo has used a higher-order predicate calculus, and Dubarle and Dos, a second-order Boolean framework. S. K. Thomason has adapted the predicate calculus so that $\sim(p \cap \sim p)$ is valid but $(p \cdot \sim p) \to q$ is not, and applied this to Hegel. G. Gunther has based his presentation on a trivalent sentential logic derived from Lukasiewicz. R. Routley and R. Meyer have used a sentential relevance logic. Michael Kosok has attempted to formulate the dialectic as a "modern temporal logic of non-identity." Paul Thagard has used the Sneed-Stegmuller formalization of scientific theory change. Finally, Thomas Seebohm has elaborated the Kantian logic of concepts to show how Hegel's procedure builds on it.[5]

These strategies, with the exception of Seebohm's, are of course anachronistic. The predicate calculus, to say nothing of its more complex modifications, was uninvented in Hegel's day. But they run into more serious problems than that as accounts of how Hegel actually constructed his System. Thagard's treatment is keyed to the *Phenomenology*, and Kosok's is formulated without specific reference to any of Hegel's texts. All the rest attempt to construe Hegel's System as, basically, a set of assertions, and this leads to a familiar problem. An assertion is generally supposed to describe the world somehow—that is, to be true of a state of affairs which is other than it. Of what sort of state of affairs would the assertions in Hegel's system be true? If they describe the actual phenomena of nature and history, Hegel's System is open to the charge that both history and our interpretations of nature are open-ended matters, and a definitive description of either domain is impossible. If on the other hand the System is to describe some sort of objective but nonempirical realm, Hegel seems guilty of hypostatizing an ideal Absolute, leaving reality behind. Both readings have often been given: the former by Kierkegaard, Marx, and Left Hegelians in general; the latter

paradigmatically by Iwan Iljin and the Right-wing British "Hegelians."
We are back at the Left-Right split, which reveals itself to be an artifact of
what I have called assertionism: both sides in the dispute take the view
that Hegel's System must describe, be true of, something, and differ only
as to what. But no sentence can describe itself: there is always an otherness between word and object, or assertion and fact. Neither position,
then, allows for Hegel's claims, at the end of the *Phenomenology* and the
beginning of the *Science of Logic*, that *all* otherness to thought has been
overcome and that thinking can, in the System, develop purely in its own
element.[6]

Behind the apparent diversity of approaches, then, is a single un-
stated presupposition: that the element of Hegelian thought, the basic
constituent of the dialectic, is the assertion. And, presumably because all
assertions share a single general form, it follows that there is only one
kind of Hegelian dialectic—or that, if there is not, there probably should
be, as Hintikka implies. I will by contrast give here brief accounts of two
types of Hegelian dialectic: the "historical" dialectic of the rise to the
absolute standpoint, and the "Systematic" dialectic of that standpoint
itself. These are quite different. True, dialectic is present both in the rise
to the absolute standpoint (of which the standard example is the *Phenomenology*) and within that standpoint itself (as represented by such systematic works as the *Science of Logic* and the *Encyclopedia*). But the former
process is enmeshed in contingency, both in its procedures and its results.[7] Change must, so to speak, be forced upon historical dialectics by
the randomness with which it must deal. In the *Phenomenology*, resistance
to change is at such a pitch that revision is viewed as a "loss of self"; the
"way to science" is a "path of despair,"[8] treatment of which I will rele-
gate to an appendix to this chapter. Such is not the case in Systematic
dialectics, where as we will see content is not negated in the same way
and revision is not resisted.

If assertions function paradigmatically in descriptions and a
descriptivist reading of Hegel's system is impossible, some sort of nonassertional framework must be found for explicating his dialectical
method. Thomas Seebohm has provided it from Kant's logic of concepts.[9] There, as the previous narrative showed, concepts are viewed, not
in terms of their extensions—of what they are in the assertional sense
true of—but in terms of the aggregates of subconcepts (*Teilbegriffe*)
which constitute (or, as I will say, define) them. Falsity, and therefore
truth, are defined strictly in terms of conceptual interrelations, rather
than as relations of thought to some external reality: a concept is "false"
if it is defined by two subconcepts which are logical complements of each

other.[10] If "soul," for example, is defined as both mortal and immortal, then it is what Seebohm would call a false concept.

Seebohm's reconstruction of Hegel, proceeding on this basis, is able to present his dialectic as a procedure which "says nothing about facts, but seeks only to explicate concepts in its own way."[11] The question of assertionism arises again, however, if we ask whether the concepts thus explicated are themselves other than their own Systematic analyses: are we simply replacing the view that Hegel's system establishes truths about reality with the view that it establishes truths about concepts, as Locke perhaps replaced the view that words name things with the view that they signify ideas?[12] The Kantian answer would be yes: a concept is a representation, not a word.[13] But Hegel's answer is no, because for him thinking is essentially linguistic: "it is in names that we think," he writes.[14] If we think in the names in which the Logic is written, and if all otherness to thought is overcome at the beginning of the Logic, then it seems that Systematic thought is not other than Systematic language for Hegel: the words of the System *are* the System. That such is the case will be argued in more detail later. For the moment, I simply note that it follows that a philosophical concept for Hegel can be nothing other than its own enunciation in his System. My reconstruction of Hegel's procedure will be keyed to the vehicles of such enunciation: to the philosophical "names we think in."

We find the limits of Seebohm's approach to Hegel through Kant, and complete our aporia, by recognizing that one characteristic of philosophical names can be assimilated to a basic distinction in Hegel's thought: that of "in itself" (*an sich*) and "for itself" (*für sich*). As is well known, Hegel criticizes Kant's view of the thing-in-itself as constituting a realm beyond experience. He does so, I suggest, in the spirit of Aristotle's attack on Plato's Theory of Forms. Hegel does not deny the notion of the "in-itself," any more than Aristotle denied the existence of *eidê*; rather, he rejects what might be called the Kantian *chorismos*: the separation of the in-itself from experience. Thus, for Hegel, "all things are in the first instance *an sich*"; the Hegelian in-itself is not an indeterminable something beyond experience, but an indeterminacy—a potentiality—which is found as such within experience and which we call such because it goes on to determine, or actualize, itself within appearances.[15]

Seebohm, ignoring this revision in Kantian terminology, argues that two absolutes are present at the beginning of Hegel's System, one concrete and one abstract. The former, according to him, is substitutable for the latter. But the logical complement of the abstract absolute is also itself a moment of the concrete absolute—that is, occurs in its logical explication. In virtue of the substitutability of the two absolutes, the logical complement of the abstract absolute is then also a moment of the abstract absolute itself, and this makes of it a contradictory or "false" concept: its explication contains its own logical complement. Hegel's system is then trapped from the outset in a contradiction from which, Seebohm says, nothing positive can result.[16]

But Hegel, in the passage Seebohm cites, says that the concrete absolute is present in the beginning only in-itself; it is the "goal and business of the further development."[17] The abstract absolute cannot then be substituted for it, any more than an embryo can be "substituted" for a philosopher. The movement of the Logic as a whole can have as "positive" result, not a contradictory set of assertions about two absolutes both present from the start, but the raising of the concrete absolute from its status as merely in-itself to the full explicitness of the for-itself.[18] While retaining Seebohm's Kantian vocabulary of "markers" (*Merkmale*), which covers both concepts and subconcepts, I will therefore amend his account in two ways. The markers will be considered not to signify concepts, but to stand in for philosophical names.[19] And I will key my presentation to the role of the moments of the "in-itself" and the "for-itself" as functionally constitutive for philosophical names.[20]

The main exegetical device I will use to present Hegel's various forms of dialectic will be to rewrite in arbitrary symbols some of the global gestures of dialectics—gestures that, as far as I can tell, are repeated throughout the System. This effort has three main purposes.

First, Hegel himself, as I have noted, eschewed arbitrary symbols. He expressed his thought in the sounds and inscriptions of the German language, to which he assigned his own, philosophically constructed, meanings. His reasons for this will become clear in the sequel, as will the extent to which my rewriting, like the formalizations I have discussed, manipulates Hegel's intentions. The manipulation is necessary because the meanings Hegel provides for the moments of his System are often quite different from the meanings associated with those words in German. The result is constant distraction, when not actual misunderstanding and angry rejection; and these problems are only magnified when Hegel is translated into English. By presenting Hegel's basic dialectical gestures in arbitrary symbols, I hope to focus attention on the gestures themselves, and to avoid entanglements occasioned by the words in which he himself makes them.

Second, one of my main contentions will be that the System is much more supple than has previously been thought. Not only could Hegel have developed it in directions other than those it actually takes in his writings, but it has enormous capacities for revision. This can be shown by liberating its basic gestures from the words in which Hegel's writings couch them. The result will be a Hegel who is not ultimately committed to *any* of the specific doctrines he develops in the course of the System, any more than scientists are ultimately committed to any of the specific views they may currently hold on the basis of available evidence. In both cases revision is always possible, and *Hegel is among the most ontologically uncommitted of philosophers*. This, in turn, is crucial to our evaluation of the long-term viability of his System, since so many of its specific claims have been amply refuted by subsequent science and history.

Third, I hope by this to begin to make clear how the System can develop unconditioned by anything outside itself, purely by grouping and regrouping already defined terms so as to produce new ones. Because it (or its writer, Hegel himself) freely chooses *which* sounds from German to use for any moment, and could in principle choose or invent others, the System is not conditioned by the German language. But because the sounds it freely chooses are in fact those of German, the System is responsive to that language—and to the world which that language forms and is formed by. Full discussion of how this works must await chapters 7 and 10, which finally will answer the question of the Hegelian Left and Right—the question of how the System can respond to concrete reality without being conditioned by it.

The account I will give, by its use of symbols, may resemble the kinds of system with which formal logicians deal. It should not be mistaken for one, for several reasons. It is, in the first place, a mere exegetical device, not a full-blown logic. I will discuss the symbols I use in enough detail, I hope, to make those uses clear. But I will not attempt to give fully rigorous definitions, of the kind that would enable a thinker to use those symbols in contexts other than the present project. Whether various infelicities would arise in such extension is beyond my concern here. Indeed, the infelicities which will inevitably arise even in these few pages—I am no logician—will not greatly concern me, for my aim is merely to convey Hegel's general idea as tidily as I can.

Second, since my aim is exegesis, I will try to keep my account simple. This is almost the opposite to the concern of formal approaches, where "power" is often considered to be the capacity of a system to generate logical complexity. In part, this emphasis on simplicity is true to Hegel. For Carnap in the *Logical Structure of the World*, to take one example, anything which is not formal is merely subjective and individualistic. Hence he wants to develop as much formal structure as possible—to the extent that he undertakes to construct purely formal (or "structural") definite descriptions.[21] For Hegel, what is not purely formal is, because of constraints introduced by his view of history, not individual and "subjective" but social and communal. His aim, unlike that of Carnap, is not to replace this "content" with formal structure, but simply to organize it. The simpler its principles, the more economical and comprehensive the organization: Hegel's dialectical procedures will tend, not to the complex, but to the simple. My rewriting will be even simpler than Hegel's original version, for I will restrict myself to only those of his gestures which are the most generalized and basic. Though I will allude to some further complexities, the three goals I set myself above can be met without unraveling all the complexities of Hegelian dialectics. That is a matter for Hegelian logicians, should any ever exist.

Third, as with my use of symbolism generally in this book, I will attempt to remain as close as possible to the overt structures of the expressions they rewrite. It is quite possible that Hegel's dialectics can be written more economically, with more elegant and sophisticated symbolic tools than the ones I am developing. But the results would not look much like what is on a page of Hegel, and it is those pages which I want to understand.

Fourth, the expressions I will generate, couched in arbitrary symbols, will perhaps look a bit like an uninterpreted, purely syntactic calculus. But those expressions will not serve for a syntax. They will have nothing to do, for example, with ordinary grammatical categories, such as noun and verb, or even with logical ones such as conjunction, disjunction, and implication. Nor will they at any later stage receive a traditional semantics. For one thing, as Hegel actually writes the System, its intended "interpretation" is there from the start: it is the few hundred terms from German expert discourse whose sounds he uses for his own Systematic constructions.

Even to call this an "interpretation" may be misleading, however. In the mathematical sense of a domain for which its expressions are true, Hegel's System can of course have no interpretation: it contains no propositions and does not state or preserve truth. If we understand "interpretation" in its loosest hermeneutical sense, we come a bit closer: the System offers us a scheme in terms of which to make concrete sense of our cultural world. But even this is not very close unless we stress the active, organizing function of Hegel's System. Hegel's basic claim will be that, if Germans do not use their words with the meanings his System gives them, they ought to. Only so can they articulate their world and themselves in a well-defined, well-organized vocabulary: only so can they attain and make use of a company of words. The point of the System, then, is not simply to capture certain features of discourse, but to provide a basis for organizing it. On the other hand, the System's interpretive basis should come as close as possible to the meanings already established in German for the terms it contains. If a closer approach is possible, it must be devised, either by remodeling the language or by revising the System. Where neither of these is possible, the differences between the two must be clearly stated. The relation between the System and the language in whose sounds it is expressed is thus a process, one of establishing differences while growing together: a dynamic of Nobility, not a capture of truth.

Systematic Dialectics

Hegel maintains that the copula in a judgment is "empty," and that this renders judgments (to say nothing, we saw, of propositions or sentences) an inadequate way of expressing the development of his System. The "empty is" of the copula emphasizes the identity of subject and predicate at the expense of their diversity:

> In fact, a speculative meaning does not allow itself to be correctly [*richtig*] expressed in the form of such a sentence: it is the unity *in* the diversity, which itself is at once present and posited, that is to be grasped.[22]

Hegel goes on here to say that the "true expression" of the unity of Being and Nothing is not a judgment at all, but a single word: *Werden,* becoming. This somewhat mysterious claim follows from his view of the function of names in thinking:

> The name is the simple sign for the genuine representation, i.e., the *simple* one which has not been resolved into its determinations and put together again out of them. . . . The basic requirement of language as such, that for names, is the need to have, for the immediate representation, an immediate, simple sign as well. . . . Thinking sums up [*resumiert*] in the form of a simple thought the concrete content of analyses in which the content has been reduced to a connection of a number of determinations.[23]

A common name, as a sign, is a simple unit. It presents a complex of content in a simple, immediate way: as an "abstract universal," or *an sich*. But:

> Just as when I say *"all* animals" the phrase cannot pass for a zoology, so we realize immediately that the words divine, absolute, eternal, etc. do not express what is contained in them.[24]

This relates to my previous discussion of Hegelian truth in the following way. Suppose the set of terms which define a name is called the "content" of that name, so that (for example) "rational animal" is the content of "man." Such content can be presented in two ways: first, merely uttering the name itself can, in a sense, call it up or render it accessible (though not actually accessed), as when hearing the sound "man" disposes us to act toward its referent as if that referent were a rational animal. A complex of content thus rendered accessible is present in a simple, immediate way. But it is a truism for Hegel that what is explicitly, or "for itself", simple is implicitly, or "in itself," complex: what is thus rendered accessible is not ipso facto accessed or displayed. The content abbreviated by the name is, we may say, present "in itself"; when the name is explicated, it is displayed and becomes "for itself." The movement from "in itself" to "for itself" and back again—what I will call "explication" and "abbreviation"—is basic to Hegel's thought. It is, he tells us, the movement of education; of science itself; and in fact of any being.[25] It is the capacity of names to present such a movement in their function of abbreviating content that make them so basic to thinking in Hegel's view: they are not *merely* immediate unities, but unities which have an intrinsic pull to bring forth other contents.

Hegelian Systematic dialectic, proceeding in names rather than assertions, is thus a kind of calling-up, or accessing, of information: the name itself is a code for a certain set of contents which it sums up in simple form. If systematic thought is to be unconditioned from outside, this content must be other names from the System. Such names do not, like the copula, disguise the complexity they signify; they rather point to it as what is necessary to understand them. In virtue of this pointing, names of this sort are for Hegel essentially abbreviations which require explication of their latent content. That for Hegel we think *in* such names, rather than in sentences or propositions,[26] indicates that *Hegel's system is constructed as a series of explications of the content contained within (or abbreviated by) the philosophical names which it, itself, introduces.* As I will discuss below, Hegel also makes continuous use of assertion and predication in his expositions of his System; but in view of his recognition of their inadequacy, these are perhaps best regarded as a "surface structure" of his Systematic dialectic.

My rewriting of its depths, which are not static structures but dyamic gestures of thought, will make use of a number of symbols which I will introduce here, adding some remarks below. Both the introduction and the remarks are provisional: no symbol in Systematic dialectics can be understood apart from its function in the construction of the System—its meaning, to coin a phrase, is its use. These symbols, then, cannot really be understood until they are seen in action. They include:

1. A set of simple markers, or as Hegel calls them, names. I will keep them straight with subscripts: "M_1, M_2, M_3, . . . "

The dialectic moves by regrouping markers and then naming the groups with new markers, which in turn become subject to regrouping themselves. The various groups thus constituted will be indicated by:

2. The usual levels of parenthesis, here playing an unusual role: as denoting previously formed unities, they are to be respected where possible (as in law, *stare decisis*). But they can always be dissolved if necessary, and their components treated separately.
3. The symbol "•" will denote simple aggregation, and is used as follows: if M_x and M_y have occurred previously in the development, we are allowed to write "$M_x • M_y$" ("conjunction"). If we already have "$M_x • M_y$," we are allowed to write either M_x or M_y ("disjunction").

Any two markers or groupings can be conjoined and disjoined in this way. Two more restricted types of connective will also be used. First, a single marker can be conjoined with a complex set of markers in either of two ways:

4. $M_{n+1} \Leftarrow (M_{n-x} . . . M_n)$, where n>x ("explication").
5. $(M_{n-x} . . . M_n) \Rightarrow M_{n+1}$, where n>x ("abbreviation").

Simple markers or complex markers, or a combination of both, can be conjoined by the connective ⇑ if and only if they have already occurred as conjoined by both "$\Leftarrow$" and "$\Rightarrow$." This gives us another Systematic gesture:

6. "$(M_{n-x} ⇑ . . . ⇑ M_n) \Rightarrow M_{n+1}$" and "$M_{n+1} \Leftarrow (M_{n-x} ⇑ . . . ⇑ M_n)$,"

where n>x, allow us to write "$(M_m \Uparrow \ldots \Uparrow M_{n+1})$" ("reflection," for reasons to be discussed below).

Also needed is the opposite of reflection:

7. "$(M_{n-x} \Uparrow \ldots \Uparrow M_{n+1})$" allows us to write "$(M_{n-x} \Uparrow \ldots \Uparrow M_n) \Rightarrow M_{n+1}$" • "$M_{n+1} \Leftarrow (M_{n-x} \Uparrow \ldots \Uparrow M_n)$," where n>x (counterreflection). This can be performed on any instance of $\Uparrow$, whether within a longer sequence of symbols or not.

Four more gestures complete the picture:

8. "M_{n+1}" allows us to write "$M_{n+1} \Leftarrow (M_1 \Uparrow \ldots \Uparrow M_n)$" ("full mediation") or "$M_{n+1} \Leftarrow \{M_n\}$," where $\{M_n\}$ lists any subset, including connectives, of $\{M_1 \ldots M_{n-1}\}$ ("partial mediation").
9. "M_{n+1}" allows us to write "$M_1 \Uparrow \ldots \Uparrow M_n$" ("transition").
10. "$(M_m \Uparrow \ldots \Uparrow M_n) \Rightarrow M_{n+1}$" allows us to write: "$M_{n+1}$" ("immediation").
11. "$(M_m \Uparrow \ldots \Uparrow M_{n+1})$" warrants to write "$(M \Uparrow \ldots \Uparrow M_{n+1}) \Rightarrow M_{n+2}$" ("introduction").

Discussion

Ad 1. "Markers" (a term whose history I partially traced in chapter 3) are, as I have noted, philosophical names; such a name becomes a "marker" by being "introduced" as an abbreviation for a set of other markers. As I will argue in chapter 7, philosophical names for Hegel have a complex and elusive nature. In general they can be understood as individual utterances, sounding words. As such, they are tokens, not types; each disappears as uttered. Philosophical names, then, are not the kind of symbol with which philosophers are familiar. For one thing, they cannot be written down without falsifying their nature: inscription gives them a static character which they should not have. (My own precedent for writing them is, of course, Hegel himself.) The markers I use in my rewriting are thus inscriptions of philosophical names (e.g., the sound of "M"); they are not variables for which other names (such as those Hegel actually uses) could be substituted. Hence, my rewriting does not directly give the formal structure of the Hegelian dialectic. It presents, instead, another dialectical system, a schematization which resembles Hegel's System in its basic gestures and is less confusing in its individual symbols.

Ad 4 and 5. "⇐" can be read as "is explicated by" and "⇒" as "is abbreviated by." Normally, abbreviation and explication are specific forms of substitution: when a relatively short formula is substituted for a relatively long one, the latter is "abbreviated" by the former; when a longer formula is substituted for a shorter one, the latter is "explicated" into the former. In the present notation, the expression at the point of the arrow, being simple, would be shorter than the other one. (A restriction which, I will argue, does not hold for the first triad of the *Logic*.) In common logical parlance, substitution preserves truth-value: replacing an abbreviation with its abbreviatum in any sentence should not change the truth-value of that sentence. As we would expect from Hegel's indifference to assertional truth, abbreviation and explication may, but need not, preserve truth-value; they are better looked at in terms of computer "accessing," in which a single simple code may cue a variety of complex displays, rather than in the assertionistic terms of logical substitution.

The gesture of explication has an important set of analogues in nonphilosophical discourse. In the System, "explication" is a relation between one marker—one momentary vocalization—and a set of such vocalizations. This makes it an inherently dynamic relation: by the time we arrive at the set of markers that are abbreviated, for example by the word "becoming," "becoming" itself has died away. In "finite" reality, things are not fleeting moments of a larger whole, but isolated and independent;[27] as such, they seem also to be static and enduring. Thus, the "finite"analogue to abbreviation would be a situation in which a simple entity did not die away but persisted, coexisting with a set of other entities which it unified—as precisely the kind of substrate which Hegel, chapter 1 showed, wanted to eliminate from philosophy. The "content" of such a substrate would be its parts or properties. Hence, a particular grouping of Systematic markers provides us with an analogue to a corresponding sort of being—one in which the properties corresponding to those markers actually exist as unified: the Systematic group enables us to conceive of a particular sort of entity in the finite world. I will give examples of this where helpful.

Ad 6. The connective " ⇑ " can first be viewed in terms of "⇒" and "⇐." These are both dialectical transitions in thought, and as such are themselves contents that, when both present, can be abbreviated by a single, simpler marker. " ⇑ " serves as such a marker, abbreviating these two transitions. " ⇑ " is thus a sort of meta-abbreviation: it converts the operations of explicating and abbreviating into a single abbreviated content: when "⇐" and "⇒" are replaced by " ⇑ ," something *done* is replaced by something *thought about*. In thus unifying and objectifying previously existing material, the replacement conveys the important Hegelian moment of "reflection."[28]

Ad 8. Mediation may be full or partial. In partial mediation, I explicate a given moment of the System by writing only some of the markers it abbreviates. Thus, if "man" were a name in Hegel's System which abbreviated the term "rational animal," a mediation of it would be either full (consisting of "rational animal") or partial (consisting of either "rational" or "animal"). This holds no matter what connectives or parentheses govern that marker: at any stage, any subset of previously introduced markers, however connected, is available for further developments. It is this trait of Systematic dialectics which is largely responsible for the System's capacity to generate complexity, as well as for its ability to revise itself by dissolving and regrouping markers previously introduced. Since I will prefer to do these jobs, here, more slowly by using counterreflection and disjunction together to dissolve previous groupings, partial mediation will be largely absent from my examples. But Hegel makes almost constant use of it.

In addition to being "full" or "partial," a mediation can be to varying degrees "adequate," depending on whether it also includes mediations of the explicating terms. Thus, to continue the example above, suppose "animal" abbreviates "living thing capable of motion in space." "Man" can thus be given a more adequate, though still partial, mediation if we write (as we are warranted to do) that formula instead of "animal." Such a relatively adequate mediation of "man" would be "rational living thing capable of motion in space."

Ad 9. "Transition" seeks to capture the Hegelian notion of *Übergehen*, in which a process of mediation is independent of what it mediates—of its own beginning point—to the extent that that beginning point is not only gone but forgotten as it gets mediated.[29] As forgotten, it cannot be written down, as it can with mediation. But transition is very close to mediation, and in a more elegant presentation of the dialectic might be defined in terms of it. Transition has its uses here in understanding Hegel's text.

The concluding sections of Hegel's *Science of Logic*, on the "Absolute Idea," contain some general remarks on what Hegel considered Systematic dialectics to be, and before discussing specific examples I will measure my proposed tools against this account.

This is, it should be pointed out, an unusual undertaking.[30] The strategies of the Logic are usually understood in terms of the discussion of the "speculative sentence" in the Preface to the *Phenomenology*, to which are added some passages from the Preface to the first edition of the *Science of*

Logic—passages which do not, however, actually use the phrase *spekulativer Satz*. That phrase is, in fact, wholly missing from the *Logic*; it occurs only once after the *Phenomenology*, in an *Anmerkung* to *Encyclopedia* #88.[31] It seems more reliable to turn, not to the *Phenomenology* (the status of whose Preface I indicated in the Introduction) but to the *Logic's* own discussion of "The Method." This discussion, on the present analysis, gives a complete account of the gestures by which the System is constructed, and does so without appeal to speculative sentences.

On the present reading, the speculative sentence is, as Rüdiger Bubner takes it to be, a means of overcoming certain ways of thinking peculiar to the Understanding; this is the context in which it is mentioned at *Encyclopedia*. #88 Anm. Even in the *Logic* itself, then, it belongs to what I call historical dialectics: more properly, in view of the resistance present to each stage of its complex development, to the "phenomenological" version of these.[32] Efforts to understand the development of the System in terms of speculative sentences, applying a category from historical dialectics to the System itself, predictably lead to problems with the immanence Hegel claims for the System's development. Thus Bubner is prone to make the System nothing more than the overcoming of the Understanding, and hence conditioned by something outside the System—by the Understanding itself. Bubner gets around this by postulating a pure, or abstract, negativity which can neither be dispensed with nor explained by the Logic, as the source of the "movement of the Concept." As Erich Puntel subsequently pointed out, such an abstract source of motion leads only to new Systematic moments—not to the inherently richer ones that Hegel actually produces.[33] This is a problem which Bubner pronounced himself able to see, but not to solve. My solution is that the "movement of the concept" is nothing more than the demand on the part of a Systematic name—itself, as will be seen in chapter 7, something which disappears as it arises, and hence intrinsically dynamic—for its meaning.[34]

In "The Absolute Idea," Hegel characterizes the beginning of what I call Systematic dialectics as simple and universal.[35] For him, as I have noted, the linguistic simple is the name; and his *Logic* "represents the self-movement of the Absolute Idea only as the original *word*."[36] We thus begin with a word:

1. M_k.

The universality of this beginning word, however, means that a variety of content "comes under" it; its simplicity is "in itself the concrete totality, but . . . not yet for itself."[37] Hence the name contains (or abbreviates) latent content. Since the System is to contain nothing from outside,[38] the latent content in question must have been developed previously by Systematic dialectics. True to the circularity of Hegel's system, then (1) is not a complete beginning but *immediates* an earlier stage, at which M_k was introduced as abbreviating a developed aggregate of content markers:

0. $(M_1 \Uparrow \ldots \Uparrow M_j) \Rightarrow M_k.$[39]
1. $M_k.$

Thought moves forward from its simple-but-universal beginning in (1), says Hegel, by negating it—but in a negation which *preserves* its content.[40] If the negation here is not of content, it must be of form; and since the form is simple, it must be negated in favor of complexity. This first negation is thus a mediation, a development of determinacy and distinction.[41] The only content we have at this point is that already distinguished in (0), and we can write a full mediation, which mediates (1) as follows:

2. $M_k \Leftarrow (M_1 \Uparrow \ldots \Uparrow M_j).$

In a partial mediation, some of the markers and connectives $(M_1 \Uparrow \ldots \Uparrow M_j)$ would be missing. Whether full or partial, this stage is, as Hegel remarks, "analytic" with respect to content and "synthetic" in that it introduces distinction as such—that is, in respect of form.[42] Both abbreviation and explication have now been introduced, and as transitions they set up a formal opposition between the simple unity of the name and the plurality of contents it abbreviates. This opposition itself becomes an abbreviated content,[43] and by *reflection* we can write:

3. $(M_1 \Uparrow \ldots \Uparrow M_j) \Uparrow M_k$

This completes the gesture of explication. The different contents abbreviated by M_k have been set out explicitly, and the very process of explication (together with the preceding abbreviation) has been set out with them as a specific content in its own right. At this point, says Hegel, the dialectical move consists in seeing what has been thus set apart as unified.[44] A new negation of form, this time in favor of simplicity, is in order. This will *introduce* a new term abbreviating all the previously developed content:

4. $(M_1 \Uparrow \dots \Uparrow M_j \Uparrow M_k) \Rightarrow M_m,$

which can serve as (0) for the next stage of the system. This step, the "negation of the negation,"[45] negates the complex form of the previous negation, again without negating content.

The System thus develops entirely from "within," in that new content merely regroups old. If we want to call the old content regrouped by a new term the "meaning" of that term, then Hegel's Logic is, as Terry Pinkard has written, a "constructive logic of concepts" in which meaning of each term is simply what that term does: how it regroups earlier content, and the roles it plays as it is regrouped by later terms.[46]

It should be noted, again, that this account of Systematic dialectics is incomplete in several ways. For one thing, it is designed to leave two important steps unwarranted. One is the choice of which markers to set out in (2). In a full mediation, all markers written in (0) would be written in (2) as well; but whether to make (2) a full or partial mediation, and in case of the latter what to include in it, are up to the philosopher. This does not mean that these decisions are entirely unwarranted; the way these choices are made will be discussed in chapter 10. Also up to the philosopher is the choice of which marker to introduce in (4). For as I will argue in chapter 7, the "symbols" in which Hegel writes his System are not a set of markers that are neatly ordered by subscripts, but simply the sounds of words in the German language. Hence, there is not really any M_4 to come after M_3 and before M_5, or any M_s to come after M_r and before M_t: the philosopher's array of possible new symbols is all the sounds of German words, minus only those she has already used for previous moments. These two circumstances together show that my rewriting leaves a great deal out at each step. But they also mean that Hegel's System is, as will be seen in the ensuing "demarcation," much more open and supple than it is generally thought to be.

In addition to this incompleteness in principle, the account I have given here is too basic to capture many of the complexities of Hegel's actual Systematic constructions. In order to capture the movements in the "Logic of Essence," for example, we would have to introduce the idea of sublists of markers. Thus, among the content abbreviated by "ground," for example, would be "grounded," and this would abbreviate a sublist of its own. Every item on that sublist would, in the first instance, be the negation of an item in the original content of "ground" itself. The general movement in the Logic of Essence is then, as Michael Theunissen has argued (though in different terminology), to explicate members of both lists to show that the further markers they prove, on more adequate mediation, to contain belong equally to both lists.[47]

Complexities at least as great would be needed to capture many of the intricate types of relation that we often consider concepts to have with one another. The Aristotelian hierarchy of genus and species, for example, is replaced here by a linear derivation, so that the concept of "triangle," for example, would not be treated in the System as having "under" it the species equilateral, isosceles, and scalene. A Systematic approach would first have to develop the concept of triangle as a closed three-sided figure in Euclidean space. Then it would have to replay, for each pair of sides, part of the dialectic of identity and difference from the Logic.[48] Defining all three sides as equal, and then progressively developing their inequality (in accordance with the Logic) would yield the progression "triangle—equilateral—isosceles—scalene." The species are thus derived from each other, rather than standing in the mutual externality for which Hegel criticizes Aristotle.[49]

It is worth noting, however, that Hegel never actually deals Systematically with the concept of "triangle." This is because he views it as dependent on intuitive givens. Because of this, geometry's definitions, as well as its proofs and theorems, are "empirically" warranted and cannot be appropriated by Systematic thought.[50] That the System cannot (and need not) deal with concepts as important as those in which the Pythagorean Theorem is formulated deserves emphasis: it was not only Herr Krug's pen that Hegel could not "deduce" in his System, but some of Herr Krug's most basic concepts as well.[51]

What other nonsensory—that is, "conceptual"—relations may exist among our concepts, and the extent to which Hegel's dialectical gestures could be enriched to deal with them, remain open. What seems clear is that the enrichments will be elaborations of the basic gestures of abbreviation and explication. Because of the dynamism fundamental to dialectics, the primary way in which concepts can relate to one another is succession in time. Dialectic is just succession patterned in certain ways in the System by abbreviation and explication. It is with these that Hegel seeks to replace the older philosophical picture, dominant for example in Kant, of one idea "containing" another.[52] The replacement is well motivated: in contrast to the static privacy of the Kantian picture, abbreviation and explication are dynamic and public.

Once we understand the basic gestures of Systematic dialectics, it is easy to find them being carried through in the Science of Logic. Just prior to the "Absolute Idea," in "Objectivity," we are first presented with the individual object as merely mechanical, interacting with others in a spatiotemporal way. But the idea of a Determinate Property has already been developed earlier in the *Logic*. When it is applied here, we get objects related through determinate differences, or Chemical Objects (e.g., for Hegel, acids, bases, and salts). I rewrite this as follows, using "C" for chemical object and "D" for chemical determinacies:

0.	$(D_1 \Uparrow \ldots \Uparrow D_n) \Rightarrow C^{53}$	introduction
1.	C	immediation
2.	$C \Leftarrow (D_1 \Uparrow \ldots \Uparrow D_n)$	mediation
3.	$(D_1 \Uparrow \ldots \Uparrow D_n) \Uparrow C$	reflection on 0, 2
4.	$(D_1 \Uparrow \ldots \Uparrow D_n \Uparrow C) \Rightarrow T$	introduction

The idea of the determinate transition between the chemical object and the plurality of chemically interacting determinations permits us, then, to conceive of a spatiotemporal unit in the finite world containing chemical interactions. Indeed, we can now go on to conceive of such a unit as *developing* chemical reactions within itself (attributing to it the transition in step 2), and of these as *contributing* to the maintenance of that individual (the transition in 0). Such, for Hegel, is the cellular differentiation and self-preservation of a living organism. The simple unity of such a being ("T") is the individuality which it is the goal of this activity to bring into being and preserve; the immanent telos Hegel examines in "teleology."[54]

Compared to the fabulous complexity of contemporary biology, and indeed to Hegel's own discussion in section 3 of the *Philosophy of Nature*, this is unilluminating indeed. But, in addition to locating the concept of teleology in a larger conceptual economy of mechanism and chemism, it does specify at least one of its important features. For it tells us that to conceive of an entity as teleological means to conceive of it as a manifold of chemical reactions which confine themselves to a single object, as that term is defined mechanically. A chemical reaction is, in principle, capable of expanding indefinitely through space: we can bring together any volumes of oxygen and hydrogen, and as long as their ratio is correct, they will produce water. When such a reaction is contained within a determinate space, not by any external container but by some factor within that space itself, we have a telos. This does not teach us about nature: as I noted in chapter 1, we do not know from it, in Hegel's view, if there are in fact any such internally contained reactions, or any teleology. But we have learned something about the concept of the teleological itself: teleology is on this account the immanent power of the mechanical to contain the chemical, and not the kind of purpose with which it is often confused.

It is de rigueur to measure any account of Hegelian dialectics against the opening moves of the *Science of Logic*. Those moves, however, are troublesome—for this rewriting and, as his numerous explanatory notes and remarks indicate, for Hegel himself. Being, we may say, is explicated by Nothing—or, rather, fails to be explicated since it has no determinate content and, as beginning, abbreviates—nothing. The transition from Being to Nothing and back, understood with regard to its specific terminal points, is Becoming.[55] I rewrite this as follows. Since Being ("B") is the first moment of the System, it abbreviates the empty set ∅. Since this is the beginning, there is no (0) stage (in later stages, it will usually come at the end of the previous section):

*0.	$\emptyset \Rightarrow B$	introduction
1.	B	immediation
2.	$B \Leftarrow \emptyset$	mediation
3.	$B \Uparrow \emptyset$	reflection on *0, 2
4.	$(B \Uparrow \emptyset) \Rightarrow W$	introduction

We now have "*Werden*" or "Becoming." But according to my discussion above above, (2) is ill-formed: the expression to the right of $\Leftarrow$ should contain more markers than the expression to the left. The same goes for (*0). Hence, the beginning of the Logic contains, not a true immediation and mediation, but what Dieter Henrich has called an "immediate transition" between Being and Nothing.[56]

We can continue this into "Determinate Being," which is a more typical stage of the dialectic.[57] Let (4) above be taken as (0) for the next stage. Then:

5.	W	immediation
6.	$W \Leftarrow (B \Uparrow \emptyset)$	mediation
7.	$(B \Uparrow \emptyset \Uparrow W)$	reflection on 4, 6
8.	$(B \Uparrow \emptyset) \Uparrow (B \Uparrow \emptyset)$	transition on "W" in 7

This gives us W as a unity of Being and Nothing which, in Hegel's phrasing, does not merely abstract from the two of them but is itself Being and Nothing:

9.	$(B \Leftarrow \emptyset) \cdot (\emptyset \Rightarrow B) \Uparrow (B \Uparrow \emptyset),$	counterreflection on the first occurrence of "$B \Uparrow \emptyset$" in 8.

This gives us coming to be ($\emptyset \Rightarrow B$) and passing away ($B \Leftarrow \emptyset$) as moments of Becoming:

10.	$[(B \Leftarrow \emptyset) \bullet (\emptyset \Rightarrow B)] \Uparrow [(B \Leftarrow \emptyset) \bullet (\emptyset \Rightarrow B)]$	counterreflection on "$B \Uparrow \emptyset$" in 9.
11.	$[(B \Leftarrow \emptyset) \bullet (\emptyset \Rightarrow B)] \Uparrow (\emptyset \Rightarrow B)$	disjunction on second occurrence of "$(B \Rightarrow \emptyset) \bullet (\emptyset \Leftarrow B)$" in 10.
12.	$[(B \Leftarrow \emptyset) \bullet (\emptyset \Rightarrow B)] \Uparrow B$	immediation on "$\emptyset \Rightarrow B$" in 11.
13.	$\{[(B \Leftarrow \emptyset) \bullet (\emptyset \Rightarrow B)] \Uparrow B\} \Rightarrow$ *Dasein*	introduction

This is the disappearance of arising and passing away into a single Being, a "tranquil unity" which is *Dasein* or Determinate Being. Determinate Being is thus a marker which abbreviates the markers for a Becoming which begins and ends with Being and passes through a Nothing—or of a Being which is an enduring process requiring reference to something wholly indeterminate but other than it and not itself process: what Hegel calls "Being with Not-being," or "Being at a certain (nonspatial) place."[58]

    To the extent that it can be captured with the above tools, Hegel's logic is what we may call a logic of abbreviation. Such a logic may have uses beyond Hegel; the discussion I give here aims to be sufficient only for my current purpose, which is neither to give a complete (or elegant) account of the logic of abbreviation nor one of Hegel's System, but simply to use the former to illuminate the latter: to show how Hegel's System exhibits a nonassertional kind of dialectic. Since the basic elements of such dialectic are not assertions but mere names, the dialectic does not inform us about reality: it does not serve truth. But insofar as it is the organized introduction of new markers into an already established System, it exhibits order over (increasing) size: the longer it continues, the more Noble it gets—and in a disciplined, step-by-step way. It is this step-by-step feature that permits the overall organization, and thus constitutes the rationality of the development.

    A pair of expressions in such a logic can be both similar to and different from one another in two basic ways. In the first place their content may be the same while their form differs. "Sir Walter Scott" (to take an example from Russell),[59] should it appear in systematic dialectics, would not be equivalent to "the author of *Waverly*." If in fact the former phrase is the abbreviation of the latter, then for Hegel both possess the same content-markers; but the former possesses them implicitly, as a name; the latter, explicitly as a description. If we are assertionists, whose only concern is propositional truth, this difference in form is of small account; the reason for using abbreviations is convenience, and Hegel's system can be viewed as providing no more than a set of structured conveniences for philosophers and other thinkers.

But, as cognitive scientists have discovered,[60] the need for these is a real one. Though a shorter formula is logically eliminable in favor of a longer one, it may not be eliminable *in real time*: to take an extreme example, $2^{1000^{1000}}$ can be written out in ordinary notation—but to do so would take ages. Much less extreme, but similarly (as in chapter 2), "she is a genuine friend" can perhaps be unpacked into a number of propositions—but the number is an unhappily large one. We live under circumstances of limited time, and of limiting times. Whether or not names as abbreviations for other names are as Hegel claims the "fundamental need" of language, the sort of role they play in enabling us to dispense with long expressions in favor of shorter ones is a crucial one. Even on this abstract and formal level, then, the System is useful.

Historical Dialectics

The other main type of dialectics in Hegel concerns the rise of Spirit to the absolute standpoint. The extended paradigm of this rise is his *Phenomenology*. But that book, Hegel later writes, presents only the "formal" side of Spirit's rise; the more general rise is to be found in Spirit's progress toward philosophical science in all its ramifications.[61] Hegel, like other Germans before and since, uses "science" (*Wissenschaft*) in a sense embracing most fields of human reason—in his case explicitly including ethics, social morality (*Sittlichkeit*), art, and religion. This suggests that the wider rise of "science" falls together with rational progress as such, and is in turn coextensive with Hegel's view of history as Spirit's "apprehension of itself as interpreting itself to itself."[62] The realms of history and science, and their respective forms of dialectic, thus seem to coincide rather than contrast. Without claiming that this has been definitively established for Hegel, I will take it as a preliminary hint for my reconstruction of historical dialectics, which will begin with Hegel's account of scientific procedure in general.

Nonphilosophical sciences are for Hegel "finite."[63] His account of "finite cognition" in the *Science of Logic* divides it into two types, "analytic" and "synthetic."[64] The former starts from concretely given objects and analyzes them descriptively into their abstract components. Being thus subject to what is immediately given, such cognition cannot accommodate the critical reflection inherent in scientific advance and is "undialectical."[65] Undialectical in itself, analytic cognition submits to dialectical supersession by another type of cognition, "synthetic" cognition. This type of cognition does not remain with given objects but finds universal assertions and laws, and demonstrates their coherence with other such laws, which is for Hegel essentially a process of mediation.[66]

In the first of its three aspects, "definition," synthetic cognition seeks not the basic components of a given entity, but universal aspects of kinds of entity, features which are always empirically found together in certain beings.[67] Once those higher universals (Hegel calls them *Merkmale*) have been reached, they can be taken as "objective foundations" for cognition—that is, as scientific domains which can be subdivided (as the domain of molecules can be divided into organic and nonorganic); this is "classification" or "division" (*Einteilung*).[68] A proposition or theorem (*Lehrsatz*), the third type of synthetic cognition, is then the relating of acquired universal laws to individual cases and objects. In the empirical sciences, this stage is the application of a theory to new data.[69] Such application often fails, and the final move (in the Systematic progression) is not to keep improving theory but to improve reality: the structure of cognition passes over into that of action.[70]

What is perhaps unclear from this brief sketch is that Hegel's presentation of finite cognition is resolutely ahistorical; in no part of the discussion does he refer to progress in finite cognition. But this does not mean that dialectical advance, in the sense of critical reflection on previous results, is absent; at *Encyclopedia*. #81 Zus., for example, dialectic is said to apply to "all nonphilosophical consciousness and to all experience," and to hold "in all the particular regions and forms of the natural and spiritual world."[71] That it is present within finite cognition is suggested by Hegel's emphasis on anomalies encountered by all three of its branches. With respect to definition, for example, Hegel adduces anencephalic infants as anomalous to any definition of "man" which refers to our unique brains. The anomalies to classification are species which (like the duckbilled platypus) do not fall under established genera and which require the formulation of new genera. And the anomalies to propositions or theorems are their unsuccessful applications.[72] Hegel thus recognizes that the empirical scientist, engaged in "finite cognition," continually encounters exceptions to her generalizations and must continually revise those generalizations to cope with them. We may express the dialectical nature of scientific procedure by assimilating an early definition, classification, or theorem to a dialectical thesis, its anomalies to the contradictions encountered by such a thesis, and the revised version to a new synthesis.[73]

This is certainly a minimalist account of dialectics, but no more than some of Hegel's. The dialectics of the history of philosophy, for example, result (he tells us in the Introduction to *The Philosophy of History*) from the fact that a philosophical system, simply by existing, is determinate. But its very determinateness means that it is inadequate to express the "Idea," which *contains* all determinacies and which it is the business of philosophy to express. The system must therefore "perish":

> The guiding force is the inner dialectic of the forms [of philosophy]. For what has form is determinate. . . . But then it is something finite; and what is finite is not true, is not what it ought to be. It contradicts its content, the Idea; it must perish. That it can exist, of course, means that it has the Idea in it. But because it is determinate, its form is finite and its existence is one-sided and limited. The Idea as its inner [meaning] must shatter this form and destroy the one-sided existence in order to give itself the absolute form which is identical with its content. In this dialectic of the Idea, infinite in itself but existing in a one-sided form and which must sublate that existence, lies the guiding force. This is the one point which must orient us in the history of philosophy.[74]

This account can, without much trouble, be paraphrased for scientific theories. Such a theory does not have the "infinitude" of philosophy, and is not inadequate to its domain simply by being stated in determinate or "one-sided" form. But it is determinate in that it is one scientific theory among others, which means that it is supposed to account for a certain domain of observed fact. When a fact for which it does not account is discovered in that domain, the theory no longer does what it is supposed to do and must "perish"—or at least submit to revision or expansion. In contrast to philosophy, then, "determinacy" does not of itself mean that a scientific theory is inadequate, but only that it may prove to be so: that it is falsifiable. In this respect, the dialectics of science are even looser than those here attributed to philosophy.

In empirical definition as Hegel presents it in the *Science of Logic*, the definiendum is considered to be composed of a number of characteristics or determinations—what I am calling "markers"—connected in the definition in a contingent way.[75] Because of this contingency, $\Uparrow$ has no place here, and I will use •, taken from Seebohm[76] and denoting what I have called simple aggregation. I write a definition as here required as the "introduction" of a new term into scientific discourse:

$$D_0. \ (M_1 \bullet \ldots \bullet M_j) \Rightarrow M_k$$

It can readily be seen that, given a definition in such form, only three types of revision are possible: a marker (or markers) may be (1) dropped, (2) added, or (3) replaced by a different marker. The third is a compound of the first two. I write them as follows:

$$D_1. \ (M_1 \bullet \ldots \bullet M_i) \Rightarrow M_k \ (M_j \text{ is dropped})$$
$$D_2. \ (M_1 \bullet \ldots \bullet M_j \bullet M_m) \Rightarrow M_k \ (M_m \text{ is added})$$

Perhaps the most striking thing about this rewriting is its poverty, which exceeds even that of Systematic dialectics. This is an advantage, since all sorts of historical developments have to be fitted into historical dialectics,[77] but I will enrich it slightly by noting that the revision of content in historical dialectics must be forced: in order for D_1 or D_2 to be adopted, some deficiency must be found in D_0. As might be expected, contradiction is such a deficiency, and D_0 can be contradicted in two ways, leading respectively to D_1 and D_2.

The contradiction of D_0 leading to D_1 is provoked by a counterexample to D_0 in the form of something which we (for whatever reasons) wish to designate by M_k but which fails to have some characteristic specified by one of the markers contained in M_k. (A black swan would be such a counterexample, if "white" were previously included in the definition of "swan.") The contradicting formula would then be:

$$D_1'. \ (M_1 \bullet \ldots \bullet M_i \bullet {\sim}M_j) \Rightarrow M_k$$

The counterexample leading to D_2 would be something with all the characteristics previously attributed to the definiendum, but which we are (for whatever reason) not disposed to call by that name.[78] We would then have:

$$D_2'. \ (M_1 \bullet \ldots \bullet M_i \bullet M_j) \Rightarrow {\sim}M_k$$

It can readily be seen that D_1' and D_2' are complementary. Given that *none* of a plurality of characteristics asserted to be abbreviated by a content is simply a misdescription (e.g., asserting that swans are purple), only two sorts of deficiency are possible: we have included either too many markers in our definition or too few. In the first case, we are likely to find an object which we are disposed to designate by that name defined, but with some allegedly essential characteristic missing (D_1'); or we may find all the desired characteristics but have them somehow fail to add up into the whole (D_2'). In the former case we drop the missing characteristic(s) from our definition; in the latter we add characteristics so as to specify the whole more fully. We may, on successive occasions, do both, thereby gradually transforming our concept.

In neither case do we simply accept the contradiction (D') at the expense of D_0: we do not, that is, change M_j in D_0 for $\sim M_j$, as D_1' has it. That happens, for example, in the third case, in which the final definition is identical with the contradicting one:

$$D_3. (M_1 \bullet \ldots \bullet M_i \bullet \sim M_j) \Rightarrow M_k$$

Here, D_0 has retained no rights over against D_3: it ceased to be asserted when the mistake was discovered. D is thus replaced by D_3 in what the *Phenomenology* would call an "abstract negation," one which, like death, does not preserve what it negates.[79]

This is scarcely a complete account of historical dialectics. From any posited definition containing n markers, n different immediate revisions are possible in the sense of D_1; the number of possible revisions involving more than one marker is no fewer than n!, depending on which conjunction of markers comes to be excluded. For revisions in sense D_2, only one is possible at each stage—but it is impossible to predict what that revision will be, and where the succession of them will lead; the number of markers that must be added to escape anomalies seems entirely fortuitous. It appears that the mass of historical recapitulation that such dialectics must contain serves, for all its bulk, to limit the much freer play of dialectical thought—to keep our understanding anchored in past or present worlds, rather than turning it lose to wander among merely possible ones.

Historical dialectics, we may say, has turned out to be the dialectics of the Hegelian Left, stripped of those features in it which are peculiar to the *Phenomenology*.[80] Systematic dialectics approximates to the kind of thing practiced by the Hegelian Right, but—far from being a theology of the Absolute—makes no claims that the entities it constructs correspond to anything outside themselves. Its relation to what is outside itself, to be discussed in chapter 10, will turn out to be one of mutual

transformation, rather than correspondence. The anchoring of historical dialectics in history itself is also not to be confused with any simple
mirroring. Its statements are condensations and reorderings, not assertions—however much they resemble them. For even in the most disci-
plined areas of science, new markers tend to come in packets rather than
one by one as in historical dialectics (a Heideggerian point to which I will
devote a future work). The claim of historical dialectics is not that history
actually happened as it says: like social contract theory, it makes claims
about the present rather than the past. The most general of these is that
not only the assertions but also the major terms of contemporary *Wissenschaft* (and not just science) can be validated as rational, if each of the
markers which define them can be seen as having entered that definition
for good reasons. In order to do this, a sequence must be set up in which
markers enter and leave terms in proper order, in each case again for
good reasons. Each such reason, moreover, may have only a family resemblance with the good reasons that precede or follow it in the development: the reason for dropping M_n, say, may be of an entirely different
order from the reason for adding M_3: the grounds for one may, for example, have to do with empirical accuracy, while those for the other are
political in nature. *No single guiding concern or set of rules needs to direct the
development,* other than the very general one of having as few as possible
of the "wrong" markers, and not too few of the "right" ones, so that the
markers—and the terms themselves, for markers of course are terms—
are neither too many nor too few.[81] Historical dialectics thus undertakes
to reconstruct history as a Noble enterprise, and in so doing to make
plain the Nobility of the present: its ongoing power to reconcile past
oppositions.[82]

Appendix: History, Science, and Hegel's *Phenomenology of Spirit*

I have discussed historical dialectics in connection with Hegel's account
of finite cognition, exemplified in natural science. Errol Harris has suggested that the *Phenomenology* as well is related to such science as we
understand it today, and this view has been worked out in some detail by
Paul Thagard.[83] The approach seems of interest for the philosophy of
science because of the increasing contemporary awareness that empirical science is not based simply on "value-free" observations, but incorporates critical reflection on previous theories, and hence—like the

Phenomenology—has a processual and indeed historical dimension. The relation between the *Phenomenology* and certain broad views of scientific progress also, I will argue here, sheds light on the nature of the *Phenomenology* itself.

As Thagard notes, there are major differences between the *Phenomenology* and the history of science. The book's Introduction, in fact, suggests four major discrepancies between the kinds of advance the two present. In the first place, the dialectical necessity of the *Phenomenology* requires that each succeeding stage (or its constitutive "object") be viewed as internally generated by its predecessor, rather than as motivated by the discovery (often fortuitous) of anomalous data.[84] Anomalies like platypuses and anencephalic children are not "generated" by the theories to which they are anomalies; though the recognition of them *as* anomalies clearly depends on our possession of the theory to which they are anomalous, in the final analysis they are found in the world.

Second, it is implicit in Hegel's doctrine of determinate negation that each new stage of the *Phenomenology* be the unique resolution of the problems generated by the previous stage; in science, several new theories may account equally well for a given anomaly.

Third, to be a "determinate negation," the new stage in the *Phenomenology* must resolve only the problem at hand; if it solves others as well, it is generic rather than determinate. But given the fortuitousness of anomalies, a whole series of them would presumably be removed by every change in a definition. There is no requirement in science that a revised definition (or classification or theory) should solve only the problems present at an earlier stage.

Finally, of course, the *Phenomenology* issues in the Absolute. Whatever one thinks that is, it is by now wholly naive to think that science will ever issue in any set of truths that cannot later be surpassed. Science's goal, it seems, can never be reached; the *Phenomenology*'s not only can be, but (somehow) is.

My account in chapter 4 of historical dialectics, based on Hegel's account of finite cognition, is much less constrained than the *Phenomenology* itself, and is better than the *Phenomenology* at capturing certain obvious features of empirical science. The question arises as to the source of, and motivation for, the *Phenomenology*'s dialectical stringency: whence these four restrictions on what I will call phenomenological, as opposed to historical and Systematic, dialectics?

It may be, of course, that empirical science is for Hegel a particularly "loose" kind of history, and that the broader scope of what he calls "world history" would contain more rigor. But there are some considerations against this view. In the first place, Hegel's broad conception of science as embracing most fields of human reason suggests that the wider rise of science concerns rational progress as such, and this is co-extensive with Hegel's view of history as Spirit's "apprehension of itself as interpreting itself to itself."[85] The realms of history and science, and their respective forms of dialectic, thus seem to coincide rather than contrast.

More specifically, doctrines such as "internal generation" and "determinate negation" seem to be as absent from Hegel's account of the dialectics of world history as they are from his account of finite cognition. In the Introduction to the *Lectures on the Philosophy of World History*, Hegel tells us that contradictions arise in history because a people's image of itself as expressed in its laws, customs, and artistic achievements does not encompass all the varied, unreflective experiences of the individuals in that society. These experiences turn those individuals away from their culture and eventually destroy it, but they are not "generated" by it:

> This spiritual consciousness a people has of itself is . . . as universal, merely ideal [*ideell*] and is in form distinct from real effectiveness, from real accomplishment and life. . . . So we see a people at such a time finding satisfaction in the representation and talk of virtue, which in part complements and in part supplants virtue itself. The *latter* is produced by Spirit; and Spirit can also bring the unreflected and merely factical side to reflection upon itself. In this, it becomes conscious of the limited character of such determinate principles as faith, trust, ethical practice—and thus consciousness obtains grounds for declaring itself free of them and their laws. . . . With this there enters the isolation of individuals from one another and from the whole. . . . Passion and self-interest thus emerge, set free as [social] destruction. This is then not the natural death of the spirit of a people, but its internal rupture. . . . The resolution of this through thought is necessarily at the same time the coming-forth of a new principle.[86]

Similarly, the new historical principle to which this leads can hardly be uniquely determined, since the unreflective experiences it seeks to comprehend are, if only because they are unreflective, heterogenous in nature. For the same reason, any new principle introduced into history will be likely to resolve a variety of individual problems. And the goal of all this is not the end of historical development as such, but simply the recognition that any such development can only be a rational progress:

> This process, this sequence of stages, seems to be an infinite one in accordance with the principle of perfectibility, a progress which always remains far from its goal. . . . But no limited content can remain recalcitrant to thought and to the concept. If there were something which the concept could not digest or resolve, it would be the highest rupture and wretchedness. But if there were something like this, it could only be thought itself as it grasps itself. For only thought is unlimited in itself, and all reality is determinate through it. So the rupture would cease and thought would be satisfied in itself. Here would be the final goal of the world. . . . The concept of Spirit is to return to itself, to make itself its own object; thus, the progress is not an indeterminate one to infinity, but a goal is present, namely, return to self. So there is a certain circularity there, Spirit seeks itself.[87]

If *that* is reaching the Absolute, then it is trivially true that science has reached it, for it amounts only to saying that further "scientific" progress will be, in a broad sense, "rational."

The peculiar nature of the dialectics of the *Phenomenology* thus cannot be understood in terms of Hegel's view of the rationality of science; of history; or the formal features of historical dialectic in general. I will argue here that the distinguishing features of phenomenological dialectics result from the structure of the communicative situation presupposed by the book, a structure which is not shared by historical dialectics generally.

The importance of communication, and more precisely of pedagogy, to Hegel's thought can hardly be overstated.[88] For Hegel, communication is not just an important, or even a necessary, activity of our species but constitutes its nature, which "only exists in an attained community of minds."[89] The *Phenomenology* itself, of course, is an instance of communication; in Hegel's metaphor, it is the "ladder to the absolute standpoint" handed to the individual.[90] But what did Hegel consider communication to be, and how does the *Phenomenology* fit under that general heading?

In his *Science of Logic*, Hegel discusses two types of communication, under the heading "Mechanical Process" but with specific references to "spiritual" analogues.[91] First is Formal Communication, in which a determinacy "continues undisturbed from one person to another and generalizes itself without being changed."[92] Examples of such "determinacies" are the "laws, customs, and rational representations as a whole which permeate the individual in an unconscious way and assert themselves in her."[93] Formal communication thus includes the process of acculturation in the widest sense, by which an individual comes from early childhood to exemplify the mores and outlook of her society without (perhaps) even being aware that she does so. When individuals begin to resist the imparting of "determinacy," we have the next stage, the "Real Mechanical Process." Communication of a determinacy must here overcome resistance, and this overcoming is "power." The individual's ultimate submission to power is her "fate."[94] When this fate is no longer seen as an external force compelling the individual to be what she is not, but is viewed as her own true nature, the "real" process passes over into the "absolute" one, in which determinacy is no longer posited through communication.[95]

It is evident from this brief sketch that "communication" for Hegel is the imparting to an individual of a determinacy that is, or at first seems to be, foreign to that individual. That Hegel saw the *Phenomenology* in such terms is evident from its Introduction, where he writes that because natural consciousness

> immediately considers itself to be real knowing, the path [of
> the *Phenomenology*] has a negative meaning for it, and signifies
> for it the loss of itself . . . for in this way it does lose its
> truth.[96]

We can also see from this which type of communication the *Phenomenology* presents: it is communication that is resisted as a loss of self, or what the *Science of Logic* calls real communication.

The *Phenomenology* is an attempt, then, to communicate the absolute standpoint to an individual who is resistant to the message, who attempts to remain in one's "impenetrable independence."[97] But because real communication presupposes the formal variety, it requires an individual who has been acculturated (presumably into the culture of Hegel's own Germany)[98] and who is thus, willy-nilly, not "impenetrably independent," but already permeated by the universal. She is attempting to maintain her isolated ego not only against the Absolute, but against the "universal" culture already communicated to her, and from which she has alienated herself.[99]

It seems clear that this is the sort of consciousness described in the opening pages of the *Phenomenology*, in the section on "Sense-

Certainty." Consciousness there, though insistent that "sense-certainty" is the whole truth, is able to recognize and talk about trees and houses—natural and cultural objects of a very complex kind. On the temporal side, consciousness also has the complex notions of "night" and "noon." Similarly, though in the next stage consciousness declares its own individual ego to be the truth, it is cognizant of its similarity to other egos.[100] Thus, sense-certain consciousness is in possession of a developed language, from which it alienates itself in claiming that the sensory as such is not merely the source but the repository of all truth. The whole section then portrays the resistance of consciousness to the move to the next level, "Perception."

Given this special sort of communicative situation, we can readily see why the dialectics of the *Phenomenology* take the form that they do. Contradictions must be internally generated because only a contradiction actually produced by consciousness at a given stage will prevent it from going about its business as usual. An externally derived anomaly could simply be ignored, as anomalies often are, by a consciousness whose main purpose is to avoid change. Similarly, any new stage must be the sole resolution of problems with the previous one, not in the sense that no other solutions are possible (after all, any higher stage will presumably resolve the problems in lower ones), but in the sense that consciousness will advance only as far as necessary to overcome those problems and will resist further leaps.

Consciousness, moreover, is threatened at each stage with a loss of self. In such circumstances, to argue that a proposed resolution would also solve other, as yet unknown, problems would be as irrelevant as pointing out to a drowning woman that the life preserver one is throwing her would also make a good wall decoration. There are, in fact, many places in the *Phenomenology* where the resolution proposed for a current crisis would also solve other puzzles (one such is the introduction of linguistic universals at the end of "Sense-Certainty"). But it would be beside the point for Hegel to say so.

Consciousness must be able to arrive at a stage where its real communication turns into what I would call absolute communication: where the individual no longer resists the message or seeks to halt her own development. This can come about, however, only when she no longer views further development as an alien "fate," but as her own true nature; and this in turn requires recognizing that all possible standpoints to which she might come (and, a fortiori, to which she already has come) are not external to her but only various expressions of herself. This requirement is presumably fulfilled by the "reconciliation of Spirit with its own consciousness" presented in the *Phenomenology*'s concluding section on "Absolute Knowing."[101]

The peculiar characteristics of the dialectical progression in the *Phenomenology of Spirit* can thus be seen to issue from the context of communication it presupposes. This context is not merely a matter of psychology and rhetoric, but has a structure brought forth in Hegel's *Logic,* a structure whose Systematic version I will discuss further in chapter 10. For the moment, I take it as clear that the communicative process which structures the *Phenomenology* is radically different from the pursuit of private ends which characterizes much of world history, and from the disinterested pursuit of truth which distinguishes science at its best. It is also different from the communicative situation in the *Encyclopedia,* by which time the individual has reached the absolute standpoint and no longer resists the message. This resistance, and the argumentation required to overcome it, partly explains the enormous compression of the *Encyclopedia* "Phenomenology" compared to the original.[102]

Hegelian Thought: Demarcation

S is P

The previous demarcation aimed to distinguish Hegel from other approaches with respect to his view of truth, itself understood as the goal of his own philosophy. Philosophical thought for Hegel is meant to provide us with something other than a set of true assertions, I argued, and this means that it need not be packaged as "S is P," and so forth, in order to be valid. This does not entail that standard logic is impotent to capture Hegelian dialectics, or that there is some feature of those dialectics that inevitably slips past logical form. Also possible is that the moves of Hegelian dialectic can indeed be put into standard assertionistic logic, but that in that form they become too cumbersome and time-consuming to achieve their own goals. In either case, I will argue here, Hegelian dialectical logic need not be put into assertionistic terms in order to function and be understood.

Assertionism as I have presented it claims that truth is linguistically packaged as "S is P" and compounds, and this suggests certain obvious questions. What is "S is P" anyway? Is it *merely* a package? Or is it a package which admits only certain kinds of content—certain kinds of thought, or of truth? Does it perhaps not merely contain but transform what is put into it, and in more than just "form"? What is it not to need it? What are its ontological implications? Shall we say that if "S is P" is basic, then the fundamental relation in the universe is that between a property and the thing whose property it is—an S-P relation? Must other kinds of relation—S-S relations among things, P-P relations among properties—then be reduced to this scheme? Instead of simply discussing P-P relations, must we rephrase them as pairs of S-P relations? (Introducing an S which has P_1 only if it has P_2 would be an example of this—as well as of inventing the precise sort of "substrate" Hegel wishes in his System to jettison.)[1] And how do we talk about S-S relations without construing relations themselves as P's—as properties of some individual subject? (As if Phoenix's being west of Houston were a property of Phoenix alone or in some privileged way, not at all or secondarily a fact about Houston. Or perhaps it is about the "Phoenix-Houston state of affairs"? Or even, in Donald Davidson's words, about the One Great Fact?)[2] And if we do not construe our relations as "P's," are we not perhaps construing them as "S's"? (The claim that not things but states of affairs are ultimate, far fom dispensing with such substrates, may actually be a way to salvage them, for such relations, like the Aristotelian substances from which they derive, have their forms as well as their matter, or content. Are they not eminently "S's"?)[3]

Again: What is the scope of "S is P"? Is Jack's love for Julie in the form "S is P"? What about the taste of a pineapple, or proton decay? Are they things with properties? Combinations of properties? Properties with things? ("P is S," à la the speculative sentence?)[4] Is the universe a giant all-containing "S is P"? Again: "S is P," as a package, hardly seems to create what goes into it—"S" and "P." But then must not "S" and "P" somehow exist prior to entering that package? If so, how could "S is P" itself be basic to cognition? Perhaps the prior existence of "S" and "P" was as components of *other* "S is P's," of other assertions? To ask after the meaning of "S" or "P" is then to launch a search for other assertions containing or entailing them, a long and often tangled chain of filiations. Again: we still have not begun to ask the traditional questions of *where* "S" and "P" are—Are they concepts *in* our minds? Things *in* the world? Facts *about* the world?

What about linguistic forms, such as beliefs about unknown or nonexistent objects—opacities and counterfactuals, indexicals and paradoxes—dynamic uses of words? Are not these so many linguistic instances, *Bei-spiele* in Hegel's sense,[5] which play into the regime of "S is P" in different ways, captured and recaptured in a literature which solves and resolves everything again and again?

Assertional packaging is clearly an important and indispensable phenomenon (if "phenomenon" it is); the questions concerning it are well worth answering. I can hardly undertake even to discuss them here. But perhaps we could be clearer about propositional form and related notions if we knew of alternatives to assertionistic packaging—of goals thinking can have other than truth, and of other forms it can take to reach them. Perhaps Hegel (and, after him, Heidegger) can place us outside assertionism long enough to permit us to get a grasp of what it is and is not, what it does and does not do, so that moderate views of it begin to emerge.

Let us start, not with thought as such, but again from truth. Must the various stages of a Systematic dialectical development as I have presented be viewed as so many truth-claims? I will take them in sequence:

(0), like (4), does not claim truth, because it merely introduces a new symbol (M_k). M_k does not preexist (0), which rather than making a truth-claim simply states how that symbol will be used. It is not, to speak roughly, constative but performative: a promise.

(1) is even more clearly bereft of a truth-claim: it is merely the writing of a single symbol, without any predication at all.

(2) is a bit trickier. Unlike (0), the symbols contained in (2) have all been introduced previously. (2) seems then to assert a fact about M_k—namely, that all markers listed in its explication (the part of [2] to the right of $\Leftarrow$) occurred in the original introduction of M_k, at (0). Thus, (2) could be construed as a proposition about the state of affairs instituted in (1).

I et us examine this more closely. We could replace (2) with such a proposition:

•2. The markers ($M_1, \ldots M_j$) all occurred in the original introduction of M_k in (0).

This certainly makes a truth-claim; but it does not do exactly what (2) does, which is include some (perhaps all) of the markers in (0) while excluding some (perhaps none) of them. To capture the exclusionary effect we would have to write:

•2'. The markers ($M_1 \ldots M_j$) occurred together with others (or with no others) in the original introduction of M_k in (0).

But now we are no longer merely reporting on (0): we are reporting selectively, and this is evident on the face of our report. Moreover, the selection (2) makes among the markers of (0) is as we saw what usually generates the further development, not simply the fact that the markers were there in the first place.

What makes (*2′) true, on this account, is that it mentions no markers that were not to the left of $\Rightarrow$ in (0). But we can capture this without making the truth-claim, simply by always constructing (2) so that no element occurring to the right of $\Leftarrow$ in (2) is missing from the left of $\Rightarrow$ in (0). (2) can be construed as stating precisely this, as yielding a rule such that a line which did not conform to that rule would be, not false, but wrongly written: like an illegal move in chess, or a gaffe at dinner. So viewed, the set {M} of markers to the left of $\Rightarrow$ in (0) formulates a repertoire on which (2) draws. But (2) is no more "true" of that repertoire than a melody is true of the key in which it is written:

(3), then, abbreviates (0) and (2); since neither of them makes a truth-claim, neither can it.

It thus appears that there is a way to construe the dialectics of Hegel's System which does not see it as making assertionistic truth-claims. But this turns out, perhaps surprisingly, not to answer the original question. Whether the System makes a truth-claim is not, in fact, the same issue as whether it can be put into the form "S is P." For there is one sense of "is," derived like the copula from a well-known use of the "equals" sign, which can apply to Hegel's dialectical usage. I will discuss it briefly, for it shows that the package "S is P" is in fact not a single package but a whole family of them, not all of them assertionistic.

(0) can be viewed as assigning a value to M_k—namely, the value $(M_1 \Uparrow \ldots \Uparrow M_j)$. Some computer languages indicate this sort of assignment with the equals sign. In Basic, for example, "x=3" is not read "x equals 3," which would have a truth-value determinable on the basis of whatever else we know about x (e.g., that 3x=9). Instead, it is read "let x equal 3." This is sometimes referred to as the "assignment" use of the equal sign. On that use—as in Basic—"x=x+1" is well-formed; it tells the computer to add 1 to whatever value x already has.

We could use this sense of "=" to write:

0′. $(M \Uparrow \ldots \Uparrow M_j) = M_k.$

This would capture something of (0); what it would not capture is that M_k must be shorter than $(M_1 \ldots M_j)$. But this restriction is, as I noted in the preceding analysis, not present in the System's first transition, from Being to Nothing. Hence, the assignment use of the equals sign is very apposite there:

0″. B=∅

One ordinary way of reading occurrences of the equals sign is to use the copula, so we can read the inscription "x=3" as "x is 3." If we do the same with the assignment sense of that sign in (0″), we will get Hegel's famous "Being is Nothing." The "is" in this, then, is—though Hegel does not have this way of articulating it—what we may call an "assignative is."[6] Using this sort of "is" enables us to put a moment of the System into the package "S is P." But is that package itself, then, not misleading? Does it not cover over the distinction between the "is" of assignment and that of identity? To see which "is" we are dealing with is in fact to get the utterance *out* of the ambiguous package "Being is Nothing," and into some other form—such as, for example, "Being ⇐ Nothing." And then we see that Hegel's Systematic dialectic is nothing other than an assignment of old markers to new markers: a truthless fugue of stipulations.

It seems, of course, to be something else. Because it concerns itself with the order of terms it looks, for example, like a syntax. Because their order yields their meaning, it appears to become a semantics. Because the meanings it constitutes are radically dynamic, it seems to end in pragmatics. But it is none of these kinds of inquiry, because it is not *true* of language (as it is not *true* of History, the World Spirit, God before creating the world, our conceptual structures, or of anything else). It is rather a development into and out of other discourses,[7] a development which is itself rationally organized and can help organize them.

Concepts I: Aprioricity, Contradiction, Necessity

I take it that none of the steps of Hegelian Systematic dialectics makes assertionistic truth-claims and that such dialectics do not need to be put into the package "S is P," though perhaps of course they can, given sufficient ingenuity on the part of logicians. I will now expand on this by giving, in this section, nonassertionistic acounts of three of the System's fabled properties: aprioricity (together with univeral validity), dialectical contradiction, and necessity. The following section will add two more:

completeness and circularity. These notions are all normally thought of as applying to assertions. Thus, for example, an assertion (be it a belief, judgment, proposition, sentence, or whatever) is *a priori* if its truth can be known independently of experience; *necessary* if it holds in all possible worlds. A set of assertions is *circular* if two of them can be derived only from each other, and *contradictory* if at least one of its members entails the negation of at least one other. The Hegelian meanings for these terms will be rather different.

Hegel says that his system is a priori, that in it thought remains universal, "in its own element," and refers to nothing beyond itself.[8] As I have presented systematic dialectics, the beginning of the system is "Being," which has no empirical content because it has no content at all. The system then enriches itself further purely by regrouping previously introduced content, without appeal to experience. The entire sequence is thus a priori.

Because it is thus a priori, it is also universally valid for all speaking beings—not because there is a body of truths which they can know independently of experience, or which would be accessible to a disembodied being, but because it is a way of thinking upon which they can embark regardless of their experience. The universality of thought for Hegel then does not mean that there are certain ideas which all humans share, or certain formal structures which they would all accept (such as *modus ponens*), or certain basic truths no one would deny (such as that she has a body). Rather, what is universal is just the fluent indeterminacy of thought itself, as it groups and regroups markers into new moments, a movement which nothing and no one can resist:

> If there were something which the Concept could not digest or resolve [i.e., could not raise to its own universal validity], it would be the highest rupture and wretchedness. But if there were something like this, it could only be thought itself as it grasps itself. For only thought is unlimited in itself, and all reality is determinate through it.[9]

Thought, as it explicates ("digests") and abbreviates ("resolves") contents, can do this with any of the determinations it produces—because, precisely, abbreviation and explication are the basic gestures of such production. Hence, I may not share any determinate mental content with others. But if they can group and regroup the words in their language, I share with them thought itself. The claim is that, if I and they have the desire, we can construct whole panoplies of such shared content by applying and reapplying a few basic procedures.

This Hegelian view of the universality of thought cuts between a Kantian or Cartesian view, according to which I share with all other humans a certain set of known propositions or innate ideas, and Sartrean abstractness in which the only characteristic shared by all humanity is the ability to negate all determinacy, to be what one is not.[10] The reason is Hegel's emphasis on determinate, or as I prefer to call it, "minimal" negation.[11] Instead of the willed "wrenching free" of any and all social (and epistemic) codes of which Ferry and Renaut write, this is a step-by-step revision of concrete aspects of such codes. The distinguishing feature of humankind is thus the capacity to enter into a history which can be reconstructed as a sequence of such revisions. Such a history, in Hegel's view, can account for the genesis of language itself, because dealing in symbols (and eventually signs) itself "revises" the practice of dealing with things themselves.[12] Humans are constantly changing language in this sort of way, and we are not (as the tradition formulates it) *to zoon logon echon*, the animal possessing language. We are instead, for Hegel, *to zoon logon metaballon*, the animal which transforms language.

Hegel's notion of dialectical contradiction can be clarified by modifying my rewriting in the direction of set theory. By virtue of (0) the set $(M_1, M_2, \ldots M_j, M_k)$ contains all the symbols currently available to the System, and thus exhausts the Systematic universe of discourse. This means that $(M_1, M_2 \ldots M_j)$ is equivalent to $\{\overline{M_k}\}$, the logical complement of M_k: it contains everything in the (current) universe of discourse except M_k. The step from (1) to (2) can then be written as one from M_k to $\{\overline{M_k}\}$. Step (3) would be $M_k \Uparrow \{\overline{M_k}\}$, which could then be abbreviated by introducing the symbol "M_m" to produce (not: designate) a new and expanded set $\{M_m\}$. $\{M_m\}$, then, was previously present only latently or in itself, and is not mutually substitutable with $\{\overline{M_k}\}$, as Seebohm's view (discussed in chapter 4) would entail; M_k and $\{\overline{M_k}\}$ are not moments of each other, but are complementary components of the universe of discourse. Nor do they "contradict" one another in the ordinary sense, for they are not mutually exclusive propositions, but mutually exclusive sets of markers, which is quite a different thing. By their dialectical interaction, they enlarge the universe of discourse with their positive result, which is M_m itself.

This approach is obviously congenial to many of Hegel's discussions of dialectic, perhaps because it has the advantage of showing that the dialectic progresses by a sort of minimal change at each stage, with each new step either abbreviating just the contents present before or adding a single new element to the universe of Systematic discourse. And this enables us to clear up a further Hegelian enigma, for if, as Hegel likes to write, a result "negates" that of which it is the result, then M_m negates $\{\overline{M_k}\}$ and does so minimally, by adding a single new moment to it: it is thus what Hegel calls a "determinate negation."[13]

If to take a moment of the System out of the onward development—to regard M_k, for example, independently of the markers which explicate it—is to "finitize" it, then we can see why Hegel associates contradiction with finitude, and indeed with all finite things.[14] For a Systematic moment openly shows its dependence on a set of other moments—those which it abbreviates, and which provide its content. Any finite thing is similarly dependent on a variety of other finite things—conditions for its existence, perhaps its own physical parts, its own "content." All such conditions are to some degree other than it, and in manifesting this otherness it "negates" them. Indeed, as an individual in space and time, the finite thing may *appear* not to be dependent on anything else at all: to manifest, not dependence, but independence. Hence, it is not merely other than the conditions for its existence, but seems to deny them. It denies them especially (the *Phenomenology* tells us) if it is a living thing, which intrinsically presents itself as independent of other beings. Animal locomotion is one such denial. (Kantian morality, the pitch of what Hegel calls "externalization," is another.)[15] Hence, as Hegel puts matters more generally in the *Science of Logic*:

> But everything which is manifold is determined both *in itself* and *as against others*, and has negation in it [*an ihm*]; but [such] indifferent variety in general turns into opposition; and opposition is contradiction. Therefore everything is . . . contradictory and impossible.[16]

In all cases, the dependence of the individual being on its environing conditions will reassert itself: conditions will change, and the finite being dependent on them will perish.

Hegel's expression *Widerspruch* is thus, as Vittorio Hösle and others have noted, ambiguous.[17] But it is systematically so. In the System, "contradiction" is just the relation between a newly introduced term and the rest of the universe of discourse—the terms it abbreviates. In the finite world, it is the relation between a being and the conditions for its existence.

Hegel's claims of "necessity" for his System cannot be viewed here as applying to assertions true in all possible worlds, deduced from self-evident premises, or otherwise "necessarily true."[18] Hegel himself, in the places cited, refers to necessity of "content," and we can interpret this quite straightforwardly as the claim that any moment in the System has the content systematically assigned to it: that it is defined solely in terms of moments which have preceded it, regrouped according to the kind of moves I have sketched. So generated, the content of a moment of the System is unaffected by contingencies of nature and life, which could not make it be other than it is. The necessity of the System, then, is just the claim that it has been generated in accordance with a set of rules: that it has a certain order, which is one side of its basic Nobility.

Completeness and Circularity

The other main claim of the System is its completeness claim. This presents a variety of issues, for there is a variety of senses in which the System could be thought to be "complete." They fall into two groups. In one, the System is what I will call immanently complete: it exhausts its own domain of pure thought by developing every structure of pure thought that is possible at all. The other group of senses holds that the System is somehow complete in its relation to the extraphilosophical world: that it provides a complete grasp of history, culture, or of humanity itself.

I will begin discussing immanent completeness by noting that the content abbreviated in Systematic dialectics quickly becomes enormously complex. Let an "adequate" explication of M_k be one which explicates all its content markers, and all of theirs, back to M_1 ("Being") itself. Such an adequate explication would consist in a series of occurrences of "Being," grouped by parentheses and connectives which showed how they had been grouped and regrouped as the System developed. But, as we have seen repeatedly, Systematic dialectics is nothing other than the unimpeded movement of thought, and thought is precisely the grouping and regrouping of achieved content. Hence, as I noted in chapter 4, in Systematic dialectics we are free to place our parentheses in any way we wish (though we should respect previous place-ments where possible: *stare decisis*). It follows that the number of possible directions the System can take is enormously larger than its linear presentation suggests. For k = 7, for example, it would be 2^7-1, or 127 possibilities, for seven markers can be grouped in 127 different ways.

It can be seen that the number of partial mediations possible at any stage of the logic is in principle equivalent to the number of these possible combinations, so by the time 7 moments have been traversed, the logician has no fewer than 127 possibilities open to her for the next development. The System thus presents, at any stage, the actualization of only one of an enormous, exponentially increasing, set of possibilities. I will call the set of all possible groupings of markers the Systematic "field," and the set actually written the "path." It is clear that an immense number of alternative paths is available, and that Systematic dialectics is much more flexible than is often supposed.[19]

The famous legend of "thesis, antithesis, synthesis," for example, suggests that, given the thesis and the antithesis, only one synthesis can follow.[20] But such unequivocality of result holds only for full mediation, in which there is no selection of which markers to include as explicating the next marker to be introduced. In partial mediation, the System's necessity claim does not require that each stage have one and only one successor,[21] but allows for a greater number, perhaps much greater. This fact no more impeaches the necessity of the derivation of each stage than does the fact that a conventional logician, having proved one theorem, normally has a choice about which theorem to prove next.[22]

A glance at any passage of either *Logic* will show that Hegel's explications are normally partial rather than full: that is, the traits of any moment brought out in its unfolding are not all of those which were, so to speak, placed into it previously. That Hegel was aware of this is indicated by the obvious discrepancies among the various versions of his *Logic*: a comparison of their tables of contents shows that he revised without compunction or embarrassment, presumably because he knew that a variety of equally valid developments was possible.[23] Indeed, that words, being merely conventional, can be altered in meaning to suit new discoveries and changed views is, Hegel says, one of their strengths, and makes alphabets better than hieroglyphs; we can now see that this applies to Hegel's own System.[24] The System is infinitely revisable, or (as I will argue in a moment) almost so: the "abstract absolute" which Seebohm mentions, and which is explicitly present at the beginning of the System, is to be understood primarily in terms of what it is absolved *from*, and this is precisely the need to hold any specific doctrine at all about the world.[25]

This explains our inability, noted in the Introduction, to get beyond Hegel's System. We cannot, as Christian Topp has noted, reject the System *globally*, because to do so we must ourselves think systematically.[26] Since we are rejecting Hegel, our thinking would have to be in terms of some other, alternate System. But because Hegel, as I present him, is not committed to any of the determinate contents his System develops, but could countenance alternatives, the "other System" in question cannot be shown to be any less Hegelian than Hegel's own. We also cannot reject the System *piecemeal*, arguing that some part of it is either immanently wrong because it was improperly derived, or that it fails to capture extrasystematic reality. For in both cases, the System will simply regroup so as to remedy the defect. Hence, each rejection of Hegelianism leads in practice *only* to another Hegelianism. This does not mean that we are forever trapped inside Hegelianism, as I will show in a future work. But it does mean that rejection of the System is impossible: it needs to be understood and used, not fought against.

It also follows that the famous Hegelian "end to history" has to be understood in a very special way. If history is the struggle of humans to find and hold firm some certain and immutable standpoint, then "history"—like the *Phenomenology*—has indeed come to an end, with the recognition by philosophy (of all things) that no such standpoint is possible. If history is the gradual introduction of rationality, or Nobility, into more and more corners of human life, then it is far from over. Indeed, it cannot end unless human beings do, for each new moment brings new content which has to be integrated into the (almost) infinitely flexible self-revisions of systematic thinking.

There are, however, at least two restraints on this flexibility. One is that, as I will argue in part 3, when Hegel actually writes his System he uses the sounds of German words, and this helps to constrain the path the development takes. At stage 4 of the System, for example, there may be 2^4-1, or 31, possible paths the System can take; but if it is going to shed light on the German term *Dasein*, the range of options shrinks notably. The breadth of the Systematic field thus tends to be hidden by Hegel's own procedure in his writings, because the reader is recurrently tempted to see it as "about" some named domain (Being, the Absolute, Discourse, History, and so on). Bringing out the nature of the Systematic field, and the immense revisability of the System as actually written, was one of the main motives for my rewriting of Systematic dialectics in chapter 4.

Second, of the possible combinations of markers that would be present in a complete and full explication, some of them will actually have been used in constructing the System, but most will not; at stage 7, of the 127 possibilities, just 6 will have been actualized. The interests of economy suggest that it would be best to base further developments on those 6, for use of any of the other 121 would require going back and introducing that particular combination at its proper place. Hence my appeal, in chapter 4, to *stare decisis*: parentheses should be preserved if possible, but need not be. Indeed, the more Hegel succeeds in building a System in which each moment depends on others for its meaning, the more any revision in it will require changes in earlier moments (as well as later ones). The degree of Hegel's success can be seen from Dieter Henrich's documentation of the changes in earlier parts of the system that would be necessary to accommodate a single change in Hegel's explication of the "state."[27]

   That the sort of revision I have just sketched was often made by Hegel in the construction of the various versions of his System I have no doubt. Unfortunately, the alternative versions of it with which he presents us each runs in linear fashion: except for the way moments come in pairs during the Logic of Essence, which I mentioned in the preceding analysis, Hegel never actually shows us the System developing simultaneously in two different directions. Though not, apparently, threatened by the diversity of possible systems—he certainly made no effort to hide it—Hegel chose not to pursue it: his System does seem to embody the attempt to construct a single "master narrative" which I have discussed elsewhere in connection with the *Phenomenology*.[28]

   In sum: rendering Hegel's System at all plausible, by the standards not only of our day but of his own, requires us to detach the overall project of his System from the various specific contents it generates. Hegel himself did this, I claim, but did not discuss it. The closest he comes to acknowledging the need for revision, to say nothing of his System's enormous capacity for it, is in the Introduction to the *Science of Logic*:

> How could I not believe that the method which I follow in this
> System of logic—or rather which this System itself follows—is
> not capable of much improvement, of much development in
> detail? But I know as well that it is the only true method.[29]

The defects of the Logic, then, are not merely those of Hegel the man, but of the "method," the path of the Logic itself;[30] and yet that path is, the man knows, the only possible one for philosophy.

The completeness of Hegel's System, like its necessity and its contradictions, is thus of a strange sort—or sorts, for there are at least four different senses in which the System could be said to be complete. In the one just discussed, it exhausts the possibilities for its own kind of construction, the Systematic field. The System is far indeed from such immanent completeness, for as I have argued it presents only a tiny fraction of what could have been developed via its dialectical procedures. It seems, then, that we could attribute to Hegel's System at most a second sort of completeness: given a beginning and an end, it will get from one to the other by adding just one marker at a time, and hence will omit no intervening stages, as in Proclus's Law of Mean Terms.[31]

But no end is as yet in sight: there seems to be nothing preventing us from going on forever, grouping and regouping content into ever more complex structures, thus giving Systematic dialectics over to what Hegel calls the "bad infinite."[32] This raises the issue of the beginning and end of Hegel's System, and since these are the same, of its circularity—and of a third sense in which it may be thought to be "complete."

I will not claim here to exhaust this complex issue. It is clear from the above, however, that system must assume circular form, if only because the set of German terms which can be used in its construction will at some point have been exhausted by previous developments. At that point, we would have an aggregate of contents ($M_1 \ldots M_k$) but no further M's to abbreviate it. If the development is not to come to a halt, we must return to one of the previous M's and reuse it. The most appropriate one for this purpose is M_1, "Being"—for it and the M required here share the characteristic of abbreviating nothing determinate: M_1 abbreviates nothing at all, and the M needed here abbreviates everything equally. Both, as abbreviations, refer to a realm of "abbreviata"; but in neither case is it possible to specify what these abbreviata are to the exclusion of others. This operational equivalence of the beginning and end of the System, then, necessitates its circular form. It also means that the System could, in principle, be expanded to cover "new" moments—provided that these new contents can be defined in terms of what has gone before them in the System, and that there are not an infinite number of them. Circularity is thus the product, not of a complacent System coming to rest in its own well-rounded self, but (at least in part) of the excess of thought over the words at its disposal: having used all of the appropriate ones up, it has no alternative but to reuse them, in circular fashion.

In a fourth and final sense, the System can be said to be complete if it somehow exhausts, not merely all the German terms at its disposal, but the extraphilosophical world itself. As stated at *Encyclopedia* #24 Zus. 3,[33] this claim is as follows:

> The totality of the forms [*die sämtlichen Formen*] of finite think-
> ing will occur in the course of the logical development, and in
> that manner in which they appear according to necessity.

This—as clear a claim of Nobility as Hegel ever makes—is daring in-deed: Who could ever enumerate, much less construct according to rules, all the categories of Hegelian "finite thinking," which among other things would include all our empirical concepts?

The provenance of this, like that of many Hegelian *Zusätze*, is un-clear. In the Preface to the second edition of the *Science of Logic* (1831) the claim is more circumspect:

> Therefore logical science, in treating the thought determina-
> tions which instinctively and unconsciously permeate our spirit
> and even when they enter into language remain unobjective
> and unexamined, will also be the reconstruction of those which
> have been singled out through reflection and fixed by it as sub-
> jective, in the material and form of external forms.[34]

The latter group of determinations is obviously finite; and so, appar-ently, is the former.[35] For Hegel has just specified those instinctive thought determinations as the *universals* which are displayed in lan-guage. Since the set of all utterances is finite, so presumably is the set of all universals displayed in those utterances.

The other parts of the System do not deal with ordinary language but are explicitly oriented to the *Wissenschaft* of Hegel's day, which the Preface to the second edition of the *Encyclopedia* tells us provides philos-ophy with its *Faktum*. This *Faktum* is the given element which philosophy must take into account, as "already prepared knowledge" (*die schon zubereitete Erkenntnis*); and the *Science of Logic* tells us that the prepara-tion is done by "the progress of culture itself, and particularly of the sciences."[36] Hence, *only the universals of ordinary language and thought determinations which have been previously treated by science and reflection will find their way into the System.* Further, as presented in the *Encyclopedia*, the System is only an outline, "limited" to the "starting points and basic concepts of the special sciences."[37] The "historical completeness" of Hegel's System is not a direct comprehension of history in all its motley manifold, but simply the exhaustive appropriation of a certain class of terms: those which have been worked up, consciously or not, over time and which play central roles in organizing science, culture, and ordinary language. It is the forming of these Noble terms into a company of words.

A Logic of Access?

One important feature of assertionistic logic, of course, is that it actually captures important features of how we behave—how we state truths about the world, and how we reason from one truth to another. Is there some sort of human activity which Hegelian logic can claim to capture, in a way not requiring its reduction to assertionistic procedures? Uncovering such a phenomenon would enable us further to demarcate Hegelian thought from more familiar kinds, by pointing out a different domain of symbolic activity which it can capture. It would be beyond the scope of the present investigation to attempt a rigorous exploration of any such phenomenal domain, but a candidate for the title of "domain" of Systematic dialectics can at least be introduced. I will begin the introduction with a thought experiment.

Suppose two capable logicians—call them Bertrand and Rudolf—want to have a conversation in arbitrary symbols. They design their artificial language (as I do throughout this book) to stay close to English syntax and word order. They begin by deciding that a will stand for "the zoo," b for "monkeys," c for Beth, g for "1983 Ford," h for "Mary's son's grandmother's house," i for "monkey house," n for "Mary," p for "office," s for "rain," t for "Mary's son," and v for "Mary's son's uncle"; also D for "closed" and J for "ill"; also β for "is at," η for "has, possesses," and ρ for "returns to." They begin their conversation:

> Bertrand: I guess that $((n\beta p) \bullet (c\beta p)) \supset ((t\beta h) \lor ((t\beta a) \bullet (v\beta a)))$.
> Rudolf: Well, $((t\beta a) \bullet (v\beta a) \bullet (s\beta a)) \supset ((t\beta i) \bullet (v\beta i))$.
> Bertrand: But did you know that (b) $(b\beta a) \supset J(b)$? And, of
> course, $(\exists b)$ $(b\beta a)$. So (iD).
> Rudolf: But then $\sim(t\beta a) \bullet \sim(v\beta a)$.
> Bertrand: So presumably, $(t\rho h) \bullet (v\rho h) \lor t\beta h$.
> Rudolf: I recall that $v\eta g$, and—look! $g\beta h$!

Bertrand's obvious response, as the reader may have noted, is "$t\beta h$." But we need not ask why he and Rudolf are so concerned with the boy's whereabouts, because my main points lie elsewhere. First of these is the obvious fact that whatever an arbitrary symbol system may be, it is not a medium for conversation, a point the reader can make still plainer by asking two friends to read the above symbolic representation aloud while she tries to follow it. The same holds, it would appear, for any other depiction of thought which uses arbitrary symbols, unless we are willing to adopt some pre-Wittgensteinian (and pre-Hegelian) model on which thought takes place independently of speech and language. The predicate calculus, for example, cannot be the medium of our thought, and it seems that modern logic in general is primarily a way not of speaking and thinking but of writing, a mode of what the French call *écriture* (this is perhaps why logicans are always running for blackboards).

If the reader replaces the Roman letters in the above symbolic representation with the letters immediately preceding them in the alphabet (and z for a), the conversation may get easier to follow. Its first line will read, for example, "I guess that $((m\beta o) \cdot (b\beta o)) \supset ((s\beta g) \vee ((s\beta z) \cdot (u\beta z)))$." Replacing these by the words they stand for would make it easier yet: "I guess that if Mary and Beth are both at the office, Mary's son is either at his grandmother's house or he and his uncle are at the zoo."

These arbitrary symbols, of course, "refer" to objects just as do the ordinary names of those objects. Why, then, can we not converse with them? Does something happen, in our ordinary conversations, over and above conventional "reference"? Is that extra something necessary for the comprehensibility of those conversations?

One thing which words in ordinary language do, and arbitrary symbols do not, is convey background information acquired over the lifetimes of their users. Indeed, as I have argued elsewhere,[38] even arbitrary symbols generally convey at least one item of information about the objects or properties they designate: that those objects or properties belong to that very select group of entities important enough to have names. Pike's Peak, for example, has one; the individual stones which lie at its summit do not. Dogs usually have names; chickens usually do not. Colors are important: our color vocabulary is highly ramified, compared to that for odors.

The importance of background information to the mind has led Graeme Forbes to the illuminating metaphor of a referential cognitive "operating system." Suppose that every time the mind receives information about an object that seems to be worth retaining, it creates or adds to a file in which that information is held. The proper name of the object, if it has one, may also be the name of that file. When I hear a name uttered by someone else, all or some of the information in that file is activated, and it is partly in virtue of this that I understand the utterance.

A name in current use in a language, then, is likely to be double: it names both an object and a file in the referential "operating system" of those who understand it.[39]

Traditional accounts of reference simply omit the files, and consider reference to be a binary relation between word and object. This is a highly idealized view of the way we actually use words to refer, for as Quine writes, background information is in fact incapable of being cut away from the referential capacities of words.[40] Indeed, it performs at least one valuable function as regards language, for as Gareth Evans has pointed out, to eliminate it means we fail to allow for a very basic distinction:

> If one has a dossier of information associated with the name
> "NN," and fails to bring it to bear in understanding "NN is
> F," going no further than the thought "someone named 'NN'
> is F," one has surely failed to do what it was the point of the
> utterance that one should do.[41]

In many cases, then (and I suspect in almost all), there appear to be two jobs that a name does. On the one hand, it designates the entity which it names, and on the other it activates a "file" of background information. What the above thought experiment suggests is that the background information in a file does not all function merely to help in the task of referring—as Fregean *Sinn*, for example, helps specify reference. Nor is all the information there in order to provide us with further helpful background information about the entity referred to.[42] For the problem with arbitrary symbols is not that we cannot unequivocally fix their referents, or that they do not convey much information about how those referents present themselves. It is that we cannot even keep the symbols straight. Who is c? What is i? Can i be f? And so on.

The thought experiment reminds us, then, that the most basic thing we do with words, or with arbitrary symbols, is not to use them to talk about the world. The most basic thing we do with them is keep them straight: recognize them when they recur. This is not as easy as it seems. Simple physical resemblance, for example, does not suffice: all occurrences of a's in the thought experiment above look alike, but that does not of itself enable a reader or hearer of the conversation to remember who or what a was originally introduced to designate. Linguistic symbols, it seems, are so inextricable from the background information they convey that we cannot even recognize symbols which do not convey such information—even when, as in the thought experiment, those symbols are used consistently.[43] And so, I suggest, it is the background information our words convey to us that enables us to keep them straight.

If we had no knowledge at all of a symbol or word—did not even know what it looked or sounded like—we obviously could not use it. If we do know its shape or sound, and what it designates, we still cannot use it in conversation (though it may perhaps serve for writing on blackboards). In order to keep any term straight, we need still more information about it. Such knowledge is supplied by the background information activated by a term. For this can be viewed as information, not about what that term designates, but about that term itself. Thus, the name "Mary," unlike the symbol n, may remind me of the boy's mother, and of a good many facts about her—about how she looks and acts.

But the relevant information about a term includes more than facts about the entity designated by that term. The name "Mary" may also remind me of my cousin Mary, whom I have always liked but with whom I had a spat at the last family reunion; of a sunset I saw with my first love, Mary; of the mother of God to whom I was so devoted as a child; of Mary Poppins; and so on. In terms of standard theories of reference, such information is not about the person currently being referred to by the name, and plays no role in the current referring; and this, on the present view, may be entirely correct. But the background information I associate with "Mary" helps me to be able to fix and focus on the name itself: it makes it something I can recognize and use more readily than an arbitrary symbol. I will call this the "background information" view of referential terms. It does not compete with standard philosophical theories of reference, for it presupposes that something like one of them is right: the recognition of a grapheme or morpheme as "denoting" something in the world is not denied, but seen as part of a larger process which is psychological and, more importantly, cultural in nature.

The relation of this to Hegelian Systematic dialectics can be clarified via an analogy with computers. I can type a true proposition into my computer and, with the right program, get the computer to deduce other true propositions. But I can also set my computer up to return *any symbol whatever* as a value for any symbol I type in, so that if I type in "cat" it returns to me "dog." If the second symbol is longer than the first, the computer is carrying out something very similar to the dialectical function of explication: it returns a longer string when cued by a shorter one.

My suggestion, then, is that (in spite of some differences which I will discuss shortly) Hegel's systematic dialectics of abbreviation and explication stand to this sort of accessing in something like the way that formal logic is related to description and inference: it captures the basic steps in our performance of the actions in question.

Many philosophical approaches to our linguistic operations, while not denying that the processing of background information is basic to our use of language, assume that such accessing can be captured with the standard tools of assertionistic logic.[44] But assertionistic approaches, whatever their ultimate value in this context, tend to cloud things by excluding one relevant fact and introducing one irrelevant issue. The relevant fact is that often the information I access with a term is not, as I have noted, about the entity or entities currently referred to by that term. That I once saw a lovely sunset with a very dear person named Mary is unrelated to the fact that "Mary," here and now, refers to someone quite different. But that does not mean that the information is altogether irrelevant. What it is relevant to is the status in my mind of the name "Mary" itself. This dimension—the realm in which we keep symbols straight—thus tends to be occluded by assertionistic approaches.

The irrelevant issue—actually a whole family of them—concerns the ontological status of the entities that assertions are about. "Mary" is just as much the name of Mary Poppins as it is of Mary my friend, and I can access information about Mary Poppins just as easily as about, say, the back of my right knee: the accessing is faster and the information accessed is obviously richer and more interesting. Yet the back of my right knee exists, and Mary Poppins does not. As long as we construe the accessing operation assertionistically, a sentence such as "Mary Poppins can fly" seems to correspond to some state of affairs holding somewhere, and we have all sorts of questions about where. If we view "can fly" as a partial explication of the name "Mary Poppins," no such questions arise: "can fly" is merely one of the symbols strings we are disposed to return when asked about Mary Poppins. Hegelian Systematic dialectics, since it is not concerned with how our thoughts relate to the objects of which they are thoughts, can give an elegant account of certain basic structures of how we access information. Since it is restricted to the relations of terms to other terms, it does not leave out relevant facts: it does not instate the fact that this particular term, on this particular occasion, refers to that particular entity as the only key fact about that term, but allows us to see that adducing all sorts of background information is part of keeping our terms straight. And it does not persistently direct our attention away from the terms themselves to the entities they designate. It thus affords a clearer view of the phenomena in question.

Since the accessing of background information in general is noncombinatorial, it occurs differently for different terms; its general structures and rules are, as my rewriting of Systematic dialectics would suggest, relatively uninformative—or, to put it in a more Hegelian way, the form of accessing cannot be considered apart from the contents accessed. The interesting issues involve the contents accessed, because those contents vary, of course, from person to person. Consider the case of Cinderella and her two sisters. In terms of my suggestion above, "two sisters" could be viewed as a partial explication of the content "abbreviated" by the term "Cinderella"; but this content is most unsystematic, and indeed may be idiosyncratic: perhaps my parents always deleted Prunella when they read me "Cinderella," so I think she has only one sister. Perhaps I have picked up pieces of information that are unique to me: perhaps I have got it into my head that she has an evil stepbrother, who is away at college. In either case, as I become more widely acquainted with my culture, such idiosyncratic items will be edited out of my file, as I discover in various ways that the people around me—and others whom I may read and hear about—do not share them. Keeping my symbols straight is thus part of becoming integrated into my culture.

When the background information I access in response to a word is sufficiently like what others around me access, the information turns, indeed, from being mere subjective connotation to being an interpersonal coordinating medium of some importance. That entire cultures access the background information "mother of God" when they hear the name Mary, for example, is an important fact about those cultures. It is bound up with an enormous web of social practices and mores, such as belief in God; belief that God had a mother; belief that motherhood is the highest calling for women; belief that the mother of God is all-loving, ready to intercede with her son on our behalf; belief that interceding on behalf of others is basic to womanhood; and many others, more savory or less.

Hegel's ultimate concern, then, is not with capturing the formal features of how background information coordinates behavior, but with the far more important matter of defining the content of that information itself. The method Hegel uses to construct his System is a step-by-step programming of meanings (information) to be accessed through (abbreviated by) certain key words. The point of his System, in this perspective, is to produce a set of terms which:

> —access similar information in everyone who understands them;
> —are central to the broader systems of cuing and accessing (abbreviating and explicating) which permeate and structure discourse and, thereby, culture itself.

This explains why Hegel is less interested in overall accounts of how he operates (though as we saw he finally gives one, in the "Absolute Method" section of the *Logic*) than he is in formulating and justifying his basic categories themselves. It also explains Hegel's two restrictions on the kinds of content he is willing to discuss and admit into his System. One, I noted above, is that he will discuss only the "universals" of language, the basic categories that are exemplified and used across a wide variety of utterances. The other is that, in more concrete parts of the System, he will limit himself to concepts that have been through the institutionalized reflective procedures of *Wissenschaft*. The effect of both is, first, to eliminate what Quine might call stimulus-specific background information: Hegel will be treating, not for example what I know about "Mary" today or even in general, but the "standing information" accessible across the most important (or at least the most expert) segments of the linguistic community. Further, this standing information, common to a variety of utterances in a language and often the result of institutionalized educational procedures, is not merely individualistic or subjective. It is information that is contained in many minds—either all minds or, to paraphrase Aristotle, the best (most *wissenschaftlich*) ones.[45] Accessing in general, as Hegel would understand it, is thus not always merely "psychological," but can be "social" in nature. In organizing it, Hegel undertakes to organize the culture itself: he provides a basic background of shared information in which members of that culture can understand and articulate themselves, a company of words.

Traditional logic not only captures some of the ways we actually think, but also provides a way to evaluate the performances of actual thinkers. Similarly, though in a much more concrete way, Hegel has undertaken to construct a standard for the background information members of a culture should share. That standard, to be sure, is not developed by Hegel as a formal one: it consists in Systematic definitions for the basic notions of a given culture, definitions which (as universal) can be shared by all, and which (as necessary) can be efficiently accessed and their interrelationships displayed.

Historical Dialectics

Historical dialectics are more like our familiar assertionist approaches than are the Systematic variety. To begin with, they are, in contrast to the Systematic type, a posteriori: they reconstruct certain features of something that actually happened—namely, certain basic transformations in expert discourse. Hence, they begin from definitions that have at some time actually been agreed to, or at least propounded, by the discursive community. In such cases, D_0 should be a true report of some definition propounded by someone somewhere in the finite world. The contradictions such reported definitions encounter must have been agreed upon as well, which means that the report of that anomaly also claims to be a true proposition. If it is revised through merely conceptual reflection—because two of its markers turn out in some way to be incompatible—it remains a true report of a contradictory definition: historical dialectics are on this level uncommitted to the view that reality itself is contradictory, requiring only that the concepts in terms of which we attempt to conceive of reality may be inconsistent, with reality or (presumably) with themselves or other definitions.[46]

On the other hand, though reposing upon the truth of the propositions constituting each of its stages, historical dialectics organizes them differently than did the actual historical process by which they came to be asserted and, perhaps, subsequently falsified. In the first place, as I mentioned in chapter 4, leaps can occur in which several new markers enter or leave the definition of a basic term at once.[47] The dialectical reconstruction of such a situation will have to present those markers as entering, and others perhaps as leaving, not together but in serial order, so that the warrant for including (or excluding) each can be assessed. Hence, it is also possible for historical dialectics to include D_0's which were never actually propounded by anyone—as long as they can (like Hume's missing shade of blue)[48] be reconstructed, step-by-step, as lying between other definitions which were actually propounded.

Moreover, as Hegel recognizes in several places, history tends to stall: anomalies may go undiscovered or unrecognized for centuries, and the debates (not to say the wars) over how to resolve them may go back and forth unproductively for just as long. Hence, though various of the stages of historical dialectics claim assertional truth, the overall development does not.[49] It claims, rather, to be a step-by-step reconstruction, over time, of the movement between such truths as we have: omitting no intervening stage, and ordering them correctly. It claims Nobility, then, not truth.

We can understand the standing of historical dialectics with respect to universality and the a priori by noting that the fundamental definition of a historical dialectical development, the one from which it begins, is as such a beginning a sort of "principle," and an empirical one. It is not a "first principle" in the traditional philosophical sense of something valid for all humans (or indeed all rational beings), but merely a beginning point, to some degree contingent, for a specific set of further developments. Insofar as such a principle underlies, as it well may, not merely a scientific research program or an individual's exploration of the world (as in the *Phenomenology*) but the entirety of a culture or society, all the practices, laws, and so on, which are founded on that basic defining principle will be unintelligible to members of other societies unless that principle itself is understood: the members of other societies will be unable to access important information about them. Hence, historical dialectics are not only a posteriori, they are also nonuniversal. Though, for example, Germany, in Hegel's view, is more advanced than ancient India, it is nonetheless impossible to express in German the worldview of the Bhagavad Gita:

> A word of our language gives us *our* determinate representation of such an object, and precisely because of this does not give that of another people, which has not only another langauge but also other representations.[50]

What cannot be expressed to a people cannot be understood by them;[51] Germans and ancient Indians thus live in worlds which are, in something like the contemporary sense, "incommensurable" to each other (though not, presumably, to the System itself which, in ways still to be seen, comprehends both).

Moreover, the "necessity" of historical dialectics is hypothetical: starting from an actual definition, it has an end in view. The purpose of formulating definitions is after all to "get it right": to come up with a definition that includes all and only necessary characteristics of the definiendum, so that further revisions are unnecessary.[52] The actual goal of historical dialectics is not, however, the attainment of such definitions, which would put an end to historical development as such, but simply the recognition that any such development can only be a rational progress; true to the basic revisability of Systematic dialectics, the absolute standpoint as the "goal of history" is not to be regarded as a final statement of how reality is, but as that standpoint where further scientific progress will be, in a dialectical sense, rational.[53]

Finally, because new markers are viewed in historical dialectics as coming into definitions, and old ones as leaving, singly, such dialectics are, like Systematic dialectics, narratively complete: given the starting point and the goal, no intervening stage is skipped. But this does not mean that historical dialectics—beginning from a given and working toward an ideal goal—are ordered from simple to complex. It is impossible to tell, before anomalies are brought forward, whether a proposed definition will require revision by adding a marker or by dropping one; in the latter case it would get more complex, but in the former it would get simpler.[54] As with Systematic dialectics, then, but for different reasons, no stage uniquely determines the nature of the succeeding stage, and historical dialectics, though it recounts a development in time, cannot be used to predict.

Historical dialectics claims, because of its step-by-step reconstructive strategy, to be both complete and rationally warranted: to be Noble. As I have presented it here, it is not an immanent, necessary development like the dialectics of the System. It is not a set of general theses—false, probabilistic, or apodictic—about history, and is too empty to be a Procrustean bed for historical understanding. It is rather the organized portrayal of a set of disorganized tendencies in human history. The portrayal, like the history, is open, empirical, contextualized—and, at its best, radically, painfully self-critical.

Hegelian Thought: Narrative

B asic to Hegelian thinking as analyzed in chapter 4 is its bifurcation into two quite different sorts of activity—systematic dialectics, an activity of a priori conceptual construction, and historical dialectics, a rational reconstruction of *Wissenschaft*'s continual conceptual revision in light of new evidence. Philosophy requires both, as we will see, and philosophical thought is thus double. The doubleness of thinking, the ways it takes active and passive or reconstructive forms, will form the focus of the present narrative. Passing through Aristotle, Hume, and Kant, it will begin not far from where the previous narrative did: at *Philebus* 17a, in Socrates' account of the "noble road" to speech (or, as *kallion hodos* has been translated, less literally but more safely, "attractive method": *Phil.* 16b1, 5).[1]

Plato's *Philebus*

Two apparently distinct methods are presented there; in both, thought begins in constraint (*dein*, 16c10 and *dei*, 18a8; *anagkasthai* 18b1). In the first method, which is exemplified by Protarchus learning his letters and which I will call "Protarchan," thought is confronted with the chaos and flux of the Platonic sensory world, and begins by positing a single form (*idea*) as contained in that chaos. It then goes on actually to find such a form—for all things, we recall, are composed of both unity and plurality, and unity is never wholly absent from any portion of the sensory flux.[2] But in virtue of this very identity of one and many, the single form posited and found is also a plurality. Hence, thought can—and must—proceed from any unit it has reached to investigate the plurality proper to that unit until the *determinate* plurality that stands "between the innumerable and the one" has been delimited. The aim here (one disdained by Socrates' contemporaries, 17a) is to allow none of those intermediates to escape.

This method, we are told, is important. Every single rational productive practice (*techné*) originated with it (16c2f), and its ultimate use is for "investigating and learning and teaching one another" (16e). At every stage, it seeks—in the first instance—truth. For if the Form which is at first posited or hypothesized is then actually discovered existing in the experienced things, subsequent investigation must be true to that discovery—that is, cannot state falsehoods about that Form. The investigation also seeks, in addition to faithfulness to the givens, order and completeness, for its aim is not merely to establish some facts about the one-and-many in question, but to arrive at an ordering of all the elements which come under the original unity and are unified by it. The investigation aims, then, for an account of the way the unifying principle operates, and what it operates on: it seeks to treat of order over size, or of Nobility.

The completeness and unity of the list it produces will exhibit that same quality, which is then a goal of the investigation itself. The art of letters (*hê grammatikê*) is a case in point. The sounds which come out of our mouths are, as parts of our voice, one; and yet they are also an unlimited plurality of individual sounds, perhaps no two exactly alike (17b3f). Knowing the phenomenon of voice as either a one or an indeterminate many will not yield an art of letters; only knowledge of the determinate multiplicity that structures the variety of sounds actually produced by the human vocal apparatus can qualify as *hê grammatikê*. The art of letters must then be true to the sounds we make—the alphabet must be an accurate symbolization of them. And, as a systematic whole, it must exhibit the same plurality and unity as our vocalization.

But human beings, even the "godlike" among us (18b7f) may also be compelled to begin in the opposite way: not by simply positing a unity, but by working toward one—toward, that is, a determinate and comprehensive classification—from the unlimited multiplicity that presents itself to our senses. This, apparently, is a different procedure, indeed one "opposite" to the other. We are told (18a6–b2) that this method begins

with a many and works toward a one, while the previous one begins with
a unit and works toward a plurality. But the exemplification of the second method, supposedly of a movement from a many to a one, sounds
suspiciously like a movement from one to many. The example is Theuth,
the godlike Egyptian who (by legend) recognized the diversity of sounds
in our speech and proceeded to discriminate them into vowels, consonants, and mutes. The first, Protarchan method began with a unity, posited (*themenos,* 16d2) or selected (*helês,* 17e2); so did Theuth, for his first
step was to notice (*katenoêsen*) that the sounds we make are many and not
one (18b8f), and to do this he must have begun with some perception of
sounds as an undifferentiated mass, or unity. The further process by
which Theuth recognized his three main classes of sound is, moreover,
one of discrimination, indeed of "division" (*diêrei,* 18c3), which finally
arrived at three classes of vocalization: vowels, consonants, and mutes.

On both the Theuthian and Protarchan methods, then, we begin
with the positing, selection, or perception of some unity (an *idea* or a
shared quality), and move to a rational discrimination of its types. The
goals of the two methods, however, clearly differ: the Protarchan
method ended with a determinate plurality, the different letters and
sounds. The Theuthian method does arrive finally at a unity, for we are
told that Theuth, having finished his classification of sounds, proceeded
to name them, one and all, "letter." And this reveals a second difference
between the two methods: in giving them that single name, Theuth instituted a bond (*desmon . . . logisamenos, mian . . . technên . . . poiounta*)[3]
connecting those sounds together so that they could be addressed by a
single grammatical art. The complex set of vowels, consonants, and
mutes that Theuth has discriminated is not itself a unit, other than in the
relatively trivial sense that all are noises producible by the human vocal
apparatus—the sense Theuth began with. Thus, the *Philebus* suggests (at
18c7–d2) that the ultimate unity expressed in the name "grammar" is to
some degree brought about or enhanced *by the name itself,* when it is applied to what comes under the various categories Theuth had uncovered.
Like the "mixing" that produced a formula for the good life, and which I
discussed in chapter 3, Theuthian thinking is creative—and in a way Protarchan thinking is not. The letters by themselves are what we might call
a system *quo ad nos,* in that it makes no sense to learn any member of the
classification without learning all—a state of affairs which reflects facts
about us (such as that we have inherited Theuth's classification in the
first place, and that learning only part of it wold have no purpose in our
lives), as well as facts about the sounds made by our vocal apparatus. The
Theuthian statement that "vowels, mutes, and consonants together con-

stitute letters" would hence be no true report of some antecedently existing state of affairs, but the creation of a new state of affairs via the introduction into the language of a new name—and with that of a new art, and thence of various practices associated with learning and applying that art.

Theuth thought up his verbal "bond," with the new art and practices it makes possible, for our sakes, seeing that none of us would learn any of the sounds without learning all of them (presumably because such fragmentary knowledge would serve no purpose). In particular, he did this for Protarchus, who would learn the letters in his youth.

Positing, or hypothesizing, is not creating: in the account of Protarchan thinking there is no mention of any freedom of the thinker with regard to what is, or is not, part of the determinate plurality covered by the single Form it hypothesizes and then finds. Consider Protarchus and the alphabet. Upon hearing the cue (perhaps the word *grammata*), he proceeds to write out his letters. Some of them he may omit, not having learned them yet; and he may include some designs which do not count as letters (because, perhaps, they are letters incorrectly made). As with historical dialectics in the *Phenomenology*, then, his list of letters must be corrected: some of its members must be dropped and others, more appropriate, must be added. Hence, the Protarchan formula:

$$\text{letters} \Leftarrow (\alpha \bullet \beta \bullet \gamma \bullet \ldots \bullet \omega)$$

would be an expression from what Hegel would consider historical dialectics (if not from the peculiar variety presented in the *Phenomenology*). It is a list of contents accessed by a single cue, a list which may well have imperfections—which contains wrong, insufficient or unneeded members, and which (should that be the case) would have to be corrected in ways suggested by historical dialectics: dropping some components and adding others. Such thought seeks to conform to a pregiven model: it is, then, uncreative and unfree, though it may be what Hegel calls "correct."

If, somehow, the various letters could be shown to stand in nonarbitrary relation to one another, the dialectic would become in Hegel's sense systematic. But it cannot, first because the order in which the letters of the alphabet are written is in fact wholly arbitrary, and second because the figures which have over time come to constitute our letters were originally an aggregate of pictures—*a*, for example, originally depicting an ox, and *b* a house. As such, they were selected from among the infinite variety of possible depictions, presumably because the names as-

sociated with what they depicted happened to contain unmistakable occurrences of the sounds the letters were to represent (as Beth, for
example, or house, contains an unmistakable *b*). The selection, then, was
more or less accidental: each letter counts as a letter only because of its
relationship to an indeterminate multiplicity of *depictabilia*, other members of which would qualify just as well. This accidentality remains inscribed in the nature of each letter and the order of all; and Protarchus
must remain true to it, mimicking in his own writing the irrationality of
the letters he learns. The alphabet, like other given entities, cannot be
wholly comprehended, systematically because its components are discovered existing in the world, each with its own history, unique and to some
degree irrational.[4] Protarchan thought seeks to remain accurate to such
irrationalities. Only if it freed itself from them—from the histories and
absurdities of things actually existing in the world—could it become
truly Systematic in the Hegelian sense.

Such freedom is adumbrated, if only that, by the Theuthian
method, which we can now see is the opposite of the Protarchan one in
several senses. In the first place, though it does begin from a unity, that
unity is comparatively indeterminate. For Protarchan thought, the unity
of the letters exists in quite determinate form: as an *idea*. It is the familiar
list of the members of the Greek alphabet, divided into vowels, mutes,
and consonants. The problem for young Protarchus is simply that it does
not exist in that form in *his* mind, for he cannot as yet access what his
teacher does with the term "letter." But for Theuth the unity present at
the beginning was merely that all our vocalizations can be viewed as belonging to our human "voice": he had to think up the more determinate
unity by discriminating vowels, mutes, and consonants, and then binding
them into a higher class, that of "letters." In so doing, he carried out
what we can recognize as step (0) of systematic dialectics, and I will write
it as:

$$\text{(mutes} \Uparrow \text{ consonants} \Uparrow \text{ vowels)} \Rightarrow \text{letters.}$$

This would permit, by the rules of such dialectics:

$$\text{letters} \Leftarrow \text{(mutes} \Uparrow \text{ consonants} \Uparrow \text{ vowels)}$$

which could itself, presumably, lead to some further category:

$$\text{(mutes} \Uparrow \text{ consonants} \Uparrow \text{ vowels} \Uparrow \text{ letters)} \Rightarrow \text{category x.}$$

The Hegelian movement from immediate to mediated, or from in-itself to for-itself, thus captures the Platonic move from one to many and back again. Given Hegel's view of mediation itself as the establishment of a narrative,[5] we can in fact see his statement at the beginning of the *Logic* that "there is nothing, nothing in heaven or in nature or in spirit or wherever it may be, which does not contain immediacy just as much as mediation"[6] as a transformation and reiteration of the *Philebus*'s paradox that the one and the many are identical, telling us that unity and plurality do not exist side by side but as stages in a narrative.

Theuthian thinking, dealing not with individual letters but with classes of sounds, approximates more closely than Protarchan thought to Hegelian Systematic dialectics. But Hegel is not Plato. Theuthian thinking, like Protarchan, does not present what Hegel would recognize as a fully Systematic dialectic. As a classificatory system, mutes, consonants, and vowels exhibit more systematic structure than the set of individual letters themselves (the classification is based on whether the mouth is open or closed, and on whether or not the vocal chords vibrate); but its members are still not developed out of one another the way the category of "letter" is developed out of them (and hence my use of ⇑ above was improper). Thus, Theuthian thinking is in Hegelian terms not a purely systematic dialectic, but a sort of combination of systematic and historical dialectics.[7] In going beyond the givens to connect them in ways that our experience of them does not, Theuthian thinking does not remain wholly subservient to the contingencies of nature and history inscribed in them; but it does not wholly free itself from those contingencies either. There remains within it, in other words, a residual doubleness: some of its contents—the basic ones—are given to it, and it then constructs more complex ones (as, in the example analyzed in chapter 3, Measure and Beauty are mixed together to form Good). Those simple contents themselves were not created solely in order to enter into the more complex structures built out of them—as is shown in the *Philebus*, by the fact that truth, the unifying force, must be added by the interlocutors at every stage.[8] They have, rather, independent natures of their own, and insofar as it claims to investigate these simple independent entitites, Phileban thinking is metaphysical (though not exactly Protarchan, because the Forms exist in reality rather than in the mind of an instructor).

Hegelian systematic dialectics can then overcome the doubleness still resident within Theuthian thinking by including within itself *only* entities which are themselves created through its own dialectical advance. But the entities created must still, it seems, be expressed; and for this,

Hegel must presumably use vowels, mutes, and consonants. The contrast with Theuthian thought thus opens up the problem of how, given that we can think the Hegelian System, we could ever hope to express it. This question will occupy chapters 7 and 10.

Unlike the Hegelian System, Theuthian thinking can be evaluated with respect to truth—with respect to whether it is being faithful to entities which it did not create. But it cannot be evaluated with respect to truth alone: when it becomes creative it serves other goals, such as Nobility and, ultimately, learnability. This latter goal means, in turn, that thinking may be undertaken with reference to a community: Theuth thought up his classification in private, but the purpose of it is to enable him to contribute to the education of others. This goal, the ultimate goal of thought (chapter 11 will show how it coincides with Hegelian philosophical truth), cannot be achieved within an individual mind: what happens within any single head is at most a means to the greater end of communal learning and teaching—that is, to a social activity. If Protarchan thought belongs to what we might call the context of teaching, Theuthian thought belongs to that of creating what is subsequently taught.

For Plato from the *Meno* on, as for Hegel, thinking is a way of remembering rather than of inferring. But in the earlier Platonic writings, thinking as a social process of inquiry reduces to the recollection of objects already seen, and hence to an individual process. If, asking questions of a slave child in the *Meno*, Socrates invites the child to "seek the truth in company with me" (*Meno* 84c9), the child brings the answers to Socrates' questions "up out of himself" (*Meno* 85d). The soul in the *Phaedo*, in its final attainment of wisdom, is separated even from its own body, to say nothing of other embodied souls (*Phaedo* 79d). In the *Symposium*, though wisdom directed to the ordering of society is the most noble and important (209a5–b1), the highest wisdom is attained in the privacy of the vision of Beauty itself (*Symposium* 211a seq.). In the *Philebus*, by contrast, remembered content must not only be entered into memory (learning one's letters is clearly not like recollecting a Form in the earlier dialogues), but it must be organized within memory. The doubleness of thought in the *Philebus* lies in its not merely remembering, then, but in organizing memory as well. Such organizing is, we have seen, the function of Theuthian thinking, which creates connections among various pieces of information. It does not "see" its final objects but thinks them up, in order to pass over into the activity of teaching, without which it would not operate.

Aristotle's *Analytics*

At *Prior Analytics* 1.31 (46a32–b37), Aristotle argues that Platonic division is "weaker" than his own sort of demonstration. An example may best clarify this: given that all living things are either mortal or immortal, and that man belongs to the class of living things, division cannot tell us whether man belongs in the class of mortal or immortal beings: it tells us only that one or the other of these possibilities must obtain. Aristotle's solution—and what renders his doctrine of the syllogism a "strong" version of division—is to begin with the premise that man is mortal, from which we can conclude that man is living: as Aristotle puts it, we need to make "mortal," rather than "man," the "middle" term in our investigation. Division, by contrast, uses the most universal term—"living thing"—as its middle term, dividing it into the classes of mortal and immortal. For Aristotle, the middle term is not the most inclusive term in the syllogism but the one in the middle of his hierarchy of extensions: the one whose extension includes that of one of the other terms, and is included within that of the remaining term.[9]

The focus of Aristotle's critique of division, on the role of the middle term, yields three guidelines for the present narrative. First, his logic will be a logic of terms, not propositions: it will examine what we might call conceptual relationships, not assertions. Second, one way in which Platonic division is "weak" (or at least appears so to the young: *Philebus* 16d) is, as has been seen, that it cannot deal with the "many," but remains on the terrain of determinate plurality. If Aristotle does not mention *this* weakness in his critique of Platonic division, it is perhaps because his own view of the syllogism shares it: like Platonic division, syllogizing does not concern the vast and indeterminate realm of existing individuals but merely the well-ordered domain of essences (though not, of course, separate Forms). So, as numerous writers remind us,[10] a true Aristotelian syllogism contains no statements about individuals. Hence, the famous

> All men are mortal.
> Socrates is a man.
> Therefore Socrates is mortal

is very misleading as an example of an "Aristotelian" syllogism, for it purports to deduce a truth about Socrates, an individual and in Phileban terms one of the "many."

The third guideline concerns what we might call the conceptual environment of the syllogism: What kind of thing is it, and what kind of activity is syllogizing? In spite of the large body of often useful literature devoted to exploring the syllogistic as a device for proving assertions and hence as akin to modern logic, it is clear that Aristotle himself viewed it differently.[11] Jonathan Barnes has argued persuasively that the job of the Aristotelian syllogism is not to establish new truths about the world, but to teach truths already known. Since it does not teach us about individuals, it must teach us about essences; and, as Johannes Lohmann has put it (replacing "essence" with *Begriff*):

> Its aim is to lift a merely assumed relation of two concepts out
> of the realm of mere opinion into that of secure knowledge by
> adducing an intermediate concept to connect the two.[12]

Thus, in general, thinking is for Aristotle as for the *Philebus* a form of organizing known content, of displaying rather than establishing the truth of assertions; it therefore operates with terms, rather than with propositions, and is a social, in this case a didactic, activity.

Though it is primarily a teaching device, the syllogism is not unrelated to another context of practices, those of inquiry (*zêtêsis*); that context alone allows us fully to understand the role of the middle term in the Aristotelian syllogism. The role is that of an object of search: the production of a syllogism is said to begin with the predicate of its conclusion and the subject of its minor premise, and to seek a middle term which can warrant their connection in a judgment.[13] Thus, given the concepts of man and living thing, the syllogistic connection of the two is established by finding a term—in this case, "mortal"—which will connect them. The syllogism is thus produced by a process that can be sketched as follows:

1. "Human" is possibly conjoined with "living thing."
2. Try "mortal" as a middle term.
3. All humans are mortal;
4. All mortal things are living things;
5. All humans are living things.

If the formulation of an argument ("inquiry") is the search for a middle term, step 2 is the crucial one, for it is the adduction of the correct middle term—one which will unite the other two. Such adduction is of more than the word "mortal" itself, of course, because we have to remember, not merely the word "mortal," but its meaning: the rules specifying its position in the conceptual hierarchy. Here, those rules tell us that if anything is human, it is mortal, and that if anything is mortal, it is a living thing. In general, as Aristotle puts it in his definition of the middle term, they establish that it contains the minor term and is contained in the major. It is only knowledge of such rules—memory—that warrants lines (3) and (4).[14] The formation of a syllogism is then an accessing of what Aristotle would call knowledge of essences, and what I will style the "semantic" rules associated with "mortal." Those rules, like language itself, operate in two ways: within my own mind and memory, they have a psychological manifestation, while as rules governing my interactions with others they are socially based. Though the syllogism for Aristotle has metaphysical grounding via the knowledge of essences to which it appeals, the process of inquiry that produces a syllogism is psychosocial in nature; and the primary way in which the individual gets purposely aligned with the social is via teaching.

Aristotle's standard way of presenting the result of this process—the syllogism itself—simply omits the first two steps:[15]

1. All H is M ("All humans are mortal").
2. All M is L ("All mortals are living things").
3. All H is L ("All humans are living things").

On this formulation, the middle term is not presented as searched for: it is simply given in the first line, which asserts that it denotes a quality such that everything which has H, also has it. The second line tells us that everything which has it, also has L. Neither of these premises is "warranted" by memory, or indeed at all: both are simply given, and someone with no prior knowledge of the terms "human," "mortal," and "living thing" could accept them—provided he accepted the authority of whoever expounded the syllogism to him. It is this version which is captured in modern notations, such as:

$(x) (Hx \rightarrow Mx)$
$(x) (Mx \rightarrow Lx)$
$(x) (Hx \rightarrow Lx)$

It is the middle term in the Aristotelian syllogism which allows us to "take as one" the other two terms, not (he is careful to say) in the sense of being a one-plus-a-many but in that of authorizing us to predicate them both of the same entity.[16] Standard depictions of inference, even those Aristotle himself gives, tend to occlude this, because it is more economical to do so: the second depiction of the inferential process enables us to reach the conclusion in three steps instead of five. But the economy has a price, for the original psychosocial contexts of the syllogism in inquiry and teaching are lost, and what remains can only appear as the apprehension of a necessary truth.

This leads to two further ways in which the "economical" syllogism is untrue to our experience. One is that, in argumentative practice, argument does almost always begin with its conclusion: the propositions that get proved in law courts and legislatures, in ethical disputes, and even in philosophy classes are usually propositions someone intends to prove. We start with our conclusions, and search out proofs—a process for which the "economical" syllogism can give no guidance. The other departure from reality is that many of our inferences are in fact warranted, not by the laws of logic plus stipulations openly made in the course of the argument, but by the grammar of the words in our language—their relation to other words as stored in semantic memory, or what Aristotle would call knowledge of essences.

These prices are worth paying if the sole goal of thought is truth, for from that point of view nothing is lost by replacing the first formulation with the second, more economical one; both, after all, have the same truth conditions. And for Aristotle himself, truth is indeed the only goal of (theoretical) thinking, that genre to which demonstrative science belongs.[17] But the prices are too high if we want to use logical argumentation in our daily life, for we inescapably think in words rather than in arbitrary symbols, and as I have argued in chapter 5, semantic memory is essential to our thought. And in daily life (as I suggested above, and *Posterior Analytics* 1.34 endorses) the ability to come up with the right middle term is of extreme importance. Hegel's various versions of dialectic, on the present reading, are rationalized ways of doing so.

The syllogism, and in particular the role of the middle term within it, thus point us beyond truth-oriented logic to the domain of relations among terms, which I have called "semantic." But where do the middle terms themselves originate? How do they get into semantic memory? In the *Philebus*, we saw, one place they can originate is the creative activity of Theuthian thinking, which authorizes us to take as one a determinate diversity of things. For Aristotle, in spite of the affinities of middle terms for the logical, semantic, and social realms, the origin is ultimately psychological: in the mind of the individual, alone before nature. The original discovery of middle terms, indeed of contents of thought, comes not through a communal process of inquiry, but through processes immanent to a single individual mind.[18]

De Anima, like the Platonic texts, does not strictly separate inference from memory, and views thinking as primarily the reorganization of remembered content. In this reorganization, thinking takes on a double aspect, as it did for Plato. But the account of the double nature of thinking in the final book of *De Anima*—the distinction of active from passive intellect—leaves no room for Theuthian thinking.[19] Passive intellect, to begin with, is entirely receptive: all it can do is take in the forms of sensible objects. These forms are impressed upon the mind via repeated encounters with entities bearing them, which means that the various contingent features of those entities—those which are not regularly repeated in our experience—do not get impressed as deeply and drop away; hence, the passive intellect gradually and automatically comes to be filled with a set of impressions (*typoi*) which are ever-more accurate, and ever-more general, representations of the forms it encounters through its senses.[20]

These impressions themselves may be quite complex—the one given us by our repeated experiences of human beings would presumably include such subsidiary impressions as bipedal, largely hairless, and able to talk. Thus, we find again the one/many identity of the *Philebus*: the *typos* itself is the one, and the features composing it are the many. As I get to know more human beings and to know them better, certain features may, presumably, get dropped and others added to my overall impression: the people I am exposed to as a child, for example, might all have brown eyes and be rather solemn, so that subsequent acquaintance with Nordic comedians could induce the deletion of "brown-eyed" and the addition of "risible" to my impression of humanity.

Aristotelian passive intellect thus exhibits the adding and dropping of markers that we saw to characterize Hegelian historical dialectics—only in this case the "markers" are not symbols but features of impressions. It is in this similar to Protarchan thought, differing from it in its greater generality: passive intellect does not merely learn things from teachers, and seek to conform to models the teacher presents, but learns from nature itself, which is the model for its own impressions.[21] And, because of its generality, it is individual in nature: the learning unit is not ultimately composed of a pupil and a teacher, or of a community of scientists, but is the mind of an individual taking the entire universe as the model for its thoughts.

The receptivity of the intellect here is so great that the mind does not even have the capacity to order impressions that it has gained from outside. Their organization within the mind simply mirrors their organization outside it: the hierarchies of genera and species, in terms of which impressions are organized inside the mind, are simply copied from nature by the process just described, and this holds even for the sophisticated form of organization Aristotle calls "science."[22] Hence, for *De Anima*, the mind's only true activity is the capacity to initiate thought; this is assigned to the mysterious active intellect, which is what calls up or actualizes the impressions stored in the passive intellect. Able to actualize any content whatever, the active intellect is wholly indeterminate, without any principles of its own in terms of which it might organize the impressions it actualizes. Aristotle compares it, among other things, to light which, having no color of its own, can make any color visible. Thus, the intellect as a whole contains nothing other than the impressions it copies from the sensible world; that is why, in thinking them, the intellect is able to think itself.[23] Further, actualization is not motion: in actualizing an impression, the intellect does not move from one thought to another, but remains with the impression it has raised to actuality. Except in the sense of that elevation, then, the object of Aristotelian intellect has no before and after: it is wholly nonnarrative in character, which is consonant with the Aristotelian emphasis on truth alone as the goal of thought.

Intellect, however—here, perhaps, the cooperative activity of active and passive intellect—is capable of unifying the impressions the mind receives in order to produce judgments. In such a case, it need not merely activate two aspects of some single impression stored within it, but may combine impressions which are stored separately in the passive intellect, perhaps because—like the Lockean mixed modes I will discuss in chapter 9—they did not in fact enter the mind together from sensory experience on repeated occasions. But this power of synthesis, where precisely the mind can depart from sensory givens, is at the disposal of truth. Thus, I may well not see, every time I see the diagonal of a square, that it is incommensurate with the sides. But that fact can be proved to me, which then enables me to unite the two impressions of "diagonality" and "incommensurateness." Because such a connection can be established only by proof, proof too is ultimately a mirroring operation: demonstration enables the mind to mirror features of reality which are not always obvious to the senses.[24] Those features are the Aristotelian essences, and the role of Aristotelian metaphysics (here) is to provide entities for the mind to be copying when it does not *seem* to be copying anything.

If the workings of the passive intellect, in which subsidiary forms are dropped from and added to larger unities called "impressions," recall the Hegelian account of historical dialectics, there is nothing in the Aristotelian texts to correspond to Systematic dialectics except for the abstract activity of actualizing whatever contents are there to be actualized, according to the needs of the moment; and those contents are themselves reflections of essences. Hence, in spite of the importance of Nobility in Aristotle's aesthetics, ethics, and politics—an importance documented in chapter 3—the human intellect has been placed firmly in the service of truth. Together with this go a number of innovations on Plato which place the Aristotelian intellect at a further remove from Hegelian dialectics than was the Phileban account. For one thing, the Aristotelian intellect remains basically the same in all its operations: the Aristotelian account of thinking is more general than either the Phileban or Hegelian accounts. From this generality it follows that, as I have noted, the thinking unit is conceived as a decontextualized individual mind, rather than a community; the goal of thinking is ultimately not teaching or common life, but the individual's awareness of truths.[25] This emphasis on truth means that, though thinking remains for Aristotle in part at least an accessing of remembered content, his own accounts of it tend to obscure this; and it means that he does not endow the thinking unit with any capacity to organize, or even reorganize, the contents remembered. The mind has truly become, in Richard Rorty's phrase, the mirror of nature.[26]

The Aristotelian account of thinking obscures the entire Hegelian problematic by relegating it to "inquiry" rather than "science." But if we prescind from Aristotle's view that every (rational) content of the mind originally exists outside that mind, we can get clearer on the relation of Hegel to the Theuthian thought of the *Philebus*. Without that view, the middle term is no longer itself a mirror of something outside, and can be something *made* rather than merely *found* or hit upon. And with that, we can view Hegelian systematic dialectics as an ordered invention of Theuthian middle terms. This is evident from the treatment of contradiction in the preceding demarcation, where step (3) in the systematic dialectical development was $(\{M_k\} \Uparrow \{\overline{M_k}\})$. The new term M_m introduced to abbreviate this would function as a universal term embracing both. If, for example, M_k is taken as "mortal" and $\overline{M_k}$ as "immortal," then the introduction of M_m would be the systematic genesis of the Aristotelian category of living thing.

One of the apparent virtues in the present narrative's account of the origin of the syllogism is that the logical and psychological writings of Aristotle cohere almost effortlessly.[27] *De Anima* describes the process by which the mind accesses previously acquired contents, while the two *Analytics* discuss the norms for such accessing—via connections established by middle terms which themselves are copies of actually existing essences. The account in the *Analytics* thus deals with phenomena that belong to the wider class of processes discussed in the *De Anima*, of which they are normatively correct examples.[28]

Hume's *Enquiries* and *Treatise*

The Aristotelian metaphysical categories have had their vicissitudes since his day, and Hume offers an account of thinking which is free of them but which aims to retain the generality and asociality of the Aristotelian account. It also retains the Aristotelian emphasis on truth: for Hume the normed operation of thought is reason, and reason is nothing other than "the discovery of truth or falsehood"—that is, of the agreement or disagreement of an idea to something real—to an "object of reason."[29] Thought, for Hume, can grasp truth in one of two senses, and is again double in nature. Restrictions on these senses lead him to formulate an aporia for philosophy, which turns out to be unable to grasp significant truth at all. This destroys philosophy's traditional forms and, mainly because it has still not been fully understood, has kept it from finding new ones: "the Humean predicament," Quine could write in 1969 "is the human predicament."[30] Narrating Hegel's thought as a response to Hume—a way Hegel himself did not take[31]—will, I suggest, shed enough light on the "Hum(e)an predicament" to get us, at last, beyond it.

The wider category in terms of which Hume seeks to articulate the operations of reason will be, not ontological, but epistemological: thinking for Hume is one species of the basic stance of the knowing subject, which turns out to be simply beholding some object. Since beholding is a generally passive affair, it will be hard to find any sense at all in which reason is active for Hume. My account of its doubleness will be a series of attempts to locate such activity in the Humean framework, and to see how Hume conceives the doubleness of thought in its apparent absence.

In the extraordinary Appendix to the *Treatise*, and yet more forcefully in the *Enquiry Concerning Human Understanding*, Hume argues that we cannot be aware of any power that our mind may have to actualize ideas.[32] The argument in the *Enquiry*, more developed than that of the *Treatise*, is twofold. First, if our minds did have such a power, we could not know it, for the production of an idea is a creation ex nihilo, from nothing, and this is not something finite minds can ever comprehend.

We can indeed know that production of ideas occurs: that we will our-selves to think something, and an idea of that thing is produced. But *how* this happens, if it is a *creatio* ex nihilo, we cannot begin to fathom. Sec-ond, we do not in fact have as much control over our minds as we might think. We cannot control the passions or sentiments we feel, and our powers of concentration—to control the succession of our thoughts—vary with time of day, whether we have eaten, and so forth: they consti-tute a set of limits on the mind that can be known only imperfectly and empirically. In short, the nature of our minds is sufficiently mysterious to us that we can hardly hope to understand the relation between the mind, as cause, and the ideas which are said to be its effects.[33]

As far as we can know, then, the mind has no power to actualize its ideas; without such power the mind can only behold them, and all acts of the human understanding reduce to the "simple survey of one or more ideas." Reasoning is not, as it has been thought to be (e.g., as we saw, by Aristotle) "the separating or uniting of ideas by the interposition of oth-ers which show the relation they bear to each other," partly because some inferences only require two ideas and partly because reason does not separate or unite ideas any more than it creates them. It only ob-serves them, compares, them, and becomes aware of—beholds—the re-lations they have to one another.[34] Thinking in general is not syllogistically seeking or adducing (to say nothing of creating) middle terms, but merely becoming aware of similarities. As such, it is not gener-ically different from sense perception itself, which is the activity of com-paring objects which are all present to the senses and hence cognized, not as "ideas," but as "impressions."[35]

Sense perception, for Hume as for Aristotle, begins with the "mere passive admission of the impressions thro' the organs of sensa-tion."[36] But in the absence of thinking as actualization of ideas, sense perception differs from reason, not in the way it operates but in the kind of objects it has. The same holds for the double structure of thought itself: there are two sorts of object of reason for Hume, two sorts of entity to which we can discover that our ideas do or do not correspond: matters of fact, which are the existence or nonexistence of objects and their qualities;[37] and relations of ideas, which are brought out by com-paring ideas with one another.[38]

This account of the doubleness of thought in terms of the double-ness of its objects alone produces the "Humean predicament," the fa-mous aporia to which Hume consigns philosophy and whose genesis I will now reconstruct, beginning with his account of relations of ideas. These, insofar as they can philosophically ground knowledge, fall under four general headings: resemblance, contrariety, degree in quality (e.g., the relation of warm to hot), and finally proportion and quantity. The first three of these are intuitively rather than discursively discovered: whether two ideas are the same or different, or of similar nature but differing intensity, is obvious to the mind from simple surveys.[39] Demonstration thus applies to matters of quantity and number, and it is only with regard to such matters that we can have knowledge which is certain but not obvious. Such demonstration is possible because quantitative relations are grounded on the resemblance of their relata (which are all units and in that respect all alike); it is necessary because those relations can get quite complex:

> As the component parts of quantity and number are entirely similar, their relationships become intricate and involved; and nothing can be more curious, as well as useful, than to trace, by a variety of mediums, their equality or inequality, through their different appearances.[40]

But all ideas other than those of quantitative units are

> clearly distinct and different from one another, [and] we can never advance further, by our utmost scrutiny, than to observe this diversity and, by an obvious reflection, pronounce one thing not to be another.[41]

As far as relations of ideas are concerned, then, mathematics alone can be informative. Matters of fact, by contrast, are known only through sense experience: as far as reason can tell us, anything at all may equally well exist or not exist, and only the evidence of our senses can tell us which.[42] This does not mean that an object must be directly present to the senses in order for us to decide that it exists, for we can also reason from objects to their absent causes and effects. But such inferences, to summarize the main argument of the *Enquiry Concerning Human Understanding* and of part 3 of Book 1 of the *Treatise*, are not strictly rational: the only warrant for thinking that A (an object or event) causes B, for example, is that our impressions of A (or of objects or events similar to A) have in the past often been followed by impressions of B (or of objects or events similar to B). This is not a *rational* warrant, for it provides no reason to think that the B-follows-A pattern will continue to replicate itself in the future. All it does is set up in us the habit of expecting, on experiencing A (or A-like impressions), that we will soon experience B (or B-like impressions)—or that, if we experience B, something like A must have been there to cause it.[43] Hence, it is not truth or rational inquiry but habit or custom which is the principle of all our inferences about matters of fact and is the "great guide of life" except in moral matters, where the inborn moral sentiment—likewise natural and similarly irrational—takes over.[44]

Beginning with the passive reception of an impression and formed through the repetition of such impressions, Humean habit is similar in effect to the Aristotelian passive intellect: it results in a set of components of the mind which are not arbitrary, but reflect the normal course of events. These components, however, are not for Hume static impressions but movements of the mind from one idea to another. Hence, in spite of the philosophical diffidence we noted earlier, Hume does make a small inroad into explaining how ideas get actualized: by the natural power of habit, which as an ultimate principle of the association of ideas cannot itself be further explained.[45]

The doubleness of thought has now been articulated in such a way that all certainty lies on one side, and (except for mathematics) all informativeness lies on the other. Concerning relations of ideas other than those treated in mathematics, reason can only say that no idea is another idea; concerning matters of fact, it can only follow custom, its (and our) great guide: "philosophical decisions are nothing but the reflections of common life, methodized and corrected."[46] The upshot of this view, for the present narrative, is that Nobility is impossible for thought: if reason is comprehensive it conforms, not merely to matters of fact, but to the temporal contingencies and general disorganization with which these present themselves to us; if reason is ordered, it is a repetition of one and the same thing. Order over size is impossible, and this destroys philosophy itself, as traditionally practiced. As Hume writes in the famous closing words of *Enquiry Concerning Human Understanding*:

> When we run over libraries . . . what havoc must we make? If we take in our hand any volume; of divinity or school metaphysics, for instance; let us ask, *does it contain any abstract reasoning concerning quantity or number?* No. *Does it contain any experimental reasoning concerning matter of fact or existence?* No. Commit it then to the flames: for it can contain nothing but sophistry and illusion.[47]

The aim of reason is truth, and philosophy cannot achieve this aim. As Robert Fogelin has put it:

> Pyrrhonism is the natural outcome of philosophical reflection.
> It is also the final outcome of intense reflection, for we do not
> overcome it by reflecting more deeply but by bringing our re-
> flection to an end.[48]

Two practices of traditional philosophers have in fact been thrown out.
One—call it the bathwater—is the activity of demonstrating truths supposedly holding in realms of Being which humans can never experience
sensibly. The other—call it the baby—is the tendency of philosophers,
qua philosophers, to stand out like Socrates against the iniquity of their
time, even or especially when that iniquity is so pervasive as to express
itself in "common life." With baby and bathwater both gone, Hume has
small use for the basin—philosophy itself—except as an antidote to su-
perstitious speculations.[49]

Philosophy thus cannot progress, and is in the classical sense at an
aporia. The aporia has traditionally evoked two sorts of critical response.
One is to maintain, in the face of empiricism and skepticism, that not all
our knowledge comes from sensory experience: that we are possessed of
innate ideas which teach us things independently of experience.[50] The
other has been to deny the passivity of reason: to maintain that Hume
has not given a full account of the "active powers" of the human mind,
and that such an account can in fact be given; this is the road taken, as
will be seen, by Kant. The former road does not give philosophy a new,
post-Humean form, but maintains that Hume has failed to destroy at
least one of its older forms.

The other line of critique—that Hume has ignored the active
powers of the human mind—is simply false, for there is indeed such a
power for Hume: imagination. Indeed, in imagination thought seems
not only powerful but unbounded: it not only escapes all political and
social control, but "is not even restrained by the limits of nature and
reality." It is as easy for us to imagine monsters of every kind as the most
familiar and natural objects; we can imagine ourselves at the edge of the
cosmos or even beyond:

> What never was seen, or heard of, may yet be conceived; nor is
> anything beyond the power of thought, except what implies an
> absolute contradiction.[51]

But this seeming power is illusory, for in all our imaginative vagaries we
are only operating upon fundamental ideas, themselves derived from
sense impressions: compounding, transposing, augmenting, or diminish-

ing the materials the senses afford. Our imagination thus in fact operates within "very narrow limits."[52]

The ability of the imagination to function even within these limits, to reorganize sensory data so as to form compound ideas out of simple ones, would seem to be an important one. For the *Treatise* tells us that though some complex ideas originate in complex impressions, other such ideas have never had sense impressions that corresponded to them—unike simple ideas, which always resemble the simple impressions which cause them.[53] Thus, the idea of a substance is, to begin with,

> nothing but a collection of ideas, that are unified by the imagination, and have a particular name assigned to them, by which we are able to recall, either to ourselves or others, that collection.[54]

More strictly put: when the principle of unity in the collection is considered to be the ontological foundation for the rest of its members,[55] we have the idea of a substance; when it is not, we have that of a mode.[56] In both cases, the explicit recall of the plurality—the enumeration of the components of an idea—is the definition,[57] and the imagination in uniting ideas thus produces the higher levels of language itself.[58]

The activity of the imagination extends still further. In the *Treatise* it is also the imagination which not only *compounds* ideas but *associates* them by the three laws of contiguity, resemblance, and cause and effect; the understanding itself is said to be nothing other than the imagination operating by these three "permanent, irresistable, and universal" principles. According to the *Enquiry*, what habit does is guide the imagination from the conception of one idea to that of another; imagination itself then seems to be the "actualizing" power of the mind of which Hume had disclaimed all understanding.[59]

But if compounding new ideas and associating old ones are both carried out by the imagination, how are the two activities different from one another? What is the difference, for example, between conceiving of A, a cause, and B, its effect, as two separate ideas and conceiving them as two parts of one complex idea AB? I can conceive of the coil in an electric oven as heating the oven's walls; but I can just as easily conceive of a hot stove. We may admit with Hume that it is often difficult to draw the line between resemblance or succession and identity; but he clearly thinks that there is a line to be drawn, for he cautions against drawing it wrongly and confounding the two.[60] What, then, is to be the difference between compounding a single complex idea and associating simpler ones?

Hume is in fact unable to formulate any detailed or consistent views about the capacity of the mind to form compound ideas. Indeed, he sometimes denies this capacity altogether, asserting in the *Enquiry* that "all our ideas are nothing but copies of our impressions"[61]—an assertion which directly contradicts the passages cited above but which (apart from that) saves Hume from a number of problems: for if all our ideas are merely fainter copies of impressions, their nature and existence is easily comprehensible and cannot, as he says in the *Treatise*, "imply any very great mystery."[62]

Hume's inability to theorize about our capacity to form complex ideas goes along with what Patrick Gardiner has called, with respect to his treatment of the passions, his "persistent tendency to construe the implications of what are in fact logically complex notions in terms of correlations between atomistically conceived impressions."[63] Complex ideas, however produced, seem to be something on which Hume—unlike Locke, as we will see in chapter 9—cannot focus. This refusal to take complex ideas seriously cannot result from Hume's well-known atomism, which as Ralph Church puts it is the view that "in principle, any discriminable experience may be separated without alteration from any other such." This principle tells us that all complex ideas can be resolved into simple ones which can be presented to us independently of each other, but it does not follow that complex ideas are unimportant.[64] A more likely source is that for Hume, as Barry Stroud has pointed out, it is only simple ideas which can be known to correspond to impressions, and hence it is only in its reception of such ideas that the mind can confidently attain truth about things other than itself.[65] Since, as I have noted, Hume takes the assertionistic view that reason is "nothing other than the discovery of truth or falsehood," it follows that reason has to do, most crucially, with simple ideas.

We have already seen two cases in which Hume seems to forget about complex ideas. The first of these was in his statement that the actualization of thought could only be a creation ex nihilo. Such would of course be the case for a purely simple idea, which must come into being all at once. But the production of a complex idea could be, in contrast to a pure creation, merely the assembling of its parts—the kind of creativity Plato assigned to Theuthian thinking, and which Hume himself assigns to the imagination. This gives us another reason why Hume so often fails to deal with complex ideas. For his basically epistemological stance suggests that the mind merely beholds its objects, rather than creating or organizing them, and such beholding obtains in the first instance when the object beheld is and remains simple—for then, as Aristotle notes, there is nothing for the mind to do except either behold or not, and there is no question of its doing other things.[66]

The other case, tellingly enough, is the *Enquiry*'s statement of the aporia of philosophy. The possibility of demonstration depends, we saw, upon whether the ideas being dealt with are alike or unlike; in the former case, mathematics is possible; in the latter, only the "obvious reflection" that one idea is not another. But why this stark alternative? Why are all ideas, in the *Enquiry*'s words, either "entirely similar" or "clearly distinct and different from one another?" It is an obvious truth, and one which the *Treatise* states, that resemblance does have degrees.[67] Even simple impressions can exhibit this: the taste of a grapefruit resembles the taste of a lemon more than it resembles that of butter. Hume, presumably, would answer that such degrees of resembance are not things that can be reasoned about: they are, as we saw resemblance in general to be, matters for intuition, not for reason.

When ideas get complex, however, there seems no reason why the degrees of their resemblance cannot be examined discursively. Suppose that two nonmathematical ideas, such as those of "tiger" and "lion," are compared, even by Humean "surveying" reason. It will become obvious that they resemble each other more than those of "lion" and "chocolate cake"; and since all three ideas are complex, they can be defined and their differences and similarities, which may not always be so obvious, laid out clearly. Such thought would, it is true, tell us nothing about the world: it would not tell us whether or not objects existed corresponding to the ideas thus analyzed. But it would educate us about the nature of our ideas and about how those ideas relate to each other. We can adumbrate such a program by parodying one of the Humean passages quoted above:

> As the component parts of complex ideas are similar and different in specifiable ways, their relationships become intricate and involved; and nothing can be more curious, as well as useful, than to trace, by a variety of mediums, their similarities and differences, through their different appearances.

It is possible, then, to accept Hume's empiricism and his skepticism about reason without falling prey to the scientism often associated with these: to the view that all rational inquiry belongs to empirical science, and that philosophy must somehow fit itself into the scientific enterprise or rest content with merely negative reflections.[68] Hume's statement of the aporia of philosophy overlooks this possibility, not because it refuses to countenance innate ideas or active powers in the human mind, but because it assumes that all ideas must be either wholly alike or else different in ways that cannot be further articulated—a circumstance which in fact holds only for simple ideas. Hume's aporia is a result, not of limitations inherent in human reasoning, but of his own tendency to simplify—oversimplify—the nature of the ideas we have.

Once the complexity of conceptual configurations is recognized—if, in my terms, it is admitted that abbreviation and explication are possible—the dilemma of philosophy in its stark Humean form can be overcome. Systematic dialectics, as I have presented it, provides a set of ideas (or moments of the System) that exhibit much richer and more determinate differences among themselves than Hume allows for. As we have seen, the treatment of these *Denkbestimmungen* will lead to no true assertions, and so Hume could not countenance it as (in his sense) "rational." But if we are interested in the kind of efficiency of accessing that Hegel's System is to provide, then it is extremely important. And it does lead to Nobility, to a set of "ideas" exhibiting order over magnitude. That is why philosophy became impossible for Hume, as was seen, at the same moment that Nobility was overlooked as a goal of inquiry, and the unity over size that it instills fell apart into the simplicity of ideas and the contingency of customs.

While retaining the Aristotelian orientation on truth and on the thinking unit as a human individual rather than a social unit, Hume reinterprets it within an epistemological, rather than an ontological, perspective. This enables him to detach thought from reality in ways that Aristotle did not: even though we gain our Humean ideas the same way we gain our Aristotelian impressions, those ideas are not informative of reality in the same way. This means that the ultimate principle of our cognition is not a set of essences somehow resident within material things, but nothing more than habit: though habit is for Hume "nothing but one of the principles of nature, and derives all its force from that origin," this tells us nothing at all about nature, for we can know nature only through our experience and this means through the habits it instills in us.[69]

Herbert Marcuse has it that Hume, in formulating his aporia for philosophy, "confined men within the limits of 'the given,' within the existing order of things and events."[70] But Hegel's own account of habit suggests that to consign men to custom as ground of the "existing order" is to make that order precarious. For all we know, the patterns which nature presents to us can, at any time, be overturned.[71] The history of the twentieth century would bear that out: Humean customs may be guides to life at Oxbridge and Edinburgh, but they were of little use at Auschwitz, Hiroshima, Soweto, and in other inhuman predicaments.

Kant's *Critique of Pure Reason*

The Kantian response to Hume is thus of peculiarly contemporary import, for as I will narrate it from the *Critique of Pure Reason* it aims at vindicating reason (and philosophy) as guides to life against custom and moral sentiment. In the course of this double battle, Kant formulates anew the doubleness of thought. Against custom as the basic principle of our cognitive functioning, he urges the rights of the understanding, which—so argues the "Transcendental Analytic"—structures our sensory data in terms of twelve, and only twelve, categories. These are, like Humean relations of ideas, given a priori; but they are not merely objects of passive rational survey. Rather they are rules for uniting diverse ideas (*Vorstellungen*) into single judgments. Thus, the category of causality, though not justified from the sensible characteristics of objects I perceive, can nonetheless be seen, upon reflection, to structure my experience. It is more than a mere habit, for I can conceive of a habit being broken, even if I have never seen it broken: I may never have run a red light nor seen anyone do so, but I can easily conceive of doing it. That a sensory object should come into being without a cause, however, is for Kant something that I cannot admit could ever happen. Similarly, he argues, for the other eleven categories. Though they do not, in Humean terms, give us certain truth about matters of fact—about the existence of objects—they do give us information about objects as we will perceive them, since the categories express the basic structure of our own minds and this structure itself organizes all our experiences. Hence, sense perception is not merely the passive reception of impressions from within, but includes an active organizing of those impressions by our minds in terms of twelve and only twelve categories.

The understanding for Kant is thus active, as it was not for Hume; and its activity is determinate, as it was not for Aristotle. But this organizing is not free, even in the limited sense that Theuthian thinking was for Plato: we have, and will always have, just these twelve categories and no others, and we must always apply them, following rules given in the "Analytic of Principles" and most especially in the "Schematism of the Pure

Concepts of the Understanding." If the exemplar for the mind was in external nature, for Aristotle and Hume, or in the mind of another, for Protarchus, here it is within one's own mind itself, which brings the chaos of the sensory manifold into conformity with the categories. What in this is added to, and what dropped from, the sensory manifold we are not told, nor can we be: intelligibility for Kant *begins* with the synthesis of the chaotic sensory manifold via the categories, and we cannot know or discuss what precedes this. Adding and dropping of markers from terms (or, to use Kant's phrase, from representations) is a contingent and empirical activity of comparison,[72] without interest on the transcendental level.

But there is another cognitive faculty—Reason—which operates very differently. In its "logical employment," which Kant claims has long been known, reason is a faculty of inference, the basic form of which is the syllogism.[73] As with Aristotle, and against the normal assertionist understanding, the rational purpose of syllogisms, even in reason's logical employment, is not to discover new truths about the sensory realm but to connect true sentences with one another.[74] Hence, the *rational* point of the "Socrates" syllogism previously discussed is not to prove that Socrates is mortal, for that is a fact that can be ascertained only by watching him die (until that point, it is possible that he was, say, an angel in human form). It is to show, given that Socrates is mortal, why he is so: because he is a human. The interest of reason is not to produce, then, what Aristotle calls "knowledge of the fact"; in Kant's terms, reason "prescribes no laws to the objects" but is a "subjective law of housekeeping" (*Gesetz der Haushaltung*)—that is, it aims at keeping straight the empirical knowledge provided by the understanding. It does this, as the syllogism did for Aristotle, by finding the middle term which connects the subject and the predicate in the conclusion.[75] Syllogizing is thus for Kant a kind of unification (or, to use his term, synthesis); and, we may say, reason for Kant aims at what I call Nobility:

> It seeks, in inferring, to reduce the great manifold of cognition
> of the understanding to the smallest number of principles . . .
> and through this to bring about their highest unity.[76]

It is up to the understanding, not reason, to deal with individual propositions and their truth or falsity. Reason does not aim to equip us with new truths about the world, because it does not properly deal with objects of experience at all, but only with operations of the understanding, which it tidies up, as we have seen.[77] Moreover, though Kant does not say so or exploit the idea, reason does so with reference to the same sort of psychosocial context it had for Aristotle—that of teaching. As Jonathan Bennett puts it, in a remark that would hold for Aristotle and, indeed, for anyone who takes the syllogism to be a search for a middle term:

> It cannot be a logical fact that R can be deduced from P only by moving from P to Q and thence to R. If the lemma Q is needed, it is needed *by someone*—someone who cannot see that P entails R except by being brought to see that P entails Q and Q entails R.[78]

In reason's other, transcendental employment, it is not merely a "householder" or "subaltern faculty" of giving a certain organized form to given cognitions whose validity derives from elsewhere, but is an independent source of concepts of its own. It is such a source in that it can itself create concepts.[79] It does this in virtue of its syllogistic form. A syllogism, in Kant's view, states not simply that its conclusion is true (a fact, we have seen, that the syllogistic form is not even geared toward establishing), but that it is true upon certain conditions—conditions given in the premises.[80] Thus, the traditional Socratic syllogism can be viewed as asserting that Socrates is mortal *if* he is a human, and *if* all humans are mortal. If the syllogism is valid and we actually assert its conclusion to be true, we are supposing that the conditions the syllogism states have in fact been met.[81]

But the syllogism as stated, with just three lines, does not give *all* the conditions necessary for the truth of its conclusion: all humans are mortal, for example, only if all humans are living things; they are living things only if there are certain processes, such as the replication of DNA, going on inside them; and so on, perhaps without end. On the individual level, Socrates is human only if his parents were, and so on—also, perhaps (for Kant), without end. Thus, the assertion of the conclusion of a syllogism presupposes, not only that the conditions stated by its major and minor premises have been met, but that whatever conditions are necessary for those conditions have also been fulfilled. The mere statement of a syllogism implies that there is such a thing as the totality of conditions for its conclusion, and the truth of that conclusion entails that all those conditions do in fact hold. It is then the nature of reason itself, in its construction of syllogisms, to yield the concept of a totality of conditions; and it does this through characteristics of the syllogistic form alone, without appeal to the content that is being reasoned about.[82]

Since all the conditions for the truth of the conclusion are contained within that totality, the totality itself cannot be conditioned by anything further: it must itself be unconditioned, and the concept of that totality of conditions is the concept of something which is not conditioned by anything else. But no such thing, and hence no such totality, can ever be met with in experience, for all sensory objects are conditioned—for one thing, as the understanding tells us, they have other sensory objects for their causes. Hence, the concepts of unconditioned totalities thus generated are not susceptible of empirical instantiation: no object of experience can ever correspond to them, and they are non-empirical.[83] But they are not mere arbitrary fantasies, because they are arrived at through a succession of necessary operations of formal reason, a sort of transcendental recipe. As thus formal and necessary:

> They are not arbitrarily thought up [erdichtet] but are yielded by the nature of reason itself, and necessarily relate to the entire employment of the understanding."[84]

The concepts of Kantian reason, like those of Theuthian thought, are created by it. But Theuthian thought, we now see, remained on the level of "housekeeping": it organized manifolds of empirical data so as to render them teachable. The concepts formed by Kantian reason according to the transcendental recipes imposed by its syllogistic form have nothing to do with empirical data, and are in Kant's terminology "ideas."[85]

The logic of Kant's day recognized only three different forms of syllogism—categorical, hypothetical, and disjunctive—so the transcendental ideas derived from them constitute a fixed and denumerable system. Thus, for example, according to Kant the disjunctive syllogism:

$$A \lor B$$
$$\sim B$$
$$\therefore A$$

if extended to infinity, gives—so Kant—the concept of the set of all possible predicates $(A \lor B \lor C \ldots)$, and says in effect that each of these does or does not apply to every entity in the universe.[86] The set of all possible predicates is not something we will ever run across empirically, and so this concept is for Kant a priori. When, further, we look at possible predicates, we find that some of them are merely derivatives of others (as "hearing-impaired" derives from "deaf"), while others are "transcendental negations" of others—that is, designate the privation of their positive counterparts (as "deafness" designates the privation of "hear-ing"). Eliminating such predicates yields a concept which itself contains either every possible basic, positive predicate or its opposite; and elimi-nating predicates which cannot stand together in favor of those which do cohere yields a concept which, containing no contradictory markers, could in principle be the concept *of* something. When we view all these predicates as inherent within a "transcendental substrate" conceived by our reason, we arrive at the traditional idea of an "all of reality"; we know it is traditional because Kant gives us the Latin name for it (*om-nitudo realitatis*). Conceived as an individual thing—as an "ideal" rather than merely as an "idea"[87]—this "all of reality" is the *prototypon* (Kant transliterates the Greek for "protoype") of all things, which are but frag-mentary copies of it. They are fragmentary because, unlike it, they do contain negative predicates—that is, there are some coherent positive predicates that do not apply to them. Other things are what they are as a result, then, of excluding some predicates of the protoype of all things, and so that protoype is also the original thing (*ens originarium*); since it contains all positive predicates, it is also the highest being (*ens summum*) and the essence of essences (*ens entium*). The concept of such a being is none other, finally, than that of God (*Deus*).[88] It is also, of course, that of the Hegelian "Absolute."

Kant has thus constructed an ideal of reason which turns out to capture a concept very familiar to the philosophical tradition: that of the "God of the philosophers." As such, that ideal can be the object of "transcendental theology." But the expressions *prototypon, ens summum, ens entium*, and so on, do not, Kant is careful to say, refer to anything—still less to the relation of that thing to other, finite things: for everything thus arrived at remains merely a conceptual construct, while we remain "in complete ignorance" of whether such a thing actually exists.[89]

The process by which this ideal was constructed clearly falls rather short of the necessity Kant seems to claim for it. Eliminating negative, derived, and incompatible predicates; viewing the whole as an ideal rather than as merely an idea; and considering it as having a "transcendental substrate," are not moves that *have* to be carried out the way the formal structure of the syllogism requires us to presuppose that the totality of its conditions holds in reality. Nor do they consti-tute the kind of step-by-step sequence that Hegel would use to consti-tute the moments of his System. They are moves made, we suspect, with an end in view: that of setting up a form of theology by providing a "subjective instruction" (*subjektive Anleitung*)[90] for it, a recipe which shows how the concept of God can be constructed (if not how it must be: for the philosophical tradition did not, of course, arrive at its concepts of God in just this way).

In sum, thought is double for Kant in that it can be attributed either to the understanding, which produces judgments or propositions in accordance with the categories and does so in a predetermined, unfree way; or to reason, which constructs its own "objects" with much greater freedom. Reason and the understanding differ not only in their procedures, but also in their objects: the former constructs ideas, while the latter cognizes things. The ideas thus constructed are complex, unlike those in terms of which Hume formulated his aporia of philosophy; and they are also, like "original being" and "highest being," in different yet determinate relations to one another. As constructed by reason, which as we have seen aims at systematic unity rather than truth, the ideas of reason themselves constitute a system, the exact number of whose members, Kant is careful to tell us, can be known.[91]

For Kant, reason is no longer impotent: it, and not the imagination alone, can compound ideas. Another way of saying this is that compounding ideas can for Kant be conducted in accordance with rules; for Hume the imagination had no rules, and when it operated in patterned ways it became the understanding, which did not compound ideas but associated them.[92] Insofar as Kantian reason, in its logical employment, unifies cognitions established in their truth by the understanding, it operates as did Theuthian thinking for the *Philebus*; like such thinking, it presupposes truth and seeks Nobility. When it takes as the basis for its constructive work characteristics of its own syllogistic form, it is articulating new categories (in the service, ultimately, of morality). The cognitive activity of the understanding—attempting accurately to represent sensory experience in accordance with preexisting notions of space and time—is then as close as Kant, with his very active view of the human mind, can come to Protarchan thinking. The constructing of ideas of reason is his expansion of Theuthian thinking into a realm of pure a priori invention, aiming not at truth but at the "absolute unity" of totalities of conditions.[93]

Conclusions

Several important philosophical texts prior to Hegel's (and there are doubtless others) took the view that thought falls into two general classes: that which aims to mirror the world and is directed upon truth as its goal, and that which aims to organize the results of the former and aims at Nobility. The *Philebus* adumbrated, but did not theoretically articulate, a kind of thinking in which the mind did not merely represent reality (as it did in Protarchan thinking) but created categories with a view to such things as teaching and communal life in general. Theuthian thinking did this by taking pluralities as units; and it took them thus by calling them all by the same name. In so doing, it organized them for easy access—ready teaching and learning.

The Aristotelian texts, dispensing with the separation of Forms from sensibles, embarked upon a full theoretical account of the human mind, something the Platonic dialogues never even attempt. That account, however, viewed the mind primarily in terms of just one function: that of mirroring, or trying to obtain true assertions about, reality. This led to another overrich ontology, as the Platonic realm of separate Forms was replaced by a realm of essences immanent to sensibles, which reason always merely mirrored when taking together any plurality of given things (be these sensibles, in induction, or terms, in syllogism).[94]

Hume's *Treatise* and *Enquiry* dispensed with the ontological thematic of actuality and potentiality in terms of which Aristotle had articulated his account of thinking, both active and passive. This was an abrogation of largely untenable ontological commitments and a gain in clarity. But Hume's epistemological vocabulary led him to view thinking as at bottom a type of beholding, with the doubleness of reason consisting only in the two different types of object reason could have: matters of fact and relations of ideas. This went together with a view of the mind as essentially passive, and thence to an emphasis throughout Hume's thought on simple ideas. This, finally, led him to think that, having destroyed the pretensions of philosophers to produce true assertions about nonsensible entities, he had destroyed all nonscientific inquiry. What Hume failed to see, thanks to his emphasis on assertionistic truth and the simple ideas through which alone we can achieve true perceptions, was that we really have ways of *compounding* ideas much richer than his three principles for *associating* them.

Kant, reacting to Hume's confinement of philosophy to common sense and the given order of things, began to develop such alternative ways of compounding ideas. In so doing, he freed reason from all dependence on sensory givens and made of it a truly free compounding of elements which it posited itself, rather than somehow found in the world: the elements of the totality of conditions the syllogism implies, for example, are not copied from reality and may in fact—as the Third Antinomy suggests—not exist. But in doing this, Kant divorced reason wholly from the sensory realm, a move which was to have fateful implications for his own moral philosophy.[95] Moreover, he failed to divorce his own account of reason sufficiently from the conceptual order of his time—that is, from the three forms of the syllogism recognized by the logicians of his day.

Three aspects of Hegel's complex response to Kant will be of importance here. First, while as we have seen Systematic dialectics retains the basic idea of a rational construction of ideas, Kant's actual procedures in constructing them are jettisoned. Not only are the steps in the construction impressionistic; the first step in the strategy is to take the forms of the syllogism over from the logic of the day. Kant had also done this in formulating his list of the categories of the understanding, and (as Hans Friedrich Fulda has pointed out) Hegel will have none of it,[96] instituting as was seen a very different sort of constructive procedure.

Second, Hegel will not accept the view that the ideas constructed by reason are merely subjective. The subjectivity of the ideas—the fact that no empirical instance of them can ever be found—is however the key difference, as Fulda notes, between an idea of reason and a category of the understanding; it is what made it necessary to "ground" the ideas of reason in what I have called "transcendental recipes," rather than in reflection upon experience.[97] Hence, for Hegel to deny the subjectivity of the ideas of reason means for him to undercut the distinction between such ideas and the categories of the understanding themselves. This will eventually lead, as succeeding sections of this book will argue, to the view that the ideas constructed a priori by Systematic dialectics also have a historical origin in expert reflection on sense experience—in *Wissenschaft*.

This move of Hegel's seems to reinstate the supersensible world of God, the soul, and other supersensible entities as objects of true assertions, and thus to restore metaphysics in all its traditional dogmatism. But it does not do so, because it is inseparable from another Hegelian move, which I noted at the beginning of the chapter 4. This move is to reinterpret the Kantian concept of the "thing in itself" as a dimension of sensory experience, rather than as something lying beyond all such experience. Thus, even God is for Hegel the object of a particular kind of sense experience: that in which the world itself, with all its manifold configurations of meaning, becomes meaningless to us. Religion, he writes, is the "water of forgetfulness." When all human and natural matters sink away into this forgetfulness, we confront God as the "clenched core" (*geballter Kern*) of the world itself: *deus* and *mundus*, we might say, abbreviate and explicate each other. God is the in-itself of the world, is all things taken together, *Hen-panta*.[98]

Hegel has thus completed the *Philebus*'s articulation of Theuthian thought, by freeing it from *all* the extraintellectual domains that conditioned it in the earlier thinkers. It does not get content from any realm of Forms or essences, from ideas it beholds or from transcendental categories it either contains or constructs in total disregard of empirical data. Ultimately, it must derive its content from various sorts of convergence of systematic and historical dialectics. Before we can understand this convergence, we must see how each side of Hegelian thought gets expressed: we must look to the linguistic media of systematic and historical dialectics.

PART   3

A

PHILOSOPHY

OF   WORDS

7

Hegelian Words: Analysis

Aporia

The preceding analyses have attempted to show what it means to say that philosophical truth for Hegel is the self-development of thought. But philosophical thought develops itself in something—in words, to which *Encyclopedia* #462 Zus. tells us thought in general is essentially tied: "to want to think without words . . . thus appears as wholly irrational [*eine Unvernunft*]." The dilemma of the Hegelian Left and Right appears, once again, in the question of the relation of Hegelian thought to the words in which it develops. The issues involved are not raised by Hegel himself, who proceeds as if innocently—indeed, aggravatingly—confident that his System has achieved an absolutely pellucid expression.[1] What I will call Hegel's "problem of expression" has been posed for him by secondary writers: first by G. R. G. Mure, who is followed in this by Malcolm Clark and Josef Simon, and also, in a different way, by Theodor Bodammer. After presenting their views, and the problems those views attribute to Hegel, I will discuss two types of linguistic entity, both presented in the section on "Psychology" in Hegel's *Encyclopedia*: representational names and names as such. I will then argue that none of the problems brought out in the secondary literature affects both kinds of name. My conclusion will be that while neither by itself is an adequate medium for Hegelian philosophical thought, both together may be. In chapter 10, I will show how the required complementarity actually works in the complex process of Hegelian philosophical expression.

Because thought develops itself within language, philosophy's encounter with its own time must be linguistic: philosophy must conduct a dialogue with its times.[2] Such dialogue would be impossible if philosophy were expressed in a vocabulary which was either indifferent or somehow antagonistic to the languages we actually speak. Thus, argues Mure, philosophy for Hegel must be expressed, not in an artificial symbolism, but in words actually used by "educated men." Because of this, Hegel's expression of his System falls victim to a doctrine that Mure calls "incomplete sublation." This is the general, indeed vague, view that at any stage of the dialectic previous phases still exist, "subserving their successors but not fully absorbed by them."[3] Applied to language, which precedes thought, this means that language retains a reality of its own:

> Even philosophical thought is an incomplete synthesis of language with thought. It can never quite pass from meaning to truth, from reference to an object to utter self-identification with its object.[4]

Thought that must refer to an Other is bound to the nature of what it is about, and so cannot develop itself: the Hegelian system does not find a truly adequate linguistic expression. In particular, for Mure, language always retains "emotion and imagery," including metaphors more or less buried. And it is rigid: a linguistic sign always has the same meaning, while Hegelian thought is in perpetual self-transformation. This, again, means that the philosopher must "continually remodel, adjust, and expand his language" in order to make it do what it was never supposed to do: express the wholly fluid, entirely immanent development of meaning that is Hegel's System.[5]

Accepting Mure's view that Hegel's philosophy must be expressed in an actual language that is basically inadequate to the task, Malcolm Clark attempts not to solve the problem, but to justify in Hegelian terms the absence of any solution. While Mure concludes that the expression of Hegel's philosophy is never adequate but that its shortcomings "hardly justify a complete reversal of direction" from profundity to clarity,[6] Clark seeks to redefine "adequacy" itself by tracing the difficulties he sees in Hegel's expression of his System back to one of Hegel's own fundamental ideas: that the true identity of anything is attained only in and through that thing's "other." It follows that the true nature of thought can be attained only in the other of thought, or language.[7] Clark argues that the relation of language to philosophical thought is one of "speculative identity" in which "one's true meaning is always the identity of a meaning simply identified with its language and a meaning still opposed to its language."[8] Because speculative identity is one of Hegel's own basic ideas, we cannot in Clark's view quarrel with Hegel's application of it to philosophy. But it leaves the intelligible expression of the System unattainable, for thought opposed to its own expression cannot be understood. One of Hegel's merits for Clark is that, instead of pushing the unintelligible back into a "beyond," he posited it, as the speculative identity between a philosophical assertion and its meaning, as the very principle of intelligibility.[9]

Clark offers two main considerations to support the idea that language, as the other of thought, necessarily resists its expression. One is the intense effort that Hegel must make to draw upon the resources of the German language in order to express his philosophy.[10] The other consideration is more extended. Clark argues that the passage of thought into language "illustrates" the more general passage of logic into nature.[11] Nature is for Hegel "impotent," incapable of fully manifesting the Concept. And if Clark is right in taking language for Hegel to be strictly a natural phenomenon, it would follow that language, too, is incapable of expressing philosophical thought.[12]

Josef Simon also attempts to show that the lack of a solution to Mure's problem is something Hegel can live with by maintaining that the dialectical function of language in Hegel is, precisely, to be the externality of thought and in so being to be itself one-sided.[13] Agreeing with Mure that language for Hegel always fixes thought into rigid categories, Simon claims that language for Hegel is always and essentially a "dissimulation" (*Verstellung*) of thought: "when thought is expressed, the medium of thought has already been given up and dissimulated in a positive, fixed objective concept, or a category."[14]

But for Simon, who is here truer to Hegel than Clark or Mure, philosophical thought need not "struggle" to express itself in language, for such thought has no content to which language must be accommodated. It is pure negativity, the abstract movement from one linguistic determination (or dissimulation of itself) to another: it gains content only by contrasting itself against determinate intuition, and is inexpressible except as dissimulated in this contrast.[15]

At this point, we seem to have a scholarly consensus that language cannot adequately express Hegelian thought because it is representational: rigid in form and one-sided in content. But the issue does not rest there. Theodor Bodammer, on the basis of a careful and thorough investigation of Hegel's texts, has defended the absolute "neutrality" of Hegel's language at the expense of its historical relevance. For Bodammer, the meanings of Hegelian philosophical terms are indeed wholly developed from within, by thought itself. The fact, for example, that Hegel's expressions for philosophical concepts are often taken from ordinary language is, Bodammer concludes, "uninteresting" for Hegel. Only because of such indifference to everyday language, Bodammer continues, can philosophical language express a universal Spirit.[16]

Bodammer arrives at this view because he recognizes the importance of what I will call names as such to the expression of Hegel's thought.[17] These—I will discuss them in detail later in this chapter—reside in what Hegel calls "Mechanical Memory." They are words of some spoken language which have been stripped of all meaning, as when we run through a text we have memorized in purely mechanical fashion and pay no attention whatsoever to the meaning of what we are saying. Being thus meaningless, as Bodammer notes, names as such are free to receive all their significance from philosophical thought itself, from the Concept in its self-determination. Philosophical thought, expressed in such names, is expressed in what amounts to a universal medium; its meanings, provided by thought alone, can be understood by anyone who can think. By virtue of such expression, philosophy can claim to be the "categorial presentation of the one, universal, and truly infinite reason."[18]

These alternatives—Mure, Clark, and Simon on the one hand, and Bodammer on the other—constitute yet another form of what I call the problem of the Left and the Right, and what Emil Fackenheim has called the "central problem of the Hegelian system."[19] As Fackenheim formulates the problem, Hegel's thought must be "comprehensively systematic": it must be able to comprehend all real content philosophically, and must, to be truly systematic, show such content as developed through the self-development of pure thought. But it must also be "totally open," able and willing to confront the partial truths of extraphilosophical reality on their own terms.[20] In order to achieve the latter in its expression, it seems that philosophical language must be an everyday, particular language, as Mure, Clark, and Simon claim; but in order to achieve the former, philosophy must also, it would seem, generate its expression out of itself and speak a sort of "artificial language." The two demands, in the words of Richard Dien Winfield, mean that

> there is no other alternative but this: either the validity of
> thought is conditioned by language, consciousness, or some

> other factor, in which case neither this nor anything else could
> be known with any authority, or the truth of thinking is utterly
> unlimited by the preconditions of thought and the medium in
> which it expresses itself.[21]

The writers I have mentioned take one or the other of these alternatives
to be the case for Hegel, and explore (or deplore) the consequences for
his thought on that basis.

Fackenheim notes that there are two ways in which Hegel's system
may fail.[22] One is if the Hegelians of the Left are correct and Hegel's
thought remains "bound to the life above which it seeks to rise, unable to
live up to its vast speculative pretensions": if, in the present case, the
System itself is, as Mure, Clark, and Simon argue, infected with the particularity and representational finitude of the language in which it is expressed. On the other hand, Hegel's thought "may, after all, rise only at
the cost of its foothold in life": it may, as Right Hegelians and Bodammer
think, manage to achieve an "absolute expression" which leaves it unable to relate to everyday language, and unable to dialogue with its time.
There are many ways to articulate such failure. In Kantian terms,
thought may either lose itself among the empirical, or flee into the transcendental. In Humean terms, it may remain embedded in its customary
world, or limit itself to the beholding of relations among ideas. In Aristotelian language, it may associate itself too closely with either the passive
or the active intellect. And in my terms, it may give itself immanence and
necessity by leaving out content, or increase its scope at the expense of
Systematic order. The failure, however formulated, is failure to achieve
Nobility.

In sum: though Hegel's System is supposed to be an absolute
unity, human languages come as a diverse plurality. Even to speak of the
relation of thought to language is misleading, because no one thinks in
or speaks "language"; we all speak one or more particular, historical
languages. Such languages, be they German, Chinese, or Urdu, grow up
in the articulation by a particular linguistic community of its particular
standpoint in, and on, life. If philosophy is to relate to its times in the way
Hegel deems necessary, it cannot dispense with those languages; it must
accept and appropriate their particularity and finitude, just as it must
other forms of particularity and finitude. But thought's immanent and
necessary self-development seems to require that philosophical language
be determined purely by Systematic dialectics, unconditioned by the representational and particularistic languages worked up in history and
present in the prephilosophical world. Is Hegel to avail himself of some

sort of artificial, ahistorical words in which to express his philosophy? Or does he accept the "actual" languages actually spoken by various peoples—including, of course, his native German—as providing appropriate vehicles for philosophical truth? Is Hegel on the Left, on the Right, or somewhere else?

Representational Language in the *Encyclopedia*

To begin locating him, I turn to the *Encyclopedia* discussion of language (*Enz.* ##451–64); I seek to show that, in fact, two types of philosophical words are treated there. What I call "representational" names, which form one side of philosophical expression for Hegel, are treated at *Encyclopedia* ##459–62.[23] A radically different kind of name, the "name as such" to which I have referred, is discussed at *Encyclopedia* ##463–64, plus a few other places which must be determined with some care. In order to understand those sections, however, I will briefly recapitulate "Representation" in general.

"Representation" is the second section of Hegel's Psychology, and forms a lengthy transition from "Intuition" to "Thinking." This transition takes the form of a progressive interiorization and universalization: the externality, both to each other and to the intuiting subject, of intuitions in space and time is gradually replaced by mind's occupation with its own universal meanings. In Representation, those meanings, though "within" the mind, remain conditioned by their derivation from external intuition. To that extent, they retain the externality of intuition, in the form of their separation from one another and from the mind which thinks them.[24]

The internalization and universalization which take place in Representation have three levels. In the first, Recollection (*Erinnerung*), an intuition is brought within the subject's own inner space and time as an "image" (*Bild*). It is thus torn out of the spatiotemporal, and especially causal, contexts in which it was first encountered. Stripped of these, it is present in the mind as wholly unrelated to what comes before and after it, in that mind or outside it: as arbitrary and contingent. It is retained in the Intelligence (Hegel's word for the active subject throughout this section), which is here a universal, shadowy "storehouse" of images. Once stored away there, the image can be reawakened when the subject again perceives the intuition which originally occasioned it. This is what, according to Hegel, enables us to recognize objects as things we have seen before.[25]

That an intuition can call up its image from the "storehouse" of the Intelligence is grounded in the fact that both have the same content: my image of my friend, like my friend herself, "has" brown hair.[26] When the Intelligence reflects upon the relation of image to intuition, we may say, it becomes aware of such content (e.g., "brown") as identical for both: it becomes aware of it as universal. The Intelligence can then occupy itself with that universal only as it is instantiated in the image, and can dispense with the original external intuition. At this level, I can think about the color brown without being actually confronted by a brown object—but only by virtue of my mental image of such an object.

Once the image is "within" the Intelligence in this way, it is under its power: the Intelligence can call it up at will, and can associate it with other images or dissociate its different aspects from one another so that it loses the arbitrariness it earlier had. I can, for example, compare my image of brown hair with those of brown houses, brown eyes, horses, cattle, and so on. I can also compare it with my images of red, blue, gray, and other colors. In all this, I get gradually clearer on the nature of "brown." Some features (or "markers") of my original image, for example, may turn out to have been specific to hair, and may have to be dropped. By comparing brown to other colors, I become clearer on its generic nature, including in my representation properties which differentiate it from other colors. This clarifying activity operates on concepts of all sorts. When I imaginatively conjoin, say, the images of two people, I do so under some such rubric as that both are human beings; and, in so doing, I become explicitly aware of "humanity" itself. Conversely, when I separate from my image of Socrates his paleness, or from my image of his nose its snubness, I isolate what are again universal qualities, and by that act become aware of those qualities.

This sort of activity occurs in the second stage of "Representation," "Imagination,"[27] and so Imagination is essentially and simultaneously a clarifying, connecting, and universalizing activity. The *Phenomenology* shows this universalizing to be not merely an individual, psychological process, but a social one. It becomes so because representations are, as will be seen, connected to utterances. It is characteristic of the spoken word, in contrast to other types of entity, to annihilate itself as it comes into being: a word vanishes as it sounds. This sort of annihilation is the peculiar, negative sort of being that a word has: "it is *not* a real existence, and through this vanishing it *is* a real existence."[28] The result of this manner of being is that everything about the act of utterance vanishes except the understanding that it elicits in those who hear it: "that it is perceived or heard means that its *real existence dies away* . . . and through this vanishing it *is* a real existence."[29]

An utterance's unique form of existence is thus to be perceived, heard and understood, by others. But when someone gives utterance to an idea, those who hear it change and appropriate it—just as the master, earlier in the *Phenomenology*, appropriated the products of the bondsman. Taken up and interpreted by my community in ways that cannot be exactly what I intended, my words acquire a new significance, more universal because shared. Once expressed to others, then, my message is no longer my own: it exists in their interpretations, and becomes what they make of it. The original idea that was "in my head" and which, in its uniqueness, made that head itself unique, is lost. What counts in the various interpretations my hearers produce are just the features those interpretations share: whatever those who hear me understand, not according to their own idiosyncrasies, but all in the same way. Again, such interpretation is, like Imagination (which is the part of the process that goes on in a single individual) a "universalizing" activity.

When one's words are thus "taken away" from her and disseminated through her community, and in the process are transformed, the utterer is transformed as well. Utterance, and its interpretation by others, takes the form of a double transition: "it is at once the . . . transition, both of the thought-form of substance into actuality and conversely of the specific individuality into essentiality."[30] What is lost is not as important as the self which is now attributed to the speaker, "a self that has passed over into another self that has been perceived and is universal."[31] It is only as such a "universal" self that the cultured individual counts, or is recognized, at all. As applied to the present case, Hegel tells us that it is by means of culture and education that

> what is *implicit* in the substance [i.e., the vocabulary of the language] acquires a recognized real existence. The process by which the individual moulds itself by culture is, therefore, at the same time the development of it as the universal, objective essence, i.e., the development of the actual world.[32]

One side of externalization as a social process is thus the explication, in human interaction, of the "implicit substance," or the unexpressed side of Reason: the development of more general or abstract concepts and of the words which express them. The other side is the effect this has in producing a certain sort of self. This is a self who, to be sure, is unable to communicate her precise meaning to others: she knows she cannot get her own representations and mental images unchanged into other people's minds. But she is willing to relinquish that precision, and the original self to which it sought to be accurate, in favor of a self which is communicable to, and hence in community with, others.[33] Hence, language for Hegel is never "natural," or even a mirror of nature. It is the deposit of a historical process by which individuals have sought to make sense *to each other* of the world in which they live. Those who use it, because they use it, are another such historical deposit.

Returning to the *Encyclopedia*'s account of this as a psychological process: when the Imagination acts in this way, the identity in content between the image with which it begins and the universal which it works up can be attenuated. Though, for example, my image of Socrates has (if I am personally acquainted with him) generally the same content as my intuitions of the man himself, the universal content of, say, "humanity" is not to be found within that image; nor can the content "fruit" be found by mere inspection of one's images of apples, peaches, pears. Universal and image do remain "identified" with one another, but only in that both function as parts of the same totality: the image brings forth the thought of the universal, and the universal is explicitly present only as so brought forth.[34] The distinction in content between image and universal thus remains within what we could call their "functional" identity. It is the capacity of the Intelligence to retain such identity in spite of increasing diversity of content which, for Hegel, leads to symbols, signs, and ultimately to language.

The image now occasions the thought of the universal which has been worked up from it by the Imagination. When this function of an image is seized upon by the Intelligence so that it uses the image to call forth the universal, the image becomes a "symbol." Socrates' nose, then, can occasion me to think "snubness"; when this comes to be its main function, the nose is a "symbol" of snubness. But the identity in content between symbol and symbolized can diminish and even disappear: Socrates' nose can occasion, for example, the thought of his good humor, or even that of human "good-humoredness" itself. When the identity of content between symbol and symbolized wholly disappears, the symbol has become a sign.[35] At this stage, since all likeness between symbol and symbolized is gone, Socrates' nose can occasion any universal thought I want it to; conversely, given some universal, any intuition or image whatsoever can signify it. Indeed, the poorest of intuitions, mere vocalizations which do not persist beyond the moment of their utterance, can signify the most complex of ideas: "God," "truth," "beauty." This, for Hegel, is language, considered under its representational aspect.[36]

Words are thus for Hegel the highest achievements of the Imagination, the attachment of individual spoken sounds to universal representations; written language, alphabetic or hieroglyphic, is derivative.[37] The spoken sound here is, though intuited, not strictly speaking an intuition; it is a "sign." The relationship of signs to intuitions for Hegel is rather intricate. A sign is, first of all, an intuition which, in being intuited, reveals itself to have no significance of its own and by so doing presents (*vorstellt*) something else—its meaning.[38] The sign is thus not a mere intuition, but functions as the attaching of an intuition, which itself is of an external existent, to a universal meaning. As Hegel puts it in the *Philosophical Propadeutic*:

> The arbitrary attaching of an external existent to a representa-
> tion which does not correspond to it, but is distinct from it
> even according to content, makes that existent into a sign.[39]

The distinction in content between sign and signified means that the concrete intuitional content of the former is entirely irrelevant to the sign as such: it makes absolutely no difference, for example, that the English word for camel is composed of the sounds of *c, a, m, e,* and *l*. The sign is thus not an intuition, but an intuition negated: the concrete unity of sensuous determinacy found in the individual intuition is disregarded in favor of the simple movement of the mind to a representation. This movement is then the "attaching" of the intuition to its meaning. Because the specific intuitional content of the sign is irrelevant to this, we can say that such "attaching" exhausts the nature of the sign as sign. This is why Hegel can say not merely that the sign is instituted by attaching an intuition to a representation, but can actually identify it as that attaching itself.[40] In being constituted by the mind as a sign, an intuition negates its own intuitional content; and this negation presupposes the representation which, in that negation, the sign presents.

Spoken words, which die away as they are uttered and thus negate themselves straightaway, are the most appropriate form of sign for Hegel;[41] and the simplest form of linguistic sign is the name, the "simple sign for the simple representation." Qua intuition, a name is complex; it consists in vowels and consonants, perhaps in several syllables. Qua sign, this complexity is irrelevant: the name is considered by the Intelligence as simple, and can thus present a simple representation as its meaning. Such a "simple" representation can, like the name, have a complex content of its own. Insofar as the representation is considered as "named" by its name, this content is brought together into simple form. The same can happen, Hegel is careful to note, with the contents of thought: like representational contents, they can be summed up by thinking in simple form.[42] This capacity to reduce complex content to simple thought-determinations—what, in chapter 4, I called "immediation"—is not unimportant: in the *Phenomenology*, it is said to be one of the reasons why the individual can, in her own lifetime, recapitulate the entire history of Spirit's rise to the Absolute.[43]

Language as now brought forth is hardly fit for the expression of thought, in general or in its philosophical variety. For that, the Intelligence must first gain control of its names, just as in Imagination it got control of its images. This is part of the concern of the next stage of "Representation," Verbal Memory (*Gedächtnis*).[44] Verbal Memory, says Hegel, operates on the word in the same way that Recollection (*Erinnerung*) operates on the first, immediate intuition.[45]

A mere word, as a disappearing intuited individual, cannot stand in any enduring relationship to the representation which is its meaning. In order for a representation, which is an enduring mental content, to achieve an expression which is likewise enduring, it cannot be connected to such a fleeting intuition. It must rather be attached to a sign which itself endures. In order for such an enduring sign to be under the power of the Intelligence, it cannot be a structure in external space and time; it must be something existing within the Intelligence. It must then be another representation. Just as Imagination first universalized intuitions by reflecting upon what connected them with the images they called up, so Verbal Memory reflects upon the relation between the sign and the universal signified—on the "name" as their mutual attachment.[46] The sound of the name is thus itself universalized: it becomes a representation—the representation of the sound of the name, or as I will call it the "representation of the name"—and can be retained within the Intelligence.[47]

Such a representation is able to occasion the mind to think an entirely different representation, its meaning; and it is what gives existence to that other representation within the Intelligence. In spite of their difference in content, then, the two universals are identified and come to constitute a single representation.[48] Verbal Memory can then dispense with the external intuition which constituted the original sign: it "has and recognizes the thing in its name, and with the thing the name, without intuition and image."[49] Further, these unified representations are under the power of the Intelligence in the sense that the Intelligence can combine them with, and separate them from, one another—just as did the Imagination in its working up of universals.[50] Such combination and dissociation of names is, at this level, thinking; and these names are the names in which, according to Hegel here, we think.

The "names we think in" are least one medium for the expression of thought. They are, in the first place, representations: single, enduring universals. But this unity contains a good deal of complexity. In the first place, such a name has "within" it, or functions in virtue of, two further representations which themselves share no common content. One is the universalized name (a type, not a token), which could perhaps be called the name's "mental sound." It is this which gives the name its existence within the Intelligence—that is, which occasions the Intelligence to think the universal it signifies. This "mental sound" is regarded by the Intelligence as simple; in fact (on analogy to the intuition from which it is derived), it is complex. Its complexity consists in the universalized forms of the vowels and consonants which made up the intuited utterance from which it is derived: the c, a, m, e, and l sounds of the name "camel," for instance. These "mental sounds" remain identical in content with that original utterance; this permits the name to be uttered and to acquire existence for others.

The other side of the name is its meaning; in the present example, since we are within Representation, it is the representation itself of "camelhood." This, too, is posited in the name as simple. But it is in itself complex, and its complexity survives as the different connections in which the name can be thought (and which Hegel says "lie in" the meaning).[51] I can think "camel" in connection with "desert," "hump," or "quadruped"; I cannot think it in the same sort of connection with "cosine," "middle C," or "freedom." This side of the name is also worked up from intuition and remains dependent on what I have encountered in the external world. If I have never heard of a Bactrian camel, I will not think "camel" together with "two-humped" (except to deny the connection). Similarly, if my culture has never encountered camels at all and has no word for them, I will be unable to focus reflectively on them at all—or, if I somehow do, my reflections will remain private and idiosyncratic.

The "names in which we think" (or, as I call them, representational names) are as Hegel presents them *fully* representational: they are names which have been worked up by the Understanding so that they have completely articulated their representational meaning and then coincided with that meaning. As representational, those names—on one of their two sides—provide a cultural mirror for an objective world. Precisely because they are, if only to a degree, representational, they remain related to the sensuous domain from which we saw them develop—here, in the relation between the universal meanings of those words and the sensory experiences from which they are derived. This relation is "external" in that the rich contextual nature of sensory experience is first ignored (in the "image") and then attenuated by abstraction, which simply leaves aside parts of it.[52] Hence, the only general category which is said to govern the process of working up universals at *Encyclopedia ##453–56* is resemblance—the selective (that is, abstract) similarity of intuitions to one another and to the universals under which they eventually come.

Because they refer to external reality, the names in representational language remain in fixed determinacy against other names: their meaning resides not primarily in their relations to other words, but in their reference. Representational language is thus the proper domain of representational truth—that is, correspondence. Because of this, the individual syntactical units of language—in particular, the "subjects" and "predicates" of its sentences—will stand in merely external relations to one another, the way their referents are found, unsystematically, in experience—not in the identity of each with the whole characteristic of thought.[53]

On their other side, the names in a language, the sum of what it can articulate, are the result of a social working up of meaning from sensory experience, and are thus relative to the experience of a particular people. Other languages, expressing the experiences of other peoples, will have different words expressing different content, as Arabic famously has six hundred words for "camel," and Eskimo dialects dozens of words for "snow." These contents, varying with culture rather than with the "objective" world, constitute a dimension entirely different from that of truth and representationality. Hegel was well aware of this cultural variation in language; indeed, at one stage of the development of Spirit—that of art—the content of language which is significant to Spirit is this limited content; only when Spirit moves on to religion is this particularity supplemented by a content considered to be universal.[54] As a social phenomenon, representational communication possesses dialectical power of its own. It is, as I noted above, able to compel consciousness to abandon its (idiosyncratic) views of things and to force it to move on not only to new (more universal) opinions but to new (more universal) selves. Language has this power, not only in the passage discussed above, but from the earliest stages of the *Phenomenology*.[55]

Representational language is thus at once a representation of the world and the expression of a culture. It is tempting to identify such language with what analytical philosophers call "natural language," meaning the sort of language which people speak in the world and to whose workings they have some degree of intuitive access. Though I will return to this in the ensuing "demarcation," three differences should be mentioned here. First, since the process which produces these representations is in part a process of universalization, the representations it produces are no longer bound to particular places and times: indexicality has been omitted.[56] This means, in turn, that ostensive definition is not needed here: any representational name can be defined in terms of other representations. Second, this "language" lacks syntax and grammar: it is a vocabulary, rather than a true language. And third, its universals are not only worked up from sensory intuition, but are *fully* worked up.[57] Such language possesses, so to speak, a "state of the art" set of representations, and is in this more akin to Hilary Putnam's notion of "expert" language than to the language we all speak. Hence my name for it: "expert discourse."[58]

To summarize the significance of all this for the Left-Right split: the terms of representational language are not simply given from heaven or worked up unaided by the individual mind, so as to constitute a perfect mirror of the world. They belong to the historical, particular languages of humankind, originate socially, and have histories. Representational names thus remain conditioned by the contingency of sense even as, in their very universality, they oppose it. If the development of thought is to be truly a self-development, representational language cannot impel it or determine it, for such impulse or determination, even by the "interior externality" of language, would mean that the development of thought was affected by something exterior to thought—and something particular and representational besides.

It seems that the various languages found in the world, even "expert" ones, are multiply inadequate to express philosophical truth. Philosophy, it would appear, requires an "absolute language," radically other than those particular languages. But Hegel refuses to supply any such thing, claiming instead that philosophy can and must be expressed in the particular languages of particular peoples:

> But one can first say . . . that a science finally belongs to a people when that people possesses it in its own [the people's] language; and this, in the case of philosophy, is most necessary.[59]

Hegel has, moreover, compelling reasons for maintaining this. For him, philosophy can be neither indifferent nor antagonistic to reality

which is outside it: it is the prerogative of representational, not philosophical, thinking to reduce its Other to mere appearance or abstract
from it altogether. Philosophy, by contrast, must seek to comprehend
the actual, extraphilosophical world—including, most particularly, its
own historical situation. In so doing, philosophy must be open to its
time—to the extent, says Hegel in the Berlin Introduction to the *Lectures
on the History of Philosophy*, of accepting even the limitations of that time
as its own.[60] Thus Plato was bound to portray, in his *Republic*, the slavery
and infanticides of the Greece he knew as features of his ideal state. To
have done otherwise would have been not merely inauthentic philosophy, but simply impossible.[61] How are we to reconcile this view of language with the view, discussed several times earlier, that Systematic
thought is to be entirely unconditioned by anything but itself?

Names as Such

The language so far brought forth spans the range of Spirit's functioning
from the intuitive to the fully representational, and thus should (for
Hegel) cover all the linguistic phenomena of the representational world.
It is time, one would think, for the Psychology to move to the next stage
of the System, "Thinking" (*das Denken*).

But it does not do so. Hegel mysteriously interposes another
stage in Verbal Memory: "Mechanical Memory." This stage is quite confusing and, to the commentator, even embarrassing: for the concrete
unity of meaning and expression, so laboriously achieved in the preceding sections, is here abandoned in favor of recitation by heart—in which,
Hegel is careful to note at *Encyclopedia* #463 Anm.,[62] one attaches no
meaning to one's words. Yet this *Geistverlassenes* is, in #464,[63] asserted to
constitute the very transition into the activity of thinking. What can possibly be happening here?

Philological considerations are in order. There appears to be an
ambiguity in Hegel's use of the term "name" in "Mechanical Memory"
and the preceding sections of "Verbal Memory." At #460, Hegel refers
to the name as "the attaching together of an intuition and its meaning";
this attaching is at first external because the intuition which serves as
sign is "outside" the Intelligence, while the universal meaning is within
it. By #462, the intuition itself has been internalized and universalized
into a representation so that the name is the thing, a "simple imageless
representation." In the very next paragraph, on Mechanical Memory,

however, Hegel speaks of the attachment of meaning to a name and refers to it as a "synthesis," which indicates that it is still, to some degree, external.[64]

There are two striking things about this assertion in #463. In the first place, it speaks of the attachment of a meaning to a name, instead of continuing to speak of the name as the attachment of a meaning to an intuition. It would, of course, be wrong for Hegel to continue, here, to regard names as the attachment of meanings to intuitions, because by #462 both sign and signified are representations. But in what sense are meanings to be regarded in #463 as attaching to names, if a name is already the attachment of a meaning to a representationalized mental sound? Does such a complex of sign and signified receive, in #463, yet another layer of universality?

Second, the reappearance of externality is surprising; #451 states that the stage of mere synthesis is overcome in thought, and we are already here on the level of the "names we think in." How can they still be synthetically related to their meanings?

"Name" as Hegel uses it in these two paragraphs seems then to refer (a) to the unified complex of sign and signified, and (b) to something which is attached, externally, to a universal meaning. There appears to be a similar ambiguity at #459,[65] where Hegel refers to "what names as such are, namely for themselves simple externalities which first have meaning as signs," and then goes on to characterize the name as "the simple sign for authentic, i.e., simple representation."[66] The second quote refers to "names" as "signs," while the first seems to regard them as some sort of intuition which is not yet a sign. Is this second ambiguity related to the one I have already adduced? How many meanings of "name" are in play here? Two? Three? Four?

One side of both ambiguities equates "names" with signs: this is stated in the second of my quotes above from #459, and ##460–61 refer to both names and signs as attachments of meanings to intuitions, which attachment is internalized into the sense of "name" in #462. It appears that the other sides of the two ambiguities could be identical as well. For the "senseless externalities" which, in #459, are not yet signs, still stand in need of attachment to meanings. This attachment could be the mere "synthesis" referred to in #463. The link between these sides of the two ambiguities becomes yet closer when we look at Hegel's exact language in both cases. Names as not yet signs are, in #459, designated as "names as such"; names which stand in synthetic attachment to their meanings in #463 are referred to as "Being as name." Are we entitled to take these two locutions as different ways of referring to the same thing?

Hegel partially establishes the connection further on in #463, where he refers to the Intelligence in Mechanical Memory as "Being, the universal space of names as such, i.e., of senseless words."[67] This passage then identifies "names as such" with names "in" Being as an internal "space." Can the referent of this latter phrasing be identified with "Being as name," to complete the link between the two ambiguities?

It seems that it can. For if names, which are concrete intuitions or representations, are said to be "in" Being, then they come under consideration only to the extent that they come under Being, the first and poorest category of the Logic. But this abstraction from the concreteness of a name to its Being can also be viewed as a specification of Being itself: the category is considered only insofar as "names" come under it. Such a specification is not possible, of course, within the realm of Being itself, which is empty and indeterminate; but it would be legitimate as an external specification, performed by a thinker at a later stage of the System.

"Being as name" and names as "in" Being thus work out to the same thing. The sentence I have quoted from #463, identifying names "in" Being with "names as such," thus yields the further identification of "names as such" with "Being as name." The sides of the two ambiguities which referred to names as not (or not yet) signs thus turn out to be identical; there are only two senses of "name" here, and just one ambiguity. This ambiguity, presented at two different places in Hegel's discussion of language, is probably not a mere looseness of language or slip of Hegel's. The question arises of whether coherent accounts of two different kinds of name can be drawn from Hegel's texts. If they can, these philological considerations have philosophical significance.

It can be seen that every time Hegel, in his discussion of language in the *Encyclopedia*, refers either to "names as such" or to names in connection with Being, he is referring to names apart from the attachment to universals which makes signs of them. Such names, as we have already seen, are not yet signs but are mere senseless externalities, which can be connected to their meanings via synthesis and are "in" Being as their internal "space." Hegel also tells us that such a name, "as a being gives, for itself, nothing to think,"[68] and that such a "being as name needs an other, the meaning of the representational Intelligence."[69]

The reference in #463 to names as such as "senseless words" suggests that the "word," for Hegel, can be a name as such as well as a representational name. This opens up another passage where Hegel seems to discuss names as such: the *Zusatz* to #462.[70] This passage concerns words as "articulated tones," as sounds which disappear in time but whose "true, concrete negativity" is the Intelligence itself, within which they arise and disappear. The passage thus cannot deal with the kind of name discussed in #462 proper; those names are representational and, so far from "disappearing," are "enduring attachments" (*bleibende Verknüpfungen—Enz.* #461)[71] of name and meaning. They are also "without intuition and image," and therefore cannot be "tones."[72]

"Tone" is for Hegel in the "Philosophy of Mind" an anthropological phenomenon, proper to the soul which is not yet distinct from nature. It is the expression of interiority as such, which can include representations but also takes in feelings and emotions. Such externalization belongs to the anthropological process of Sensation (*Empfindung*) and can be found in bird songs, animal cries, and music as well as in human speech.[73] If #462 *Zus.* deals with "words," which as I have argued can for Hegel be "senseless," and deals with them primarily as "tones"—that is, as anthropological—it would be hasty to read it as a discussion of representational names without some textual warrant to do so. The text provides no such warrant: there is no reference to representations as meanings of names, indeed no reference to "representation" at all. The same holds for *Encyclopedia* #444 Zus.,[74] which refers to words as "transient, disappearing, completely ideal realizations which follow forth in an element which offers no resistance." Here again, such words cannot themselves be representational names, and there is no mention of representations as being their meanings. The addition of #462 Zus. and #444 Zus. to the list of passages in which Hegel may discuss names as such uncovers, I believe, his full exposition of such names.

Hegel's terminology in distinguishing names as such from representational names is so unclear as to require rather intricate philological reasoning to show that distinction, and it is not surprising that it has occasioned numerous misunderstandings.[75] In any case, the distinction between the two kinds of name is, though obscurely phrased, not I think open to much doubt. Hegel clearly asserts, in #462, that names *tout court* are signs which, in the course of Verbal Memory, become representations. He clearly says elsewhere, as I have argued, that "names as such" are not signs and are senseless, and that names as Being are senseless and in need of meaning. His discussion in #462 Zus. clearly begins by limiting itself to names as tones, and expands this only to note that the Intelligence is their true negativity; it does not discuss representations as their meanings.

When Mechanical Memory abandons the meanings worked up by and expressed in representational language, it remains an expression of what is internal. The general expression of subjective internality, of which languge as the *articulate* expression of *determinate* internality is a development, is for Hegel the anthropological process of Sensation (*Empfindung*).[76] Names as such can be understood more clearly by contrasting them, not merely with representational names, but also with the type of expression which takes place in sensation, as well as in intuition.

Unlike the shrieks and cries of animalian sensation, names as such are explicitly located by the Intelligence in "space" and "time." As tones, they disappear in time and are temporal; and they stand to one another in the utterly external type of relationship proper to space—in the internal "space of names."[77] Hegel identifies the faculty which externalizes sensations into an explicitly present space and time as intuition;[78] and we can say that names as such are objects, not merely of sensation, but of a sort of internal intuition. Those objects would then be individuals, as are all objects of intuition—precisely those individual utterances we run through in recitation by heart.[79]

If names as such are individuals, then they must not only have the spatiotemporal forms of intuition, but must preserve as well the distinguishing feature of intuitional content: that it is "found" by the mind. For the mind cannot arrive at what is sheerly individual by any process of reasoning, dialectical or other; such a process would have to proceed via universal determinations, and can arrive at an individual only insofar as it is universally determined. Hegel does in fact say that names as such are "found" by the Intelligence, and this could be explained by the inviduality which they have, in virtue of being objects of a sort of intuition. Conversely, whatever can only be "found" by the Intelligence and cannot be worked up by it must be either a completely isolated individual or one standing in the least determinate type of relation with its other: that of space. The "foundness" of the names in Mechanical Memory, which Hegel stresses, thus goes together with their individuality, which he does not.[80]

The names externalized in Mechanical Memory thus differ from the externalizations of sensation in that they are externalized into space and time in such a way that they appear to be found there, as is the case with intuitions. But in contrast to intuitions, the space and time in which they are found are internal. The time is the "time" of the subject running through names as such in mechanical recitation; the "space" is merely the sheer externality of each name's relations to other names.[81]

The externalization which takes place in Mechanical Memory differs from that of sensations and intuitions in another way. Such externalization is not into shrieks and cries, as it is in sensation, or into any sort of immediate sense datum as it is in Intuition, but into words: into the same

names which, as signs, were internalized and universalized by Verbal
Memory and which now return, within the Intelligence, to the kind of
senseless individuality from which they took their start outside it.[82] They
retain in this the same intuitional content as the representational names
from which they come; and it would appear that, as is the case with such
names, this content is disregarded by the Intelligence, which posits
names as such as simple.[83]

Names as such are thus indeed "names," not merely vocal externalities. I will say that they are "homonymous" with the names of representational language. *But they have abandoned all representationality*: the
meaning to which representational names, as signs, are attached is missing. So is the representationalization of the sound of such names which
was, I have argued, demanded by those universal meanings. Names as
such are individual, interior utterances which would, if they signified
representations, fall under the universalized sounds of representational
names. We can say that they develop out of representational names; but
this development incorporates a return to, rather than a reappropria-
tion of, an earlier stage of the dialectic. It is not a sublation, in which
something of the immediately previous stage is retained, but a death—
the death of meaning.[84]

What names as such regain by this fatal return to a previous stage
is the "true, concrete negativity of the linguistic sign." They are "negative" in the sense that they disappear even as they arise.[85] Their status as
"found" within Mechanical Memory is thus a constant "becoming
found" (*Gefundenwerden*).[86] Names as such thus occupy fleeting positions
within the space of names; we might say that, since they have no determinate relation to anything beyond themselves, they *are* such positions and
nothing more. Each such name constitutes, within the Mechanical Memory, an individual "here" and "now." And we might suggest that "Being
as name" in Mechanical Memory is the linguistic equivalent of "pure
sensuous Being" in the *Phenomenology*'s section on Sense-Certainty:[87]
both present series of individual "heres" and "nows" without further
significance.

In presenting what they present, names as such operate as do
signs; but they do not have the representational meaning which signs
present. Their intuitional content, we may say, is simply a disappearing
word which, in disappearing, reveals itself as insignificant in itself and
should, therefore, bring forth the thought of a universal representation;
this, it appears, is what Hegel means when he says that a name as such
"requires" the meaning of the representational Intelligence.[88] But there
is only one "universal" which can be said to be presented by such a

name, and that is the Intelligence itself, "the universal, the simple truth of its own particular utterances."[89] The only significance, we may say, to names run through in Mechanical Memory is precisely that they are being run through by the Intelligence, which itself is just the universal power of running through them and the "empty connective band" which keeps them in order.[90] That the intelligence, as a universal activity, is the only universal called up by names as such appears to be what Hegel means when he says that it becomes their "meaning."[91]

But if the Intelligence can be said to be the meaning of names as such, it is not at all the same kind of meaning that a representational name has, because the Intelligence is not a fixed and determinate universal. It is, rather, precisely the process by which names as such arise and disappear: their "external objectivity itself."[92] Their meaning is just this process, then; and the process is nothing other than the existence they attain as they are run through in succession. For the name as such to have the Intelligence for its meaning means for it to follow on, and trigger, other such names. A name as such thus comes to mean precisely its own kind of existence; and the meaning of the set of all names as such is identical with its being. "In this way," says Hegel, "Verbal Memory is the transition into the activity of thinking, which has no more meaning—i.e., from whose objectivity the subjective is no longer something distinct."[93]

Parmenides once expressed the unity of being and thought in often quoted words: *t'auto d'esti noein te kai ouneken esti noêma.*[94] The words which follow are only rarely quoted:[95] *ou gar aneu tou ontos, en ôi pephitasmenon estin, heureseis to noein.* "For you will not find thinking apart from the being [i.e., the word] in which it is enunciated." It appears that, for Hegel, names as such are the "being in which thought is enunciated," and that they embody the "unity of being and thought" with which all philosophical science must begin.[96] In order to understand this more fully, we must look more closely at the reasons for his recurrent references to such names in connection with "Being."[97]

Being is, of course, the first and poorest category of Hegel's Logic. It is nothing other than pure, indeterminate immediacy which, in its very emptiness, drives thought onward to greater concretion.[98] Names as such, being found rather than worked up, are immediate; and, being mere senseless externalities, they are also indeterminate, in the sense that—as far as Mechanical Memory itself is concerned—they exhibit no general features (*Bestimmtheiten*) which connect them with each other. No two names as such, as far as Mechanical Memory can tell, resemble each other more than any other two, because any aspect in which they resembled each other would be a universal, which would connect them with one another, taking them out of the sheer externality of the space of names. They are thus beings, and nothing more. The set of all of them can be characterized, as we have seen Hegel characterize it, as "Being" itself; conversely, it is hardly surprising to find Hegel (criticizing Jacobi) say: "Being, taken as it immediately is, belongs to a subject, is something uttered."[99]

Hegel goes into somewhat more detail on this in the *Jenaer Realphilosophie*. In the section of that work entitled "Language" (*die Sprache*), he says that "the name itself is at first only the very superficial spiritual being," and immediately gives some examples. Very often, he says, when we ask what a thing is, we are satisfied to be told its name. To the question:

> What is this? we answer, "it is a lion, donkey," etc. It is—that
> means that it is not a yellow thing that has feet, etc., something
> independent on its own, but a name, a tone of my voice—
> something completely different from what it is in the intuition.
> And this is [its] true Being.[100]

The reference here to "tones" suggests that the passage can be applied to the names as such of the Mechanical Memory; and we can see that those names constitute "spiritual Being" for Hegel: a Being which, as internal, is identical with thought itself. The "interior externality" of names as such within the Mechanical Memory is then the identity of Being and Thought. In it, Hegel says, thought attains its "objectivity"—an objectivity which is, there, united with subjectivity (both, to be sure, here in impoverished form).

The contrast between the kind of universal presented by the Intelligence and representational universals shows, finally, why Hegel attached "Mechanical Memory" to "Representation," and how it is the "transition into the activity of Thinking" which he claimed it to be.[101] Representational universals, I have argued, are derived from intuition and remain bound to the externality of their source. The Intelligence, however, has not been worked up from intuition in this way. It has been present from the start as a universal, but under various guises. First it was the universal "nocturnal storehouse" in which images were preserved when the Intelligence was not aware of them;[102] then the "power" which separated and conjoined them in Imagination;[103] then the "negativity" of the linguistic sign.[104] In all these previous appearances, the nature of the Intelligence was understood in terms of the kind of images and representations it contained and from its manner of operating with them.

The final form of the Intelligence prior to "Mechanical Memory" is as containing representational names, a set of determinate universals which it connects according to their meaning.[105] To understand the Intelligence in terms of such universals would, one presumes, be to grasp it as their universal significance: as their *summum genus*. This would miss its essential nature as negative, as the very process of the arising and disappearance of those determinations. It would also see it as "worked up" from those universals, and as dependent on them in the same way that a representational universal is dependent on the external intuitions from which it is worked up. Thus, the stumbling block to awareness of the true nature of the Intelligence is the presence within it of precisely those representational meanings which it has worked up:

> Insofar as the connection of names lies in their meaning, the
> attachment of that meaning to Being as a name is still a synthe-
> sis, and the intelligence is, in this its externality, not simply re-
> turned into itself.[106]

These representational meanings must be sacrificed and die away, in order for the Intelligence to come forth in its true nature as the most universal and the "most internal" factor in representation. It is Mechanical Memory which sacrifices such meaning and allows the Intelligence to stand forth in its own right; and such memory is necessary in order that the entire process of internalization and universalization presented in "Representation" can come to an end. "Mechanical Memory" is then properly placed where Hegel has placed it—at the end of "Representation."

Mechanical Memory has, then, two functions in the transition to Thinking. In the first place, by sacrificing the representational meaning worked up by finite mind in its historical encounters with external reality, it clears the ground for the development of content from within thought itself, without that development being infected by content externally derived. Its job, as Hegel puts it, is

> to flatten the ground [*Boden*] of interiority to pure Being, to
> pure space, in which the matter itself, the content which is in
> itself, can grant itself and explicate itself without opposition
> from a subjective interiority.[107]

Second, the very flatness of this internal ground poses the demand for the development of content. When the names in Mechanical Memory posit a demand for significance, they first attach themselves to the Intelligence itself, as I have argued. But this is completely abstract, and contains only the utter externality of the space of names. What is abstract always, for Hegel, demands further differentiation; and the presence of names poses a demand for a differentiated meaningfulness within the Intelligence. But, because names as such do not have meanings derived from "outside," this cannot be a demand for more representational meaning. It must be instead a demand for a meaning which will come from "within," from the abstract universality of the Intelligence. Mechanical memory thus both makes possible and demands the development of content from within thought.[108] We can then say that Mechanical Memory makes both possible and necessary the full development of thought itself.

Two Philosophical Media

The nature of Verbal Memory and its significance for thinking make up, Hegel says, one of the most difficult points in the entire philosophy of mind.[109] I can hardly claim, in these few pages, to have done it justice. But I hope to have established that Hegel's own discussion of language leaves him with *two* media for the expression of philosophical thought. One is names as such: vanishing, individual, internal utterances which are "homonymous" with representational names and which demand, but do not possess, determinate meanings. They are free, it seems, to receive such meanings from the immanent development of philosophical thought itself. For a complex of Systematically developed content—what stands to the left of $\Rightarrow$ in step (0) of my rewriting of Systematic dialectics—can be abbreviated by a name in Mechanical Memory. That name, as a token, retains its evanescent quality; but it loses its meaninglessness. The "meaning" it gains, again, is not a representation, but simply the set of contents it abbreviates. The "meaning" of any name as such in the System is thus the set of other names as such it abbreviates; to gain a Systematic meaning is to gain a place in the System.

Representational names, by contrast, are achieved identities of name and representation; they are enduring and universal types. Their meanings are worked up by the Intelligence in its dependence on intuition and, therefore, are historical and conditional upon the particular experiences of a historical people. Such language contains, Hegel says, the names we (experts) think in; but it now appears that this is true, first and foremost, of thinking which is prephilosophical, finite, and representational:[110]

> As Homer says of a few things that they have two names, one in the language of the gods and the other in the language of ephemeral humans, so there are for [the common content of religion and philosophy] two languages: the one a language of feeling, representation, and of understanding-type thinking which nests in finite categories and one-sided abstractions; the other, the language of the concrete Concept.[111]

In representational names, the language of the Understanding, we have an expression which is adequate to the historically achieved meanings of the extraphilosophical world, because it simply *is* those achieved meanings. In names as such, we have a linguistic medium which can express the self-determination of the Concept. Philosophical science must make use of both media:

> The language of representation is different from the language of the Concept, and man not merely recognizes the truth in the first instance in the representational name, but it is in this name that he is first, as a living man, at home with it. The task of philosophical science is not to write its figurations into . . . abstract realms only; it is also to establish and record for each figuration, immediately and for itself, the existence which it maintains in actual spirit—and this is the representation.[112]

Other texts of Hegel expand on these. In the Berlin transcription of the Introduction to the *Lectures on the History of Philosophy*, he distinguishes the understanding of something which is already part of the true nature of the person who understands from the understanding of something which remains external to her. In the first case, to "understand" something is to see it as already one's own, as

> the substantial foundation of the content which, coming to Spirit as the absolute essence of Spirit, touches its innermost [nature], finds its echo in it and thereby obtains testimonial from it. This is the first absolute condition of understanding; what is not in [Spirit] cannot come into it, cannot be for it— such content, namely, as is eternal and infinite.[113]

In order to be explicitly, and hence comprehensibly, present to Spirit, what is purely interior to Spirit must be expressed in words.[114] We can take the type of understanding referred to here to be the understanding of infinite thought as expressed in the "language of the Concept," in a name as such, and thus as getting its entire significance from within. This suggestion is supported by the fact that the kind of understanding with which Hegel contrasts this first type is clearly the understanding of representational language. For as "infinite," the significance obtained by the first type of understanding does not fall under the subject-object dichotomy, and thus cannot properly be considered an object of consciousness; it is then "unconscious." In order for content to arrive in consciousness, Hegel says, it must be presented as an "object" for consciousness; and, in order to be truly understood as such an object, it must be present via a representation (rather than, for example, via an intuition or sensation): for representation provides the "common, accustomed" medium of consciousness.[115]

The opposition of these two media seems to be yet more heavily stressed in the Introduction to the *Lectures on the Philosophy of Religion*.[116] Hegel there distinguishes two ways in which we ask what something "signifies." In one sense, we possess already an awareness of it as something other than a determination of thought, and we seek to know what it is "according to the Concept." In Hegel's example here, we already have a representation of God when we ask for the philosophical meaning of the name. It also seems that this would apply to the case when we have merely an intuition of the thing, or of a name, as well.[117] Such would, for example, be the case in the question "What is this?" where we expect, as an answer, a philosophical thought-determination. "Meaning" in this case, Hegel says, is the Concept itself.[118] On the other hand, we can also ask for the "meaning" of something in an opposed sense. For we can already have a "pure thought" of something, a concrete moment of the "unity of subject and object" (and thus, as expressed, a name as such), and yet be unclear about its precise meaning. We then demand as "meaning" a representation, an example of the content as something "external" to ourselves. We ask, in my terms, for the externalization of the thought content into a representational name.

All these passages appear to refer to the two types of expression present in Hegel's discussion in the *Encyclopedia*—names as such and representational names. They present both as deriving from Spirit and as needing, each, reconciliation with the other in the full expression of the System. It thus seems that philosophical expression for Hegel must take place in both representational names and in names as such; and we can presume, in virtue of his claims for the full intelligibility of his System,[119] that he thought both together sufficient. This all suggests three things:

1. Both types of expression are necessary: neither on its own is sufficient, but has inadequacies which render it alone incapable of expressing philosophical truth.
2. Since both types of expression together are sufficient for philosophical expression, the inadequacies of each cannot be found in the other. For if both types of expression share some deficiency, then all philosophical expression is affected by it, and it cannot be overcome.
3. The two types of expression can be brought together in philosophical expression so that the disadvantages of each are canceled out and the advantages preserved.

Complementary Deficiencies of these Media

In the remainder of this analysis, I will discuss the first two of these claims in terms of the secondary literature referred to at the beginning of the chapter; I will deal with the third in chapter 10.

Bodammer, Clark, Mure, and Simon all hold, we saw, that Hegel's philosophy is to be expressed in a single medium. All, I argue, are wrong: only together can names as such and representational names provide adequate vehicles for the expression of Hegel's philosophy. But of the four writers, the last three do not recognize any role at all for names as such or for Mechanical Memory in the expression of Hegel's System. The first lesson learned here is that all three take a Left Hegelian attitude toward Hegelian philosophical expression: it must be in the words of history and the world. The strategies with which the philosopher tries to cope with recalcitrant language—Murean readjustment, Clarkian speculative identity, and Simonian dissimulation—are really so many ways of coping with history.

Mure's argument depends, I noted, on his general doctrine of incomplete sublation. In a complete sublation, apparently, the lower levels sublated would either disappear altogether or would come to be wholly determined by the higher, later levels. Since this never happens, all sublation is what Mure calls "incomplete," and this means that lower levels persist, in unaltered form, after higher levels have (so to speak) tried to appropriate them. In the present case, this means that language is not completely sublated by thought: it persists in what we saw to be its peculiar referentiality, emotionality, and rigidity. Hence it is unable to provide the immanent plasticity of philosophical thought as Hegel conceives it.

In fact thought does not, in the *Encyclopedia*, sublate language—either completely or incompletely. In between the two is Mechanical Memory, which moves from representational names toward thought not by sublating them into higher unities but by discarding all their meaning. Mure's only mention of Mechanical Memory is to remark, in a footnote, that it is "not a phase of the dialectic,"[120] a point which Hegel explicitly denies when, as I have noted, he refers to it as the "most difficult point" in (not: ancillary to) the Philosophy of Mind.[121] Names as such are thus not sublations of representational names, and do not have the external origin which renders such names rigid in form as well as abstract and particular in content, and in these ways deficient for the expression of philosophical thought.

Lacking names as such, Mure's Hegel must use representational language to express his System; and, as Mure rightly sees, expression so limited leads to two problems. If ordinary language, like mathematics but in lower degree, is representational, then it is fixed and static: its meanings do not change and are "finite."[122] They cannot change fast enough, then, to keep up with Systematic dialectics. The philosopher must, in Mure's words, "continually remodel, readjust and expand . . . language" in order to force it to even a partial expression of her thought.[123] The only alternative to such tinkering is abstractness: the fixed and stable meanings of representational names are adequate to the most general and abstract features of experience and thought—those which do not change—and to them alone.

But this criticism of the inadequate "plasticity" and resultant abstractness, primarily of artificial symbolism but also of representational names in general, does not apply to names as such. For such a name is not a representational name, in which the signifier—like the meaning—has been generalized into something that can be retained in memory and, as a universal, can have a plurality of actual utterances as its instances. A name as such, we saw, is an individual: a token not a type, which can occur only once. What seem to be recurrences of names as such in the presentation of the System are recognizable as such only by representational thought reflecting on the System—as when hearers realize that they have heard a particular word before. For resemblance is, in Hegel's Psychology, an association of ideas by the Imagination, and to recognize one word as similar to words we have heard before would mean seeing the two individuals as coming under the same representation—in this case, under the "universalized sound" of the name.[124] In the "space" of names as such, however, no two names resemble each other more than any other two; otherwise the space would not be entirely indeterminate but would contain, as well as names, their relations of similarity to one another. Hence, there is no way within that space to discriminate recurrences of old names from fresh occurrences of new ones. When, for example, Hegel calls the Absolute Idea "Being,"[125] this name, as a name as such, is a fresh utterance and can have a fresh meaning—in this case, that of immediacy as starting point of the (now explicit) speculative method. That it also retains to some extent the meaning of its homonym at the beginning of the Logic ("indeterminate immediacy" *tout court*) would be a matter for reflective representational awareness, itself also part of the wider Systematic procedure. Such awareness, focusing merely on the observed similarity of names as such, operates with regard to the sound of the name, not its meaning: it does not of itself import any of the partial, historically based representations that the Understanding also works up.

Names as such, unlike representational names, are fresh and newly meaningless each time they are uttered. They are then able to receive new meanings at each stage of the dialectic. Because they disappear as they are uttered, they do not retard thought—one can run mentally through even "antidisestablishmentarianism" in an instant. And they are not restricted merely to the "abstract," fixed and enduring, features of existence, since they speed in and out of being as quickly as anything perceptible. Finally, there is no content worked up by representational language that remains exempt from appropriation by the System. For in order for a word to be unsublatable into the System, it would have to be undefinable by other words already introduced into that System. This cannot mean that it is wholly indefinable, susceptible only of ostensive definition, for as we saw, no terms in representational language are like that. So the word would have to be definable, but only by words which themselves are not in the System. In which case we would have not one but two systems, each wholly closed in upon itself, not merely as a matter of fact without links to the other but somehow incapable of ever developing such links—and known, somehow, to be such. Unless we want to defend this implausible sort of knowledge claim, we must accept that names as such are in principle adequate to cover the full concreteness of the world, insofar as that is expressible in representational names.[126]

Like Mure, Malcolm Clark dismisses Hegel's account of Mechanical Memory—as "somewhat imaginative."[127] Clark's first argument for the necessity that Hegel's System be couched in what I call representational names appeals, as was seen earlier, to the efforts Hegel made to draw gleams of speculation from ordinary language. While those efforts cannot be denied, it does not follow that Hegel is restricted to the resources available in representational language: he could well have (as I believe he does) another form of expression available and still, on occasion, be drawn into the kind of serious wordplay that Clark alludes to—for reasons which will be suggested by chapter 10. Clark's second argument, as was also seen, attributes to language something of what Hegel calls the "impotence of nature": language, like nature in general, is a resistant medium for thought. But this misses Hegel's careful distinction, at #444 Zus.,[128] between nature, which exists as "external resistant matter" in space and time, and names which exist in the Intelligence as transient realizations of thought. It is the word, Hegel writes, that can bring about "the unlimited freedom and reconciliation of Spirit with itself"; external matter must constantly be struggled against. In particular, the name as such in Mechanical Memory receives both its meaning and its being from thought, and disappears as it is uttered: it is wholly bereft of the "external resistant individuality" of material objects. There is thus a crucial distinction between nature and language as externalities of thought; and (as Hegel puts it in the *Lectures on the History of Philosophy*) "the rational exists only as language."[129]

Given this resistance of language to thought, the only relation the two can have, for Clark, is one of speculative identity: "one's true meaning is always the identity of a meaning simply identified with its language with a meaning still opposed to its language."[130] This ingenious application of one of Hegel's basic concepts to his own language is not, Clark notes, true to Hegel's own view of his thought; Hegel believed himself to have attained complete intelligibility.[131] On Clark's view, he has attained the precise opposite. The concrete relations of unity and disunity between a philosophical utterance and its meaning cannot even come under general rules of interpretation, for then we would lose the "otherness" involved: our rules would provide a steady bridge for moving, allegorically, from statement to meaning. But without such rules, we have on Clark's scheme no way at all to move from utterance to meaning: no way to understand any expression in Hegel's System. Unintelligibility is thus not only an inescapable feature of Hegelian philosophical expression but is on Clark's view basic to the way it works.[132] As a general strategy of "saving" Hegel, this scorches the conceptual earth, and is not only dubious but unnecessary if Hegel's System has at its disposal the unresisting medium of names as such.

My final representative of the Hegelian linguistic Left, Josef Simon, makes only a very brief reference to Verbal Memory and none at all to Mechanical Memory.[133] The main problem for Simon, given his view that thought has no content other than what is presented to it by the representational language in which it is expressed, is that of how to do justice to Hegel's repeated claims that philosophical thought can develop content from "within" itself. How can content develop within something which is essentially unnameable and abstract? Simon's answer to this is torturous, but it appears to be a Kantianizing, so to speak, of Hegel:

> When thought determines itself, it brings forth its determinations in the manner of synthetic a priori judgments. This means that it posits something which does not lie in its concept and is not taken from experience. This positing as a synthesis occurs outside of thought. . . . The concept of the determinate thought does not lie within the formal concept of thought.[134]

Simon is, apparently, driven to deny that Hegelian thought has any immanent content because he agrees with Clark and Mure that representational language alone must express philosophical thought, but disagrees with their view that philosophy never finds a complete expression. It is clear, I think, that this view does not do justice to what we saw, in chapter 4, to be Hegel's view of the Concept as the concrete, self-determining totality of thought which admits no content, so to speak, from outside but develops plenty from within. And it should be clear by now that names as such do not "dissimulate" thought: in Hegel's terms, they enable thought to "follow forth in a resistanceless element" that "remains completely by itself," eventually to reach the form of conceptual knowledge.[135] But Simon opens up another question, to which the present reading of Hegel must respond: Granted that thought has a developing content, what makes names as such adequate to express that development? What would it mean for philosophical language to "manifest" the development of thought rather than "displace" it?

As chapter 4 argued, the development of thought is a progressive bestowal of meaning: thought develops when a plurality of markers finds itself abbreviated by a single new one, or when a single new marker finds itself explicated into such a plurality. As couched in names as such, which arise and disappear in time, this is a temporal phenomenon: the meaning of a term is the previously introduced markers that it abbreviates, and a name manifests thought by virtue of its relation to what went before and what comes after in the System. Representational language is indeed incapable of such relation, because of the externality and fixity of its meanings: each representational name is ultimately, we saw, the arbitrary but fixed connection of two representations, one of which (the meaning) has been worked up cognitively from sense experience, while the other (what I call "the representation of the name") is the universalization of a set of arbitrary sounds. Both components are then derived from external realities; any relation that either would have to what went before it, and what comes after, in a philosophical system would be secondary and after the fact—perhaps, indeed, "dissimulative."

But a name as such does have, as its nature, to be related to what went before and to what comes after. This intrinsic relation takes the form of a disappearing demand. The name, as meaningless, "requires" a meaning.[136] For Hegel, this means that the name disappears in favor of something else: it is the nature of the name to disappear, while the meaning takes its place. But for names as such there is no fixed and stable meaning before which they can efface themselves, no representational presence to which they can be subjected. There are only other names as such, forever becoming found in the intelligence which, as their presumed "meaning," is nothing over and above them. Hence, the name as such, disappearing in time, effaces itself before other names as such— the markers which explicate it; and they do the same, according to the gestures discussed in chapter 4. The meaning of a name as such is simply those other names which it abbreviates or explicates, and this ordered movement is the "development of thought."[137]

Any attempt to construe Hegel's philosophical language along the lines of Mure, Clark, and Simon, no matter how learned or ingenious, makes hash of Hegel. It yields a Hegel who can never really say anything, who makes unintelligibility into an explanatory principle, or who views philosophical thought as empty and dissimulative. A final, and positive, lesson is that the expression of philosophy in names as such can avoid all the problems which Mure, Clark, and Simon have raised for Hegel. Their objections, where valid, apply to representational names alone.

I have argued already that names as such overcome the formal problem of how to stay plastic enough not to fix or dissimulate thought. Theodor Bodammer shows how names as such are also free from the problems with content that representational language brings with it. Too free, in fact, for Bodammer seems to leave no role for representational names in philosophical expression. He maintains that the meanings of terms in representational language must, in the strict presentation of logical science, "on principle be abstracted from." Though it is possible to recognize "shadowings" (*Schattierungen*) of representational language in the language of the Concept, the two spheres are "in principle distinct." It was for Hegel "uninteresting" that philosophy uses for its presentation words from historical languages.[138]

There are several problems with Bodammer's restriction of philosophical expression in Hegel to names as such alone. If it were for Hegel "uninteresting" that philosophy uses words from historical languages, then what can we make of his intense efforts to draw "gleams of reason" from words in ordinary German, to which we saw Malcolm Clark appeal—efforts manifest throughout Hegel's writings?[139] Indeed, the presence in Logic of *Schattierungen* of representational words seems for Hegel to have been neither uninteresting nor a mere pedagogical device. He even refers to his Logic as the *Reich der Schatten*, the "realm of shadows" which is "free" from sensuous concretion in not being determined by it—but which constitutes the inmost rational nature of such concretion, and therefore remains, in its own inmost nature, essentially related to it.[140] Indeed, a philosophy expressed solely in words wholly other than and indifferent to the languages actually spoken around it would be unable to enter into the dialogue with its times which is necessary to philosophy for Hegel. This dialogue requires that the meanings provided by philosophical thought somehow "comprehend" the meanings worked up by the extraphilosophical world. Such extraphilosophical meanings must then be present themselves, clearly and precisely, in philosophical thought. Their expression, in representational names, must somehow be integrated into the expression of the System itself.

A philosophy which aims to present the "one, universal, and truly infinite reason," but does not undertake any dialogue with its times, is a Right Hegelianism. Attributing it to Hegel leads to problems, not just in the dialogue with history, but within the expressed System itself. Names as such, we saw, are perfectly senseless individuals; each of them is, as far as Mechanical Memory is concerned, as well-equipped as any other to express a given determination of thought. If the expression of the System takes place with reference only to such names, there will be no reason for any moment of thought to be expressed in one such name rather than in another, and the expression of thought will be entirely haphazard. This, in turn, leads to two absurdities. First, the same moment of thought could be expected to be expressed, at the same time but in different thinkers, by different words. What "came into" Hegel's mind as *Sein*, for example, could as well come into his hearer's minds as *Nichts,* or *Dasein*—or as *Friedrich*, or *Georg*, or *Kamel*. Thought would be unable, in other words, to find a standard expression which would be the same for a number of different people. There is no evidence in the transcriptions of Hegel's lectures that he thought of himself as confronting such a situation, and there is no discussion in Bodammer of how such an unstandardized philosophy could qualify as the presentation of a universal reason.

Moreover, as we have seen, because a name as such is a disappearing individual, there is no way for it to recur at different stages of the development. If it did "recur" in the sense that one moment of thought could be expressed at different times by two individual utterances which resembled one another, the fact could not be recognized within philosophical thinking itself. For, as I noted earlier, the universalized sound which enables us to recognize a name as one that we have heard before belongs to the representational name. The manifest fact that the word "Being," for example, occurs on many different levels of the Logic would either not be a fact at all (since what seem to be recurrences are really fresh occurrences of new names as such) or would be inexplicable (since the resemblance of such names to one another is discerned by the Imagination—that is, by Representation). Philosophical thought would thus be unable to achieve a uniform, enduring expression. It is obvious that Hegel thought that he had, indeed, found a standard and uniform expression of philosophical thought. To attain this, however, it would seem that the choice of a name for a given moment of thought must be made, not with reference merely to names as such, but to names which have enduring "sounds" and determinate meanings—to representational names.[141]

It seems then that names as such, distinct from the names occurring in historical languages, are necessary for the System to be expressed in a way unconditioned by the particular natures of those languages and, therefore, universally valid. But they must be supplemented by representational names, in order to achieve a uniform and standard expression for philosophy within its own domain and to enable it to carry on its "dialogue with its times." In short—the next chapter will show the final story to be considerably longer—philosophical thought must be expressed *in* names as such, and *with regard to* representational names. The philosopher must produce at each stage, from her Mechanical Memory, a name as such homophonic with the name from representational language whose meaning her current Systematic construction is designed to capture—and she must explicate it with other names as such which can also be recognized to be themselves homophonic with representational names already comprehended by the System.

In terms of my rewriting of Systematic dialectics in chapter 4, the philosopher arrives at a complex of content—a set of previously introduced names as such (step 4). She then chooses another name as such from Mechanical Memory to abbreviate that (0). The dialectics then play forth as I wrote them earlier. Representational Intelligence does two further things: it recognizes the similarity of names as such currently being uttered with previous names as such (e.g., that of "Being" as uttered in developing the "Absolute Idea" and "Being" as uttered at the beginning), noting similarities and differences. And it notes the homophony of the current name with the appropriate representational name.

Two main deficiencies in representational names as the expression of philosophical thought have emerged from this discussion. Their meaning, which is worked up from sense intuition, remains conditioned by the externality and contingency which affects its origin. And in form, representational names are not "plastic" enough to keep up with the movement of the dialectic. They cannot take on new meanings, so to speak, with the speed at which thought develops itself in philosophical discourse.

I have argued that names as such do not have these deficiencies. Since they receive both their meaning and their being from the Intelligence itself, they are not affected by the externality and contingency of representational language. As negative, disappearing individual utterances, they are capable of keeping up with the movement of thought and are incapable of "dissimulating" thought in Simon's sense. Meaning nothing other than a moment of thought, they do not hinder the expression of its concrete development from previous moments and into later moments, and so can express fully concrete philosophical thought. Finally, because they are homonyms of representational names, they are in principle able to express all the concrete content which Representation works up from Intuition. The sounds of names as such can serve as mediating links between representational language and philosophical meaning, because they express the latter and are homonymous with the former. These two forms of expression can—perhaps—be brought together in a way which preserves the advantages of each and cancels the disadvantages of both.

In such a unification, philosophy would find an expression which enables it (through names as such) to be both universal and plastic, its presentation unaffected by the particularities and finitudes of representational language. And (via representational names) philosophy would achieve an expression which is both uniform and standard, as well as intelligibly related to the words of the nonphilosophical world. So expressed, philosophy would be able to carry on its "dialogue with its times": to unite System and representation, philosophy and history, time and rationality. Its names would, in the reconciliation of such mighty oppositions, be the Noblest words of all. It is to this dynamic of unification of two philosophical media—this Systematic version of Nobility—which I will turn in the next "Analysis."

8

Hegelian Words: Demarcation

I s Hegel's System (granted the reading of it developed so far) of merely the general kind of utility I sketched in the Introduction? Or can it be a way of pursuing, specifically, linguistic philosophy? Is it, as a System in and of words, entirely without relation to the enormous amount of work that has been done in that area in the twentieth century? Or is it capable of fitting into, or passing beyond, certain definite spaces opened up in and among other approaches?

Consider two concepts of meaning, which I will call "narrow" and "broad." On the "narrow" view, the meaning of an utterance is what we need to know in order to assign a truth-value to it. The "broad" concept views meaning as what can be done with a word. On the narrow view, the meaning of a word works out to the conditions under which it can be used to assert a truth; on the broad view, a word's meaning is its function in a larger context of activity. The narrow view, together with many of its implications, has been systematically set forth—and then startlingly deconstructed—in the writings of Donald Davidson;[1] the broad view resonates through the mysteriously compelling aphorisms of Wittgenstein's *Philosophical Investigations*.[2] Do these two paradigms encounter one another at all? Do they unite under the dominance of truth, as John Searle thinks?[3] Or do they engage one another in such a way as to open up terrain between and beyond themselves, terrain into which may fit still other ways of handling language?

I undertake here to demarcate such terrain by recounting Davidson in such a way as to show how the thought of Wittgenstein points to
certain gaps in his work, and vice versa. Into the gaps will fit a further
approach, complementary to and in some respects beyond both: the Hegelian one which I am sketching here. The task is on the level of project,
not thesis, and hence is unrefined. It seeks not to show that either Davidson or Wittgenstein is wrong (on the *essentials* of each's undertaking, I
think both are largely right), but to show that neither, nor both together,
has done all there is to do. I approach both thinkers, then, as a sympa-
thetic outsider; those who, from the inside, read this and find Davidson
and Wittgenstein presented in ways too strange to be right, engage that
sympathy. They are invited to read the discussion in chapter 7 of universalization as a social procedure, and to contemplate in discussions like
this one the price of their philosophical success.

The Unity of Language

Davidson's claim that language is amenable to systematic treatment has
many levels. One is motivated,[4] generally, by a concern that languages
not be unlearnable. A language is unlearnable if it contains sentences
whose meanings cannot be contructed from a set of basic terms ("semantic primitives") and rules for combining them. In such a case

> no matter how many sentences a would-be speaker learns to
> produce and understand, there will remain others whose mean-
> ings are not given by the rules already mastered.

Hence Davidson's oft-repeated claim that to know a language is to be
able to tell, for *any* arbitrary sentence in it, what the meaning of that
sentence is.[5]

To learn a language is thus, in theory, a finite, completable undertaking. Language is amenable to this because it has a structure borrowed
from (or akin to, or the occasion for) that of logic: the infinite possible
utterances which compose a language are all formed from recursive operations on a finite set of primitives, and the number of types of such
operation is itself finite. One can in principle learn all the grammatical
rules and semantic primitives of a language, and this will amount to the
kind of learnability for which Davidson wishes to account.

Our mastery of a particular language is given, then, by our knowledge of a theoretical structure: to understand the language is to have a theory for it. The theory by which we understand a language is smaller than the language, and so the language is unified by its theoretical structure. Any of its sentences will, if it is a well-formed sentence, have the kind of structure (and meaning) the theory prescribes.

Davidson would presumably agree that complete mastery of any language is never really exemplified. There are any number of English sentences which a competent speaker of the language may not understand, such as:

1. "Long term potentiation in dentate dyrae can be induced by asynchronous volleys in separate afferents."
2. "The moral law is the fact of reason."

That neither of these sentences is likely to be comprehensible to the average competent English speaker is, I take it, an empirical fact; the reasons differ slightly. The first sentence contains some of the specialized scientific vocabulary of murine neurology.[6] Since it is grammatically well-formed, Davidson will attribute an English speaker's failure to understand it to ignorance of the words it contains. Either those unknown words are semantic primitives—that is, cannot be removed by paraphrase with any other words of English; or they are not semantic primitives, can be paraphrased with other English words, and the hearer has not learned how to do this.[7] Which is the case can be decided, presumably, only by undertaking to paraphrase: if all attempts fail, we are dealing with semantic primitives. In any case, the lesson for Davidson will presumably be, though he does not say so, that our languages are expanding all the time, especially with the growth of scientific vocabularies, and that the number of primitive terms-plus-paraphases which would give the whole vocabulary of the language may (probably has) become too large for any human being to master in one lifetime. The lesson for us is that "semantic primitives" can be hard to recognize. Paraphrasability is a complicated property, and recognizing the semanically primitive may require sophisticated testing.

Example (2) uses terms from ordinary English, but uses them in their specifically Kantian senses. The lesson here is that words which are, in themselves, quite well-known may have other senses with which a given average speaker is quite unfamiliar. Some of these, again, may be paraphrasable and some not. That a word may have some senses which admit of paraphrase by other words in the language, and others which do not, makes it even harder to tell what is or is not a semantic primitive.

Indeed, it would seem that in the last instance we must attempt paraphrase with every other word in the language before we can tell whether
or not this particular word is semantically primitive.

My aim here is not to suggest that Davidson cannot accommodate
these examples, but to point out a danger that they show his program to
run: that of explaining our mysterious ability to understand any member
of an enormously large, even infinite set of utterances by an implicit appeal to an equally mysterious ability to recognize and learn semantic
primitives.[8] The danger points us toward Wittgenstein.[9] For his thought,
also keyed to the learnability of language, avoids the notion of a "semantic primitive" that can be recognized as such only via sophisticated testing. What is "primitive" for Wittgenstein is not sentences or sentence
components, but certain language games: those in which "one can command a clear view of the aim and functioning of the words."[10] The primitiveness in question is also different: Wittgenstein's "primitives" are not
objects of recursive procedures, but simply particularly lucid examples.
There will be no problem, then, about how to recognize primitiveness
when it occurs, because recognizability is built into its definition: primitiveness evidences itself to those monitoring a language game (including
those playing it) in that all goes smoothly and there is nothing that they
feel they do not understand. In terms of Wittgenstein's beloved analogy
to music, there are no false notes.[11] This may be mysterious, but it is no
more mysterious than other capacities involved in understanding utterances, because it is the same: to recognize a linguistic primitive is to understand a language game.

Linguistic rules, for Wittgenstein, are to be understood in terms
of language games, and not vice versa. Indeed, he avoids formal appeal
to rules altogether. They function differently, he says, in different language games and at different times. They may serve as aids in learning
the game, or as moves in the game itself (as when a football coach argues
with a referee to give his team a brief rest); as general patterns read off
the play by observers who do not know the game; and so on.[12] Moreover,
rules do not univocally prescribe actions, but merely indicate the general
sort of thing that may or may not be done.[13]

For present purposes, what Wittgenstein is denying with his many
examples and reminders is twofold: (a) that language is learnable in Davidson's sense, and (b) that the concept of learnability tells us very much
about language and how we speak and understand it. For Wittgenstein,
"language" is an open-textured concept: we can give examples that clearly
are examples of language use, but we cannot achieve lasting clarity at the
edges. There are all sorts of activity which are borderline linguistic, bor-

derline nonlinguistic, or "linguistic" in a sense not suggested by whatever examples we may have given.[14] And new language games are always coming into being, while old ones fall into disuse.[15] Since we cannot understand a word except in terms of its functioning within a language game, there will always be sentences that we do not understand—even in languages which we have, in all reasonable senses, "mastered."

If learning a language is thus for Wittgenstein partial and always incomplete, how does it come about? What do persons know when they have mastered a language? As we might expect, there are for Wittgenstein many ways to learn a language. We may have its rules taught to us in a classroom. We may learn one language game from having played other, similar (perhaps simpler) language games, picking up the new details as we go along.[16] In all cases, what we learn is chunks of verbal behavior, which we are eventually able to produce without explicit awareness, either of the patterns which provoke them or of the rules by which they are produced.[17] To put it slightly differently: for Wittgenstein a word has meaning if and only if it can be used in a language game—that is, woven into a pattern of interpersonal activity.[18] And a language game is itself part of a "form of life," which (as J. F. M. Hunter has shown) is for Wittgenstein a learned response that we come to produce as if instinctively, so that eventually (in Wittgenstein's words), "it is natural for us to say a sentence in such-and-such a context, and unnatural to say it in isolation."[19] The capacity to perform without attention actions which had previously to be learned is precisely what Hegel calls a "habit" (and Wittgenstein calls a *Gepflogenheit*);[20] in the *Philosophical Investigations* (¶508), Wittgenstein refers to a failure to be habituated (*gewöhnt*) into a particular language as a failure to "master" it. Indeed, one of Wittgenstein's standard ways of referring to the language we all speak is as *die gewöhnliche Sprache*, usually translated as "ordinary language" but also translatable as "customary language."[21]

For Davidson, to know a language is to have mastered a set of primitives and rules; for Wittgenstein, though he never actually puts it that way, it is to have acquired a set of habits—a set that, as linguistic, includes verbal behavior shared with others. For Hegel, the set of habits (*Gewohnheiten*) that a person has acquired is in large part a mass of unrelated propensities, contingently developed and each isolable from the rest. Applying this to Wittgenstein leads us to ask: What sort of unity can he attribute to language as he conceives it? Is language for him anything over and above the various individual language games that are played?

The answers, several commentators have urged, are none and

no.[22] Even one of the simplest and most impoverished of Wittgenstein's language games—the "slab" game which opens the *Philosophical Investigations*—is he says to be conceived as a complete (*vollständig*) language, and may indeed be viewed as the whole language of an entire tribe.[23] It follows that what "slab" means in this particular language game will not be illuminated by what it means, for example, on a menu ("a juicy slab of aged roast beef"), in forestry ("Slab that log!"), and baseball ("The pitcher just stepped off the slab"). Not merely are such extraneous uses not illuminating; they can be positively misleading. Many of the philosophical errors that Wittgenstein wishes to exorcise derive from mixing up language games, carrying what is proper to one over to another: thinking of the language of sensations, for example, in terms of the language which we use to describe physical objects.[24] Any language game—any sufficiently primitive one, at least—is thus capable of being played and understood in complete isolation from all other language, and this is what needs to be understood about it; holistic approaches to language and meaning are bound to mislead.

There is room to doubt whether Wittgenstein can have intended this degree of isolation. His statements at ¶¶2 and 7 really say nothing more than that the slab game is a primitive one, since as we have seen "primitive" language games are by definition intelligible in themselves, independently of all else. And certainly to deny *all* unity to language would run counter both to the account of learning I noted in ¶31 (which made explicit appeal to carry-overs from one language game to another), and to the general "family resemblance" type of identity Wittgenstein wants to apply to language, which I will discuss later in this chapter.[25]

But a key dimension of Wittgenstein's philosophy is its therapeutic side, which aims to free philosophers from various puzzles they have gotten themselves into. It is clear that some of those puzzles result from philosophers approaching questions of meaning at too high a level of generality.[26] For the view that a word means the same thing on all occasions of its use licenses the kind of indiscriminate and misleading carry-over from one language game to another that Wittgenstein is concerned to expose. In that regard, as Charles Hardwick has put it, Wittgenstein's key insight is that

> we have a precise understanding of the particular use of a
> word [within a particular language game] and at best only a
> vague understanding of its general use.[27]

Or, as Wittgenstein himself puts a similar point:

> The inexpressible [*unsägliche*] diversity of all the everyday language games escapes our consciousness because the clothing of our language makes everything alike.[28]

There are now two issues between Davidson and Wittgenstein. Davidson views our knowledge of meaning narrowly, as a theoretical matter: to understand a language is to have a theory for it, one consisting of primitive terms and rules for combining these into more complex expressions. For Wittgenstein, the meaning of a term is broader: a pattern of habitual activity, the term's use in a language game. And for Davidson the rules of a language, being a finite and determinate set, give that language a kind of unity: they can operate on its semantic primitives to generate every expression possible in the language. For Wittgenstein, a language ultimately reduces to a mass of habits, "forms of life," which have no discernible unity.

Unification as theory, fragmentation as practice: a pair of ancient oppositions surfaces here again. What if the kind of unity that Davidson attributes to language could be vindicated also for a Wittgensteinian view that language is practical? What if Wittgenstein's insight that language is disunified could be vindicated for Davidson's view that it is theoretical? The latter task, I will argue, is accomplished by Davidson's own "A Nice Derangement of Epitaphs."[29] The former conduces to the Hegelian paradigm sketched here.

Wittgenstein has not, simply by relocating meaning from the theoretical to the practical level, successfully avoided the problem of the unity of language. Davidson's holism has, I suggested, many levels. Consider, as a second level, that which concerns the reduction of words to sentences. Since it is only in a sentence that a word can have meaning, Davidson can define a word as "an aspect of a sentence that recurs in other sentences, and can be assigned identical roles in other sentences."[30] There is thus no way to give the meaning of a word except by giving the meanings of the various sentences in which it occurs. And this means that we can give the meaning of a single word only in the course of giving the meaning of every word or sentence in the language.[31] For as I reconstruct Davidson here, if we leave one word out, then we will leave undetermined the meaning of every sentence in which it occurs; and since the meaning of the sentence determines that of the words in it, we will leave undetermined the meaning of every other word in that sentence. But that means, in turn, that we will leave undetermined the

meaning of that larger set of sentences which contains occurrences of
those other words; and so on. The spreading indeterminacy is unstoppa-
ble, and is generated by the conjunction of these two claims:

1. Meaning is exhibited only by complex linguistic entities (sentences).
2. The components of such entities (words) can migrate from entity to
   entity.

But Wittgenstein would not deny either of these. If in (1) we substitute "language game" for "sentence," we have the familiar dictum
that a word only has meaning in the context of a language game.[32] And in
spite of Wittgenstein's concern about the danger of indiscriminate carry-
over of meaning from one language game to another, he did allow that
such carry-overs exist, as is shown by comparing the language games
given in the *Philosophical Investigations* at ¶¶2 and 8, for example, or
¶¶48 and 64: in both cases the latter game is a modification of the former and contains some of its moves. There is then no way to give the full
meaning of a word except by showing how it functions in *all* the language games in which it occurs. To do this is to clarify what Wittgenstein
calls the "grammar" of the word. This is not the same thing as the word's
use, its role in a specific language game: Wittgenstein recurrently relates
the "grammar" of a word to its connections with other words, not just in
this or that language game, but in the language as a whole, so that the
"grammar" of a word is the sum of its functions within the various language games where it can be used.[33] In order to trace such a grammar
out, we must give the meanings of whatever other expressions occur in
the same language games as the word we are trying to understand; until
we have achieved that, we have not understood the word with which we
started. But in order to clarify the grammar of those further expressions,
we must go to a further set of language games in which those expressions
occur not with our original word, but with still others, and so on: "*Einen
Satz verstehen*," writes Wittgenstein with supreme ambiguity, "*heißt, eine
Sprache verstehen*."[34] He presumably does not mean by this that a language, as an object of understanding, can only be a single assertion. Also
possible, and suggested by the parallels to Davidson's argument, is that
short of learning a whole language, we have not understood our original
language game.

True, there is less migration of component expressions from one
complex to another in Wittgenstein than in Davidson. It is more common, in fact de rigueur, for Davidsonian words to recur in other sentences than for Wittgensteinian expressions to recur in other language

games; indeed, it is hard to call a phoneme which only occurs in one sentence a "word" at all. So the spread of indeterminacy is slower for Wittgenstein; but it is there, and for both thinkers there is a sense in which a language must be learned as a whole. Only Davidson, however, formulates this holism explicitly and draws its consequences. It remains in the background for Wittgenstein, presumably because of his interest in therapy—in rooting out cases in which words are unconsciously, and misleadingly, carried over from one language game to another. This therapeutic concern gives Wittgenstein his characteristic focus on primitive—that is, independently intelligible—language games; but elevated from its polemical context into a general theory of language, it leads us to underestimate language's unity. Davidson, then, wins this first round, and we must return to see more clearly how he articulates what Wittgenstein misses: the unity of language.

One kind of unity that might be attributed to language is suggested by David Pole:

> Language is unitary by reason of certain structural concepts
> that appear constantly throughout the plurality of its parts or
> departments; it is these which hold it together.[35]

It is just such structural unity which Davidson, in his earlier writings,[36] finds in language, and the single "structural concept" that gives it is that of truth.

Truth and Language

The centrality of the concept of truth in Davidson's philosophy—a centrality in which, as he notes, he excels even Quine[37]—has played its role on the levels of holism that I have already discussed. Davidson's analogy between the structure of logical systems and that of language as a whole implies it, for the business of logical systems has since Aristotle been to preserve truth: to yield true conclusions from true premises.[38] And it lies behind Davidson's reduction of words to sentences, since the dictum that "a word has meaning only in a sentence" is grounded in the view that to mean something is to be true or false, and only sentences can do that. And, in fact, Davidson's usual way of referring to the theory which one must have mastered to know a language is as a "theory of truth." His central insight is that a theory of truth can function as a theory of meaning for a language.

The concept of truth defines not only Davidson's concept of meaning but that of language itself: "An action counts as linguistic," we read, "only if literal meaning is relevant."[39] If a language is a sign system in actual use (a view for which Davidson thinks there is "much to be said"), the use speakers make of it is to interpret sentences: to speak the same language as others is to expect them to interpret your sentences in the same way you do, and to interpret a sentence is just to specify the conditions under which it would be true.[40] A language is thus a set of signs to which truth-values can be assigned; we distinguish languages from one another by the ways in which we make the assignments. Truth, then, functions as precisely the kind of "structural unifier" to which we saw Pole refer.

Davidson's account of truth, one of the most subtle ever given, has two features which make it suitable for such a central role: truth, according to him, is both uniform and thin. By "uniform" I mean that Davidson would reject any Wittgensteinian family resemblance account of truth: "Truth," he writes, "is a single property which attaches, or fails to attach, to utterances." In particular, it can apply to any sentence, and holding a sentence for true is "a single attitude applicable to all sentences." Being thus general, Davidson's theory of truth is also "thin" in that it is ontologically highly uncommitted. In "True to the Facts" Davidson argues against the commonplace version of the correspondence theory which holds that the universe contains packets of reality called "facts," and that a given sentence is true (or false) of one of these packets. A normal or "genuine" sentence is true not if it corresponds to some particular portion of the universe, but if the universe itself as a whole—in Davidson's phrase, the "Great Fact"—supports it. We need not have an ontology of things with properties, or of substances outside the mind and ideas in it, or indeed any determinate ontology at all, in order to have Davidsonian truth. We need only to dwell among creatures who assent to, and dissent from, sentences in ways consistently related to what is going on around them. The really functional aspect of a sentence's truth, then—the aspect of it which makes truth convertible into meaning—is not the relation of that sentence to reality. It is rather a matter of human behavior: that speakers of a language hold that sentence for true. The truth theory for a language takes its empirical purchase not from true sentences, but from someone's holding sentences for true.

Holding for true is thus the evidentiary basis for a theory of interpretation: we learn to interpret a language by seeing what utterances speakers of it hold for true, and in what circumstances.[41] As such a basis, holding for true must be (at least in part, and at least sometimes) empirically accessible: a public phenomenon. Because of this, whether someone holds a given sentence for true is determinable independently of whatever beliefs and attitudes, or mental states generally, a person may have, and it can serve as the basis for attributing such states to her.[42] For Davidson as for Wittgenstein, then (and for Hegel), meaning is intrinsically public; it is not a set of private thoughts to which we attach public words. One cannot have a language—cannot even think—unless one is an interpreter of the language of others.[43] While to know a language is for Davidson to have a theoretical kind of knowledge, that theory is ultimately a theory of the practices of others: of what they are holding for true. Whatever the criteria are by which we recognize others to hold sentences for true, they constitute rules for the use of language, and holding for true is a sort of language game. But it is not one independent of all others; rather, it is basic to all of them.[44]

Thus again, for Davidson as for Wittgenstein, language is essentially a set of human activities. For Davidson, unlike for Wittgenstein, these activities are united by the fact that they all, in one way or another, depend on or reduce to assenting to sentences. But granted that Davidson has clarified and accounted for one structurally unifying concept of language, are we to say that he has achieved a complete account of language? Davidson himself is careful to note some limitations of his theories.

On the one hand, we have seen, holding for true is a basic linguistic activity, and if to learn a language is to formulate a theory of truth for that language, holding for true is basic to our learning: it is the fundamental datum from which theory formation begins, or, as Davidson puts it:

> All the evidence for or against a theory of truth (interpreta-
> tion, translation) comes in the form of facts about what events
> or situations in the world cause, or would cause, speakers to as-
> sent to, or dissent from, each sentence in the speaker's
> repertoire.[45]

So held Davidson in 1979. But by 1981 we read that contexts of honest assertion are not indispensable to learning language because "much language learning takes place during games, in hearing stories and in pretence."[46] Indeed, much learning, as a form of initiation into practice or ultimately of habit formation, takes place via imitation,[47] and here it seems that truth conditions may play no role at all. Suppose that Little George is playing while his father cooks dinner. He observes the adult touch a round coil (which, unbeknownst to George, is a hot burner), pull his hand back with a sharp cry, suck his finger, roll his eyes, and cry "It's hot!" Little George then reaches out, touches the refrigerator, pulls his hand back, sucks his finger, rolls his eyes, and cries "It's hot!"

We cannot, I think, say that Little George's utterance exhibits the kind of structure to which Davidson refers to on p. 272 of "Communication and Convention": that it is composed of a speech act (descriptive) plus an "ulterior purpose" (communicating pain). Little George clearly does not know what is, and is not, hot; he is unable to use the sentence descriptively, and knows nothing, or almost nothing, about its truth conditions;[48] its literal meaning is in fact irrelevant to him, he has no intention to communicate pain by means of it, and in Davidson's view he performs, strictly speaking, no *linguistic* act at all (whence it also follows that George's purpose, whatever it may be, cannot be ulterior to such an act). What Little George does learn is how the words "It's hot" fit into larger activities of behavior: he has begun to master a language game. Davidson must say that such knowledge has nothing to do with the meaning of the term "hot," and that the behavioral context of the term is not linguistic at all. Little George has, it appears, learned nothing about language.

But this raises questions about the status of "holding for true." Suppose I am constructing a theory of truth for a sentence in a language I hardly know. I want to see if a speaker of that language holds that sentence to be true, so I cause it to be uttered in her presence and observe her reactions. Like Little George observing his father, I do not know what in the ambient circumstances (other than hearing the sentence) provokes the reaction; but I do know what the reaction is. Little George, of course, did the same thing while observing his father: he heard the words "It's hot!" and then observed his father's subsequent behavior. What Little George does is in fact rather similar to what Davidson would call "learning a language." It would *be* learning a language if George were concerned to figure out exactly what in the ambient circumstances provoked his father's reaction, rather than with imitating that reaction.

It therefore seems that, as Wittgenstein argued with respect to ostension,[49] the first thing we do with any utterance, before we can even recognize that another person views it as sentential at all, is fit it into the ongoing context of her behavior. This, then, is the behavioral dimension to what, in chapter 5, I called "keeping symbols straight." To keep a symbol straight was, as I expounded it there, to fit it into a larger context of information. But the larger contexts into which we fit symbols are not necessarily restricted to merely the kind of cognitive informedness I discussed there; parts of them may be public and behavioral as well: a set of practices triggered by the word or utterance. Indeed, we may regard "behavior" itself as a sort of public display of background information—the "informed" movements of the bodies of those who hear a word or utterance.[50]

Only when an utterance has been thus fitted into a larger behavioral context do we know that another person assents to it or dissents from it, and only thence do we get the behavioral data for our theory of truth. It seems that a wider account of language is necessary on Davidson's own terms—one which recognizes what we might call, using a non-Wittgensteinian term for a Wittgensteinian notion, the "practical meaning" of expressions—to supplement the account Davidson has given of their cognitive meaning. The practical meaning of a term is then the set of practices associated with it—that trigger, it, accompany it, or are triggered by it.[51] Such practical meaning is linguistic in the sense that it uses words; but for Davidson it must be ultimately nonlinguistic, because it is not reducible to the truth of the sentences formed with those words.

A certain price has thus been paid for the kind of unity Davidson has attributed to language. In the first place, much that we might call (and Wittgenstein certainly would call) "linguistic" has to be excluded from what is thus unified. Second, what is excluded includes cases strangely similar to what Davidson considers the basic linguistic attitude: that of seeing someone else hold something for true. Holding for true is thus parasitic upon a larger class of ways to deal with words—namely, to see them as woven into practices. So this second round goes to Wittgenstein, and we have an aporia: Davidson must be right that language has more unity than Wittgenstein explicitly allows, but wrong to think that the unity can be entirely accounted for if we make holding for true the basic behavior underlying all our understanding of language. Wittgenstein is right to think that truth telling cannot structurally unify language, but wrong to disregard the unity language must have, even on his own view. A truly holistic account of language would have to see it as unified, then, on the behavioral level. A Hegelian approach would aim not merely to "see" such unity, but to highlight and enhance it by defining the most general and basic terms of a language in terms of one another.

Language, Time, and History

Wittgenstein is concerned with fragmenting timeless essences; eventually, in his therapeutic practice, he dissolves language into diverse, independent games whose structural unity is recognized but never articulated. Another important insight left undeveloped in Wittgenstein's philosophical practice is that language games are not eternal, that they are born and die. I have mentioned that for Wittgenstein new language games are always coming into being, while others are passing away.[52] But this is not for him a *philosophically* relevant fact. This is not unrelated to my previous point about the unity of language. It is, as David Pole has argued, Wittgenstein's tendency to treat language games as self-contained entities that gives him problems with accounting for language change. For such change—extension or revision of language games—is brought about, in the main, by inadequacies in the presently existing games: somebody finds herself unable to say what she wants to say, and invents a new way of speaking to convey herself. But the idea that a language game is somehow inadequate cannot be accommodated by Wittgenstein's conceptual framework:

> If we refer to the rules of the present language game, it [our
> new way of speaking] will simply be counted as wrong; other-
> wise we must think of it as belonging to another language game
> of its own.[53]

An example of this is Wittgenstein's famous account of family resemblance in the *Philosophical Investigations*, at (roughly) ¶¶66–76. In spite of reservations expressed elsewhere about vision as a model for knowledge,[54] at ¶66 Wittgenstein uses just such a model, asking us to take examples of activities we call "games" and "see" (*schau*) if there is any common element to them:

> And the result of this observation [*Betrachtung*] runs like this:
> We see [*sehen*] a complicated net of similarities that overlap
> [*übergreifen*] and cross one another. Similarities in large and
> small matters.

The visionary nature of both method and result here means that temporal differences among the different types of game are obscured: the facts that ball games preceded board games, and board games preceded card

games; that games played for fun predate games played for money; and
so on.

This leads to a telling irony in ¶67, where games are said to form a
"family" because of the kind of resemblances they have to one another:

> I can think of no better expression to characterize these simi-
> larities than "family resemblances"; for the various resem-
> blances between the members of a family: build, features, color
> of eyes, gait, temperament, etc., etc. overlap and crisscross in
> the same way.—And I shall say: "games" form a family.

As the rest of ¶67 goes on paradoxically to highlight, however, a "family" is just what Wittgenstein has not *seen*. Suppose we view a picture of a
number of people, some of whom share the same shape of eye, others of
mouth, others coloration, and so on, all overlapping and crisscrossing in
the way Wittgenstein specifies. We would not, I think, be tempted to call
them a "family" unless some of them were obviously much older than
others; if all the people were about the same age, we might suspect that
the picture is of a group of siblings or cousins. But a family includes
descent, and has more than one generation.[55] And a picture will not normally be taken to portray a family unless some people in it look old
enough to be parents of others.

A point of which the rest of ¶67 shows itself to be aware. For it
adverts to the *history* of the concept of number, and its gradual extension, as mathematics progressed, to new sorts of entity.[56] Words acquire
new meanings by being spun out in time; to have a family of meanings is
to be engaged in a temporal development. To be true to the situation
with respect to "game," we would have to consider its various meanings
in the historical order in which they present themselves, reconstructing
the history of the concept across the language games which have been
played with it. Our description would have, in other words, to become a
narrative. As I will show in chapter 11, Wittgenstein does view language
games as, in a sense, narratively given. A language game, I will argue
there, must for Wittgenstein be more than a simple sequence of utterances, because unless it manifests some sort of development over time,
we would be unable to recognize "wrong" moves. But this sort of narrative awareness is in any case confined to individual language games. It
does not extend to the perception of such games themselves as evolving
from one another in a comprehensible history, as opposed to simply following one another arbitrarily. Hence, in ¶67 as elsewhere, Wittgenstein's gaze is decisively fixed on what happens within the individual

language game; he does not consider the possibility of narrative development from one language game to another. While he is willing to recognize that those mathematicians who extended the concept of number did
not begin wholly new language games but extended old ones, he is reluc-
tant to apply this sort of insight to his discussions of ordinary language.

We can understand that reluctance further by recalling the specific context for the discussion of family resemblance, given at ¶65. It
was an accusation: that Wittgenstein had nowhere given the "essence" of
language games (*das Wesentliche des Sprachspiels, und also der Sprache*). By
"essence" here, as ¶92 tells us, Wittgenstein means quite specifically
something unitary, hidden, and fixed for all time. The concept of family
resemblance, one of Wittgenstein's most profound and revolutionary innovations, is thus introduced not as part of a general theory of meaning
but therapeutically, to combat a specific sort of essentialism. His fundamental claim is that what we "see" in "observing" language games gives
us no reason to postulate timeless essences. But timeless essences are not
the only alternatives to Wittgenstein's own practice. Also possible is that
the manifold diversity of games now present in our world can be seen to
be reconstructible historically, to some degree, so that they manifest, not
a timeless essence, but an intelligible development of the type I documented in Hegelian historical dialectics (chapter 4).[57] In such development, change is minimal at each stage (determinate negation). It is also
rationally warranted at each stage—but, as was seen, by warrants which
may not be even generically similar to one another. Hence, no set of
rules persists through and governs the entire development: no single
warrant or essence guides the whole manifold.

This possibility is not impeached by Wittgenstein's arguments,
and indeed is underwitten by most of ¶67, for it amounts to family resemblances unfolding over time. Articulating it philosophically is, to be
sure, not relevant to Wittgenstein's concern, which is the refutation of
timeless essences. But it is a possibility to be taken seriously by those who
seek to expand Wittgenstein's insights into a philosophy of language. To
ignore it is to ignore the "intergenerational" filiations among the various meanings of a word: to show ourselves unable to appreciate the difference between a collection of orphaned linguistic siblings and a
linguistic family.

Davidson's thought is equally resistant to history, but from a different direction: from the urge to consider language, not in terms of
unrelated instances, but as a formal whole. Truth for Davidson, we saw, is
a single property which any sentence either does or does not have; in
itself it appears to be timeless—as timeless as the kind of truth that we

saw Solomon, in chapter 1, attribute to Hegel. But it is a property whose instances can change. Truth-values must, indeed, be constantly redistributed over the sentences of a language, as the world turns: or, as Davidson puts it, "truth (in a given natural language) is not a property of sentences; it is a relation between sentences, speakers, and dates."[58]

If truth is a single, unchanging property, then redistributing it among sentences is much easier if the truth *conditions* for those sentences also are unchanging. If, a few moments ago, I said that "The sky is blue," and now I have to redistribute truth-values because of an approaching storm and say that the sky is gray, the meanings of "sky," "gray," and "blue" have not, I must hope, changed in the meantime. If they have, I have a double task: on the one hand, I must sort out the new meanings for the terms, and on the other hand must assign truth-values to the sentences in which they now occur. Moreover, these are not for Davidson two separate tasks: the new meaning of the word will be evident only in that I assign a new truth-value to a sentence containing it. But then it becomes impossible to separate redistributing truth-values from redefining terms, and the norms of language are endangered by the passing of time. Thus, if someone says "The sky is blue" when in fact it is gray, there are only two possibilities: either she is speaking falsely, or the meaning of "gray" has changed without my knowledge. I have no easy way to tell which is the case. I may, as Davidson has recommended, be charitable and suppose the other person is telling the truth.[59] But I cannot do that always, lest I arrive at a world in which languages change very fast and no one is ever mistaken. So I may decide, as Davidson also recommends,[60] to dismiss her utterance as false or idiosyncratic until its pattern is repeated, thus holding the meanings of its terms—the ways they affect truth conditions of the sentences in which they occur—as unitary, unchanging, and "identical" as possible.

It is this latter tack that seems to motivate Davidson's stringent criterion for the identity of a word. Words are, Davidson tells us, "aspects of sentences that recur in other sentences, and can be assigned identical roles in other sentences." Those roles are "their systematic effect on the meanings of the sentences in which they occur" (i.e., the way in which they make the sentences that contain them true or false).[61] The roles are "identical," not similar; a word has a "systematic effect," not "effects." It is this singularity of effect that makes the word's roles in various sentences identical, and thus makes it *a* word at all. The strictness of this rules out much of the open-texturedness to which Wittgenstein likes to appeal, and to the extent that those appeals are valid, it is theoretically suspect. Its motivation, I have argued, is practical: we can redistribute truth-values intelligently only as long as we have stable truth conditions in terms of which to do so.

However motivated, the demand leads to difficulties, as Wittgenstein would point out, in being elevated to a general theory of language. In addition to Wittgenstein's basic point that language is open textured, so that a word does not in fact make an "identical" contribution even to the truth of all the sentences in which it occurs, Davidson's adoption of singularity of effect as the criterion for the identity of a word leaves unclear why it is that, so far as we know, every single word in every single natural language has a multitude of meanings—sometimes united by family resemblance, sometimes not obviously even by that. Polysemy is so widespread in language as to be prima facie essential to it.[62] Knowing the variety of ways in which a given utterance might be construed by its hearers is necessary to using that utterance effectively, and hence is part of knowing the language in which that sentence occurs. Any theory of language that leaves out polysemy is thus in danger of serious incompleteness.

Because a word can never change meaning if it has "identical" roles in all the sentences in which it occurs, Davidson also has problems with the phenomenon of meaning change—problems which have led to some of his most startlingly original insights. Because of his strong emphasis on the social nature of language, meaning change is revealed for Davidson in the fact that

> we are very good at arriving at a correct interpretation of words we have not heard before, or of words we have not heard before with meanings a speaker is giving them.[63]

In "Radical Interpretation" (1973), this was viewed as a problem of translation: the strange utterance is perceived to be in an unknown language, and must be translated into a known one.[64] In "A Nice Derangement," the strange utterance is viewed as itself possibly unique and momentary, and so not part of a "language" in the ordinary sense; our reaction to it passes beyond translation to sheer invention. In this context, Davidson distinguishes between what he calls the "prior theory" of a language, which contains our knowledge about what its terms mean for our interlocutor and which we bring to our encounter with her, and the "passing theories" which result from our improvisations as we attempt to understand her on individual occasions. This introduces a third possibility into what was earlier a dichotomy, for I no longer have to decide whether my interlocutor is speaking falsely or "the" meaning of her words has changed. Now open is that the meaning has indeed changed, but only for the moment and only for my interlocutor.

Since the passing theory responds to all sorts of momentary deviations from normal usage, it is not itself a "linguistic" theory, and we do not form it by "linguistic competence." It turns out, moreover, that the passing theory does all the work: two interlocutors do not need to have the same linguistic starting point to understand each other, so long as at the end of their exchange they have learned enough about each other to make their passing theories sufficiently similar. Hence, there is no such thing as a body of linguistic knowledge which must be *shared in advance* of any particular interchange and then employed in the act of communicating. Since, in the tradition that Davidson wants to criticize, "language" is defined, precisely, as a theory of meaning shared by speakers in advance of any case of their interaction, he arrives at the paradoxical conclusion that there is no such thing as a language.

It now seems that Davidson has fragmented language as thoroughly as did Wittgenstein; that instead of an indeterminate variety of language games, we have an indeterminate variety of prior and passing theories. Certainly Davidson, in "A Nice Derangement," sounds this way:

> We have discovered no common core of consistent behavior,
> no shared grammar or rules, no portable interpreting machine
> set to grind out the meaning of an arbitrary utterance. (p. 445)

But this would be premature. My phrase "shared in advance" was intended to suggest that what Davidson has refuted here is the notion of a static, learnable language with which he (and others) began—a language whose terms retain their meanings over repeated use. For Wittgenstein, though as we saw he does not develop the insight, we must continually improvise new rules for language games—making rules up, sometimes, as we go along (*PI*, ¶83). For "A Nice Derangement," our linguistic knowledge retains its primarily theoretical structure: it is just that the theories can change, radically, from moment to moment. It seems that Davidson has fragmented language into the kind of disunity evident in Wittgenstein, without revoking the theoretical character it had in his earlier writings.

That is not quite the case; in fact Davidson leaves us with a general characterization of language—a structurally unifying concept, but now a dynamic one. For the theory of truth with which a hearer operates is no longer, if it ever was, something she merely learns or possesses. It is something she actively changes, from moment to moment. Speaker and hearer start with a body of knowledge, which to some degree differs for each: their prior theories. And, as they talk, these prior theories—and passing theories—become, if their communication is successful, more and more alike. So language does have, even for the Davidson of "A Nice Derangement," a basic unity: it is the convergence of speakers and interpreters, from time to time, on a passing theory.[65] This unity, then, is no longer something given by language's logical structure. It is actively brought about by the formation, and reformation, of passing theories.

The intergenerationality of a Wittgensteinian language game, and the convergence of Davidsonian passing theories, open up what I call the "essential temporality" of language. By this I do not mean the simple fact that utterances come and go in time, or that their truth-value often (even always) depends partly on the times at which they are uttered. Such views are perfectly compatible with the view that grammar and meaning persist unchanged. What I have in mind is rather the broadly Heideggerian point that everything about language is mortal: in particular that words, like people, are born of pain and hope; that, like people, they grow and find their place, perhaps flourish and contribute; that eventually they lose force and die. Trying to understand language without taking this dimension of it into account is like trying to study only those qualities of human beings that they would have if they were immortal. If some types of logic can be viewed as linguisticized metaphysics, this type of study would have to be seen as linguistic angelology. Not that it is therefore a waste of time: we share, I hope, many qualities with the angels (if they exist); and those qualities are what is best in us. But we share them only briefly, and that makes an enormous difference.

"History" is the sum of temporal developments which last longer than single human lives, which they can contain and to some degree govern. The temporality of language, which Wittgenstein and Davidson broach, leads to its historicality, which they do not. Wittgenstein, as chapter 11 will argue, recognizes the temporality of individual language games—that it is essential to them to unroll in time. But this temporality, I have argued here, is kept within strict bounds—the bounds of a single language game. Similarly for "A Nice Derangement." The convergence of speaker and hearer is clearly a *temporal* phenomenon, beginning as it does from divergent prior theories which each speaker/interpreter modifies as the occasion demands, and against which each measures those same demands. But the kind of modification Davidson is talking about takes place over minutes or at the most a lifetime, as opposed to the longer trends we normally associate with the "historical." "A Nice Derangement" recognizes the temporality of language in ways its writer earlier did not; but, like the *Philosophical Investigations*, it keeps that temporality within narrow bounds so that it cannot become historical.

Is it certain that convergence of the type Davidson calls to our attention can be held within such bounds? Is it not possible that it is a longer term, historical phenomenon?

The passing theory is transient, and hence not a "language," certainly not one that anyone would want to learn. But in order to maintain that language is not historical, we would have to maintain that the transient improvisations peculiar to passing theories were without larger effects on the speech community.[66] A prior theory, on Davidson's account, is also, since it is geared to a concrete individual, relatively transient. But Davidson's account of prior theories is unduly narrow, and can be broadened in two steps. First, as Davidson points out, prior theories can be more or less detailed, depending on how much I know about my interlocutor. In some cases (Davidson's examples include ordering in a restaurant and giving directions to a taxi driver), we may know so little about her that we can do no better than to assume that she

> will interpret our speech along what we take to be standard lines. But all this is relative. In fact we always have the interpreter in mind; there is no such thing as how we expect, in the abstract, to be interpreted. We inhibit our higher vocabulary, or encourage it, depending on the most general considerations, and we cannot fail to have premonitions as to which of the proper names we know are apt to be correctly understood.[67]

Prior theories, it seems, stand along a continuum. At one end are cases where we are confronting, and trying to understand, someone who, we may have reason to believe, is very individualistic in her use of words (as, for example, is Sheridan's Mrs. Malaprop). At the other end are cases in which we assume no more about our interlocutor than that she goes by the most general rules of interpretation that our culture contains, or (as Davidson would once have said), that she "speaks our language." Quine keys his entire philosophy of language to the latter sort of case—to what he calls the "language of the marketplace."[68] Davidson's version of it is the closest he comes to the traditional idea of a language. Between these two, but unmentioned by Davidson, are cases where my expectations about others are formed, not from what I know about them as individuals, or from my general expectation that they speak my language, but on the basis of my beliefs about the category of person to which I assign them. If, in the middle of a conversation, I learn that my interlocutor belongs to some highly defined group, such as that he is a Catholic priest or a member of Congress, my expectations as to how he will interpret my utterances will change, perhaps so quickly as to leave me giddy. Taken in this direction, Davidson's conception of prior theories begins to gain political and ethical significance, because if I simply accept without qualm these changes in expectation, I am prejudiced.

The second step in broadening Davidson's view of passing theories is to see that the kind of "mid-level" prior theory I just mentioned may not only be *about* categories of individuals: it may be formulated *by* them as well. To grow up in a culture, to learn its language (which, as Davidson notes, now means to learn, more generally, how to find one's way around in that culture)[69] means to imbibe a number of expectations about how other groups of people will react to my utterances. If I am a Catholic, my prior theory about priests will differ from the corresponding theory in a Northern Irish Protestant. Prior theories, functioning on this mid-level, are thus historical phenomena: they pass on, though not usually without changes, from generation to generation. For each generation of speakers, they implant certain expectations about how certain others will respond to them, and thus to some extent govern their interactions with those others. When I understand someone who is different from me, more than our prior and passing theories may converge. Our cultures may as well.

Further New Terrain: Public and Political Language

The historicality of language, as an extension of the temporality that Davidson and Wittgenstein broach, is possibly fruitful terrain for philosophical treatment of language. Certainly Hegel thought so, for much of his concrete philosophical activity—the kind of thing he did in his lecture courses, and which I cannot discuss here—centered on reconstructing the historical developments of, and practices associated with, certain key words or parameters (such as "God," "art," and "the state"). But the terrain opened up by these reflections on Davidson is I think more than historical. Consider again Quine's "language of the marketplace": the language that passes between myself and people whom I do not know, about whom I have no expectation other than they will "speak my language." That Quine was able to build an entire philosophy of language around such speech indicates that it is an important phenomenon. But on Davidson's views, there is something mysterious about it. If all I have in the way of "linguistic" competence, outside of transient improvisations, is prior theories about individuals and groups, what justifies me in walking up to someone I have never seen before and speaking English to him or her, confident of a reply? Why, moreover, am I justified in this behavior if I am in Los Angeles, but not if I am in Marseilles or Hamburg?

The answer can only be political: English is the language of the United States, French that of France, German that of Germany; and Los Angeles, Marseilles, and Hamburg happen to be in those countries respectively. National languages exist because of the governments that sustain and promote, even enforce, them; before the rise of the nation-state they did not exist, and in many parts of the world they still do not. Where they do exist, it is not by nature but because government policy, in particular educational policy, has encouraged or enforced them. There is no other reason why I do not encounter Spanish everywhere in Los Angeles, or Provençal in Marseilles, or Plattdeutsch in Hamburg.

This political dimension has never been wholly ignored. But as long as language, the set of linguistic expectations shared among all members of a society, was given some other sort of reality—as a copy of nature, as transcendentally hard-wired in the human mind, as a set of games that just happen to be played around here, or as an interpreted logical system—the political aspect of language could be demoted and consideration of it deferred. Thus, in "Communication and Convention," Davidson could distinguish linguistic skill from whatever we gain by acculturation, and maintain that consideration of the latter had no useful light to shed on the nature of the former. After "A Nice Derangement" abolishes the distinction between linguistic and other skills, such separation is no longer possible.[70]

The concept of a prior theory thus makes the nature of national languages into a philosophical problem: for if all we have at our disposal are the theories we have formulated for individual speakers, our assumption that everyone we see, whether we know them or not, can understand what we say becomes quite mysterious. It also makes it hard to see how the explanation and justification of that assumption can be anything but political.

In sum: mid-level prior theories are often formed by, and used for and against, various groups in society; high-level prior theories are formulated, promoted, and occasionally enforced, by groups within society who claim, sometimes quite literally, to speak for it. The only "apolitical" use of language would be in encounters to which neither mid-level nor high-level prior theories were relevant. And such encounters are difficult to conceive: the parties to them would have, for example, to be genderless.

All this suggests a question for Wittgenstein. If we open almost any of his books, we see on one page a text in High German, which is a sort of Teutonic Esperanto largely invented by Martin Luther. Facing it will be a text in the King's English. What tempts Wittgenstein to call these "ordinary language" (*gewöhnliche Sprache*)? Both are, as a matter of empirical fact, brilliant creations of the human spirit; each is shot through with the best insights of Aristotle, Goethe, Shakespeare, and countless others famous and unknown. Nothing, in fact, could be less "ordinary" than our everyday language: the English word "hammer," for example, is an artifact so ancient that it once meant "stone." It is a museum-quality word.

Wittgenstein might respond that we are not normally aware of this extraordinary heritage of everyday language. Though words do commonly, as J. L. Austin put it, "trail clouds of etymology,"[71] when I walk down the road to buy groceries I do not normally recall that Shakespeare invented the word "road" or that grocers deal in things by the gross. But that we are not normally aware of the extraordinariness of ordinary language does not mean that we can investigate such language adequately by restricting ourselves to those of its aspects of which we normally *are* aware. If someone understood a supercomputer only well enough to run a word processing program, we would not say that she therefore understood supercomputers.

Wittgenstein would presumably answer that he is not in the business of attaining a general understanding of language, and that in fact he only discusses language in terms of his therapeutic project: the point is not that ordinary language is not a near-miraculous creation of the human spirit, but that it is *gewöhnlich* in the sense of "habitual." This response abandons the practice of using "ordinary language" as a paradigm for all language—a project which probably was never Wittgenstein's anyway—and in so doing opens up several types of new terrain for investigation.

Both Wittgenstein and Davidson, for example, understand language primarily through its use in private encounters. Almost all of Wittgenstein's examples of language use, in the *Philosophical Investigations*, are from the private sphere: political, literary, and other public

types of language are simply not dealt with. This is perhaps the result of
the atrophy of public discourse in the Vienna of Wittgenstein's formative years, which is comparable in scope to what occurred in the Red-
hunting America in which Davidson came of age.[72] But, like so much else
in the book, it also makes good sense in terms of Wittgenstein's therapeutic project, for the incursions of metaphysical essentialism into the
more intimate uses of language are surely among its most damaging effects. In "A Nice Derangement," language is also understood solely
through its operations in private encounters, the least intimate of which
are ordering coffee and giving directions to a taxi driver.[73] Davidson's
inattention to public language can be traced back through his writing, at
least to "True to the Facts" (1969). There, startlingly enough, the first
example given of a true sentence is quite false. French is not the official
language of Mauritius, though it is the language in which much of that
island's elite conducts its private affairs. The public, political, *official* language of Mauritius is English.[74]

But the public language of a society is not only political, and together with Davidson's avoidance of political matters goes a curious
change in attitude toward another major type of public language: literature. It is not until "What Metaphors Mean" (1978) that Davidson gives
other than passing mention to literary works; such works figure promi-
nently in that article and are central to "A Nice Derangement of Epitaphs" (1986). The reason for this change in attitude is given by
Davidson himself: metaphors and malapropisms become important to
him, not when he is developing his central theory of truth and meaning
(or of truth as meaning), but when he comes to reflect upon its limits.[75]
The surprising thing is that Davidson's reflections on literary language
(in a sense including that of Richard Sheridan's Mrs. Malaprop as well as
the sitcoms of Goodman Ace, an essay by Mark Singer, "Jabberwocky,"
and Shakespeare) should reveal a defect at the core of his previous theory—the hypostatization of language against which "A Nice Derangement" argues so brilliantly.

One of the morals of this is that language strange enough to require passing theories very different from our prior theories (and hence
able to suggest that distinction in a powerful way) occurs paradigmatically in literature.[76] And this point is not unconnected with one type of
meaning change I discussed earlier: that in which what is at first a strange
use of words eventually becomes integrated into the language and gains
"literal" meaning. For if you and I are talking, and you utter a brilliant
metaphor which I, coming to understand it, admire and repeat, your
new meanings have some chance of being taken up into community us-

age. But if you are a Shakespeare or even a Goodman Ace, and your metaphors are heard by thousands or millions of intelligent people, they have a much better chance of adoption. Hence, public language may change more dynamically than private language. It is not surprising that Davidson's later stress on language as dynamic, as continually transforming itself, should go together with a reduction of his earlier emphasis on the private sphere of language, and take its cue from the public language of literature. This emphasis on public language could be extended into investigations of other public languages, such as those of politics, religion, and science.[77]

Conclusions

It is now time to sketch out the space opened up by my demarcation of Wittgenstein and Davidson, a space into which can fit, perhaps not alone, the Hegelian paradigm I have been developing. It is a space which opens up with, between, and beyond Davidson and Wittgenstein.

With Davidson. For Hegel as for the Davidson of "A Nice Derangement," language does not so much exhibit unification as achieve it, again and again, as its speakers gradually create a company of words with which to understand one another. Hence the resemblance between what, in chapter 7, I called "universalization as a social process" and what Davidson comes to call "the convergence of passing theories." True, Hegel's version begins with a speaker who discovers that her hearers understand her utterances differently than she does herself, while Davidson begins with a hearer who suspects that a speaker understands what she herself says differently than does the hearer. But are these anything more than different sides of the same process? Both could be rewritten (though perhaps not interestingly captured) in terms of my rewriting, in chapter 4, of historical dialectics. One person would begin with one set of defining markers for a term (or, for Davidson, of truth conditions for it); the other would begin with a different set. They would then, by argument and experiment, add or drop members of those sets until their definitions converged. So construed, Hegelian historical dialectics would be largely a reconstruction of various processes of convergence that have resulted historically in the language we now have.

With Wittgenstein. But Davidson is not a reinvention of Hegel, because Hegel ultimately—in the case of the System itself—opts for a quasi-Wittgensteinian concept of meaning. For the meaning of a term in the System is, I have argued, simply its role in the System—the way it functions to abbreviate and explicate certain other Systematic words. The System, as an overall totality of words, then functions as the language game in which individual terms make sense.

Between Davidson and Wittgenstein, 1. But what is ultimate, for Hegel, is always *merely* ultimate. At other levels of culture, the kind of immanent meaning the System constructs is not possible, and words cannot be understood merely in terms of their relation to other words. They also refer and describe. We cannot, for Hegel, Systematize nature, for example: we can only describe it, in all its contingency. But the terms we use to describe it can converge with those that other individuals, other discourses, and other cultures, use, so that we are here close indeed to the kind of account Davidson might give of the function of a term. In general then, Hegel stands between Wittgenstein and Davidson in that he views meaning as not exclusively either theoretical or practical, but as a mixture of the two, depending on the type of discourse in which it is being used: a matter for detailed and localized investigation, as is (on Hegel's view) what he calls "truth."

Between Davidson and Wittgenstein, 2. Hegel believes that language not only recurrently attains unity, but that in many ways it has already attained it and so, as the earlier Davidson holds, exhibits it. Unlike the earlier Davidson, Hegel does not believe that this unity can be furnished by truth: as Wittgenstein argued, truth-telling is simply not that basic to language. For Hegel, then, language is unified in that it always involves, not some basic concept, but a basic practice. And that practice is nothing other than what the later Davidson calls convergence. For it is the many processes of convergence that have occurred among speakers in the past that have produced, over millennia, the languages that we speak today. Nor should we be surprised at *this* convergence of two philosophers who seem on the surface so different from one another. For the result of the various kinds of discourse with which Hegel deals will inevitably be a company of words that is at once diverse, because the original standpoints of its speakers are diverse, and organized, because those speakers have come over time to harmonize their vocabularies. The key notion of the Hegelian approach is thus, as one would expect, not truth but Nobility. It is this that Hegel always seeks to find in language—and if it cannot be found, to create.

Because it seeks Nobility rather than truth, the Hegelian approach sees itself not as a set of theses but as a unification of opposites. This places it beyond both Davidson and Wittgenstein, in ways I will discuss in chapter 11. Here, I will discuss two less radical ways in which Hegel differs from both Wittgenstein and Davidson.

Beyond Davidson and Wittgenstein, 1. Hegel focuses not on private, but on public, even "expert," language. Convergence can be found, I argued, far beyond the private encounters with which Davidson deals. There are political forms, in which citizens come together to articulate their common (and not so common) goals and interests. There are religious forms, in which people come together to articulate themselves in (one hopes) disinterested ways. There are artistic forms, in which an entire culture articulates and converges with itself, or sends a message to another place and time. Simply to call all these "convergence" is dangerous, for it risks masking important differences among them. Here is wide room for further investigation, which would begin with a careful reading of the entire Hegelian corpus to see just how Hegel treats the manifold phenomena he discusses as discourses rather than as extralinguistic phenomena, as a prelude to understanding and evaluating the different forms of convergence he locates in them.

Beyond Davidson and Wittgenstein, 2. Hegel, I have suggested, examines long-term cases of convergence, extending the temporality of language to the scale of history itself. Does not history manifest such convergences everywhere and always, even at the same moment that it shows us inexpressible (*unsäglich*) divergence, proliferation, and even conflict? We do not need to believe, as so many think Hegel did, that convergence is the single necessary pattern of human history, or that it is being realized in any sort of final sense, to see that it is a phenomenon of language worth studying, a study which can complement the thought of Wittgenstein and Davidson. To investigate language with respect to such convergence: Can this not be to view it as possessing an occasional dynamic, an intermittent essence? Is it not to view it in many of its forms as bringing about, intentionally or not, the unification of opposites, harmony over diversity? Is this investigation anything other than the investigation of language from the point of view, not of truth or success, but of Nobility? Is it not the questioning and articulation of the Nobility of words? And to create, via Systematic dialectics, a set of words arranged so as to display their own interdefinability, thus to highlight the deep conceptual ecology that binds and rebinds them together—Is this not to articulate the company of words, the highest pitch of such Nobility?

Or does that highest pitch come in Systematic dynamics, when we bring together the Systematic and the actual use of words?

9

Hegelian Words:
Narrative

The previous narrative traced the duality of thought from Plato on. The theme of the duality of language—the idea that it divides into two types, one fit to express the highest truths and the other not— is even older. It hearks back beyond St. Paul's fantasy of speaking with the tongues of men and angels, and beyond Plato's view (at *Timaeus* 29b seq.) of the bastard logos to, at least, the very distinction between Sanskrit and Prakrit. Chapter 7 saw Hegel trace it to Homer and it continues, as chapter 11 will show, into Davidson. In its more ancient forms the distinction between types of language tended to be aligned with that between ordinary and sacred reality, so that one sort of language is adequate to religious truth and the other not. In modern philosophy it became bound up with the (no less sacred) boundary between the inner and the outer, between consciousness and the body-in-society. Because ordinary language developed out of, and for, one's commerce with others, commerce always at least partly physical, it was held to be inadequate to express the phenomena of the self, found as these were strictly through our inner intellectual eye.

Thus, for example, in Descartes's *Principia Philosophiae*[1] language is a sort of subrepository into which drip cognitive evils, themselves several times distilled. From others and our bodies, in the naivety of our youth, we imbibe prejudices, beliefs which do not truthfully convey reality. Memory adds its own distortions, and the memory of a prejudice is worse than the original prejudice itself.[2] For it is by means of words that we commit our prejudices to memory: these doubly distorted beliefs are what language conveys and indeed makes possible. Language is not merely an impediment to thought, then, but its deepest enemy, for it distills prejudice and permits the weight of the past to bear, prejudicially, on the present. Always present to us as a medium for our thought, it is—like Descartes's evil demon—a continuous deceiver.[3]

Adequate expression of the truth is given, not linguistically but to the eye—the inner eye of the intellect, *sicut clare . . . videri dicimus.*[4] The discourse most fitting for this is mathematics, and in particular that form of it which, as Berkeley would later notice, makes most "constant use of the eye": geometry.[5] Descartes's own early hopes for an ideal language, voiced in his letter to Mersenne,[6] aim (as did Leibniz's efforts at an *ars characteristica*, which will not concern me here) at giving language the perspicacity and clarity of mathematics, thus freeing it from the heritage of tradition and prejudice that it imposes on us. This is possible through the arbitrariness of names: once the "true philosophy" has distinguished and clarified our ideas, they can be associated with whatever verbal sound one pleases. Such a language—one whose significations come wholly from philosophy—will be able not merely to express thoughts but to enumerate them, put them into order beginning with the simplest. The names used for this must be new coinages: for the language must be, in addition to conceptually transparent, easy to pronounce and to learn, and common to all humankind, no matter what languages are already spoken.

If language as we ordinarily use it is the archenemy of thought because of its origin in past, carnally conditioned interpersonal discourse, then, it need not always be so antagonistic: the arbitrariness of names gives hope of reform—hope for a language that would be capable of expressing adequately not only the various ideas which are its contents but their (numerical) relations to other ideas. Hegel's System, we have seen, makes the same claims and proceeds in broadly the same ways, though without reference to "ideas." It is a self-contained order of words.

Locke's *Essay Concerning Human Understanding*

But all this is a side issue for Descartes. It is with Locke, who surprises himself by discovering the supreme importance of language for thought, that the present narrative begins.[7] Though Locke, as an empiricist, distances himself from the kind of pure knowledge conveyed for Descartes by mathematics,[8] he sees language as deficient in a way strangely similar to Descartes: words are inherently an "obscurity and disorder," and

> interpose themselves so much between our understanding and
> the truth which it would contemplate that . . . the obscurity
> and disorder do not seldom cast a mist before our eyes, and
> impose upon our understandings.[9]

For Descartes, it is not *essential* to words that they enable prejudices to persist, and it is no fault of theirs if the memory of which they are vehicles is faulty. The early hopes of the letter to Mersenne, though later silenced, are not repudiated, and it remains possible in principle, because of the arbitrariness of names, to come up with a language sufficiently similar to mathematics to be transparent to thought. For Locke, language is not only essential to (much) thought, as we will see, but imperfection lies "in the very nature of words." Indeed, the abuses of language that Locke discusses, and for which he proposes remedies, consist mainly in willful efforts to turn the intrinsic imperfections of language to one's own ends.[10] Those imperfections are not merely inescapable, but intrinsic; they result not from the prejudiced understandings of those who use words or from the faultiness of their memories, but from the very fact that, in Locke's famous phrase, "words stand for ideas."[11] For the relation of "standing for," seemingly innocent, transgresses the deepest of all modern clefts, that between the subject and the object. Words are social sounds learned in youth, material phenomena; and yet their meanings are private ideas. Locke's account of "standing for" is predictably polymorphous, allusive, and fraught.

With regard to simple ideas, the relation is one of "voluntary connection" by which a sound becomes the mark of an idea: once we have experienced a simple idea, we associate it with a sound. This level of language gives rise to few problems, because either we have ourselves had the simple idea signified by a sound or we have not, and we generally know which is the case. It can of course happen that we use words without having had the simple ideas they signify, as when a blind person talks about colors, and such a speaker is using words she does not understand. Or we may mistakenly associate a word with the wrong idea, as if I call "green" what others call "red." But this does not result from any imperfections in language itself, any more than a mathematical proof is impeached by the fact that some people may find it difficult to understand. To understand the *essential* defects of language, and indeed the essence itself of language, we must turn to the names of complex ideas. These are divided into substances and mixed modes, and it is the latter that are important for my narrative.[12] In their case, the relation of "standing for" is generically different from what holds for simple ideas.

A "mixed mode" is a collection of simpler, and ultimately simple, ideas which are unlike one another. It is formed freely by the mind because those simpler ideas are not found together in experience.[13] If the subideas thus collected were similar to one another (as in what Hume calls "resemblance"), we would have a "simple" rather than a "mixed" mode.[14] If they had any kind of archetype in nature, which in that case would present them together in what Hume would call "contiguity," they would be ideas of substance (for which, see below).

Among the mixed modes are thus what we may style fantasy categories—unicorns, griffins, brains in vats, and the like. But the range of mixed modes is much greater and more important, because for Locke the idea of anything that progresses over time, especially if the time is relatively long (long enough to escape what Hume will call "succession" or causality), is a mixed mode. Its parts, being successive and lengthy, are not found together, and must be brought together by the mind. Not only historical developments but actions, Locke points out, are of this type. Including as they do our vocabulary concerning action, the names of mixed modes comprise "the greatest part of the words made use of in divinity, ethics, law, and politics, and several other sciences."[15]

Though produced by a free conflation of "scattered and independent" ideas, and hence without any representative function, mixed modes are not (fantasy categories aside) invented arbitrarily. Out of all possible collections of simple ideas the mind selects a few to be made into mixed modes, and this with a view to convenience in communication:

> The use of language is, by short sounds, to signify with ease
> and dispatch general conceptions, [which may contain] a great
> variety of independent ideas collected into one complex one.[16]

The names of simple ideas are not, then, the paradigm case of names for Locke; language achieves its full purpose only with names it has bestowed on complex (and "general") ideas. The primary function of the names of mixed modes is to achieve such quick communication by abbreviation:

> What a number of different ideas are by this means wrapped
> up in one short sound, and how much of our time and breath

are thereby saved, anyone will see, who will but take the pains
to enumerate all the ideas that either *reprieve* or *appeal* stand
for.[17]

The formation of mixed modes is thus essential to language, if it is to
serve its purpose. But language, conversely, is essential to mixed modes
if they are to serve theirs—indeed, if they are to persist over time at all.
For the combination of scattered ideas by the mind is of itself "fleeting
and transient," and the mixed modes thus produced have "but a short
existence anywhere but in the minds of men, and there too have no
longer any existence than whilst they are thought on."[18] It is the name
which, by associating the aggregate of simpler ideas with a single sound,
makes the aggregate repeatable and gives it stability: "though therefore
it be the mind that makes the connection, it is the name as it were that is
the knot that ties them fast together."[19]

It is only when it has been given such repeatability and stability
that a mixed mode can be taught to others—that is, become part of the
language. Hence, in order to serve the purpose which animates its formation (and indeed, we saw, informs all of language for Locke), a mixed
mode must be given a name. The name not only "marks" the union of
simpler ideas into a single one but "completes" it:

> No such species are taken notice of, or supposed to be, unless
> a name be joined to it, as the sign of man's having combined
> into one idea several loose ones; and by that name giving a last-
> ing union to the parts which would otherwise cease to have
> any, as soon as the mind laid by that abstract idea, and ceased
> actually to think on it.[20]

Like the name of a simple idea, that of a mixed mode is attached to, or
associated with, an idea; and this association is, we saw, a "voluntary connection." But in the case of a simple idea, the connection is established
between two things that exist independently of one another: a sound and
an idea. In the case of a mixed mode, the name becomes a condition for
the linguistic existence of the idea to which it is attached. This dependence is what Locke is trying to articulate with his metaphorical talk of
the name "knotting together" the component ideas of a mixed mode. It
is not that a mixed mode cannot exist at all without a name; but it cannot
exist *as linguistic,* since to be linguistic it must last long enough to be
communicable to others.

This gives named mixed modes (to which I will now restrict myself) a peculiar ontological status. For one thing, it is possible that a mixed mode preexists the realities which it designates. There was, for example, no such thing as "adultery" before it was made a crime, and it was not made a crime without being discussed first: legislation, for Locke, involves the creation of the entities to which legal terms refer.[21] More: "adultery" (which designates a hodgepodge of distinct activities and indeed kinds of activity) had to have not just any meaning, but a clear and settled meaning in the minds of the legislators—clear enough to enable them to make inferences about it and the consequences of outlawing it. Locke is not afraid to label such inference "discovering the certain truths" about the (as yet nonexistent) object.[22]

Thus, though the names of mixed modes "lead our thoughts to the mind, and no farther,"[23] it does not follow that they always, like fantasy categories, designate something merely subjective or unreal. They designate things whose original pattern is in the mind, and—as long as there is a possibility of something existing in conformity to them (that is, as long as they do not contain incompatible predicates)[24]—they signify in this "*real* essences":

> For these abstract essences being the workmanship of the mind
> . . . there is no supposition of anything more signified by that
> name, but barely that complex idea the mind itself has formed
> . . . and [which] is that on which all the properties of the spe-
> cies depend, and from which alone they all flow.[25]

It is, then, only of such abstract ideas and their relations that we can have "general and certain truth."[26] This does not hold for Locke's other main kind of name, that of substances. The mind forms these names in a way intermediate between the narrowly circumscribed ways it names simple ideas and the latitude with which it names, and constitutes, mixed modes.

Unlike a simple idea, that of a substance is complex. Unlike a mixed mode, such an idea is copied from nature—in particular, from our experiences of ideas which occur and recur in concatenation. We are prone to explain the repeated co-occurrence of such ideas by assuming a substratum, outside ourselves, in which they inhere.[27] As the supporter of the ideas we experience, this substratum is not one of those ideas: it is beyond experience, a featureless "x I know not what," from which the observable set of attributes is held to be derived. Since the substratum, or substance itself, is unknowable as such, any features we attribute to a substance are themselves derived from the original ideas—those ideas whose concatenation first led us to conceive them as inhering in a substance. And the members of that list of attributes will vary—not merely with the substance in question, but according to the nature of our experience, our care and industry in seeing just what ideas are recurring when and where, and so on. Hence, the definition of a substance does not give its essence—what characteristics really constitute it—but only what appear to someone to be such.[28]

Names of mixed modes, then, can in a way afford us truth and certainty, and are the names of real essences: those of substances always retain relation to unknowable substrates outside the mind, and must continually be revised as those substrates, in their mysterious ways, produce new appearances. We are very close here to the motivation for Hegel's demand (see chapter 1) that the philosophical treatment of language dispense with the "substrates" of predicates. For Locke, such dispensation would result in the reflectively self-aware discussion of mixed modes, and this if anything would seem to be "ideal language" for him. But in fact it is with respect to names of mixed modes that the imperfections intrinsic to language come to the fore, and it is there that language is most open to abuse. For in mixed modes the external standards are not only unknowable (as with substances) but entirely missing.[29] This causes varying degrees of trouble, and has several remedies.

Two characteristics that might cause problems do not do so, in Locke's view. Both follow from the fact that names for mixed modes are language relative. Different languages, with different names, will have different stocks of them; within a single language they will vary over time. But the latter is an advantage, since it gives language the flexibility to deal with changes of custom and opinion.[30] The former is also not a problem, because Locke, like many Anglo-Saxons, is culturally incurious: communication is for him utilitarian, and therefore primarily an intracultural matter. As he says regarding the ancients,

> There being no writings we have any great concernment to be
> very solicitous about the meaning of, but those that contain
> either truths we are required to believe or laws we are to
> obey . . . we may safely be ignorant of their notions.[31]

Where the laxity of mixed modes gives us trouble is in the here and now, and this occasions from Locke a major lament:

> But as for mixed modes, especially the most material of them,
> *moral words*, the sounds are usually learned first; and then, to

> know what complex ideas they stand for, [children] are either
> beholden to the explication of others or (which happens for
> the most part) are left to their own observation and industry;
> which being little laid out in the search of the true and precise
> meaning of names, these moral words are in most men's
> mouths little more than bare sounds. . . . Where shall one find
> any, either controversial debate or familiar discourse, concern-
> ing honor, faith, grace, religion, church, &c., wherein it is not
> easy to observe the different notions men have of them? Which
> is nothing but this, that they are not agreed in the signification
> of those words, nor have in their minds the same complex
> ideas which they make them stand for, and so all the contests
> that follow thereupon are only about the meaning of a sound.[32]

The problem, inherent in the nature of language itself, is that in order to
serve the purpose of communication—which is, after all, its own purpose—language must contain a large number of complex terms for
which there are no standards in nature. Both the complexity and the lack
of standards pose problems. The greater the number of simple ideas
combined into a single mixed mode, the harder it is to be sure that its
name excites exactly the same idea in everyone who hears it. And if the
components of the two complex ideas diverge, speaker and hearer attach
different ideas—that is, meanings—to the term and inevitably misun-
derstand one another.[33]

In addition to the sheer multitude of ideas that may be included
under a single mixed mode, there is the lack of pattern in the way the
mind puts them together:

> [Mixed modes] are an assemblage of ideas put together at the
> pleasure of the mind. . . . They have their union and combina-
> tion only from the understanding, which unites them under
> one name: but, *uniting them without any rule or pattern*, it cannot
> but be that the signification of the name that stands for such
> voluntary collections should be often various in the minds of
> different men.[34]

There are two sorts of remedy for this state of affairs. One strategy, discussed in Locke's chapter on "Remedies of the Foregoing Imperfection
and Abuse of Words," consists in making words dependably subordinate
to ideas. With respect to mixed modes, to which I will limit myself, there
are two main ways to do this. One is to conform to common usage, which
can be learned from study of the clearest writers and speakers; such con-

formity will enable us to communicate with others in our speech community.[35] But faithfulness to common usage is not enough, because many
terms in such speech are confused. Those who are actively interested in
improving their knowledge frequently reach the limits of what can be
said, at which point they must either invent new words or use old ones
with new significations. In such cases the remedy is to "declare" one's
meaning, in the case of mixed modes by defining the term—enumerat-
ing the simpler ideas it abbreviates.[36]

These strategies will not, however, resolve the ultimate problem,
the imperfection of names of mixed modes, which as has been seen resulted from the great number of ideas contained in a mixed mode and in
the disorder of their combination. To cope with these problems, we must
introduce restrictions on the ideas themselves, not merely on our use of
the names which denote them. Locke discusses these restrictions in his
chapter on distinct and confused ideas.[37] In forming a mixed mode,
enough simpler ideas should be included to differentiate it from all others. The simpler ideas should also be introduced in an organized way,
and not be all "jumbled together."[38] In this way, we can render our ideas
themselves more distinct:

> When a man designs, by any name, a sort of things, or one par-
> ticular thing, distinct from all others, the complex idea he an-
> nexes to that name is the more distinct, the more particular
> the ideas are, and the greater and more determinate the order
> of them is, whereof it is made up.[39]

Though he suggests elsewhere that mathematics may offer us a model of
how to introduce such order into our mixed modes, Locke never discusses the issue for itself.[40] He cannot, because his account of the disorder in our complex ideas is itself highly confused, predicated as it is on
the notion that "our ideas are, as it were, the pictures of things"—a view
which, if adhered to in the succeeding book of the *Essay*, would have
meant that there is no such thing as a mixed mode in the first place.[41] But
enough is clear here to show us that the answer to the problems with
mixed modes is what I call Nobility: a mixed mode ought to contain the
right number of simpler ideas, arranged in the proper order.

The nature of language is for Locke, then, most fully achieved in
the names of complex ideas. Of these, mixed modes, we have seen, are
the most prone to defects. Like Cartesian prejudices, they do not reveal
the nature of things as they are. Like such prejudices, they must be
learned from others; and because they have no archetypes in nature,

they are often mislearned, with resulting empty controversies and witless discourses. But unlike prejudices, the names of mixed modes do not claim cognitive status: they do not even appear to tell us what the world is like. Once this is understood, their status changes from most defective to, potentially at least, most perfect. They are knowable generally and with certainty, and the "essences" they posit are, as posited, wholly real and even "objective." Unlike names for substances, which are shadowed by the obscure realities to which they are referentially bound, the names of mixed modes would be both rationally transparent, if defined with care, and in perfect touch with such reality as they can relate to at all. They constitute, with one restriction, an ideal language. That restriction is that they do not tell us anything about nature; and about ourselves, they tell us at most what complex practices and phenomena we have, in the past, found it convenient to give names to.

Among the various problems with Locke's thought in general, three will be of significance to my narrative. The first two are pointed out by Berkeley; the third will be shown by Hamann. All have ramifications for Locke's theory of meaning in general.

The first concerns the strange role played in Locke's philosophy by his concept of substance. As has been seen, the real essences of substances are unknown to us, for we perceive only recurring concatenations of ideas. What is the epistemological or ontological gain of assuming, over and above such concatenations, substances supporting them? Epistemologically there is an obvious loss: in addition to the concatenated ideas which are the objects of our knowledge, there is one more idea, and an inherently obscure one. How, indeed, can an idea—the object of our knowledge, safe within the confines of consciousness—be inherently obscure? Ontologically, all the concept of substance does is provide an explanation for the observed fact that some ideas are always found together with certain others. But is this the only possible explanation? Why cannot such concatenation be taken for a brute datum (as Hume will do), or explained by appeal to God (as Berkeley will do)? Locke wavers on this point: at *Essay* 2.23.1f., the attribution of a substrate as a principle of explanation is said to be a matter of "custom" and "supposition," which suggests that the idea of substance could be entirely dispensed with—an attractive move, in view of the epistemological problems it puts to rest. But when challenged on this ground by Stillingfleet, who thought that Locke was indeed making substance an optional concept, Locke responded that any other explanation for the subsistence of concatenated ideas is "inconceivable."[42]

Berkeley's *Principles*

Through the obscurities and otiosity of Locke's account of substance, Berkeley drives the ethereal chariot of his subjective idealism.[43] The qualities we sense cannot in fact be shown to be caused by external substances, or at least by unintelligent ones: they are all caused directly by God.[44] But if an intelligent God is the sole cause of our sensations, then those sensations count as a sort of divine, visual language in which the Author of Nature instructs us about what to expect, especially in the way of tactile impressions: I see the fire from a distance, in order that I not be burned. The tactile impression, following regularly upon the visual one, is, so to speak, its "meaning."[45]

That sense ideas are a kind of language is argued, in "Towards a New Theory of Vision," as early as 1709. It is said that the way some sense impressions signify others is, as with humanly instituted signs, a matter not of resemblance but of "habitual connection."[46] Only in the third edition does Berkeley identify this language as that of the "Author of Nature," of God.[47] The move is a fateful one, for if our sensations are divine utterances geared to our moral guidance, the natural vocabulary in which they are uttered cannot be wrong or incomplete. Though nature, as divine language, requires "deciphering" by natural philosophers,[48] they will not have to supplement or reform it by creating terms of their own, as we do for Locke. Hence, while the concept of an ideal language gains power in Berkeley, he loses the possibility of construing that language as freely constructed by the human mind. For, presumably, no creation of ours could ever match, much less replace, the divine language which God has already given us. Thus, while Berkeley allows to our mind an arbitrary power of collecting ideas, combining them into one, and assigning a name to that unit,[49] he neither considers that aptitude in itself nor draws any major consequences from it. Nor, indeed, does he phrase the point with any care: it arises tangentially, in connection with the argument that a blind man, if suddenly granted sight, would not see the same objects that the rest of us do. Elsewhere the combination of ideas is said to be for the purpose of providing causal information about the world; it remains, then, merely imitative of nature.[50]

With the combinatory powers of the human mind thus restricted and devalued, Berkeley cannot recuperate Locke's insight that we define moral terms for ourselves. With this goes the possibility, for Berkeley, of any *philosophical* account of morals. For an adequate moral vocabulary would have to be grounded in the "deciphering" of the language of nature—an implausible enterprise, even before Hume argued that you cannot deduce what ought to be from what is.[51] Morals, then, are best left to scripture and the church, and philosophers—especially those who are also bishops—promulgate their doctrines.

Berkeley's reinstatement of the imitation of nature as the main (and best) cognitive occupation for our minds brings us to the second problem with Locke, and to Berkeley's second major criticism of him. This concerns the status of abstract ideas. Simple ideas, the foundation and "materials of all our knowledge,"[52] are not, for Locke, what we immediately perceive. Qualities are, in the things themselves, "so united and blended, that there is no separation, no distance between them."[53] The ideas which first come to be in the mind are those of "particular things," not ideas *tout court* but ideas *as* of such things, and hence "united and blended" themselves.[54] So, as for Carnap in chapter 2:

> It requires pains and assiduity to examine [the mind's] ideas,
> till it resolves them into those clear and distinct simple ones
> out of which they are compounded.[55]

Simple ideas are thus products of abstraction.[56] But, as for Carnap, this throws doubt upon their status as foundational material for knowledge. For if a process is as painful and laborious as abstraction, how universal or dependable can its results be? And what can it then mean to say, as Locke does, that ideas enter the mind "simple and unmixed"?[57]

Again, Berkeley attacks Locke's irresolution—here by denying, in his famous polemic against abstract ideas,[58] that abstraction ever reaches the kind of ultimate dissociation of ideas it achieved for Locke. This restricts, again, the capacity of the mind to rearrange our ideas and thereby freely to form mixed modes: for Locke, it was ultimately simples that could be rearranged and recombined; for Berkeley, it is concretes. The Berkeleyan mind, in comparison to the Lockean, is like a painter who must combine on her canvas, not pigments, but whole pictures.

To the extent that the divine language model of nature imposes itself on Berkeley, he can have no basic quarrel with language itself: for according to that model, some language is divine. The problem is rather with how we understand language: as William McGowan has put it, "where Locke worried about words, Berkeley worried about the *doctrine* of words."[59] The prevailing doctrine includes the belief, for example, that every name has, or should have, a single meaning—a view conducive to the postulation of abstract ideas as the single meanings needed.[60] Unfortunately, that belief has itself given rise to a large number of words—

those which purport to name abstract ideas. Such words are unreal and unneeded, and Berkeley proposes in his philosophizing to dispense with (human) language altogether—an aim which Locke thought wholly impractical, but which Berkeley thinks is quite attainable if we realize that along with the words will go a number of "ideas" they purport to name:

> I cannot be deceived in thinking I have an idea which I have not. It is not possible for me to imagine that any of my own ideas are alike or unlike that are not truly so. To discern the agreements or disagreements there are between my ideas, to see what ideas are included in my compound idea and what not, there is nothing more requisite than an attentive perception of what passes in my own understanding. . . . But the attainment of all these advantages presupposes an entire deliverance from the deception of words. . . . It were, therefore, much to be wished that everyone would use his utmost endeavours to obtain a clear view of the ideas he would consider; separating them from all that dress and incumbrance of words which so much contribute to blind the judgment and divide the attention. . . . We need only draw the curtain of words, to behold the fairest tree of knowledge, whose fruit is excellent, and within the reach of our hand.[61]

That tree, of course, is also linguistic: our "naked" ideas, the language of God.

Hamann's *Metacritique*

It is a Berkeleyan conception of sense impressions as a divine language that Hamann takes over and uses against Kant. This is evident from the first pages of his *Metacritique: on the Purism of Pure Reason*, a seven-page essay Hamann wrote in 1784 but which was not published until after his death in 1800.[62] Hamann begins this work by giving what for him is the core lesson of the Empiricists, citing Hume's version of Berkeley's critique of Locke:

> Ein großer Philosoph hat behauptet, daß allgemeine und abstrakte Ideen nichts als Besondere sind, aber an ein gewisses Wort *gebunden*, welches ihrer Bedeutung mehr Umfang oder Ausdehnung giebt und zugleich uns jener bei einzelnen Dingen erinnert.[63]

I have quoted the German because it contains a pregnant mistranslation. In the passage Hamann quotes, Hume speaks—as did Locke—of an idea being "annexed" to a term. For Locke,[64] such annexation is the "voluntary connection" of a word and a complex idea. It is not an association of equals, for as we have seen, the idea, especially if it is a mixed mode, depends on the name for its enduring existence as linguistic. But annexation is not bondage: it can voluntarily be undone. Similarly for Hume: "the word," he writes, "raises up an individual idea, along with a certain custom."[65] The custom is, again, not created by the name, for it is here just the habit of referring to a variety of different impressions with a single name and is due, not to the name, but to an original association of similar ideas. Nor is the annexation necessarily permanent: the same idea may at different times be annexed to different words.[66]

This use of "annexation" calls for investigations I cannot pursue here; but it is clear that, for Locke and Hume, to say that an idea is "annexed" to a name means that though the idea may in a sense be dependent on the name for its existence, the connection can be undone so that we can, as Berkeley advocates, break through to "naked ideas." But Hamann, fatefully, translates "annexed" not, for example, with *beigefügt*, but with *gebunden*, so that general ideas are *bound* to the words which stand for them. General ideas are thus, from the start, word-bound for Hamann, as they are not for Hume and Locke: to think without words, which is precisely what *ein großer Philosoph*, Berkeley, made essential to philosophical method, is for Hamann senseless.

The degree of binding Hamann has in mind is illustrated, two pages later, by the word "metaphysics." Hamann accepts the traditional view, now discredited, that the name is a mistake: that early editors of Aristotle introduced it to cover a number of treatises they placed following ("meta") the *Physics* in the order of his works. Once the name was in place, however, it inevitably resulted in those treatises being viewed as constituting a single investigation, aiming at completing the *Physics*'s account of natural phenomena by investigating what lies beyond (again, "meta") them.[67] The name thus created its idea—one of the central ideas in the Western tradition.

Hamann's own "metacritique" aims at continuing Kant's "critique" of reason by exposing and investigating what lies beyond the purity of Kantian pure reason: language itself.[68] We become aware of this, Hamann argues, by seeing that pure reason is not simply given but has been constituted by a twofold purification.[69] The first was the attempt, associated with Descartes,[70] to make reason independent of all tradition, including cultural heritage and religious faith. The second, "more transcendent" and clearly attempted by Kant, was to make reason independent of experience altogether. But these two purifications cannot be completed without a third: reason must be made independent of language, for a language conveys the tradition and heritage of its speakers (Cartesian "prejudices"), as well as the more or less scientific results of the inductions they have performed over history. Thus, when Kant claims, for example, that freedom can be given no sensible display, and hence that the concept of it is entirely independent of sensory experience, it is inconsistent of him to go on and define it in the ancient words of philosophical German. At least as wrong was the idea of deriving the "pure concepts of the Understanding," or the categories, from a consideration of the basic forms of predication; for language, writes Hamann, has no other credentials than usage and tradition.[71]

Hence, as Günter Wohlfahrt points out, none of the three purifications is possible for Hamann.[72] Reason for Hamann is never pure, but at most a concrete formative power whose material is language. Philosophical discourse, therefore, is not a pure description or argumentative consideration of ultimate facts, but a series of transformations of words, the rekneading of old leaven.[73] It is this creative transformation of language that is carried out by what Josef Simon calls the "concrete reason" that Hamann defends against what he sees as the artificially purified version put forward by Kant.[74] Such reason takes its "pure a priori forms," or its elements, from words and letters[75]—or, for Hamann, as we will see, from the basic sounds and visual forms of the sensory world. Articulating these into what we ordinarily understand as words, it creates something midway between sense and intellect:

> Words thus have [both] aesthetic and logical capacities. As visible and sensible objects, they belong with their elements to sensibility and intuition, but according to the spirit of their institutionalization [Einsetzung] and meaning, to the Understanding and to concepts.[76]

It is thus language which heals the great split in Kant's account of the human mind—that between sensibility, on the one hand, and reason and the Understanding on the other. But the capacity of language to heal dualisms goes beyond this. For it seems that Hamann goes on to cross and undo two basic Kantian dichotomies: that between the empirical and the a priori, on the one hand, and between intuition and concepts on the other. As empirical intuitions, words are the sounds and visual forms we experience, and as such they direct the distinctions we form. But as set up or "instituted" by human beings, words are also pure intuitions, because they have no role in determining the meaning attached to them: the arbitrariness of the designator is thus its purity from the very empirical distinctions that its meaning aims to capture. But in their arbitrary meaninglessness, words are merely "indeterminate objects of empirical concepts": it is only through their association with such concepts that they become determinate objects for the Understanding.[77] Hence, the only sense in which words can be "pure" or "a priori" follows from their arbitrariness. The view that there is a truly a priori realm, in Kant's sense, is the *proton pseudos*, the first falsehood, of his transcendental philosophy.[78]

Words thus play their unifying role for Hamann in virtue of a deeper doubleness in their nature: on the one hand, as associated with concepts or meanings, they grow up from the basic elementary forms of sensory experience, and direct the formation of concepts. On the other, they are entirely subservient to concepts because as mere sounds they cannot determine the meanings they are given. These two aspects of language coincide for Hamann. In one of the most demented moments of the *Metacritique* (itself a far more demented text than my account here dares to portray it), he asks the reader to imagine a ladder on which armies of intuitions climb into the "fortress" of reason, while armies of concepts descend into the "deepest abysses of the most intensely felt sensibility." When the two hosts meet, they fall upon one another with "wanton need"—a hypostatic union whose manifest image is to be found, Hamann claims, in the dynamics of ordinary language.[79]

But how can words be going both ways at once? If ideas are "bound to" words, how can words be unable to determine their own meaning? To see this, we must arrive at the deepest of language's healing powers: its capacity to close the gap between God and man. I have said that the elements of language for Hamann are the basic visual and aural forms of our sensory experience: it is this language, Berkeley's language of the Author of Nature, which ascends the ladder, guiding our empirical distinctions. This is the origin of all language, and was taught to Adam in the Garden of Eden. There,

> every appearance of nature was a word—the sign, sensible image, and pledge of a new, secret, ineffable, but all the more internal unification, communication, and community of divine energies and ideas. Everything that man in the beginning heard, saw, contemplated and touched was a living word: for God was the word.[80]

It is in this final move that Hamann undoes the subservience that language had to ideas in Locke and Berkeley. For now the two are no longer radically different sorts of thing, as they were even for Berkeley, but the same: where Berkeley viewed divine language (ideas) as radically other than human language, Hamann has merged the two—and into words, not ideas. The one ultimate word of this divine language of nature, which is also its one definite meaning, is God.[81] As such, God unites all oppositions, and is the "coincidence of opposites"—including the hypostatic union of sensible and intellectual which humans achieve in meaningful speech. But human theory, as opposed to human speech, cannot achieve this. Our language is only a "translation" from the divine language of nature,[82] and goes astray when transcendentalists like Kant create abstract terms which Berkeley had shown were impossible, in the service of a reason which Hume had shown to be impotent. All that human reason can do is highlight the oppositions that run through our existence, while pointing beyond them to God.[83] Hence, philosophy as a rational development—as a systematic unfolding of the unity of the Word behind the plurality of words—is impossible. The human mind can deliver only the "balled fist" of the truth, in the form of images and words which cannot be brought together into any kind of unity. No human, not even the philosopher, can unfold the fingers.[84]

To say that thoughts are "bound" to words is thus to say that they are bound to mysterious and partial manifestations of God. To say that words cannot determine their own meanings is not to contradict this, but in a way to repeat it: for it is to say that the arbitrary signs of human language are bound to the meanings given by God in the original, divine language. But—in a final twist—human language and divine language are not wholly separate types, or even strata, of language. For if God speaks to us in the sights and sounds of sensory experience, he also does so in human language, in the Bible: "Holy scripture should be our dictionary, our art of language, on which are founded all concepts and discourse of the Christian."[85]

Hamann's mistranslation of Hume is thus religiously motivated. At the beginning of the *Metacritique*, Hamann suggests that Hume's skepticism has an infinite debt to Berkeley's idealism (*Mk*, 285/215). We now see that Hamann has in fact accepted Hume's demonstration of the impotence of reason,[86] and has combined with it Berkeley's view of nature as a divine language—with the result that the language is not for "natural philosophers," or anyone else, to decipher.

But we can see what such deciphering would look like, if it were possible. As Erwin Metzge has pointed out, in order to clarify the presence of God in language, the divine language of sensory experience must be seen as at once fragmented (from the human side) and yet unitary (from the side of the divine word), in such a way as to reconcile everyday fragmentation with divine unity.[87] Linguistically conceived, this can only consist, on one level, in showing how the manifold of diverse and incompatible words contained in a given language can be ordered into a single dynamic whole. On a higher level will go a demonstration of the inner unity of the various human languages themselves, and this will have to be accomplished via a *communicatio* between the (many) human languages and the (one) divine language. Since divine language does not merely tell us what is, but informs us of what to do, the dichotomy of practical and theoretical must also be overcome, so that words are not neutrally theoretical but are grasped as deeds.[88] In this, the language of nature—purified sounds and forms, themselves united into unitary wholes—will be shown to have an identity with the freely instituted meanings created by human reason.[89]

Metzge concludes his statement of how things would have to be for the Hamannian program to be fulfilled with the words, "The great tasks which Hamann imposed upon thought . . . have not been brought notably nearer a solution by anyone."[90] Metzge's account is persuasive, and its irony saddening: the fulfillment of Hamann's program has been standing before us for almost one hundred sixty years. It is Hegel's System.

With one exception. As with Berkeley, and in the words of Fritz Blanke,

> Hamann's "philosophy" of language is entirely in the service
> of theology. The Magus hardly occupied himself with the social
> side of language, and its psychological basic concepts.[91]

For Hegel, as for Locke, words are of social use and importance, and as such are our doing: created by us. Meaning is a set of social habits, or practices, and the unity of language is not divine, but humanly thoughtful. It lies in the interdefinability of the words in any language, and is elicited by the philosopher.

Conclusions

The dream of a company of words is thus an ancient one. Plato, whom I have not discussed here, mistook it for an order of things—Forms—and

Aristotle consolidated this in his hierarchies of genera and species. The dream became clearer only with modernity, when the objects of discourse became private ideas and language, as our only means of communicating them, had to do jobs it did not have to do for the ancients: hence Descartes's dream of a reformed language, which was actually a set of reformed meanings or ideas. It took Locke to realize how essential language was to all of this, and that the needed reforms could not be concentrated (assertionistically) on the referential capacities of words but should deal with how meanings (for Locke, still, ideas) related to one another.

Berkeley then purified Locke of the residual concept of substance, viewing sensible ideas as direct relations, not to "substrates," but to God; and since God is a spiritual being, these ideas were not God's properties but God's words, radically other than the human kind. Hamann retained Berkeley's vision of a single divine source for language, but denied the radical otherness of human and divine words. The words which became the objects of Hamann's heated religious consciousness were thus at once human and divine, unified and diverse, sensual and intellectual, deed and insight.

Hegel restored to this religous vision the Lockean view that words are human creations, and thus subject to rational critique and reformation. This critique will employ the two methods of thinking inherited from the tradition: on the one hand, a reconstruction of vocabularies changing over history, and on the other, a free construction of words in their own sphere. Each of these, as has been seen, exhibits Nobility in itself. As I will argue in chapter 10, the two will possess it to a still greater degree when they are brought together in the final company of words.

Herder's *Fragments*

But if Hegel would undertake to unclench the "balled fist" of Hamann's prose[92] into a set of rational definitions, he was not the only one. Johann Gottfried Herder, as Isaiah Berlin points out, had a generation before Hegel already expressed in a coherent and systematic way the kind of insight Hamann spills forth.[93] Outside the *Aesthetics* Hegel speaks of Herder only rarely,[94] and usually condescendingly. But, as he well knew, Hegel himself was very much a child of this time; and the degree to which Hegel's times, and his own response to them, were shaped by Herder will be evident to anyone who reads the first chapter of Charles Taylor's

Hegel.[95] Herder stands no closer to Hegel than does Hamann, however, and his relation to Hamann is more one of similarity rather than creative derivation. Hence I do not include Herder in my narrative.

Herder's efforts to restate Hamann show that at least one person was aware that explicating Hamann as an alternative to Kant meant making what Richard Rorty, two hundred years later, would call the "linguistic turn." That turn, Rorty wrote in 1967, consisted in two claims: that all philosophical problems are problems of language, and that they can all be dealt with by reforming language or by understanding it better.[96] This is precisely the program advocated by Herder in the third collection of his *Fragments*, published in 1769.[97]

We learn to think, writes Herder, by means of language, and we cannot think without words. The "treasury of concepts" that a language provides us is thus attached to, and indeed identified with, its words. These verbal concepts are in the first instance, Herder writes, "sensibly clear" (*sinnlich klar*), where "clarity" is understood as a complement to "distinct." We can know the word "horse" with sensible clarity when we can use it to distinguish horses from other objects, even if we cannot define the term. But in its full conceptual richness, the term "horse" does not function alone: it picks out horses in virtue of a set of other terms, subordinate to it in this activity, which designate various features of horses and which Herder calls *Teilbegriffe*, which I will translate as "subconcepts." Philosophy is to deliver, then, knowledge of such subconcepts:

> It takes the objects, which we already know with sensible clarity; and lays out the . . . ideas that lie in them, which everyone can understand and no one can deny; [it] rises to ever more refined [*immer feineren*] ones, until it arrives at the definition.[98]

Where prior to philosophical analysis we are able to distinguish one thing from another by means of our words, as a result of it we can understand reflectively those distinctions themselves, because such analysis makes us aware of the subconcepts—or, as Herder also calls them, markers (*Merkmale*)—through which they are made. On this level, the philosopher seeks to dissolve philosophical problems (clear but not distinct words) by understanding language better. But she is not restricted to this, because understanding ordinary language inevitably, for Herder, moves us away from it. It is precisely the function of words to be simple and quick, and hence *not* to present explicitly the subconcepts associated with them. By explicating those subconcepts, philosophical analysis dispenses with the ordinary forms of language in favor of forms which, for its purposes, are better: it tends, inescapably, toward reform. In it, we transform and exchange (*umsetzen* and *wechseln*) our words until they are distinctly known.[99]

Such is what Herder calls "the true and only method of philosophy."[100] Its field of application is not restricted to ordinary language:

> There is a fundamental science of physics, mathematics, logic,
> and morals which takes the concepts of the sciences from their
> clear comprehensibility back to the simplest distinctions and is
> therefore a wealth of clear concepts.[101]

The name of this analytical, linguistic superscience is, Herder tells us, "metaphysics." So construed, metaphysics does for physics (and other sciences) what Hamann's "metacritique" did for Kantian critique: it clarifies and investigates the linguistic medium which other investigators presuppose. Metaphysics, writes Herder, "now becomes a *philosophy of human language*."[102]

In becoming this, philosophy also becomes intrinsically historical. This is because, for Herder, language *never* simply mirrors reality, but is always the deposit of previous interactions with it. For all the features that distinguish beings from other beings are not taken up into our language; the formation of general terms requires us to select out certain characteristics of a thing as the "essential" markers by which it will be remembered when it is seen again.[103] It is only for these few characteristics that we coin names; and our choice of them is thus dictated, not merely by the properties of the objects we are naming (and classifying), but by numerous factors which enhance the obviousness, or the importance for us, of one characteristic over others: the kinds of bodies we have, the natural surroundings and climate, the type of society we live in, our position within that society, and other such factors.

Given this sort of freedom of selection, even at the rawest level of designation, languages will inevitably develop and articulate different conceptual systems:[104]

> A people has no idea for which it has no word; the liveliest in-
> tuition remains an obscure feeling until the soul has found a
> marker and incorporated it, via the word, into the memory
> [*Gedächtnis*], the reminiscence, the understanding of humanity
> itself: a pure reason without language is, in all the earth, a uto-
> pian land.[105]

"We all come to reason only through language, and to language only through tradition, through faith in the word of our fathers." Through language, my individual soul is connected to those of the first, and perhaps the last, thinking beings.[106] Any "philosophy of human language—that is, any metaphysics—must take this side of language into account. There are two ways in which to do so.

The first, synchronic, is to extend the analysis of words into a philosophical comparison of a number of different languages. How many abstract terms does a language contain? How are more concrete terms related to them? Does a language exhibit characteristic pathways of word formation, such that some sorts of idea remain systematically underdeveloped when compared with other languages? To lay these out comparatively is to sketch the "general physiognomic of peoples" from their languages, a project wished for by many thinkers (presumably most intensely by Leibniz) but advanced by none.[107] The diachronic complement to this is the investigation of the transformations of a single language over history, again providing a comparative study of analytical paths and the basic terms which end them.[108]

However, there are limits to this sort of investigation. One pair of problems it can encounter leads[109] to defective philosophy: when the words from which analysis begins are not only historically and culturally conditioned, but capricious (*eigensinnig*). By this Herder presumably means that philosophers should direct their analyses to words used by the culture in general, not by particular subgroups or individuals, and to words which show by their history that they have staying power. The second problem is when the higher order subconcepts to which analysis leads are jargonistic, "barbarian coinages" which express contempt for the ordinary language from which investigation starts. The end points of analysis, then, should be words in general circulation, just as much as are its beginning points.

The remaining limitation is inherent in all philosophy, good and bad. There is a plurality of simple words, and hence of unanalyzable concepts: Herder mentions space, time, and force as three which are contained within what has traditionally been regarded as the simplest concept, Being.[110] But these snares and limitations do not for Herder impeach his main point: that philosophy must make the linguistic turn: "to develop concepts from given words, and make them distinct—that is philosophy."[111]

PART 4

THE DYNAMICS OF PHILOSOPHICAL EXPRESSION

10

The Expression of the System: Analysis

Aporia

Philosophical expression for Hegel, I have argued, requires *two* linguistic media which are not merely radically different, but opposed: one is reached by working representations up into full meaningfulness as universals, and the other by abandoning all such meaning. These two media are now to find a higher unity in the full expression of Hegel's philosophy, and the unity to be attained is that of the Hegelian linguistic Left and the Hegelian linguistic Right: the one maintaining that philosophy should be expressed in representational words worked up over history, the other demanding an expression that is entirely immanent and necessary. The unity (or unities, for we will see there are several forms of convergence between the two media) sought must be one of equals. For if it is dominated by representational names, we revert to Left Hegelianism; if by names as such we are, once again, Right Hegelians. These alternatives are presented respectively by Jean Hyppolite and Werner Marx, in whom we will encounter—for the last time—the dilemma of the Hegelian Left and Right.

Both writers maintain that representational names and names as such are brought together in what Hegel would call an "immediate" way, prior to philosophy and to the process of philosophical expression. The site of their conjunction must then be in the sort of representational name which most closely approaches the sheer meaninglessness of names as such. This will be the simplest, least meaningful type of representational name, or what Hegel refers to as "the simple sign for the simple representation."[1] Hyppolite and Marx both take the view that Mechanical Memory in fact contains such simplified representational names. But they differ as to what sort.

For Hyppolite, Recollection (*Erinnerung*) internalizes the richness of the sensory world, while Verbal Memory (*Gedächtnis*) reduces that richness to simplicity by externalizing it into a name:

> This memory which internalizes the world only exists in virtue
> of the other memory which externalizes the Ego. The *Erin-*
> *nerung* exists only in virtue of the *Gedächtnis*.[2]

Mechanical Memory for Hyppolite does not contain mere names as such, for the two processes of internalization and externalization "melt together" (*se confondent*) and are "the same."[3] At the end of "Representation," then, the subject "has transposed into the element of her universality all sensible diversity," via *Erinnerung*;[4] but as "expressed" by the Ego, signification is present in immediacy and externality.[5] Thought thus begins for Hyppolite, not with representational names and names as such held apart through their radical disparity, but with them already brought together into the simplest (i.e., most immediate) form of representational language.

Such language, though simple and immediate, is still representational, and Hyppolite's view of Hegel is ultimately from the Left. The meanings of words in Mechanical Memory are not the work of philosophical thought, but "precede as well as express it;"[6] and, insofar as they precede it, it exhibits a "universal reference which, however, remains reflection and sense."[7] Once Hyppolite has established that the union of names as such and representational names is basically representational, the rest of his exposition of the problem of philosophical expression follows Mure's. Like Mure, Hyppolite concludes that Hegel did not solve the problem. His merit lies in having seen it.[8]

The view that representational names and names as such are reconciled prior to thinking depends on the view that the language reached by Mechanical Memory is the same as that reached by the preceding phases of Verbal Memory. Both processes then converge on a single result. Hyppolite's way of expressing that convergence is to label one process "externalization" and the other "internalization," and then to assert that they are identical. This cuts, however, across Hegel's text. Hegel indeed refers to the identity of internalization and externalization at both #462 and #463—the latter concerned with Mechanical Memory and the former with Reproductive Memory. But Hegel distinguishes the two identities by referring to names as such in Mechanical Memory as the *highest* internalization and externalization of the Intelligence; the representational names of Reproductive Memory are merely an internalization (*Erinnerung*) which is an externalization (*Entäusserung*). *Each* phase is at once an internalization and an externalization; to assign the former moment exclusively to *Erinnerung* and the latter to *Gedächtnis* is untenable. More than that, however: by calling the internalization-externalization of Intelligence in Mechanical Memory its "highest" internalization-externalization, Hegel indicates quite clearly that it is dialectically posterior to the internalization-externalization of Reproductive Memory. Names as such, then, belong to a higher dialectical development than representational names. The two types of name cannot be the same, and no convergence is possible in the processes which produce them. The unification must come later, and be accomplished thoughtfully rather than immediately.

Werner Marx, in *Absolute Reflexion und Sprache*, stresses that language is to be, totally, the "servant" of thought. Not only must the structures of meaning of individual, representational sentences and names be "emptied out" so that they do not dialectically influence language by their limitations of form and content;[9] but this "empty" language itself must be produced by Spirit (specifically, says Marx, by the Mechanical Memory),[10] so that language is in no sense an "external" dimension which thought must take into account, but is simply its expression and nothing else besides. Marx agrees with Mure, Clark, Simon, and Hyppolite that names can have only representational meaning. But for him, thought has not one but two ways in which it can express itself nonrepresentationally. On the one hand, he maintains that some "words" for Hegel are not names, but go beyond the merely representational in their signifying power to mean "concepts."[11] On the other hand, thought for Hegel also has, Marx says, the power to transform the meanings of representational language into the meanings of thought; whatever other meaning the name as representational may have is then mere *Eigensinn*, its own stubborn sense, which is unimportant to philosophical expression.[12] This power of thought to transform representational language by disregarding its meanings places Marx, like Bodammer, on the Hegelian Right. For Bodammer, names as such were alone relevant to philosophical expression, while for Marx such expression is carried out in representational names which have been transformed, or somehow overlain, by thought.

Having suggested that meaning, though expressed in names and thus expressed representationally, can be the meaning provided by thought itself, Marx then asks about the very demand for "expression" of thought at all. Is this not an external demand, since the language in which it takes place, though a mere "elementary being-external," is itself still undeniably external to thought?[13] Here, Marx calls in Mechanical Memory: names as present in Verbal Memory, and chiefly in Mechanical Memory, have their existence within the intelligence; they are purely products of the intelligence, and are not in any sense "external" to thought. This view of (representational) language as purely a product of the Intelligence occurs, says Marx, only in the *Encyclopedia*; he makes no attempt to justify it, either for Hegel or in itself, and in effect gives Mechanical Memory the status of deus ex machina.

Indeed, on Marx's view of it, Mechanical Memory could hardly be other than adventitious; as an externalization of names, it is for Marx an externalization of representational language—of the very same language which in the preceding sections of "Representation" was so laboriously worked up from external intuition. If the very same words can also be produced from within, purely by the immediate self-externalization of the Intelligence, then that entire process—indeed, history itself—is unnecessary to philosophical expression. For the historical process of working up representations culminates not (as Hegel and, indeed, Marx say) in the "names we think in,"[14] but in a set of names whose only function is to have their meanings transformed into those which thought provides for them.

Hyppolite and Marx thus pose, once again, the Left-Right split. What both have in common is that they do not believe the split, in its linguistic form, can be mediated philosophically. The convergence between names as such and representational names is for them established prior to philosophy, which simply takes its medium of expression over ready-made. But this poses a problem: if the immediate self-externalization of the intelligence (in Mechanical Memory) and the laborious working up of representations by the mind over history both yield the same result, the process which produces each type is unintelligible from the side of the other. The working up of representational meaning is, from the point of view of Mechanical Memory, unnecessary; and Mechanical Memory, after that working up, appears on the scene as an ad hoc solution. If, however, the names in Mechanical Memory are not simply representational names but are names as such, which arise not from a deus ex machina but develop from representational names through an abandonment of representationality itself, then the unification of the two forms of expression must be carried out by thought, and in particular by the System itself. Reunification would then take the form of uniting the plasticity of the latter with the content of the former. Such unification—the rational establishment of its own medium of expression—would then be the way the System works: its own dynamics.

The Process of Philosophical Expression: "The Object"

I have argued that each of the two forms of expression so far discovered, that in names as such and that in representational names, has its advantages and its disadvantages for philosophical expression. These advantages and disadvantages, I have also argued, are complementary. Names as such, "spiritual Being," permit the universal and plastic expression of the development of philosophical content from within. Representational names permit philosophy to carry on its dialogue with its times. Hyppolite and Marx have shown that the two forms of expression cannot be unified prior to thought without reawakening the Left/Right dilemma, and the question now is that of how they can be brought together—ways which will preserve the advantages and cancel the disadvantages of each.

Representational names, which have meaning derived from Intuition, are more "external" to the thinking subject than are names as such. To the extent that philosophical expression is truly, for Hegel, "expression," it would seem that it ought to move from the less external to the more external, and that it ought first to occur in names as such. This would accord with the passage I adduced, in chapter 7, from the Berlin transcription of the Introduction to the *Lectures on the History of Philosophy*, where what seemed to be this type of expression was referred to as "the first absolute condition of understanding," and representational expression was assigned a subsequent position.[15] Expressed in names as such, prior to any further expression into representational names, philosophical truth would be presented in a way fully adequate to the interiority and universality of its meanings, and to the "plasticity" of their development. But the externalization of thought into names as such alone would be an externalization into individual utterances, each haphazardly "chosen." As I have argued, a given moment of thought cannot achieve standard and uniform expression without reference to a representational realm. Moreover, philosophy cannot carry on its dialogue with its times or express itself as understanding unless its expression in names as such somehow *bears on* representational meanings. But how is such bearing possible?

A name as such receives both its meaning and its Being, as I have argued, entirely from within. If either of these moments brought with it reference to what is "without," the immanence and freedom of philosophical thought would be externally conditioned, and thought would be in truth neither immanent nor free. But there is one element in the name as such which does not come from "within," and *that is its concrete sound.* For this sound remains, as I have argued, homophonic with that of the representational name from which the particular name as such is derived.

In the *Encyclopedia* of 1817, Hegel refers to the externality in the Mechanical Memory as "intuition made subjective," and this intuitive side is (as we would expect) said to be for itself completely inessential.[16] It is only in virtue of its status as a sign, then—a status in which its sound is arbitrary—that the name as such expresses thought. At this first stage in philosophical expression, any similarity such a name may have, through its concrete sound, to a representational name would lie completely outside its significance for the Mechanical Memory, and hence for philosophical expression. The likeness is merely that of one externality to another; it cannot interfere with the internality of thought's expression in names as such. Names as such, then, can safely bear upon representational names through their homonymity with them.

Further, a plurality of individually uttered names as such can be homophonic with a given representational name. As I pointed out in chapter 7, such homophony cannot be recognized by thinking insofar as it externalizes itself immediately into a name as such, because for such thought the name is significant only as an individual utterance, not as the token of a type. But it can be recognized by thinking which, as understanding, "hears" those names and relates them (a) to each other, and (b) to the representational names of which they are homophones, thereby giving philosophical thought a uniform, iterable expression. If names as such bear upon representational names through their homophony with them, then the haphazardness of expression into mere names as such can be overcome without impeaching the ability of those names to express thought in a plastic and universal way.

What makes any given name as such more appropriate than the rest for the expression of a given moment of thought is then its homophony with some representational name. What makes the representational name itself appropriate for *its* role in this—for being the representational name whose homonym is, at this particular stage, the best one for the expression of thought—cannot be its mental sound; that would hardly remove the arbitrariness which we saw to be the problem with names as such. Its appropriateness must lie in its other side—in its meaning, the specific representation it signifies. This representation must, in general, be a historical given: it must be the case that the expert language of the time has come up with it, for otherwise, capturing it philosophically will not advance philosophy's dialogue with its times. Since it is the ultimate business of the System to give, in senses yet to be determined, the "final truth" of the names it comprehends, I advance the hypothesis that *each moment of thought is, in the first instance, expressed by a name as such homophonic with the name of the particular representation of which that moment will prove to be the final truth within the System.*

This leaves much unanswered; indeed, the hypothesis has not yet been stated fully, because the sense of "identity" (or "final truth") on which it trades has not been specified. Before undertaking that, I will seek preliminary verification by considering an example of what is happening here that does not presuppose any particularly Hegelian sense of "identity." In the beginning of the *Science of Logic*, Hegel considers three possible ways of characterizing the first moment of his System: as "Being," "Ego," or "God."[17] All three terms are, here at the beginning, on a par—they all mean no more than "Being":

> What may be contained or expressed, beyond Being, in the
> richer forms of representation of God or the Absolute is, in
> the beginning, only an empty word and only Being; this simple
> thing, that otherwise has no meaning, this emptiness, is there-
> fore most completely the beginning of Philosophy.[18]

"Ego" and "God," as mere beings (i.e., "empty words") can express the beginning. But, Hegel continues, they also bring with them richer representational meanings. "Ego" would, if used, trouble the reader with a flood of misconceptions from everyday life.[19] "God" would bring content from the even richer sphere of religious life.[20] Only "Being," as it is ordinarily understood, can appropriately express the poverty and emptiness of the beginning of Science. The choice is thus made among the three on the basis of the representational meanings they have in historically situated discourse: more specifically, on the basis of the background information associated with those representational meanings. The fewer the associations presented by a representational name, the more appropriate is its homophone to express the beginning of the System. The identity of representation and thought can hardly be reduced to lack of associations, however, for philosophy must go onward to appropriate much more complex representations—such as, precisely, "Ego" and "God." To spell out the dynamics of the System in a more general and rigorous way, I will turn to the section of the *Encyclopedia* Logic entitled "The Object."[21] The reasons for this choice deserve some discussion.

The task of philosophy, says Hegel, is overcoming the opposition of subject and object through thought.[22] Philosophical expression is the externalization of the subjectivity of thought into a linguistic "objectivity,"[23] and can therefore be viewed as the overcoming of a subject-object opposition. Because philosophy is the *final* form of theoretical Spirit, we might expect to find the discussion of thought's externalization into language in the section on "Practical Spirit" which immediately follows "Thinking" in Hegel's Psychology: philosophical expression would then be the first practical move onward from pure theory. But philosophical expression is not practical because it deals not with the external resistant matter of the real world, but only with the "disappearing, resistanceless" objectivity of language. In this sense, it remains a purely theoretical phenomenon,[24] and we will not find it discussed for itself either in "Practical Spirit" or in the section on "Objective Spirit" which follows that.

But we *can* expect to find the purely theoretical overcoming of the subject-object opposition in that part of the System which presents, in the Logic's realm of "pure thought," the fundamental structures of the "Concept's self-determination into objectivity."[25] This occurs in the Logic's section on "The Object," which begins from the full development of the subjective Concept in syllogism and leads to Hegel's discussion of the fully realized Concept, the Idea (or, as I argued in chapter 1, philosophical "truth"). Indeed, since as I have noted thought for Hegel finds complete realization only in language, when that section presents the *complete* realization of the Concept we must view it as presenting such realization in language: as presenting Hegel's view of how philosophical expression proceeds.

Philosophy remains, nonetheless, just one of the ways thought realizes itself in objectivity. The entire activity of Spirit, as the return-to-self of the Absolute from its externalization in Nature, can be viewed as another way, or ways; and the basic structures of all of them are to be found in one part or another of the passage I will discuss. To approach this passage with just one of its more concrete manifestations in mind is, in terms I discuss elsewhere, to analyze rather than expound it.[26] This does not mean dealing with Hegel's texts in an un-Hegelian way; for, precisely, one of the things that we are supposed to do with his Logic is recognize its forms in their more concrete articulations.[27]

I will do this here in two stages: first I will give a short summary of the text; then, using clues the text itself provides, I will identify names as such and representational names as two forms of "the object." The result will be a process of unification of those names which successfully meets the requirements I have derived from secondary literature for philosophical expression. Philosophical communication is, one presumes, a purposive activity; and this means that I will pay particular attention to the last section of "The Object," "Teleology." But I will also look briefly at the first two sections, "Mechanism" and "Chemism," if only because they reappear in the third. I will make use primarily of the *Encyclopedia Logic*, but will refer to the *Science of Logic* as necessary for further detail and clarification.

At the beginning of "The Object," then, we have the "subjective Concept," a self-determining totality of thought whose activity is articulated, not merely into judgment, but into syllogism.[28] This thought now considers itself to confront an "object" other than it—an object which is, because other, precisely *not* a self-determining totality but an "immediate, unaffected" indeterminate manifold of individual existents.[29] In the first form which this object takes, these existents stand in the poorest and most external type of relationship with one another possible: that of objects coexisting in space and time. As comprised of such, the object is the "mechanical object."[30]

Hegel refers to the process of interrelation among mechanical objects as "communication"—in the sense in which mechanical properties (heat, for example, or velocity) can be "communicated" by one object to another.[31] This process of mechanical communication overcomes the sheer externality of the mechanical objects to one another. For the temperature, impetus, or other property communicated by one such object to others is, itself, a determinacy. When the other objects receive it, they become determined, and in this determinacy are related to the original object from which the determinacy came. When, for example, one billiard ball sets five others in motion, those five—for the duration of their motion—receive a determinate mechanical property and are, in their common possession of it, related to one another and to the original ball; they are differentiated from other billiard balls which have not received that motion. When this relation ceases to be, as it is with billiard balls, a process which runs through in time and ends with the objects resuming their original indeterminate indifference to one another, but becomes a constant application of force or an equilibrium of moving bodies, we have "absolute mechanism."[32] In this, the different objects remain in their determinate relation to one another and to the original source of motion; this is the case, for example, with the sun and the planets.[33] When this relation to a central body ceases altogether to be external to the objects and becomes part of their very nature, mechanism has passed over into chemism—in which, for example, acids and bases are essentially related to each other and to the neutral compounds in which they are united.[34]

It is the nature of chemical substances, then, to be classifiable in various complementary ways (e.g, as acids, bases, and salts).[35] The interrelation of these objects is no longer the mere mechanical communication of properties from one to another, but a constant conjoining and disjoining which is part of the very essence of the objects themselves. In this conjoining and disjoining, each chemical object shows its dependence on its opposite (e.g., acids on bases; the unification of both, the salt, on the disjunction into the other two). But the interdependence does not develop, in chemistry, into a dynamic unification: when the result of the chemical process is present, the beginning is gone. The unity, for example, which is the salt does not contain within itself any features of "acidity" and "baseness"; these have disappeared, and the salt cannot properly be said to "unify" them. Salts are then merely another class of chemical objects, which stand in opposition to the class of "nonsalts"— that is, acids and bases.[36] Thus, each part of a chemical process of combination and disjunction reveals itself to be dependent on its opposite: "dependent" because it came to be from something else, which is "opposed" to it in that the two cannot coexist. The chemical process is thus the demonstration, by the individual chemical object, of the instability of its fixed determinacy: that it is compounded out of, and resolves back into, something with which it is incompatible.[37]

When the two sides of the chemical process—the conjoining and disjoining of chemical objects—are viewed together as both brought forth by the moment of unity, which itself then has the active property of separating its elements from one another and reuniting them, we have moved from "Chemism" to "Teleology." Since it is in "Teleology" that "Mechanism" and "Chemism" find their unity as moments of a larger whole, it will be worthwhile to examine this section in some detail.

At the end of the "chemical process," we have returned to the situation at the beginning of "The Object": the Concept, as subjective, has opposed to itself an object. The latter is, however, no longer a mere immediate totality of existing individuals, but an object which has become both mechanical and chemical.[38] Because the Concept is at this point in the Logic fully operational, it can (and does) develop its own content within itself by particularizing itself.[39] In teleology, this self-determination has two sides. On the one hand, the Concept takes on determinate content which is its own and remains within it;[40] on the other hand, it is directed through this determinacy to an object presupposed by the Concept as lying outside it:[41]

> Thus, the primal interior externality of the Concept, through which it is the self-repulsing unity or end, and its struggle outward to objectivication, is [as well] the immediate positing or presupposing of an external object.[42]

In the first of these aspects, the Concept's determinacy remains "included in the simple unity of the Concept." But the determinacy has, in its "interior externality," objectivity within it; and this objectivity lies, Hegel says, in the indifference which its individual determinations have to one another and to the Concept itself. As included in the self-determining of the Concept, these moments do not stand determinately against one another, as do for example subject and predicate of a merely formal judgment; we can say that they are the moments of a *philosophical* judgment, in which the Concept separates itself immediately into determinate moments—which moments, because of that immediacy, remain indifferent to one another and to the Concept itself.[43]

This judgment is the "first premise" of the syllogism which, for Hegel, will constitute the entire structure of teleology. It is the relation of the subjective Concept, as end, to the means it will use for its realization.[44] In this relation, the Concept assumes "power" (*Macht*) over the means;[45] but the means, nonetheless, remains in the state of indifference which I have argued to characterize it. This retention of its externality makes the means into a mechanical object—but a mechanical object which is "completely permeable" to the Concept, totally "receptive to this communication" of determinacy to it.[46] Though under the power of the Concept, and thus fit to serve in its externalization, the means thus remains external to it.[47]

The externality persisting in the means brings with it the relation of that means to an objectivity still not "under the power" of the Concept—another object which is still external to the Concept and must be worked on by the Concept through the means.[48] This relation of the means to the still external object is for Hegel the "second premise" of the syllogism of teleology.[49] It is a relation among objects, and the process by which the means operates on the remaining externality is a mechanical or chemical process; these processes are thus here reinstated within teleology and proceed under the "dominance" of the Concept (a process Hegel refers to here as the "cunning of reason").[50]

The connection between the end and the object was at first the mere externality of the means; and we can say that this was an empty, merely formal connection.[51] But in the operation of the means on the object under the guidance of the Concept, the connection becomes concrete; and in this concretion, content (our old friend from chapter 1) emerges as what all three moments have in common. The concrete content of the Concept, of the means under its power, and of the object was the same all along; for the Concept contains all possible determinacy, and hence all possible content, within itself. This is the content which was externalized into the means, and now the content of the object can also, ultimately, be none other. In the operation of the means on the object, then, this implicit identity in content becomes explicated and acquires determinate existence.[52]

We have now seen the Concept externalize itself immediately into a mechanical object which it takes as means; seen that the means, via its own externality, presupposes a further objectivity, both mechanical and chemical; and seen it work on that objectivity until its identity with the Concept becomes explicit. The final stage in the teleological process is for Hegel the reunification of means, end, and object with one another. The external objectivity on which the end operated via the means shows itself to be nothing on its own account; as mechanical object, it is entirely unable to resist the objectification of the Concept, and as chemical object its process is a demonstration by its moments of their own untenability as fixed.[53] The object thus proves to be no more resistant to the Concept than was the means, and collapses into it. Because the means and the object are thus identified, the activity which brings the means under the Concept is the same as that which brings the object under the means: the latter activity is no longer assigned to the means, as distinct from the Concept. And, in bringing the means under it, the Concept as end shows itself to be no more than this same activity: it thus gives up its one-sided subjectivity.[54] It shows itself, like the object, to be identical with the means.[55] The end and the object thus turn out to be forms of the means; in taking on such forms, the means separates them from itself and then reunites them under itself. It is the means, then, and not the end, which in truth functions as does the Concept—and thereby gives itself, as the Concept, its presentation in the objective realm. In this way, the means turns out to be the Idea, or (philosophical) truth.[56]

"Teleology" thus presents the subjective Concept giving itself a first externalization in the means, using that means to work on the remaining presupposed objectivity, and finally bringing forth the fact that the means, as Idea, actually contained the content of the whole. How does this illuminate the process of philosophical expression as I have hypothesized it to be?

The Process of Philosophical Expression as Derived from "The Object"

Mechanism, says Hegel, is a very superficial category of objective interrelation, even within Nature. Its importance to the spiritual world is even more restricted, being limited to such mechanical mental operations as reading, writing—and Mechanical Memory.[57] If Mechanical Memory is an instance of mechanism, then the indeterminate manifold of names as such within it must function as mechanical objects. The communication of "determinacy" to them in the "first premise" of the teleological syllogism is then the communication of differentiated, determinate Systematic meaning.[58]

The "second premise," the process by which a chemical object demonstrates the instability of its own fixed determinacy, proper in the objective world to chemistry, extends, like the mechanical process, beyond Nature into Spirit. Hegel finds it not only in the sexual relation, but in friendship and love as well.[59] But he also notes that "the sign" and "language" function, like water, as a universal medium within which chemical processes take place and in which, as a universal "neutral," chemical objects have their unity.[60] Since the objects of chemistry are fixed determinacies, it seems that Hegel is here thinking of something like representational language as the field in which representational names constitute themselves and are worked up. A representational name is, like a chemical object, unified with its own determinacy in the form of its meaning. Such names can be considered to fall under the category of "chemical objects" for Hegel, just as names as such can be viewed as mechanical objects.

Thus, what Hegel says about the subjective Concept realizing itself in a mechanical object can apply to the expression of philosophical thought in a name as such, while the complicated relation of this to the chemical object can be viewed as the System's relation to representational names, and through them to the representational world itself. The first externalization of the Concept is, as I have noted, a (Hegelian) premise, or judgment. It externalizes thought into a "mechanical object" which Hegel calls an "interior externality" to the Concept—into, as I have argued, names as such. In terms of my previous rewriting of Systematic dialectics, we can say that meaning is communicated to a name in step (0) of the dialectic: when M_j is asserted to abbreviate a previous sequence of markers. The "meaning" thus received is simply the set of those other markers—of other names as such, homophones of which were previously introduced into the System. Because those names, and the configurations by means of which earlier terms define later ones, are mere meaningless sounds from which thought chooses freely, the whole process is internally directed, unconditioned from outside. Because the meanings thus bestowed are entirely internal to thought, they can be understood equally well by anyone who can think—who can group and regroup content. And because it is expressed in names as such, which are not bound to fixed grammars and meanings but disappear as they are uttered, the process is "plastic."

But this first externalization is, the *Logic* tells us, into an object which, as mechanical, is utterly indifferent to the Concept and to other such objects; as Hegel puts it, the means is at this stage the "formal middle of a formal syllogism," and any other object could serve equally well as means.[61] This is then the *Logic*'s version of the haphazardness I argued earlier to characterize the externalization of thought into names as such without reference to a representational realm. It cannot be mitigated within this first externality of the Concept. We cannot make an intelligent selection of tools, or names, until we know not merely what we are going to produce with them, but the nature of the material on which we are to work. Further externality is needed.

The *Logic* here says that such further externality is presupposed by the very "externality" of the means to the Concept. I have argued that the mental sound of a name as such is "external" to it because it is utterly indifferent to that name's character as a sign. Indeed, its mental sound is the most external aspect of such a name and is, I argued, the only aspect of such a name that can have any relation to further externality. That relation is, then, the only one that can be established by the sound alone of a name as such: the relation to a representation of which it is the homonym. Since representational names are both temporally and systematically prior to philosophical thought,[62] this reference is to an object which is posited as already existing—that is, is indeed "presupposed."[63]

The means, says Hegel, works on the remaining objectivity by "dominating" (his word is *Herrschaft*) that objectivity's own mechanical and chemical processes. If we can take representations as instances of chemical objects, then chemical processes must be analogous to what I earlier called historical dialectics. In them, the set of markers defining some representation—the "fixed determinacy" of its name—runs up against an anomaly, in the form of entities in the world which are either missing some defining markers they ought to have, or possess some they ought not to have. In theoretical pursuits, the representations are then modified to fit the objects; in practical ones, the objects are modified to fit the representations.[64] In both cases, the original discrepancy disappears completely: markers which do not conform to the object are not "sublated" into some higher sequence, but simply thrown away.[65] In this, the process remains "chemical."

Hegel's statement that the chemical (and mechanical) processes of the second objectivity proceed "under the domination" of the means is supremely important. On the present reading, it is to be understood as follows. Both representational names and names as such, once they have been taken up into the System, have determinate "content." This content is, respectively, other representational names and sets of defining markers. The "domination" here is teleological, and so what Hegel is saying is that the adding and dropping of markers from representational definitions is carried out with a view to arriving at definitions similar to those of names as such. To put this another way: a name as such is "identical" with a representational name if and only if every marker of the former is a homonym of a marker of the latter, and vice versa. This is not a given but a goal to which Systematic and historical dialectics are directed: the one, freely grouping and regrouping old content to generate new; the other, adding and dropping markers in response to anomalies. In particular, historical dialectics can stop when it reaches that goal, instead of remaining in the aimless negations of skepticism and sophistry.[66]

That the alternative to stopping the dialectic is sophistry shows that there is, for Hegel, such an alternative: he does not believe, then, that his thought puts an end to the historical development of representation. New historical events, he predicts, will keep on happening, such as a possible war between North and South America;[67] indeed, not only new wars but new representations will arise from the progress of the sciences, representations which will be have to be taken up into an expanded and modified System.[68] As I argued in chapter 4, the System is open to radical revision to accommodate such new contents, and is anything but the final and definitive exposition of the Absolute—or of anything. It is a creative enterprise.

At the beginning of the *Encyclopedia,* discussing the two languages of the Concept and of Representation, Hegel says that their content (*Gehalt*) is the same.[69] This identity is not always present when a moment of the System is expressed. Indeed, the Logic here tells us that the reference of the means to the object is at first purely external, a mere indication of their true relationship—on my reading, a mere similarity in sound. It is only in the operation of the means on the remaining objectivity that the mediating factor ceases to be merely external and becomes the content, which is identical in means, end, and object. The directing operation of the means on the object can thus be viewed, in terms of philosophical expression, as the movement from a relationship in which their identity is merely indicated via the homophony of their names to an identity which is established through the dialectical process of the representational name itself, as its constituent markers approach those of the guiding moment of the System.

Finally, in the completion of philosophical expression, all three sides—thought as "end," names as such as "means," and representational names as "remaining object"—are seen to be founded in the nature of the means, which reveals itself as the true nature of the whole. The means, as I have argued, is the thought expressed in names as such. That thought is identical with its expression is insisted upon by Hegel in *Encyclopedia* #462 Zus.;[70] that representations themselves have identical content with the thought of the System is the burden of the System itself.

The function of names as such as determinate middles connecting representational names with philosophical meanings suggests that philosophical expression itself has the form of a Hegelian syllogism, with each of its three aspects—thought, names as such, and representational names—functioning in turn as the middle term connecting the other two. It is easy to see that this is the case, and that the triad of syllogisms which results stands in close accord with the "threefold mediation" which, according to Hegel, makes up the final nature of philosophy.[71] The first part of that mediation is accomplished by Nature, the externality of Thought, as "immediate totality" linking Logic and Spirit; here we find that names as such, through their natural existence as "mental sounds," first link thought to representation. In the second mediation of philosophy, Spirit is the mediating factor, for it "raises nature to its essence" and thus connects it with the logical structures which constitute its own inmost nature. This process can be viewed in terms of philosophi-

cal expression as the activity of the Understanding, which "separates the
essential from the unessential" via the "chemical process." This process,
as historical dialectics, culminates in precise and determinate representational names, which, through their content, mediate thought and
names as such.[72] Finally, the expressed System itself—no longer an expression *of* thought but simply concrete determinate thought—is seen to
have been the producer of the whole process; this can be viewed as corresponding to the third mediation of Philosophy, in which logical
thought reveals itself as "the absolute substance of Spirit, the Universal
and all-permeating."[73]

All three mediations exhibit the characteristic I am calling Nobility. The meanings assigned to names as such in the first mediation, as I
argued in the preceding section on thought, are composed of the right
number of markers: each is necessary and all are sufficient to distinguish
that term from others. Any systematic definition thus exhibits order over
size, and hence is Noble. When, in the second mediation, historical dialectics adds and subtracts representations from the meanings of representational names, those names gradually approach the kind of
definition that the System can provide: the dialectical clarification of
names thus en-Nobles each name. Further, the concrete terms used in
everyday representational language are in this shown to express basic
structures of thought and the world: the gap between logical structure
and the contingent "prose of the world" is overcome, as names themselves en-Noble our lives, showing them to be at once material and spiritual, contingent and necessary, logical and irrational. And, finally, the
en-Nobled words take their place in the System, which aspires to define
them all sequentially in such a way as to leave out no term which ought to
intervene between two others and to include no term which has not itself
been en-Nobled (i.e., which still retains unnecessary markers in its definition or omits needed ones). In the compactness of its order and the
reach of its comprehension, the System is the company of words which
Hegel sought; and Philosophy, which can bring thought, nature, and
spirit into reciprocating company with each other, is the noblest speech
of all.

To sum up: Philosophical expression for Hegel is a complex undertaking, of which I have so far discussed three aspects. The first of
these is the abbreviation of a complex of Systematically produced content by a name as such, creating a new "determination" for the System.
Second, the name as such used for this is a homonym of some word from

representational language: from the culture and historical epoch the System seeks to comprehend. Third, the two—representational name and Systematic thought-determination—proceed to show that they are not merely homophonic but that they have as well the same "meaning"—that is, that the markers abbreviated by the Systematic thought content are themselves all homophones of the words included in the definition of the representational name.

Much remains to be clarified. But it can already be seen that at its first stage, carried out in names as such, philosophical expression satisfies Mure's criteria of plasticity, concreteness, and internality. It is able to meet the demand, derived from Simon's writings, that it express the nature of thought itself as the immanent development of its own content. And it can meet the need, seen in my consideration of Clark, for some sort of rule or indicator which will enable the mind to move from representational language to philosophical meaning. Carried out with bearing on representational names, philosophy is also able, as I will argue in more detail shortly, to carry on the dialogue with its times that Bodammer's views failed to articulate. Further, because the final expression of the System is the "means"—that is, what is midway between the interior goal and the externality of representational language—both Hyppolite and Marx obtain satisfaction. The System appropriates representational names for its expression, as Marx suggests, but it is not indifferent to what it appropriates: representational names, as what is to be appropriated, guide the System in the choice of its tools and the direction of its development. In the process of philosophical expression as presented in "The Object," philosophical truth finds an expression which is adequate not merely to Hegel's own implicit requirements, but to criteria developed by or implicit in the secondary writers I have considered.

The Rights of Representation

The account I have so far given may suggest that Systematic comprehension is a form of identity—in the sense of marker-for-marker homophony—between representational names and Systematic names. In fact, the situation is more complex. Representation—and the historical, nonphilosophical world generally—has certain rights over and against the System, and these determine the nature of the "dialogue" between the two. My aim here is to spell them out in some detail.

The relation between a representational name and the Systematic thought content which comprehends it can be thought of in terms of a continuum. They may, at one extreme, share only their sound. At the other, all markers of each may be homophones of markers of the other. The "second premise" of philosophical expression, we saw, consists in moving from the first of these situations toward the second. This movement is facilitated, first, by the highly flexible rules of Systematic dialectic. The philosopher arranges her sequential developments so that the contents she produces come as close as possible to the representational names to be comprehended: this is what I mean by saying that the System "bears upon" representational names. And historical dialectics, operating from the other side, can add and drop markers from the definitions of representational terms to converge on the nearest Systematic moment.

Rationally impelled from both sides, *the coincidence of System and history actually turns out to be a trivial truth.* For it is achieved by adding and dropping markers, from both the Systematic side and the historical or representational side. By such means, any representational name can in fact be brought to coincide with any moment of the System: all we need to do is, one by one, drop all the markers in its definition and substitute the markers of the Systematic moment.

There are, however, constraints. The more economically the philosopher can construct her System—the fewer dialectical steps she needs to construct a Systematic explication which will match the meaning of some representational name or, in terms of my rewriting, the less she has to change the parentheses already in place—the more Noble is that System. But Nobility constrains more than Systematic dialectics. The rights of representation begin when we add the constraint that any representational name be brought into the System with as few changes in its definition as possible. This, too, is a form of Nobility, of order over size; here, the expanse to be ordered is the gap between the Systematic thought content and the representational name closest to it, and Nobility dictates that this distance be bridged in as few steps as possible. This amounts to no more than saying that the System is to be a minimal, or determinate, negation of representational language, and is prefigured in the Preface to the *Phenomenology* when Hegel says that the "individual has the right to demand that science at least provide her with the ladder" to the absolute standpoint.[74] The ladder must reach to where we historically conditioned beings are, not to where someone else is—or no one.

When a representational name, as defined in its language, comes to correspond marker for marker with the Systematic definition of some

term, we can say that philosophy has achieved its Hegelian goal of "puri-
fying" and "raising to freedom and truth" the forms of thought found in
historical language.[75] Philosophy has then "comprehended" the term
and given it a "confirmed definition," one whose content "is not simply
taken up as we merely find it in front of us, but is cognized as grounded
in free thought, and that means on itself."[76] This does happen, for
Hegel—sometimes. In the case of the Christian religion, for example, he
argues repeatedly that the content is already there and needs only a
change in form to be brought into the System.[77]

But there are times when a given word simply cannot, as it stands
or with modifications that would remain at all true to the way the word is
actually used, be brought to full identity with its Systematic analogue. In
such cases, writes Hegel:

> Philosophy has the right to choose from the language of com-
> mon life, a langage made for the world of representations, such
> expressions as *seem to come close* to the determinations of the
> Concept. There cannot here be a question of showing, for a
> word from the language of common life, that in such life we
> connect it to the same concept for which philosophy uses it;
> for common life has representations, not concepts, and philos-
> ophy itself is just the grasping of the Concept of what is other-
> wise mere representation.[78]

Hegel thus recognizes that there are irreducible gaps between the
System and what it is to comprehend; and, as his language here suggests,
in such cases the System assumes a normative dimension over against
representational language. For in the conceptual configuration which
explicates a name as such in the System, each defining marker is present
by dialectical necessity, and all together constitute a complete specification of the moment they explicate. The System thus provides a formula
for the necessary and sufficient definition of a name, one which tells us
what markers need to be included in the definition of that term, which
are unnecessary, and how they all contribute to defining one another.
These "Systematic formulas" are logically produced, comprehensive,
economical, a priori, and universal (in the sense discussed in chapter 5).
Above all, they are coherent with one another. But the representational
definition of a name, even in expert discourse (to say nothing of "common life"), is unlikely to match this standard. It is formed by history and
conditioned by chance, and presumably contains unnecessary markers
while omitting needed ones.

Aligning representational names with Systematic ones may, then, mean notable departures from actual uses. In such cases, Hegel proceeds in two different ways. One is simply to list the discrepancies between the System and the historical language.[79] This amounts, from Hegel's point of view, to listing the deficiencies of historical language vis-à-vis the System, but there is no indication that he is undertaking to revise the former. A representational definition may, however, be several dialectical steps removed from its Systematic standard form: it may be that to align the two by determinate negation, markers must be added or dropped in a certain order. A mere list of divergencies would be unable, in many cases, to convey this, and may in fact tell us relatively little. A more precise way to state the disparity between a term from historical language and a moment of the System would be to list, not merely the different content markers of the two, but the dialectical steps that would be necessary to bring the historical representation into line with the System. It is not surprising to find Hegel giving, on occasion, such "dialectical programs" for representational languages.[80] It is possible that he believes that history will eventually follow the programs he sets forth; but he would have no philosophical warrant for such belief—rather the opposite, for as the extended quotation above says, representation cannot be reduced to Concept. In view also of Hegel's well-known and generalized avoidance of predictions, it is more likely that he views such dialectical programs as precise statements of the discrepancies between the System and the representational world (so that the issue does not, for philosophy, swim in the vaguenes that it does for representation).[81]

The final task of Hegelian philosophy, on this analysis, is not to annihilate the disparities between the System and nonphilosophical language, but to state them clearly. It is in fact the *lack* of identity between the two which gives Hegel's philosophy its broad comprehensive power. For where System and world cannot coincide, a precise account of the failure can be given, either as a list or as a "dialectical program." Hegel does this in many of his *Anmerkungen* and *Zusätze*.[82] These are valuable, not because they dictate revisions to the German language or predict its future evolution, but because they give precise statements of the disparities between it and the System. Those statements are properly placed in subsidiary texts. For that the identity between it and representational language actually obtains cannot be stated by the System itself; such a statement would not be an explication or an abbreviation, or the dropping or adding of a defining marker. The System is never a set of assertions "about" representational language, or about anything: it is never a "metalanguage" which takes representational language for its object. And so it cannot assert, but only display, its comprehension of historical language and (thence) of the historical world. It is for the student to verify the exhibition.[83]

It seems clear that, in German anyway, the exhibition is in large part successful. As Klaus Hartmann writes:

> We see a major achievement on the part of Hegel in the fact
> that he tells us—or, rather, retells us in an explanatory fash-
> ion—what such and such is. . . . He succeeds in supplying "on-
> tological" meaning to all manner of content.[84]

That those who study Hegel in languages other than German re-act much more skeptically to it than does Hartmann can readily be explained. In regard to the expression of Logic, Hegel counts it an advantage of certain (historical, representational) languages to have already in them a "richness of logical expression"; it is an advantage of German in particular that it has these in the form of nouns and verbs. Further, because many terms in German have contrary meanings, the "chemical process" of representational words is clearer in it.[85] The System is then most adequately expressed in German. The distance between the System and Hegel's German—the number of times markers must be added or dropped to bring the two together—is, we may say, generally shorter than in other languages. But the predominance of German is only an "advantage" (*Vorzug*); the System can be expressed as well in any other language which has the required representational development. The first moment of the System could then, one presumes, be equally well expressed as *Sein*, Being, *l'être*, *esse*, or *to on*.

But this does not solve all problems. An early moment of Hegel's Logic is something he calls *Dasein*. English, close kin to Hegel's own German, has no name for this; translators of the Logic must make do with "determinate being," which is not a name but a phrase. Does this mean that English lacks a representation that its cousin, German, possesses?

Let us assume that it does, for even the phrase "determinate being" is hardly current in English the way *Dasein* is in German. There are then two possibilities for a Hegelian philosopher who is trying to philosophize in English. Either she can modify the development of the System at some point prior to the introduction of *Dasein* into the German version, so that she does not need to find a representation analogous to it; or she can find some representation in English and, by adding and dropping markers, transform it into the needed analogue. What she cannot do—if she wants to be true to Hegel's philosophical procedures—is *translate* the System, as it stands on Hegel's pages, into English; for it must take different paths in each language.

The Communicative Context

I noted above that it is for the student to verify whether the Hegelian comprehension of a representational content has been successful. Philosophical expression for Hegel has been conceived, by the authors I have discussed, as a binary relation: one between philosophical thought and its externality, language. I have so far argued that it is, in fact, a triadic relation: one among thought itself (the "end"), names as such (the "means"), and representational language (the "object"). But two more terms must be added to the relations: those of philosophical speaker and hearer.

The ultimate unity of the three factors presented in "The Object" was the Idea itself—the Means as containing within it both of the other two terms of the syllogism of Teleology. But, at previous levels of the process of philosophical expression, other unifying factors were present. The first and poorest, I argued, was the mere homophony of the Systematic name as such with a representational name, which permitted the first externalization of thought into a name as such to bear upon a further, representational externality. The second unifying factor was the identical content: that of the name as such with that of the representation on which the thought expressed in that name operated.

The essential communicative dimension of philosophical expression for Hegel becomes evident when we examine the relation of these two earlier unifications. In the presentation of the System, the unification of homonymity *precedes* the unification by content; and yet it *presupposes* it as well. This is because of the intrinsically haphazard nature of the expression of thought into names as such. Since all such names are equally senseless, any of them will serve as well as any other for the expression of a given moment of thought. In order for thought to be able to make a selection of the best name as such for its own expression, reference was necessary to some sort of determinate linguistic meaning. Such meaning we saw for Hegel to be the meaning of a representational name which, on the side of its sound, was homophonic with some name as such and which came, in its content, to be identical with the moment of thought being expressed.

Identity in content thus guides the choice of the name as such for the expression of thought; and that identity must, to some extent, exist explicitly *for* thought in order so to guide it. It is in this sense that the identity of content between thought and representations is presupposed by philosophical expression. The thinker, in other words, must know, prior to abbreviating a set of markers by a name as such, which representational name those markers will come closest to defining.

But if this identity of content is presupposed by the unification through homonymity, then it is difficult to see why the latter is necessary at all. For the reason for the homonymity was to enable the expressed thought to work on the representation, to bring out precisely that representation's identity as a moment of the System. If the content of the representation is already known to be identical with that of thought, there would seem to be no need for philosophical thought to use *appropriate* names as such as means of its expression.

In order to explain the need for the first expression of philosophical thought to develop its identity with representatonal names, then, it is necessary somehow to *deny* the explicit existence for thought of the identity of its own content with that of any particular representation. If we deny this identity completely, we return to the original arbitrariness of the externalization of thought in names as such. Can we take a middle way, and suggest that the identity of content between thought and representation is only partially or vaguely accessible to thought prior to its expression, but achieves clarity and precision when a moment of thought is given a name homophonic with that of the representation of which it is the final truth? The identity of content is then, prior to such expression, like the content of thought itself: something "brewing" and unclear, which only gains clarity when expressed.[86]

This solution, however, fails. For on my above account, both thought content and representational content can attain full precision *independently*: the former in the process of its development from the self-determination of the Concept, the latter in being worked up by the Understanding. As possessed of such clarity, each would retain it no matter what "mental sounds" were used to express them. They could be compared, and their final identity ascertained, with different names used for each. The problem then remains. If philosophical thought, at a given stage of its development, is totally unaware of the identity of its content with that of any representation, it cannot give it a name which will both relate it to that representation and constitute a uniform and standard externalization for that moment itself. If such thought is to any degree aware of the identity, then giving itself such a uniform and standard externalization becomes unnecessary.

The dilemma thus amounts to a contradiction between two types of awareness on the part of philosophizing thought. On the one hand, it must be to some degree aware of the identity of its content with that of representations—and on the other, it must not. The only way, I think, to resolve this dilemma is to distribute the sides of it to two different thinkers.[87] For one thinker—we may call her the "teacher"—the unity of content between thought and representation is already present. Her thought is not bound to the arbitrary externalization of itself in indifferent names as such, but can achieve a uniform and standard expression—though, precisely because that unity of content is present, it has no need to. (The first such teacher, of course, was Hegel himself. He was also the last.)

For the other thinker—let us call her "the student"—the identity of content is not yet present. Her philosophical thought is either still "brewing," not having achieved any expression, or has achieved some sort of expression which does not enable her to see how it relates to representational content. Such a thinker will need a first indication of that relation in order to be able to explicate it for herself; and such an indication would be the mere homonymity of an expression of thought and a representational name. Once this homonymity has been recognized, thought can then proceed to operate on representation to explicate the full identity, as Hegel shows in "Teleology."

Hegel distinguishes understanding philosophical thought in its own immanent development from understanding it in relation to the more concrete world. In the Introduction to the *Science of Logic*, we read:

> Logic must at first be learned as something which one doubtless understands and appreciates, but in which comprehensiveness, profundity, and further significance are, in the beginning, missed. Only from a deepened acquaintance with the other sciences does the logical exalt itself for the subjective Spirit as, not merely an abstract universal, but the universal which contains within itself the realm of the particular.[88]

Only from knowledge of mathematics, then, can we hope to understand the Logic of "Quantity" in its relation to the prephilosophical particularities of which it is the final truth. Only from an understanding of metaphysics can we understand the Logic of "Being."[89] The same is true not only of Logic, but of the whole of philosophical science:

> Philosophy can thus doubtless presuppose an acquaintance
> with its objects—indeed, it must, just as [it must presuppose]

an interest in them—if only because consciousness makes representations of things earlier, in a temporal sense, than it
makes concepts of them, and even thinking knowledge and
conceptual comprehension come only through representation
and by applying itself to representation.[90]

"Conceptual comprehension" of the extraphilosophical world by the System can only come about when the meanings of that world are clearly understood, and their identity with (or their final identity as) moments of
thought is clearly seen. But this identity may be far from obvious; and when
it is not, the student needs some sort of guide or indication which will enable her to move from representational name to the truth of that representation within the System. This indication is provided, afresh and with justice
to the concrete form of the "speculative identity" between thought and
representation, by the particular name each moment receives.[91]

It thus takes at least two, for Hegel, to philosophize; the philosophical community contains two roles, teacher and student.[92] Philosophers playing these roles must contain the same "elements": the
self-developing activity of thought; a set of precise representational
names; and a set of names as such, developed from the representational
names, which can give that thought a universal and "plastic" expression.
In one thinker, thought has externalized itself into names as such which
are the homonyms of the representations of which the respective moments of thought are the final truth; she is able to express thought in
appropriate names as such. In the other(s), the elements are separate:
thought is still merely "fermenting," has not yet found appropriate expression. Names as such are merely internal sounds that she runs
through in her Mechanical Memory. Representational contents, present
in her Recollection (*Erinnerung*)[93] and expressed by the representational
names provided by her "Name-Retaining Memory," function only in her
nonphilosophical thought about the natural and social worlds.

The dynamics of philosophical expression are such, then, that it
requires not only the three terms of ends, means, and object but also
that these be interrelated in two different ways—one constitutive of the
teacher, the other of the student. If the Absolute is not other than the
System which expresses it; and if the System is not other than that expression itself; then we can see just how self-referential Hegelian philosophy is. For the Absolute is not other than the teacher (Hegel) lecturing
to (his) students. It is one, very special, language game.

As such an interpersonal relation—or language game—the Absolute is of course confronted by contingency. If it were not, in the purest possible expression of the System, new names as such, connected dialectically and hence internally to what had gone before, would not even need the copula of the philosophical judgment to connect them; their very utterance would be their connection. The "pure" expression of the System would consist in nothing other than the succession of names which express these concrete developments. It would hold throughout to the criterion Hegel posits for the strict expression of the System's beginning: that it consist merely in "simple expressions of the Simple, without the addition of any other word whatsoever."[94]

But readers capable of following such a strict presentation, Hegel knows, do not exist; misunderstandings, in themselves intrusions of contingency, can occur, and to avoid them Hegel must make concessions to his readers. Because they are not "plastic enough to hold to the movement of pure thought,"[95] we can say that they will tend to grasp logical transitions in representational terms. To counteract this, Hegel must *argue* that the transitions take place as he presents them and not otherwise.[96] Because his readers are "unaccustomed" to abstract thought, Hegel must warn them away from mixing in inappropriate representations.[97] Because they are "impatient" with thought, and thus prone to think of earlier phases in representational terms, Hegel must recapitulate those phases in the form of thought.[98] Because they will tend to regard the part of the development with which they are concerned separately from the whole, he must add general titles and summaries, as well as recapitulations.[99] Because they may have what to him is an imperfect understanding of even the correct representational meanings of terms, he must draw out those meanings via historical discussions.[100]

I have presented these weaknesses in Hegel's readers as due to the inappropriate presence in them of representational thinking. The development of thought itself, as expressed in names as such, *va de soi* for Hegel: all difficulties in the comprehension of the System must arise in the form of intrusions from the representational side. Because they arise from representational thinking, these difficulties must be met in representational language.[101] The use of such language, which accounts I think for the bulk of Hegel's published writings, runs up against all the difficulties I have argued such language to pose for the expression of the System. If guarding against the representational "intrusions" which can impeach it constitutes the bulk of Hegel's writings, it is nonetheless *philosophically* unimportant:

> Such intrusions into the simple immanent course of the devel-
> opment are, however, for themselves contingent, and the effort
> to fend them off is thus encumbered with this contingency.[102]

The misunderstanding of the System by individuals is then, it appears, contingent for Hegel; and the successful communication of it will, given the full and distinct presence of representational language and names as such at its outset, come about of itself.

However, the student's relation to Hegelian philosophy is more than the removal of contingencies of representation. The student consists (qua student) in the ferment of thought, names as such in Mechanical Memory, and a stock of representations—all more or less disunified. Without their unification—absent, that is, an active engagement with philosophy—this second type of philosopher is dependent on the representational language she has learned, which remains unchallenged in its own sphere. This language, we have seen, expresses the history of her particular culture. If she is an Eskimo, it will have numerous words for snow and, presumably, none for "camel" or "quark." At higher levels of abstraction, the variations may be even wider: if she is French, for example, her language will have no word for "mind"; if she is English, none for *Dasein*; and so on.

She is also dependent on the language *as she has learned it*. Some of the ways she understands terms will be peculiar to her—or, as we are more likely to say, there are terms in her own language whose meaning she does not fully understand. Both she and the language may be lacking terms in some areas, and have an overabundance in others.

When such a philosopher hears thought expressed appropriately by another philosopher, she is introduced to her own language as a coherent whole, containing parts (moments or words) that are distinct from one another and yet interdefinable. She is enabled to see how concrete terms—later moments of the System such as "disease," state," and "religion"—are definable by the simple and more general terms with which the System begins (e.g., Being, Nothing, Becoming). In this, she is en-Nobled in two ways.

First, when she hears a word uttered by the other philosopher, she is aware that it can be understood in two ways: either as denoting a representation, or as meaning a moment of the System. The Hegelian philosophical utterance is thus what I have elsewhere called a "normal poetic elicitor," one which can be understood in two ways. And the process of understanding it is the process of unifying those two meanings, in a response which poetically unifies the self of the respondent. Thus, the philosopher achieves the kind of freedom I have called unification of the self, which is one form of Nobility.[103]

Because this informs her about her own language, she receives a rich and organized vocabulary and is freed of the deficiencies of her own language—both those which are peculiar to her, and (as I have argued above) at least some of those which are shared by her culture and the lexicon of her community. She learns words which enable her to articulate herself in ways others can understand, ways which enhance her life in her community. She thereby ceases to be a merely contingent, or inarticulate, being, and becomes an individual of universal import—one from whom others can learn. This, then, is what Hegel refers to as the "history which repeats itself for every human being."[104] The history will never, of course, be complete. Even at his most messianic, Hegel never denies that new individuals will continue to be born and enter into all the difficult oppositions of life. And, as I have noted, he is also aware that new representations will arise. Revisions are not only possible but continual: an adequate vocabulary is something that the philosopher, no matter what her culture and even in her early years, must help create as well as passively learn.

11

The Expression
of the System:
Demarcation

egel's System, if I am right about it, never claims to be "true" of
extraphilosophical discourse, to say nothing of extralinguistic reality itself. It is a linguistic ideal, constructed with regard to Nobility and engaging in various types of interplay with discourses
outside it. Those interplays proceed via a double set of meaning transformations, in which both the System and historical language drop and add
markers from the definitions of the words they contain or form. Where
the identity of System and history is not achieved, this process remains
incomplete: the two meanings, Systematic and historical, are alike or an-
alogical, but not identical, and the movement between them is accordingly a carrying over. When this carrying over is between languages, as it
was in Hegel's account of representational and conceptual languages in
chapter 7, it is what Hegel calls an *Übersetzen*, a translation from one
language to another.[1] When it moves between two sets of meanings
which have coincided enough to constitute a single medium of philosophical expression—the goal of the syllogistic process of philosophical
expression discussed in the previous chapter—we can call it (though
Hegel does not) a metaphor, though it is a very precise one. In exhibiting
its own metaphorical relation to historical language, Hegel's System
highlights a feature also present, but also backgrounded, by the thought

of Davidson and Wittgenstein. For them as well, the relation between the different types of language with which they deal is one of metaphor, and metaphoricality is central to the status of their own theories.

In chapter 8, I presented Davidson's conception of learnability. The requirement is, I noted, extremely, perhaps unrealistically, strong as regards the languages we actually speak. It is, however, eminently plausible when applied to formal languages, which are constructed in just the way Davidson's theory suggests: a set of primitive terms is constituted and a finite number of rules is applied, recursively, to generate sentences. Anyone knowing the primitives and the rules has learned the language: is in a position to understand the meaning of any sentence that can be formulated in that language. The type of truth theory to which Davidson appeals was originally formulated by Tarski for such formal languages, and Tarski did not think it would apply to "natural languages" such as English.[2] In Tarski's doubts, Davidson's thought encounters the ancient tension between language which is formal or ideal, and language which is spoken or merely "natural"—the tension between, as the ancients had it, sacred and profane language. What justifies the hope that this tension can be overcome: that truth theory, developed for ideal languages, can apply to languages actually spoken in the world? Certainly our written and spoken languages do not ordinarily look or sound like the objects of a Davidsonian truth theory.

In "Truth and Meaning," Davidson adverts to a number of characteristics of actual languages that pose difficulties for the kind of theory he envisions, and he has several different ways of dealing with them. One—the fact that the number of utterances possible in any given language is infinite while the resources of any theory are only finite—is obviated by the design of the theory itself: such, indeed, is the point of the design. Another, ambiguity, is not a problem for the theory but rather part of what is to be captured (though not, as follows from my remarks on polysemy in chapter 8, explained) by it. It achieves this quite faithfully: the truth conditions for an ambiguous word will be ambiguous in just the ways that the word is.[3] Other syntactical phenomena, such as adverbial and adjectival modification, propositional attitudes, counterfactuals, and the like, are calls to action.[4] And the semantic paradoxes (which actual languages run into when formalized but Tarski's formalized languages, because of their hierarchy of metalanguages, do not) are admitted to be unanswerable, at least for the moment.[5]

These discrepancies between formal and actual languages point to a tension in Davidson's approach. On the one hand, he wants to minimize the independence of formal language from actual languages, the

better to bring them together in an achieved theory of meaning for a
natural language. Thus, unlike Quine, Davidson does not view regi-
mented languages—languages which have submitted to the demands of
logical theory—as improvements upon actual languages, but merely as
tools for understanding them. Formal language is no more than a statement of the formal properties of various structures which themselves are
abstracted from, and part of, actual language:[6]

> Since I am not interested in improving upon natural language
> but in understanding it, I view formal languages as devices for
> exploring the structure of natural language . . . standard for-
> mal languages are intermediate devices to assist us in treating
> natural languages.[7]

On the other hand, it turns out that an actual language must be changed
quite a bit in order to be understood by applying to it a truth theory
originally designed for formal languages; and if we regard such intel-
ligiblity as desirable, the changes will indeed be improvements. In any
case, there is a series of them.

First, according to Davidson, a theory of truth is to be formulated
for a language as similar to English as we can make it. Indeed, if we can
explain this language in English, and its words sound and function like
English words, then the language is not merely like English, it is English—presumably its "indicative core."[8] But the gap is not quite closed:
before the indicative core of spoken English really matches up with this
theoretical model, it has to undergo some remodeling of its own to
make it exhibit the logical forms of its own sentences. Davidson refers to
this as "semantic taming" and "gerrymandering."[9] This, whatever
nonmetaphorical terms we might use to describe it, is clearly more than
merely abstracting. To take just one concrete example: suppose someone
at work picks up a hammer, grunts "too heavy!" and reaches for a
smaller one.[10] It would take a fair, though not an enormous, amount of
remodeling to get that utterance—itself apparently descriptive—to exhibit the logical form by which it has been constructed, via recursive
rules, from semantic primitives. Finally, the nondescriptive sentences
still outside this remodeled core must also be, in some way, "systematically transformed" into sentences that also exhibit their logical form.[11]

Given that actual languages exist, and that (since Tarski anyway)
the required kind of formal ones do as well, what Davidson gives us here
is an account of the possible *convergence* between the two. Davidson does
not actually carry the project out; it would require large-scale coopera-

tion among linguists and philosophers.[12] As matters stand, then, any sentence of the type: "Tarski-type theory of truth X applies to actual language Y" is false. What does this tell us about the status of Davidson's own views?

There is a recurrent rhetorical gesture in the passages where Davidson discusses the applicability of theories of truth to actual language. Consider the following (emphasis added):

> Insofar as we succeed in giving such a theory for a natural language, we see the natural language *as* a formal system.[13]

> Interpreted formal systems are best seen *as* extensions or fragments of the natural languages from which they draw life.[14]

> We may think of the sentences to which the first stage of the theory applies *as* giving the logical form, or deep structure, of all sentences.[15]

> I view formal languages *as* devices for exploring the structure of natural language.[16]

> [Formal languages] assist us in treating natural languages *as* more complex formal languages.[17]

The gesture is carried through in other terms as well:

> As a result of [Frege and Tarski] we have gained a deep *insight* into the structure of our mother tongues.[18]

> We may welcome the *insight* that comes when we understand language well enough to apply [the semantic theory of truth].[19]

In these sentences, Davidson is advocating a program; his recommendations are grounded pragmatically, in some cases because they yield "insight." But is insight truth? If I see formal languages *as* parts of actual languages, am I presupposing that they *are* parts of actual language? Denying it? Remaining neutral on the matter? Neutral with a bias toward the truth of the assertion? Neutral with hopes? Davidson's answer is:

> Seeing as is not seeing that. Metaphor makes us see one thing *as* another by making some literal statement that inspires or prompts the *insight*.[20]

A metaphor, for Davidson, is not a sentence with a literal plus a figurative meaning. It is a sentence with a literal meaning, usually false,[21] which invites us to seek the likeness that inspired it and elicited its utterance. This account applies perfectly, then, to Davidson's own theory: to see actual languages *as* formal systems is to see them in terms of a metaphor—to investigate the likenesses between actual languages and formal systems. To see formal systems *as* tools for exploring actual languages is to view the other side of the same metaphor. Davidson's theory thus claims to be, not true, but insightful: it is itself a metaphor.[22] Moreover, this metaphorical status is not something that Davidson can easily dispense with. For eliminating the metaphor would just be to achieve the convergence of formal and natural language. And then the statement that "Tarskian truth theories apply to natural languages" would be, not a theory at all, but an established fact: one that *we* had established, by formulating our theory and by remodeling its object. It would be, not merely theory laden, but practice ridden.

As the language of Hegel's System stands to historical language, then, so Davidsonian formal languages stand to natural languages (which are just historical languages viewed ahistorically). They are metaphors for understanding them and are also, for both thinkers, standards in terms of which to reshape them. But for Hegel, who views historical language as temporal, the convergence of the two types of language is actually coming to pass, on all fronts. Language remodels itself, and one job of the philosopher of language is to reconstruct this process—as well as to help it along. In the passages I have cited from Davidson on the transformation of "natural language," it is presented as an object of taming and gerrymandering, as wild or inert.

The other difference is that in Hegel's view, convergence is not a necessary condition for insight. Providing a baseline from which to measure word meanings, and a measure as well of their distance from that baseline, Hegel's philosophical definitions can provide useful information about words in representational language even where the two kinds of language do not coincide. Could the same be true of Davidson's kind of theory? What would it mean for the theory to yield insight where it does not apply—where, for example, the "meaning" of a sentence cannot be derived from its truth conditions, perhaps because it has no very determinate truth conditions? Can Davidson say more, in such cases, than that the sentence is "vague"? And how does *this* apply to the metaphors in which Davidson's own theory is articulated? After his discussions of convergence, are we very clear on what must happen for the sentence "Tarski's theory of truth applies to actual languages" to become true? What precisely is this remodeling, gerrymandering, taming that will take place? As an activity, does it come under any of the traditional models for action that philosophers have advanced? Is it possibly a Fichtean attempt to realize an ideal, as moral imperative? Or an Aristotelian introduction of form onto the burgeoning matter of our everyday utterances? Or is it, not the imposition, but the elicitation of a form somehow already there in our speech, awaiting the efforts of the semanticist as the statue in the stone awaits the sculptor or as historical language, sometimes, moves toward Hegel? Does Davidsonian remodeling have other alternatives than to be either a moral impositon of form or an aesthetic elicitation of it? And whatever we do, must we not take account of our sensory experiences as we remodel? In remodeling, are we not somehow, morally or aesthetically, bringing together our senses—the sounds and sights of our language—with our intellects, the abstract forms of our logical acumen? Can Davidson's theory, and our response to it, be anything other than what I call "normal poetic interaction"?[23]

Davidson certainly, perhaps felicitously, does not talk that way. Those regions of language which do not come under the theory, at any stage of the convergence process Davidson sketches, are simply areas to be dealt with in the future; if they cannot be subdued, the theory fails. This demand in turn means that the distance between the Hegelian and Davidsonian approaches is actually rather wide. For it places Davidson within a threefold procedure that has, fatefully, characterized philosophy almost since its inception:

1. Theoretically, one part of some domain is articulated and described; call it "F."
2. Theoretico-practically, the rest of that domain—which in some respects differs from F, and which I will call "M"—is understood, or seen, as F.
3. Practically, those parts of M that cannot be seen as F are transformed into members of F.

This procedure, as I have shown elsewhere, has been basic to metaphysics since Aristotle. It is the gesture by which his ontology can explore being as such by focusing on the Prime Mover, or ethical life by focusing on the *phronimos*.[24] The antimetaphysical gesture would be to show that one's own theory yields insights even where it does not apply, by showing the other in a specific way what it is not and thereby highlighting, in a specific way, what it is. Conceiving of this, as the case of

Davidson shows, is hard to do on an assertionistic basis—or, as we might say, when a vestigial assertionism kicks sand in our eyes.

For Davidson's assertionism cannot be anything more than vestigial. In the first place, to make truth do the job of meaning (and for other, Quinean reasons), Davidson has, as I noted in chapter 8, thinned its concept to an ontological minimum: it specifies the goal of inquiry very broadly indeed. In the second place, Davidson has shown that, even so attenuated, the concept of truth cannot give the goal of at least one important species of rational inquiry: his own. But as regards the aim of his own inquiry, in the passages quoted above, Davidson continues to speak as if the basic metaphor he propounds will yield insight only where it proves true: where the resemblances it suggests actually obtain. Where falsified, it will be uninformative (except, presumably, in the sense that it will show us paths not to try again). Insight remains, then, theoretically subordinate to truth. It is Davidson's *practice* which belies this: just by advancing his theory in metaphorical form, he implicitly suggests that it has value, here and now, in such form; that the areas where it is not true—whether they will eventually be transformed into areas where it does apply or not—are areas worth knowing about; that the ability to inform us about ourselves is not coextensive with the ability to state truths about what we are, and what our language is.

Hence, what I call Davidson's residual assertionism has not impeached his theory as much as it has impeded his own understanding of that theory. Attaining such understanding will place the Davidsonian paradigm explicitly into the proximity with Hegel that it already shows but does not say.[25]

For Wittgenstein, philosophy is not to advance theories about language but to describe language games: his invitation to his reader is not "remodel language," but *beschreibe Sprachspiele*, "describe language games."[26] Since description is obviously itself a language game, we have here a situation in which one such game relates to another. There is more to this relation than family resemblance.

"Description" denotes for Wittgenstein, as we would expect, a family of related activities, undertaken for different purposes and with different standards for success and failure. There is, however, one trait that runs through this entire family, a necessary condition for something to be a "description" at all. It is a negative one: a "description" does not generate (*erzeugen*) what it describes.[27] As applied to philosophy, this works out to the view that philosophy is to leave untouched (*antasten*) what it describes: it "leaves everything as it is."[28] I will call this the *noli tangere* requirement on description in general and on philosophy in particular. As applied to description in general, it is, Wittgenstein says, a "conceptual claim" (*begriffliche Feststelllung*),[29] and as such it is for him to be viewed as, like all grammatical claims, arbitrary.[30] Why? If the *noli tangere* requirement is arbitrarily related to "description," is the relation of description to philosophy equally arbitrary?

There is, in fact, a gap between the *noli tangere* requirement as applied to description generally and its philosophical version: it is a long way from "not generating" one's object to "leaving everything as it is." It is quite possible that a description can alter its object without generating it. An example of this is suggested in the *Philosophical Investigations* at ¶254, which refers to the philosophical propensity for substituting "identical" for "like" (*gleich*). This is in fact the very move which sets up the metaphysical search for essences; Wittgenstein's aim in describing it is not merely to change, but indeed to end, that particular language game—and to transform any larger games in which it is a move.[31]

Wittgenstein's own practice, in the *Philosophical Investigations*, is also not purely descriptive. It diverges from description, in fact, in two ways. First, it contains, for therapeutic purposes, a comparative dimension. Metaphysical uses of words must be traced back to—that is, compared with and differentiated from—ordinary uses.[32] There are thus, we might say, at least three separate language games at play in a piece of Wittgensteinian philosophical analysis: the metaphysical language game in which a word is given an essentialistic meaning, the ordinary game in which it does not have that meaning, and the therapeutic game in which the analysis is conducted.[33] The therapeutic game, then, depends on the other two for its existence, and the metaphysical game (presumably) depends on the ordinary game. For Wittgenstein, the ordinary game ought to be linguistic bedrock, but in fact it cannot be independent of the other two: it is an empirical fact that ordinary language is stuffed with the rubble of dead metaphysics, and the point of therapy is to restore it to its true status after the war philosophy has made against it. So the three types of language games stand in a circular relationship of mutual conditioning.

Wittgenstein's practice also requires a certain dimension of narrative. Narrative, as I define it, is a linguistic exercise in which *post hoc ergo propter hoc* is not a fallacy: in which some things occur because others have occurred. I alluded in chapter 8 to Wittgenstein's awareness of the temporality of language—of the fact that language games unroll in time. If language games had no narrative structure in the present sense, they could not thus "unroll": for we would not be able to distinguish a language game from a nonsense conversation such as the following:

Emma: "How are you?"
Joe: "Is my ball red?"
Emma: "Down with numismatism!"
Joe: "Your toe hurts."

This, I take it, is not immediately recognizable as anything except silly or even insane babble, at least partly because the utterances do not come in any *meaningful* order: any of them could occur at any place in the exchange. It seems, then, essential to a language game that certain things cannot be said (or done) in it until other things have been said; otherwise we will be unable to recognize wrong or nonsensical moves.[34] Such a game must unroll in a way which is in principle recognizable, and so must have a kind of unity over time.

Wittgenstein refers to the unity of a language game as its *Witz*, literally its "wit" or "humor": its point.[35] But while he recognizes that a language game has a kind of unifying principle, he has strong reservations about what that unity can consist in. First, it should not be teleological, in that the various moves are all seen to contribute to some larger purpose. We can attribute teleological unity to a language game only if we know, independently of our knowledge of what happens in the game, what its purpose is, or if we can ascribe some purpose or purposes to the participants.[36] Second, it certainly cannot be archetypical—that is, evident in that the various moves conform to and confirm some preknown pattern or set of rules; such patterns are, as essences, of a very troublesome status for Wittgenstein, and he explicitly distinguishes the *Witz* from rules at ¶564.

Third, the *Witz* may be merely habitual: constituted simply by the fact that we have heard those utterances in that order before. This is not only attractive to Wittgenstein, but plausible in itself: if we have heard Joe and Emma repeat their bizarre conversation several times in the past, for example, we will expect the current conversation to unroll in the way that it does, and it will make sense to us. Our expectation will be grounded in what we saw Wittgenstein instate as a basic linguistic phenomenon: our habits. But in order to recognize a game, we must have already seen it played: we must be able to compare the description of the present game with other, previous playings in order even to recognize it as a description of a language game.

In all three cases, a simple description of an exchange is not enough to show that it is a language game. In all, it is difficult to account for the unity of a language game except with reference to something over and above that game: a purpose, an archetype, other games previously experienced. In the first two cases, the "something over and above" that must be appealed to is a metaphysical construct, a purpose or pattern: precisely the kind of general essence against which Wittgenstein's therapy is directed. In the third case, a language game is a language game because it repeats other langage games. Repeats them how? Repeats what in them? It cannot *simply* make use of individual moves in the earlier games, for the whole point is to see how individual moves come together to constitute a unified game. It must repeat not the moves of previous games, but their *Witz*. But how do those earlier games show their *Witz*, so that we can recognize the repetitions? Do we want to begin an infinite regress? Or a Derridean loss of origin, so that language games repeat other language games in ways we cannot understand?[37] What if we cannot tell whether a bizarre conversation, like Joe's and Emma's above, is a language game until we see it repeated a certain number of times? Then how can we distinguish nonsense from sense? If "sense" just means repeatability, anything we hear may turn out someday to be sensible, if we hear it often enough, including talk about metaphysical essences. The therapeutic project is in great danger if any "disease" that is repeated enough turns into health.

Wittgenstein's answer is closest, it seems at first, to the Derridean: it is possible for us to recognize a conversation as repeating an earlier language game, without our being able to say exactly how. But Derrida goes on to say that it is also impossible for us to say *which* language game, or games, or in his own word "texts," the present one repeats. Where for Derrida the present text relates repetitively to an indeterminate range of previous texts, Wittgenstein would want to keep the set as determinate as possible, because of his concern with learning language games. On both thinkers' view, we cannot learn by formula, by memorizing the rules of language games; but on Derrida's view, if it were pushed with consistency, we would not even be able to teach by example, because we would never have a clear example of anything. And that is precisely how Wittgenstein wants us to be able to teach.[38] We learn a language game by seeing its resemblance to a determinate set of other linguistic exchanges that we can recognize as language games because we perceive their *Witz*, though not as a purpose or a set of rules. From this, indeed, follows Wittgenstein's own strategy of appealing to "primitive" language games, which I discussed in chapter 8.

This, for Wittgenstein, is possible because the *Witz* of the earlier game was indeed given to us, but in ways we cannot articulate. The view that we can perceive a unity that is nonetheless ineffable is central, of course, to Kant's doctrine of aesthetic judgment.[39] So it is perhaps not surprising that Wittgenstein tends to refer to this narrative dimension of a language game in terms which approximate it to perceptual feel—to music:

> Understanding a sentence of a language is much more akin to understanding a musical theme than one often thinks. . . . Why just this movement of loudness and tempo? One would like to say, "I know what that all means." But what does it mean? I would not know what to say.[40]

> What happens when we learn to *perceive* the ending of a church mode as an *ending*?[41]

Here, again, theory comes down to metaphor. In this case, eliminating the metaphor would mean either identifying the unity of language games as unities of Kantian reflective judgment, or destroying the analogy between the two by somehow articulating the *Witz* of a language game, so that it would no longer be a matter of perceptual feel. But the former would mean completely sacrificing the descriptive claim of philosophy: philosophy would articulate language games much the way criticism articulates music and art in general—and would fall victim to all the subjectivity of such articulation: *de linguis non sit disputandum*. The latter is precisely what Wittgenstein wants to prevent, because then the language game would gain an essence, would achieve a governing purpose or set of rules.

Hence, the metaphoricity of his account of *Witz* is essential to Wittgenstein's project: if one were to eliminate it, one would land either in art criticism or in metaphysics, while to unpack it *is* to land back in metaphysics. This is all right for specific purposes, says Wittgenstein, but not as a general procedure.[42]

Is there a way out of this bind? Is it possible to articulate the unity of language games not as an unchanging essence or from the standpoint of one's own individual feelings but as, perhaps, having structures which change step by step, so that each move revokes some but not all aspects of the previous move? Could such reconstruction be, in virtue of its step-by-step form, intersubjectively justifiable and yet not the imposition of a previously existing, unchanging essence? Could such a procedure yield, in short, not a description of a game in previously existing terms (very ordinary language used for a very special purpose), but create the very words which were adequate to it? Would we not be able to articulate *Witz* without subjecting it to previously existing categories? In such a case, would our sacrifice of description not lead to an interplay between our (ordinary, extraordinary) language and the game we describe, so that we gain content—the words for newly comprehended langage games—as those games gain articulation? And would not this particular resolution of the snarl leave us, again, in proximity to Hegel?

I have said that my account of Hegel would leave standing the approaches and achievements of Wittgenstein and Davidson, among others. I did not say that it would leave intact the assertionistic rhetoric in which they, like Hegel, have been covered over. If we openly admit our metaphors, forsaking theory's ancient truth-claims in the interests of new and richer claims (such as Nobility)—are we anything other than Hegelian? Is there any way to do philosophy of language without resorting either to metaphor or to Hegel? And if we resort to Hegel, what do we do about what I call the *diakena*—the gaping absences that yawn, as Heidegger and others teach us, in all our experience, that undo the textures of our lives and languages? Hegel never saw them. Another book must accredit them.

12

The Expression
of the System:
Narrative

T he dynamics of Hegelian Systematic expression, as I have outlined
them, are virtually unprecedented in philosophy—as unprecedented as Hegel's radical break with assertionism and his radical
turn toward language. In place of a narrative, I can offer only an
analogy.

Consider all of history as a giant Platonic dialogue. Alcibiades
(consciousness or science, or humanity itself) puts forward, from his felt
needs, a definition of something—anything. Socrates (nature, history,
the Other) refutes it. Alcibiades then formulates a new definition which
keeps the valid features of the old, changing it only as needed to accommodate the new. At the end of the process, which will be only provisional, waits Diotima, philosophy: able in her sacred wisdom to take
words that have refined and proved themselves and to tie them together,
showing their deep interrelatedness. In so doing, she is not fixated either
upon an ineffable vision of essence or on rigid accounts of it, but in what
Hamann called *Herablassung* she descends, and transforms Heaven itself
to reach out to what Socrates and Alcibiades, so laboriously, are building
up out of history. For Diotima's Heaven is, after all, just a company of
words.

And when others arrive—Plato's lost mother Perictione, or

Phaedo, the freed slave—to cry that their needs are still wordless, Diotima has the strength and resources, one way or another, to wrench Heaven, and enlarge it as well, to accommodate them, too.

And so we wander forward, all of us in company and separately, but less separately after than before.

Such, if I am right, is Hegel's view of the cosmos and humanity's philosophical activity in it. Is there any truth in that view? Not much. But it certainly is Noble.

Notes

Introduction

[1]For a trenchant summary of the ongoing and splendid chaos in Hegel interpretation, see Robert B. Pippin, *Hegel's Idealism* (Cambridge: Cambridge University Press, 1989), 3–6.

[2]Who saw the Concept (*Begriff*) as "the other side of the empirical": Hegel, letter to Schelling of February 23, 1807, in Johannes Hoffmeister, ed., *Briefe von und an Hegel*, (Hamburg: Meiner, 1952–1960), 1:151 (#90); *Hegel: The Letters*, trans. Clark Butler and Christiane Seiler (Bloomington: University of Indiana Press, 1984), 77.

[3]As I will argue in chapter 1.

[4]I will explore affinities between Hegel and various Analytical philosophers in the "demarcations" of this book.

[5]See the argument in William Desmond, "Hegel, Dialectic, and Deconstruction," *Philosophy and Rhetoric* 18 (1985): 260f., and the suspicions of Irene Harvey, "The Linguistic Basis of Truth for Hegel," *Man and World* 15 (1982): 295. For a very different statement of the general postmodern point that intelligibility and totality do not go together (a view which Hegel, on my interpretation, would accept—provided the "intelligibility" in question is not asserted to be "scientific" or "philosophical"), see Joseph Flay, *Hegel's Quest for Certainty* (Albany: SUNY Press, 1984), 249–67.

[6]On this see John McCumber, *Poetic Interaction* (Chicago: University of Chicago Press, 1989), 210ff.

[7]David Hume, *A Treatise of Human Nature*, ed. L. A. Selby-Bigge (Oxford: Oxford University Press, 1888), 251ff.

[8]*KRV* B 823–58 ("The Canon of Pure Reason").

[9]Kant, *Werke* 5:171; *Prolegomena to Any Future Metaphysics,* ed. L. W. Beck (Indianapolis: Bobbs-Merrill, 1950), 52.

[10]Gilles Deleuze, *La philosophie critique de Kant* (Paris: Presses Universitaires de France, 1963), 39f.

[11]*KRV* B25, B89, B860; *Prolegomena,* in Kant, *Werke* 5:192/69f.

[12]*KRV* B 836ff.

[13]*KRV* B 860f.

[14]Friedrich Nietzsche, *Götzendämmerung,* in *Sämtliche Werke,* ed. Alfred Bäumler, (Stuttgart: Kohlhammer, 1964), 8:64.

[15]*KRV* B 862.

[16]*KRV* B xxiiif.

[17]*Werke* 10:16f.; *Critique of Judgment,* trans. Werner S. Pluhar (Indianapolis: Hackett, 1987), 392f.

[18]As claims Vittorio Hösle in *Hegels System* (Hamburg: Meiner, 1987); but on Hösle see n. 54 below.

[19]Preface to the second edition of the *Encyclopedia,* VIII 38; not translated. It is in the spirit of the view that philosophy *simply is* the final end of human reason that Hegel so often assures us that it *simply must be* a system; for a discussion of such passages, see Manfred Baum, "Anmerkungen zum Verhältnis von Systematik und Dialektik bei Hegel," in Dieter Henrich, ed., *Hegels Wissenschaft der Logik: Formation und Rekonstruktion* (Stuttgart: Klett-Cotta, 1986), 65ff.

[20]See the letter to van Ghert of December 16, 1809, in *Briefe* 1:299 (#152)/588.

[21]XI 331; also 280, 346.

[22]Kant, *Werke* 10:226f./160f.

[23]XI 318, 332, 336; also see 318, 320f.

[24]XI 309, 323.

[25]XI 323f.

[26]XI 317.

[27]For the importance of friendship to Hegel's Hamann, see XI 285ff., 294, 297f., 310f.

[28]XI 297.

[29]XI 285ff., 308f., 314.

[30]XI 309.

[31]XI 343f.

[32]XI 327, 329. These writings will be discussed in chapter 9.

[33]Hegel, "Solgers Nachgelassene Schriften und Briefwechsel," XI 248f.

[34]XI 246.

[35]III (*PHG*) 82–92/58–66.

[36]VIII 51f. (*Enz.* #8 Anm.)/12.

[37]See McCumber, *Poetic Interaction,* 301ff.

[38]XVII 250.

[39]Anthony Storr, *Solitude* (New York: Ballantine Books, 1988), 7ff. It is noteworthy that many of the most important examples Storr uses to argue *against* this view are philosophers such as Kant, Spinoza, and Wittgenstein. In this respect Hegel, who as we will see was in many ways a veritable sphinx, remained true to his profession: he perhaps exalted the value of intimate friendships because he himself had so few of them.

[40]See the essays in Jürgen Habermas, *Communication and the Evolution of Society,* trans. Thomas McCarthy (Boston: Beacon, 1979); also Habermas, *Theory of Communicative Action,* trans. Thomas McCarthy, 2 vols. (Boston: Beacon, 1984–87).

[41]VII 463f., 469f. (*Rechtsphil.* ##295 Anm., 296, 301 Anm.)/192f., 196.

[42]Wolfgang Sünkel, "Hegel und der Mut zur Bildung," in Wilhelm Raimund Beyer, ed., *Die Logik des Wissens und das Problem der Erziehung* (Hamburg: Meiner, 1982), 205f. Also see the thorough account of Siegfried Reuss, interpreting Hegel's philosophy as "an affirmative, emancipatory concept of education developed with a view to state pedagogy": Reuss, *Die Verwirklichung der Vernunft* (Frankfurt: Max Planck Institut für Bildungsforschung, 1982), 5–297, esp. 18; and also the very interesting discussion of Ursula Krautkrämer, *Staat und Erziehung* (Munich: Johannes Beichmann, 1979), 182–249.

[43]III (*PHG*) 65/43.

[44]David Hull, *Science as a Process* (Chicago: University of Chicago Press, 1988).

[45]As notes Willem A. deVries in *Hegel's Theory of Mental Activity* (Ithaca: Cornell University Press, 1988), xii. But see the efforts of M. J. Petry, in his editions of the *Philosophy of Nature* (London: Allen and Unwin, 1970), and the *Philosophy of Subjective Spirit*

(The Hague: Reidel, 1979). De Vries has done an excellent job of relating Hegel's views on subjective spirit to contemporary philosophy of mind and psychology; for a discussion of Hegel's relation to empirical science in general, see pp. 13–18, as well as the essays in Robert Cohen and Marx Wartofsky, eds., *Hegel and the Sciences* (Dordrecht: Reidel, 1984), especially Gerd Buchdahl, "Conceptual Analysis and Scientific Theory in Hegel's Philosophy of Nature (With Special Reference to Hegel's Optics)," 13–36.

[46]VIII 51 (*Enz.* #8)/12.

[47]VIII 56 (*Enz.* #12)/18.

[48]XVIII (*Hist. Phil.*) 76f./57.

[49]V (*WDL*) 20/31f.

[50]V (*WDL*) 19/31.

[51]III (*PHG*) 464ff./383ff.

[52]*Glauben and Wissen* (hereinafter *GW*) II 288; *Faith and Knowledge*, trans. Walter Cerf and H. S. Harris (Albany: SUNY Press, 1977), 55f.

[53]See Jacques Derrida, *De la grammatologie* (Paris: Minuit, 1967), 208f.; *Of Grammatology*, trans. Gayatri Chakravorty Spivak (Baltimore: Johns Hopkins University Press, 1974), 144. True, Hegel speaks, both in the *Differenzschrift* and in *Faith and Knowledge*, as if he had a principle; but his formulations of it are invariably vapid, nonsensical, or both (e.g., in the former text, "the identity of identity and non-identity," II 96/156). Hence, I cannot agree with Dieter Henrich that philosophy for Hegel must have a single principle; and since that belief is the only motivation I can find for Henrich's claim that negation and the negation of the negation have the same object and are but two sides of the same *Grundoperation*, I cannot accept that either: Henrich, "Hegels Grundoperation," in Ute Guzzoni et al., *Der Idealismus und seine Gegenwart* (Hamburg: Meiner, 1976), 208–30. For an approach to Hegelian dialectic which sees it not as the application of a single "basic operation" but as the confluence of an irreducible plurality of gestures, see chapter 4.

[54]II *GW* 398/157; see the commentary by Walther Zimmerli in "Die Frage nach der Philosophie. Interpretationen zu Hegels 'Differenzschrift,' " *Hegel-Studien* Beifheft 12 (2d ed. 1986): 137–46, and also that of Heinz Röttges, *Der Begriff der Methode in der Philosophie Hegels* (Meisenheim/Glan, 1976), 12f. For Hegel's rejection of principled foundationalism, see chapter 3 of Tom Rockmore, *Hegel's Circular Epistemology* (Bloomington: Indiana University Press, 1986), 44–77, and Michael Forster, *Hegel and Skepticism* (Cambridge, Mass.: Harvard University Press, 1989), 130f. Manfred Baum has brought this critique of principles into illuminating connection with Hegel's early doubts about propositional form: Baum, *Die Entstehung der Hegelschen Dialektik*, 2d ed. (Bonn: Bouvier, 1989), 49f. For a brief account of the point of view from which Hegel criticizes Fichte, see Frithjof Bergmann, "The Purpose of Hegel's System," *Journal of the History of Philosophy* 2 (1964): 196. Vittorio Hösle's claim that Hegel criticizes not the core of Fichte's systematic program but only the way he carried it through, a claim for which Hösle admits he cannot find any textual warrant (Hösle, *Hegel's System*, 28 and n. 29), thus cannot be correct. With this claim falls much of the basis for Hösle's claim to be interpreting Hegel as a "transcendental philosopher" (p. 12), though his book is a noteworthy achievement in its own right.

[55]II (*GW*) 398/157.

[56]II (*GW*) 413f./172. Reinhard Lauth argues that Hegel is wrong to claim that Fichte conflates the two levels; indeed, Fichte himself denied this doubleness, claiming that his *Wissenschaftslehre* never claimed that the ego as found and perceived was its principle. The principle of Fichte's philosophy was instead the ego as a free, a priori construction. But Hegel's deeper point remains: even a "pure" ego, if used as the sort

of principle that Fichte uses it, must be at once plenary and defective. Lauth, *Hegel vor der Wissenschaftslehre* (Wiesbaden: Franz Steiner Verlag, 1987), 146f.

[57]Hegel, letter to Sinclair of early 1813, *Briefe* 2:4 (#218)/293.

[58]Hegel, *Differenzschrift*, II 81; *The Difference Between Fichte's and Schelling's System of Philosophy*, trans. Walter Cerf and H. S. Harris (Albany: SUNY Press, 1977), 144.

[59]II (*GW*) 425/183.

[60]II 87/148f.

[61]II (*GW*) 426f./184.

[62]II 89f./151.

[63]Isaiah Berlin, "On the Pursuit of the Ideal," *New York Review of Books*, March 17, 1988, 11.

[64]II 187/148.

[65]Søren Kierkegaard, *Concluding Unscientific Postscript*, trans. David F. Swenson and Walter Lowrie (Princeton: Princeton University Press, 1941), 100n.

[66]For the "metaphysical" Hegel, see J. N. Findlay, *Hegel: A Re-examination* (London: Allen & Unwin, 1958); also Iwan Iljin, *Die Philosophie Hegels als kontemplative Gotteslehre* (Bern: Francke, 1946). For the historicized Absolute, see Charles Taylor, *Hegel* (Cambridge: Cambridge University Press, 1975); Hegel's view of language, which on my reading is all there is to Hegel, is discussed on p. 568. For criticism of "large-entity" intepretations in general, see David Kolb, *The Critique of Pure Modernity* (Chicago: University of Chicago Press, 1986).

[67]See Rodolphe Gasché, *The Tain of the Mirror* (Cambridge, Mass.: Harvard University Press, 1986); Alan White, *Absolute Knowledge: Hegel and the Problem of Metaphysics* (Athens: Ohio University Press, 1983). Also Paul Guyer, "Dialektik als Methodologie," in Henrich, *Hegels Wissenschaft*, 164–77.

[68]V 44/50. For remarks of this sort, see also III (*PHG*) 28, 46, 588/14, 27, 490f.; V (*WDL*) 19, 57, 67f./31, 60, 69; VI (*WDL*) 264/592; VIII 14f., 57 (*Enz.* #12 Anm.), 307 (*Enz.* #160 Zus.), 368 (*Enz.* #213 Anm.)/not translated, 16ff., 223f., 275. In my refusal to pursue "large entity" interpretation, I generally follow David Kolb, *Critique,* and such thinkers as Kenley R. Dove, "Hegel's Phenomenological Method," in Warren Steinkraus, ed., *New Studies in Hegel's Philosophy* (New York: Holt, Rinehart & Winston, 1971), 34–56; Klaus Hartmann, *Die Ontologische Option* (Berlin: de Gruyter, 1976); Alexandre Koyré, "Notes sur la langue et la terminologie hégéliennes," in *Études d'histoire de la pensée philosophique* (Paris: Colin, 1961), 175–204; William Maker, "Understanding Hegel Today," *Journal of the History of Philosophy* 9 (1981): 343–75; Terry Pinkard, *Hegel's Dialectic* (Philadelphia: Temple University Press, 1988); and Richard Dien Winfield, *Overcoming Foundations* (New York: Columbia University Press, 1989), especially the first four essays (pp. 13–89). See also the strong arguments in Winfield, "The Method of Hegel's *Science of Logic,*" in George di Giovanni, ed., *Essays on Hegel's Logic* (Albany: SUNY Press, 1990), 46–50, and in Thomas J. Bole, "Contradiction in Hegel," *Review of Metaphysics* 40 (1987): 532f. Robert Pippin, in the footnotes to *Hegel's Idealism,* conducts an excellent critique of such interpretations. His view is that Hegel critically completes the Kantian project by showing that, for subjectivity to be truly spontaneous, it must determine its own categories (see pp. 166ff., 200). My account of thought and language here can be read as an attempt to show, in more detail than Pippin, exactly how this goes on throughout the System; how those categories are determined without appeal to what they may categorize; and how this happens as what Pippin recognizes it must be: as the determination, *by a community*, of what its categories are to be. For the relative weakenss of Pippin's account of the System, as opposed to the

strengths of his account of the *Phenomenology*, see Terry Pinkard, "How Kantian was Hegel?" *Review of Metaphysics* 43 (1990): 831–38.

[69]Richard Rorty, *The Linguistic Turn* (Chicago: University of Chicago Press, 1967), 1ff.

[70]Hegel himself later dismissed the *Phenomenology* as a "peculiar early work": see the Editor's Note in Hegel, *Phänomenologie des Geistes*, ed. Johannes Hoffmeister, 6th ed. (Hamburg: Meiner, 1952), 578. Given the circumstances of the book's composition, this seems largely justified; but see my appendix to chapter 4. For an account of the stresses Hegel was under during the final composition of the *Phenomenology* and the "sudden" addition to it of the preface, see Walter Kaufmann, *Hegel: A Reinterpretation* (Garden City, N.J.: Anchor Books, 1966), 90–93.

[71]For some of Hegel's problems with the Kaiser, see my review article of Clark Butler et al., *Hegel's Letters*, in *Queen's Quarterly* (Canada) 93 (1986): 637–44.

[72]V (*WDL*) 44/50. This line has rolled around the Hegel literature from the start, a loose canon, and has been the basis for all manner of theological readings. But it is an unflagged citation, from Spinoza's *On the Improvement of the Intellect* at Spinoza, *de Intellectus Emendatione* in Spinoza, *Opera*, ed. C. Gebhard, (Heidelberg: Winter, 1925), 2:27; *The Collected Works of Spinoza*, ed. Edwin Curley (Princeton: Princeton University Press, 1985), 31f. Spinoza refers to the presentation of the thoughts of God before the creation of the world as a thought-experiment for a philosophical project, not as something that could actually be carried out. For him, as well as prima facie for the Hegel who quotes him, the idea is a counterfactual: the God who is nature (*deus sive natura*) cannot have created nature: see on this Ephraim Schmueli, "Some Similarities between Hegel and Spinoza on Substance," *The Thomist* 36 (1972): 654f. What Hegel writes/cites, then, is perhaps that there is no God before he created the world: that his Logic presents nothing, is as far removed from traditional theology as its God is removed, not from his creation, but from the nothingness that preceded it. For examples of the use of this quote by writers who themselves are *not* concerned to establish a theological reading of Hegel, see John Burbidge, *On Hegel's Logic: Fragments of a Commentary* (Highland Heights, N.J.: Humanities Press, 1981), 214; Michael Forster, *Skepticism*, 97, 121; Erroll Harris, *An Interpretation of the Logic of Hegel* (Lanham, Md.: University Press of America, 1983), 10; Peter Rohs, "Der Grund der Bewegung des Begriffs," *Hegel-Studien* Beiheft 18 (1978): 43; Michael Rosen, *Hegel's Dialectic and its Criticism* (Cambridge: Cambridge University Press, 1982), 69; Charles Taylor, *Hegel*, 251 (where the line, though attributed to Hegel, is recognized as "somewhat misleading"). Pierre-Jean Labarrière locates it as representational, i.e., nonspeculative and nonphilosophical, in Labarrière, "L'esprit absolu n'est pas l'absolu de l'esprit," in Labarrière and Gwendoline Jarczyk, *Hegeliana* (Paris: Presses Universitaires de France, 1986), 298ff. Robert Pippin quotes it, with distaste, in *Hegel's Idealism*, 177, and Vittorio Hösle, with distance, in *Hegel's System*, 67.

[73]This unitarian presupposition is not without some plausibility. L. B. Puntel has noted that the terms in which Hegel describes his method are extremely general ("element of thought," "thought determination," "form of thought," etc.) and thus must be intended to apply to the entire System: Puntel, "Was ist logisch in Hegels Logik," in Beyer, *Logik des Wissens*, 40–51. What Puntel sees as a leap from a "structural" logic (in the "Objective Logic") to a "model" which fills out that structure (the "Subjective Logic") I would see as the effect of a gradual gain in concreteness as the Logic progresses. Gwendoline Jarczyk has aptly stated the relation between Logic and *Realphilosophie*, "Nature and Spirit are *the Logic itself* which comes, by its own dynamic, to oppose itself to spatiotemporal exteriority and then to the interiorizing recollection

of that exteriority": Jarczyk, *Système et liberté dans la logique de Hegel* (Paris: Aubier Montaigne, 1980), 15. The structures of Nature and Spirit cannot, it seems, be other than those of the Logic, though they may be complications of them; and it is worthy of at least prima facie acceptance that the *Realphilosophie* deals with the results of natural science and history in the same general way that the Logic deals with the history of logic and metaphysics.

[74]For historical accounts of this split see Karl Löwith, *From Hegel to Nietzsche*, trans. David E. Green (Garden City, N.J.: Anchor Books, 1967), and John R. Toews, *Hegelianism* (Cambridge: Cambridge University Press, 1980), 203ff.; for an approach to it as a philosophical problem, see E. L. Fackenheim, *The Religious Dimension in Hegel's Thought* (Boston: Beacon, 1967); also valuable is the Introduction to Lawrence S. Stepelevich, ed., *The Young Hegelians: An Anthology* (Cambridge: Cambridge University Press, 1983), 1–15. Texts are collected there and also in Karl Löwith, ed., *Die Hegelsche Linke*, 2d ed. (Stuttgart: Frommann, 1988); Hermann Lübbe, *Die Hegelsche Rechte* (Stuttgart: Frommann, 1962). The issues are concisely formulated from a purely systematic standpoint, without regard to intellectual history, in Christian Topp, *Philosophie als Wissenschaft* (Berlin: de Gruyter, 1982), 261ff.

[75]Fackenheim, *Religious Dimension*, 237f.

[76]The quotes are, respectively, from Jean Hyppolite, *Studies in Marx and Hegel*, trans. John O'Neill (New York: Harper Torchbooks, 1973), 169; Herbert Marcuse, *Reason and Revolution* (Boston: Beacon Press, 1960), xiii; Alexandre Kojève, *Introduction à la lecture de Hegel* (Paris: Gallimard, 1947), 39; Kierkegaard, *Postscript*, 100, 295.

[77]XVIII 74; *Hegel's Idea of Philosophy*, trans. Quentin Lauer (New York: Fordham University Press, 1974), 95.

[78]V (*WDL*) 44f./50.

[79]VIII 106–12/60–65. David Hume, *Enquiry Concerning Human Understanding*, 2d ed. (La Salle, Ill.: Open Court, 1966), 182f. For more on Hume's aporia, see chapter 6.

[80]XVIII 275–81; VIII 106–12. Hegel's followers have also been tardy to respond to Hume: the extensive bibliography concerning Hegel's relationship to other thinkers by Joseph C. Flay, in Joseph O'Malley, Keith Algozin, and Frederick G. Weiss, eds., *Hegel and the History of Philosophy* (The Hague: Martinus Nijhoff, 1974), 194–236, does not list a single work concerning Hegel and Hume.

[81]Bernard Williams, *Descartes: The Project of Pure Enquiry* (Penguin, 1978), 10.

[82]Michael Inwood, Introduction to Inwood, ed., *Hegel* (Oxford: Oxford University Press, 1985), 2–10.

[83]My doubts about the theoretical/practical distinction are Hegelian in inspiration: see chapter 8 below.

Chapter 1

[1]Michael Inwood, "Solomon, Hegel, and Truth," *Review of Metaphysics* 31 (1977): 272–82, which responds to Robert C. Solomon, "Truth and Self-Satisfaction," *Review of Metaphysics* 28 (1975): 698–724. For the existence of Hegel's theory of truth, see Solomon, passim, and Inwood, much more reticently, p. 280.

[2]Solomon, "Truth," 703f., 713; III (*PHG*) 41ff./23ff.

[3]Inwood, "Solomon," 273f.

[4]Ibid., 282.

[5]III (*PHG*) 45/26.

⁶III (*PHG*) 40/23; also 23/10.

⁷Solomon, "Truth," 701.

⁸This suggestion is also made by J. N Findlay in "The Contemporary Relevance of Hegel," in Alasdair Macintyre, ed., *Hegel: A Collection of Critical Essays* (Garden City, N.J.: Anchor Books, 1972), 4ff.

⁹Perhaps the best nontechnical introduction to these issues is in W. V. Quine, "The Ways of Paradox," in *The Ways of Paradox and Other Essays*, 2d ed., rev. (Cambridge, Mass.: Harvard University Press, 1976), 6ff.

¹⁰Solomon, "Truth," 705, 716; Inwood, "Solomon," 278, 280; Alfred Tarski, "The Concept of Truth in Formalized Languages," in Tarski, *Logic, Semantics, and Metamathematics*, ed. J. H. Woodger, 2d ed., rev. (Indianapolis: Hackett, 1983), 152–278, esp. 253f., 273f.

¹¹And this fact would hold whether attempts to read the *Phenomenology* as itself a series of metalinguistic reflections are valid or, as Inwood shows very well, not.

¹²It is this sort of faith which Tom Rockmore has found at the heart of Hegel's thought: *Circular Epistemology*, 153ff.; my response to Rockmore's subtle critique will become evident in chapter 7.

¹³Solomon, "Truth," 706, 710f.; Inwood, "Solomon," 277; VIII 317f. (*Enz. #166 Zus.*), 323f. (*Enz. #172 Anm.*)/231f., 237.

¹⁴IV 104f., 142; VI (*WDL*) 37, 305/410, 626; VIII 319 (*Enz. #167 Anm.*)/233. *EGP* 31/19 stands as commentary on the "rose is red" example. For Hegel's account of the relative completeness claim of judgments, see VI (*WDL*) 305/626 and VIII 319 (*Enz. #167 Anm.*)/233. As Walther Zimmerli has pointed out, this kind of consideration pushes Hegel's account of the Judgment (as opposed to the assertion) in the direction of pragmatics: Hegelian logic, for Zimmerli, is a unification of syntax, semantics, and pragmatics. As I will argue in chapter 4, Hegelian logic is actually different from all these, but mistakable for any of them. Zimmerli, "Aus der Logik lernen? Zur Entwicklungsgeschichte der Hegelschen Logik-Konzeption," in Beyer, *Logik des Wissens*, 66–79.

¹⁵As it is not in the wagon example, where much of the individuating is done by "that."

¹⁶Solomon, "Truth," 708f.

¹⁷At VI (*WDL*) 127/482, belief is said to be a "*merely* immediate consciousness," i.e., no "likeness that has come to be"; at XI 46, it is said to be a mere "holding-for-true [*Fürwahrhalten*]" which can apply to any content whatsoever.

¹⁸Inwood, "Solomon," 277.

¹⁹Both in important discussions of truth and in asides; see II 460f./(Natural Law) 76; V (*WDL*) 29f., 36ff./38f., 44ff.; VI (*WDL*) 264–68/592–95; VIII 86 (*Enz. #24 Zus.* 2)/41, XIII (*Aesth.*) 105/74; XX (*Hist. Phil.*) 206/III 311f.; *Phil. Rel.* 131, 139f./223, 230.

²⁰V (*WDL*) 29/39; VI (*WDL*) 93f./454f.; VIII 264f. (*Enz. #133*)/189f. See the extended commentary on "Form and Content" in the *Science of Logic* given by Peter Rohs, *Form und Grund, Hegel-Studien* Beiheft 6 (3d ed., 1982): 181–95.

²¹All content resides in the predicate for Hegel because the "subject" of a genuine judgment, as opposed to a *Satz*, is for Hegel—as in contemporary logic—nothing but an unknown "x." See IV 144f.; VIII 320 (*Enz. #169*)/234; and the passages cited in n. 13.

²²VI (*WDL*) 302/623; VIII 316 (*Enz. #136 Anm.*)/231.

²³Note the way Kant can presuppose the truth of mathematics in the *Prolegomena* of 1783: "Here is now a great and verified [body of] cognition, which . . . carries with it

through and through apodictic certainty, i.e., absolute necessity." Kant, *Prolegomena*, in *Werke* 5:142.

[24]Solomon, "Truth," 702f.; for the pragmatic turn, see pp. 722f.

[25]Inwood, "Solomon," 273.

[26]See ibid., 279.

[27]Solomon, "Truth," 722; Arthur Fine, *The Shaky Game* (Chicago: University of Chicago Press, 1986), 112–50.

[28]See III (*PHG*) 76ff./53ff. for the general account of this.

[29]*Phil. Rel.* 136/227 n. 115; also see VI (*WDL*) 13/389; VIII 202 (*Enz.* #95 Anm.), 204 (*Enz.* #96 Zus.)/140, 141, etc.

[30]III (*PHG*) 26/12; VIII 14/not translated; X 203 (*Enz.* #416)/157; XII 413/341; XIII (*Aesth.*) 138/100; *EGP* 14, 91/11, 62.

[31]See III (*PHG*) 68–70/46–48; VI (*WDL*) 262f., 434/590ff., 779f.; *EGP* 86, 100/58f., 70.

[32]*EGP* 39/25f.

[33]IV 157; VI (*WDL*) 265, 464/593, 756; VII 73f. (*Philosophy of Right* #21 Zus.)/231f; VIII 85 (*Enz.* #24 Zus. 2), 323 (*Enz.* #172 Zus.)/41, 236f.; X 15 (*Enz.* #379 Zus.), 228f. (*Enz.* #438)/6, 178; XIII (*Aesth.*) 138, 151/100, 110, XIX (*Hist. Phil.*) 250/ II 233.

[34]VI (*WDL*) 245/577.

[35]VIII 63f. (*Enz.* #18)/23f.; see H. S. Harris, *Night Thoughts* (Oxford: Oxford University Press, 1983), xlix–liii and passim.

[36]V (*WDL*) 23/34; see also VIII 67ff. (*Enz.* #19)/25ff.

[37]V (*WDL*) 20/31f.; see also the Introduction to this book.

[38]V (*WDL*) 26f./36f.; Hegel refers to his logic as "authentic metaphysics" (*die eigentliche Metaphysik*) at V (*WDL*) 16/27. Also see VIII 52f. (*Enz.* #9), 80f. (*Enz.* #24), 93–105 (*Enz.* ##26–36)/13f., 36f., 47–59.

[39]VI (*WDL*) 464/756.

[40]VIII 181 (*Enz.* #84)/123.

[41]VIII 231 (*Enz.* #112)/162. See Michael Theunissen, *Sein und Schein* (Frankfurt: Suhrkamp, 1980), esp. 301ff.; G. R. G. Mure, *A Study of Hegel's Logic* (Oxford: Clarendon, 1950), 79–92; Erroll Harris, *Interpretation*, 153ff.

[42]VIII 303 (*Enz.* #158)/220.

[43]This—and this alone—gives the sequence what I call *narrative* character.

[44]VIII 307 (*Enz.* #160)/223.

[45]The "wealth of all content": VIII 294 (*Enz.* #151)/213.

[46]Hegel makes this point in his discussion of the Idea at VI (*WDL*) 464/756; with regard to the Concept itself, at VI (*WDL*) 251ff./582ff.

[47]VI (*WDL*) 264f./591f., VIII 307 (*Enz.* #160)/223. My use of *an sich* and *für sich* follows VIII 255 (*Enz.* #124 Zus.), 347 (*Enz.* #193 Anm.)/181, 257f., as well as *EGP* 101–11/71–86.

[48]VIII 303 (*Enz.* #158)/220. For the necessary order of logical determinations, see V (*WDL*) 48f./53; VIII 59f. (*Enz.* #14 Anm.)/90.

[49]VI (*WDL*) 253/583; see VIII 72f. (*Enz.* #20 Anm.)/29f.

[50]By considering the Concept in terms of the Ego, Hegel is also able here to assimilate it to Kant's transcendental unity of apperception, which is the unitary awareness, in all the manifold of my determinate awareness, that it is "I" who think. See Kant, *KRV* B 131ff.

[51]G. E. Moore, "The Refutation of Idealism," in Morris Weitz, ed., *20th Century Philosophy: The Analytical Tradition* (New York: Free Press [Macmillan] 1966), 28–36.

⁵²III (*PHG*) 137f./104f.; see also X 205f. (*Enz.* #418), 213 (*Enz.* #424)/158f., 165.

⁵³A position Lucio Colletti wrongly attributes to Hegel: see "Hegel and the 'Dialectic of Matter,' " in Colletti, *Studies in Marx and Hegel*, trans. Lawrence Garner (London: Verso, 1979), 7–27.

⁵⁴XIII (*Aesth.*) 138/100.

⁵⁵Ibid.; see also XIX (*Hist. Phil.*)110/II 95. The latter sort of finitude, we may note, is not merely a deficiency of the finite thing: if the Concept, or Idea, remains other than the individual, it does so partly through its *own* lack of identity with the totality—in which case, of course, it is not truly Concept or Idea. See chapter 10.

⁵⁶More exactly, real-causal: VI (*WDL*) 225–32/560–66.

⁵⁷IX 55f. (*Enz.* #260)/441f.

⁵⁸See IX 483ff. (*Enz.* #365)/397ff., X 25f. (*Enz.* #382)/15; also V (*WDL*) 20/31f., XVIII (*Hist. Phil.*) 88/67f. The contrast appears to be between the total loss of self the animal undergoes in the attempt to realize its essence (which, as a mere abstraction, cannot in fact be realized in any existent individual) and the limited loss which the human being undergoes when she is educated out of her old beliefs—an education which, at its most intense, is for Hegel the *Verlust seiner selbst* of consciousness in the *Phenomenology* (III 72/49).

⁵⁹III (*PHG*) 137f./104ff.

⁶⁰The Master can be said not to realize his true humanity in that his lordship ultimately leaves him alone and helpless before "death, the absolute master"; the Slave, insofar as (in the absence of any recognition from the Master) he flees into a freedom which is purely inward and intellectual: III (*PHG*) 150–55/115–19.

⁶¹X 393 (*Enz.* #574)/313f. Note that the replacement of animal species by human community—a transformation which is obviously due to language—means that for Hegel, even here in his later "Systematic" works, no final statement of the human essence—of the nature of Spirit itself—is possible: Spirit is in fact defined as that which can change itself radically without dying. This does not impeach the "absolute" character of the System; indeed, as I will argue in chapter 10, it is what makes it possible.

⁶²Hence, the Hegelian philosophical project, to be really carried out, would have to be socially located in a type of institution which was (1) educational, and (2) seen as the heart of society. I will abstain from further speculation on this point.

⁶³VI (*WDL*) 464/756.

⁶⁴An example would be someone who makes no contribution at all to the community, living a life of significance only to himself; what the Athenians called an "idiot" (*idiotês*).

⁶⁵See G. R. G. Mure's discussion in *An Introduction to Hegel* (Oxford: Clarendon, 1940), 165f.

⁶⁶VIII 84ff. (*Enz.* #24 Zus. 3)/39ff.

⁶⁷In ways to be discussed in chapters 5 and 10.

⁶⁸VIII 369 (*Enz.* #213 Zus.)/276 (my emphasis).

⁶⁹At VIII 84ff. (*Enz.* #24 Zus. 2)/39ff.

⁷⁰VI (*WDL*) 464/756, XX (*Hist. Phil.*) 408f./III 499ff.; H. S. Harris, "Hegelians of the 'Right' and 'Left,' " *Review of Metaphysics* 11 (1958): 603–9.

⁷¹IX 34 (*Enz.* #250)/22; see also VI (*WDL*) 464/756. That Hegel did not deny contingency or the necessity for philosophical thought to confront it is shown by Dieter Henrich in "Hegels Theorie Über den Zufall," *Kant-Studien* 50 (1958): 131–48.

⁷²*Phil. Rel.* 147f./238 n. 144; XVIII (*Hist. Phil.*) 102f./81f.

⁷³Hence, F. H. Bradley thought that truth is fully attained by the Absolute; he denied that it could be attained by us. If I am right, both views, along with the distinction

between "us" and "the Absolute," are antithetical to Hegel. F. H. Bradley, *Appearance and Reality* 9th ed., rev. and ext. (Oxford: Oxford University Press, 1930).

[74]III (*PHG*) 41/23.

[75]Ibid.

[76]III (*PHG*) 40f./22f.

[77]In chapter 11, in connection with Donald Davidson, I will call this "convergence." Willem deVries has admirably summed up the role of the Concept in this: "what Hegel calls a concept is a prescriptive ideal that is part of a system of such ideals that the world is striving to realize and in terms of which we can make sense of what is happening in the world": Willem deVries, *Mental Activity,* 173. My only emendation would be to replace the first occurrence of "the world" with "language."

[78]II 96.

[79]It is, Hegel says, "the correspondence which eternally perfects and has perfected itself. . . . Only so is the idea truth, and all truth." XIII (*Aesth.*) 150/110. See also VIII 367 (*Enz. #213* Zus.)/274 for a general statement of the Idea as the object's "corresponding" with the Concept as "Purpose." This process will be examined in terms of Hegel's logical treatment of "Teleology" in chapter 10.

[80]VIII 367ff. (*Enz. #213*)/274ff.

[81]III (*PHG*) 24, 46f./11, 27f. Thus, for example, Hegel implies that philosophy itself is the history of philosophy correctly understood. VIII 58ff. (*Enz. ##13f.*)/18ff.; *EGP* 24ff., 94ff./15f., 65ff. It would follow that, since the final result of philosophy is Hegel's entire System, which incorporates the results of the developments of other fields such as religion and the special sciences, any science is identical with the history of its development. Hegel, however, distinguishes between the "internal" development presented by the history of philosophy and the "external" histories possessed by other fields (*EGP* 16f., 126/12f., 94), so the history of the system of science would present, presumably, only the "inner" history of those other regions.

[82]XIII (*Aesth.*) 137/99f.

[83]II 512 (Natural Law)/118; IV 291; X 204 (*Enz. #416*) Zus./157; *Phil. Rel.* III 220/203; *EGP* 86/58.

[84]VIII 86 (*Enz. #24* Zus. 2), 369 (*Enz. #213* Zus.)/39f., 276.

[85]VII 172 (*Rechtsphil. #82*)/64; IX 520ff. (*Enz. #371*)/428ff.

[86]XI 55; XIII (*Aesth.*) 150f./110f.

[87]Aristotle, *Metaphysics* 3.2, 12.1.

[88]XX (*Hist. Phil.*) 460/III 551; see also X 354f. (*Enz. #552* Anm.)/282ff. It is not possible here even to begin to discuss Hegel's concept of "Spirit" (*Geist*). It perhaps suffices for the present to characterize it as the Idea, insofar as this is aware of itself as an historical process. See III (*PHG*) 498, 572, 576/412, 476, 480; X 354ff. (*Enz. #552* Anm.)/282ff. This self-knowledge, however, must be understood to embrace the self-knowledge of each individual (human) spirit, insofar as such a spirit recognizes itself to convey the Idea.

[89]XIII (*Aesth.*) 205, 151/155,111; X 367 (*Enz. #556*)/293.

[90]X 368f. (*Enz. #559*)/294; XIII (*Aesth.*) 23, 29, 105/9f., 13, 74.

[91]XIV (*Aesth.*) 261f., 223f., 239f./626, 959f., 972f.

[92]X 278 (*Enz. #422* Anm.)/219f.

[93]XIII (*Aesth.*) 141f./102f.

[94]*Phil. Rel.* 14f./205.

[95]See Fackenheim, *Religious Dimension,* 22ff., 122f., and 154ff. for an account of the nature of religious representation and its relation to representation in general.

[96]See *Phil. Rel.* 293f./398.

[97]*Phil. Rel.* 150/240 n. 149.

[98]*Phil. Rel.* 300f./405f.; see III (*PHG*) 553–57/459–63. Such thought is "philosophical" in that it gives the rational determination of the finite, and is a concrete form of logical thought (*Phil. Rel.* 205/301). The rational "concept of God" is given at *Phil. Rel.* 266ff./366f.

[99]*Phil. Rel.* 53f., 211ff./139f., 307f.

[100]X 378 (*Enz.* #572)/302; see XIII (*Aesth.*) 143/104. Bernard Quelquejeu argues at length that the language in which Hegel presents his System must, since it is constitutive of human nature itself, be considered as poetic: Quelquejeu, *La volonté dans la philosophie de Hegel* (Paris: Editions du Seuil, 1972), 331–40.

[101]X 249ff. (*Enz.* #448)/195ff. For art as such an externalization, see XIII (*Aesth.*) 27f./12f.

[102]X 280 (*Enz.* #462 Zus.)/220. Michael Rosen has stressed the intuitive nature of philosophical thinking for Hegel, but has failed to see the linguistic character of that intuition, asserting it to be merely private and hence subjective in nature: Rosen, *Hegel's Dialectic,* 72–77, 179f. The same holds for Stanley Rosen, *G. W. F. Hegel* (New Haven: Yale University Press, 1974), 267–73, esp. 272f.

[103]X 278 (*Enz.* #462 Anm.)/219f.; XVIII (*Hist. Phil.*) 109/88; see also V (*WDL*) 386/325.

[104]*Phil. Rel.* 114f., 325f./205, 436f.

[105]*Phil. Rel.* 159f., 212f./ 250f., 308 n. 97.

[106]III (*PHG*) 82/60; XVIII (*Hist. Phil.*) 527/457.

[107]*EGP* 151/113f.; *Phil. Rel.* III 96f./162.

[108]In a formulation of Gwendoline Jarczyk, which anticipates some of the results of the current discussion, "by itself [truth] is nothing; it is only the fact that whatever is, as such, comes to itself": Jarczyk, "Une approche de la vérité logique chez Hegel," in Labarrière and Jarczyk, *Hegeliana,* 162.

Chapter 2

[1]VIII 86 (*Enz.* #24 Zus. 2), 323 (*Enz.* #172 Anm., Zus.)/39f., 236f.; X 228 (*Enz.* #438 Zus.)/177f.; XIII (*Aesth.*) 105/74. For the pre-Hegelian use of *richtig* in connection with truth, see Reinhold Aschenberg, "Der Wahrheitsbegriff in Hegels *Phänomenologie des Geistes,*" in Hartmann, *Option,* 221 n. 10. The traditional philosophical meaning of *richtig* was not, Aschenberg points out, "corresponds to its object" but "is consonant with the laws of logic." Aschenberg notes that Heidegger shares Hegel's unusual usage: "The truth of an assertion is always, and always only, this correctness [*Richtigkeit*]": Martin Heidegger, "Der Ursprung des Kunstwerkes," in *Holzwege,* 4th ed. (Frankfurt: Klostermann, 1963), 40; "The Origin of the Work of Art," in *Poetry, Language, Thought,* trans. Albert Hofstadter (New York: Harper and Row, 1971), 51.

[2]IV 213, 291; V (*WDL*) 37/44f.; VIII 86 (*Enz.* #24 Zus. 2), 323 (*Enz.* #172 Anm., Zus.)/39f., 237; XIX (*Hist. Phil.*) 165/II 180.

[3]VIII 368 (*Enz.* #213 Anm.)/275; with this also see the general treatment of "representation" at X 257–83 (*Enz.* ##451–64)/201–23.

[4]IV 213ff.; V (*WDL*) 37/44f.; VIII 86 (*Enz.* #24 Zus. 2), 323 (*Enz.* #172 Anm., Zus.)/39f., 237; XIX (*Hist. Phil.*) 165/180.

[5]XI 378; XIX (*Hist. Phil.*)165/II 180; also see X 97 (*Enz.* #400)/73.

[6]IV 214f.; VIII 86 (*Enz.* #24 Zus. 2)/39f.

[7]IV 213; XIII (*Aesth.*) 153/112.

[8]VI (*WDL*) 498ff./783ff.; VIII 379ff. (*Enz.* #227)/284ff.

[9]III (*PHG*) 575-91/479-93.

[10]Some writers, such as Michael Theunissen, have undertaken this for him: Theunissen, "Begriff und Realität: Hegels Aufhebung des metaphysischen Wahrheitsbegriffs," in Rolf Horstmann, ed., *Seminar: Dialektik in der Philosophie Hegels* (Frankfurt: Suhrkamp, 1978), 324-59. Theunissen emphasizes the dynamic and concrete nature of "corresponding" for Hegel. Aschenberg, searching for such an *Aufhebung*, appeals only to the passage where Hegel denies that qualitative judgments can be true, and which I discussed in chapter 1: Aschenberg, "Wahrheitsbegriff," 223.

[11]VIII 86 (*Enz.* #24 Zus. 2), 369 (*Enz.* #213 Zus.)/39f., 276.

[12]IV 213.

[13]Solomon, "Truth," 703.

[14]VI (*WDL*) 28f./402f.

[15]A similar point is made by Robert Hanna in "Hegel's Critique of the Common Logic," *Review of Metaphysics* 40 (1986): 311f. Hanna's account of Hegel's criticism of attempts to read the structures of ordinary (or "common") logic directly into the nature of reality assumes that Hegel's thought itself also has such direct relevance. On the present interpretation, Hegel's thought gains "ontological" relevance, indeed relevance of any kind, only insofar as it is relevant to language, and insofar as our language structures our world. In proclaiming his Logic to coincide with "metaphysics" (e.g., at VIII 81 [*Enz.* #24 Anm.]/36), Hegel claims that it *comprehends* the concepts of traditional metaphysics—not that it *uses* them the way metaphysicians did (see Hanna, 305).

[16]II 512; Hegel, *Natural Law*, trans. T. M. Knox (Philadelphia: University of Pennsylvania Press, 1974), 118; also see IV 209f.; VIII 111 (*Enz.* #39), 119 (*Enz.* #42 Zus. 3)/64, 70. We might express this in more contemporary language by saying that the objects to which representations must correspond are theory-laden. But a general property is not for Hegel a "theory," and different objects bear their theoretical burdens in different ways. A more flexible way to express it would be that such objects are already conceptualized.

[17]See VIII 86 (*Enz.* #24 Zus. 2)/39f.

[18]Karl Marx, *Theses on Feuerbach*, in Allen Wood, ed., *Marx: Selections* (New York: Macmillan, 1988), 80.

[19]VI (*WDL*) 266, 499/593f., 783f.; XIII (*Aesth.*) 105/74.

[20]The coherence theory, of course, generally views truth as ranging over sentences and beliefs; that Hegel held it in this sense has long been a staple of Anglo-Saxon philosophical folklore, as evidenced by Alan R. White, "The Coherence Theory of Truth," in Paul Edwards, ed., *Encyclopedia of Philosophy* (New York: Macmillan, 1967), 2:130; and by Bertrand Russell, "The Monistic Theory of Truth," in *Philosophical Essays* (London: Longman's, Green, 1910), 156; also see p. 172 and Russell, "Truth and Falsehood," in Robert Egner and Lester Denonn, eds., *Basic Writings of Bertrand Russell 1903–1959* (New York: Simon & Schuster, 1961), 328. The misattribution is occasioned by the so-called British Hegelians, for whose views see Bradley, *Appearance and Reality*, 319f.; Bradley, *Essays on Truth and Reality* (Oxford: Clarendon, 1914), 314f., 325f.; and H. H. Joachim, *The Nature of Truth* (Oxford: Clarendon, 1906). Joachim, like others of his approach, hardly mentions Hegel except to complain of the sloppy misuse (by others!) of his name: 5, 84n. L. Jonathan Cohen has concisely traced the vicissitudes of the coherence theory from Joachim through Blanshard, Bradley, McTaggart, and Rescher. If I am right, this all has nothing to do with Hegel (whom Cohen, discussing these "Hegelians," wisely never cites): Cohen, "The Coherence Theory of Truth," *Philosophical Studies* 34

(1978): 351–60. For an illuminating account of why Hegel was not committed to the coherence theory, see Winfield, *Overcoming Foundations*, 81. The view that Hegel held a doctrine of internal relations is another part of the same folklore, which falls once we realize that he in fact held a correspondence theory of (assertional) truth: see Richard Rorty, "Relations, Internal and External," *Encyclopedia of Philosophy* 7:125–33 for a summary of the general issue; misattribution to Hegel occurs on p. 126.

[21]VI (*WDL*) 267/594; VIII 86 (*Enz.* #24 Zus. 2)/39f.

[22]V (*WDL*) 29/39, 44/50; VI (*WDL*) 266f./593f.; in a similar vein, Hegel warns us that the Idea is not the Idea *of* anything at all: VIII 368 (*Enz.* #213 Anm., Zus.)/276.

[23]Hegel's discussion of this is at VI (*WDL*) 437f./734f. Also see the discussions of matter, at IX 117 (*Enz.* #276)/91, and of electricity at IX 274 (*Enz.* #323 Zus.)/222. Also see Hösle, *Hegels System*, 82f.

[24]Thus, the point of Hegel's Logic is not to take a stand on traditional issues such as idealism and materialism, but to clarify the terms in which such views are couched: see Hegel's letter to Niethammer of October 23, 1812, reproduced in Hegel, *Sämtliche Werke*, ed. H. Glockner (Stuttgart: Frohmann, 1965–68), 3:301–6; *Hegel: The Letters*, ed. and trans. Clark Butler and Christiane Seiler (Bloomington, Indiana: Indiana University Press, 1984), 277. This is why, as I noted in the preceding chapter, Moore did not envisage Hegel's brand of idealism when he refuted the kinds based on the proposition that *esse est percipi*.

[25]Hence, Hegel is very far indeed from the wholesale rejection of the correspondence theory imputed to him by Hermann Schmitz—and Schmitz's point that Hegel's works are full of sentences which at least claim to correspond to something is, while obviously accurate, in no way a criticism of Hegel—far less what Schmitz calls it, an "aporia" in the dialectical concept of truth: Hermann Schmitz, "Das dialektische Warheitsverständnis und seine Aporie," *Hegel-Studien* Beiheft 17 (1977): 241–54.

[26]J. L. Austin, *Sense and Sensibilia* (Oxford: Oxford University Press, 1962), 62–83.

[27]Ibid., 68f.

[28]Ibid.

[29]Ibid., 70.

[30]VIII 86 (*Enz.* #24 Zus. 2), 369 (*Enz.* #213 Zus.)/39f., 276.

[31]I will qualify this later.

[32]In this I follow G. R. G. Mure's usage in *Introduction*, 165.

[33]One of the rare formulations of this is in Martin Heidegger, *Sein und Zeit* (Tübingen: Niemeyer, 1927), 212–30; also see Heidegger, "Vom Wesen der Wahrheit" (Frankfurt: Klostermann), 1943. Heidegger does not, however, discuss the function of the concept of truth in designating the goal of inquiry. Hilary Putnam argues that to say that science aims at truth is vacuous, and that in order to understand science we need to know the standards of "rational acceptability" scientists use. But he remains a type of assertionist insofar as (a) "rational acceptability" is the "bottom line" for scientific inquiry, and (b) the bearers of rational acceptability are beliefs, i.e., entities in the form "*S* is *P*": Hilary Putnam, *Reason, Truth and History* (Cambridge: Cambridge University Press, 1981), 129f.

[34]I intend "package," a word best left supple, in somewhat the sense of Bentham's "import": "For the giving expression and conveyance to any thought that ever was entertained . . . nothing less than the *import* of an entire proposition . . . ever was, or ever could be, made to serve. . . . Words may be considered as the result of a sort of analysis." Jeremy Bentham, "Theory of Fictions," in C. K. Ogden, *Bentham's Theory of Fictions* (London: Kegan Paul, Trench, Trubner & Co., 1932), 67f. A thought for Bentham is here the "assertion of the existence of a matter of fact external to the speaker," and so

his sweeping statement is apparently tautologous. For the seminal character of Bentham's theory of fictions see W. V. Quine, "What Is It All About?," *The American Scholar* 50 (Winter 1980–81): 47.

[35]Perhaps by way of Quine's "lo, a rabbit!" in W. V. Quine, *Word and Object* (Cambridge: MIT Press, 1960), 29ff.

[36]Gottlob Frege, *Begriffsschrift*, ed. Ignacio Angelelli. (Hildesheim: Georg Olms, 1964); the diversions from "*S* is *P*" begin on p. 2.

[37]Thomas Baldwin, "The Identity Theory of Truth," *Mind* 100 (January 1991): 35–52; later in his fascinating article, Baldwin goes on to suggest that the identity theory applies to what he calls "content," and that it is a theory of "actuality," not truth.

[38]See Hans Reichenbach, *The Rise of Scientific Philosophy* (Berkeley: University of California Press, 1951), 3–73 for a compendium of such reductions. The unattributed quote with which the book opens is, of course, from Hegel: see p. 67. Also Karl Popper, "What is Dialectic?" in Popper, *Conjectures and Refutations* (New York: Basic Books, 1965), 312–35.

[39]W. V. Quine, *Methods of Logic*, 2d ed. (Cambridge, Mass.: Harvard University Press, 1982), 1. For a more recent affirmation of assertionism by Quine, see p. 77 of his *Pursuit of Truth* (Cambridge, Mass.: Harvard University Press, 1990) in conjunction with, of course, the book's title.

[40]Quine, *Methods*, 9. Similarly, Donald Davidson, in his 1981 account of the coherence theory, restricts it to "beliefs, or sentences held true by someone who understands them": Davidson, "A Coherence Theory of Truth and Knowledge," in Dieter Henrich, ed., *Kant oder Hegel?* (Stuttgart: Klett-Cotta Verlag, 1983), 423–38 (the sentence quoted is from the top of p. 424). Also see Davidson, "True to the Facts," *Journal of Philosophy*, 66 (1969): 748–62; Davidson's articles do not contain explicit statements of assertionism's thesis (a), which will be of importance for chapter 11.

[41]Nicholas Rescher, *The Coherence Theory of Truth* (Oxford: Clarendon, 1973), 1.

[42]Alfred Tarski, "The Semantic Conception of Truth," *Philosophy and Phenomenological Research* 4 (1943–44), 342, 366f.

[43]Tarski, "Concept of Truth," in *Metamathematics*, 152, 167.

[44]Gottlob Frege, "Der Gedanke," in Frege, *Kleine Schriften*, ed. Ignacio Angelleli (Hildesheim: Georg Olms Verlag, 1967), 343; an English translation, varying widely from my own here, is given in Frege, *Logical Investigations*, trans. Peter Geach, ed. Geach and R. H. Stoothoff (New Haven: Yale University Press, 1977), 2.

[45]Rudolf Carnap, *Der logische Aufbau der Welt* (Berlin: Weltkreis Verlag, 1928); the quote is from the preface to the second edition of the English translation, *The Logical Structure of the World*, trans. Rolf George (Berkeley: University of California Press, 1967), v.

[46]Carnap, *Aufbau*, 1/5.

[47]Ibid., 64/78.

[48]Ibid., 51/65.

[49]Ibid., 53/67.

[50]Similarly, when A. J. Ayer insisted that philosophers provide, not true assertions, but definitions, his norm for a good philosophical definition was that it preserve truth: that it show "how the sentences in which [a symbol] significantly occurs can be translated into equivalent sentences." A. J. Ayer, *Language, Truth, and Logic* (New York: Dover, n.d.), 60.

[51]Hence, as Hans Friedrich Fulda points out, to "define" a term in Systematic dialectics is to show not how that term can be eliminated, but why it cannot be. For the set of other terms which "define" it *are* its meaning—are the patterned responses it evokes

in the language game of Systematic dialectics. And they, in turn, evoke a set of patterned responses different from themselves; hence, they cannot have the same "meaning" as the term they "define." Fulda, "Unzulängliche Bemerkungen zur Dialektik," in Horstmann, *Seminar*, 33–69, 47.

[52]*Phil. Rel.* 353/464. Even what Hegel sometimes calls the "so-called proofs of the existence of God" are examined, not for the truth of their conclusion, but in terms of what they accomplish for us: they raise our minds to the thought of God. See *Phil. Rel.* 28, 88, 308ff./110, 179, 414ff.

[53]Carnap, *Aufbau*, 47–49, 51f., 54/61f., 65f., 78.

[54]Tom Rockmore, "Hegel and the Unity of Science Program," *History of Philosophy Quarterly* 61 (1989): 338f.

[55]Ibid., 340ff.

[56]In addition to Quine's *Word and Object*, see, for example, Richard Rorty, *Philosophy and the Mirror of Nature* (Princeton: Princeton University Press, 1979).

[57]Carnap, *Aufbau*, 93/108f.

[58]Ibid., 93f./109–12.

[59]And which I will discuss in chapter 7.

[60]Carnap, *Aufbau*, 11/19.

[61]See Quine, *Word and Object*, esp. chapter 1.

[62]Carnap, *Aufbau*, 2f./7.

[63]And with that would go the view that science as practiced in the West can be detached from the surrounding culture and set down to work anywhere in the world. Science may prove to be inextricable from such larger cultural characteristics as the institutionalization of assertionism in the university (where certain views can be evaluated with respect to their truth alone), or from the capacity of a society to undergo paradigm changes without resorting to violence.

[64]Edmund Husserl, *Logische Untersuchungen* (Tübingen: Niemyer, 1921), 3:120ff.; Heidegger, *Sein und Zeit*; also see Ernst Tugendhat, *Der Wahrheitsbegriff bei Husserl und Heidegger* (Berlin: de Gruyter, 1967), 96–101, 331–62.

[65]Tarski, "Semantic Conception," 155f.

[66]If we take Rescher's claim as the empirical one that *philosophical* theories of truth are all exclusively assertionistic, then it is patently false; the succeeding narrative will only multiply evidence for its falsity.

[67]Gerold Prauss, "Zum Wahrheitsproblem bei Kant," *Kant-Studien* 60 (1969): 171 n. 28.

[68]Alan White has treated Schelling's critique, as given in the *Grundlegung der positiven Philosophie*, insightfully from an Hegelian point of view, arguing that the Hegelian Absolute is a matter, not of theology, but of "ideal ontology": *Absolute Knowledge*, 84–90. Also see Schelling, *Geschichte der neueren Philosophie*, in *Sämtliche Werke* (Stuttgart & Augsburg: Cotta, 1856–61), 10:126–64, esp. p. 140, where Schelling claims that concepts are posterior to nature and that Hegel should not have begun with them.

[69]I have argued for emancipation as such a goal for ordinary language in my *Poetic Interaction*.

[70]John Locke, *Essay Concerning Human Understanding* (New York: Dover, 1959), 2:32.1–4.

[71]Except that, as we have seen, the Hegelian Concept is not to be *merely* in our minds.

[72]Bernard Bolzano, *Wissenschaftslehre*, ed. Jen Berg (Stuttgart: Friedrich Frohmann Verlag, 1835, 1985) 2:133–36.

[73]We do not yet understand, even roughly, what Hegel thinks "right" criteria would be, and I will treat this set of issues later.

[74]See Eleanor Rosch, "Principles of Categorization" in Rosch and Barbara Lloyd, eds., *Cognition and Categorization* (Hillsdale, N.J.: Erlbaum, 1978), 30–36, 40f., 42.

[75]Quine, *Word and Object*, 8, 13f., 94.

[76]This is in fact Locke's main argument, the point about metaphysical truth being presented in a sort of aside.

[77]Locke, *Essay*, 1:32 (Introduction, ¶8); also see E. J. Ashworthy, "Locke on Language," *Canadian Journal of Philosophy* 14 (1984): 45–74, esp. 46–48; Stephen Nathanson, "Locke's Theory of Ideas," *Journal of the History of Philosophy* 11 (1973): 29–42.

[78]Tarski, "Semantic Conception," 342f.; Heidegger, *Sein und Zeit*, 214f.

[79]E.g., *Phaedo* 100a, *Theaetetus* 161c seq.; in the *Cratylus*, the view that propositions are true is taken, without argument, to entail that the ultimate constituents of propositions—names—are true: 385 b seq. For references to truth as the most real reality and as, simultaneously, the goal of inquiry, see *Phaedrus* 248b, *Republic* 475b, 573d, 581b, *Sophist* 254a, *Theaetetus* 173e.

[80]St. Augustine, *Soliloquien*, ed. Hanspeter Müller (Bern: Benteli, 1954), 177; St. Anselm, *de Veritate*, in *Truth, Freedom and Evil*, eds. Jasper Hopkins and Herbert Richardson (New York: Harper Torchbooks, 1967), 93ff.; also see Editors' Introduction, 12–25.

[81]See Proclus, *in Timaeo* 2:287, 3–5: *kai dia touto kai alêtheia einai hê pros to gignoskomenon epharmogê tou gignoskontos*; cited at Werner Beierwaltes, *Proklos: Grundzüge seiner Metaphysik* (Frankfurt: Klostermann, 1965), 129; but see 337f.

[82]See Evanghelos A. Moutsopoulos, "The Idea of False in Proclus," in R. Baine Harris, ed., *The Structure of Being: A Neoplatonic Approach* (Albany: SUNY Press, 1982), 137ff.

[83]St. Thomas Aquinas, *The Disputed Questions on Truth*, trans. R. W. Mulligan, S. J. (Chicago: Regnery, 1956), 1:11.

[84]St. Thomas Aquinas, *Summa Theologica*, Question 16, Article 2, cited from Anton C. Pegis, ed., *Basic Writings of St. Thomas Aquinas* (New York: Random House, 1945), 1:170f.

[85]Benedict de Spinoza, *Ethica*, in *Opera*, 2:47, 116f./410, 472f.

[86]*KRV* B 82f.; see Prauss, "Wahrheitsproblem," 167f.

Chapter 3

[1]*Philebus* 15a1ff.

[2]*Philebus* 15a seq.; see *Parmenides* 141a seq.

[3]*Phaedrus* 230e seq.

[4]See H. S. Harris, *Hegel's Development: Toward the Sunlight, 1770–1801* (Oxford: Clarendon Press, 1972), 97–105.

[5]Cynthia Hampton, "Pleasure, Truth and Being in Plato's *Philebus*: A Reply to Professor Frede," *Phronesis* 32 (1987): 257.

[6]*Philebus* 45a–e; 47c; see 52d6. The ordinariness of the conception of pleasure in terms of magnitude is attested at 45a2 ("everyone would agree with what you say") and 47b9f. ("everything that most people think"). The second conception of the truth of pleasure, of course, regards it in purely quantitative terms: as a sudden diminution of pain.

[7]Hence, the view that the Forms are without admixture of opposites is very important in the *Phaedo* (74c, 102d, 103b), but is undergoing some revision here. In any case, we do not need the Theory of Forms to prefer purity as opposed to magnitude as the criterion of pleasure or anything else: Epicurus, for example, did the same: *Kyriai Doxai* 19, in *Epicurus: The Extant Remains,* ed. Cyril Bailey (Oxford: Clarendon, 1926), 98; also see the "Letter to Menoeceus," 86. For this type of metaphysical warrant in Plato, which I call "hegemonic," see my *Poetic Interaction,* 201ff.

[8]*Philebus* 57a seq., 58a, 58c2f., 59b10f., c2; also 59a11f., c2f.

[9]Hampton, "Pleasure," 255.

[10]*Republic* 508e.

[11]Rudolf Schmitz, *Sein Wahrheit Wort* (Munster: Lit, 1984), 3–16, 22f.; also see Robert Gregg Bury, ed., *The Philebus of Plato* (Cambridge: Cambridge University Press, 1897), Appendix F.

[12]The same holds for each of its properties, if we want to attribute an object/property distinction to Plato.

[13]*Philebus* 64b; I here read *metriotês* for *symmetria* at 65a1, so as to harmonize it with 64e5f. and 65b7f.; for *symmetria* is, as Bury has noted, to be read in the sense of "commensurate," i.e., measured by the measure, *metriotês;* Bury, *Philebus,* 176, and see *Timaeus* 87d.

[14]As is said of the soul at *Phaedo* 67c, 83b.

[15]As Henri Joly puts it, comparing the views of purity put forth in the *Philebus* and in earlier dialogues: "From purity without mixture, it has become purity in view of mixture": Henri Joly, *Le renversement platonicien,* 2d ed., rev. and cor. (Paris: Jean Vrin, 1985), 72; also see *Sophist* 226d.

[16]That Plato was at least aware of this possibility is established by *Republic* VI 508e seq., which makes the Good other than, yet the cause of, all determinate Forms; also see *Republic* VII 517b, 534b seq.

[17]For which also see *Sophist* 260a.

[18]*De Interpretatione* 1; *De Anima* 3:6, 430a26f ; 3.8, 432a11; *Metaphysics* 4.8 1012b8.

[19]Joseph Owens, *The Doctrine of Being in the Aristotelian Metaphysics,* 2d. ed., rev. (Toronto: Pontifical Institute of Medieval Studies, 1963), 411–14.

[20]See Franz Brentano, *On the Several Senses of Being in Aristotle* (Berkeley: University of California Press, 1975), 23; also, F. P. Ramsey, "Facts and Propositions," in George T. Pitcher, ed., *Truth* (Englewood Cliffs, N. J.: Prentice-Hall, 1964), 16f.

[21]For which see *Metaphysics* 4.2, 1003a35, and 11.3, 1061a3–7.

[22]*Metaphysics* 5.29, 1024b32; see 6.4, 1027b30ff.

[23]Pierre Aubenque, *Le problème de l'être chez Aristotle* (Paris: Presses Universitaires de France, 1962), 167.

[24]*Metaphysics* 9.10, 1051a2ff.

[25]XIX (*Hist. Phil.*) 164/II 149f.

[26]See *Analytica Posteriora* 2.3, 2.10; *Metaphysics* 7.12 1038a5ff.

[27]Explored in most detail at Owens, *Doctrine;* also see my *Poetic Interaction,* 205–12, and Martin Heidegger, "Die Onto-theologische Verfassung der Metaphysik," in *Identität und Differenz* (Pfullingen: Neske, 1957), 51–67.

[28]Thomas Hobbes, *Logica* 3.7, in *Opera philosophica quae Latine scripsit,* ed. William Molesworth (London: John Bohn, 1839), 1.32; G. W. Leibniz, *Nouveaux essais sur l'entendement humain,* ed. André Robinet and Heinrich Schepers (Berlin: Akademie-Verlag, 1962), 254–63/*New Essays on Human Understanding,* trans. and ed. Peter Remnant and Jonathan Bennett (Cambridge: Cambridge University Press, repr. 1982), 397f.; Benedict de Spinoza, "Appendix containing Metaphysical Thoughts" to *Descartes's Prin-*

ciples of Philosophy, in *Opera,* 1:247/*On the Improvement of the Intellect* in *Collected Works,* 213f.; Locke, *Essay* 2:23 (but see chapter 9 for more on Locke and substance); for Descartes see Josef Pieper, *Wahrheit der Dinge* (Munich: Kösel Velag, 1957), 17; for Kant, *KRV* B 113f.; also see Pieper, 19.

[29]Descartes, *Meditationes de prima philosophia,* ed. Geneviève Rodis-Lewis (Paris: Jean Vrin, 1970), 23f./*The Philosophical Works of Descartes,* trans. Elizabeth Haldane and G. R. T. Ross (Cambridge: Cambridge University Press, 1931), 1:148f.

[30]Locke, *Essay* 2:23.29f.; see 2:23, passim.

[31]Spinoza, *Opera* 2:56, 110f./420, 468f.; for similarities with Hegel on the nature of truth, see Schmueli, "Similarities," 654f.

[32]G. W. Leibniz, "De modo distinguendi phaenomena realia ab imaginariis," in *Die philosophischen Schriften,* ed. C. J. Gebhardt (Hildesheim: Georg Olms, 1966), (hereinafter: *Phil. Schriften*) 7:319ff./*Philosophical Papers and Letters,* ed. Leroy Loemker, 2d ed. (Dordrecht: Reidel, 1969), 363–66.

[33]*KRV* B 102ff.

[34]Even Spinoza's view, which I will not discuss here, has not escaped assimilation to the correspondence theory, for which see Spinoza, *Ethics* in *Opera* 2:47/410, and Edwin Curley, *Spinoza's Metaphysics* (Cambridge, Mass.: Harvard University Press, 1969), 122ff.

[35]René Descartes, *Les principes de la philosophie (le partie),* ed. Guy Durandin (Paris: Jean Vrin, 1970), 49f./Haldane and Ross, *Philosophical Works,* 1:219.

[36]Descartes, *Principes,* #4f., 51ff.; #43, 83/220,236.

[37]See Spinoza, *Descartes's Principles of Philosophy* 1:171f./256; *De emendatione intellectu* 2:24, 34/29, 38.

[38]Again, I will prescind in discussing Leibniz from much that is of importance. In particular, Leibniz's account of a universal harmony, which contains the greatest possible variety with the greatest possible order, developed for example in the *Monadology,* would be of importance for a full understanding of Hegelian truth; but it lies off the path of the present narrative. "The Meditation" can be found at Leibniz, *Phil. Schriften* 4:422–26/291–95.

[39]*Phil. Schriften* 4:422/291. The translation in Loemker uses "recognize" for both *agnoscere* and *recognoscere,* obscuring the point at issue here.

[40]The term *nota* will play an important role in what is to come. In German, it becomes *Merkmal* and is treated, chapter 6 will show, in Kant's *Logic.* Chapter 4 will give it a central role in Hegel's dialectics, though Hegel does not use the term in the sense I will give it there. I will translate both *nota* and *Merkmal* as "marker," though the translation I cite here renders it "mark," and the one I will cite for Kant renders it "attribute."

[41]See "Meditation," 424/293. The point is stated more clearly in Leibniz, "Two Dialogues on Religion," *Revue de métaphysique et de morale* 13 (1905): 1–38/219.

[42]*Phil. Schriften* 7:261f./167; also see *Monadologie* ##41ff., in *Phil. Schriften* 6:613f./646f. and Loemker, Introduction to *Philosophical Papers,* 52.

[43]*Monadologie* #31, *Phil. Schriften* 6:612/646; see "The Principles of Nature and of Grace, Based on Reason," *Phil. Schriften* 6:602f./639; "On First Truths," in Louis Couturat, ed., *Opuscules e fragments inédits de Leibniz,* repr. *Phil. Schriften* 8:518f./267f. We may note that the rule of perfection—that God always employs the simplest of means to achieve the richest of effects, or that he causes the greatest harmony together with the greatest order—does not tell us anything about the properties of God himself: *Monadologie, Phil. Schriften* 6:616/648; *Discours de metaphysique, Phil. Schriften* 4:430f./305f.

[44]XX (*Hist. Phil.*) 203f./not translated.

[45]Locke, *Essay*, "Epistle to the Reader," 1:22. The book was first published in 1690; this section of the "Epistle" dates from 1699. Locke, however, seems to have no acquaintance with Leibniz's "Meditation on Knowledge, Truth, and Ideas" of 1684: see Fraser 21 n. 2, 23 n. 1, and 486 n. 1. I will not avail myself of Locke's terminological innovations, which did not find acceptance.

[46]Locke, *Essay* 3:9.21.

[47]Ibid., 2:29.5-9.

[48]Ibid., 2:29.5.

[49]Ibid., 3:3.6; also see 2:32.8.

[50]Leibniz, *Nouveaux essais*, 254-63/397ff.; also see "Dialogue," *Phil. Schriften* 7:190-93/182-85, and "On Universal Synthesis and Analysis, or the Art of Discovery and Judgment," *Phil. Schriften* 7:295/231.

[51]Locke, *Essay* 3:5; Leibniz's point against this is that the important thing about the ideas of mixed modes is not that they are arbitrarily created by the human mind, but that they have reference to a possibility and are, in the sense we have seen, "true": *Nouveaux essais*, 304-29. I will discuss Locke on mixed modes further in chapter 9.

[52]Locke, *Essay* 2:29.10.

[53]For this "deontologizing" of the discussion of ideas, see John Yolton, "Ideas and Knowledge in Seventeenth-Century Philosophy," *Journal of the History of Philosophy* 13 (1975): 158-61.

[54]Locke, *Essay* 4:5.2; "Epistle to the Reader," 22ff.

[55]Kant, *Werke* 6:434-37; 442f./*Logic*, trans. Robert Harman and Wolfgang Schwartz (Indianapolis: Bobbs-Merrill, 1974), 15-18, 23.

[56]Ibid., 6:464/44.

[57]Ibid., 6:461, 476/41, 55.

[58]Ibid., 6:457f., 491/37ff., 69.

[59]Ibid., 6:526/101f.

[60]Ibid., 6:521/96.

[61]Ibid., 6:485, 521, 526, 572/64, 96, 101f., 141f.

[62]The following paragraphs discuss Kant, *Werke* 6:486f./65ff.

[63]Kant, *Werke* 6:488-90/66-68.

[64]E.g., by Hegel and Heidegger, as Gerold Prauss notes: Prauss, "Wahrheitsproblem," 167; my account will largely follow Prauss.

[65]Kant, *Werke* 6:476ff./55f.

[66]Ibid., 6:477f./56f.

[67]Ibid.

[68]The analogy is stated at *Metaphysics* 12.10, 1075a12-24.

[69]The line between substances and *kalon* is not hard and fast: the inherence of a form in its matter is for Aristotle *kalon*, as in the case of reason in the good man, the *phronimos*, for which see below. Hence, for Hegel to identify his own concept of truth with substance alone, if that is what he is up to, would be to absolutize what for Aristotle is a merely relative distinction. It would also be to ignore one of Hegel's own major innovations. In general, as Heinz Röttges has put it, "subjectivity which merely rests within itself and does not refer beyond itself, is substantiality in the traditional sense": Röttges, *Begriff der Method*, 63. Subjectivity is thus substance transcending itself, recognizing its inability to "rest within itself," and establishing itself only through its relation to others—a relation which, holding among substances, exhibits for Aristotle the weaker grade of unity proper to what is *kalon*. Hence when Hegel says, in one of his more famous slogans, that substance must become subject (III 23, 28/10, 14) he is implying that the "strong" unity exhibited by substance is to be displaced in favor of the weaker

unity proper to what is *kalon*. See also Gwendoline Jarczyk, "Approche," in Labarrière and Jarczyk, *Hegeliana*, 159–68.

[70]Aristotle, *Nicomachean Ethics* (hereinafter: *NE*) 2.6 1106a26–1106b8; 2.7 1107b1 seq.; 2.9 1109a24–29; 3.6–9 passim; see A. L. Peck's approximation of the biological notion of symmetry with virtue in *NE* in Aristotle, *De Generatione Animalium*, trans. A. L. Peck (Cambridge, Mass.: Harvard University Press [Loeb Classical Library]), 1vff.

[71]*Metaphysics* 12.10, 1075a 12–24; *NE* 3.1 1110b9–11; 3.5 113b8–14; 3.7 115b13; 4.1 1120a22–24; 4.2 1122b6f.; 7.14 1333a32–37.

[72]*NE* 9.8 1169a8–11.

[73]*NE* 8.1 1155a29–32; also see *Rhetoric* 2:13 1390a1 seq.

[74]Joseph Owens, "Nature and Ethical Norm in Aristotle," in *Aristotle*, ed. John R. Catan (Albany: SUNY Press, 1981), 166f.

[75]*Metaphysics* 13.3 1078b1f.; *NE* 5.15 1138a6; *De Partibus Animalium* 1.1 641b18; *De Generatione Animalium* 5.1 778b4.

[76]*Metaphysics* 5.1 1013a22; 13.3 1078b2–6.

[77]*De Generatione Animalium* 2.1 731b26 seq.

[78]*Metaphysics* 12.7 1072a26–b11.

[79]This solution is suggested (for example) by *De Generatione Animalium*, where it is said that each animal, desiring eternality but unable to achieve it as an individual, achieves it as a species—by reproducing: *De Generatione Animalium* 2.1 731b32–732a2.

[80]*Metaphysics* 12.10 1075a12–24.

[81]X 395 (after *Enz.* #577)/315.

[82]*Posterior Analytics* 2.10 93b28–99a19; 2.13, 96b15–24.

[83]*Poetics* 1450b35–51a5; *Politics* 7.3 1325a29–35.

[84]And he applies this even to static works of art, considering them only as they are progressively appreciated by their audience: for this in connection with a general account of reconciliation in Hegel, see my *Poetic Interaction*, 63–86.

[85]See Dieter Henrich, "Hegels Theorie," 131–48.

[86]For the distinction between Kant and Leibniz on this issue, see Nicholas Rescher, "Leibniz and the Concept of System," *Studia Leibnitiana* 13 (1981): 114–20.

[87]*Metaphysics* 12.10 1075a14–16.

Chapter 4

[1]See the survey in Andries Sarlemijn, *Hegelsche Dialektik* (Berlin: de Gruyter, 1971), 82–95.

[2]Jaako Hintikka, "On the Common Factors of Dialectic," in Werner Becker and Wilhelm Essler, eds., *Konzepte der Dialektik* (Frankfurt: Klostermann, 1981), 109f. In the mid-1970s, Dieter Henrich had noted that there had been no accepted answer at all to the question, "what is dialectic": Henrich, "Hegels Grundoperation," in Guzzoni, et al., *Idealismus*, 208–30. For a brief summary of the major recent viewpoints, see Fulda, "Unzulängliche," in Horstmann, *Seminar*, 33ff.

[3]V (*WDL*) 245/213f. For reservations on Hegel's view see Howard P. Kainz, *Paradox, Dialectic and System* (University Park: Pennsylvania State University Press, 1988), 33f. My own "rewriting" will avoid what Kainz poses as the basic problem: that traditional formalizations repose on the subject-object split, or are what I call assertionistic. Robert Pippin also presents some reservations, which I share, about the usefulness of overall accounts of Hegelian dialectic, in view of the very different forms it takes in dif-

ferent parts of the System: Pippin, *Hegel's Idealism*, 255, and n. 73 to the introduction to this book. For further reservations see Topp, *Philosophie*, 261ff.

⁴X 283 (*Enz.* #465)/224. This insight has been amply confirmed by some of the classical work in artificial intelligence: see Marvin Minsky, "A Framework for Representing Knowledge," in P. H. Winston, ed., *The Psychology of Computer Vision* (New York: McGraw Hill, 1975), 211–77; Roger Schank and Robert Abelson, *Scripts, Plans, Goals, and Understanding* (Hillsdale, N.J.: Erlbaum, 1977), 17ff.; for an overview, see George Lakoff, *Women, Fire, and Dangerous Things* (Chicago: University of Chicago Press, 1987).

⁵See F. G. Asenjo, "Dialectical Logic," *Logique et analyse* 8 (1965): 321–26; Clark Butler, "On the Reducibility of Dialectical to Standard Logic," *The Personalist* 6 (1975): 414–31; D. Dubarle and A. Dos, *Logique et dialectique* (Paris: Larousse, 1971); Yvon Gauthier, "Logique hegelienne et formalization," *Dialogue* 6 (1967), 151–65; G. Günther, "Das Problem einer Formalisierung der transzendentaldialektischen Logik," in *Hegel-Tage*, Hrsg. Hans-Georg Gadamer, *Hegel-Studien*, Beiheft 1 (1964): 65–113; Michael Kosok, "The Formalization of Hegel's Dialectical Logic," *International Philosophical Quarterly* 6 (1966); R. Routley and R. Meyer, "Dialectic Logic, Classical Logic, and the Consistency of the World," *Studies in Soviet Thought* (1976): 1–25; Thomas Seebohm, "The Grammar of Hegel's Dialectic," *Hegel-Studien* 11 (1975): 149–80; Paul Thagard, "Hegel, Science, and Set Theory," *Erkenntnis* 18 (1982): 397–410; S. K. Thomason, "Towards a Formalization of Dialectical Logic," *Journal of Symbolic Logic* 39 (1974): 204.

⁶V (*WDL*) 44/50. For remarks of this sort, see also III (*PHG*) 28, 46, 588/14, 27, 490f.; V (*WDL*) 19, 57, 67f./31, 60, 69; VI (*WDL*) 264/592; VIII 14f., 57 (*Enz.* #12 Anm.), 307 (*Enz.* #160 Zus.), 368 (*Enz.* #213 Anm.)/not translated, 16ff., 223f., 275. Yirmiahu Yovel has concisely stated the basic warrant for the assertionist view: "Hegel's problem with predicative language is that he can have no alternative to it": Yovel, "Hegel's Dictum that the Rational is Actual and Actual is Rational," in Becker and Essler, *Konzepte*, 111–23. Yovel is right that there is no *alternative* to predicative language if one is in the business of stating and justifying assertions. But predicative language can be *complemented*, for such truth is not the only goal of speech. As Hans-Martin Sass has put it,

> While traditional logic entertains symbols or words in the game of *predication*, speculative logic encourages movement, dialogues, and intercourse within language itself. It calls itself a business of *emancipation*.

Sass, "Speculative Logic (Dialectics) as Conflict Theory," in Becker and Essler, *Konzepte*, 66f., 68.

⁷VII 55–58 (*Enz.* ##12f.)/16–18.

⁸III (*PHG*) 72–49.

⁹Seebohm's basic work on this topic is "Das Widerspruchsprinzip in der Kantischen Logik und der Hegelschen Dialektik" (hereinafter cited as WP), in *Akten des 4. Internationalen Kant-Kongresses Mainz 1974*, 862–74. Also see his "Grammar."

¹⁰WP 862–66.

¹¹WP 870.

¹²But see Norman Kretzmann, "The Main Thesis of Locke's Semantic Theory," *Philosophical Review* 77 (1968): 175–96 for nuances in this, and n. 12 to chapter 9 for critical comments on Kretzmann.

¹³Kant never even discusses language in his *Logic*, or changes his early view that words only bring to mind concepts, and that—as with Lockean ideas—it is these which

the thinker must keep before his mind: Kant, *Werke* 6:521; also see "Untersuchung über die Deutlichkeit der Grundsätze der natürlichen Theologie und der Moral," *Werke* 2:762.

[14]X 278ff. (*Enz.* #462 Anm.)/220ff. Peter Ruben has seen that Hegelian dialectic moves, not via assertions, but via terms *(Termini)*. Reading this in terms of the "elementary judgment of sense-certainty" in the first phase of the *Phenomenology*, Ruben concludes that the Logic is subject to a "serious weakness." Just what that weakness is need not concern us for, as will become clear in the appendix to this chapter, the predications in "Sense-Certainty" are not elementary, and do not form any sort of basis for understanding Systematic developments: Peter Ruben, "Von der 'Wissenschaft der Logik' und dem Verhältnis der Dialektik zur Logik," in Horstmann, *Seminar*, 70–100.

[15]VIII 255 (*Enz.* #124 Zus.); see also VIII 275f. (*Enz.* #140 Zus.)/181, 198–200; III *(PHG)* 25/12; and, more generally, III *(PHG)* 51f./31f.

[16]WP 869f.

[17]VI *(WDL)* 553ff./827ff.

[18]Such a result is, of course, unthinkable from the standpoint of the Kantian chorismos: things in themselves cannot be raised to the level of appearances.

[19]Even this will have to be modified in the next section: the markers do not signify, but are, the names.

[20]From an investigation of the *Phenomenology*, Reinhold Aschenberg has shown that even there truth is conceived as a relation between what is in-itself and what is for-itself: Aschenberg, "Wahrheitsbegriff," in Hartmann, *Option*, 220–23, 249–53. This, Aschenberg argues, is motivated by a desire to overcome the "epistemological" concept of truth, according to which it is the relation, ultimately unfathomable, between something subjective and something objective. Hegel revises this by locating truth in the relation between two different phases of the same thing. This motivation, of course, would only be stronger in the System itself.

[21]Rudolf Carnap, *Logical Structure*, 22–27.

[22]VIII 260f. (*Enz.* #130), 191 (*Enz.* #88 Anm. 4)/185f., 131. Also see VI *(WDL)* 93f./91f.

[23]X 275f. (*Enz.* #459 Anm.)/217f.

[24]III *(PHG)* 24f./11.

[25]VIII 275ff. (*Enz.* #140 Zus.)/198–200; III *(PHG)* 19, 25, 51f./7, 11f., 31f.

[26]"It is in names that we *think*," X 278 (*Enz.* #462 Anm.)/220; the import of this dictum will be discussed in chapter 7.

[27]See my discussion of finite things in chapter 1, and the application to Hegel's concept of contradiction in chapter 5.

[28]It will be noticed that one device of contemporary logic not required here is the infamous hierarchy of metalanguages. For a discussion of Hegel in such terms, see J. N. Findlay, "Contemporary Relevance," in *Collection*, MacIntyre, 4ff. Hegel is not open to the various paradoxes which the device of metalanguage avoids, since the dialectic as here presented is nonpropositional: it *asserts* nothing, whether paradoxical or not.

[29]V 97/93; VIII 229 (*Enz.* #111 Zus.), 308 (*Enz.* #161)/161, 224.

[30]Rolf-Peter Horstmann, writing in 1977, called it "remarkable" that no one had thought to measure the account of dialectics in "The Absolute Idea" against Hegel's own practice elsewhere in the *Logic*. I cannot claim to make more than a small beginning of this here, though I hope the beginning is a promising one. Contrary to Horstmann's doubt, describing the dialectical method is indeed at least a partial justification of it, for it shows that the method at least exists: Horstmann, "Einleitung" to Horstmann, *Seminar*, 14 and n. 9. In 1979, Heinz Kimmerle undertook just such a project,

and remains my main predecessor in this. His account differs from mine in that he does not view the development in terms of names, but sees it as moving assertionistically. This renders his account much more complex than mine—and, if my account is sufficient, needlessly so: Heinz Kimmerle, "Die allgemeine Strukturen der dialektischen Methode," *Zeitschrift für philosophishche Forschung* 33 (1979): 184–209. Klaus Düsing has noted that speculative sentences are dropped by Hegel in favor of "speculative content," which is the dialectical movement of the Concept in syllogistic terms: Düsing, "Syllogistik und Dialektik in Hegels spekulative Logik," in Henrich, *Hegels Wissenschaft*, 15–38. For my own syllogistic reconstruction of the dynamics of Hegel's System, see chapter 10.

    [31]VIII 190/130, where *spekulativer Satz* is mysteriously translated as "speculative truth." For the absence of the phrase in the *Science of Logic*, see Günter Wohlfahrt, *Der spekulative Satz* (Berlin: de Gruyter, 1981), xiii: "to my knowledge, the *Science of Logic* does not speak, in so many words, of the 'speculative sentence.' "

    [32]III 59-63/38–41; Rüdiger Bubner, "Strukturprobleme dialektischer Logik," in Bubner, *Zur Sache der Dialektik* (Stuttgart: Reklam, 1980), 8–39. For the nature of phenomenological dialectics, see the appendix to this chapter.

    [33]Bubner, "Strukturprobleme," 24; Puntel, cited in Bubner, 36.

    [34]For more on the "movement of the Concept," see chapter 7, n. 85.

    [35]VI (*WDL*) 554f./828f.

    [36]Ibid. 550/825.

    [37]Ibid. 554ff./828ff.

    [38]V (*WDL*) 31f./40.

    [39]This stage is usually given in the *Wissenschaft der Logik* at the end of the preceding stage: see VI (*WDL*) 123, 185, 240, 448, 486f./478, 528, 571, 742f., 774, etc.

    [40]VI (*WDL*) 561/833.

    [41]Ibid. 556/830.

    [42]Ibid. 557/831.

    [43]Ibid. 560/832f.

    [44]Ibid. 562f./834f.

    [45]Ibid. 563f./835f.

    [46]On my reading, of course, the moments of the System should not be called "concepts" in any ordinary sense, because Hegel is not worried about reference or, here, about how his System permits us to talk about objects: Terry Pinkard, "The Logic of Hegel's Logic," in Inwood, *Hegel*, 85–109.

    [47]Michael Theunissen, *Sein und Schein*, 28ff. The present interpretation cannot agree with Theunissen that Hegel's Logic "finds philosophical truth prefigured in the dialectical movement of the assertion [*Satz*]" (13), except insofar as, for Hegel, logical truth is "prefigured" throughout nature and the human world; Theunissen's support for this comes from the *Phenomenology*, not the Systematic works themselves. At p. 54, Theunissen notes that the orientation to assertions is clearer in the first edition of Hegel's *Logic* than in the second; the quotes he gives there from the second edition are not, as he says, part of the "foundation laying for logical science," but occur in a Remark *(Anmerkung)*, for which see V (*WDL*) 92f./90.

    [48]See VI (*WDL*) 49, together with 38f. and 46f./419f., 411f., 418f.

    [49]XIX *(Hist. Phil.)* 239f., 242/II 221f., 229. Klaus Hartmann has argued that Aristotelian genus-species relations are not only not to be found in Hegel's System, but that the System yields a critique of them: Hartmann, "Die ontologische Option," in Hartmann, *Die Option*, 10–13. In general, my interpretation is close to Hartmann's, except that the "ontological" relevance of Hegel's System is mediated by language: Hegel's Sys-

tematic moments are ontologically relevant only insofar as they clarify a language which structures a world. For an instance of problems caused by reading Aristotelian genera and species directly into Hegel, see Manfred Baum, "Anmerkungen," in Henrich, *Hegels Wissenschaft*, 74–76. Determinate negation, as the unity of a previous moment with its opposite, is understood by Baum to produce a new, more general concept. But in the Aristotelian hierarchy, "more general" means "emptier," which cannot be right since determinate negation for Hegel is also supposed to enrich content. Baum gives a solution to this, which is unnecessary if Aristotelian hierarchies do not apply at all to the Logic.

[50]VI (*WDL*) 535f./813f.

[51]II 194–98/not translated.

[52]Kant, *KRV* B 10–19.

[53]Given at VI (*WDL*) 429/727.

[54]VI (*WDL*) 436ff./734.

[55]V (*WDL*) 82f./734.

[56]Dieter Henrich, "Anfang und Methode der Logik," *Hegel-Studien* Beiheft 1 (1964): 19–35.

[57]V (*WDL*) 111–13/105f.

[58]V (*WDL*) 116/109f. Determinate Being thus does not arise, as Peter Rohs has it, through successive sublations of the difference between Being and Nothing. Since according to Rohs it is impossible to sublate something twice in two successive moves of the Logic—it is gone after the first—the "mediated immediacy" which supposedly results from such a double sublation is impossible, and since mediated immediacy is essential to Hegel's method as expounded in "The Absolute Idea," that method cannot work. My own account of "mediated immediacy" would see it as resulting, not from a double mediation, but from what I have called the gesture of "immediation": Peter Rohs, "Das Problem der vermittelten Unmittelbarkeit in der Hegelschen Logik," *Philosophisches Jahrbuch* 81 (1974): 331–80.

[59]Bertrand Russell, "On Denoting," in Russell, *Logic and Knowledge*, ed. Robert C. Marsh (London: Allen and Unwin, 1956), 39–56.

[60]See Terry Winograd, "Formalisms for Knowledge," in P. N. Johnson-Laird and P. C. Wason, eds., *Thinking* (Cambridge: Cambridge University Press, 1978) 64f.

[61]VIII 92 (*Enz.* #25 Anm.)/46.

[62]VII (*Philosophy of Right*) 504/216.

[63]VIII 60–62 (*Enz.* #16 Anm.)/20–22.

[64]VI (*WDL*) 502–41/786–818.

[65]VI (*WDL*) 503f./787f.

[66]VI (*WDL*) 511f./793f.

[67]VI (*WDL*) 512/794.

[68]VI (*WDL*) 519f./800f.

[69]VI (*WDL*) 532/811.

[70]VI (*WDL*) 540f./819f.

[71]VIII 174f. (*Enz.* #81 Zus.)/118.

[72]See respectively VI (*WDL*) 518, 524f., 532/789f., 804f., 811.

[73]See Paul Thagard, "Set Theory," 397–410, which I will discuss in the following appendix.

[74]*EGP* 126/94.

[75]VI (*WDL*) 513/795f.

[76]Seebohm, "Grammar," 154.

[77]This sort of adding and dropping of markers could also be applied to the adding

and dropping of properties from my conception of a "friend," and to my complex conception of a person I am coming to know as a friend: it can reconstruct the characteristics of "genuineness" discussed in chapter 2. But Hegel never uses it that way; what is philosophically "genuine" for him is only the concepts, not the entities to which they apply.

[78]See VI (WDL) 516f./798—if we accepted the definition of "man" mentioned there as "animal with earlobes," and then found another such animal.

[79]III (PHG) 150/114f.

[80]In line, for example, with Alexandre Kojève's Introduction. For the "special" nature of the Phenomenology, see the appendix to this chapter.

[81]This puts Hegel at some remove from traditional views of essence, according to which an essence is an unchanging, determinate substrate grounding the observable properties of a thing. That markers may enter and leave definitions with no overall rule or pattern means that any specification of a single "essence" governing the development inevitably distorts reality, and is as false as it is true. Hence, Robert Pippin has brought Hegel's account of contradiction into illuminating proximity to his account of essence: Pippin, "Hegel's Metaphysics and the Problem of Contradiction," Journal of the History of Philosophy 16 (1978): 301–12. See also my discussion of Wittgensteinian family resemblance from a Hegelian perspective in chapter 11. This may seem at odds with Hegelian teleology: if there is no unified, guiding essence to history, how can it "culminate" in, for example, Hegel's System? The answer, I suggest, is just that the telos of history is a state of affairs in which philosophy can proceed without postulating such essences: see the discussion of the "end of history" in chapter 5, and of the "attainment of the Absolute" in the appendix to this chapter.

[82]See Clark Butler, "Hermeneutic Hegelianism," Idealistic Studies 15 (1985): 121–36.

[83]Errol Harris, "Dialectic and Scientific Method," Idealistic Studies III (1973): 1–17; also see Harris's presentation of similar theses at Cohen and Wartofsky, eds., Hegel and the Sciences, 195–213, and the response by Ernan McMullin, pp. 215–39, which takes a far more "necessitarian" view of Hegelian dialectic than what I defend here. Paul Thagard, "Set-Theory," 397–410.

[84]III (PHG) 78f./55f.

[85]VII (Philosophy of Right) 504/216.

[86]PWG 177–79.

[87]PWG 180f.

[88]As H. S. Harris has put it, "deep concern with what might be called the 'education of humanity' in the widest sense forms the main nerve of Hegel's earliest philosophical speculation, and this concern remained always one of his fundamental interests": H. S. Harris, Hegel's Development, 4. See also the essays in Beyer, Logik des Wissens, and the treatments of Hegel's views on education in Ursula Krautkrämer, Staat und Erziehung (Munich: Johannes Beichmann, 1979), 182–249, and Siegfried Reuss, Die verwirklichung der vernunft (Frankfurt: Max Planck Institut für Bildungsforschung, 1982).

[89]III (PHG) 65/43.

[90]III (PHG) 29/14f.

[91]VI (WDL) 415ff./716ff.

[92]VI (WDL) 416/716.

[93]Ibid.

[94]VI (WDL) 421/720.

[95]VI (WDL) 423f./721f.

[96]III (*PHG*) 72/49.

[97]VI (*WDL*) 419/719. Hence the *Phenomenology* has the status of what W. H. Bossart calls an "exoteric" dialectic, as opposed to the immanent dialectic of the System itself: in Bossart's words, "The former seeks to conceive the essential structures which are hidden in experience. At the same time, however, it points the way to the *logos* which substitutes an ideal genesis of those structures for their actual genesis": William H. Bossart, "Exoteric and Esoteric in Hegel's Dialectic," *The Personalist* 58 (1977): 271. For my answer to Bossart's main problem—how the "infinite" thought of esoteric dialectic can be actualized in a finite mind—see chapter 10, n. 87.

[98]This, presumably, is why Hegel was so willing in 1831 to admit that the *Phenomenology* was conditioned essentially by the time in which it was written. As pedagogy, it would have to take different forms, to some extent at least, when addressed to individuals of different times and cultures. See Lasson's note in his "Zur Feststellung des Texts," in Hegel, *Phänomenologie des Geistes*, 578.

[99]VI (*WDL*) 421f./720f.

[100]III (*PHG*) 83/58ff. Charles Taylor's view that "Sense-Certainty" does not specify the objects of consciousness is thus incorrect. Hegel specifies them, but in such a way as to render suspect any reading of the section as containing a straightforward account of empiricism: "The Opening Arguments of the *Phenomenology*," in MacIntyre, *Collection*, 161.

[101]III (*PHG*) 578f./481f.

[102]This explanation is partial because the *Phenomenology* probably owes much of its nature to the difficult circumstances under which Hegel wrote it: see Walter Kaufmann, *Reinterpretation*, 87–95.

Chapter Five

[1]See chapter 1.

[2]I will discuss Davidson's project in chapters 8 and 11.

[3]See chapter 2 for remarks on this move in Carnap.

[4]III (*PHG*) 38ff./59ff.

[5]Ibid., 83/59.

[6]Hegel, I take it, attempts to express this by declaring that the copula is itself here dynamic: "Being is Nothing" is supposed to mean "Being turns into Nothing, thanks to the development itself"; or, as he puts it, "Das Sein . . . ist *in der Tat* Nichts." (V [*WDL*] 83/82, my emphasis); also see V (*WDL*) 92/90, which however introduces the complicated phrasing "Being and Nothing is one and the same." The other way to express this dynamic sense of "is" would be, as Hegel notes, to complement the sentence which expresses the completed assignment ("Being is nothing") with one which expresses the state of affairs before the assignment is made ("Being and Nothing are not the same"): V (*WDL*) 94/91. But this, Hegel notes, is clumsy (*ungeschickt*) and leads to unneeded complexity in presenting the dialectic.

[7]As chapter 10 will discuss in more detail.

[8]VIII 57 (*Enz.* #211 Anm., Zus.)/17.

[9]Hegel, *PWG*, 180f.

[10]For a recent defense of what I call "Sartrean abstractness" against the "postmodernity" often attributed to Heidegger, see Luc Ferry and Alain Renaut, *Heidegger and Modernity*, trans. Franklin Philip (Chicago: University of Chicago Press,

1990), 94–110. For a Hegel-inspired critique, see my review of that book in *International Studies in Philosophy*, forthcoming.

[11]See below.

[12]See my recounting of the genesis of language in the *Phenomenology* in my *Poetic Interaction*, 33–38.

[13]For which see III (*PHG*) 74/51; V (*WDL*) 49/54.

[14]VI (*WDL*) 74, 203/439, 543; XI 472 (Review of Ohlert), 540 (1822 fragment on the philosophy of Spirit), XIII (*Aesth.*) 134/97; also Hösle, *Hegel's System*, 165ff., 179, and Paul Guyer, "Hegel, Leibniz, and the Contradiction in the Finite," *Philosophy and Phenomenological Research* 40 (1979–80): 75–98. Hegel is thus not doing here what Guyer and Hans Friedrich Fulda, among others, think he is doing: formulating a point about the structure of concepts and then projecting it upon the world. Hegel's point is formulated, in the Logic, not with regard to "concepts" (in the ordinary philosophical sense which Guyer observes), but for Systematic moments; nor, on the present reading, do those moments have anything to do with what Fulda, also conforming to traditional usage, calls the *wahrheitsgemäß*: Fulda, "Unzulängliche," in Horstmann, *Seminar*, 33–69. As I will show in chapter 10, the movement from Systematic moments to extraphilosophical realities is not a simple projection, but a complex set of interplays which (sometimes) involves a change in kind: what I here call "finitization."

[15]III (*PHG*) 1412/107; for an account of "externalization" as the denial of conditions, see my *Poetic Interaction*, 46–62.

[16]VI (*WDL*) 302/543. The Logic's *comprehension* of this type of contradiction, as opposed to the type which the Logic itself *exhibits* and which I have discussed above, relies on the general structures of the Logic of Essence. In such contradiction, two opposed determinacies each claim to be the "essence" of some larger entity, which requires for each reducing the other to a mere appearance or *Schein*. Since the essence of anything cannot be for Hegel definitively specified, neither determinacy can win this argument, and compromise (here, *Aufhebung*) is inevitable. Such a situation is a moment of the Logic of Essence and cannot apply to the System as a whole, which is structured by the Logic of the Concept. Systematic moments do not claim to be the "essences" of anything, and Systematic "contradiction" is a harmonious expansion of the universe of discourse. See on this Pippin, "Hegel's Metaphysics," 301–12, and Theunissen, "Begriff und Realität," in Horstmann, *Seminar*, 324–59.

[17]Hösle, *Hegel's System*, 176; Andries Sarlemijn, *Hegelsche Dialektik*, 95–98.

[18]VIII 41, 52, 55ff., 86, 91 (*Enz.* ##1, 9, 12, 24 Zus. 3)/3, 13, 16ff., 41–45. For a perceptive discussion of different senses of "necessity" and their application to Hegel, see John Burbidge, *On Hegel's Logic*, 195–203.

[19]Heinz Kimmerle has argued that the vast quantity of empirical material Hegel found himself working into his lectures eventually produced a switch in his view of the System: in the Berlin lectures, the Logic is no longer a foundation for later developments but can be transformed by them. Logic and *Realphilosophie* (and, through that, reality itself) thus enter into a reciprocal dynamic. If I am right, the possibility of this was present from the start, whether or not Hegel allowed himself to recognize it. Heinz Kimmerle, "Hegels 'Logik' als Grundlegung des Systems der Philosophie," in Beyer, *Logik des Wissens*, 52–60.

[20]See Gustav E. Mueller, "The Hegel Legend of Thesis-Antithesis-Synthesis," *Journal of the History of Ideas* 19 (1958): 411–14; something like the view that the synthesis in a triad is unique is suggested in Mure's view that it is the "coincidence" of the thesis and antithesis; see Mure, *Study*, 325; also see pp. 302 and 350f., where Mure criticizes Hegel for failing to achieve this: "There will be a continual possibility, nay certainty, of

alternative and partially discrepant statement in the formulation even of logical categories," p. 355. On my view, such alternative statements are not, as Mure thinks (p. 354) due to the fact that the synthesis does not fully follow from the other two moments but always adds something of its own, but are permitted because the explication (step 2), being partial, actually contains *less* than did the previous abbreviation (0). Terry Pinkard has argued at length against construing the dialectic as unequivocally determining, at each stage, its next stage; but he maintains that this point was not understood by Hegel himself, who saw each category as the only possible outcome of the preceding development (Pinkard, *Hegel's Dialectic*, 15f., 27, 172). On the pages where he argues this, however, Pinkard does not cite any texts of Hegel to the effect that he saw things in so "rigorous" a way; as a general impression picked up from Hegel's own rhetoric, the view contradicts both the immanent nature of Hegelian Systematic dialectic and, as I will discuss below, Hegel's own practice.

²¹As John Burbidge notes: see Burbidge, *Hegel's Logic*, 48, 200.

²²Inwood gives three arguments why this cannot be the case for Hegel in *Hegel*, 510ff.:

1. For Hegel, the steps leading up to a result are contained in the result itself; hence, there is only one way to achieve that result. I fully agree with this; it is in fact exactly the kind of necessity I attribute to Systematic dialectics. But it is only once the result has been stated that the previous steps lead up to it. Before that they may lead to any of a number of still unrealized possibilities.

2. Alternative routes through the System would mean a mind over and above the concrete development of the System, choosing its paths arbitrarily. The choice, I will argue in chapter 10, is guided by the specific results to be obtained and, though not warranted by Systematic dialectics, is far from arbitrary: it is made by the concrete mind of the philosopher, as she chooses how to develop a thought which is, as we saw, "unlimited in itself."

3. It would leave too much for philosophers after Hegel to do. Precisely!

²³Robert Pippin claims that Hegel, in his 1831 revision of the *Science of Logic*, actually reaffirmed the organization of the 1812–16 edition, in spite of the very different versions given in intervening editions of the *Encyclopedia* (Pippin, *Hegel's Idealism*, 213). The fallibility of the *Logic* at each stage explains how it can be at once a spontaneous self-determination of thought, as each stage is formulated, and yet be guided by a telos which is to some degree ulterior: the telos is what determines *which* spontaneous self-determinations are actually made. Hegel was, on the present reading, much less confident of the details of his System, and could correspondingly be more confident about its overall success, than Pippin concludes. This actually places Hegel closer to what Pippin rightly desires: a Hegel who recognizes that "many [Systematic] concepts are what they are because the world is as it is" (Pippin, 259f.), and that genuine empirical and moral discoveries are possible.

²⁴X (*Enz.* #459 Anm.) 273/215; also see the need for philosophical treatment of the (continuing) discoveries of empirical science at VIII 17f./not translated.

²⁵See Dove, "Hegel's Phenomenological Method," in Steinkraus, *New Studies*, 34–56.

²⁶Topp, *Philosophie*, 5.

²⁷Dieter Henrich, Introduction to Hegel, *Philosophie des Rechts: die Vorlesungen von 1819/20*, ed. Dieter Henrich (Frankfurt: Suhrkamp, 1983), 30–38.

²⁸See my *Poetic Interaction*, 302–4.

²⁹V (*WDL*) 50/54.

³⁰For the view of the Logic's "method" as its "path" (a view inspired by the Greek

etymology of *methodos,* "road after"), see VI (*WDL*) 551f./826f., VIII 392 *(Enz. #243)/* 296.

[31]Proclus Diadochus, *Elements of Theology,* ed. and trans. E. R. Dodds (Oxford: Clarendon Press, 1963), Prop. 29, 32f. Mure suggests that because (in his view, not mine: see n. 20 above) the synthesis adds something to the thesis and antithesis, and because the latter two moments, being to some extent "syntheses" themselves, share this character of the synthesis, a third term can be placed between any two terms of the development. Mure concedes this, but will not allow it to impugn Hegel, for it is he says a characteristic of all thought: "thinking cannot proceed at any level if the identity which it asserts has no stability in its differences" (Mure, *Study,* 354f.). This passage, with its anticipation of Derrida, points us to two issues that must be distinguished. Given my presentation (in chapter 7) of Systematic dialectics in the medium of "simple signs," each of which does nothing but bear the meaning it is assigned to bear, Mure's argument as stated does not hold; the discrepant developments of the System are due not to a surplus of meaning at each stage, but to a lack of meaning in the partial explications. However, if a sign is not simple—if a marker brings with it a complexity of its own and is not reducible to a mere designation of its Systematically assigned meaning—then Mure may be right.

[32]V (*WDL*) 149ff./137ff.

[33]VIII 87/43.

[34]V (*WDL*) 30/39f.

[35]The former is further reduced, writes Hegel just prior to what I have quoted, because a universal thought form only qualifies as such, ultimately, if it can be immanently developed by the Logic itself: the System's completeness would then consist in its including whatever it includes, which reduces the completeness claim to triviality.

[36]V (*WDL*) 21/32; VIII 17/not translated.

[37]VIII 60 (*Enz. #16*)/20.

[38]*Poetic Interaction,* 133f.

[39]Graeme Forbes, "The Indispensibility of *Sinn,*" *Philosophical Review* 99 (1990): 535f. I am using the term "information" here, not in the sense of Fregean *Sinn* but in the wide, and nonassertionistic, sense given in Claude Shannon and Warren Weaver, *The Mathematical Theory of Communication* (Urbana: University of Illinois Press, 1959): as a deviation from random noise. "Collateral information" is simply whatever responsory patterns a term accesses in, or for, someone who hears it.

[40]Quine, *Word and Object,* 37f.

[41]Gareth Evans, *The Varieties of Reference* (Oxford: Clarendon, 1982), 399.

[42]For Frege's concept of *Sinn* as conveying not merely the object designated by a word, but the way that object presents itself, see Gottlob Frege, "On Sense and Meaning," in Frege, *Selections from the Philosophical Writings of Gottlob Frege,* ed. Peter Geach and Max Black, 3d ed. (Oxford: Blackwell, 1980), 56–78.

[43]It may be that familiarity with the symbol, not background information activated by it, is the crucial parameter. Bertrand and Rudolf, being logicians themselves, are able simply to set their system up and use it. Perhaps, over time, the reader would become sufficiently accustomed to it to use it as well. But, again, how do we become "accustomed" to something without in the process developing a store of information about it? An account of familiarity that made no appeal to background information may be possible; I doubt that it would be easy.

[44]What Lakoff calls the "objectivist" and Winograd and Flores the "rationalist" paradigm: George Lakoff, *Women, Fire,* 157–84; Terry Winograd and Fernando Flores, *Understanding Computers and Cognition* (Reading, Mass.: Addison-Wesley, 1987), 14–20.

[45]Aristotle, *Nicomachean Ethics* 1.4 1095a16f.

[46]Hence, on the present reading Hegel's philosophy is not open to the main objection of Charles Taylor. Taylor takes Hegel to "characterize or describe the Absolute" (in *Hegel*, 472). The various features developed in the Logic are thus properties of the Absolute, which results for Taylor in Hegel's maintaining that reality itself is contradictory—a claim for which Taylor, rightly, has little sympathy (230f., 233–39). On the present reading, Hegel's development of contradiction as a moment in the Logic tells us strictly nothing about the world independently of our encounters with it: a contradiction is always a contra*diction* or Wider*spruch*, a claim made in opposition to another claim: VI (*WDL*) 64–70/431–35. Hegel's *Alle Dinge sind ein Widerspruch* (VI [*WDL*] 74/439; quoted by Taylor, *Hegel*, 105) tells us only that if we call something a *Ding* we are committed to calling it contradictory. (In any case, the passage in question is not strictly part of Hegel's System, but a "Remark" in which he says how the results of the previous section would look if expressed propositionally—how "contradiction" would look if viewed as a property of the universe rather than as part of the System.) See the discussion of "contradiction" earlier in this chapter, and its n. 16.

[47]This possibility will be invoked by Heidegger, which makes him the most radical challenge to Hegel since Hegel himself. I plan to argue this in a forthcoming work, *Diakena*.

[48]David Hume, *Treatise*, 6.

[49]XII (*Philosophy of History*) 81–85/60–65; for an account of the discrepancies between the course of the *Phenomenology* and the historical realities of which it supposedly treats, see my *Poetic Interaction*, 43f.

[50]Hegel, "Über die unter dem Namen Bhagavad-Gita bekannte Episode des Mahabharata: Von Wilhelm von Humboldt," XI 149/not translated.

[51]"One can only say that a science belongs to a people when it possesses it in its own language": XX (*Hist. Phil.*) 259/351f.

[52]The fact that this end is abstract and unattainable for empirical science (see VI [*WDL*] 518/799) does not mean that it is not "in view."

[53]Hegel locates the final goal of thought in Spirit's maintenance of the rationality of its own development, not in any final set of contents, at *PWG* 180f./translated in the appendix to chapter 4.

[54]The progress of the *Phenomenology* could, perhaps, be viewed as a simplification in content from the apparent concrete (but inexpressible) richness of sense-certainty (III [*PHG*] 82/58) to the emptiness of the "immediate unity of self-consciousness" (III (*PHG*) 588f./490f.)—the empty "Being" with which the System begins.

Chapter 6

[1]See R. Hackforth, in Edith Hamilton and Huntington Cairns, ed., *Plato: Collected Dialogues* (Princeton, N.J.: Bollingen, 1961), 1092.

[2]See *Philebus* 16c9–d2 and chapter 3.

[3]I thus view Theuth's "thinking up" the bond as the same sort of activity by which the interlocutors in the *Philebus* construct a recipe for the good life; see chapter 3. Also possible, admittedly, is the reading that J. C. B. Gosling gives, in which *desmon . . . logisamenos* is to be understood as "he concluded that this constituted a single bond": Plato, *Philebus*, trans. J. S. B. Gosling (Oxford: Oxford University Press, 1975), 9. In any

case, the kind of thinking to which I refer clearly occurs in the *Philebus*; at issue here is whether I am right to see this sentence as exemplifying it via Theuth.

⁴Those who think that Hegel undertook a totalistic logical comprehension of all reality should realize that the System is incapable of comprehending logically even the humble letters in which it is written—and that Hegel explicitly recognized this, in his refusal to organize the *Encyclopedia* alphabetically: see IV 10; VIII 61 (*Enz.* #16 Anm.)/21.

⁵"Mediation is having made a transition from a first to a second and a coming forth from opposites," where the first and the second may be taken as the opposites in question and the development from one to the other as the "coming forth": VIII 183 (#86 Anm.)/125.

⁶"With What Must the Science Begin," V (*WDL*) 66/68.

⁷That such a combination of historical and Systematic dialectics is the only possibility really open to thought is another way of stating the conclusion of Fackenheim's *Religious Dimension*. The brute givens—here, the categories of mute, vowel, and consonant—would stand as the "existential matrix" which Fackenheim thinks Hegel's thought needs, while the bond supplied by the word "letter" would enable us to go beyond their given diversity and comprehend them all as one: "The new metaphysics is a thought which remains bound to existing man and his world even as it seeks the transcending comprehension of both": Fackenheim, *Religious Dimension*, 238f.

⁸See the narrative in chapter 6.

⁹See *Prior Analytics* 1.4 25b32 for this definition of the middle term, to which I will recur.

¹⁰Jan Lukasiewicz, *Aristotle's Syllogistic* (Oxford: Clarendon Press, 1957), 1, 205f.; also see Günther Patzig, *Aristotle's Theory of the Syllogism*, trans. Jonathan Barnes (Dordrecht: Reidel, 1968), 4–8; George Engelbretsen, "On Propositional Form," *Notre Dame Journal of Formal Logic* 21 (1980): 101–10.

¹¹Thus, Lukasiewicz, for all the vigor and subtlety of his treatment of Aristotle "from the standpoint of modern formal logic" (as his subtitle has it), never gets around to discussing the all-important middle term; while Patzig's decision to view Aristotle's logic as independent of his metaphysics led to so many misunderstandings that he was compelled to qualify it in the preface to the second edition as "historically speaking, evidently false." In neither of these cases is viewing Aristotle's syllogistic as a modern formal system anything other than the introduction into Aristotle of distinctions he did not himself make: Patzig, *Aristotle's Theory*, xvif. An instructive example of how easy it is to assume that Aristotle's syllogistic is something akin to contemporary logic is offered by Jonathan Lear, who asserts that "a proof, for Aristotle, is a syllogism which enables one, simply by grasping it, to gain knowledge of the conclusion" (Jonathan Lear, *Aristotle's Syllogistic* [Cambridge: Cambridge University Press, 1980], 10). The passage Lear adduces for this—*Posterior Analytics* 1.2, 71b18ff.—does not speak of "gaining knowledge of the conclusion," but of gaining "scientific" knowledge, as opposed not to ignorance but to the "accidental" knowledge of the sophist (71b8–10). Sophists and scientists, in other words, both know conclusions; demonstration enables the scientist to know conclusions through their causes, i.e., essences. For a general summary of the literature on Aristotle and contemporary logic, see Joseph A. Novak, "Some Recent Work on the Aristotelian Syllogistic," *Notre Dame Journal of Formal Logic* 21 (1980): 229–42.

¹²Johannes Lohmann, "Vom Ursprung und Sinn der Aristotelischen Syllogistik," in Hans-Peter Hager, ed., *Logik und Erkenntnislehre des Aristoteles* (Darmstadt: Wissenschaftliche Buchgesellschaft, 1972); Jonathan Barnes, "Aristotle's Theory of Demonstration," *Phronesis* 14 (1969): 123–52.

¹³See *Prior Analytics* 1.27–31 (cited by Barnes) and the examples at 1.23,

40b30–41a20; 2.23, 68b33–36; *Posterior Analytics* 2.1, 2 (also cited by Barnes) and 1.34, 89b10–20.

[14]Aristotle, *Prior Analytics* 1.4, 25b32. For accounts of semantic memory, see George A. Miller, "Semantic Relations among Words," in Morris Halle, Joan Breshan, and George A. Miller, eds., *Linguistic Theory and Psychological Reality* (Cambridge, Mass.: MIT Press, 1978), 60–64, 74ff.; also Schank and Abelson, *Scripts, Plans,* 17–19, and the further references there. It should be noted that I am using the concept of semantic memory as a heuristic device: in spite of its anachronistic features, it seems to capture something of what is going on in the texts.

[15]E.g., at *Prior Analytics* 1.4, 1.15 79b1–5; 2.4, passim. For complications with this, see Patzig, *Aristotle's Theory,* 12–14, 88–118.

[16]*Posterior Analytics* 1.11, 77a5–9; also see, again, the various examples at *Posterior Analytics* 2.4.

[17]For the prescriptive role of truth in Aristotle, see my *Poetic Interaction,* 216f.

[18]Ibid., 235ff.

[19]*De Anima* 3.4–6.

[20]See *De Memoria* 1, and *Metaphysics* 1.1.

[21]The account is, indeed, more general even than Hegel's, which is restricted to the history of rational progress.

[22]See *Posterior Analytics* 1.28.

[23]*De Anima* 3.4, 429b9. Aristotle also compares active intellect to an art, which suggests that it has rules of thumb, at least, which it uses to organize its subject matter. But such is not the case: if the active intellect is an art, it is the art of making *everything,* and hence is nothing more than the abstract power of intellectual actualization itself: *De Anima* 3.5, 430a10ff. For the passive intellect as also without content of its own see *De Anima* 3.4, 429a18–28.

[24]*De Anima* 3.6, 430a27–b5.

[25]This interpretation of active intellect as a strictly human, finite reason is not the traditional one; I follow Michael Wedin, who has ingeniously shown that it is at least as plausible to attribute it to Aristotle as accounts which would interpret active intellect as a supra-individual mind or even as the Prime Mover itself: Michael V. Wedin, "Tracking Aristotle's *Nous,*" in Alan Donagan, Anthony N. Perovich Jr., and Michael V. Wedin, eds., *Human Nature and Natural Knowledge* (Dordrecht: Reidel, 1986), 167–97.

[26]Richard Rorty, *Philosophy and the Mirror of Nature* (Princeton: Princeton University Press, 1979).

[27]Such harmony is difficult to achieve if the syllogism is taken to be the establishment of new truth rather than the accessing of old information.

[28]That psychological account is in turn located within a wider genus: true to Aristotle's basically metaphysical perspective, this genus is an ontological one in which thinking is the actualization of potentialities, of the contents of the passive intellect.

[29]Hume, *Treatise,* 463, 625; also 415, 448.

[30]W. V. Quine, "Epistemology Naturalized," in Quine, *Ontological Relativity and Other Essays* (New York: Columbia University Press, 1969), 72.

[31]As I mentioned in the Introduction, Hegel regarded Hume as notable chiefly for having impelled Kant to work out his transcendental philosophy: XX (*Hist. Phil.*) 275–81/III 369–75. Eugène Fleischmann, however, has argued that Hegel's critique of Kant shows a high, if covert, regard for Hume: "Hegel thus seems to believe that Kant not only did not refute Hume's argument, but develops his own theory of knowledge in a way true to Hume's spirit": Fleischmann, "Hegels Umgestaltung der Kantischen Logik," *Hegel-Studien* Beiheft 3 (1965): 187. Both Hume and Kant, Fleischmann points

out, deny that general concepts such as causality can be grounded in experience, and neither attempts to show where and how they do arise. Hume then claims that they are illegitimate, and Kant that they are "objective"—but both claims are for Hegel equally "groundless." Fleischmann's masterly treatment of Kant and Hegel, carried out without specific reference to Kant's *Logic*, can serve as background to the present, more highly focused, narrative.

[32]The issue is important for him because if such awareness could be vindicated, we would have an idea of causal power, and hence might be able to talk rationally of such things as the "cause" of the universe.

[33]Hume, *Human Understanding*, in Hume, *Enquiries*, 67–69; *Treatise*, 632f.; also the puzzling argument that motion is the cause of thought at *Treatise*, 248.

[34]Hume, *Treatise*, 73, 96n., 157; also see Norman Kemp Smith, *The Philosophy of David Hume* (London: Macmillan, 1941), 101–3 for a critique of Hume on this point.

[35]Hume, *Treatise*, 73; for the distinction between impressions and ideas, see *Treatise*, 1f., *Human Understanding*, 17f., and Barry Stroud, *Hume* (London: Routledge and Kegan Paul, 1977), 17f., 27–33.

[36]Hume, *Treatise*, 173f.

[37]Ibid., 94.

[38]Ibid., 463; also see Farhang Zabeeh, *Hume: Precursor of Modern Empiricism* (The Hague: Martinus Nijhoff, 1973), 113–225 for a thorough account of Hume on inductive and deductive reasoning, and Barbara Winters, "Hume on Reason,"*Hume Studies* 5 (1979): 20–35.

[39]Hume, *Treatise*, 70, 463.

[40]Hume, *Human Understanding*, 163, 25.

[41]Ibid., 193.

[42]Ibid., 164, 25f.

[43]See Ibid., 60–79; *Treatise*, 98f., 283, 343.

[44]Hume, *Human Understanding*, 43f.; for the moral sentiment, see Hume, *An Enquiry Concerning the Principles of Morals*, in *Enquiries*, 285–94.

[45]Hume, *Human Understanding*, 43.

[46]Ibid., 162.

[47]Ibid., 165.

[48]Robert Fogelin, *Hume's Scepticism in the Treatise of Human Nature* (Boston: Routledge and Kegan Paul, 1985), 92.

[49]Hume, *Treatise*, 270–72; also see Terence Penelhum, *Hume* (London: Macmillan 1973), 21ff.

[50]For some contemporary debate, see Stephen Stich, ed., *Innate Ideas* (Berkeley: University of California Press, 1975).

[51]Hume, *Human Understanding*, 18; also see 47, 49.

[52]Ibid., 19.

[53]Hume, *Treatise*, 3f., 157; as Kemp Smith notes, Hume basically follows Locke in his account of simple and compound ideas: Kemp Smith, *Philosophy of Hume*, 250f.; see pp. 459–63 for a discussion of Hume on imagination; also Barry Stroud, *Hume*, 34–37. Chapter 9 will discuss Locke on simple and complex ideas.

[54]Hume, *Treatise*, 16.

[55]Which it ought not to be: see Hume, *Treatise*, 16, 219–22 for Hume's critique of Aristotle's metaphysics, grounded in Hume's denial of the discursiveness of our experience.

[56]Hume, *Treatise*, 17.

[57]Hume, *Human Understanding,* 62; this idea of definition is operative but not stated at *Treatise,* 277, 329, 399.

[58]Hume, *Treatise,* 10f.

[59]Ibid., 10f. 225, 267; for habit guiding the imagination see *Human Understanding,* 49.

[60]See Hume, *Treatise,* 203f.

[61]Hume, *Human Understanding,* 62.

[62]Hume, *Treatise,* 72f.

[63]Patrick L. Gardiner, "Hume's Theory of the Passions," in D. F. Pears, ed., *David Hume: A Symposium* (New York: St. Martin's Press, 1966), 31–42. It is not satisfying to a historian of philosophy to appeal to "persistent tendencies" in order to explain the defects of a thinker; one would rather be able to uncover philosophical reasons why Hume so continually loses sight of the existence of complex ideas. I suggest two below, but the blatant contradictions in Hume's texts testify as well to a simple lack of assiduity in applying his mind to something uncongenial to it.

[64]Ralph Church, *Hume's Theory of the Understanding* (Ithaca: Cornell University Press, 1935), 218.

[65]Barry Stroud, *Hume,* 20f., 225f.

[66]*De Anima* 3.6, passim; also see *Metaphysics* 9.10, 1051b18–1052a4.

[67]Hume, *Treatise,* 142; see Stroud, *Hume,* 47–50.

[68]Stroud, *Hume,* 221f., 246f.

[69]Hume, *Treatise,* 179; *Human Understanding,* 54f.

[70]Marcuse, *Reason and Revolution,* 20; see the whole discussion at pp. 16–28; also see my "Hegel on Habit," *Owl of Minerva* 21 (1990): 155–65.

[71]Hume, *Treatise,* 89; *Human Understanding,* 32–39.

[72]Kant, *Logik,* at Kant, *Werke,* 524, 573/*Logic,* ed. Robert Hartman and Wolfgang Schwartz (Indianapolis: Bobbs-Merrill, 1974), 99, 141f.

[73]*KRV* B 355, 357; the general discussion of the logical employment of reason is at *KRV* B 359–61.

[74]I am here following Jonathan Bennett, who assigns greatest importance in Kant's account of the syllogism to what Bennett calls the "ascending" function of reason, in which the syllogism begins with its conclusion accepted as true and, by uniting the terms of that conclusion with other ones, seeks (as did the Aristotelian syllogism) not to deduce the conclusion but to place it in a "wider intellectual structure." Bennett also sees a more traditionally assertionistic "descending" function of the Kantian syllogism, in which it deduces its conclusion in the sense of proving it. This contrast, however, is not all that clear in Kant's text: the paragraph which speaks about what Bennett calls the "descending function" of reason begins with the words "in *every* syllogism of reason" (emphasis added), and the end of the succeeding paragraph—which according to Bennett discusses the "ascending" function of reason—ends with the words: "it seeks, in inferring, to reduce the great manifold of cognition of the understanding to the smallest number of principles . . . and through this to bring about their highest unity" (*KRV* B 360f.). Given the manifold confusions and unclarities Bennett has attributed to Kant here, including the failure to formulate a proper distinction between reason and understanding or a proper definition of the syllogism, it would perhaps be surprising if the text were clear about the distinction of "ascending" and "descending" reason. Bennett's main point remains, however: the business of the syllogism is not to prove propositions. Jonathan Bennett, *Kant's Dialectic* (Cambridge: Cambridge University Press, 1974), 260ff.

[75]*KRV* B 362f; see Aristotle, *Posterior Analytics* 1.13 for the distinction; for Kantian reason as a search for a middle term, see *KRV* B 378.

[76]*KRV* B 361.

[77]*KRV* B 359, 362–64, 382f.; also see *KRV* B 384f.

[78]Bennett, *Kant's Dialectic*, 259.

[79]*KRV* B 362. It is remarkable that Lukasiewicz, without ever mentioning Kant, attributes this view to Aristotle: Lukasiewicz, *Aristotle's Syllogistic*, 2f.

[80]*KRV* B 364, 387.

[81]*KRV* B 388f.

[82]*KRV* B 364f., 379, 388f.

[83]*KRV* B 364f., 367.

[84]*KRV* B 384; also 390, 397.

[85]*KRV* B 368–76.

[86]*KRV* B 601.

[87]For which move see *KRV* B 595–99.

[88]This whole construction occupies *KRV* B 601–8.

[89]*KRV* B 607.

[90]*KRV* B 393. Hence, the "ideal of reason," though in form like the Kantian "logical essence" I discussed in chapter 3, is not really one: first, in view of its totalized or unconditional character, and secondly because in virtue of that unconditionality it cannot serve as a "ground of cognition" for anything.

[91]*KRV* B 394f.

[92]See Hume, *Treatise*, 225, 267.

[93]*KRV* B 391.

[94]For a more complete account of Aristotle's handling of the Platonic "separation" of Forms and sensibles, see my *Poetic Interaction*, 235ff.

[95]The most thorough short account of Hegel's complex response to Kantian moral philosophy is Olivier Reboul, "Hegel, Critique de la morale de Kant," *Revue de métaphysique et de morale* 80 (1975): 85–100; also see Adrian Peperzaak, *Le jeune Hegel: Ou, la vision morale du monde* (The Hague: Nijhoff, 1969); and André Stanguennec, *Hegel critique de Kant* (Paris: Presses Universitaires de France, 1985), 194–213.

[96]Hans Friedrich Fulda, "Über den Ursprung der Hegelschen Dialektik," *Aquinas* 24 (1981): 378f.

[97]Fulda, "Ursprung," 379f.

[98]XI 330; *Phil. Rel.* 4f., 31f., 61f.

Chapter 7

[1]Mure, *Introduction*, 21; Malcolm Clark, *Logic and System* (The Hague: Martinus Nijhoff, 1971), 46, 66. Kierkegaard had already recognized the problem in his journals: "if the claim of philosophers to be unbiased were all it pretends to be, it would also have to take account of language and its whole significance to speculation, for therein speculation has a medium which it did not itself choose." Søren Kierkegaard, "Journals", in Robert Bretall, ed., *A Kierkegaard Anthology* (New York: Modern Library, 1963), 12f. Also see Hermann J. Cloeren, "The Linguistic Turn in Kierkegaard's Attack on Hegel," *International Studies in Philosophy* 17 (1985): 1–13.

[2]If we substitute "history" for "science," Gerd Buchdahl has admirably captured the general nature of such dialogue: it must be "a living dialogue between the problem-

atical stages of science in flux and a mind that attempts to interpret these stages in the light of an underlying structure that is meant to bestow a relative degree of intelligibility as well as legitimacy upon a shifting scene": Buchdahl, "Hegel's Philosophy," in Inwood, *Hegel,* 111.

[3]Mure, *Introduction,* 7. The unretrieved vagueness alone of this formulation ought to render the doctrine suspect.

[4]Ibid., 22.

[5]Ibid., 17, 22f.

[6]Ibid., 19.

[7]Clark, *Logic,* xi.

[8]Ibid., 97.

[9]Ibid., x.

[10]Ibid., 12.

[11]See the allusion to Hegel's "struggle for expression in a resisting language of space and time," Ibid., xi.

[12]IX 34–36 (*Enz.* #250)/ 22–24; for a lucid treatment of nature and its impotence, see Fackenheim, *Religious Dimension,* 112–15.

[13]Josef Simon, *Das Problem der Sprache bei Hegel* (Stuttgart: Kohlhammer, 1966), 13, 203; "Die Kategorien im 'Gewöhnlichen' und im 'Spekulativen' Satz," *Wiener Jahrbuch für Philosophie* 3 (1970): 31, 34.

[14]Simon, "Kategorien," 34.

[15]Simon, *Problem,* 181, 189f., 203.

[16]Theodor Bodammer, *Hegel's Deutung der Sprache* (Hamburg: Meiner, 1969), 238.

[17]Ibid., 66f., 172.

[18]Ibid., 173, 236ff.

[19]Fackenheim, *Religious Dimension,* 22.

[20]Ibid., 16ff.

[21]Winfield, *Overcoming Foundations,* 88f.

[22]Fackenheim, *Religious Dimension,* 24.

[23]With this, see the general accounts at Günter Wohlfahrt, *Denken der Sprache* (Freiburg/Munich: Alber, 1984), 208–13; and deVries, *Mental Activity,* 135–63.

[24]See VIII 72–75 (*Enz.* #20)/29–31; X 257 (*Enz.* #451 Anm.)/201f. The highest form of such separation is the separation of God from man and the mutual contradictoriness of God's attributes, which I discussed briefly in chapter 1 in connection with representation's culminating, religious variety.

[25]X 258–52 (*Enz.* ##452–54)/203–6.

[26]Though that of the image is less determinate: X 261 (*Enz.* #454) 205.

[27]X 206–18 (*Enz.* ##455–60)/262–77.

[28]III (*PHG*) 376/308f.

[29]Ibid.

[30]III (*PHG*) 364/298f.

[31]III (*PHG*) 376/309.

[32]III (*PHG*) 365/299.

[33]See my *Poetic Interaction,* 53–55, for a longer account of this. In terms of the Introduction, Hamann's problem was his inability to "relinquish" himself in this way.

[34]X 265f. (*Enz.* #456)/209.

[35]X 270 (*Enz.* #458 Anm.)/213.

[36]X 271 (*Enz.* #459 Anm.)/214.

[37]X 272f. (*Enz.* #459 Anm.)/215.

[38]X 270f. (*Enz.* #458 Anm.)/213.

[39]IV 51; *The Philosophical Propadeutic*, trans. A. V. Miller (Oxford: Blackwell, 1986), 156.

[40]E.g., at X 277f. (*Enz. #461*)/219).

[41]X 274f. (*Enz. #459 Anm.*)/216f.

[42]Ibid.

[43]III (*PHG*) 34/17.

[44]I translate *Gedächtnis* standing alone as "Verbal Memory" in order to distinguish it from *Erinnerung*, which I translate as "Recollection." When it occurs in the combination *mechanisches Gedächtnis*, I translate it as "Mechanical Memory."

[45]X 277f. (*Enz. ##460, 461*)/218f.

[46]X 277 (*Enz. #460*)/218.

[47]X 277f. (*Enz. #461*)/219.

[48]Ibid.

[49]X 278f. (*Enz. #462*)/219f.

[50]X 266f. (*Enz. #456*)/209.

[51]Ibid.; at X 281f. (*Enz. #463*)/221f., Hegel also refers to meaning at this stage as the *Zusammenhang der Namen*, the "connection of the names."

[52]X 277, 282f. (*Enz. ##460, 464*)/218, 223.

[53]See the discussion of nonspeculative language at III (*PHG*) 57ff./36ff.

[54]X 368f., 372 (*Enz. ##559, 563*)/294, 297; also see Joseph Derbolav, "Hegel und die Sprache," in *Sprache: Schlüssel zur Welt: Festschrift für Leo Weisgerber* (Düsseldorf: Schwann, 1959), 71f.

[55]In the *Phenomenology*'s section on "Sense-Certainty," for example, consciousness cannot retain the certainty of the "here and now" because such certainty is incompatible with its own linguistic expression: III (*PHG*) 91f./65f.; see Daniel Cook, *Language in the Philosophy of Hegel* (The Hague: Mouton, 1973), 49; also Jacob Loewenberg, *Hegel's "Phenomenology": Dialogues on the Life of the Mind* (La Salle, Ill.: Open Court, 1965), 39, and "The Comedy of Immediacy in Hegel's 'Phenomenology,'" *Mind* 44 (1935): 21–38. Possessed of this power, it is language which in fact accomplishes for Hegel what Michael Theunissen mistakenly thinks the System lacks: the recognition of a third thing, over and above subject and object, which unites them. Michael Theunissen, "Die verdrängte Intersubjektivität in Hegel's Philosophie des Rechts," in Dieter Henrich and Rolf-Peter Horstmann, eds., *Hegel's Philosophie des Rechts* (Stuttgart: Kohlhammer, 1982), 317–81.

[56]Already in the *Phenomenology*, the reduction of indexicality is said to be a function of language itself: III (*PHG*) 85/87, 91f./60, 62, 65f.

[57]In Hegel's words, the Intelligence "purifies the [sensory] object of whatever in it turns out to be merely external, contingent, and worthless" (X 244 [*Enz. #445 Zus.*]/191). As regards the historical origins of representational or expert discourse, I can do no better than quote Eugène Fleischmann: "science is the ripe fruit of the intellectual labor of innumerable generations who have reduced the empirical chaos of their more or less limited world to generalized concepts, principles, or truths, in brief, to thought": Fleischmann, *La science universelle* (Paris: Plon, 1968), 354.

[58]Hilary Putnam, "Meaning and Reference," in Stephen P. Schwartz, ed., *Naming, Necessity, and Natural Kinds* (Ithaca: Cornell University Press, 1977), 125ff. For a case, from the *Philosophy of Nature*, of Hegel rejecting scientific representations as still unripe for philosophical treatment, i.e., as not yet worked up to true "expert" status, see IX 13 (*Enz. #280 Anm.*)/103.

[59]XX (*Hist. Phil.*) 259/III 351; see also XX (*Hist. Phil.*) 52f./III 150; V (*WDL*) 20/31f.; Cook, *Language*, 66–70, 161ff.

[60]XX (*Hist. Phil.*) 483, 516/III 25f., 49f.

[61]XIX (*Hist. Phil.*) 111/II 95.

[62]X 281f./222.

[63]X 282f./223.

[64]The externality of "syntheses" is referred to at X 257 (*Enz.* #451)/201f.

[65]X 274/216.

[66]X 275/217.

[67]"*Being*, the universal space of names as such, i.e. of senseless words." X 281 (*Enz.* #463)/222.

[68]X 275 (*Enz.* #459 Anm.)/217—where the words *als ein Sein* are mysteriously translated as "for its own sake."

[69]X 282 (*Enz.* #464)/223—where *das Seiende als Name* is mysteriously translated as "the mere name as an existent."

[70]X 279f./220f.

[71]X 278/219.

[72]X 278 (*Enz.* #462)/219.

[73]X 109–17 (*Enz.* #401 Zus.)/82–88.

[74]X 239f./187f.

[75]The first such misunderstanding, perhaps, was the misplacement of the *Zusatz* to #462; as concerned with language as the expression of thinking, rather than merely of representation, it should have come after #464.

[76]X 109–17 (*Enz.* #401 Zus.)/82–88.

[77]For the temporal side, see X 279f. (*Enz.* #462 Zus.)/219f.; for the "space of names," see X 281. (*Enz.* #463)/221f.

[78]X 249–53 (*Enz.* #448 and Zus.)/195–98. See also my discussion of linguistic intuition in chapter 1.

[79]For the individuality of intuited objects, see X 243–45 (*Enz.* #445 Zus.)/190–92.

[80]For the "foundness" of intuitional or "felt" content, see X 246, 256, 257 (*Enz.* ##446, 450, 451)/192f., 200f., 201f. For the interior "foundness" of names as such, see X 281 (*Enz.* #463 Anm.)/222. This is of course a recovery of the indexicality which was lacking in representational language.

[81]For the bringing of intuitional content into the subjective space and time of the Intelligence, see X 258f. (*Enz.* #452 and Zus.)/203f.; for the general "subjective" character of certain types of space and time, see X 249–53 (*Enz.* #448 Zus.)/195–98.

[82]Such senselessness is referred to in *Enz.* #463; Hegel connects it with individuality at V (*WDL*) 126–27: "the individual name is however something senseless in that it does not express a universal."

[83]At X 276 (*Enz.* #459, Anm.)/217, Hegel refers to names as "simple signs, consisting in a plurality of letters or syllables, and also divided into them"; his point is presumably that the simplicity which such names have for the Intelligence in spite of their manifold of concrete content enables each to express a simple representation, and not the multiplicity of representations which would correspond to the complexity of their sensuous content.

[84]Hence, Jacques Derrida to the contrary notwithstanding, Hegel does not understand the nature of the sign strictly in terms of sublation: Derrida, "Le puits et la pyramide," in Derrida, *Marges* (Paris: Minuit, 1972), 79–127, esp. 110f.; *Glas* (Paris: Denoël-Gonthier, 1981), 10. This is not the only place where Hegel makes this type of advance, which is a loss of structure (or, in terms of my rewriting, of parentheses). I have elsewhere called it "death from habit": see my "Hegel on Habit," 155–65. Because he takes sublation to be the single basic gesture of Hegel's thought, Jean-Luc

Nancy—who is well aware, in general terms, of the role of Mechanical Memory in speculation—concludes that Mechanical Memory "resists and disarticulates" sublation. In fact sublation is not thus basic, and hence is not necessarily being "resisted" when other kinds of dialectical progress occur: Jean-Luc Nancy, *La remarque spéculative* (Paris: Galilée, 1973), 124ff. For the dangers of taking sublation to be the *Einundalles* of the dialectic, see Hans Friedrich Fulda, "Dialektik in Konfrontation mit Hegel," in Henrich, *Hegels Wissenschaft*, 328–49, esp. 341.

[85]X 279f. (*Enz. #462* Zus.)/220f. When Hegel's System is construed linguistically, the "movement of the Concept," which has been problematic since Trendelenberg's 1840 *Logische Untersuchungen*, is not a problem at all: it is merely the demand of a name for its meaning. Since the name itself is something which disappears as it arises, this demand is posed temporally: the name disappears in favor of the other Systematic names which are its meaning. The Concept is nothing other than the totality of such names, and hence is itself intrinsically dynamic. Thus, as Eugène Fleischmann puts it, "the real problem is not to know how thought 'passes' from one determination to another, but how it happens that it stops and crystallizes in a determination that would be stable": Fleischmann, *Science Universelle*, 29.

Such crystallization is in part what in chapter 4 I called "immediation"; in other cases it is performed by Representation, which as will be seen has its own role in giving uniformity and stability to the System. Peter Rohs's question about the ground of the movement of the Concept is thus doubly misplaced. First because, as Josef Simon points out, "Ground" is a category within the Logic, and not one that can be applied to its totality (the one passage that Rohs cites speaks, not of the "ground" of the movement, but of its "source" (*Quelle*): VI (*WDL*) 563/835. Second because, once the verbal nature of the Concept is seen, its movement is intrinsic to it. Rohs, "Grund," 43–62; Simon, "Die Bewegung des Begriffs in Hegels Logik" (response to Rohs), *Hegel-Studien* Beiheft 18 (1978): 63–73. Rohs's worry that the movement of the Concept must somehow be atemporal is also not a problem if we attribute to Hegel a broadly Neoplatonic view of time, in which time is disorganized movement and eternity is organized movement; the same holds for Harald Holz, "Anfang, Identität, und Widerspruch," *Tijdschrift voor Filosofie* 37 (1974): 742ff. Such a Neoplatonic view of time, though not under that title, is sketched for Hegel by Klaus Hedwig, "Hegel on Time and Eternity," *Dialogue* (Can.) 9 (1970): 139–53. For further remarks on the movement of the Concept, see Terry Pinkard, "Hegel's Idealism and Hegel's Logic," *Zeitschrift für philosophische Forschung* 33 (1979): 210–26, esp. 214. For a brief history of the controversy, see Rüdiger Bubner, "Strukturprobleme," in Bubner, *Sache*, 7–36.

[86]X 282 (*Enz. #463* Anm.)/222.

[87]III (*PHG*) 82–85/58–61.

[88]X 282 (*Enz. #464*)/223.

[89]X 281 (*Enz. #463*)/221.

[90]Ibid.

[91]X 282 (*Enz. #464*)/223.

[92]Ibid.

[93]Ibid. It will be recognized that, so understood, Mechanical Memory presents what Hans Friedrich Fulda isolates as the essential qualities of what Hegel calls "the element of thought" but never identifies with names as such: it is a medium which is simple, pure, and wholly "abstract" (i.e., without sensory meaning): Fulda, "Dialektik in Konfrontation," 334.

[94]Parmenides, Fragment 8, lines 34–36, from Hermann Diels and Walther Kranz, eds., *Fragmente der Vorsokratiker*, 6th ed. (Zürich: Weidmann, 1951), 1:238.

[95]But see the discussion at Martin Heidegger, "Moira (Parmenides, Fragment VIII, 34–41)," in Heidegger, *Vorträge und Aufsätze* (Pfullingen: Neske, 1954), 223–48.

[96]III *(PHG)* 32, 554/16, 461; V *(WDL)* 43f./49f.; VIII 155–60 *(Enz. ##64–70)/* 99–105. This can help us understand Hegel's answer to what Michael Forster, in his account of Hegel's concern with skepticism, calls the "concept instantiation problem." Ancient skepticism, with which alone Hegel was seriously concerned, radically distinguished concepts from their instances, so that it was possible for us to have concepts for which there were no instances in reality. As Forster notes, Hegel seeks to maintain that this cannot be the case for his own System: the being of the System and its concept are one and the same. Attention to names as such as intellectual Being shows that the "being of the System" is nothing more than its existence as a set of names as such, while its "concept" is nothing more than the meaning of those names—which, in each case, is just the rest of them, i. e., the ordered totality of other names as such. In the "internal/external" medium of names as such, the language of concept and instance must be replaced by talk of part and whole—more precisely, moment and System. Whence, by a logic as old as Plato's *Parmenides,* we cannot have either without the other. (See Forster, *Skepticism,* 26f., 122–25.) Thus, the unity of thought and Being is not present at the beginning of the System, as Tom Rockmore argues, in the form of mere faith in reason's ability to know Being (though such faith was clearly an important part of Hegel's own psychology). It is achieved rationally in the System itself, when a new moment is introduced in a name as such and its identity with a representational name is, in ways to be discussed in chapter 10, brought out, thus achieving a mediated identity: Rockmore, *Circular Epistemology,* 156f. For a critique of Rockmore on this score, see Kainz, *Paradox, Dialectic,* 99f.

[97]Via a consideration of the requirements of the beginning of the System for Hegel, Georg Römpp has reached the conclusion that Being must be "a saying without saying anything" and that Being as an "empty word" must be the beginning of the System. What Römpp does not see is that names as such in Mechanical Memory meet these requirements: Römpp, "Sein als Genesis von Bedeutung," *Zeitschrift für philosophische Forschung* 43 (1989): 58–80.

[98]V *(WDL)* 82/82; VIII 182f. *(Enz. #86)/124f.*

[99]V *(WDL)* 106/101; emphasis added.

[100]Hegel, *Jenaer Realphilosophie,* ed. Johannes Hoffmeister (Hamburg: Meiner, 1931), 183. Also see this passage from the *Logic:* in cases where one asks,

> What is this, of what sort of plant is this, etc., by the *Being* which is asked for is often understood merely the *name,* and when one has learned this one is satisfied and now knows "what" the thing is. This is Being in the sense of the subject. But the Concept, or at least the essence and the universal as such, is only given by the predicate, and it is this which is asked for in the sense of a judgment.—*God, Spirit, Nature,* or whatever it may be is thus . . . only present according to the concept in the predicate. (VI *[WDL]* 303/624)

[101]X 283 *(Enz. #464* Anm.)/223; on this topic, see Iring Fetscher, *Hegels Lehre vom Menschen* (Stuttgart: Frommann, 1970), 180f.

[102]X 260 *(Enz. #453* Anm.)/204.

[103]X 262 *(Enz. #455)/206.*

[104]X 271 *(Enz. #459)/213.*

[105]X 278 *(Enz. #462)/220.*

[106]X 281 (*Enz.* #463)/221.

[107]X 282 (*Enz.* #464 Anm.)/223.

[108]Such development is syllogism, the highest form of thinking for Hegel: X 285–87 (*Enz.* #467 and Zus.)/225–27.

[109]X 263 (*Enz.* #464 Anm.)/223.

[110]Theodor Bodammer also argues this point, in more detail, in *Hegels Deutung*, 56.

[111]VIII 24/not translated.

[112]Hegel, "Review of Göschel," XI 378. See Fackenheim, *Religious Dimension*, 193n.

[113]XX 493/33.

[114]As *Enz.* #462 Zus. says: X 280/221.

[115]Ibid.

[116]*Phil. Rel.* I 34–39/117–40.

[117]See V (*WDL*) 72/73; VI (*WDL*) 303/624.

[118]VI (*WDL*) 303/624.

[119]As evidenced, for example, in *Enz.* #462 Zus.

[120]Mure, *Introduction*, 14n.

[121]Where Hegel does discuss language in terms of incomplete "synthesis"—at *Enz.* #451 (X 257/201f.)—it is to restrict such synthesis to representational language. As *Enz.* #463 (X 281/221f.) makes clear, in Mechanical Memory that very "synthetic" feature of previous meaningfulness is overcome.

[122]Mure, *Introduction*, 18, 20, 22. For Hegel's own account of all attempts, mathematical or otherwise, to express the Absolute in "finite" categories, see V (*WDL*) 386/325.

[123]Mure, *Introduction*, 23.

[124]See VIII 262 (*Enz.* ##455–56)/206–10.

[125]VIII 390 (*Enz.* #238)/293.

[126]See III (*PHG*) 86f., 92/61f., 65f.

[127]Clark, *Logic*, 63.

[128]X 239f./187f.

[129]XVIII 527/457; see the discussion of language as the "actuality of reason" at Wohlfahrt, *Denken*, 215–20.

[130]Clark, *Logic*, 97. Jère Paul Surber arrives at the same view through his discussion of the "speculative sentence" in the Preface to the *Phenomenology* in "Hegel's Speculative Sentence," *Hegel-Studien* 10 (1975): 211–29.

[131]Clark, *Logic*, 44, 66; see X 279f. (*Enz.* #462 Zus.)/220f.

[132]Clark, *Logic*, x.

[133]Simon, *Problem*, 174, 181.

[134]Ibids., 196 (my translation).

[135]X 239 (*Enz.* #444 Zus.)/187.

[136]X 262 (*Enz.* #464)/223.

[137]That "into which" and "out of which" a determinate moment of the System develops are both, ultimately, the same thing: the circular System in its entirety, from Being to Philosophy and back to Being.This enables us to see how Hegel's philosophical language avoids a problem, similar to Simon's, raised by Theodor Litt: that any name in philosophical discourse expresses only that moment whose "time has come," thereby pushing the *whole* of the System into the background. Here, we must distinguish two senses in which the whole System can be considered to be "pushed into the background": one acceptable to Hegel and the other not. It is the nature of the Hegelian Concept to bring forth determinate content within itself via its dynamic moment of

what Hegel calls "self-repulsion." This must in each case mean a certain corresponding "retreat" or "pushing back" of the rest of the System. To maintain that *all* the determinacies of the System must always be fully explicit would not only deny this moment of self-repulsion but would, in fact, render the whole merely static. This kind of "pushing the whole into the background" is a necessary concomitant of the dynamism of the Concept and, presumably, acceptable to Hegel. What is then not acceptable would be to move from the whole as inexplicitly present to the whole as irrelevant: to look at a given moment of the System, not as part of a momentarily unarticulated but articulable whole, but rather as something entirely independent in its own right—as a finite being, and in particular as a representation. A name as such, disappearing as it arises, manifests its meaning as itself a fleeting negativity, a mere moment of something else; and in this very manifestation, the System as a whole can be said to have an undeniable—if inexplicit—presence. A name as such, then, does not "push the whole" into the background in an unacceptable way, but in precisely the way in which, in the self-repulsion of the Concept, the whole *must* be "pushed back." The Hegelian System, like the whole of Absolute Spirit, is as I have phrased it elsewhere (see my *Poetic Interaction*, 296) not a full presence but a "free play of occlusions." Theodor Litt, *Hegel: Versuch einer Kritischen Erneuerung* (Heidelberg: Quelle & Meyer, 1953), 17.

[138]Bodammer, *Hegels Deutung*, 238.

[139]Clark, *Logic*, 12; see V (*WDL*) 20f./31f.

[140]V (*WDL*) 55/58.

[141]These general criticisms of Bodammer's view can be supplemented with a more specific one. If names as such are sufficient to the expression of philosophical thought, and if "Mechanical Memory" presents us with such names and no others, then that section cannot be differentiated from the beginning of the Logic. For it presents the fundamental "Being" out of which the System develops, and presents nothing else. Bodammer's view is, in fact, that the "Mechanical Memory" belongs not to the Psychology where Hegel located it, but to his Logic: Bodammer, *Hegels Deutung*, 67. Fetscher also expands Mechanical Memory so as to equate it with thought itself, which would entail that names in it have meanings—for thought is not meaningless for Hegel: Fetscher, *Hegels Lehre*, 182. If, on the other hand, *two* sorts of expression are necessary for the presentation of the System, and only one of them—names as such—is treated in "Mechanical Memory," we can readily see that the expression reached in that section is not identical with that of the System itself, in the Logic or elsewhere.

Chapter 8

[1]These will be cited by title, with pagination after Donald Davidson, *Inquiries into Truth and Interpretation* (Oxford: Clarendon, 1984; hereinafter *T & I*).

[2]Ludwig Wittgenstein, *Philosophical Investigations*, trans. G. E. M. Anscombe, 3d. ed. (New York: MacMillan, 1958; hereinafter *PI*). Citations will be to paragraph number for part 1, to page number for part 2.

[3]John Searle, *Speech Acts* (Cambridge: Cambridge University Press, 1969), 55f.; for predication as a basic dimension of speech acts, see 121–23; for the connection to truth, see 125.

[4]In the 1964 "Theories of Meaning and Learnable Languages"; the following quote is from *T & I*, 18.

[5]See *T & I*, 7f.; also 17, 55, 56, 61, 127, 160f.

[6]See my *Poetic Interaction*, 437 n. 5.

[7]Davidson's definition of a "semantic primitive" is that it is a term for which the rules which give the meaning for the sentences in which it does not appear do not suffice to give the meaning of the sentences in which it does appear: "Theories of Meaning and Learnable Languages," *T&I*, 9. To eliminate the occurrence of a word in a sentence without changing the meaning of the sentence is to "paraphrase"; hence my version of Davidson's definition.

[8]Or, perhaps, to learn and use them without recognizing them for what they are.

[9]For a general comparison of Wittgenstein and Hegel, see David Lamb, *Hegel: From Foundation to System* (The Hague: Martinus Nijhoff, 1980), 177–87.

[10]*PI*, ¶5.

[11]*PI*, ¶¶341, 527, 529, 535, p. 182.

[12]*PI*, ¶53; also 82.

[13]*PI*, ¶¶80–85; also 204, 208, 567.

[14]*PI*, ¶¶68–71.

[15]*PI*, ¶23.

[16]*PI*, ¶31.

[17]See *PI*, ¶¶306–8, and the general attack on meaning as a mental process at, e.g., ¶¶36, 547, 598–604, 611ff., etc.

[18]*PI*, ¶7.

[19]J. F. M. Hunter, "Forms of Life in Wittgenstein's *Philosophical Investigations*," in *Ludwig Wittgenstein: Critical Assessments*, ed. Stuart Shanker (London: Croom Helm, 1986), 2:106–24; *PI*, ¶595.

[20]*Werke*, X 182–91 (*Enz.* ##409f.)/139–47; for a closer analysis, see my "Hegel on Habit," 155–65, and *PI*, ¶¶198ff.

[21]See, e.g., *PI*, ¶¶132, 402, 494.

[22]See, for example, Charles S. Hardwick, *Language Learning in Wittgenstein's Later Philosophy* (The Hague: Mouton, 1971) (*Janua Linguarum* #104); Jean-François Lyotard and Jeann-Loup Thébaud, *Just Gaming*, trans. Wlad Godzich (Minneapolis: University of Minnesota Press, 1985), 50f.; David Pole, *The Later Philosophy of Wittgenstein* (London: University of London [Athlone] Press, 1958), 80, 92; Rush Rhees, "Wittgenstein's Builders," in Rhees, *Discussions of Wittgenstein* (New York: Schocken Books, 1970), 71–84.

[23]*PI*, ¶¶2, 6.

[24]Pole, *Later Philosophy*, 93; *PI*, ¶¶24, 180, 577, 662, 665, pp. 186–90, 222.

[25]*PI*, ¶¶65–67.

[26]See *PI*, ¶¶107, 209.

[27]Hardwick, *Language Learning*, 69.

[28]*PI*, 224.

[29]Donald Davidson, "A Nice Derangement of Epitaphs," in Ernest LePore, ed., *Truth and Interpretation: Perspectives on the Philosophy of Donald Davidson* (Oxford: Blackwell, 1986), 433–46.

[30]"Truth and Meaning," *T & I*, 25.

[31]Ibid., 22.

[32]The difference with Davidson would be that Wittgenstein would not hold that language games have meanings as sentences do; they *are* meanings, but cannot themselves be asserted to have meaning in the context of (other, presumably wider) language games.

[33]See, e.g., *PI*, ¶¶29, 182, 199, 496f., p. 18n.

[34]*PI*, ¶182.

[35]Pole, *Later Philosophy*, 93.

[36]Those prior to "Communication and Convention" and "A Nice Derangement of Epitaphs," which will be discussed later.

[37]"The Method of Truth in Metaphysics," *T & I*, 203.

[38]In terms of my discussion of Aristotle in chapter 6, this means that his doctrine of the syllogism cannot be reduced to talk about the kind of "logical system" presented, for example, in the *Analytica Posteriora*.

[39]"True to the Facts," *T & I*, 45; "Communication and Convention," *T & I*, 272.

[40]"Radical Interpretation," *T & I*, 125; "Belief and the Basis of Meaning," *T & I*, 141; "Thought and Talk," *T & I*, 157f.

[41]"Belief and the Basis of Meaning," 144, 152.

[42]"Belief and the Basis of Meaning," 144, 152; also see "Thought and Talk," 161f.

[43]"Thought and Talk," passim.

[44]As holding for true is a basic language game, so interpreting sentences others hold for true is a set of language games, presumably a diverse one: see "Introduction," *T & I*, xixf.

[45]"The Inscrutability of Reference," *T & I*, 230.

[46]"Communication and Convention," 274.

[47]"Truth and Meaning," 6.

[48]If little George recognizes his father's activity as pain behavior, he may know that "It's hot" is true if and only if something is painful. This is false, but a good start. However, he may not recognize the behavior as pain behavior; children are prone to understand minor injuries (to others) as jokes.

[49]"One can sensibly ask about a denomination only when one already knows how to do something with it": *PI*, ¶31; see *PI* ¶¶27–32 for the argumentative context.

[50]The Shannon-Weaver definition of "information," on which chapter 5 trades, is much broader than the assertionistic views which see information as, basically, a set of true beliefs about something. On the Shannon/Weaver view, anything nonrandom counts as information: a dance, for example, is information.

[51]See ¶486: "An inference is the transition to an affirmation; and also, therefore, to the behavior that corresponds to the affirmation. 'I draw the consequences' not only in words, but also in deeds."

[52]*PI*, ¶23.

[53]Pole, *Later Philosophy*, 57; also see 95.

[54]*PI*, ¶¶113, 200.

[55]Unless it is just a married, childless couple, in which case there will be no "family resemblance."

[56]Wittgenstein also refers to the history of mathematics as a paradigm of language change at *PI*, ¶23.

[57]For Hegel's distance from the traditional view of essence, see Pippin, "Hegel's Metaphysics," 301–12.

[58]"True to the Facts," 43.

[59]E.g., at "Belief and the Basis of Meaning," 152; "Thought and Talk," 168f.; "On the Very Idea of a Conceptual Scheme," *T & I*, 196f.

[60]"Belief and the Basis of Meaning," 152.

[61]"Truth and Meaning," 18, 25.

[62]I have argued elsewhere that leaving it out is an effect of approaching language assertionistically, as if truth were its only goal. Polysemy is in fact essential to freedom as an intrinsic goal of language: see my *Poetic Interaction*, passim.

[63]"Communication and Convention," 277.

⁶⁴"Radical Interpretation," 130.

⁶⁵"A Nice Derangement," 442, 445.

⁶⁶An example of such an effect—of a strange remark becoming normal usage— occurs, as philosophers from Aristotle to Richard Rorty have noticed, in metaphor. Davidson's account of metaphor, however, is silent on the role it plays in language change. It is Rorty who develops Davidson's account of metaphor into one of language change: see Rorty, *Contingency, Irony, and Solidarity* (Cambridge: Cambridge University Press, 1989), 18ff.

⁶⁷"A Nice Derangement," 443.

⁶⁸Quine, *Word and Object*, 234, 272.

⁶⁹"A Nice Derangement," 445f.

⁷⁰"Communication and Convention," 272; "A Nice Derangement," 445.

⁷¹See J. L. Austin, "A Plea for Excuses," in Austin, *Philosophical Papers* (Oxford: Clarendon, 1961), 149f.: "a word never—well, hardly ever—shakes off its etymology and formation. In spite of all changes in and extensions of and additions to its meanings, and indeed rather pervading and governing these, there will still persist the old idea."

⁷²See Allan Janik and Stephen Toulmin, *Wittgenstein's Vienna* (New York: Simon and Schuster, 1973), and my "Time in the Ditch: American Philosophy in the McCarthy Era," forthcoming.

⁷³"A Nice Derangement," 443.

⁷⁴"True to the Facts," 38.

⁷⁵"Preface," xix.

⁷⁶Though, as I have argued elsewhere, not only: see my *Poetic Interaction*, 388f., 392f.

⁷⁷For an illuminating account of science as a form of what I am here calling public discourse, see Hull, *Science as a Process*.

Chapter 9

¹The discussion is at Descartes, *Principia Philosophiae*, in Descartes, *Oeuvres*, ed. Charles Adam and Paul Tannery (Paris: Cerf, 1905), 7:35–37; English translation in Haldane and Ross, *Philosophical Works*, 7:249–52.

²See the account of how to get memory out of one's cognitive functioning at Descartes, *Regulae* XI, in *Oeuvres* 10:407f./1:34.

³For the evil demon, see Descartes, *Principia Philosophiae* 6/220.

⁴Descartes, *Principa Philosophiae* 45:22/*Philosophical Works*, 237.

⁵Descartes, letter to Mersenne of July 27, 1638: "toute ma physique n'est autre chose que la géométrie," in *Oeuvres* 2:268.

⁶Descartes, letter to Mersenne of November 20, 1629, in *Oeuvres* 1:76–82; also see the letter of December 18, 1629, for the arbitrariness of names as opposed to cries and laughter, at *Oeuvres* 1:103.

⁷Locke, *Essay* 2:33.19. Locke's account of language in general draws little attention, partly because of its undeniable looseness: "As one reads Book III and compares it with the drafts, one cannot but feel that the theory is being developed in the very act of writing the book": Richard Aaron, *John Locke*, 3rd ed. (Oxford: Clarendon Press, 1971), 202. Language, in the form of *écriture*, has apparently taken over the formulation of the theory, even as Locke strives to articulate that very dominance. Of enormous general

help is Norman Kretzmann's essay "Semantics, History of," in Edwards, *Encyclopedia of Philosophy*, 7:359–406.

[8]*Essay* 4:12.7, 4:12.15.

[9]*Essay* 2:9.21.

[10]*Essay* 3:9.1, 3:10 passim.

[11]*Essay* 3.2.1.

[12]Locke's account of the language of mixed modes is even more neglected than other aspects of his theory of language, perhaps because, from an assertionistic perspective, mixed modes are useless: the ideas of mixed modes do not "mean" anything in the external world, and their names do not refer beyond the mind, so they yield no assertionistic truth. Hence, Charles Landesmann could write an entire essay ("Locke on Meaning," *Journal of the History of Philosophy* 14 [1976]: 23–35) without ever mentioning that there is such a thing as a mixed mode. The difficulty of assimilating Locke to the standard assertionistic framework is illustrated by Kretzmann, "Locke's Semantic Theory." Kretzmann argues that names for Locke "signify" ideas, which in turn "represent" things. It is only when the latter point, as well as the former, is kept in mind that the "full details" of Locke's semantic theory can be appreciated. But an important part of Locke's theory of meaning (that concerning mixed modes) deals, precisely, with ideas that do *not* represent things, while—as Kretzmann notes—Locke himself never bothers to explain what it is for an idea to "represent a thing." The moral is that what Kretzmann finds essential to "the full details of" Locke's thesis is of suspiciously lesser importance for Locke, while an extended part of Locke's theory concerns matters of no importance to Kretzmann. For general discussions of mixed modes, see David L. Perry, "Locke on Mixed Modes, Relations, and Knowledge," *Journal of the History of Philosophy* 5 (1967): 219–35, and the critical notice of this at Christopher Aronson and Douglas Lewis, "Locke on Mixed Modes, Knowledge, and Substances," *Journal of History of Philosophy* 8 (1970): 193–99.

[13]*Essay* 2:22, passim.

[14]*Essay* 2:12.5, 2:13.1.

[15]*Essay* 2:22.12. For a discussion of Locke's analysis of property as—loosely—based on his views about mixed modes, see John Yolton, *Locke and the Way of Ideas* (Cambridge: Cambridge University Press, 1970), 181–95.

[16]*Essay* 3:5.7; also see 2:22.5.

[17]*Essay* 2:22.7.

[18]*Essay* 2:22.8.

[19]*Essay* 3:5.10.

[20]*Essay* 3:5.11.

[21]*Essay* 2:22.2; 3:5.5.

[22]*Essay* 3:5.5.

[23]Thus, Locke's own account of meaning, restricted to how names "signify" ideas and uninterested in how ideas "represent" things, turns out to include just enough to explain the significance of mixed modes, and no more: see the discussion of Kretzmann in n. 12 above.

[24]*Essay* 2:30.4.

[25]*Essay* 2:5.14.

[26]*Essay* 4:12.7.

[27]*Essay* 2:23.1f.; 3:6.29.

[28]*Essay* 2:23.1f. 2:6.9, 2:6.21.

[29]*Essay* 3:9.5.

[30]*Essay* 2:22.7.

[31]*Essay* 3:9.10.

[32]*Essay* 3:9.9.

[33]*Essay* 3:9.6.

[34]*Essay* 3:9.7; emphasis added.

[35]*Essay* 3:11.11.

[36]*Essay* 3:11.12. Once the meaning has been declared, the term must be used in conformity to the declaration (*Essay* 3:11.26).

[37]*Essay* 2:29.7-12.

[38]Especially when such jumbling includes the assigning to an idea of incompatible predicates: *Essay* 2:30.4.

[39]*Essay* 2:29.10.

[40]*Essay* 4:12.8.

[41]*Essay* 2:29.8.

[42]See the editor's remark at *Essay* 1:390 n. 3.

[43]See, e.g., George Berkeley, *The Principles of Human Knowledge* (hereinafter *P*), in *Berkeley's Philosophical Writings*, ed. David M. Armstrong (New York: Collier, 1965), 74-96. All references to Berkeley's works will be to this collection.

[44]*P*, 71f.

[45]See Berkeley, "Towards a New Theory of Vision" (hereinafter *TV*), in *Philosophical Writings*, 343f.

[46]*TV*, 344.

[47]In an extended and illuminating account of Berkeley's view of nature as a divine language, Paul Olscamp shows that the idea of divine language is first introduced by Berkeley as a metaphor, and is taken increasingly literally as time goes on: Paul Olscamp, *The Moral Philosophy of George Berkeley* (The Hague: Nijhoff, 1970), 10-46.

[48]*P*, 88.

[49]*TV*, 328.

[50]*P*, 88; at *P*, 81, Berkeley allows that false assertions can have pragmatic value, even though they do not mirror nature; but a false assertion is not a mixed mode. In general, though Berkeley recognizes noncognitive uses of language, he restricts them to the arousal of passions, attitudes, and actions in the individual (*P*, 19, 56f.). The social dimension of language, as we will see, escapes him.

[51]Hume, *Treatise*, 455-70.

[52]*Essay* 2:2.2.

[53]*Essay* 2:2.1.

[54]*Essay* 4:7.9.

[55]*Essay* 2:13.28.

[56]*Essay* 3:4.2. See the illuminating remarks at J. O. Urmson, "Ideas," in Edwards, *Encyclopedia of Philosophy*, 4:120.

[57]*Essay* 2:2.1; see also 2:3.1.

[58]In the Introduction to *P*.

[59]William H. McGowan, "Berkeley's Doctrine of Signs," in Colin Turbayne, ed., *Berkeley: Critical and Interpretive Essays* (Minneapolis: University of Minneapolis Press, 1982), 242.

[60]*P*, 56f.

[61]*P*, 58-60.

[62]The *Metakritique* (hereinafter *Mk*) can be found at Johann Georg Hamann, *Sämtliche Werke*, ed. Josef Nadler (Vienna: Herder Verlag, 1949-1953), 4:283-89. All references to Hamann's works will be to this edition, the pagination of which is maintained in the useful collection Hamann, *Schriften zur Sprache*, ed. Josef Simon (Frankfurt:

Suhrkamp, 1967). For an English translation of some of the major texts see R. G. Smith, *J. G. Hamann* (London: Collins, 1960), 213–21. All translations here, as elsewhere in this book, remain my own.

63*Mk*, 283/213; emphasis added.

64Hume, *Treatise*. See *Essay* 2:29.10.

65Hume, *Treatise*, 20f.

66Ibid., 21.

67*Mk*, 285/215. For this tradition and its fate, see Owens, *Doctrine*, 74, and the literature referred to there in n. 18.

68Günter Wohlfahrt has illuminated the degree of Kant's blindness to language, and listed some of the isolated themes in Kant's *Critique of Judgment* which might have been brought together had Kant, like Hamann, understood the linguistic nature of reason. These themes include such important ones as the (linguistic) inner continuity of reflection and determination, the (linguistic) interchanges between intuition and concept, the *comprehensio aesthetica* (bringing together in an intuition) and the *comprehensio logica* (bringing together in a concept), etc. Wohlfahrt, *Denken*.

69*Mk*, 284/214f.

70Günter Wohlfahrt, "Hamanns Kantkritik," *Kant-Studien* 75 (1984): 408.

71See, for example, Kant, *KRV* B 369ff., 95–109; *Mk* 284/215.

72Wohlfahrt, *Denken*, 147. Focusing on Kierkegaard's critique of Hegel, Hermann J. Cloeren has traced its background in an entire "analytical" tradition in eighteenth- and nineteenth-century German philosophy, including Hamann and O. F. Gruppe: Cloeren, "Kierkegaard's Attack on Hegel," 1–13.

73*Mk*, 284f./215.

74Josef Simon, Introduction to Hamann, *Schriften zur Sprache*, 71ff.

75*Mk*, 286/217.

76*Mk*, 288/219.

77*Mk*, 288/219.

78*Mk*, 289/220.

79*Mk*, 287/218f.

80Hamann, "Des Ritters von Rosenkreuz Letzte Willensmeinung," in Hamann, *Werke* 3:32; also in Hamann, *Schriften zur Sprache*.

81See Robert E. Butts, "The Grammar of Reason: Hamann's Challenge to Kant," *Synthese* 75 (1988): 251–83.

82Hamann, *Aesthetica in Nuce*, in Hamann, *Werke* 2:261; also, with identical pagination, in Hamann, *Schriften zur Sprache*.

83For more on this, see H. A. Salmony, *J. G. Hamanns metakritische Philosophie* (Zollikon: Evangelischer Verlag, 1958), 185–92.

84*Mk*, 289/220.

85Hamann, *Werke* 1:243; also see Fritz Blanke, "Gottessprache und Menschensprache bei J. G. Hamann," in Blanke, *Hamann-Studien* (Zürich: Zwingli-Verlag, 1956), 53–97.

86For Hamann and Hume, see James C. O'Flaherty, *Unity and Language: A Study in the Philosophy of Johann Georg Hamann* (Chapel Hill: University of North Carolina Press, 1952), 60f.

87Erwin Metzge, *J. G. Hamanns Stellung in der Philosophie des 18. Jahrhunderts* (Darmstadt: Wissenschaftliche Buchgesellschaft, 1967), 243.

88Ibid., 251.

89Ibid., 242.

90Ibid., 252.

[91]Blanke, "Gottessprache and Menschensprache," 96f. For a partial corrective, see Butts, "Grammar of Reason," 262f.

[92]XI 330.

[93]Isaiah Berlin, "The Counter-Enlightenment," in Berlin, *Against the Current* (London: Hogarth, 1979), 10.

[94]E.g., at I 201, 215; II 357; VIII 270 (*Enz.* #136 Anm.)/193; XI 279; XVIII (*Hist. Phil.*) 21/not translated.

[95]Taylor, *Hegel*, 19f. Interestingly for Taylor's account of Hegel's "expressivism" (24ff.), Hegel's philosophical criticisms of Herder center precisely on what, for Herder, most primally expresses itself: *Kraft* or force: II 357; VIII 269f. (*Enz.* #136 Anm.)/193. This is not unexpected: if, as I argue in this book, "large entity" interpretations do not capture Hegel, then there cannot ultimately be a "thing" which expresses itself in and by means of an entire language. Hegel in fact recognizes *only* the expression, without substrate; that which is unexpressed is not unclear, but nonexistent.

[96]Rorty, *Linguistic Turn*, 3.

[97]These (hereinafter: *F3*) have been collected, along with other of Herder's writings on language, in *Herders Sprachphilosophie*, ed. Erich Heintel, 2d ed. (Hamburg: Meiner, 1964).

[98]*F3*, 154.

[99]*F3*, 155.

[100]*F3*, 154.

[101]*F3*, 156.

[102]Herder, "Eine Metakritik zur Kritik der reinen Vernunft," in *Sprachphilosophie*, 184.

[103]See Herder, "Abhandlung über den Ursprung der Sprache," in *Sprachphilosophie*, 24f., for this, and Herder, "Ideen zur Philosophie der Geschichte der Menschheit," in *Sprachphilosophie*, 173f.

[104]Even the baptism of an entity with a proper name, it could be argued on Herder's behalf, is in its way highly selective, for we name only a few of the things that surround us. *Which* we name depends not only on what is around to be named, but on what we think deserves its own name. This, again, is codetermined by our climate and culture, needs, and other such factors. Two languages could be spoken in a single place and time, and yet have sets of proper names that designated different entities.

[105]"Ideen," 173.

[106]"Ideen," 175, 173.

[107]"Ideen," 176.

[108]Ibid.

[109]*F3*, 155.

[110]*F3*, 156.

[111]*F3*, 157.

Chapter 10

[1]X 275 (*Enz.* #459 Anm.)/217. Sumio Deguchi has argued forcefully that, since the terms in which the System is written are not such as to refer, the Absolute can only be linguistic: Sumio Deguchi, "Der absolute Geist als Sprache," in Dieter Henrich and Rolf-Peter Horstmann, eds., *Hegels Logik der Philosophie* (Stuttgart: Klett-Cotta, 1984), 242–60. Deguchi, however, equates thinking with Judging and locates a hidden Judgment in every word, one which reconciles the domains of Being and Essence. Such rec-

onciliation is not, then, as immediate for philosophical thought as the versions of Marx and Hyppolite—where representational names would belong to the sphere of Essence, and names as such to that of Being—would imply. On my reading, however the reconciliation is not accomplished simply by the name itself, but by the act of naming, which must take account of and respond to a complex interplay of the various types of name and the realms which produce them.

²Jean Hyppolite, *Logique et existence* (Paris: Presses Universitaires de France, 1953), 34.

³Ibid., 31, 41.

⁴Ibid., 35.

⁵Ibid., 38, 52. Like Hyppolite, Jacques Derrida, who develops his account of Hegel in terms of what he calls "an implicit and permanent appeal" to *Logique et existence* (Derrida, "Puits," 81), misses the importance of Mechanical Memory and identifies thought with an earlier stage of the Psychology, Productive Memory ("Puits," 101f.; Derrida, *Grammatologie,* 41). Thus, Derrida does not see how Mechanical Memory functions for Hegel as a kind of "mental machine," over and above mathematics, differing from it in that the units in Mechanical Memory are fleeting and unstable, and their connections wholly without rules of any kind (see "Puits," 125–27). What Derrida instates as a discourse that would destabilize the System by rendering it "mechanical" is thus, ironically, the very kind of discourse that, I have argued, Hegel takes as a condition for the System: one which, precisely as does Mechanical Memory, "multiplies words, hurls them against one another, engulfs them also in a substitution without ground whose only rule is the sovereign self-affirmation of the play beyond meaning. . . . A sort of potlatch of signs, burning, consuming, wasting words in the gay affirmation of death: a sacrifice and a challenge." Derrida, "De l'économie restreine à l'économie générale: un hégélianism sans réserve" in Derrida, *Écriture et différence* (Paris: Éditions du Seuil, 1967), 403.

⁶Hyppolite, *Logique,* 38, 52.

⁷Ibid., 57.

⁸Ibid., 3, 44, 56ff., 247; also see 92.

⁹Werner Marx, "Absolute Reflexion und Sprache," in *Natur und Geschichte: Festschrift für Karl Löwith,* ed. Braun, Heimann, Riedel, (Stuttgart: Kohlhammer, 1967), 247f.

¹⁰Ibid., 251.

¹¹Ibid., 247.

¹²Ibid., 248.

¹³Ibid., 251f.

¹⁴Ibid., 250.

¹⁵*EGP* 49/33.

¹⁶Hegel, *Enzyklopädie der Philosophischen Wissenschaften im Grundrisse* (Heidelberg, 1817) #383; to be found in Hegel, *Werke* 6:271.

¹⁷Hegel, in fact, has a variety of less-than-systematic ways of referring to the beginning of Science. Among other things, he calls it "the whole, concealed in its simplicity," "the universal ground" of the new world and "the attained concept of the whole" (all at III [*PHG*] 29/7); "the immediate unity of self-knowledge" (III [*PHG*] 588/490); "the concept of Science" (V [*WDL*] 42/48); "I=I, absolute indifference or identity, etc." (VIII 182 [*Enz.* #86 Anm.]/124); he also refers to it as the known unity of pure Concept and true Being (V [*WDL*] 57/60), and as pure thought and knowledge in general (III [*PHG*] 29/14).

¹⁸V (*WDL*) 79/78.

[19]V (*WDL*) 76/75f.

[20]V (*WDL*) 79/78.

[21]VIII 350-67 (*Enz.* ##194-212)/260-74.

[22]VIII 351 (*Enz.* #194 Zus.)/260f.

[23]X 282 (*Enz.* 464)/223.

[24]X 238-40 (*Enz.* #444, and Zus.)/186-88.

[25]VI 402f./705; VIII 345 (*Enz.* #193)/256. The translation mysteriously places quote marks around "realization," which translates the German *Realisierung*.

[26]See the "General Introduction" to my *Poetic Interaction*.

[27]VIII 84 (*Enz.* #24 Zus. 2)/39f.

[28]X 344-50 (*Enz.* ##192, 193)/255-59.

[29]X 346 (*Enz.* ##192, 193)/256.

[30]VIII 352f. (*Enz.* #195)/261f.; VI (*WDL*) 412/713.

[31]For a brief discussion of Hegel's general account of communication, see the appendix to chapter 4.

[32]VIII 355f. (*Enz.* ##197, 198)/264f.; VI 423-26/721-24.

[33]IX 82-108 (*Enz.* ##269-71)/62-84.

[34]VIII 356f. (*Enz.* ##199, 200) 265f.; VI (*WDL*) 427f./725f.

[35]VIII 357f. (*Enz.* #200)/265f.; VI (*WDL*) 429/727.

[36]VIII 358f. (*Enz.* ##202, 203)/266f.; VI (*WDL*) 431f./729.

[37]VIII 358f. (*Enz.* #203)/267; VI (*WDL*) 434f./731.

[38]VIII 358f. (*Enz.* #203)/267; VI (*WDL*) 447/742.

[39]VIII 362f. (*Enz.* ##205, 206) 269f.; VI (*WDL*) 445ff./740ff.

[40]VIII 362 (*Enz.* #205)/269f.

[41]VIII 363, 364f. (*Enz.* ##206, 208)/270f.; 271f.; VI (*WDL*) 446/741.

[42]VI (*WDL*) 460/752f.

[43]VI (*WDL*) 446/741f.

[44]VIII 363f. (*Enz.* ##207)/271; VI (*WDL*) 447f., 450/742f., 744f.

[45]VIII 364 (*Enz.* #208)/271f.

[46]VI (*WDL*) 450/745.

[47]VIII 364 (*Enz.* 208/271). For a reliable discussion of this passage, see Jan van der Meulen, *Hegel: Die Gebrochene Mitte* (Hamburg: Meiner, 1958), 118ff.

[48]VIII 365 (*Enz.* #209)/272f.; VI (*EDL*) 449f./744.

[49]VIII 452 (*Enz.* #209)/272f.; VI (*WDL*) 452/746.

[50]Ibid.

[51]VI (*WDL*) 448f./743.

[52]VIII 365f. (*Enz.* #210)/273; VI (*WDL*) 454f./747f.

[53]VIII 366f. (*Enz.* #212)/273f.; VI (*WDL*) 458-60/750-52.

[54]VIII 366f. (*Enz.* #212)/273f.; VI (*WDL*) 447/742.

[55]VI (*WDL*) 458/750f.

[56]VIII 366f. (*Enz.* #212)/273f.; VI (*WDL*) 460f./752.

[57]VIII 354 (*Enz.* #195 Zus.)/263.

[58]The original assignment of meaning to a name as such can then be seen as giving a certain determinate impetus to other names; and this can apparently happen in two ways. The names run through in Mechanical Memory are held together in sequences memorized by the Intelligence; if one of them is uttered meaningfully by thought externalizing itself, it brings others with it and can be said to "communicate" meaning to them. Suppose, for example, that someone has memorized the standard example of a syllogism, "all men are mortal; Socrates is a man; therefore Socrates is mortal" as a chain of mere names as such. If she then comes somehow to understand the meaning of

"man," she will know a bit more about the meanings of the terms "Socrates" and "mortal" than she did previously. If she comes to understand as well the meanings of "all" and "some," she will know still more.

[59]VI (*WDL*) 429/727.

[60]VI (*WDL*) 431/729.

[61]VI (*WDL*) 448, 460/743, 752f.

[62]VIII 41 (*Enz.* #1)/3.

[63]Wolfgang Nikolaus argues that in order for the Concept to develop all content from within itself, it must be the whole of the System—but that it has the "motor" for this, the drive to posit itself in objectivity, only as part of the larger Idea. Hence, Hegel's "absolute method," which is roughly what I mean by "Systematic dialectics," is contradictory from the start—and so there is no start. Nikolaus fails to distinguish, then, between the mechanical and chemical objects. The immanent development of content is objectivized in the first, mechanical object; at this stage, no special "motor" is needed for the System to objectify itself, because it is objectified from the start—in names as such. The "drive to posit" enters when the System, expressed in names as such, confronts the discourses of the representational world: the "chemical object" of philosophy. It is as first expressed in names as such, then, that the Concept is what Nikolaus calls the *terminus a quo* of dialectical development, with the entire Systematic field latent within it. Uttered in names as such which have been shown to be homophonic with the appropriate representational names, it becomes the *terminus ad quem* of historical dialectics. Wolfgang Nikolaus, *Begriff und absolute Methode* (Bonn: Bouvier, 1985), 102–6.

[64]See the illuminating discussion in the *Aesthetics*, XIII 153f./112f.

[65]Indeed, in the *Phenomenology* consciousness not only forgets the previous markers, but forgets at each stage that there even was a previous stage—a very "chemical" trait.

[66]XVIII (*Hist. Phil.*) 420f./365f.

[67]XII (*Philosophy of History*) 114/87.

[68]Which for that reason cannot be written in hieroglyphics: X 273 (*Enz.* #459 Anm.) 215.

[69]VIII 24/not translated.

[70]X 279f./220f.

[71]The threefold mediation is discussed at *Enz.* ##575–77 (X 393f./314f.) but I shall follow the lead of Fackenheim (*Religious Dimension*, 89) in centering this short treatment of it on the less-obscure statement at *Enz.* #187 Zus. (VIII 339f./251). It will be seen that this reading of Hegel amounts to a linguistic interpretation of what Fackenheim calls perhaps Hegel's single most important term: "overreaching" (*Übergreifen*). Put abstractly, philosophical thought as overreaching for Fackenheim has three stages: (1) It must recognize the reality of the world, i.e., assume a finite embodiment of its own; (2) it must raise that finitude to the infinite status of the System; and (3) in carrying out the rise, it must affirm the persistence of finite reality (Fackenheim, *Religious Dimension*, 98; also see 27, 85–106). On the present reading, thought assumes a finite embodiment in being uttered in a name as such homonymous to a representational name; it then raises that latter name to the status of the System by guiding its chemical process. It recognizes the persistence of the representional world by continuing to be expressed in names homophonic to representational names, as well as by recognizing the existence of new representations.

[72]X 286 (*Enz.* #467 Zus.)/226f.

[73]VIII 39f. (*Enz.* #187 Zus.)/251. It is only as such a "mediating element," writes Gwendoline Jarczyk, that the Logic can be the principle (*principe, Grundsatz*) of the System. The same, I would add, for Nature and Spirit: Jarczyk, "La logique de Hegel, prin-

cipe du système," in Labarrière and Jarczyk, *Hegeliana* 205–15, esp. 206; also see the account of Hegel's response to Fichte in the Introduction. I will note, finally, that my view of the end of the *Encyclopedia* corresponds in general to that of Thèodore Geraets, for whom each syllogism expresses a reading of the System: Geraets, "Les trois lectures philosophiques de l'Encyclopédie ou la réalisation du concept de la philosophie chez Hegel," *Hegel-Studien* 10 (1975): 231–54. See esp. 244–51: in the first syllogism, says Geraets, the individual reader "forgets himself" in the objective development of thought; on my view, in this syllogism the name as such, which expresses thought purely in itself without regard to any externality (including a reader) is the middle. The second syllogism, in which for Geraets the philosophizing subject is the key, is for me the "chemical process" in which thought encounters history and the thinker attempts, as Geraets puts it, "to comprehend—in assimilating the philosophical labor of previous generations—his own time"; while the third syllogism is the unification of the other two. The main difference between my view and that of Geraets is that he assumes the context of an individual philosopher "reading" the *Encyclopedia*, while on my reading the classroom lecture, rather than private reading, is the appropriate context.

[74]III (*PHG*) 29/14f.

[75]V (*WDL*) 27; also 19, 30/37, 31, 39.

[76]VIII 210 (*Enz.* #99 Zus.)/146.

[77]III (*PHG*) 556f., 580f./463, 484; X 378ff. (*Enz.* #573)/302ff.

[78]VI 406/708.

[79]See, e.g., V (*WDL*) 211, 229, 276/186, 200f., 238.

[80]E.g., at V (*WDL*) 166f./150f.

[81]VI 407/708.

[82]As notes Nancy, *Remarque spéculative*, 65f.

[83]V (*WDL*) 53–56/57–59. L. B. Puntel has interpreted Hegel's thought as a Systematic semantics, and on the present reading it is true, as Puntel suggests, that the System constructs some of the basic categories underlying discourse; in the dynamism of that construction, it can moreover be viewed as, in Puntel's phrase, a coherent set of speech acts. But the categories it treats are not those of language in general, but those of expert discourse (though it may at times use names from "common life" to designate them); and the relation between Systematic thought and and the discourse it treats is, as should be clear by now, *toto caelo* different from that between a language and the metalanguage in which its semantics is formulated. For one thing, a change in the meaning of a term in either discourse can change the meaning of terms in the other discourse; for another, the System, being nonassertional, cannot in any way "talk about" expert discourse. L. B. Puntel, "Hegels Logik."

[84]Klaus Hartmann, "Hegel: a Non-metaphysical View," in MacIntyre, *A Collection*, 101–24.

[85]V (*WDL*) 20f./32f.

[86]For the statement of this with regard to the content of thought alone, see X 280 (*Enz.* #462 Zus.)/221.

[87]This suggests an answer to the problem raised by W. H. Bossart, which I mentioned in the appendix to chapter 4. Bossart's question—that of how infinite thought can actualize itself in a (finite) individual thinker—is in fact wrongly posed: infinite thought is not actualized in "an" individual thinker, but in a group of them; its *infinitude* is the way it brings them together by transforming the words in terms of which they understand and constitute themselves. Hence, Wolfgang Wieland's earlier formulation of the same problem—in terms of "finite spirit" rather than of the "individual thinker"—remains preferable: Wolfgang Wieland, "Bemerkungen zum Anfang von

Hegels Logik," in Helmut Fahrenbach, ed., *Wirklicheit und Reflexion* (Pfullingen: Neske, 1973), 395–411. I hope it is clear that Hegel does not, as Wieland charges, wholly ignore this issue. The System is not, in Wieland's words, "written in the determinate language of a determinate time," but stands I have argued at a complex remove from such language. Nor does Hegel fail even to try and come up with a nonassertional form for his Systematic thought, though he certainly fails to explain clearly the form such thought adopts. Bossart, "Exoteric and Esoteric."

[88]V (*WDL*) 54f./58.

[89]It is then this bearing on the representation of Being, as developed in the history of metaphysics, which distinguishes the expression of the beginning of the *Logic* from the mere mechanical expression in names as such.

[90]VIII 41 (*Enz.* #1)/3.

[91]Hence, Clark's formula of the "identity and non-identity" of philosophical language and its meaning, which I discussed in chapter 7, can be given a precise statement which does not inhibit the possibility of adequate expression of the System. The "identity" of statement and meaning is furnished by the expression of thought in a name as such; the otherness, by the homophony of that name with a representational name. The student who knows the procedures of Hegelian dialectics will, on hearing the expression of the System, be able to convert the latter into the former.

[92]Thus, contrary to Hösle, Puntel, and Theunissen, Hegelian philosophical reason is intersubjective from the start. Its interpersonal context was manifested by, though never adequately thematized in, Hegel's lectures. This is presumably why, after he obtained a professorship, Hegel published only handbooks to his lectures. Hösle, *Hegels System*, 122ff.; Puntel, *Darstellung, Methode und Struktur* (Bonn: Bouvier, 1973), 342; Michael Theunissen, "Intersubjektivität," in Henrich and Horstmann, *Hegel's Philosophie*, 317–81.

[93]See VIII 284f. (*Enz.* #466)/25; III (*PHG*) 31f./16.

[94]V (*WDL*) 31/40.

[95]Ibid.

[96]See V (*WDL*) 123/115, where Hegel argues against possible misunderstandings of the sublation of the distinction of reality and negation in determinate being.

[97]See V (*WDL*) 123/115, where Hegel argues against thinking of "something" as "real" ("*ein Reelles*").

[98]An example of such recapitulation is at V (*WDL*) 124/116.

[99]V (*WDL*) 50/54f.

[100]See the discussion of Spinoza at V (*WDL*) 121/113f.

[101]As Hegel implies at VIII 44f. (*Enz.* #3 Anm.)/6.

[102]V (*WDL*) 31/40.

[103]See my *Poetic Interaction*, 390ff.

[104]VIII 89 (*Enz.* #24 Zus. 3)/43.

Chapter 11

[1]VI 454/747.

[2]Alfred Tarski, "Concept of Truth," in Tarski, *Metamathematics*, 154–65.

[3]It is noteworthy that for Davidson our use of background information (which is not built up from primitives via rules) in disambiguating sentences is not covered by the

theory and is an important limitation on it: "Truth and Meaning," 30ff.; "Semantics for Natural Languages," *T & I*, 59f.

[4]"True to the Facts," 51f.; "Radical Interpretation," 132.

[5]"Truth and Meaning," 28.

[6]"Method of Truth in Metaphysics," 203; "Semantics for Natural Languages," 59f.

[7]"Method of Truth in Metaphysics," 203; also "Truth and Meaning," 29.

[8]"Truth and Meaning," 27ff.; "Radical Interpretation," 132ff.

[9]"True to the Facts," 51; "Radical Interpretation," 133.

[10]The example is from Heidegger, *Sein und Zeit*, 154f.; this is also valid for the marginal pagination in the English translation, *Being and Time*.

[11]"Method of Truth in Metaphysics," 203; see "Moods and Performances," *T & I*, 119-21 for an example of this.

[12]"Truth and Meaning," 29; "True to the Facts," 51f., 60.

[13]"Semantics for Natural Languages," 55.

[14]"In Defense of Convention," 71.

[15]"Radical Interpretation," 133.

[16]"Method of Truth in Metaphysics," 203.

[17]Ibid.

[18]"Truth and Meaning," 30.

[19]"True to the Facts," 51.

[20]"What Metaphors Mean," 263.

[21]Ibid., 257.

[22]This is why, as I noted in chapter 2, Davidson does not assert subthesis (b) of assertionism: he avoids claiming that truth is the goal of his own inquiry.

[23]See my *Poetic Interaction*, 380–94.

[24]*Poetic Interaction*, 211f.

[25]Simon Evnine has stated the proximity concisely: "Davidson's problems are of a piece with the problems that have always affected rationalist idealists such as Plato and Hegel: how can people, as finite, limited, and material creatures, participate in the ideal?" The answer: by metaphor and dialectical transformation. Simon Evnine, *Donald Davidson* (Stanford: Stanford University Press, 1991), 154.

[26]*PI*, ¶496.

[27]The point is made at *PI*, 187 with regard to *Beobachtung*, contemplation, which is coordinated with description further on that page.

[28]*PI*, ¶124.

[29]*PI*, 187.

[30]*PI*, ¶¶372, 496f.

[31]It is also, since Foucault, possible to think of descriptions as not merely altering or destroying but as, indeed, generating their objects. Thus, Foucault argues, there was no such thing as mental illness until people started talking about it. Michel Foucault, *Madness and Civilization*, trans. Richard Howard (New York: Random House, 1965).

[32]*PI*, ¶116.

[33]And which, according to ¶120, is itself a part of ordinary language. But how can such an unusual game be played with ordinary pieces?

[34]See Pole, *Later Philosophy*, 81; *PI*, ¶136.

[35]*PI*, ¶564. Wittgenstein's use of *Witz* could be very interestingly compared with the Hegelian insights on *Witz* collected by Jean-Luc Nancy in *Remarque spéculative* 157–78.

[36]See *PI*, ¶¶5, 564 for teleological unity.

[37]See Derrida's analysis of iterability in "Signature, Evènement, Contexte" in Derrida, *Marges*, 365/393.

[38]*PI*, ¶¶208–10.

[39]*Werke* X 32–34; *Critique of Judgment*, trans. Werner S. Pluhar (Indianapolis: Hackett, 1987).

[40]*PI*, ¶527.

[41]*PI*, ¶535.

[42]*PI*, ¶¶130–32.

Select Bibliography

A. Works by Hegel (also see "A Note on the Texts")

Hegel, G. F. W. *Briefe von und an Hegel.* Edited by Johannes Hoffmeister. 4 vols. Hamburg: Meiner, 1952–1960. Translated by Clark Butler and Christiane Seiler, under the title *Hegel: The Letters.* Bloomington: University of Indiana Press, 1984.

———. *Phänomenologie des Geistes.* Edited by Johannes Hoffmeister. 6th ed. Hamburg: Meiner, 1952.

———. *Werke* (Jubiläumsausgabe). Edited by Herman Glockner. Stuttgart: Frommann, 1927.

———. *The Difference between Fichte's and Schelling's System of Philosophy.* Translated by Walter Cerf and H. S. Harris. Albany: SUNY Press, 1977.

———. *Faith and Knowledge.* Translated by Walter Cerf and H. S. Harris. Albany: SUNY Press, 1977.

———. *The Philosophical Propadeutic.* Translated by A. V. Miller. Oxford: Blackwell, 1986.

———. *Philosophy of Nature.* Edited by M. J. Petry. London: Allen and Unwin, 1970.

———. *Philosophy of Subjective Spirit.* Edited by M. J. Petry. The Hague: Reidel, 1979.

B. Works on Hegel and Hegelian topics

Aschenberg, Reinhold. "Der Wahrheitsbegriff in Hegels *Phänomenologie des Geistes.*" In *Die ontologische Option,* edited by Klaus Hartmann, 211–304. Berlin: de Gruyter, 1976.

Asenjo, F. G. "Dialectical Logic." *Logique et analyse* 8 (1965): 321–26.

Baum, Manfred. "Anmerkungen zum Verhältnis von Systematik und Dialektik bei Hegel." In *Hegels Wissenschaft der Logik: Formation und Rekonstruktion,* edited by Dieter Henrichs, 65–76. Stuttgart: Klett-Cotta, 1986.

————. *Die Entstehung der Hegelschen Dialektik.* 2d ed. Bonn: Bouvier, 1989.

Becker, Werner, and Wilhelm Essler, eds. *Konzepte der Dialektik.* Frankfurt: Klostermann, 1981.

Bergmann, Frithjof. "The Purpose of Hegel's System." *Journal of the History of Philosophy* 2 (1964): 189–204.

Beyer, Wilhelm Raimund, ed. *Die Logik des Wissens und das Problem der Erziehung.* Hamburg: Meiner, 1982.

Bodammer, Theodor. *Hegels Deutung der Sprache.* Hamburg: Meiner, 1969.

Bole, Thomas J. "Contradiction in Hegel." *Review of Metaphysics* 40 (1987): 515–34.

Bossart, William H. "Exoteric and Esoteric in Hegel's Dialectic." *The Personalist* 58 (1977): 261–76.

Bubner, Rüdiger. *Zur Sache der Dialektik.* Stuttgart: Reklam, 1980.

Buchdahl, Gerd. "Conceptual Analysis and Scientific Theory in Hegel's Philosophy of Nature (With Special Reference to Hegel's Optics)." In *Hegel and the Sciences,* edited by Robert Cohen and Marx Wartofsky, 13–36. Dordrecht: Reidel, 1984.

————. "Hegel's Philosophy of Nature and the Structure of Science." In *Hegel,* edited by Michael Inwood, 110–36. Oxford: Oxford University Press, 1985.

Burbidge, John. *On Hegel's Logic: Fragments of a Commentary.* Highland Heights, N. J.: Humanities Press, 1981.

Butler, Clark. "Hermeneutic Hegelianism." *Idealistic Studies* 15 (1985): 121–36.

————. "On the Reducibility of Dialectical to Standard Logic." *The Personalist* 6 (1975): 414–31.

Clark, Malcolm. *Logic and System.* The Hague: Martinus Nijhoff, 1971.

Cloeren, Hermann J. "The Linguistic Turn in Kierkegaard's Attack on Hegel." *International Studies in Philosophy* 17 (1985): 1–13.

Cohen, Robert, and Marx Wartofsky, eds. *Hegel and the Sciences.* Dordrecht: Reidel, 1984.

Colletti, Lucio. *Studies in Marx and Hegel.* Translated by Lawrence Garner. London: Verso, 1979.

Cook, Daniel. *Language in the Philosophy of Hegel.* The Hague: Mouton, 1973.

Deguchi, Sumio. "Der absolute Geist als Sprache." In *Hegels Logik der Philosophie,* edited by Dieter Henrich et al. Stuttgart: Klett-Cotta, 1984.

Derbolav, Joseph. *Sprache: Schlüssel zur Welt: Festschrift für Leo Weisgerber.* Düsseldorf: Schwann, 1959.

Derrida, Jacques. "Le puits et la pyramide." In *Marges,* 79–127. Paris: Minuit, 1972.

Desmond, William. "Hegel, Dialectic, and Deconstruction." *Philosophy and Rhetoric* 18 (1985): 244–63.

deVries, Willem. *Hegel's Theory of Mental Activity.* Ithaca: Cornell University Press, 1988.

di Giovanni, George, ed. *Essays on Hegel's Logic.* Albany: SUNY Press, 1990.

Dove, Kenley R. "Hegel's Phenomenological Method." In *New Studies in*

Hegel's Philosophy, edited by Warren Steinkraus, 34–56. New York: Holt, Rinehart & Winston, 1971.

Dubarle, D., and A. Dos. *Logique et dialectique*. Paris: Larousse, 1971.

Düsing, Klaus. "Syllogistik und Dialektik in Hegels spekulativer Logik." In *Hegels Wissenschaft der Logik: Formen und Rekonstruktion*, edited by Dieter Henrich, 15–38. Stuttgart: Klett-Cotta, 1986.

Fackenheim, E. L. *The Religious Dimension in Hegel's Thought*. Boston: Beacon, 1967.

Fahrenbach, Helmut, ed. *Wirklicheit und Reflexion*. Pfullingen: Neske, 1973.

Fetscher, Irving. *Hegels Lehre vom Menschen*. Stuttgart: Fromann, 1970.

Findlay, J. N. *Hegel: A Re-examination*. London: Allen & Unwin, 1958.

———. "The Contemporary Relevance of Hegel." In *Hegel: A Collection of Critical Essays*, edited by Alasdair Macintyre, 1–20. Garden City, N.J.: Anchor Books, 1972.

Flay, Joseph. "Bibliography" on Hegel and the history of philosophy. In *Hegel and the History of Philosophy*, edited by Joseph O'Malley, et al., 194–236. The Hague: Martinus Nijhoff, 1974.

———. *Hegel's Quest for Certainty*. Albany: SUNY Press, 1984.

Fleischmann, Eugène. "Hegels Umgestaltung der Kantischen Logik." *Hegel-Studien* Beiheft 3 (1965): 185–87.

———. *La science universelle*. Paris: Plon, 1968.

Forster, Michael. *Hegel and Skepticism*. Cambridge, Mass.: Harvard University Press, 1989.

Fulda, Hans Friedrich. "Unzulängliche Bemerkungen zur Dialektik." In *Seminar: Dialektik in der Philosophie Hegels*, edited by Rolf Horstmann, 33–69. Frankfurt: Suhrkamp, 1978.

———. "Über den Ursprung der Hegelshen Dialektik." *Aquinas* 24 (1981): 378f.

———. "Dialektik in Konfrontation mit Hegel." In *Hegels Wissenschaft der Logik: Formen und Rekonstruktion*, edited by Dieter Henrich, 328–49. Stuttgart: Klett-Cotta, 1986.

Gauthier, Yvon. "Logique hegelienne et formalization." *Dialogue* 6 (1967): 151–65.

Geraets, Thèodore. "Les trois lectures philosophiques de l'Encyclopédie ou la réalisation du concept de la philosophie chez Hegel." *Hegel-Studien* 10 (1975): 231–54.

Günther, G. "Das Problem einer Formalisierung der transzendentaldialektischen Logik." In *Hegel-Tage*, Hrsg. Hans-Georg Gadamer. *Hegel-Studien* Beiheft 1 (1964): 65–113.

Guyer, Paul. "Dialektik als Methodologie." In *Hegels Wissenschaft der Logik: Formation und Rekonstruktion*, edited by Dieter Henrich, 164–77. Stuttgart: Klett–Cotta, 1986.

———. "Hegel, Leibniz, and the Contradiction in the Finite." *Philosophy and Phenomenological Research* 40 (1979–80): 75–98.

Guzzoni, Ute, et al. *Der Idealismus und sein Gegenwart*. Hamburg: Meiner, 1976.

Hanna, Robert. "Hegel's Critique of the Common Logic." *Review of Metaphysics* 40 (1986): 305–38.

Harris, Errol. "Dialectic and Scientific Method." *Idealistic Studies* 3 (1973): 1–17.

———. *An Interpretation of the Logic of Hegel.* Lanham, Md.: University Press of America, 1983.

Harris, H. S. *Hegel's Development: Toward the Sunlight, 1770–1801.* Oxford: Clarendon Press, 1972.

———. "Hegelians of the 'Right' and 'Left.' " *Review of Metaphysics* 11 (1958): 603–9.

———. *Night Thoughts.* Oxford: Oxford University Press, 1983.

Hartmann, Klaus, ed. *Die ontologische Option.* Berlin: de Gruyter, 1976.

———. "Hegel: a Non-metaphysical View." In *Hegel: A Collection of Critical Essays,* edited by Alasdair MacIntyre, 101–24. Garden City: Anchor Books, 1967.

Harvey, Irene. "The Linguistic Basis of Truth for Hegel." *Man and World* 15 (1982): 285–97.

Hedwig, Klaus. "Hegel on Time and Eternity." *Dialogue* (Can.) 9 (1970): 139–53.

Henrich, Dieter. "Anfang und Methode der Logik." *Hegel-Studien* Beiheft 1 (1964): 19–35.

———. "Hegels Theorie über den Zufall." *Kant-Studien* 50 (1958): 131–48.

———. "Introduction" to G. F. W. Hegel, *Philosophie des Rechts: die Vorlesungen von 1819/20,* edited by Dieter Henrich, 30–38. Frankfurt: Suhrkamp, 1983.

———. "Hegels Grundoperation." In *Der Idealismus und sein Gegenwart,* edited by Ute Guzzoni et al., 208–30. Hamburg: Meiner, 1976.

Henrich, Dieter, ed. *Hegels Wissenschaft der Logik: Formation und Rekonstruktion.* Stuttgart: Klett-Cotta, 1986.

Henrich, Dieter, and Rolf-Peter Horstmann, eds. *Hegel's Philosophie des Rechts.* Stuttgart: Kohlhammer, 1982.

———. *Hegels Logik der Philosophie.* Stuttgart: Klett-Cotta, 1984.

Hintikka, Jaako. "On the Common Factors of Dialectic." In *Konzepte der Dialektik,* edited by Werner Becker and Wilhelm Essler. Frankfurt: Klostermann, 1981.

Holz, Harald. "Anfang, Identität und Widerspruch." *Tijdschrift voor Filosofie* 37 (1974): 707–61.

Horstmann, Rolf-Peter, ed. *Seminar: Dialektik in der Philosophie Hegels.* Frankfurt: Suhrkamp, 1978.

Hösle, Vittorio. *Hegels System.* Hamburg: Meiner, 1987.

Hyppolite, Jean. *Studies in Marx and Hegel.* Translated by John O'Neill. New York: Harper Torchbooks, 1973.

———. *Logique et existence.* Paris: Presses Universitaires de France, 1953.

Iljin, Iwan. *Die Philosophie Hegels als kontemplative Gotteslehre.* Bern: Francke, 1946.

Inwood, Michael. "Solomon, Hegel, and Truth." *Review of Metaphysics* 31 (1977): 272–82.

Inwood, Michael, ed. *Hegel*. Oxford: Oxford University Press, 1985.

Jarczyk, Gwendoline. "La logique de Hegel, principe du système." In *Hegeliana*, edited by Pierre-Jean Labarrière and Gwendoline Jarczyk, 205–15. Paris: Presses Universitaires de France, 1986.

———. *Système et liberté dans la logique de Hegel*. Paris: Aubier Montaigne, 1980.

———. "Une approche de la vérité logique chez Hegel." In *Hegeliana*, edited by Pierre-Jean Labarriére and Gwendoline Jarczyk, 159–68.

Kainz, Howard P. *Paradox, Dialectic, and System*. University Park: Pennsylvania State University Press, 1988.

Kaufmann, Walter. *Hegel: A Reinterpretation*. Garden City, N.J.: Anchor Books, 1966.

Kimmerle, Heinz. "Die allgemeine Strukturen der dialektischen Methode." *Zeitschrift für philosophishiche Forschung* 33 (1979): 184–209.

———. "Hegels 'Logik' als Grundlegung des Systems der Philosophie." In *Die Logik des Wissens und das Problem der Erziehung*, edited by Wilhelm Raimund Beyer, 52–60. Hamburg: Meiner, 1982.

Kojève, Alexandre. *Introduction à la lecture de Hegel*. Paris: Gallimard, 1940.

Kolb, David. *The Critique of Pure Modernity*. Chicago: University of Chicago Press, 1986.

Kosok, Michael. "The Formalization of Hegel's Dialectical Logic." *International Philosophical Quarterly* 6 (1966): 596–631.

Koyré, Alexandre. *Etudes d'histoire de la pensée philosophique*. Paris: Colin, 1961.

Krautkrämer, Ursula. *Staat und Erziehung*. Munich: Johannes Beichmann, 1979.

Labarrière, Pierre-Jean, and Gwendoline Jarczyk. *Hegeliana*. Paris: Presses Universitaires de France, 1986.

Lamb, David. *Hegel: From Foundation to System*. The Hague: Martinus Nijhoff, 1980.

Lauer, Quentin. *Hegel's Idea of Philosophy*. 2d rev. ed. New York: Fordham University Press, 1974.

Lauth, Reinhard. *Hegel vor der Wissenschaftslehre*. Wiesbaden: Franz Steiner Verlag, 1987.

Litt, Theodor. *Hegel: Versuch einer Kritischen Erneuerung*. Heidelberg: Quelle & Meyer, 1953.

Loewenberg, Jacob. *Hegel's "Phenomenology": Dialogues on the Life of the Mind*. La Salle, Illinois: Open Court, 1965.

———. "The Comedy of Immediacy in Hegel's "Phenomenology." *Mind* 44 (1935): 21–38.

Löwith, Karl, ed. *Die Hegelsche Linke*. Stuttgart: Frommann, 1962.

———. *From Hegel to Nietzsche*. Translated by David E. Green. Garden City, N.J.: Anchor Books, 1967.

Lübbe, Hermann, ed. *Die Hegelsche Rechte*. Stuttgart: Frommann, 1962.

McCumber, John. "Hegel on Habit." *Owl of Minerva* 21 (1990): 155–65.

———. *Poetic Interaction*. Chicago: University of Chicago Press, 1989.

———. Review article of Clark Butler, et al., *Hegel's Letters*. *Queen's Quarterly* (Canada) 93 (1986): 637–44.

Macintyre, Alasdair, ed. *Hegel: A Collection of Critical Essays*. Garden City, N.J.: Anchor Books, 1972.

Maker, William. "Understanding Hegel Today." *Journal of the History of Philosophy* 9 (1981): 343–75.

Marcuse, Herbert. *Reason and Revolution*. Boston: Beacon Press, 1960.

Marx, Werner. "Absolute Reflexion und Sprache." In *Natur und Geshcichte: Festschrift für Karl Löwith,* edited by Braun, Heimann, and Riedel, 278–97. Stuttgart: Kohlhammer, 1967.

Mueller, Gustav E. "The Hegel Legend of Thesis-Antithesis-Synthesis." *Journal of the History of Ideas* 19 (1958): 411–14.

Mure, G. R. G. *An Introduction to Hegel*. Oxford: Clarendon, 1940.

———. *A Study of Hegel's Logic*. Oxford: Clarendon, 1950.

Nancy, Jean-Luc. *La remarque spéculative*. Paris: Galilée, 1973.

Nikolaus, Wolfgang. *Begriff und absolute Methode*. Bonn: Bouvier, 1985.

Peperzaak, Adrian. *Le jeune Hegel: ou, la vision morale du monde*. The Hague: Martinus Nijhoff, 1969.

Pinkard, Terry. *Hegel's Dialectic*. Philadelphia: Temple University Press, 1988.

———. "Hegel's Idealism and Hegel's Logic." *Zeitschrift für philosophische Forschung* 33 (1979): 210–26.

———. "How Kantian was Hegel?" *Review of Metaphysics* 43 (1990): 831–38.

———. "The Logic of Hegel's Logic." In *Hegel*, edited by Michael Inwood, 85–109. Oxford: Oxford University Press, 1985.

Pippin, Robert B. *Hegel's Idealism*. Cambridge: Cambridge University Press, 1989.

———. "Hegel's Metaphysics and the Problem of Contradiction." *Journal of the History of Philosophy* 16 (19XX): 301–12.

Prauss, Gerold. "Zum Wahrheitsproblem bei Kant." *Kant-Studien* 60 (1969): 166–82.

Puntel, L. B. "Hegels Logik—eine systematische Semantik?" *Hegel-Studien* Beiheft 17 (1977): 611–22.

———. "Was ist logisch in Hegels Logik." In *Die Logik des Wissens und das Problem der Erziehung,* edited by Wilhelm Raimund Beyer, 40–51. Hamburg: Meiner, 1982.

———. *Darstellung, Methode und Struktur*. Bonn: Bouvier, 1973.

Quelquejeu, Bernard. *La volonté dans la philosophie de Hegel*. Paris: Editions du Seuil, 1972.

Reboul, Olivier. "Hegel, critique de la morale de Kant." *Revue de métaphysique et de morale* 80 (1975): 85–100.

Reuss, Siegfried. *Die Verwirklichung der Vernunft*. Frankfurt: Max Planck Institut für Bildungsforschung, 1982.

Rockmore, Tom. *Hegel's Circular Epistemology*. Bloomington: University of Indiana Press, 1986.

Rohs, Peter. *Form und Grund. Hegel-Studien* Beiheft 6 (3d ed. 1982).

———. "Das Problem der vermittelten Unmittelbarkeit in der Hegelschen Logik." *Philosophisches Jahrbuch* 81 (1974): 331–80.

———. "Der Grund der Bewegung des Begriffs." *Hegel-Studien* Beiheft 18 (1978): 43–62.

Rosen, Michael. *Hegel's Dialectic and its Criticism.* Cambridge: Cambridge University Press, 1982.

Rosen, Stanley. *G. W. F. Hegel.* New Haven: Yale University Press, 1974.

Routley, R., and R. Meyer. "Dialectic Logic, Classical Logic, and the Consistency of the World." *Studies in Soviet Thought* (1976): 1–25.

Römpp, Georg. "Sein als Genesis von Bedeutung." *Zeitschrift für philosophische Forschung* 43 (1989): 58–80.

Röttges, Heinz. *Der Begriff der Methode in der Philosophie Hegels.* Meisenheim/Glan, 1976.

Sarlemijn, Andries. *Hegelsche Dialektik.* Berlin: de Gruyter, 1971.

Sass, Hans-Martin. "Speculative Logic (Dialectics) as Conflict Theory." In *Konzepte der Dialektik,* edited by Werner Becker and Wilhelm Essler, 66–68. Frankfurt: Klostermann, 1981.

Schmitz, Hermann. "Das dialektische Warheitsverständnis und seine Aporie." *Hegel-Studien* Beiheft 17 (1977): 241–54.

Schmitz, Rudolf. *Sein Wahrheit Wort.* Munster: Lit, 1984.

Seebohm, Thomas. "Das Widerspruchsprinzip in der Kantischen Logik und der Hegelschen Dialektik." *Akten des 4. Internationalen Kant-Kongresses Mainz 1974,* 862–74.

———. "The Grammar of Hegel's Dialectic." *Hegel-Studien* 11 (1975): 149–80.

Simon, Josef. *Das Problem der Sprache bei Hegel.* Stuttgart: Kohlhammer, 1966.

———. "Die Kategorien im 'Gewöhnlichen' und im 'Spekulativen' Satz." *Wiener Jahrbuch für Philosophie* 3 (1970): 9–37.

———. "Die Bewegung des Begriffs in Hegels Logik." *Hegel-Studien* Beiheft 18 (1978): 63–73.

Solomon, Robert. "Truth and Self-Satisfaction." *Review of Metaphysics* 28 (1975): 698–724.

Stanguennec, André. *Hegel critique de Kant.* Paris: Presses Universitaires de France, 1985.

Steinkraus, Warren, ed. *New Studies in Hegel's Philosophy.* New York: Holt, Rinehart & Winston, 1971.

Stepelevich, Lawrence S., ed. *The Young Hegelians: An Anthology.* Cambridge: Cambridge University Press, 1983.

Sünkel, Wolfgang. "Hegel und der Mut zur Bildung." In *Die Logik des Wissens und das Problem der Erziehung,* edited by Wilhelm Raimund Beyer, 203–9. Hamburg: Meiner, 1982.

Surber, Jère Paul. "Hegel's Speculative Sentence." *Hegel-Studien* 10 (1975): 211–229.

Taylor, Charles. *Hegel.* Cambridge: Cambridge University Press, 1975.

Thagard, Paul. "Hegel, Science, and Set Theory." *Erkenntnis* 18 (1982): 397–410.

Theunissen, Michael. "Die verdrängte Intersubjektivität in Hegel's Philosophie des Rechts." In *Hegel's Philosophie des Rechts*, edited by Dieter Henrich and Rolf-Peter Horstmann, 317–81. Stuttgart: Kohlhammer, 1982.

———. "Begriff und Realität: Hegels Aufhebung des metaphysischen Wahrheitsbegriffs." In *Seminar: Dialektik in der Philosophie Hegels*, edited by Rolf-Peter Horstmann, 324–59. Frankfurt: Suhrkamp, 1978.

———. *Sein und Schein*. Frankfurt: Suhrkamp, 1980.

Thomason, S. K. "Towards a Formalization of Dialectic Logic." *Journal of Symbolic Logic* 39 (1974): 204.

Toews, John R. *Hegelianism*. Cambridge: Cambridge University Press, 1980.

Topp, Christian. *Philosophie als Wissenschaft*. Berlin: de Gruyter, 1982.

van der Meulen, Jan. *Hegel: Die Gebrochene Mitte*. Hamburg: Meiner, 1958.

White, Alan. *Absolute Knowledge: Hegel and the Problem of Metaphysics*. Athens: Ohio University Press, 1983.

Wieland, Wolfgang. "Bemerkungen zum Anfang von Hegels Logik." In *Wirklicheit und Reflexion*, edited by Helmut Fahrenbach, 395–411. Pfullingen: Neske, 1973.

Winfield, Richard Dien. *Overcoming Foundations*. New York: Columbia University Press, 1989.

———. "The Method of Hegel's *Science of Logic*." In *Essays on Hegel's Logic*, edited by George di Giovanni, 45–57. Albany: SUNY Press, 1990.

Wohlfahrt, Günter. *Denken der Sprache*. Freiburg/Munich: Alber, 1984.

———. *Der spekulative Satz*. Berlin: de Gruyter, 1981.

Yovel, Yirmiahu. "Hegel's Dictum that the Rational is Actual and the Actual is Rational." In *Konzepte der Dialektik*, edited by Werner Becker and Wilhelm Essler, 111–23. Frankfurt: Klostermann, 1981.

Zimmerli, Walther. "Aus der Logik lernen? Zur Entwicklungsgeschichte der Hegelschen Logik-Konzeption." In *Die Logik des Wissens*, edited by Wilhelm Raimund Beyer, 66–79. Hamburg: Meiner, 1982.

———. "Die Frage nach der Philosophie. Interpretationen zu Hegels 'Differenzschrift.' " *Hegel-Studien* Beiheft 12 (2d ed. 1986): 137–46.

c.   Works by other authors

Aaron, Richard. *John Locke*. 3d ed. Oxford: Clarendon Press, 1971.

Anselm, Saint. *De Veritate*. In *Truth, Freedom and Evil*, edited by Jasper Hopkins and Herbert Richardson. New York: Harper Torchbooks, 1967.

Aquinas, Saint Thomas. *Summa Theologica*. In *Basic Writings of St. Thomas Aquinas*, 2 vols., edited by Anton C. Pegis. New York: Random House, 1945. Translated by R. W. Mulligan, S.J., under the title *The Disputed Questions on Truth*. 3 vols. Chicago: Regnery, 1956.

Aronson, Christopher, and Douglas Lewis. "Locke on Mixed Modes, Knowledge, and Substances." *Journal of the History of Philosophy* 8 (1970): 193–99.

Ashworthy, E. J. "Locke on Language." *Canadian Journal of Philosophy* 14 (1984): 45–74.

Aubenque, Pierre. *Le problème de l'être chez Aristotle.* Paris: Presses Universitaires de France, 1962.

Augustine, Saint. *Soliloquien.* Edited by Hanspeter Müller. Bern: Benteli, 1954.

Austin, J. L. *Sense and Sensibilia.* Oxford: Oxford University Press, 1962.

——. *Philosophical Papers.* Oxford: Clarendon, 1961.

Ayer, A. J. *Language, Truth, and Logic.* New York: Dover, n.d.

Baldwin, Thomas. "The Identity Theory of Truth." *Mind* 100 (January 1991): 35–52.

Barnes, Jonathan. "Aristotle's Theory of Demonstration." *Phronesis* 14 (1969): 123–52.

Beierwaltes, Werner. *Proklos: Grundzüge seiner Metaphysik.* Frankfurt: Klostermann, 1965.

Bennett, Jonathan. *Kant's Dialectic.* Cambridge: Cambridge University Press, 1974.

Bentham, Jeremy. "Theory of Fictions." In *Bentham's Theory of Fictions,* edited by C. K. Ogden. London: Kegan Paul, Trench, Trubner, 1932.

Berkeley, George. *Berkeley's Philosophical Writings.* Edited by David M. Armstrong. New York: Collier, 1965.

Berlin, Isaiah. "On the Pursuit of the Ideal." *New York Review of Books,* March 17, 1988, 11.

——. *Against the Current.* London: Hogarth, 1979.

Blanke, Fritz. *Hamann-Studien.* Zurich: Zwingli-Verlag, 1956.

Bolzano, Bernard. *Wissenschaftslehre.* Edited by Jen Berg. 2 vols. Stuttgart: Friedrich Frohmann Verlag, 1985.

Bradley, F. H. *Appearance and Reality.* 9th ed., rev. and ext. Oxford: Oxford University Press, 1930.

——. *Essays on Truth and Reality.* Oxford: Clarendon, 1914.

Brentano, Franz. *On the Several Senses of Being in Aristotle.* Berkeley: University of California Press, 1975.

Bury, Robert Gregg, ed. *The Philebus of Plato.* Cambridge: Cambridge University Press, 1897.

Butts, Robert E. "The Grammar of Reason: Hamann's Challenge to Kant." *Synthese* 75 (1988): 251–83.

Carnap, Rudolf. *Der logische Aufbau der Welt.* Berlin: Weltkreis Verlag, 1928. Translated by Rolf George, under the title *The Logical Structure of the World.* Berkeley: University of California Press, 1967.

Church, Ralph. *Hume's Theory of the Understanding.* Ithaca: Cornell University Press, 1935.

Cohen, L. Jonathan. "The Coherence Theory of Truth." *Philosophical Studies* 34 (1978): 351–60.

Curley, Edwin. *Spinoza's Metaphysics*. Cambridge, Mass.: Harvard University Press, 1969.

Davidson, Donald. "A Coherence Theory of Truth and Knowledge." In *Kant oder Hegel?*, edited by Dieter Henrich, 423–38. Stuttgart: Klett-Cotta Verlag, 1983.

———. "A Nice Derangement of Epitaphs." In *Truth and Interpretation: Perspectives on the Philosophy of Donald Davidson*, edited by Ernest LePore, 433–46. Oxford: Blackwell, 1986.

———. *Inquiries into Truth and Interpretation*. Oxford: Clarendon, 1984.

———. "True to the Facts." *Journal of Philosophy* 66 (1969): 748–62.

Deleuze, Gilles. *La philosophie critique de Kant*. Paris: Presses Universitaires de France, 1963.

Derrida, Jacques. *De la grammatologie*. Paris: Minuit, 1967. Translated by Gayatri Chakravorty Spivak, under the title *Of Grammatology*. Baltimore: Johns Hopkins University Press, 1974.

———. *Écriture et différence*. Paris: Éditions du Seuil, 1967.

———. *Glas*. Paris: Denoël-Gonthier, 1981.

———. *Marges*. Paris: Minuit, 1972.

Descartes, René. *Meditationes de prima philosophia*. Edited by Geneviève Rodis-Lewis. Paris: Jean Vrin, 1970. Translated by Elizabeth Haldane and G. R. T. Ross, in *The Philosophical Works of Descartes*. 2 vols. Cambridge: Cambridge University Press, 1931.

———. *Oeuvres*. Edited by Charles Adam and Paul Tannery. 12 vols. Paris: Cerf, 1905.

———. *Les principes de la philosophie* (1e partie). Edited by Guy Durandin. Paris: Jean Vrin, 1970.

Diels, Hermann, and Walther Kranz, eds. *Fragmente der Vorsokratiker*. 3 vol. 6th ed. Zurich: Weidmann, 1951.

Donagan, Alan, et al., eds. *Human Nature and Natural Knowledge*. Dordrecht: Reidel, 1986.

Edwards, Paul, ed. *Encyclopedia of Philosophy*. 8 vols. New York: Macmillan, 1967.

Engelbretsen, George. "On Propositional Form." *Notre Dame Journal of Formal Logic* 21 (1980): 101–10.

Epicurus. *Epicurus: The Extant Remains*. Edited by Cyril Bailey. Oxford: Clarendon, 1926.

Evans, Gareth. *The Varieties of Reference*. Oxford: Clarendon, 1982.

Evnine, Simon. *Donald Davidson*. Stanford: Stanford University Press, 1991.

Ferry, Luc, and Alain Renaut. *Heidegger and Modernity*. Translated by Franklin Philip. Chicago: University of Chicago Press, 1990.

Fine, Arthur. *The Shaky Game*. Chicago: University of Chicago Press, 1986.

Fogelin, Robert. *Hume's Skepticism in "The Treatise of Human Nature."* Boston: Routledge & Kegan Paul, 1985.

Forbes, Graeme. "The Indispensibility of *Sinn*." *Philosophical Review* 99 (1990): 535–63.

Foucault, Michel. *Madness and Civilization*. Translated by Richard Howard. New York: Random House, 1965.

Frege, Gottlob. *Begriffschrift*. Edited by Ignacio Angelclli. Hildesheim: Georg Olms, 1964.

———. *Kleine Schriften*. Edited by Ignacio Angelleli. Hildesheim: Georg Olms Verlag, 1967.

———. "On Sense and Meaning." In *Selections from the Philosophical Writings of Gottlob Frege*, edited by Peter Geach and Max Black, 56–78. 3d ed. Oxford: Blackwell, 1980.

Gardiner, Patrick L. "Hume's Theory of the Passions." In *David Hume: A Symposium*, edited by D. F. Pears, 31–42. New York: St. Martin's Press, 1966.

Gasché, Rodolphe. *The Tain of the Mirror*. Cambridge, Mass.: Harvard University Press, 1986.

Habermas, Jürgen. *Communication and the Evolution of Society*. Translated by Thomas McCarthy. Boston: Beacon, 1979.

———. *Theory of Communicative Action*. Translated by Thomas McCarthy. 2 vols. Boston: Beacon, 1984–87.

Halle, Morris, et al., eds. *Linguistic Theory and Psychological Reality*. Cambridge, Mass.: MIT Press, 1978.

Hamann, Johann Georg. *Sämtliche Werke*. Edited by Josef Nadler. 6 vols. Vienna: Herder Verlag, 1949–53.

———. *Schriften zur Sprache*. Edited by Josef Simon. Frankfurt: Suhrkamp, 1967.

Hampton, Cynthia. "Pleasure, Truth, and Beauty in Plato's *Philebus*: A Reply to Professor Frede." *Phronesis* 32 (1987): 253–62.

Hardwick, Charles S. *Language Learning in Wittgenstein's Later Philosophy*. The Hague: Mouton, 1971.

Heidegger, Martin. "Der Ursprung des Kunstwerkes." In *Holzwege*. 4th ed. Frankfurt: Klostermann, 1963. Translated by Albert Hofstadter, under the title "The Origin of the Work of Art." In *Poetry, Language, Thought*, 15–81. Translated by Albert Hofstadter. New York: Harper and Row, 1971.

———. "Vom Wesen der Wahrheit." Frankfurt: Klostermann, 1943.

———. *Identität und Differenz*. Pfullingen: Neske, 1957.

———. *Sein und Zeit*. Tübingen: Niemeyer, 1927.

———. *Vorträge und Aufsätze*. Pfullingen: Neske, 1954.

Herder, J. G. *Herders Sprachphilosophie*. Edited by Erich Heintel. 2d ed. Hamburg: Meiner, 1964.

Hobbes, Thomas. *Opera philosophica quae Latine scripsit*. Vol. 1. Edited by William Molesworth. London: John Bohn, 1839.

Hull, David. *Science as a Process*. Chicago: University of Chicago Press, 1988.

Hume, David. *A Treatise of Human Nature*. Edited by L. A. Selby-Bigge. Oxford: Clarendon, 1896.

———. *An Enquiry Concerning the Principles of Morals*. In *Enquiries*. Edited by L. A. Selby-Bigge. Oxford: Clarendon, 1894.

————. *An Enquiry Concerning Human Understanding*. In *Enquiries*. Edited by L. A. Selby-Bigge. Oxford: Clarendon, 1894.

Hunter, J. F. M. "Forms of Life in Wittgenstein's *Philosophical Investigations*." In *Ludwig Wittgenstein: Critical Assessments*, edited by Stuart Shanker, vol. 2, 106–24. London: Croom Helm, 1986.

Husserl, Edmund. *Logische Untersuchungen*. 3 vols. Tübingen: Niemeyer, 1921.

Janik, Allan, and Stephen Toulmin. *Wittgenstein's Vienna*. New York: Simon and Schuster, 1973.

Joachim, H. H. *The Nature of Truth*. Oxford: Clarendon, 1906.

Johnson-Laird, P. N., and P. C. Wason, eds. *Thinking*. Cambridge: Cambridge University Press, 1978.

Joly, Henri. *Le renversement platonicien*. 2d ed., rev. Paris: Jean Vrin, 1985.

Kant, Immanuel. *Logic*. Translated by Robert Hartman and Wolfgang Schwartz. Indianapolis: Bobbs-Merrill, 1974.

————. *Prolegomena to Any Future Metaphysics*. Edited by L. W. Beck. Indianapolis: Bobbs-Merrill, 1950.

————. *Critique of Judgment*. Translated by Werner S. Pluhar. Indianapolis: Hackett, 1987.

————. *Werke*. Edited by Wilhelm Weschedel. 12 vols. Frankfurt: Suhrkamp, 1978.

Kemp Smith, Norman. *The Philosophy of David Hume*. London: Macmillan, 1941.

Kierkegaard, Søren. *Concluding Unscientific Postscript*. Translated by David F. Swenson. Princeton: Princeton University Press, 1941.

————. "Journals." In *A Kiekegaard Anthology*. Edited by Robert Bretall. New York: Modern Library, 1963.

Kretzmann, Norman. "Semantics, History of." *Encyclopedia of Philosophy*, vol. 7, 359–406. Edited by Paul Edwards. New York: Macmillan.

————. "The Main Thesis of Locke's Semantic Theory." *Philosophical Review* 77 (1968): 175–96.

Lakoff, George. *Women, Fire, and Dangerous Things*. Chicago: University of Chicago Press, 1987.

Landesmann, Charles. "Locke on Meaning." *Journal of the History of Philosophy* 14 (1976): 23–35.

Lear, Jonathan. *Aristotle's Syllogistic*. Cambridge: Cambridge University Press, 1980.

Leibniz, G. W. "Two Dialogues on Religion." *Revue de métaphysique et de morale* 13 (1905): 1–38.

————. *Nouveaux essais sur l'entendement humain*. Edited by André Robinet and Heinrich Schepers. Berlin: Akademie-Verlag, 1962. Translated and edited by Peter Remnant and Jonathan Bennett, under the title *New Essays on Human Understanding*. Cambridge: Cambridge University Press, 1982.

————. *Die philosophischen Schriften*. Edited by C. J. Gebhardt. 8 vols. Hildesheim: Georg Olms, 1966. Translated by Leroy Loemker, under the title *Philosophical Papers and Letters*. 2d ed. Dordrecht: Reidel, 1969.

LePore, Ernest, ed. *Truth and Interpretation: Perspectives on the Philosophy of Donald Davidson*. Oxford: Blackwell, 1986.

Lohmann, Johannes. "Vom Ursprung und Sinn der Aristotelischen Syllogistic." In *Logik und Erkenntnislehre des Aristoteles*, edited by Peter Hager. Darmstadt: Wissenschaftliche Buchgesellschaft, 1972.

Lukasiewicz, Jan. *Aristotle's Syllogistic*. Oxford: Clarendon Press, 1957.

Lyotard, Jean-François, and Jean-Loup Thébaud. *Just Gaming*. Translated by Wlad Godzich. Minneapolis: University of Minnesota Press, 1985.

Marx, Karl. *Theses on Feuerbach*. In *Marx: Selections*. Edited by Allen Wood. New York: Macmillan, 1988.

Metzge, Erwin. *J. G. Hamanns Stellung in der Philosophie des 18. Jahrhunderts*. Darmstadt: Wissenschaftliche Buchgesellschaft, 1967.

Miller, George A. "Semantic Relations among Words." In *Linguistic Theory and Psychological Reality*, edited by Morris Halle, et al., 60–64. Cambridge, Mass.: MIT Press, 1978.

Minsky, Marvin. "A Framework for Representing Knowledge." In *The Psychology of Computer Vision*, edited by P. H. Winston, 211–77. New York: McGraw Hill, 1975.

Moore, G. E. "The Refutation of Idealism." In *20th Century Philosophy: The Analytical Tradition*, edited by Morris Weitz, 28–36. New York: Free Press (Macmillan), 1966.

Moutsopoulos, Evanghelos A. "The Idea of False in Proclus." In *The Structure of Being: A Neoplatonic Approach*, edited by R. Baine Harris, 137–39. Albany: SUNY Press, 1982.

Nathanson, Stephen. "Locke's Theory of Ideas." *Journal of the History of Philosophy* 11 (1973): 29–42.

Nietzsche, Friedrich. *Götzendämmerung*. In *Sämtliche Werke*, edited by Alfred Bäumler. 12 vols. Stuttgart: Kohlhammer, 1964.

Novak, Joseph A. "Some Recent Work on the Aristotelian Syllogistic." *Notre Dame Journal of Formal Logic* 21 (1980): 229–42.

O'Flaherty, James C. *Unity and Language: A Study in the Philosophy of Johann Georg Hamann*. Chapel Hill: University of North Carolina Press, 1952.

Olscamp, Paul. *The Moral Philosophy of George Berkeley*. The Hague: Martinus Nijhoff, 1970.

Owens, Joseph. *Aristotle*. Edited by John R. Catan. Albany: SUNY Press, 1981.
———. *The Doctrine of Being in the Aristotelian Metaphysics*. 2d ed., rev. Toronto: Pontifical Institute of Medieval Studies, 1963.

Patzig, Günther. *Aristotle's Theory of the Syllogism*. Translated by Jonathan Barnes. Dordrecht: Reidel, 1968.

Penelhum, Terence. *Hume*. London: Macmillan, 1973.

Perry, David L. "Locke on Mixed Modes, Relations, and Knowledge." *Journal of the History of Philosophy* 5 (1967): 219–35.

Pieper, Josef. *Wahrheit der Dinge*. Munich: Kösel Verlag, 1957.

Pitcher, George T., ed. *Truth*. Englewood Cliffs, N. J.: Prentice-Hall, 1964.

Plato. *Philebus.* Translated by J. S. B. Gosling. Oxford: Oxford University
    Press, 1975.
———. *Philebus.* Translated by R. Hackforth. In *Plato: Collected Dialogues,* ed-
    ited by Edith Hamilton and Huntington Cairns, 1086–1150. Prince-
    ton: Bollingen, 1961.
Pole, David. *The Later Philosophy of Wittgenstein.* London: University of Lon-
    don (Athlone) Press, 1958.
Popper, Karl. "What is Dialectic?" In *Conjectures and Refutations,* 312–35. New
    York: Basic Books, 1965.
Proclus Diadochus. *Elements of Theology.* Edited and translated by E. R. Dodds.
    Oxford: Clarendon Press, 1963.
Putnam, Hilary. "Meaning and Reference." In *Naming, Necessity, and Natural
    Kinds,* edited by Stephen P. Schwartz. Ithaca: Cornell University Press,
    1977.
———. "Models and Reality." *Journal of Symbolic Logic* 45 (1980): 464–82.
———. *Reason, Truth and History.* Cambridge: Cambridge University Press,
    1981.
Quine, W. V. *Methods of Logic.* 2d ed. Cambridge, Mass.: Harvard University
    Press, 1982.
———. *Ontological Relativity and Other Essays.* New York: Columbia University
    Press, 1969.
———. *Pursuit of Truth.* Cambridge, Mass.: Harvard University Press, 1990.
———. *The Ways of Paradox and Other Essays.* 2d ed., rev. Cambridge, Mass.:
    Harvard University Press, 1976.
———. "What Is It All About?" *The American Scholar* 50, no. 1 (1980–81):
    43–54.
———. *Word and Object.* Cambridge, Mass.: MIT Press, 1960.
Ramsey, F. P. "Facts and Propositions." In *Truth,* edited by George T. Pitcher.
    Englewood Cliffs, N.J.: Prentice-Hall, 1964.
Reichenbach, Hans. *The Rise of Scientific Philosophy.* Berkeley: University of
    California Press, 1951.
Rescher, Nicholas. "Leibniz and the Concept of System." *Studia Leibnitiana*
    13 (1981): 114–20.
———. *The Coherence Theory of Truth.* Oxford: Clarendon, 1973.
Rhees, Rush. *Discussions of Wittgenstein.* New York: Schocken Books, 1970.
Rorty, Richard. *Contingency, Irony, and Solidarity.* Cambridge: Cambridge Uni-
    versity Press, 1989.
———. *Philosophy and the Mirror of Nature.* Princeton: Princeton University
    Press, 1979.
———. "Relations, Internal and External." *Encyclopedia of Philosophy,* edited
    by Paul Edwards, vol. 7, 125–33. New York: Macmillan, 1967.
———. *The Linguistic Turn.* Chicago: University of Chicago Press, 1967.
Rosch, Eleanor. "Principles of Categorization." In *Cognition and Categoriza-
    tion,* edited by Eleanor Rosch and Barbara Lloyd, 30–42. Hillsdale,
    N.J.: Erlbaum, 1978.
Russell, Bertrand. *Philosophical Essays.* London: Longman's, Green, 1910.

————. *Logic and Knowledge.* Edited by Robert C. Marsh. London: Allen and Unwin, 1956.

————. *Basic Writings of Bertrand Russell, 1903–1959.* Edited by Robert Egner and Lester Denonn. New York: Simon & Schuster, 1961.

Salmony, H. A. *J. G. Hammanns metakritische Philosophie.* Zollikon: Evangelischer Verlag, 1958.

Schank, Roger, and Robert Abelson. *Scripts, Plans, Goals, and Understanding.* Hillsdale, N. J.: Erlbaum, 1977.

Schelling, Friedrich. *Sämtliche Werke.* 14 vols. Stuttgart and Augsburg: Cotta, 1856.

Schmueli, Ephraim. "Some Similarities between Hegel and Spinoza on Substance." *The Thomist* 36 (1972): 654–57.

Schwartz, Stephen P., ed. *Naming, Necessity, and Natural Kinds.* Ithaca: Cornell University Press, 1977.

Searle, John. *Speech Acts.* Cambridge: Cambridge University Press, 1969.

Shanker, Stuart, ed. *Ludwig Wittgenstein: Critical Assessments.* 2 vols. London: Croom Helm, 1986.

Shannon, Claude, and Warren Weaver. *The Mathematical Theory of Communication.* Urbana: University of Illinois Press, 1959.

Smith, R. G. *J. G. Hamann.* London: Collins, 1960.

Spinoza. *Opera.* Edited by C. Gebhard. 4 vols. Heidelberg: Winter, 1925. Translated and edited by Edwin Curley, under the title *The Collected Works of Spinoza.* Princeton: Princeton University Press, 1985.

Stich, Stephen, ed. *Innate Ideas.* Berkeley: University of California Press, 1975.

Storr, Anthony. *Solitude.* New York: Ballantine Books, 1988.

Stroud, Barry. *Hume.* London: Routledge and Kegan Paul, 1977.

Tarski, Alfred. *Logic, Semantics, and Metamathematics.* Edited by J. H. Woodger. Translated by J. H. Woodger and edited by John Corcoran. 2d ed., rev. Indianapolis: Hackett, 1983.

————. "The Semantic Conception of Truth." *Philosophy and Phenomenological Research* 4 (1943–44): 342–67.

Tugendhat, Ernst. *Der Wahrheitsbegriff bei Husserl und Heidegger.* Berlin: de Gruyter, 1967.

Turbayne, Colin, ed. *Berkeley: Critical and Interpretive Essays.* Minneapolis: University of Minneapolis Press, 1982.

Urmson, J. O. "Ideas." *Encyclopedia of Philosophy,* vol. 4, 120. Edited by Paul Edwards. New York: Macmillan, 1967.

Wedin, Michael V. "Tracking Aristotle's *Nous.*" In *Human Nature and Natural Knowledge,* edited by Alan Donagan et al., 167–97. Dordrecht: Reidel, 1986.

Weitz, Morris, ed. *20th Century Philosophy: The Analytical Tradition.* New York: Free Press (Macmillan), 1966.

White, Alan R. "The Coherence Theory of Truth." *Encyclopedia of Philosophy,* vol. 3, edited by Paul Edwards, 13. New York: Macmillan, 1967.

Williams, Bernard. *Descartes: The Project of Pure Enquiry.* London: Penguin, 1978.

Winograd, Terry. "Formalisms for Knowledge." In *Thinking*, edited by P. N. Johnson-Laird and P. C. Wason. Cambridge: Cambridge University Press, 1978.

Winograd, Terry, and Fernando Flores. *Understanding Computers and Cognition*. Reading, Mass: Addison-Wesley, 1987.

Winters, Barbara. "Hume on Reason." *Hume Studies* 5 (1979): 20–35.

Wittgenstein, Ludwig. *Philosophical Investigations*. Translated by G. E. M. Anscombe. 3d ed. New York: MacMillan, 1958.

Wohlfahrt, Günter. "Hamanns Kantkritik." *Kant-Studien* 75 (1984): 398–419.

Yolton, John. "Ideas and Knowledge in Seventeenth Century Philosophy." *Journal of the History of Philosophy* 13 (1975): 158–61.

———. *Locke and the Way of Ideas*. Cambridge: Cambridge University Press, 1970.

Zabeeh, Farhang. *Hume: Precursor of Modern Empiricism*. The Hague: Martinus Nijhoff, 1973.

Index

—for Leibniz, 39, 92, 100, 102–4, 106, 111, 365 n.45
—for Locke, 83, 92, 100, 104–6, 111, 280, 283–84, 362 n.76
—meaning in ordinary language, 66
—for modern philosophy, 21, 100–102
—packaged as "S is P." *See* "S is P"
—for philosophical tradition, 88–90, 110–12; Hegel's view compared with, 33–40, 59–67
—for Plato, 92–98, 99–100, 106, 110–11, 114, 180, 185
—as a structural concept in language, 257–59
—syllogistic conditions for, 204–5
—theories of expressed in a meta-metalanguage, 36–37
—theory of as a theory of meaning for Davidson, 258–62, 265–71, 333–36
—*See also* coherence theory of truth; correspondence theory of truth
truth, for Hegel, 40–41, 59, 70–71, 79, 111–12, 309; bearers of as issue in, 37–39; compared with traditional views, 33–40, 59–67, 80–90; as conformation to a systematic structure, 43, 44; and consolidation of the self, 11; and correctness, 60–67; and correspondence, 46, 50–53; as a diachronic predicate, 69; expression of, 228–29, 307; as goal of inquiry, 40–41, 66, 80; highest equated with the "truth as such," 52, 53; Kantian formal truth as, 110; and Nobility (*kalon*), 112–18; as outcome of all past philosophy, 91, 110–12; philosophical, 34–36, 40–41, 53–58, 185, 215. *See also* Idea, the; positive side of, 70; as a relation between what is "in itself" and what is "for itself," 368 n.19; relationship to Aristotelian concept, 99; relationship to Systematic dialectics, 131, 157–59; relationship to the Logic, 23; terms used for, 111; Theunissen on, 369 n.47; translated as "genuineness" and "realness," 69–70
truth-values, 71, 77, 134, 158, 259; of

utterances for Davidson and Wittgenstein, 250, 266–67, 269

Übereinstimmung. See convergence; correspondence
Übergreifen (overreaching), 398 n.71
understanding, 239–40, 307–8; for Hume, 194, 198, 207; for Kant, 4, 202–7, 209, 380 n.74; for Locke, 104–5, 280, 285
Understanding, the: for Hegel, 136, 226, 239–40, 318–19, 326; for Kant, 6, 109, 292–93
unity, 101–2, 110–11, 198, 219, 244, 314; for Aristotle, 99–100, 110–11, 112; of Being and Nothing, 130; of the Concept, 313; for Kant, 4, 106–10; of language games, 340–42; of media for philosophical expression, 303, 306–7; of names, 131, 137; place in Systematic dialectics, 132; for Plato, 93, 96–97, 99–100, 179–83
unity, of language, 258, 259, 275–77, 295, 314; for Davidson, 265–66, 268–69, 275–77, 314; for Davidson and Wittgenstein, 251–58, 262, 263
universal(s), 37, 63, 144, 168, 236; abstract, 60, 131; linguistic, 153, 168, 175, 224–26, 227; presented by names as such, 231, 234–35; representational names as, 237, 238, 242; representations as, 303, 306
universality, 116–17, 160–61, 176–77; of the Idea in religion, 54; of the Intelligence, 238; as a perfection of cognition for Kant, 106–7; of representational language, 220–22, 223–24, 228; of representational names, 228, 234; of Systematic dialectics, 136–37
universal term, use as middle term, 186
unsituated reason, 26
untruth, 11, 52–53, 68. *See also* bad
Urteil(e). See judgment(s)
utterances, 72, 92, 133, 221–25, 233, 249; and background information, 170–75; for Davidson and Wittgenstein, 250–55, 259–62,